I0797852

JOSHUA HILL OF MADISON

MERCER UNIVERSITY PRESS

Endowed by

TOM WATSON BROWN

and

THE WATSON-BROWN FOUNDATION, INC.

JOSHUA HILL OF MADISON

Civil War Unionist and Georgia's First Republican Senator, 1812–1891

BRADLEY R. RICE

MERCER UNIVERSITY PRESS
Macon, Georgia

MUP/ H1051

Published by Mercer University Press
1501 Mercer University Drive
Macon, Georgia 31207

29 28 27 26 25 5 4 3 2 1

Books published by Mercer University Press are printed on acid-free paper that meets the requirements of the American National Standard for Information Sciences—Permanence of Paper for Printed Library Materials.

Printed and bound in Canada.

This book is set in Adobe Caslon and Georgia (display).

Cover/jacket design by Burt&Burt.

ISBN 978-0-88146-960-8
Cataloging-in-Publication Data is available from the Library of Congress

The publication of this book was partially supported by the Heritage Education Fund of the Morgan County Landmarks Society. All royalties will benefit the programs of Landmarks.

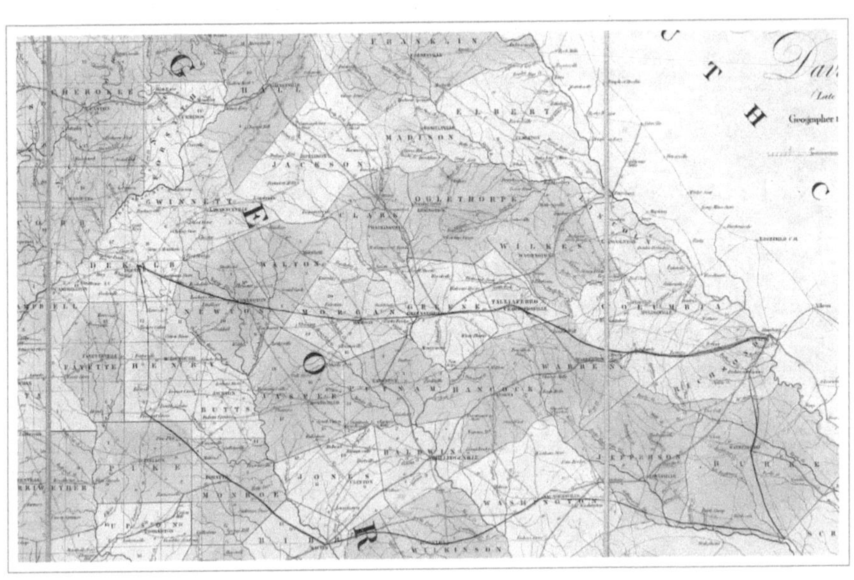

Madison and the Georgia Railroad, 1839. This detail from David Burr's map of Georgia and Alabama shows the Black Belt region of the lower Piedmont including Morgan County. The bold line indicates the planned route of the Georgia Railroad from Augusta to Atlanta.

Courtesy Library of Congress

Georgia Female College, ca. 1855. Anna Hill attended the institution just a block from the family home. In the opening days of the Civil War the young ladies of the college hosted a festive farewell as the local Panola Guards went off to war in Virginia. The president's home (left) still stands.

Joshua Hill, Representative from Georgia. Thirty-Fifth United States Congress, ca. 1857.

HARPER'S WEEKLY.
A JOURNAL OF CIVILIZATION.

Vol. V.—No. 210.] NEW YORK, SATURDAY, JANUARY 5, 1861. [Price Five Cents.

THE GEORGIA DELEGATION IN CONGRESS.

The Georgia Congressional Delegation on the Cusp of Secession, January 1861. Joshua Hill (lower right corner) resigned separately from his colleagues. Pictured L-R by horizonal rows: (Top row) Rep. J.W.H. Underwood, Rep. Peter E. Love, Rep. Lucius J. Gartrell, (Center row) Rep. Martin Crawford, Sen. Robert A. Toombs, Sen. Alfred Iverson, Rep. James Jackson (Bottom row) Rep. Thomas J. Hardeman, Rep. John J. Jones, Rep. Joshua Hill.

Harper's Weekly, Jan 5, 1861

Major General William T. Sherman with his Generals, 1865. (Seated, L-R) John A. Logan, Sherman, Henry W. Slocum. (Standing L-R) O.O. Howard, William B. Hazen, Jefferson Columbus Davis, Joseph A. Mower. Slocum led the 20th Corps through Morgan County in November 1864.

Courtesy Library of Congress

Main Street Madison as Union Troops Approached, November 1864. The accompanying story declared, "This town is said to be the most picturesque in Georgia." The Madison Baptist Church still stands albeit with grand columns and a revised steeple added in the very early 20th Century.

Harper's Weekly, January 7, 1865

Destruction of Madison Station by Union Troops, November 1864. The depot had been damaged earlier in 1864 by retreating remnants of General George Stoneman's command before General Henry Slocum's men finished the job in November. The much repaired and modified building still stands.

Harper's Weekly, January 7, 1865

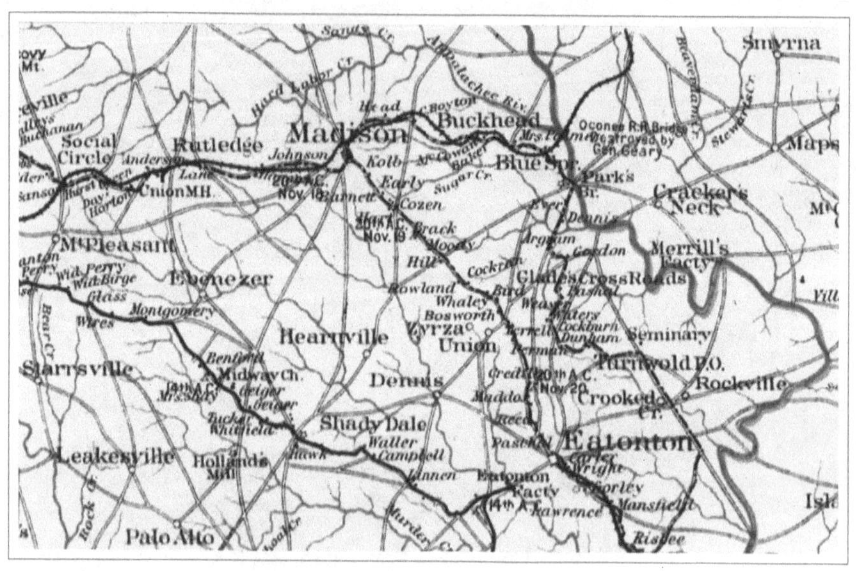

The route of the 20th Corps through Morgan & Putnam Counties. The 20th formed the left wing of Sherman's March to the Sea. The Hill plantation is identified about a third of the way from Madison to Eatonton.

Detail from a larger map in the *Atlas of the Official Records of the War of Rebellion*, p. 126

Alexander H. Stephens, ca. 1861. Best known as the Vice President of the Confederate States of America, Stephens defeated Hill for U.S. Senator in 1866; but the Senate refused to seat him. In 1868 he withdrew from the Senate race as a Democrat and threw his support to Conservative Republican Hill over Radical Republican Joe Brown. Stephens served in Congress before the Civil War and returned to the House of Representatives in 1873, the year that Hill left the Senate.

Courtesy Library of Congress

Joseph E. Brown, ca. 1880. Brown served as Governor of Georgia 1857–1865. He defeated Hill for governor in 1863. Brown turned Republican in the early days of Reconstruction but lost to Hill for U.S. Senator in 1868. He later returned to the Democratic Party and served in the U.S. Senate from 1880–1891.

Courtesy Ackland Art Museum, The Univeristy of North Carolina at Chapel Hill

Senator Joshua Hill, 1871. Finally seated in 1871 after being chosen by the Georgia General Assembly in 1868, Hill then sported a full beard in contrast to his days in the House of Representatives ten years earlier.

Biographical Directory of the United States Congress

Senator Homer Virgil Milton Miller, MD, 1871. Moderate Democrat Miller, who had served as a Confederate surgeon, sat in the Senate with Hill for a few weeks in February and March 1871.

Atlanta Medical and Surgical Journal, July 1896

Senator John B. Gordon, ca. 1873. The popular Confederate General, Democrat, and reputed head of the Ku Klux Klan in Georgia replaced Hill in the Senate in March 1873. No Republican would serve again until 1981.

Courtesy Library of Congress

Contents

Joshua Hill of Madison

Introduction

Unswerving Unionist, Conservative Republican

> "Soon the waves of oblivion seep away their faintest traces, and not a foot print will remain to show that I was of those who lingered by the stormy sea of politics."—Joshua Hill, September 1876[1]

Joshua Hill was too pessimistic about his legacy. His discernable footprints remain on the shores of the mid-nineteenth-century politics of Georgia and the nation. Along Main Street in Madison, Georgia, a historical marker points down Hill Street toward the home of the local luminary who served as a member of the US House of Representatives before the Civil War and as a Republican United States senator during Reconstruction. Though Hill was an enslaver and plantation owner, even after his state seceded, his refusal to endorse the Confederacy earned him the reputation as an unswerving Unionist. A foundation of truth covered with layers of legend identifies Hill as the man who saved Madison, "the village too beautiful to burn," from the torches of General Sherman's infamous March to the Sea.

For scholars of the Civil War and Reconstruction era, Joshua Hill is known as a prewar politician of Whiggish proclivities and as a postwar Unionist who stood at the center of the long and contentious controversy over his seating in the US Senate and the full readmission of Georgia to the Union. Along the way, Hill's path crisscrossed with all of Georgia's political leaders of the day, including Alexander H. Stephens, Robert Toombs, Joseph E. Brown, Rufus Bullock, John B. Gordon, Benjamin Hill, Henry Turner, and Jefferson Long. His path on the national shores

[1] Hill to 9th District Republican Convention, *Augusta Chronicle*, October 17, 1876.

intersected often with leading Republicans such as General William T. Sherman, General and President Ulysses S. Grant, Senator John Sherman, and Radical luminary Senator Charles Sumner.

In Georgia and Southern politics from the mid-1850s into the late 1880s, Hill was always present, persistently prominent, usually influential, and occasionally powerful. Distinguished Georgia historian Tom Dyer wrote that Hill was "Undoubtedly Georgia's most prominent wartime Unionist." Likewise, in the standard study of the state's Republicans in the Reconstruction period, Elizabeth Studley Nathans characterized the man from Madison as "Georgia's foremost Unionist." Period historians Eric Foner, Michael Perman, Gregory Downs, Anne Sarah Rubin, and others have taken note of aspects of Hill's role in their broad accounts.

In the great mid-nineteenth-century struggle between the Democratic Party and the Radical wing of the Republican Party, Joshua Hill sought to make his path down the middle. Low-key centrist politicians, especially those such as Hill, who left no trove of personal papers, receive less attention than the more successful or colorful actors who surrounded them. In the late 1930s, the *Georgia Historical Quarterly* published a mostly accurate and reasonably fair overview of Hill's political career that has stood for eighty-five years as the most comprehensive account of the public life of the antebellum representative and Reconstruction senator from Madison, Georgia. Until now, the career of Joshua Hill has not attracted the more up-to-date and more extended analysis it merits. [2]

The career of representative and later senator Joshua Hill was sometimes mentioned in passing but mostly ignored in the books written by generations of "Lost Cause" historians who had no interest in calling attention to a Georgia politician who called secession a folly, refused to pledge allegiance to the Confederacy, joined and clung to the Republican Party, and refused to get on the Democratic bandwagon of redemption.

As Georgia's first Republican senator, Joshua Hill attracted a brief flurry of attention when, after 110 years, Mack Mattingly defeated longtime Democratic senator Herman Talmadge in 1980 to become Georgia's *second* Republican to sit in the nation's upper house. Some Georgians had even forgotten that the state had *ever* had a Republican in the Senate. At

---

[2] Dyer, *Secret Yankees*, 257; Nathans, *Losing the Peace*, 13; L. Roberts, "Political Career of Joshua Hill," 50–72.

that time, a widely distributed news story described Hill's opposition to secession, his campaign for governor of Confederate Georgia in 1863, and his support of some Reconstruction measures. Using the slang of the day, the AP writer dubbed Hill "something of a peace-nik."[3]

In summer 1868, when the Georgia General Assembly chose Hill to be senator, a Radical-leading Ohio newspaper classified him as a "semi-Republican." If the Republicans of the Reconstruction era were to have used the parlance of the early twenty-first century, they would have dubbed Hill a RINO—"Republican in name only." Unlike today, however, the state's first Republican senator would have earned the RINO opprobrium not for being too liberal but for being too conservative. To many of today's readers, much late-nineteenth-century press coverage regarding matters of race would appear at first to be a gigantic misprint in which the Democratic and Republican party names were inadvertently reversed because then it was the GOP that endeavored, albeit often cautiously, to secure political rights for Black Americans. To be sure, Joshua Hill's rhetoric was sometimes tainted with racial condescension and insensitivity, but he refrained from the kind of bombastic and inflammatory race-baiting characteristic of so many of his contemporaries, especially Democrats. He may not have agreed with all the racial policies of Ulysses S. Grant, but his continued support for the president confirmed his Republican affiliation. Hill's repudiation of the Confederacy never waned, even when it would have benefitted his political aspirations to have been more circumspect in his denunciations of the "folly" of secession. To the horror of most of the state's press, Hill told the delegates of the 1867–1868 Georgia State Constitutional Convention that he would have left the South if the Confederate States had won the war. Ironically, the Morgan County monument that extols the purity of the Confederate cause stands today on the corner of a

[3] *Atlanta Constitution*, September 13, November 10 (peace-nik), 1980. In 1972, during his campaign against Sam Nunn, Republican candidate Fletcher Thompson erroneously claimed that if he won, he would become the state's first Republican senator. In response, the *Atlanta Constitution* (September 24, 1972) headlined its story, "State's 1st GOP Senator? It's Been Done, Fletcher," and profiled Hill. Much earlier a *Constitution* columnist (January 21, 1913) mistakenly wrote that Georgia had never had a Republican senator.

park named for the family of the man who wrote in 1876, "The sin of secession took away half the joys of existence."[4]

Several case studies and broad historical analyses have focused on the activities of Unionists and Confederate dissenters. Collectively, these works have disproven the lingering myth that the White people of the Deep South were fully unified and unanimous in their support of the Confederacy. The resistance of many Southerners, male and female, Black and White, was intense and sometimes violent. Some left the South. Some engaged in or supported guerilla action, and others joined the Union military. Such Unionists often faced intense persecution or at least social ostracism. Hill was in contact with a group of this nature in Atlanta, but he was not that type of Unionist. Recent historical literature has tended to give less attention to cautious Unionists of high social status like Hill, but as early as 1917, one historian in the *Journal of Negro History* cited Hill as an example of the few men of the "Southern aristocracy" who were steadfast enough to work with the Republican Party during Reconstruction. Certainly, these men were not immune from criticism and suspicion, but they knew how to navigate the political shoals of Union loyalty without posing a direct and immediate threat to the Confederacy. They knew how to support and be friendly with individual Confederates without supporting or befriending the Confederacy itself. Many of them had family members who served in the Confederate Army, and some, like Hill himself, lost sons in combat. In his memories of wartime Madison, a Baptist minister described the man he knew personally:

> [Joshua Hill was] about as much at odds with the Confederate government as one could well be without proviking the stroke of its ironhand.... Though, naturally, well hated, he stood to high for assault. Preserving an external and entirely honorable loyalty to the existing government, and giving his sons to the army, he still did not disguise his hostility to what was going on, and

[4] *Cincinnati Gazette*, July 18, 1868 (semi-Republican); *Augusta Constitutionalist*, December 19, 1867 (leave the state); *Augusta Chronicle*, October 25, 1876 (Sin of secession).

> employed a freedom of criticism which would hardly have been tolerated in a less formidable man."[5]

When the war ended, Hill and similarly situated men could ease back into political and business life more easily than those whose Unionism had been more combative.

Joshua Hill of Madison: Civi War Unionist and Georgia's Preeminent Unionist & First Republican Senator unfolds the chronology of the Madisonian's political career and personal life with chapters that provide insights into several might-have-beens in the politics of Georgia and the rest of the South. Hill was a key organizer of the Constitutional Union Party, which hoped to avoid secession and war by offering compromise and an alternative to Lincoln in 1860. After Lincoln prevailed, Hill urged a plebiscite designed to slow Georgia's stampede to secession. When secession came despite his efforts, he renounced the Confederacy. When all of his Georgia congressional colleagues and most of his fellow planters jumped on the Confederate train, Hill refused to get on board. In 1863 he stood for governor of Georgia against incumbent Joseph Brown, not with the intent of winning but rather to take measure of voter dissatisfaction with the course of the war. In the autumn of the following year, Hill carried General William T. Sherman's offers of negotiated peace to Brown and other unheeding Confederate politicians.

Always a Whig at heart who stressed national interests, abhorred disunion, and detested disruptive controversy, Hill personified Abraham Lincoln's vision of building loyal governments in the rebel states on the foundation of loyal Unionists, but that vision died in the wee hours across the street from Ford's theater. Hill attempted to cozy up to Andrew Johnson, but the new president passed him over for provisional governor in favor of a less ardent Unionist. Hill expected to win election to the United States Senate in 1866, but defiant White legislators chose former Confederate vice president Alexander H. Stephens instead. Indignant at Georgia's insolence, the Senate refused to seat Stephens. After passage of the Reconstruction Acts, Hill allied with White leaders who sought to bring Black voters into a moderate-to-conservative version of Republicanism that could defeat Democrats by offering fair and honest—though subordinate

[5] Kendrick, "A Non-Combatant's War Reminiscences," 449–63.

and separate—treatment for freed people. Hill's conservative approach temporarily triumphed in 1868 when the Democrats were forced to abandon Alexander H. Stephens and cooperate with conservative Republicans in the Georgia General Assembly to elect Hill as the compromise United States senator over the temporary Radical Joe Brown. Before Hill could take his seat in the Senate, the Georgia legislature expelled its recently elected Black members, sparking more than two years of convoluted controversy before Georgia could be fully readmitted to the Union and Hill seated in January 1871. By the time his term ended in March 1873, Democrats had "redeemed" Georgia from Republican control, and Hill's senate seat went to Confederate general and Ku Klux Klan idol John B. Gordon. In his last significant role, Hill worked diligently but only partially successfully to defend his principles and limit the excessively detailed provisions of the Constitution of 1877.

Hill's experience illustrates why those numerous might-have-beens became never-happeneds. It shows that the Lincolnesque vision of a South governed by loyal Unionists, a few particularly deserving Black men, and contrite Confederates was never a viable option in the face of intractable and mainly racist opposition. The powerful White elite prevailed by clinging tightly to its own version of state rights, White man rule, and the Democratic party. Yielding to deep, if less overt, racial attitudes and anxious to promote economic growth, the Republican Party of the North gradually lost the will and political support to carry out the Radical vision of a South based on free labor, fairly treated. Given his views on race and economics, Joshua Hill would likely have been more comfortable and accepted in the Grand Old Party of the 1890s and the early twentieth century than he was in his own era.[6]

Upon the former senator's death in March 1891, the principal newspaper in Augusta epitomized the prevailing assessment of his career by Georgia Whites: "He was a Republican, but an honest man." The widely read *New York Herald* wrote more broadly: "Joshua Hill has been one of the most unique characters politically in the South for the past twenty years and more."[7]

---

[6] On Lincoln's vision, see W. Harris, *With Charity for All.*

[7] *New York Herald,* March 7, 1891; *Augusta Chronicle,* March 8, 1891; *Chicago Tribune,* March 11, 1891, re-printed the *Chronicle* comment.

Chapter 1

South Carolina Native in the Georgia Gentry, 1812–1850s

Joshua Hill was born and raised in the Abbeville area of northwest South Carolina and then spent his entire adult life in Georgia. He grew up on a small plantation owned by his father and operated by a workforce of enslaved people. By the time Hill became a planter-lawyer-businessman-politician on his own, he had developed a self-awareness of how his standing as a Southern White man from a moderately privileged family had let an indelible imprint on his personality, politics, and perspective. Understanding this indelible imprint gave Hill the ability to put his own views in perspective, to have some empathy for opposing viewpoints, to seek compromise when he could, and to adapt as needed to the changing world about him. Despite this self-awareness and some personal evolution over many decades of experience, Joshua Hill remained always a deeply conservative man steeped in the traditional values of the Southern White gentry.

From South Carolina Boy to Georgia Lawyer

Royal land grants in northwest South Carolina date as early as 1738. To promote settlement in the remote backcountry that bordered the Savannah River and Cherokee territory, the British government offered large plots to influential colonists. Following the American Revolution, migration accelerated as farm families from Virginia and elsewhere sought opportunities in the low hills and heavy clay soil of the Ninety-sixth District, as this upstate region was then known.[1]

---

[1] L. Ware, *Chapters in the History of Abbeville County*, and *Old Abbeville: Scenes of the Past of a Town Where Old Time Things are Not Forgotten*.

Among those early migrants with Virginia roots were Joshua and Nancy Hill, who settled near Abbeville and built a prosperous small plantation. On January 10, 1812, Nancy gave birth to Joshua, her eleventh and final child. By the time Joshua was eight years old, only four of his siblings still lived at home with their little brother—three sisters and his brother Edward, who would become his future law partner and Georgia Whig politician. Joshua Hill's father arranged for his namesake to receive a fine education from the common schools and distinguished private tutors.[2]

Around 1830, Joshua Hill left his South Carolina home and migrated to Georgia where two of his brothers already lived. Striking out for better prospects further west was a hallmark of the times, and as the youngest son, Joshua likely foresaw little opportunity around Abbeville, where his father and an older brother ran the family plantation. Chances that he would ever obtain his own place nearby were not great since cotton land in the region was wearing out, and larger plantations were absorbing small operations. The Panic of 1819 and the ensuing recession hit South Carolina especially hard. For the next twenty years, the state's White population count remained essentially flat as birthrate barely matched outmigration. During that same period, Georgia gained 218,000 White residents—ten times more than South Carolina.[3]

Young Joshua Hill joined his brothers in Monticello, the seat of Jasper County in the center of Georgia. Treaties of 1802 and 1805 forced the Creek (Muskogee) Indians to surrender their lands between the Oconee

---

[2] The Hill family history in South Carolina up to 1830 is drawn mainly from Ancestry.com using the well-sourced Obear-Wood-Smith family tree of Hon. Joshua Hill. Biographical directory entries for Joshua Hill include Mellichamp, *Senators from Georgia*, 151; Nathans, "Joshua Hill," *American National Biography*, *Biographical Directory of the US Congress*; R. J. Massey, "Hon. Joshua Hill," in *Men of Mark*, 3:71–76; Knight, *Georgia's Landmarks*, 2:809–810; Allen and Dumas, *Dictionary of American Biography*, 5:42–43. The 1830 federal census for the Abbeville District lists one free male aged 15–19, presumedly Joshua, as the only child still living at home (accessed via Ancestry.com). Joshua Hill's tutelage under Messrs. Gray and Waddell is mentioned in the Morgan County Bar Memorial Tribute to Joshua Hill, 1891, typescript in Joshua Hill file, Morgan County Archives (hereafter MCA). Despite sharing his father's name, Joshua did not use the "junior" suffix.

[3] *Historical Statistics of the United States, Colonial Times to 1957*, Bicentennial Edition (Washington, DC: GPO, 1975).

and Ocmulgee rivers. The state quickly organized much of the area into Baldwin County and then later divided it into others, including Jasper and Morgan in Georgia's rich lower Piedmont. The region is defined on the south by the fall line where river shoals and falls mark the transition from coastal plains. To the north, the rolling hills and fertile river and creek beds of the lower Piedmont transition into the foothills of the Blue Ridge Mountains. By 1830, cotton reigned supreme in the region, and slaves constituted 46 percent of the population—a percentage that grew to 55 percent by 1860. Milledgeville, the new state capital, stood about thirty miles southeast of Monticello. Two-thirds of Georgia's population resided within ninety miles of that little city which thrived on politics.[4]

White settlers and their slaves poured into the region, bringing Jasper's population to over fourteen thousand by 1820. It was during this initial influx that John Hill, twenty years senior to Joshua, arrived. By 1819, John was well-established enough to marry a local girl and start a family. In the mid-1820s, Edward followed and soon married. Both older brothers quickly became locally prominent, so it can be assumed that they invited Joshua to join them. Legend has it that the youngest Hill made the whole trip on foot.[5]

In 1829 a guidebook described Monticello as boasting two churches (Methodist and Baptist) along with a female academy and fifty-five houses. There were nineteen stores, eight shops, three doctors, and five law offices. A town with that many retail and professional establishments but only fifty-five houses served a trade area of substantial size. During the twenty years between 1810 and the 1830s, Jasper County's economy shifted from independent family farming to large-scale cotton plantations, a pattern typical all across the so-called Black Belt of the lower Piedmont. Prosperous farmers and professional men like the Hills enlarged their holdings and acquired more enslaved workers, thereby pushing less successful Whites further west. The county's enslaved population more than

---

[4] Hodler and Schretter, *Atlas of Georgia*, 11–37, 74–76; Carey, *Parties, Slavery, and the Union*, 1–5.

[5] Jasper County Historical Foundation, *History of Jasper County*, 55–56; Jasper County Marriage Records in the Edward Y. Hill heading of Ancestry.com using the Obear-Wood-Smith family tree.

tripled from just under two thousand to more than six thousand—nearly half the total population.[6]

Armed with a strong combination of talent and family connections, Joshua eagerly accepted his brothers' tutelage and soon became well-established. He assisted John in the office of the Clerk of the Superior Court of the Ocmulgee Circuit and studied law under Edward, who was then solicitor general of the circuit. At the end of 1833, twenty-two-year-old Joshua became a member of the bar and entered into partnership with Edward. The following notice appeared on Christmas day in the capital city's *Southern Recorder*[7]:

LAW

THE undersigned having connected themselves
in the Practice of Law, under the firm
of E. Y. & J. Hill, will attend the Courts of the Ocmulgee Circuit, and a few of the adjacent counties.
EDWARD YOUNG HILL
JOSHUA HILL

Joshua Hill quickly set out to make himself known in the community. At Shadydale, a crossroads community about nine miles northeast of Monticello, he offered a Fourth of July toast at the local 1833 celebration; a year later he presented a "warm and patriotic" oration in the same village. By 1837, the young man's reputation was valuable enough that the nearby Indian Springs Hotel printed his name along with other endorsers in a local advertisement.[8]

Joshua's partnership with Edward dissolved five years later when the voters elected the latter to the prestigious Superior Court judgeship. Edward served as a Georgia judge for most of the next twenty-two years until he died in the midst of the secession uproar just two weeks after Abraham

---

[6] Knight, *Georgia's Landmarks*, 2:809; Mellichamp, *Senators from Georgia*, 151; Jasper County Historical Foundation, *History of Jasper County*, 8, 97.

[7] *Milledgeville Southern Recorder*, December 25, 1833.

[8] *Milledgeville Southern Recorder*, August 7, 1833, July 23, 1834; *Milledgeville Georgia Journal*, May 10, 1863; *Milledgeville Federal Union*, February 26, 1836; *Macon Telegraph*, November 19, 1831, April 5, 1833, July 25, 1837; *Augusta Constitutionalist*, April 5, 1833.

Lincoln's election. The December 1838 newspaper notice of the dissolution declared that the younger brother would "attend to the unfinished business of the firm, as well as to any new business entrusted to him." Soon Joshua Hill was indeed entrusted with much business—and much property.[9]

On January 12, 1836, while still practicing with his brother, Joshua married Miss Emily Reid, daughter of Mr. and Mrs. Samuel Reid of nearby Eatonton. The license was issued in Madison (Morgan County) where the couple would move some dozen years later. Why the marriage occurred in Madison rather than in Monticello or Eatonton is not known. Emily (born July 17, 1820) was only fifteen-and-a-half years old and was eight years junior to Joshua, so perhaps it was an elopement. The union lasted fifty-three years until Emily's death in 1889.[10]

For a brief time, Joshua and Emily maintained a residence on eleven acres near the Putnam County seat town of Eatonton, about twenty miles east of Monticello. It is unclear if Hill intended to set up his law practice permanently in that city or if he moved there only temporarily to start married life near his in-laws. In either case, it did not work out well; by May 1838, the Hills put their small farm on the market and moved to Monticello. Ever anxious to promote his reputation, Hill gave a speech at Eatonton's July 4th celebration even while his residence was up for sale. The newspaper advertisement for his property was jarringly candid: "My only reason for offering to sell is because I think I can make money faster elsewhere." Apparently, his profit-seeking strategy worked. Lawyer Hill's growing clientele soon extended well beyond Jasper and Putnam counties into several surrounding communities where his legal notices appeared in local newspapers.[11]

---

[9] *Milledgeville Southern Recorder*, December 25, 1833, December 4, 1838 (attend to); Morgan Bar Tribute, MCA.

[10] Morgan County Marriage Records 1836, MCA, Madison, GA. (Their first child, Anna, was born in 1840.)

[11] *Milledgeville Southern Recorder*, July 17, 19, 1838; *Milledgeville Georgia Journal*, November 1, 1836, December 6, 1836, June 19, 1838; *Macon Telegraph*, February 18 & April 14, 1840; *Milledgeville Federal Union*, February 4, 1840; *Savannah Republican*, May 11, 1837. See Jasper County Grantee-Grantor Index books, 1838–1849 *passim*, Office of the Court Clerk, Monticello, GA.

Hill Becomes a Whig

The biographer of United States Supreme Court justice James Moore Wayne almost threw up his hands at the challenge of explaining it all when he wrote, "The true nature of Georgia politics in the antebellum period is unknown and unknowable, but evidence suggests little was systematic and less was constant."[12] Still, it is necessary to provide some sense of the unknowable in order to put Joshua Hill's political ascent in context. Whether out of sincere conviction or opportunistic effort to promote his law practice—most likely a mixture of both—Joshua Hill thus stepped into this confusing milieu in which the names adopted by the various political factions seemed to shift with the seasons.

Hill came of age in the northwest South Carolina where John C. Calhoun was and seems to remain a favorite son in the eyes of the community's Whites well into the twenty-first century. He could hardly have escaped the towering influence of Calhoun, who was already a well-known, forty-year-old congressional "war hawk" when Hill was born in the year of the War of 1812. By the time that the youngest Hill relocated to Georgia around 1830, the old political order was beginning to break down. The catalyst for this realignment was the nullification controversy revolving around Calhoun. At the most basic level, nullifiers took the position that states were sovereign entities that could determine for themselves what national laws would be executed within their states. Throughout the 1820s, many White South Carolinians blamed federal policies on banking, internal improvement, and, especially, the protective tariff policies for the persistent economic malaise that caused young men such as Joshua and his brothers to emigrate.

Southern opponents of protective tariffs were optimistic that the 1828 election of Andrew Jackson as president with Calhoun as his vice president would bring relief, but it did not. When, in November 1832, a South Carolina convention voted to nullify the so-called tariff of "abominations," President Jackson denounced the action and declared that he would enforce national law by military force if necessary. Fortunately, Senator Henry Clay of Kentucky and others managed to negotiate a compromise tariff that diffused the crisis, but the episode irrevocably broke the Jackson-

---

[12] McMahon, *Our Good and Faithful Servant*, 72.

Calhoun alliance. Throughout the episode, slavery was a persistent subtext to the arguments ostensibly about tariffs.[13]

Hill began dabbling in politics soon after the nullification crisis. As early as summer 1833 his comments about national affairs appeared in newspapers and his public speeches. Two years later, twenty-three-year-old Hill became secretary of the Jasper County chapter of the anti-Jackson States' Rights Party, which eventually evolved into Georgia's Whig party. In the meantime, pro-Jackson forces established the Union Democratic Republican party, which would morph over time into the Democratic Party. This early decision marked the beginning of Hill's consistent and lifelong opposition to the Democratic Party. Ironically given the "States' Rights" title of his first political affiliation, loyalty to the Union and extreme opposition to the states' rights position became a bedrock of Hill's politics.[14]

In 1836, as his second term was coming to its end, Jackson endorsed Martin Van Buren of New York to be his Democratic successor. The States' Rights Party of Georgia was appalled by the nomination of a man whom they considered to be soft on the protection of slavery. Although still a small player in a small town, Joshua Hill joined in the clamor. As party secretary, he was one of six Monticello signatories to an anti-Van Buren letter that appeared in several newspapers. Georgia's States' Rights congressional candidates went down to defeat, but the anti-Van Buren presidential electoral ticket carried the state. Voter analysis by historian Anthony Gene Carey revealed that the gains for the States Rights Party in 1836 were strongest in the Black Belt region of the lower Piedmont where Hill resided. Carey emphasized that both parties stood for slavery and state rights but that they "differed most significantly in their attitudes toward the rise of national parties."[15]

Starting in 1837, Hill regularly served as a delegate to the States' Rights Party's state conventions. The next year the party's candidates made

---

[13] R. E. Ellis, *Union at Risk*; Freehling, *Prelude to Civil War*; Freehling, *The Road to Disunion*, vol. 1: *Secessionists at Bay, 1776–1854*.

[14] *Milledgeville Southern Recorder*, August 7, 1833; *Milledgeville Georgia Journal*, August 7, 1833, June 9, 1835; Carey, *Parties, Slavery, and the Union*, 25–31.

[15] *Macon Georgia Journal*, September 13, 1836; *Savannah Republican*, September 21, 23, 28, November 17, 1836; *Augusta Chronicle*, September 17, 1840; Carey, *Parties, Slavery, and the Union*, 36–44.

a clean sweep of Georgia's congressional seats by capitalizing on blaming Democrats for the Panic of 1837 and the subsequent depression. Still wary of national parties, the 1840 States' Rights convention, with Hill in attendance, declined to endorse William Henry Harrison, the Whig presidential nominee. However, as the campaign progressed, the main body of the party drifted toward Harrison and the Whigs. Hill became a member of the state Central Committee and was among the signers of a pro-Harrison letter published in several newspapers. The efforts paid off, and the unabashed Whig William Henry Harrison carried Georgia. Even with a string of victories in hand, Georgia's States' Rights Party remained hesitant to affiliate with a national movement and take full ownership of the name "Whig."[16]

When the General Assembly convened in 1840, Joshua Hill, not yet thirty, became a casualty of the struggle to organize the state senate along party lines. The upper house, about evenly divided between the Union-Democrats and the more loosely organized States' Righters, narrowly elected a States' Rights man as its presiding officer. For secretary of the senate, an important position held by a non-member of the body, the party nominated Hill. A dispute ensued over counting the ballots, which had literally been collected in a hat. The final count resulted in a deadlock between Hill and his Democratic opponent. For unexplained reasons, perhaps a forward-looking attempt at bipartisan conciliation with the opposition or perhaps just a backroom deal, the newly elected senate president, even though he was a Harrison man, broke the tie in favor of the Democrat.[17]

The thrill that national Whigs and their Georgia States' Rights Party allies experienced upon the election of President Harrison came to a shocking halt on April 4, 1841. After only thirty-one days, Harrison became the first president to die in office, and Vice President John Tyler, not an enthusiastic Whig, replaced him. The effect on the Georgia States' Rights Party was devastating. Later that year Democrats retained the

---

[16] *Milledgeville Southern Recorder*, May 2, 23, 1837, April 9, 1839; *Savannah Republican*, May 19, 1837; Carey, *Parties, Slavery, and the Union*, 46–47.

[17] *Milledgeville Southern Recorder*, May 5, June 9, August 11, 1840; *Milledgeville Georgia Journal*, May 5, July 16, August 25, September 8, 1840.

governorship, swept all of the state's congressional races, and secured effective control of both houses of the Georgia General Assembly.[18]

Despite the disappointments, Hill stuck with his party. He remained secretary of the Jasper County organization and served as a state convention delegate as the States' Rights Party eventually dropped its name and became unabashedly "Whig." Meanwhile, the Georgia Democratic Party had split between Van Buren supporters and pro-Calhoun men, so the Whigs took advantage of their opportunity. With Joshua Hill in attendance, the 1843 Whig convention nominated George W. Crawford, an Augusta lawyer. He narrowly prevailed to become Georgia's first and only Whig governor. The Whigs also won enough seats in the general assembly to gain control of both houses. It was a remarkable turnaround.[19]

After the 1843 election, Governor Crawford honored some of his most ardent supporters, including Hill, with the title of honorary aide-de-camp. Though he was not yet a first-order Whig leader, a measure of the young Monticello lawyer's rise was his election as a delegate to the 1844 national convention in Baltimore. Among Hill's fellow Whig delegates were future Confederate vice president Alexander H. Stephens and Robert Toombs, both of whom won congressional seats in 1844. In one letter to his brother Linton, Alexander Stephens referred to "Colonel Joshua Hill," indicating that the thirty-one-year-old Monticello lawyer had become prominent enough to merit the distinguished honorific so often accorded members of the Southern White gentry.[20] The political careers of Hill and the much more famous Stephens and Toombs would remain closely, and often convolutedly and bitterly, intertwined for the next three decades.

As the 1844 presidential election approached, Joshua Hill's future hometown of Madison hosted one of the year's biggest Whig rallies. The invitation proudly declared: "We have no large city into which to receive you.... We *can*, however, offer you the freedom of as good Whig soil, and

[18] *Augusta Chronicle*, September 17, 1840; *Milledgeville Georgia Journal*, November 3, 1840; Carey, *Parties, Slavery, and the Union*, 56–63.

[19] *Milledgeville Georgia Journal*, August 17, 1841; *Augusta Chronicle*, August 19, 1941, May 13, 1842; Cook, *Governors of Georgia*, 120–22.

[20] *Richmond Whig*, June 27, 1843; *Madison Southern Miscellany*, May 24, June 24, December 22, 1843; *Savannah Republican*, May 26, 1843; A. H. Stephens to Linton Stephens, May 4, 1844, in Waddell, *Biographical Sketch of Linton Stephens*, 49.

as good Whig atmosphere as can be found in this broad Union." What the local Whigs could also offer was existing connection to Augusta via the Georgia Railroad and a promise to Whigs in the northwestern part of the state that "We shall soon be tied to you by bands of iron." Indeed, the Georgia Railroad would be completed to the terminus at Marthasville (Atlanta) the following year, and with strong support from the newly elected Whig governor, the state-owned Western & Atlantic Railroad was building northward toward the Tennessee River at Chattanooga.[21]

The rally was no doubt the grandest event that Madison had hosted since its 1809 incorporation. County delegations encamped all around the outskirts of the town, which numbered fewer than two thousand residents. A pro-Whig newspaper optimistically estimated the crowd at between fifteen and twenty-five thousand people people and vividly described the scene:

> Long before reaching the town the National Flag was seen floating at an immense height, and on entering the public square, the glowing welcome of the Whigs of Madison met the eye on an immense banner suspended across the street at great height, inscribed:
>
> HENRY CLAY
> THE HOPE OF HIS COUNTRY
>
> *To you, brothers and friends, the Whigs of*
> *Morgan extend the hand of welcome;*
> *their hearts were yours before*

Bands played and the crowd consumed great quantities of food. Robert Toombs and other Georgia politicians, along with Whig orators from neighboring states, regaled the crowd during four days of festivities. Among the banners carried in the climactic parade on July 31 was that of Joshua Hill's then-home county of Jasper. One reporter characterized the Jasper Countians, with whom Hill was almost certainly marching on that

[21] *Milledgeville Southern Recorder*, June 25 (we have, we shall, *Madison Miscellany*), August 6, 1844; Russell, *Atlanta 1847–1890*, 14–21; Gagnon, *Transition to an Industrial South*, 150–56; Schott, *Alexander H. Stephens*, 18, 54–56.

grand day, as a "determined band…often defeated though never conquered or dismayed." The event concluded with an oration by Alexander H. Stephens. The Whigs, who were so excited at that summer rally in Madison, were disappointed in fall 1844 when James K. Polk bested Clay. Despite the presidential loss, Georgia Whigs and Democrats remained closely balanced for another few years.[22]

In 1847, Governor Crawford narrowly won reelection, and the Whigs managed to eke out narrow control of the Georgia General Assembly. It would be the last time that they held such power. When the legislature met to organize, Judge Edward Hill, Joshua's older brother and former law partner, administered the oath of office to the members of the senate, and the Whigs quickly elected their man president of the senate. Joshua Hill had continued to be a regular and loyal Jasper County delegate to Whig annual conventions, a position that again earned him a nomination for the position of secretary of the senate. Hill lost the race following several ballots that presaged the factionalization that would soon destroy the party.[23]

Greener Pastures in Madison

No longer content to live in a tiny town on a wagon route far from railroads, all three Hill brothers decided to pull up stakes in Jasper County and move to better prospects. John was the first to go. Around 1843, he moved east to Augusta, where he practiced law for a while and then served for several years as city clerk. Shortly after John moved away, a devastating fire swept through Monticello doing at least fifty-thousand dollars in damage. Joshua wrote John about the tragedy:

> MONTICELLO, October 22d, 1843
>
> Dear Brother—A most destructive fire occurred in this town this morning, about 4 o'clock, which we have just succeeded in subduing. The whole range, from Mr. Dyer's old corner to my house,

---

[22] *Milledgeville Southern Recorder*, June 25 (we have, we shall, *Madison Miscellany*), August 6, 1844; Cook, *Governors of Georgia*, 120–22.

[23] *Augusta Chronicle*, June 12, 1845, November 4, 1847; *Savannah Republican*, July 4, 1845, November 5, 1847; *Richmond (Virginia) Whig*, November 9, 1847; Montgomery, *Cracker Parties*, 2; Cook, *Governors of Georgia*, 122–26; Carey, *Parties, Slavery, and the Union*, 70–91. The first year Georgia elected congressmen by districts was 1844.

> embracing [several stores] are completely consumed—My house escaped most narrowly, by great exertions of the citizens; the furniture is much injured. The Court House, new and beautiful as it is, took fire, and after much injury to the upper stories, was saved.... But for the exertions of Mr. Stephen Talmadge, Mr. Doolittle, and one of my negro boys, my house must have gone, and with it Simonton's and others.

The town was slow to recover.[24]

The next Hill to leave Monticello was Edward, who relocated to LaGrange, the seat of Troup County about a year after the great fire. LaGrange stood in the rapidly expanding cotton-growing region of west Georgia, and the railroad was on its way. By 1860 Troup had become the fourth wealthiest county in the state. Soon Edward again became a Superior Court judge and stood as one of his new community's most prominent citizens.[25]

Joshua remained in Monticello for a few more years, and in May 1847 he was admitted to practice in the Georgia Supreme Court. That same month Hill laid his personal credibility on the line by submitting to the *Augusta Sentinel* his colorful description of a severe hailstorm that wreaked havoc along the Ocmulgee River west of town: "Were you not well acquainted with me," Hill wrote,

> I should hesitate in my brief account for fear of not being believed.... The hail fell as large as goose eggs, and in quantities incredible to relate.... The houses appear as if they had been assailed by an army of Davids, and each man throwing his stone as if aimed at a giant. Such a disaster as this was never before witnessed by the oldest inhabitant.

In the nineteenth-century version of a story going viral, dozens of newspapers around the state and country reprinted Hill's vivid account. The standard history of Jasper County confirms the essence of Hill's

---

[24] *Augusta Chronicle*, October 25, 1843; Jasper County Historical Foundation, *History of Jasper County*, 8, 44.

[25] Edward Y. Hill vertical file, Troup County Archives, LaGrange, GA; F. C. Johnson, "LaGrange, GA"; S. Storey, "Railroads"; Knight, *Georgia's Landmarks*, 2:810.

observations by quoting additional reports that "stones were as big as a man's fist" resulting in great losses in the area's cotton crop, stock, and timber.[26]

The new railroads that were built from Savannah and Augusta toward Atlanta bypassed Monticello. Jasper and Butts County boosters, including Joshua Hill, realized that they needed road improvements to obtain quicker access to the nearest railroad towns, so they appealed for federal help to improve and extend the Seven Islands Road mail route westward to provide a better connection with the Macon & Western Railroad at Griffin. The 1848 petition, with Hill among the signatories, ended up in a congressional committee that included Illinois representative Abraham Lincoln.[27]

Even as he was signing the petition that found its way to the desk of the future president, Joshua and Emily Hill were apparently already contemplating relocation from Monticello. Apparently the combination of fire, hail, railroad snub, and the departures of the older Hill brothers convinced them that their prospects would be better in Madison about twenty-five miles northeast. Hill's association with Madison went back as far as 1836 when he and Emily obtained their marriage license at the Morgan County courthouse. Over the ensuing years, he occasionally conducted legal work in the county, and it is certain that he had developed a collection of influential local contacts. The decision to move paid off handsomely. Within ten years of his move, Hill had transformed from being a rising young lawyer in a backwater town to being a wealthy and well-connected member of the United States Congress.

The railroad town of Madison where the Hill's would soon settle was, according to the George White's *Statistics of the State of Georgia,* "the wealthiest and most aristocratic village on the stage-coach route between Charleston and New Orleans." The village had come a long way since the early 1830s when Alexander H. Stephens obtained his first job as a teacher

---

[26] *Augusta Sentinel* quoted in *Charleston (SC) Courier*, June 4, 1847; Jasper County Historical Foundation, *History of Jasper County*, 97; *Augusta Constitutionalist*, May 13, 1847.

[27] "Petition by H. P. Kirkpatrick and others" to House Committee on Post Roads, Records of the US House of Representatives, Petitions and Memorials 1847–1848, National Archives, RG 233, Entry 367; Copy at the Abraham Lincoln Presidential Library, Springfield, IL.

at an academy in Madison. The future vice president of the Confederacy later wrote that those few months were the "most miserable" of his life, and Stephens's standard biographer concluded that the ambitious young man soon discovered "that Madison offered nothing approaching the intellectual stimulation of Athens."[28]

Around 1848 or 1849, Joshua and Emily moved to Madison and purchased a house nestled amongst the in-town homes of the county's planters, merchants, and lawyers. It stood on the corner of a tract that had earlier functioned as the militia mustering grounds and a sometime racetrack. The recently completed Georgia Railroad ran just a few hundred yards to the northwest, and the new courthouse in Madison's downtown square lay about a half mile northeast. The exact configuration of the Hill's house at the time they moved in is not known. The best interpretation of the preservation architect and the restoration contractor who worked together on an extensive renovation and enlargement in the early twenty-first century is that the original structure was a two-over-two "I-house" erected about 1842. There may have been a shed-roof addition on the rear. Outbuildings included Hill's law office, a small cotton warehouse, and various other dependencies. Indications are that the Hills later enlarged the house to a four-over-four configuration.[29]

A historical marker at the corner of Hill Street and South Main tells about Joshua Hill and directs tourists to his home, but they won't see the house as it looked in Hill's time. What one sees today is a much-enlarged structure with a neo-Classical revival façade added around 1915. Fortunately, the Madison National Register Historic District contains several considerably less modified houses from the antebellum era that provide better current visual examples of the kind of home place where Hill practiced law, managed his plantation properties, and raised his family. During the cotton boom of the 1850s, several expansive new houses were built in the neighborhood, and some older homes were enlarged and remodeled.

---

[28] White, *Statistics of the State of Georgia*, 435; Schott, *Alexander H. Stephens*, 18; Avary, *Recollections of Alexander H. Stephens*, 10; Knight, *Georgia's Landmarks*, 2:884–85; Mitchell, *Madison*, 23–26. The structure at 530 Academy St. is built partially on the foundations of the academy where Stephens taught.

[29] Typescript of interviews with Steve Huggins (former owner who restored the home); Joe Smith (restoration architect), and Curtis Whitzel (contractor) in the Hill house file at MCA and author's several conversations with all three.

Greek revival architecture predominated, but the then-stylish Italianate treatment was also often featured in both new construction and remodeling.[30]

Although he relocated to Morgan County, Hill did not abandon his previous clients and connections. An 1849 notice in the *Augusta Chronicle* announced Joshua Hill "Attorney at Law, Madison & Monticello" and promised that citizens of Morgan and Jasper counties "and those contiguous will receive prompt attention." In one 1851 instance, that prompt attention led to a fracas. The city marshal charged Hill and fellow planter William O. Saffold with engaging in an "affray." Both men, apparently contrite, entered pleas of guilty and paid their respective fines. One of the commissioners who fined the scufflers was Augustus Reese, who would sit next to Hill at the state constitutional convention a quarter-century later.[31]

At the time that the Hills moved to town, White's *Statistics* estimated Madison's population at "about 1,200" and declared, "In point of intelligence, refinement, and hospitality, this town acknowledges no superior." The Presbyterian (1842), Methodist (1844), and Baptist (1858) congregations erected sturdy masonry buildings that stand today only slightly modified. One of the two buildings of the Madison Female College, which was incorporated in 1851 and where the Hill's oldest daughter later attended, is now a residence just a couple of hundred yards from the Hill home. The prospectus for the new institution declared that "Madison is synonymous with wealth, refinement, and morality." Several small male academies and another female institution, also very near the Hill house, operated during this time, making Madison an important educational center for the sons and daughters of the lower Piedmont's gentry.[32]

The prosperity that Joshua Hill and his neighbors enjoyed was acquired mainly at the expense of the less affluent Whites who left the county and the enslaved workers who replaced them. As of 1850, the thirty-eight-year-old Hill owned significant agricultural property in Morgan County in addition to the land that he retained in Jasper County. On

---

30 Mitchell, *Madison*, 31, 70–40. See also Symmes and Hammett, *Madison, Georgia: An Architectural Guide.*

31 *Augusta Chronicle*, November 14, 1849; B. Harris, *Minutes of the Board of Commissioners*, Meeting of July 17, 1851.

32 White, *Statistics*, 435; Mitchell, *Madison*, 21–28.

those properties, Hill held thirty-two slaves. Eight years later, his enslaved workforce had nearly doubled to fifty-nine.[33]

Hill's acquisitions and Morgan County reflected a pattern typical of nearby cotton belt counties in the lower Piedmont. Morgan County's White population reached an early peak in 1820 and then entered a steady proportional decline over the next forty years as successful planters consolidated productive land into larger holdings while the percentage of the population's enslaved steadily increased. The Panic of 1837 accelerated the trend by making it even more difficult for undercapitalized marginal landowners to hold on to their property. Most displaced White farm families moved westward, many of them into the recently opened Cherokee country in Northwest Georgia. During the decade of the 1840s, when the railroad and the Hills arrived, the White population of Morgan County declined by five hundred while number of enslaved people increased by thirteen hundred, reaching 62 percent of the total by 1850. In that year Morgan County contained about thirty-eight hundred *fewer* Whites and over a thousand *more* slaves than it had counted three decades before. Meanwhile, the population of Georgia as a whole increased substantially with 58 percent White and 42 percent Black, all but a tiny number of whom were enslaved. The process accelerated in the 1850s such that by the time that the Civil War began, more than two-thirds of Morgan County's population was composed of enslaved Black people.[34]

Joshua Hill became one of the biggest boosters of his new hometown. By the mid-1850s Morgan County had thirty-one manufacturing establishments. Among the most notable was the Madison Steam Mill Company, which produced fabrics and rope at its factory along the railroad tracks on the west side of the city, not far from the Hill's house. On the northern edge of the county, the High Shoals Factory spun yarn. To the south, Winships Cotton Gin Factory employed twenty workers, producing what a testimonial described as "the best gin I've ever used." Local boosters sought even more businesses, so in 1854 they appointed a delegation including Joshua Hill, Nathaniel G. Foster, and other businessmen to attend a convention in Charleston, South Carolina. Hill was one of the founding directors of the Bank of Madison in 1856. In the same year, he joined other

---

[33] Knight, *Georgia's Landmarks*, 2:885; Allen, "For Union and Slavery," 102.

[34] Mitchell, *Madison*, 40–47; Merritt, *Masterless Men*, 29, 45–52, 341–48.

investors to incorporate the Madison Town Hall Company to engage in the "legitimate business of building and improving property for the purpose of renting same." The company built a large wooden building on the west side of Main Street just south of the square. Until destroyed in the fire of 1869, it housed offices for the municipal government and several professional men. Madison had one railroad, and its planters and businessmen coveted another one. Joshua Hill chaired an 1857 meeting that unsuccessfully urged the Georgia Railroad to extend a spur from Madison to Eatonton some twenty miles south. For over four decades from the late 1840s until his death in 1891, the identities and fortunes of Joshua Hill and his adopted hometown remained inextricably intertwined.[35]

The Demise of the Whigs

Joshua Hill carried his Whig political affiliation from Jasper County to his new home in Morgan. He expanded his role in the party until its disintegration forced him to find a new vehicle to continue his battle against the Democrats. In short, the tensions between Northern and Southern Whigs over the potential spread of slavery to the west bedeviled the party from its beginning. The course of events after the Compromise of 1850 combined finally to destroy the party.

Division within the Whigs became especially evident at the 1848 national convention where both Joshua's brother Edward Hill and his Madison associate Nathan G. Foster were delegates. Northern Whig support for the congressional proposal known as the Wilmot Proviso appalled Georgia Whigs because it proposed to bar slavery from the territory obtained as a result of the Mexican War. So desperate were the Whigs for a winner that they passed over Winfield Scott and their beloved Henry Clay in favor of war hero Zachery Taylor, a slaveholder from a Kentucky plantation family. The gambit worked. Taylor carried Georgia and the nation.

---

[35] *Augusta Chronicle*, February 2, 1848 (Winship); White, *Historical Collections of Georgia*, 555–56; *Madison Family Visitor* reprinted in the *Augusta Chronicle*, April 9, 1854; *Acts of the General Assembly of Georgia, 1855–56*, 84, 424. No connection to the current Bank of Madison; *Augusta Daily Constitutionalist*, May 7, 1857; *Savannah Morning News*, May 8, 1857.

The state also snagged a plum when Taylor selected Georgia's former Whig Governor George W. Crawford to sit in his cabinet.[36]

Despite the national victory in 1848, none of Georgia's best-known Whigs sought to run for governor against the popular Democratic incumbent in 1849. As a consequence, the party nomination went to Joshua Hill's older brother, Judge Edward Y. Hill of LaGrange. A long-time Whig loyalist with experience in the legislature and on the bench, Edward Hill was a credible but not stellar choice. Because both Georgia parties vociferously opposed the Wilmot Proviso and there were no burning state matters, little remained to argue about. There was enough residual Whig sentiment to keep the election close, but Judge Hill went down to defeat.[37]

By 1850, struggle over the potential extension of slavery into the western territories had festered to the point that rumbles of disunion began to accelerate. Seeking to avert an imminent crisis, Kentucky's Whig senator Henry Clay offered a compromise package of bills he hoped would appease both sides. It stalled at first, but several factors came together in the late summer to break the logjam. President Taylor died in July and was replaced by Vice President Millard Fillmore, who supported Clay's legislation. On the Democratic side, Illinois senator Stephen A. Douglass led the pro-compromise faction, and Howell Cobb, the Georgian who was Speaker of the House, decided to move from what one historian called "judicious silence" to cautious support. With that momentum, the Compromise became law in September 1850.[38]

In Georgia, most Georgia Whigs and many moderate Democrats forged a bipartisan alliance in support of the Compromise of 1850 under the eventual name Constitution Union Party. Opponents called themselves Southern Rights Democrats or the Resistance. The most vociferous of the resisters who leaned toward immediate secession became known as "fire eaters." In December 1850, a convention dominated by the Union group

---

[36] Murray, *Whig Party in Georgia*, 142–48; Carey, *Parties, Slavery, and the Union*, 100–10.

[37] *Charleston (SC) Courier*, June 29, 1849; *Tallahassee Floridian & Journal*, June 30, 1849; *Columbus Enquirer*, July 12, 1849 (*Savannah Republican*); *Savannah Republican*, August 21, 1849; Carey, *Parties, Slavery, and the Union*, 158; Murray, *Whig Party in Georgia*, 142–43; Miller, *Bench and Bar of Georgia*, 2:330, 376; Cook, *Governors of Georgia*, 123–24.

[38] Hubbell, "Three Georgia Unionists," 316–18.

adopted the influential Georgia Platform. The manifesto endorsed the Compromise of 1850 but included a key caveat declaring that the state's continued allegiance to the Union was dependent on Congress strictly enforcing the Fugitive Slave Act and refraining from restricting existing slavery. Thus, even the ostensibly pro-union Georgia Platform contained an ominous undertone of secession.[39]

The gubernatorial election of 1851 proved a test of the new political landscape in Georgia. The Southern Rights Party nominated a fire-eater while the Constitution Union Party (no direct connection with the later 1860 national party of the same name) nominated Howell Cobb as its standard bearer. Cobb warned that voting for a fire-eater could lead to war, and he was elected with nearly 60 percent of the vote. The Constitutional Union Party also won control of the legislature and sent Robert Toombs to the US Senate. Voter analysis shows that the Constitutional Union victory depended on overwhelming support from the Black Belt Whig counties such as Morgan. Despite the nascent party's bipartisan origin, Democrats like Cobb dominated the coalition, and the same was true in other states that formed fleeting coalitions in support of the Compromise of 1850. In an attempt to keep Whigs mollified, sixteen men from around the state, including Joshua Hill, were listed as "Senior Managers" for Governor Cobb's inauguration ball.[40]

The temporary Constitutional Union truce between Georgia Whigs and moderate Democrats quickly dissolved over the presidential election of 1852. Governor Cobb and most of the Constitutional Union leadership ended up in an alliance with the bulk of their previous Southern Rights rivals to support Democrat Franklin Pierce. Meanwhile, loyal Georgia Whigs like Joshua Hill, who refused to be subsumed within the Democrat-dominated Constitutional Union coalition, rallied to the candidacy of incumbent Millard Fillmore and the national Whig party. One of several Whig meetings around the state was in Madison, where future Congressmen Hill and Nathaniel G. Foster helped draft a resolution that endorsed Fillmore and declared, "We regard the series of laws known as the

[39] Ibid.; Murray, *Whig Party in Georgia*, 154–65; Carey, *Parties, Slavery, and the Union*, 169–73.

[40] Allen, "For Union and Slavery," *passim*–50; *Milledgeville Southern Recorder*, October 21, 1851; *Milledgeville Federal Union*, October 28, 1851; Varon, *Disunion*.

Compromise Measures as a *final* settlement...and that we will not support any candidate for the Presidency or Vice-President who does not deem such acts as *final* in all respects."[41]

In June, the Whig state convention selected about thirty delegates, including Joshua Hill, to go to the national convention solidly in support of Millard Fillmore. Pro-Fillmore Georgians like Hill were disappointed by the nomination of Gen. Winfield Scott, but they were generally pleased that the platform promised enforcement of the Compromise of 1850. The Whigs of Morgan County endorsed Scott and passed a resolution affirming that the Whig national convention had "responded manfully to all that the South asked of them." On the other hand, some Georgia Whigs refused to support Scott, so the two rival Whig factions held separate conventions. The regular party stuck with Scott while the independents put forth a ticket supporting perennial Whig Daniel Webster at the top with Georgian Charles Jenkins as the vice-presidential nominee. The two-convention Whig imbroglio split the Hill brothers. Joshua and John backed Scott, but Edward sided with the independents and was slated as an elector for the Webster ticket.[42]

Thus, in fall 1852, Georgia voters had the choice of four tickets: two Democratic tickets both supporting Franklin Pierce, one official Whig ticket endorsing Scott, and one independent Whig ticket backing Webster. In a low turnout, Georgia Democrats swept the day with the combined Pierce tickets winning about 65 percent of the vote. Nationally, the overwhelming election of Pierce and the humiliating defeat of General Scott, who carried only four states, led to the death of the Whigs.[43]

There was a final effort to revive the Whigs during Georgia's 1853 gubernatorial election. Some rallies around the state, like the one in

---

[41] *Cassville Standard*, October 21, 1852; Carey, *Parties, Slavery, and the Union*, 170–79; *Augusta Chronicle*, June 8, 1852 (We regard, italics original); *(Macon) Georgia Journal & Messenger*, June 16, 1852.

[42] *Milledgeville Southern Recorder*, June 8, 1852; *Baltimore Daily Advertiser*, June 15, 1852; *Augusta Chronicle*, June 10, August 21, 1852; *Savannah Republican*, June 10, 1852; *(Macon) Georgia Citizen*, June 12, 1852; *(Athens) Southern Banner*, June 17, 1852; *South-West Georgian* (Oglethorpe) June 11, 1852; *(Macon) Georgia Citizen* August 14, 1852.

[43] Carey, *Parties, Slavery, and the Union*, 176–80; Murray, *Whig Party in Georgia*, 166–68.

Morgan County where Hill spoke, continued to embrace the name Whig, but in most of Georgia, the Monikers Union or Conservative Union prevailed amongst the anti-Democrats. The re-unified Democrats nominated Herschel V. Johnson, who somewhat tempered his fire-eater rhetoric. Despite disarray among Whig-leaning leaders, the final count for governor was extremely close. Nevertheless, Democrats held on to the governorship, captured control of the General Assembly, and elected six of eight congressmen. The only Whig or "Union" House of Representatives winners were David A. Reese of Jasper County and the ever-popular Alexander Stephens, both of whom represented long-time cotton-belt Whig strongholds. The Whigs did not even make an effort in the following year's gubernatorial race.[44]

Georgia's Whig organization was now fully moribund, and with it died the first phase of Joshua Hill's political involvement. In the political disarray of the 1850s, Joshua Hill and men like him would have to look elsewhere for a party home, and he never found one where he was entirely comfortable. Through it all, he held to three constants: an unwavering commitment to the American union, a fundamentally conservative mindset that remained open to moderate change, and a refusal to join the Democratic Party even when it would have benefitted his political career to do so. He had exhibited Whiggish inclinations well before there was a political party of that name, and he would cling to Whig principles long after the party broke apart on sectional shoals.

---

[44] *Milledgeville Southern Recorder*, June 14, 28, 1853; *Augusta Weekly Chronicle & Sentinel*, June 9, 15, 1853; Murray, *Whig Party in Georgia*, 170–76; Carey, *Parties, Slavery, and the Union*, 179–83; DeBats, *Elites and Masses*, 110.

Chapter 2

Georgia Lawyer in the United States Congress, 1857–1861

Joshua Hill came of political age during the convoluted period of closely balanced Georgia politics from the early 1830s to early 1850s. The cotton plantation belt of the lower Piedmont formed the heart of support for the Whigs and their predecessors. Joshua Hill personified this profile of conservative Whiggish lawyer and plantation owner. By the late-1850s, that old order was dead, and the nation was on the cusp of its greatest crisis.

During the last few years before the outbreak of the Civil War, party alignment in Georgia remained in a period of flux with slavery and related sectional considerations underlying every political issue. From 1854 onward, many party-less Whigs had great difficulty finding a suitable place to land. Some became Democrats; some stayed unaffiliated, and some, including Joshua Hill, found an uneasy home in a national party that did not quite align with their Southern perspective. The politics of Georgia's Seventh District illustrated the challenge. The district included eleven counties stretching from just north of the fall line to the foothills of the Blue Ridge Mountains. Madison stood roughly in the middle. In nine of the counties, including Morgan, enslaved African Americans constituted a majority of the population. The other two lay at the northern end of the district where smaller farms with few, if any, slaves predominated. In 1857, this became the district of United States House of Representatives member Joshua Hill.[1]

---

[1] Murray, *Whig Party in Georgia*, 203, *passim*; DeBats, *Elites and Masses*, 110–11, 339.

From Whig to Know-Nothing

Most Morgan County Whigs, including Joshua Hill and his mentor Nathaniel G. Foster, ended up in the American Party, better known as the Know-Nothings. At the national level, opposition to mass European immigration, especially by Roman Catholics, was a principal driver of the Know-Nothing movement. The organization began in the 1840s as a loose collection of secret societies, but by the mid-1850s it had morphed into a full-fledged political party under the official name American. Even though relatively few of the immigrants of the 1840s and 1850s actually settled in the South, the region's Know-Nothings were nevertheless wary of increased Catholic immigration because it meant that there would be more antislavery voters in Northern states. For the most part, however, the American Party existed in Georgia and other slave states mainly as a vehicle for former Whigs to have some semblance of an organization to challenge the Democrats. The Americans, like the Whigs before them, hoped to preserve the Union by keeping discussion of slavery out of political discourse. The passage of the Kansas-Nebraska Act in 1854, however, made it nearly impossible to ignore the issue of the potential expansion of slavery to the west.[2]

In 1855 the Know-Nothings nominated Nathaniel G. Foster (1809–1869) for Congress from Georgia's Seventh District. A prominent Madison attorney and part-time preacher whose home stood near Joshua Hill's, Foster had been, in sequence, a Democrat, a Whig, and a Constitutional Unionist before affiliating with the American Party. He worked for three years as solicitor general for the Ocmulgee Circuit court, served five years in the Georgia General Assembly, and stood as a Whig elector for General Winfield Scott in 1852. Foster was a close political ally of Judge Francis Hiram Cone of nearby Greensboro, who was the founder of the Know-Nothing movement in Georgia.[3]

Foster's Democratic opponent was Linton Stephens, half-brother of Alexander Stephens. The Stephens brothers and many others who had

---

[2] Allen, "For Union and Slavery," 18–24, 56–60, 121.

[3] "N. G. Foster," *Congressional Directory*, 1856, and Foster file (#928), Hargrett Rare Books and Manuscript Library, University of Georgia, Athens (hereafter HRBML); Candler and Evans, *Georgia*, 2:73 (commonly *Cyclopedia of Georgia*).

supported the unofficial splinter Whig ticket in the 1852 presidential race soon abandoned all semblance of Whig affiliation and joined the Democratic camp. Alexander was something of a father figure to Linton; when the younger man came of age, he followed his brother into law and politics. He became an attorney in Sparta and represented Hancock County in the state senate starting in 1853. Linton Stephens realized that the race against Foster would be tight even with his high name recognition. He advised his brother, "The Know-Nothings are a great power in the State just now—greater than you may have imagined."[4]

Foster's standard stump speech argued that voters should embrace the new American Party because both the Whigs and the Democrats had become corrupt and unworthy. At one event, Joshua Hill stood in for Foster where he "labored hard and ably to sustain the 'Know-Nothing' cause." Both candidates professed to support the Georgia Platform, which cautiously endorsed the Compromise of 1850, but Stephens went even further by emphasizing the thinly veiled threat of secession embedded in the platform's fourth resolution. The fact that the Know-Nothing platform contained no such explicit pro-Southern ultimatum became his "fighting line."[5]

Joseph Addison Turner, who would soon become the publisher of the *Countryman* and the mentor of author Joel Chandler Harris, responded to Foster by charging that the Know-Nothings were more loyal to the Union than to the South because their national platform made preservation of the Union "paramount even to the existence of slavery." Despite such attacks, Foster narrowly prevailed against Stephens in the seventh, and a Know-Nothing also won in the Third District. Indicative of the trend to come, Democrats carried the rest of the state.[6]

Even in face of their state-wide weakness, the American Party did not yet go away. As the presidential election of 1856 approached, Linton cautioned Alexander, "The Know-Nothings here look chap-fallen, but they intend to fight." The Democrats nominated James Buchanan while the emerging Republican Party selected John C. Freemont. Unwilling to

---

[4] Waddell, *Biographical Sketch of Linton Stephens*, 106–16.

[5] Ibid.; *Columbus Times & Sentinel*, June 27, 1855; *Milledgeville Federal Union*, August 7, 1855.

[6] Waddell, *Biographical Sketch of Linton Stephens*, 124.

support either of the major candidates, the Americans united behind former president Millard Fillmore, who had expressed concerns about the baleful impact of immigrant votes. Joshua Hill chaired the regional American Party meeting in Morgan County where he gave "an eloquent and impressive speech." Both he and his brother Edward were delegates to the state convention in Macon. As a reward for his efforts, the younger Hill was slated as an alternate elector on the Fillmore ticket. The increasing strain between Georgia Americans and the national party was reflected in the fact that Georgia declined to send delegates to the party's national convention. Convinced that Fillmore could not win, some Know-Nothings deserted the party altogether. As expected, Buchanan easily carried Georgia and all the slave states except Maryland. Excepting a few persistently Whiggish areas like the Seventh and Third Districts, Georgia had effectively become a one-party Democratic state. One Democratic paper's sarcastic "obituary" for the Know-Nothings listed Joshua and Edward Hill among the "mourning committee."[7]

As the 1857 congressional election loomed, rumors circulated that Representative Foster would decline to seek renomination or that the American Party would not nominate him. Some loyal party members were upset because Foster had acquiesced in allowing Nathaniel Banks, an antislavery Republican, to become Speaker of the House. A Democratic paper confidently declared, "We say it in no boasting spirit, that we shall defeat Col. Foster in this District if he runs, and if he does not run, we shall beat the man who takes his place." That man would be Joshua Hill, who unanimously won the nomination over D. W. Lewis of Sparta and others. Contrasting the mild-mannered incumbent with the new nominee, a Democratic observer noted, "Josh is said to be the fighting candidate."[8]

---

[7] Linton Stephens to Alexander Stephens, June 18, 1856, in Waddell, *Biographical Sketch of Linton Stephens*, 124–25; *Madison Family Visitor*, July 5, 1856; *Augusta Daily Chronicle*, June 13, July 4, 15, September 30, 1856; *(Macon) Georgia Journal & Messenger*, July 9, 1856; *(Athens) Southern Watchman*, July 17, 1856; *Griffin Empire State*, October 15, 1856 (obit); Allen, "For Union and Slavery," 75–89; Murray, *Whig Party in Georgia*, 200; DeBats, *Elites and Masses*, 222; Carey, *Parties, Slavery, and the Union*, 203–204; Varon, *Disunion*, 287.

[8] *Sandersville Central Georgian*, April 30, May 7, 1857; *Milledgeville Federal Union*, April 14, May 12, June 16 (we say) April 28, July 28 (Josh), August 4, 1957; *(Macon) Georgia Journal & Messenger*, June 10, 1857 (in fact).

Candidate Hill had paid his dues in the Whig trenches for years, and he stuck with the Americans even after many other Whigs had fled to the Democrats. A Whiggish newspaper in Athens commented, "It is hardly necessary for us to say anything in praise of the American nominee—Col. Hill—for Congress from this District, as he is generally well and favorably known to the people.... We regret to part with Col. F. as our representative, but compelled to do so, we rejoice to have so able a successor." In his letter of acceptance, Hill claimed that he had not sought the nomination and that, in deciding whether to accept the call, he had wavered "between private interest, personal preference, and family wishes, on the one side, and the entreaties of friends, backed by arguments and appeals addressed to my patriotism and devotion to my party" on the other. In the end, he yielded to the "earnest and unceasing" pleadings of the party. The letter reflected a tension between Hill's personal interests and his political ambitions, which would remain with him throughout his career. In this case, it is inconceivable that Hill would have sought to oppose Foster unless his close friend and political ally had personally given him the green light. A Sandersville paper stated as much: "We are informed by a gentleman who has seen him that the Colonel [Foster] is pleased at the nomination of his townsman, and intends to help him canvass the District." Foster did help during Hill's campaign, and the warm relationship between the two men and their families continued for many years.[9]

Meanwhile, Linton Stephens had been equivocating about whether to run again to avenge his 1855 defeat. On the Fourth of July, he wrote Alexander, "I don't know what I shall do yet. I intend, however, to wait and see what the Know-Nothing concern may do next week, and then decide on my course." Once he knew that he would face Hill rather than the incumbent, the younger Stephens quickly accepted the Democratic nomination. A Milledgeville Democrat expressed the essence of his party's position: "How can the case be bettered by sending Mr. Joshua Hill to do the

---

[9] *Athens Southern Recorder*, July 14, 1857 (it is); *Augusta Constitutionalist*, July 11, 1857; *Athens Southern Watchman*, July 16, August 13, 1857; *Southern Recorder*, July 14, 1857 (we are); *Sandersville Central Georgian*, July 15, September 10, 1857.

very same things Mr. Foster has done?" Would not it be "the wiser course" to elect Linton Stephens instead?[10]

Joshua Hill was not the best-known man named Hill to carry the American/Know-Nothing Party banner in fall 1857. The fast-rising thirty-four-year-old Benjamin Hill snagged the gubernatorial nomination. He was no relation to the South Carolina-born Hill brothers, but he was a fellow townsman of Edward Hill in LaGrange. Like most other Know-Nothings, Ben Hill had previously been part of the Constitutional Union Party. However, unlike well-established leaders such as Howell Cobb, Robert Toombs, and Alexander Stephens, when the short-lived Constitutional Union coalition broke apart, Ben Hill joined the American/Know-Nothing camp rather than the Democrats. The LaGrange orator came to prominence in a highly-publicized series of debates in fall 1856 during which he made the case for Fillmore. The volatile Alexander Stephens challenged him to a duel, but Ben Hill wisely declined. In the governor's race, Ben Hill faced Joseph E. Brown of Northwest Georgia. Linton Stephens's assistance was key to Brown's nomination. Linton explained to Alexander that Brown was "a very effective stump-speaker" who "stands high in the upcountry." The Stephens brothers probably hoped that having such a vigorous campaigner heading the Democratic ticket would help their respective congressional campaigns.[11]

The 1857 campaign raged in the months just after the Supreme Court's infamous Dred Scott decision protected slavery and declared the Black people could not be considered citizens of the United States. The ruling did not, however, resolve the pending issue of whether Kansas would become a slave state or a free one. During the campaign, Josh Hill and Stephens refrained from personal attacks on each other and concentrated

---

[10] L. Stephens to A. H. Stephens, July 4, 1857, in Waddell, *Biographical Sketch of Linton Stephens*, 127; *Milledgeville Federal Union*, July 21, August 11, 18 (How can), 1857; *Savannah Republican*, July 16, 1857; *Columbus Enquirer*, September 29, 1857; *New Orleans Times-Picayune*, July 14, 1857; Allen, "For Union and Slavery," 95.

[11] Parks, *Joseph E. Brown*, 22–32; Montgomery, *Cracker Parties*, 193–96; Carey, *Parties, Slavery, and the Union*, 207–208; Schott, *Alexander H. Stephens* **[page?]**; Allen, "For Union and Slavery," 87–94; L. Stephens to A. H. Stephens, June 29, 1857, in Waddell, *Biographical Sketch of Linton Stephens*, 127; *Milledgeville Federal Union*, August 18, 1857.

on national issues. For example, a writer from the state capital observed, "Col. Hill has an easy and a pleasant address," but he covered "pretty much the old [Know-Nothing] track—opposition to foreigners and great anxiety for the fate of Kansas." Regarding Kansas, the American Party position advocated by both Ben and Josh Hill reflected the old Whig philosophy that slavery agitation should be avoided and that Kansas would inevitably become a free state regardless of what happened in the short run. In contrast, Linton Stephens was principal drafter of the Kansas section of the Georgia Democratic platform, which demanded that Congress guarantee the opportunity for Kansas to become a slave state. The *Milledgeville Federal Union* sneered that Georgia might "as well put a wolf to watch the shepherd's rights in his flock as to put Ben Hill in the Executive Chair or Joshua Hill in Congress to watch the South's rights in Kansas." An American Party–leaning newspaper summarized the contrary view by declaring, "It is our deliberate judgement that no sounder and safer man will be sent from the South to Congress than Joshua Hill."[12]

The highly popular Alexander Stephens promised to help Linton against Madison's Joshua Hill, but for most of the campaign, his influence was limited to just a few visits while he took care of his own heated race in the adjoining district to the east. A buggy accident involving the Stephens brothers temporarily changed the campaign dynamic. Both men were injured, but only Linton suffered badly enough to have to cancel personal appearances. Alexander promised to stand in for his brother when he could. Following one heated debate between the former political allies, the Democratic *Weekly Telegraph* of Macon proclaimed that Stephens "literally wore Josh into a frazzle—tore him all to pieces, and there was not enough of the portly, dignified and gentlemanly candidate of the opposition left to make a grease spot." Acknowledging that "Mr. Hill is a gentleman of courteous manners, fair abilities, and high character," the Democrat asserted that "he must, and should have known, that his opponent was an intellectual Colossus." It can be presumed that pro-American listeners held a more

---

[12] *Macon Weekly Telegraph*, July 15, 1856; *Savannah Republican*, July 4, 11, 14, 1856; *Milledgeville Federal Union*, September 27, 29, 1857; *Sandersville Central Georgian*, September 24, 1857 (It is); Allen, "For Union and Slavery," 78–95.

sanguine opinion of Hill's performance, but they lacked a biased local newspaper to report it.[13]

Democrats were cautiously optimistic but not entirely confident that the younger Stephens would prevail. Early in the year, Howell Cobb, the former Georgia governor and Speaker of the House, now treasury secretary, expressed his worry in a letter to Alexander Stephens. However, by September, Cobb was more optimistic, expressing that he was "much gratified" to learn of the "brightening prospects in our election. I do hope and trust that Linton will carry his district.... From what I hear of Josh Hill's position [Linton] will be able to do it. I understand that Hill openly denounces the Kansas bill." When the votes came in, Cobb's optimism turned out to be close but wrong about Joshua Hill. The Madisonian won by a scant 175 votes (4,800 to 4,625), a similarly narrow margin to Foster's of two years earlier. Democrats obtained decisive control of both houses of the Georgia General Assembly, and Brown easily bested Ben Hill for governor. The congressional victories of Joshua Hill in the Seventh District and incumbent Robert Trippe in the Third were the only bright spots for the American Party in face of the Democratic landslide of 1857.[14]

Freshman Congressman

Joshua Hill arrived in the nation's capital, then often referred to as Washington City, in December 1857 and proudly took his seat in the 35th Congress. This session was the first to have the honor of meeting in the new House of Representatives chamber in the southern wing of the United States Capitol extension. (The old chamber is now Statuary Hall.) Unlike Nathaniel Foster, Hill had no experience serving in a state legislature to help him understand intricate legislative procedures and norms, but he was a quick learner. He combined his experience as an attorney with the advice

[13] Schott, *Alexander H. Stephens*, 234–37; *Milledgeville Federal Union*, September 29, 1857; *Macon Weekly Telegraph*, October 5, 1857.

[14] Cobb to Stephens, September 3, 1857, in Phillips, *Correspondence*, 408; Cobb to John B. Lamar, July 10, 1857, in Brooks, "Howell Cobb Papers"; *Milledgeville Southern Banner*, October 15, 1857; *New York Times*, October 7, 1857; *Washington (DC) States*, October 10, 1857; *Milledgeville Federal Union*, October 20, 1857; Allen, "For Union and Slavery," 89–90; Schott, *Alexander H. Stephens*, 237–38; Carey, *Parties, Slavery, and the Union*, 209–10.

of his colleagues to become skilled at parliamentary maneuvers and legislative customs.

As Know-Nothings in a sea of Democrats and Republicans, Hill and Trippe were part of a tiny minority. One of the arguments that Democrats had used against Hill during the 1857 campaign was that the dying Know-Nothings "will have no more weight in Congress, than so many men of straw." And they were correct—only fourteen members of the American Party remained in the House, all from slave states. In the previous Congress when Foster served, there had been fifty-two Americans, a majority of whom had been Northerners and most of whom, including Foster, had voted with Republicans to organize the House. Now all but a handful were gone, and Democrats had regained control with 132 members to the Republican's ninety. Democrats also controlled the Senate.[15]

As a freshman aligned with a fringe party, Hill found himself on the relatively unimportant Committee on Public Lands. He had little time to learn the ropes before the great controversy of the day presented itself—the admission of Kansas as a slave state or free. The issue had been front and center since the 1854 debates over the Kansas-Nebraska Act, which Hill had roundly criticized while campaigning. Objectively, it was widely acknowledged that a heavy majority of the bona fide settlers of Kansas held antislavery views. However, a combination of political maneuvering by the Democrat-appointed territorial governor, election fraud by proslavery forces, and electoral boycotts by antislavery citizens had paved the way in fall 1857 for Kansas territory to submit the proslavery Lecompton Constitution to Congress for its approval. For Southern Democrats, favoring the Lecompton document and thus the admission of Kansas as a slave state became the *sine qua non* of regional loyalty. In their eyes, anyone who wavered, even on peripheral matters, was a traitor to the cause of the preservation of slavery.[16]

Joshua Hill's very first vote in Congress was on just such a peripheral concern. In December 1857, he dutifully supported fellow Know-Nothing Henry Davis Winter from the border state of Maryland for Speaker. Davis

---

[15] *Journal of the House of Representatives*, 35th Congress, 1st session, 1857, 8–9; *Milledgeville Federal Union*, September 29, 1857.

[16] Freehling, *Road to Disunion*, vol. 2, chapters 6 and 10; M. Woods, *Bleeding Kansas*; Etcheson, *Bleeding Kansas*; D. Potter, *Impending Crisis*.

harbored personal antislavery sentiments and had voted with the so-called "Black Republicans" on some Kansas-related issues. Democrats presented Hill's vote for Davis as an affront to the Deep South. The *Atlanta Intelligencer* called Hill "deluded." The *Federal Union* of Milledgeville called Davis an "open and avowed enemy of the South" and judged Hill guilty by association: "We did not expect so soon after Col. Hill's installation to find fault with him."[17]

Another of Hill's peripheral votes that seemed to depart from Southern orthodoxy led to more attacks. Critics charged that the freshman congressman's vote in the case of a disputed Ohio election had the effect of retaining an "Abolitionist in his seat against the most overwhelming proof that the said Abolitionist was elected by illegal negro votes." It was an exaggeration to call the individual whom Hill supported an "Abolitionist," but in the eyes of most Georgia Democrats, anyone who was not explicitly for protecting slavery was effectively against it. The case was a complicated one, and Hill's vote, which he claimed to be based on the facts of the case, should not reasonably have been interpreted as an endorsement of antislavery views. Such were the passions of the day.[18]

As the Kansas debate intensified, the recently defeated Linton Stephens ruminated to Alexander: "The bonds of my attachment to the Union are powerfully loosened, and if Kansas is rejected, they will be broken." A few days later, he wrote again, indicating that he was highly distressed over the possibility that Hill might not support the Lecompton bill and asking his brother's advice about a draft letter he planned to send to the new congressman. It is not known how Alexander responded or if Linton mailed the missive to Hill, but the private exchange between brothers leaves no doubt that they sensed potential seeds of disunion in the upcoming Kansas vote and that they did not think that Hill would be a strong enough advocate for the Deep South position.[19]

---

[17] *Jackson Mississippian & State Gazette*, March 19, 1858 (*Intelligencer*); *Milledgeville Federal Union*, December 22, 1857.

[18] *Milledgeville Federal Union*, February 22, 1858; *Miscellaneous Documents of the House of Representatives*, 1st Session of the 35th Congress, 1857, vol. 1, no. 29; *Globe* (hereafter, *Globe*), 35th Congress, 1st Session (hereafter 35-1), 657.

[19] L. Stephens to A. Stephens, February 9, 13, 1858, in Waddell, *Biographical Sketch of Linton Stephens*, 138–39.

Meanwhile, Northern Democrats were in the beginning stages of their own fractionalization that would become so evident in the presidential election of 1860. Needing Southern support, President James Buchanan urged his party to endorse the Lecompton Constitution and its proslavery provisions. In contrast, Senator Stephen Douglas of Illinois believed that the fraudulent votes that ushered in the Lecompton convention violated the spirit of his "popular sovereignty" concept. Douglas pulled enough Northern Democrats away from Buchanan to seriously threaten the immediate admission of Kansas. With Georgia's Robert Toombs leading the administration's forces in the Senate and Alexander Stephens doing the same in the House, Georgia Democrats were at the center of the battle.[20]

On March 23, the Lecompton Constitution finally came to the key vote in the Senate where Democrats held a comfortable majority. It passed 33 to 25. The battle then turned to the House of Representatives where the handful of American Party members, including Joshua Hill, held, in the words of the *Milledgeville Federal Union*, "the balance of power between the friends of the Lecompton Constitution, and its enemies the Abolitionists and Free Soilers." The writer claimed that he had heard from "good and responsible sources" that "Joshua Hill will vote with the enemies of the South." The strategy of the American party, like that of the Whigs before, was to avoid direct engagement with the slavery controversy and hope that the acrimony would fade away. The Lecompton vote forced a severe test of that strategy. Even the normally pro-American *Savannah Republican* urged "the few American members from the South" to vote with the Democrats of their region. "We love the Union better than we do Kansas, and more than we hate the democratic party," the editor explained. "We believe the speedy admission of Kansas is the only remedy."[21]

In the end, rumors that Hill would oppose the Lecompton bill turned out to be wrong. Shortly after the Senate vote, Hill addressed the House with an extended explanation of his decision to vote for immediate admission of Kansas as a slave state. Several Georgia papers representing both parties praised the speech, and Hill had it printed and distributed as a

[20] Freehling, *Road to Disunion*, 2:138–39; W. C. Davis, *The Union*, 72–73.

[21] *Milledgeville Federal Union*, March 30, 1858 (the few, *Savannah Republican*).

stand-alone document. Although the Madisonian's decision to support the Lecompton Constitution pleased most White Georgians, some Democrats expressed dissatisfaction with the details of his explanation. Rather than offer a ringing endorsement of slavery's potential advancement to the west, Hill's middle-of-the-road reasoning emphasized technical points. On the one hand, he argued that acceptance of the Lecompton document would affirm the Southern legal argument that Congress could neither limit slavery in the territories nor dictate to new states how their constitutions should read. But, on the other hand, he agreed with the prediction of many observers that even if Kansas were to be admitted as a slave state, it would not stay so very long. Hill's position was not that different from that of Stephens and Toombs except that he avoided lacing it with ringing endorsements of slavery.[22]

In the Whig tradition of deploring all agitation about slavery, Hill's published speech disassociated himself from the angry rhetoric of the fire eaters:

> I will not say to the North, in angry tone and defiant language, "come on and wrest these rights from us, if you dare!" I will not speak of bloody fields and desolated home; such language, in my judgment, will never convince the understanding of any man—certainly not that of a fanatic. It is not the language of a brother, and so long as we live in the Union, we are brothers.

The Georgian ardently defended his future Constitutional Union allies John Crittenden and John Bell from the vitriolic attacks that they suffered from Southern Democrats. Though he had voted differently, Hill reminded his listeners that Critten, Bell, and Douglas had acted upon nothing but "love of country, and devotion to the pacification of the land." Hill was careful to affirm his personal "advocacy of our cherished institution;" but he also strongly declared in the Whig tradition, "Properly speaking, not one word should have been said…that involves the question of slavery. It has been dragged in here most improperly. It is a thing that

---

[22] Joshua Hill, *Speech of Hon. Joshua Hill, of Georgia, on the Admission of Kansas*, 1858, *Globe*, 5–6; *Augusta Daily Constitutionalist*, April 2, 1858 (*National Intelligencer*); *Augusta Chronicle*, April 13, 1858, and *Savannah Daily Republican*, April 15–16, 1858; *Milledgeville Federal Union*, February 23, 1858; W. C. Davis, *The Union*, 70–72.

belonged exclusively to the local community."Toward the conclusion of his lengthy address, Hill gingerly raised the specter that agitation about slavery could lead to secession. He addressed his words directly to House Republicans:

> I implore you to give up and abandon this idea, which is suicidal to the Confederacy [meaning in this context the Union], of restricting the institution of slavery to its present limits.... I have seen exhibited, in the course of this discussion, unerring evidence to my mind, of a general sympathy with strong anti-slavery sentiments—ay, with abolition itself.... I desire the preservation of the Union, [but] It cannot be preserved, in my honest opinion, unless these ultra opinions are surrendered upon the altar of our country.

Georgia Democrats noticed and praised this reference to the possible "dissolution of the Union." Later, as part of his own address on the subject, Robert Trippe, Hill's fellow Georgia American Party representative, told Congress that his colleague's speech "expressed a sentiment which I have privately and publicly expressed on all occasions."[23]

Despite unified support from all Deep South Democrats and the eight Deep South Americans including Joshua Hill, the Lecompton Constitution went down to defeat 120 to 112 on April 1, 1858. The majority coalition included all Republicans plus the Douglas wing of the Democratic party and the six Americans from border states. The result made it clear that the number of Southern friends among Northern Democrats was waning.[24]

Faced with the defeat of the Lecompton Constitution, dispirited Southern Democrats sought a way to claim some semblance of victory in the form of the so-called English Bill. Alexander Stephens was the principal drafter of the legislation, but the wily Georgian knew that his name was toxic in Northern quarters, so the bill took on the name of another sponsor. The English Bill offered a convoluted compromise whereby the

---

[23] Hill, *Speech...on Admission of Kansas*, 7–8; *Globe*, 35-1, 309 (Trippe); *Columbus Times & Sentinel*, April 4, 1848; Etcheson, "'Our lives, our fortunes,'" 73.

[24] Ashworth, *Slavery, Capitalism, and Politics*, 2:540–42; Freehling, *Road to Disunion*, 2:140–42; W. C. Davis, *The Union*, 72–73; Carey, *Parties, Slavery, and the Union*, 210–11.

citizens of Kansas would conduct a vote ostensibly about land grants but, in practice, would have the effect of delaying the time when the territory could finally become a free state. It was a face-saving deal that pro-union Southerners like Stephens could accept but that fire eaters considered a sellout. When the English Bill came to a vote during the first week of May, Joshua Hill was absent. His absence led to charges that he had deliberately avoided being in Washington so that he would not have to go on record either way. In fact, Hill had arranged to pair his probable vote in favor of the English Bill with that of an absent Northerner who planned to oppose the measure. That nuanced action based on parliamentary maneuvers failed to satisfy critics on either side of the issue who demanded more explanation from the congressman. Hill explained that his goal had been "to give peace and quiet to my distracted country" and "to cut loose from the Kansas question." Despite this defense and the fact that the bill effectively ended the long-running Kansas debate, Hill's opponents would not let the matter go. His failure openly to support the English Bill became an issue in his reelection campaign.[25]

The balance of 1858 was politically uneventful for Joshua Hill. Back home he continued to practice law across the region and to acquire more property in Morgan County. He visited Milledgeville during the legislative session and no doubt talked politics in the halls of the capitol and in the taverns of the town. He did little that attracted the attention of the press. Early in 1859, a bill to admit the Territory of Oregon to the union came before the House of Representatives. Although there was never any doubt that Oregon would eventually become a free state, the case raised some of the same issues as Kansas. Hill cast his vote against immediate statehood. He justified his position by stressing the practical consideration that Oregon was peaceful whereas in Kansas people had been "cutting each others throats" and threatening to involve "the entire nation in a civil strife." In

[25] *Augusta Chronicle*, March 4, 1859 (to give); *(Athens) Southern Banner*, May 6, 1858; *Milledgeville Southern Recorder*, May 18, 1858; *Milledgeville Federal Union*, May 11, 1858, July 13, 1858; L. Roberts, "Political Career of Joshua Hill," 53; W. C. Davis, *The Union*, 73–74; Carey, *Parties, Slavery, and the Union*, 212, Etcheson, *Bleeding Kansas*, 179–84; Freehling, *Road to Disunion*, 2:142; Allen, "For Union and Slavery," 105–106; Varon, *Disunion*, 313–14.

the Know-Nothing tradition, Hill also objected to the provision of the proposed Oregon constitution that allowed aliens to vote.[26]

Reelection 1859

By the middle of 1859, it had become painfully obvious that the American Party was in the throes of death. Know-Nothing representation in Congress had already dropped from more than fifty when Nathaniel Foster served to fourteen when Hill entered the House. The division between the upper and lower South revealed by the Lecompton vote assured that the number of avowed Americans would drop even lower if any existed at all. In Hill's Seventh District of Georgia, the shell of the party kept the name "American" for its conventions as late as August 1859, but that was the exception. More and more, the term for Southern politicians who were unwilling to support the Democratic Party had come to be simply the "Opposition." In July there were Opposition meetings in at least seven Georgia counties, including Morgan. The first effort to hold a statewide Opposition convention suffered from very poor attendance, but a second try in Atlanta in August attracted more interest. Sensing the tide, Benjamin H. Hill declined to try again against incumbent governor Joseph E. Brown, so the convention nominated a former Whig lawyer from Brown's neck of the woods.[27]

Joshua Hill's renomination as the American/Opposition candidate in the Seventh faced some resistance from the southern part of the district. Contending that the incumbent had ignored their neck of the woods, a group in Hancock County nominated state legislator A. H. Kenan. Another gathering of Opposition supporters from several counties nominated Hill. Not wanting their split to open the way for Democratic victory, the two men resolved their differences and released an exchange of public letters in which Hill professed a "long standing personal friendship" with Kenan and promised to "conciliate" his supporters. In return Kenan praised Hill's "magnanimity" and resolved to "preserve, inviolate, the unity and integrity of the American party." An editor from the Kenan-leaning end of the district effused, "Two more noble-hearted, generous, high-toned,

---

[26] *Atlanta Intelligencer*, February 18, 1859; *Augusta Chronicle*, March 4, 1859.

[27] Allen, "For Union and Slavery," 107; Ashworth, *Slavery, Capitalism, and Politics*, 2:569–91.

gentlemen never met in a similar manner." He urged "Col. Kenan's friends" to give Hill "full and hearty support."[28]

After two consecutive losses, Linton Stephens chose not to try again, so the Democrats had to find a new candidate to challenge Representative Hill. Robert G. Harper, a Newton County Democrat, gained some prominence by publishing a pamphlet discussing but opposing the revival of the slave trade. No other serious candidates emerged, so in summer 1859, the Democrats settled on Harper. The *Atlanta Weekly Intelligencer* wrote, "Col. Hill is a very clever man *personally*, but *politically*, is highly objectionable, especially to the Democratic party. We expect our friends will make a gallant fight under the lead of Col. Harper and the Banner of Democracy, will be borne in his hand." In his acceptance letter, Harper called for Southern unity against the antislavery forces of the North. Without mentioning Hill by name, he charged that the American Party/Opposition constituted a threat to that unity. Both candidates spoke throughout the district, sometimes in joint appearances. Hill made speeches in Harper's own backyard in Covington and Conyers while Harper did the same in Madison. T. P. Saffold, a long-time acquaintance but political opponent of Joshua Hill, was a leader of the Morgan County Democrats. Without much else to criticize about Hill's first term, Democrats re-hashed the issue of Hill's absence on the English Bill vote. Hill wrote to editors to clarify once again that he had endorsed the convoluted English Bill compromise on Kansas as "the last hope of disposing of a worthless and irritable question." Surprisingly, even Robert Toombs, who endorsed fellow Democrat Harper, came to Hill's defense on his English bill vote.[29]

---

[28] *Macon Daily Georgia Citizen*, September 3, 9 (two more), 1859; *Macon Weekly Telegraph*, August 23, 1859; *Macon Messenger* July 13, 27, 1859; *Columbus Enquirer*, August 6, 23, 1859; *Milledgeville Southern Recorder*, September 6, 1859 (Hill-Kenan); *Columbus Daily Sun*, September 5, 1859; *Augusta Chronicle*, September 4, 1859; DeBats, *Elites and Masses*, 272.

[29] *Milledgeville Federal Union*, November 11, 1858; *Macon Georgia Citizen*, December 24, 1858 (*Augusta Dispatch*, *Augusta Daily Constitutionalist*); *(Macon) Georgia Journal and Messenger*, December 22, 1858; September 7, 1859; *Atlanta Weekly Intelligencer*, August 25 (emphasis original), September 8,1859; *Augusta Constitutionalist*, August 5 (*Madison Visitor*), 19, September 13, 1859; *Macon Weekly Telegraph*, August 23, 1859; *(Athens) Southern Banner*, August 25,

Hill squeaked to reelection by a mere 250 vote margin. As Foster and he had done in 1855 and 1857, Hill squeaked by with strong returns in Morgan, Greene, and other counties in the northern section of the district while managing to stay close enough in the south and west to prevail. Details revealed that Hill's narrow victory was personal as well as anti-Democrat. Enough Democratic voters split their tickets by voting for incumbent governor Joe Brown but against Democratic congressional nominee Harper to make the difference. In the Third District, Opposition/American candidate Thomas Hardeman, Jr., captured the seat that Robert Trippe had held, but that was the only other significant victory that did not go to the Democracy.[30]

When Joshua Hill began his second term in the House of Representatives in the first week of December 1859, the atmosphere had become especially tense. John Brown's raid on Harper's Ferry had dominated the press since shortly after Georgia's congressional election in early October, and the notorious abolitionist was hanged for his actions only three days before Congress convened. Tales of violence, concerns about abolitionism, worries about slavery in the territories, speculations about the 1860 presidential election, and murmurs of disunion abounded. Neither major party held the majority. Hill described the chaotic scene in a letter to his nephew: "The House lingers on its slow and uncertain effort at organization—and no man can guess the end. Speeches, speeches, are the order of the day."[31]

The plurality of 109 Republicans was fairly well unified, but the 101 Democrats were divided, mainly because of lingering differences over the territorial controversies. The split manifested mostly, but not exclusively, along lines of pro-Buchanan or pro-Stephen Douglas. A disorganized collection of twenty-seven members variously labeling themselves Americans, Opposition, and People's held the balance of power, and they hoped to

---

September 8, 1859; *Milledgeville Southern Recorder*, August 9, September 6, 20, 27, 1859; *Sandersville Central Georgian*, September 14, 1859; *Macon Georgia Citizen*, September 9, 1859; *Augusta Chronicle*, August 19, 26, September 20, 1859; *Savannah Morning News*, August 18, 1859; *Columbus Enquirer*, September 16, 20, 27, 1859; *New York Times*, August 25, 1859; Varon, *Disunion*, 294–95.

[30] *(Macon) Georgia Journal and Messenger*, October 12, 1859; L. Roberts, "Political Career of Joshua Hill," 53.

[31] Joshua Hill to Fleming Jordan, December 12, 1859, ms. 826, HRBML. The author's reading of the handwritten letter differs slightly from the typescript.

influence the choice for Speaker of the House. Hill told his nephew that a move was afoot for a "union of Democrats and So[uthern] Americans" to work together, but he was not sure that it could happen. The effort at unity resulted in a boomlet of interest for advancing Hill's name as the Opposition candidate for Speaker. The *Augusta Chronicle* got on board for Hill. Several other Georgia papers, plus some in Washington, Richmond, Knoxville, and further afield took note of the plan. The *New York Tribune* detected the fingerprints of Howell Cobb, secretary of the treasury, on the Hill candidacy. It speculated that if the Democrats failed, Cobb would turn his backing to his fellow Georgian. Hill's support of the Lecompton Constitution would make him a safe alternative to a Republican Speaker:

> We hear...that Secretary Cobb—who is by odds the shrewdest and most thoroughgoing politician of his party now at Washington—has decided to urge his friends in the House to take up a South-American for Speaker, and thus secure a Pro-Slavery organization if possible. Joshua Hill of Georgia, is understood to be his favorite, but any one who can be molded to his purposes...will satisfy him.

The paper predicted, correctly as it turned out, that "Mr. Cobb's scheme" would not work.[32]

Although Joshua Hill never mounted a viable candidacy for himself, he played a key role behind the scenes and on the floor in one of the most contentious and convoluted Speaker of the House elections in US history. The strategy of the American/Opposition members was either to elect one of their own as the compromise Speaker or to forge an alliance with Southern Democrats to block a "black Republican" from assuming the office. Early in the contest a Philadelphia paper reported that Hill was "regarded as a trusty and trusted leader of the South Americans." Later as the struggle neared its end, the *New York Times* penned this vivid description of the

---

[32] *New York Tribune*, October 25, 1859 (*Savannah Republican*); *Augusta Chronicle*, October 15, 25, 1859; *Washington (DC) States*, October 19, 1859; *Macon Weekly Telegraph*, December 20, 1859 (*Richmond Whig*); *Columbus Daily Enquirer*, October 27, 1859 (*Knoxville Whig*); *(Macon) Georgia Journal & Messenger*, October 12, 1859; *Athens Southern Watchman*, October 20, 1859; *Cassville Standard*, October 20, 1859.

clean-shaven Madisonian who had been for weeks among those at the center of the epic battle:

> JOSHUA HILL, of Georgia,—one of the South-American leaders—...Mr. HILL is a very marked man, with a large head made still more conspicuous by a huge tangle of brown hair bushing out on all sides.... Mr. HILL has just such a face as a sculptor would make by only using his thumb on the clay, and not his boxwood implements. It is a florid and powerful face with deep, retreating blue eyes, an oval contour, good attempts at a nose and chin, but nothing finished—nothing decisively marked out and rounded off. The nose merges into the brow without any eyebrow lines, and a pillar of throat joins the cheek, with no whiskers or beard to act as a boundary for either. His voice is deep, pleasant, and musical, but its utterance would rather suggest a hollow palate. He talks vigorously and with a polished affluence of diction: there is little fancy in what he says, but a great deal of political knowledge, using this expression in its partisan sense.[33]

On the Republican side, John Sherman quickly emerged as the consensus candidate for speaker. The popular Ohioan stood by the Whig-like philosophy that Congress should not interfere with slavery in the states where it currently existed, but, like future president Abraham Lincoln and most other Republicans, he adamantly opposed the expansion of the institution into the western territories. Democrats demonized Sherman for his being among the several dozen Republicans who lent endorsement to Hinton R. Helper's incendiary antislavery book, *The Impending Crisis* (1857). Sherman endeavored to distance himself from Helper, but he was unable to make the charge go away. Hill worked hard to block Sherman, but shortly after the fight for Speaker was over, he acknowledged to a Georgia friend, "I do not regard Sherman, even now, as an ultra anti-slavery man after all the efforts of the Democrats to make him an out and out abolitionist." Unable to fashion a majority for Sherman, Republicans attempted to use the parliamentary maneuver of electing him Speaker by plurality. The tactic had worked in a previous instance, but this time Democrats managed to block the ploy. As a result, the House entered a tedious

---

[33] *Philadelphia Press*, December 29, 1858; *New York Times*, February 3, 1860; Freehling, *Road to Disunion*, 2:205–66.

weeks-long struggle to find some sort of majority that could elect a Speaker.[34]

Meanwhile, Democrats were so divided over support of the Buchanan administration that they sought in vain to put forth a candidate who could unify the party while simultaneously attracting enough American votes to win. Early in the process, a Savannah paper normally sympathetic to the American/Opposition faction argued that if no American candidate could manage to become a compromise Speaker "it will be the duty of Mr. Hill and of every other representative of the southern Opposition…to cooperate with the Democratic party in the organization of that body." An openly Democratic journalist declared that if Hill and "his South American colleagues" would just put aside their animosity and back a Democrat that they could organize the house "in twenty-four hours" and prevent the "Black Republicans" from gaining control. Neither Hill nor most American budged.[35]

On Christmas Eve, after the House had already endured many inconclusive ballots, Hill proposed a holiday recess. He explained, "I have written home to my overseer to give my slaves one week at Christmas, and I think we should be entitled to as much." The *Globe* records that laughter followed. It was one of the very few times that day that the record of proceedings took note of such a reaction amongst the testy and exhausted members. No recess was granted, so the struggle continued into the new year.[36]

By adopting a middle-of-the-road stance, Joshua Hill invited, as he would throughout his political career, criticism from both sides. Southern Democrats criticized him for being too willing to bargain with Northerners while Republicans were appalled by his comment that he would entertain consideration of "extreme" measures if Congress prevented the spread of slavery. When pressed, Hill responded, "I did not say as to what extreme

---

[34] Jenkins and Stewart, *Fighting for tshe Speakership*, 212–24; *Globe*, 36-1, 653; Hill to "My Dear Judge," February 5, 1860, MS 4229, HRBML.

[35] Ibid.; *Augusta Chronicle & Sentinel*, December 11, 1859; *Savannah Morning News*, December 12, 1859; *Charleston (SC) Mercury*, December 13, 1859; *Augusta Constitutionalist*, December 13, 1859; *Savannah Republican*, October 13, 1859; *Globe*, 36-1, 335, and January 12, 1860, 434; D. Potter, *Impending Crisis*, 386–91; Freehling, *Road to Disunion*, 2:246–66.

[36] *Globe*, 36-1, December 24, 1859, 246.

measures I would resort," but he made it clear what it did not mean. Even if, Hill declared, "some person, disagreeable to me on account of his political sentiments, as obnoxious even as an Abolitionist, were elected constitutionally to the presidency of the United States, I would not regard it as sufficient cause for disunion." A few days later when Democrats again tried to portray Hill's position as supportive of disunion, he snapped back, "I have never yet uttered the words my colleague has put in my mouth."[37]

A major obstacle that Democrats faced in their quest for unity was that a significant number of Northern Democrats represented constituencies that held antislavery sentiments. In several of those districts much of the antislavery sentiment came from recent immigrants. Returning to a tried-and-true Know-Nothing talking point, Hill asserted, "If gentlemen will come up and say upon this floor what they say in private, they will tell this House that the reason why they cannot vote for an American, who is national in all respects, is because they have too many foreign constituents."[38]

Try as they might, the Democrats remained unable to unite among themselves and bring enough American/Opposition members with them to achieve victory. Senator Stephan A. Douglas vainly prowled the House wing of the Capitol, trying to engineer a compromise that could bring his faction into some sort of winning coalition. Finally, after many inconclusive ballots, the Douglas Democrats and the Buchanan Democrats agreed to put aside their differences and find temporary unity in support of an American/Opposition candidate. Rather than selecting Joshua Hill or another American who had been prominent in speaker fight, the transient coalition strategically chose obscure freshman William N. H. Smith of North Carolina, who had stayed quietly out of the fray. In Hill's words, the interparty negotiators settled on Smith "because of his own peculiar position—he not being exceptional, as most of us were, by reason of our American sentiments.—he was the most available man that we could present on this side of the chamber." The American-Democratic alliance almost pulled off the last-minute gambit, but Smith fell three votes short on the thirty-ninth ballot.[39]

---

[37] *Globe*, 36-1, 346, 388–98.

[38] Ibid., January 16, 1860, 466.

[39] *Globe*, 36-1, January 31, 1860, 640; Johannsen, *Stephen A. Douglas*, 718–21.

By the end of January 1860, Republicans finally conceded that there was no path that would lead to John Sherman becoming Speaker even though, like Smith, he had come as close as three votes. Many years later in his *Recollections,* Sherman blamed his defeat on the controversy over his praise of Hinton Helper's *Crisis* book and on "the abnormal excitement created by Brown's invasion and the bitterness of political antagonism existing at that time." Sherman formally withdrew from consideration on January 30. Following a strategy like the Americans had used in their nomination of Smith, the Republicans turned to the inoffensive William Pennington of New Jersey. Pennington was by no means a party leader, but he had the good fortune of not having been among the Republicans who signed the endorsement of Helper's work.[40]

After Sherman's withdrawal, the Americans tried one last time to rally votes for Smith. The *New York Times* called attention to Hill's endeavors, but observed, "the sense of the House is against him, and even his large popularity cannot redeem the effort." The Douglas Democrats were also unsuccessful in their final effort, which centered on a back bench representative from Douglas's home state of Illinois. Finally, on the forty-fourth ballot, Pennington prevailed by one vote—generally considered to be that of Southern American, soon-to-be Republican, Henry Winter Davis of Maryland. In appreciation, Pennington awarded John Sherman the powerful position of chairman of the Ways and Means Committee.[41]

Although Hill had fought hard for Smith, he grudgingly conceded that Pennington was probably the least objectionable Republican that could be found. If what his supporters have reported is correct, Hill told the House, Pennington "is not after all so very bad a man. If it be true that he is in favor of the fugitive slave law and its enforcement, and that he will not interfere with slavery in Territories where it naturally belongs, he comes very close to my views." A few days later, Hill assured a Georgia friend that Pennington had a "sincere and kindly nature" and that "The

---

[40] Sherman, *John Sherman's Recollections*, 39, 146 (the abnormal).

[41] Johannsen, *Stephen A. Douglas*, 720; *New York Times*, February 3, 1860; *Globe*, 36-1, 634 (January 30, 1860), 640 (January 31, 1860); *Journal of the House of Representatives*, 36th Congress, 1st Session, February 1, 1860, 165; *Rome Weekly Courier*, February 17, 1860; Scroggins gives Toombs partial credit for the defeat of Sherman (*Robert Toombs*, 108–109).

country will not be indignant at the election of so moderate a conservative—not even the thinking men of the South."[42]

As the first session of the 36th Congress closed in early March 1860, the nation warily eyed the upcoming presidential campaign and the sectional conflict that was sure to accompany it. The contest for Speaker was the very last gasp of American Party relevance, so Joshua Hill turned his attention to a new goal—the creation of a political party designed to protect his two greatest loves other than hearth and home: slavery and Union.

[42] *Globe*, 36-1, 653; Hill to "My Dear Judge" [specific name not indicated], February 5, 1860, ms 4229, HRBML.

The Political Parties of Joshua Hill and His Opponents to 1860

Date and Key Events	Political Parties of Joshua Hill	DEMOCRATIC PARTY
1833 After election of Andrew Jackson.	States Rights Anti-Jackson	Union Pro-Jackso
1840 President: Martin Van Buren (D) v. Wm. H. Harrison (W)	States Rights & Anti-Van Buren	Union Democrats
1842–1844 George Crawford (W) elected governor 1842; Henry Clay (W) ran for president	Whig	Democrat
1848–1850 Zachery Taylor (W) elected President. Compromise of 1850 and Georgia Platform.	Whig Georgia Whigs weakened their connection with Northern Whigs.	Two Factions: Resistance (also known as Southern Rights) and Constitutional Union (also known as Union or Union Democrat)
1852–1853 Winfield Scott (W) vs. Franklin Pierce (Demo)	Whig Whigs who did not desert to the Union Democrats split into Scott and Webster tickets.	Democrat Including many old Whigs including A. H. Stephens and R. Toombs. Dominated state government and congressional membership.
1855–1857 Foster then Hill elected to Congress. Republicans emerged nationally. Democrats nominate and elect James Buchanan.	Know-Nothing (aka American) Strained relationship with the Northern wing of Americans. Georgia Americans backed Fillmore for president in 1856.	
1859 Hill reelected	Opposition The American Party had mostly collapsed. Opposition to Democrats constituted the only affiliation.	
1860 Republican Lincoln elected president.	Constitutional Union (Bell) Hill was a leader in the formation of the party.	Two factions: Northern Democrat (Douglas) and Southern Democrat (Breckinridge)

Chapter 3

Unionist Congressman in the Secession Crisis, 1860–1861

When Congress adjourned on March 4, 1860, no one knew for sure that the United States of America would be torn asunder a year later, yet no politically astute person could have been surprised when it happened. Sectional interests deriving mainly from the institution of slavery bedeviled the nation from its very earliest days, and the potential of the institution's westward expansion dominated all other political issues from the time of the Mexican War forward. The *Southern Watchman* of Athens succinctly explained the political environment in one sentence: "All intelligent readers know that the only question between the North and South, of any practical importance, is the question of slavery in the Territories."[1]

The persistent question of whether the nation could long endure finally came to a head during the presidential election of 1860 and its aftermath. The course of events swept Joshua Hill into the Constitutional Union Party and the swirl of a heated presidential campaign. Abraham Lincoln's election resulted in a flurry of post-election secession conventions and a testy mood in Congress. Hill tried his best to influence the outcome, but when he could not, he faced the most difficult decision of his political life.

Organizing the Constitutional Union Party

With the demise of the American Party, Hill and other Whig-American-Opposition partisans who had sought to steer a middle course between Republican antislavery activism and fire-eating Democratic threats of disunion had to find a new political home. One option for these men was to

[1] *(Athens) Southern Watchman*, March 1, 1860.

attach themselves to the more moderate wing of the Democratic Party under the leadership of Stephen Douglas—and some of them did. Still, Joshua Hill and many of his Southern Know-Nothing colleagues could not bring themselves to become Democrats of any stripe, so they joined the effort to build a new "Constitutional Union" party. The key organizers came mainly from the old Whig-Know-Nothings-Opposition continuum, but they also hoped to attract a coterie of disaffected Democrats and moderate Republicans. The *Milledgeville Federal Union* mocked the Constitutional Union movement as a "conglomeration of shreds and patches, of odds and ends of all parties" that was seeking "a new party and a new name." Democrats, the writer proudly proclaimed, "do not wish to change their name or to form a new party. The old Democratic name and party are both good enough for them."[2]

In Georgia, the name "Constitutional Union" was not new. As explained in chapter 1, moderate Democrats and Whigs temporarily allied to form the Constitutional Union Party as a mechanism to support the Compromise of 1850. A study of Georgia's Know-Nothings (Americans) argued that the early 1850s group constituted "a critical link" to the 1860 party of the same name. It is important, however, not to overplay that connection. Although it is true that several Know-Nothings, including Joshua Hill, Edward Hill, and their unrelated ally Ben Hill, were involved in both efforts, Democrats dominated the first Constitutional Union alliance, and almost all of them returned to the Democratic fold rather than becoming Know-Nothings.[3]

The demise of the Know-Nothings/American Party combined with the approach of the 1860 presidential election to move the concept of a new national party from speculation to implementation. John J. Crittenden, who had served in Fillmore's Cabinet and who later became an American Party senator from Kentucky, was the key player. Late in 1859, Crittenden initiated preliminary discussions with fellow American Party members in Congress. In response, the American Party National Committee, on which Joshua Hill served, resolved to confer with political forces favorable to "the formation of a National party on the basis of the Union, the Constitution, and the enforcement of the laws." Joshua Hill was a

[2] *Milledgeville Federal Union*, May 11, 1858.
[3] Allen, "For Union and Slavery," 107–108.

member of the original ten-man exploratory group that started working out the details and drafting a statement.[4]

Early in February 1860, Hill wrote a seven-page epistle explaining the Constitutional Union movement to "My dear Judge" and asking for his support. The extant document does not indicate the recipient's name, but clearly it was one of Hill's fellow members of the American Party in Georgia. The private letter is as succinct an explanation of the origins and purposes of the Constitutional Union party as one is likely to find:

> Some of us here, with the old Roman J. J. Crittendon at our head, have attempted to get up a new party for the Union.... I am happy to be able to say that the party seems to commend itself most highly to the old national conservative Whigs everywhere—except for such as have too clearly allied themselves with the Republican organization.... Even if our efforts to build up a great party for the Constitution and the Union & the enforcement of the laws of the Union should fail—we shall have the satisfaction of knowing that already our advent before the Country as a party has had the happy effect of modifying the tone of Republicans.[5]

By the end of February 1860, the now-expanded committee was ready to publish its official lengthy statement of principles with thirty signers, including Hill. The group was deliberately cross sectional with almost half of the signatories residing in slave states. The widely-published manifesto lamented that the nation had fallen "into an organization of parties founded on the question of slavery." The "cardinal principles" were mainly platitudinous except for two specific pledges: first, to leave slavery alone in states where it existed, "and second, "to remove all obstacles from the due and faithful execution of the provisions for the rendition of fugitive slaves." Turning to practical considerations, the statement urged "immediate steps" to organize state parties and to plan a national convention. By urging "forbearance, concession, and conciliation" among men of different

---

[4] *National Intelligencer* (DC), December 24, 1859; *Boston (MA) Evening Transcript*, December 21, 1859; *Augusta Chronicle*, August, December 28, 1859. See Green, "Constitutional Unionists," 231–53; Mason, *Apostle of Union*. Everett was the CUP candidate for VP.

[5] Hill to "My Dear Judge," February 5, 1860, ms 4229, HRBML.

opinions, the Constitutional Union Party constituted, in the words of British historian John Ashworth's magisterial study of the period, "the closest thing to a resurrected Whig party that was imaginable in the final months of the antebellum republic."[6]

Ardent Democrats were rightfully fearful that the formation of the Constitutional Union Party (CUP) could have the effect of dividing the anti-Republican vote. A particularly acerbic New Orleans editor characterized the signers of the initial CUP statement as "respectable solid old fogies," and concluded, "We consider, therefore, this movement of Messrs. Crittenden & Co. as ill-timed, unwise, and calculated to destroy at the North that concert among the conservatives so necessary to the defeat of Black Republicans."[7]

The timing of the formal declaration by the CUP was critical. They intended to make their presence fully known to the public in advance of the upcoming conventions of the two major parties. In late February no one was sure who the rival nominees would be. Two things, however, were certain: the Republican nominee would ardently oppose the spread of slavery, and the Democrat nominee, whoever he might be, would face a bitter internecine battle likely to split the party.

The Democrats went first. Deep tensions within the party dating to the Kansas controversy were evident when the new Congress convened in December 1859 and could not unite on a candidate for Speaker through multiple ballots. The intraparty squabbles continued at the national convention in Charleston, South Carolina, in April 1860. The faction led by the Illinois "Little Giant," Senator Stephen Douglas, was in the majority, but they lacked the two-thirds vote necessary for nomination. The Charleston Convention rendered the Democratic Party asunder. Factions reconvened in Baltimore and Richmond, and two rival Democratic candidates emerged from the chaos. Douglas represented the official ticket with Georgian Herschel V. Johnson in the second spot. Kentuckian John C.

---

[6] *New York Times*, February 22, 1860; *New York Herald*, February 21, 1860; *Boston (MA) Advertiser*, February 22, 1860; *Augusta Chronicle*, February 25, 1860; *Milledgeville Southern Recorder*, March 6, 1860; *(Athens) Southern Watchman*, March 1, 1860; *Rome Tri-Weekly Courier*, March 1, 1860; Ashworth, *Slavery, Capitalism, and Politics*, 2:593–606.

[7] *Baton Rouge Weekly Advocate*, March 4, 1860.

Breckinridge, the sitting vice president, became the candidate of the so-called Southern Democrats.[8]

Georgia Democrats, like those in other slave states, had to make a choice. As historian William W. Freehling neatly phrased it, "Georgians reluctantly had to decide who were their true brothers, overly zealous Lower South seceders or overly compromising Upper South stay-at-homes?" Most joined the former, but not everyone was on board. Hershel V. Johnson, Douglas's vice-presidential running mate, stayed loyal to the national party as did Alexander Stephens. The intensity of the split was so marked that it resulted in long-time friends and allies Stephens and Roberts Toombs ending up on opposite sides.[9]

On May 9, 1860, the Constitutional Union Party (CUP) convention convened in Baltimore. Joshua Hill was a member of the committee that managed the event, and Hill's South Carolina friend and future mayor of Atlanta James Calhoun served as a convention vice president. When the CUP gathered, the Republicans had not yet met, and the final outcome of the Democratic mess had not yet been determined. The CUP had originally hoped that its potential strength in the border states would force Republicans to nominate what Hill called in his February letter to the Georgia judge "a moderate, conservative, national man." However, by May, that thought had faded, and the Constitutional Unionists proceeded under the reasonable assumption that the Republicans would nominate William Seward of New York, who had abolitionist leanings. Therefore, the CUP strategy was threefold: first, to run strong in the border states; second, to pick up Northern support from those who could not abide Seward, and third, to capture Unionist-leaning Democrats in the Deep South who could not accept Douglas. The third part of the plan was where Georgia came in.[10]

---

[8] Johannsen, *Stephen A. Douglas*, 717–59; M. Woods, *Bleeding Kansas*, 102; Etcheson, *Bleeding Kansas*, 222–23; D. Potter, *Impending Crisis*, 407–15; Freehling, *Road to Disunion*, 2:295–322.

[9] Freehling, *Road to Disunion*, 2:306; W. C. Davis, *The Union*, 77–81; Carey, *Parties, Slavery, and the Union*, 221–25. Johannsen says Douglass wanted Stephens for VP (*Stephen A. Douglas*, 741–42).

[10] *Boston (MA) Courier*, May 10, 1860; *Alexandria (VA) Gazette*, May 11, 12,1860; Green, "Constitutional Unionists," 231–53; Wortman, *Bonfire*, 96; Hill to "My Dear Judge."

Seventy-three-year-old Crittenden chose not to seek the nomination of the new party that he helped birth. Some party leaders engaged in "clandestine operations" to find a conservative Republican, perhaps even Abraham Lincoln, to carry the banner, but that effort failed. Without a turncoat Republican to head the ticket, it was critical to CUP strategy for the nominee to represent a border state. John Bell, a former Whig congressman, cabinet member, and United States senator, fit the bill. Moreover, as the owner of numerous slaves, Bell seemed safe on protection of the "peculiar institution." Bell, like Joshua Hill and most Southern Constitutional Unionists, believed that demanding that slavery have the option to take hold in territories and future states was politically counterproductive to the overriding goal of protecting slavery where it already existed. The Constitutional Union Party strategy hit a bump when the Republican Convention in Chicago did not go according to expectations. Seward, who tried to moderate his previous antislavery stances, led on the first ballot, but as the convention dragged on, Abraham Lincoln attracted more delegates away from the also-rans and triumphed. By nominating Lincoln, a moderate ex-Whig who opposed slavery but was no abolitionist, the Republicans effectively lessened the appeal of the middle-of-the-road CUP.[11]

The 1860 Campaign

Joshua Hill served on the Central Executive Committee that managed the Bell-Everett campaign, but chronic underfunding limited the effort. More important, the CUP seemed unable to generate the passion and enthusiasm that Lincoln, Breckinridge, and Douglas inspired among their respective followers. Adept at simultaneously defending both the supremacy of the Union and the principle that slavery was a state rather than national matter, Hill balanced his congressional duties with being a busy orator and writer for the Constitutional Union cause in Washington and nearby cities including Boston, New York, and Baltimore. For example, Hill was among the speakers at one New York meeting that endeavored "to collect and discipline the scattered rank and file of the old Know-Nothing faction throughout the state" into the new pro-Union party. At another New York

[11] Mason, *Apostle of Union*, 250 (clandestine), 263; Freehling, *Road to Disunion*, 2:326–29; D. Potter, *Impending Crisis*, 417–30; Green, "Constitutional Unionists," 239–53.

gathering, a local party member read aloud a letter from Hill along with correspondence from Crittenden and several other leading Constitutional Unionists. Hill distributed printed copies of his letter, and several sympathetic newspapers in Georgia carried his observations. Hill's statement frankly conceded that it was unlikely that the new party could ever "attract a majority of the voters of the country at large." Nevertheless, he contended that the Constitutional Union Party would be able to "consolidate the scattered forces of the old Whig party" into a coalition that "could, at least, make ourselves a balance of power, to be feared and courted by the two great rival parties." The Georgia congressman counseled patience with the slave-holding states because "it will require time to calm the excited popular mind in the South, so as to permit a dispassionate consideration" of the ideas of his new party.[12]

The sympathetic *Richmond Whig* was over-the-top effusive in its account of one Hill speech in Baltimore:

> In his clear and distinct voice [Joshua Hill] held the vast multitude spell bound for upwards of an hour, in one of the most fervent, patriotic, conservative, national, Union, speeches ever delivered by man. It had the ring of the old Clay and Webster days—a speech that does him and the State of Georgia, which he represents in Congress, great credit. At the conclusion, three cheers...were given for the eloquent speaker.[13]

As the campaign opened, Georgia press opinion was divided, but Democratic organs predominated. According to one count, thirty newspapers endorsed Breckinridge, sixteen backed Bell, and only two supported Douglas. No Georgia editor was, of course, so bold as to speak for Lincoln. State senator Benjamin H. Hill emerged as the Constitutional Union Party's principal campaigner in Georgia. Josh and Ben Hill had been fellow Know-Nothing/American Party members, so it was natural that they would find themselves together again. Over the ensuing years, the two Hills would split, re-ally, and then split again as they faced secession, the Confederacy, the gubernatorial race of 1863, and Reconstruction. Ben

---

[12] *Milledgeville Federal Union*, May 5, 1860; *Milledgeville Southern Recorder*, May 6, 29, 1860; *(Athens) Southern Watchman*, May 10, 1860; *Columbus Enquirer*, May 22, 1860; *Dawson Weekly Journal*, May 22, 1860.

[13] *Augusta Chronicle*, October 3, 1860 (*Richmond Whig*).

Hill's most widely reported speech for the CUP occurred in Macon in late June. Vice-presidential nominee Herschel Johnson had spoken on behalf of Douglas in the same auditorium the previous night, so the audience was no doubt primed to hear how the bombastic Hill would respond. He began with an extended forthright defense of owning slave property as a God-ordained right. Next, he proceeded to assert without fear of contradiction that it would be unthinkable for a Southern White man to vote for Lincoln. Finally, he turned his attention to Stephen Douglas, the official Democrat. Following a few nice words about his fellow Georgian Johnson, Ben Hill asserted that the Little Giant's squatter sovereignty theory would not only allow territories to exclude slavery but could also lead to abolition. "The issue," the Troup Countian declared, "is thus narrowed down to Mr. Bell and Mr. Breckinridge.... The election of Mr. Bell will give our principles a peaceful, quiet triumph, and disband the Republican party." On the other hand, he argued, "the election of Mr. Breckinridge will increase the strife and tend to build up the Republican party."[14]

Ben Hill's fiery oratory had the same message that Joshua Hill and other CUP spokesmen were simultaneously carrying to places like Boston, Baltimore, and New York—with one major difference. Unlike Ben Hill, Congressman Hill refrained from lacing his speeches with explicit defense of the righteousness of slavery. The more cautious of the Hills did not want to take the chance that arguments for the moral rectitude of slavery would alienate his Northern audiences. Taking note of this hypocrisy, a Columbus, Georgia, Democrat wrote snidely that when the Morgan County plantation owner spoke in Baltimore, he "forgot" to bring up proslavery arguments.[15]

Although Ben Hill headlined the Georgia effort for the Constitutional Union ticket while Joshua Hill spoke mostly to Northern and border audiences, the congressman did come home a few times during the

[14] *Albany Patriot*, July 5, 1860; *Macon Telegraph*, October 4, 1860; *Washington (DC) Evening Star*, April 13, May 11, 1860, *Boston (MA) Courier*, September 27, 1860; *Macon Telegraph*, October 2, 1860; *Augusta Chronicle*, August 16, 1860; *Baltimore Sun*, April 13, 1860; *Washington (DC) Daily National Intelligencer*, April 14, 1860; B. Hill, *Senator Benjamin H. Hill of Georgia*, 229–35; Pearce, *Benjamin H. Hill*, 36–40; Doherty, "Union Nationalism in Georgia," 30–31; Dyer found some very quiet support for Lincoln from Atlanta Unionists (*Secret Yankees*, 39–40).

[15] *Columbus Daily Times*, August 15, 1860.

campaign. In August, at a rally in Milledgeville, both Hills spoke on the same day. A crowd of some five hundred CUP supporters gathered in the afternoon as Ben Hill "addressed them in his usual forcible and eloquent manner for about two hours." Later that evening, Joshua Hill and others spoke to a crowd nearly as large in the piazza of the Milledgeville Hotel.[16]

In one typical address, Congressman Hill decried "the destruction of the government threatened by reckless partisans North and South" and defended the right of slavery to continue in the states where it existed. To those who claimed that the new party had "no chance," Hill countered by likening Bell to General Washington in the dark days of the American Revolution just before victory. Acknowledging that his own voting record sometimes diverged from the nominee's, Hill explained, "I do not agree with Mr. Bell in all things, but I do agree with him upon those questions which I esteem of vital importance." He called listeners' particular attention to the recent House Speakership contest and forcefully blamed the Democrats' lack of cooperation with Southern Americans like himself for the eventual selection of a Republican. He also faulted Democrats for "pertinaciously" keeping the slavery question agitated.[17]

When previewing an upcoming event in Augusta, the *Chronicle & Sentinel* effused, "There is not a nobler man in Georgia than Joshua Hill." Indeed, Hill's speech was temperate and genteel. He told the City Hall crowd that he was "personally well acquainted with both Mr. Douglas and Mr. Breckinridge" and that he regarded the two Democrats to be "honest, capable and patriotic" men. Thus, Hill argued, voters should "unite upon Bell," not because of the flaws of the Democratic candidates, but because the man at the top of the Constitutional Union ticket had the "best prospect of defeating Lincoln." One Democratic paper grudgingly called it "an admirable speech," and another Breckenridge supporter gave high praise to Hill's calm deportment:

> During the present campaign we have not heard [a speech] that has been so distinguished by fair and candid treatment of political opponents; or freer from the usual wholesale denunciations

---

[16] *Sandersville Central Georgian*, August 22, 1860 (addressed); *Augusta Chronicle*, August 16, 1860; *Washington (DC) National Intelligencer*, August 21, 1860.

[17] *Milledgeville Southern Recorder*, July 31, 1860 (*Madison Visitor*); *Augusta Daily Constitutionalist*, August 31, 1860; *Augusta Chronicle*, October 2, 1860.

> and clap-trap arguments of stump speakers.... Much of the vindictiveness of politics, and many of the asperities of a canvass would be avoided if all public men would take Col. Hill's manner and language as models in political discussions. Men may differ as to the merits of the cause he advocates, but no man, however wrong he may think [Hill's] opinions, can regard him except as a magnanimous and chivalrous antagonist.[18]

With few exceptions, commentors expressed similar sentiment throughout Hill's career even when they disagreed with the substance of the Madisonian's positions.

One reason that Joshua Hill was so solicitous of the good intentions of Democrats in his September speech in Augusta was that he was no doubt aware of back-channel discussions then occurring between the Douglas and Bell campaigns regarding the possible fusion of their Georgia efforts against Breckenridge. Similar machinations were underfoot in other states as well. Douglas made a tour into the Deep South, including Atlanta, Macon, and Columbus, but it was too little, too late. On the trip, he refrained from explicitly advocating fusion, but, on October 30, he spoke in Atlanta to a crowd that included many Constitutional Union supporters. By that time, Douglas and his leading in-state supporter, Alexander H. Stephens, were already resigned to the fact that Breckinridge would carry Georgia.[19]

It is understandable that the fusion efforts in Georgia, and in other states for that matter, failed to bear fruit given the acrimonious tone of the spring-summer campaign and the long pattern of distrust between Democrats and the collection of old Whigs and Americans that constituted the core of the Constitutional Unionists. As one Democratic paper put it derisively, the Constitutional Unionists consisted of "every sort of men, who for the last quarter of a century have been fighting the Democracy." Joshua Hill and Benjamin Hill were influential and persuasive politicians, yet their efforts were no match for the passions of the day and their state's

---

[18] *Augusta Chronicle*, September 4, 13, 1860; *Augusta Constitutionalist*, September 12, 1860; *(Macon) Georgia Journal and Messenger*, September 18, 1860 (during); Dyer, *Secret Yankees*, 39–42.

[19] Johannsen, *Stephen A. Douglas*, 799–800; Crofts, *Reluctant Confederates*, 76–81.

normal Democratic tendencies. Their calls for union fell flat on the ears of the many White Georgians who had already concluded that disunion was all but inevitable. Nevertheless, friendly editors and Constitutional Union politicians continued to profess upbeat opinions about their prospects in Georgia.[20]

Nationally, Bell ran fourth behind Lincoln, Douglas, and Breckenridge. However, in Georgia, he finished second with 40 percent of the vote, higher than in any other Deep South state. Douglas trailed at only 11 percent. Bell polled best in the upper South states but carried only Tennessee, Kentucky, and Virginia. To have won, or even to have thrown the election into the House of Representatives, would have required the Constitutional Union Party to carry several additional states. That would have required fusion with the Douglas Democrats in addition to a stronger showing in the North. Joshua Hill and his Constitutional Unionist partners had worked hard to make the middle viable, but it was not to be.[21]

As expected, Breckinridge carried Georgia, but he fell just shy of a majority. Despite all the rhetoric and the looming specter of secession, the 1860 vote turned out pretty much the same as other recent Georgia elections between Democrats and their opponents of the day—by whatever party name. Bell ran best in Atlanta and in the Whiggish Cotton Belt that included the Madison and LaGrange homes of both Hills. If the Breckenridge and Douglas votes are combined, the Democratic vote totaled approximately the same number that Joseph E. Brown had received for governor in 1859. On the other hand, if the number of Bell and Douglas votes could have been combined as Josh and Ben Hill had urged, the more moderate voices would have polled a narrow majority. In the end, the Georgia General Assembly chose the state's electors since no candidate had a clear majority of the popular vote. There was never any doubt that the Democratic dominated legislature would award the state's electoral votes to the

---

[20] M. P. Johnson, *Toward a Patriarchal Republic*, 14 (every sort, *Atlanta Intelligencer*); *Augusta Chronicle*, October 2, 1860; *New York Times*, September 25, 1860; Pearce, *Benjamin H. Hill*, 39; B. Hill, *Senator Benjamin H. Hill of Georgia*, 37; Green, "Constitutional Unionists," 242; Mason, *Apostle of Union*, 262; Johannsen, *Stephen A. Douglas*, 799–800; Allen, "For Union and Slavery," 118; Montgomery, *Cracker Parties*, 243; Mason, *Apostle of Union*, 262 (an air).

[21] Freehling, *Road to Disunion*, 2:338–41; Ashworth, *Slavery, Capitalism, and Politics*, 2:593–606; M. Storey, *Loyalty and Loss*, 23–29.

Breckenridge ticket. Of course, even if Georgia had gone for Bell, it would not have made a difference in the national outcome of the 1860 election.[22]

As a postscript to the election of 1860, it should be noted that Abraham Lincoln's absence from the ballot does not mean that he lacked support from a large portion of the people of Georgia and the Deep South, i.e. the Black people. To be sure, Lincoln would have received scant few votes from Southern White men, but he had acquired a deep well of support from the Black men (and women) who were held in bondage and denied the vote. Historian David Williams relates that enslaved Georgians often attended campaign events and that some Whites became alarmed at the large number of Black folks who lingered on the edge of such rallies to eavesdrop on the words of the campaigners. Speakers, regardless of which of the three candidates they backed, were wont to harangue the crowds by charging that Lincoln and the duplicitous Black Republicans were intent on bringing about the end of slavery. In the minds of the enslaved people listening to the speeches, the White orators were inadvertently planting seeds that would grow into the idea that Lincoln could be their great savior.[23] Thus, to a great extent, Southern White people had themselves to blame for the fact that Black Southerners fully understood that at its roots the Civil War was about them and their right to be free.

Secession Debated and Accomplished

The pending ascendency of a Republican to the presidency transformed the dynamic of America's long-simmering sectional tension. The breakup of the Union changed from abstract theory and veiled threat to very real possibility. Georgia senator Alfred Iverson contended that the election of Lincoln alone would justify secession, and according to one Atlanta editor that sentiment was widely shared: "The Southern masses, almost to a man, regard the simple election of Lincoln as an 'overt act,' and it is the solemn determination of the eight cotton states to secede immediately on his

---

[22] Breckinridge 51,893; Bell 42,855; and Douglas 11,580 (Coleman, *History of Georgia*, 146–49; Parks, *Joseph E. Brown*, 106–109; Carey, *Parties, Slavery, and the Union*, 223–29; M. P. Johnson, *Toward a Patriarchal Republic*, 10–9; Ashworth, *Slavery, Capitalism, and Politics*, 2:593–606; Venet, "From Gate City to Gotham," 151; Dyer, *Secret Yankees*, 40–42).

[23] Williams, *Georgia's Civil War*, 30–32.

election." The politicians of all the slave states, including Georgia, had to decide how and when to proceed. The intricate details leading to Georgia's secession are beyond the scope of a biography of Joshua Hill, but an understanding of the fundamental issues and the course of action is essential to placing the role of the sitting representative and future senator in context. While Hill remained in Washington, the crisis reached a crescendo in Georgia.[24]

The Georgia General Assembly was in session in Milledgeville in mid-November. During the day, they met for their normal business, and then in the evening, they listened to a series of speeches in which several of the state's political heavyweights confronted the crisis. Senator Robert Toombs, former Georgia Supreme Court justice Henry Benning, Thomas R. R. Cobb, and other "separatists" passionately urged the state legislature to withdraw from the Union immediately. "Strike while it is yet time," Toombs cried. Alexander Stephens, Benjamin Hill, and Herschel V. Johnson spoke for the "cooperationists"—those who counseled compromise and a more cautious course. They contended that only a convention chosen by the voters and not the General Assembly on its own would possess the requisite sovereignty to make such a weighty decision as secession from the United States of America. Governor Joseph E. Brown clearly favored secession but agreed that a convention would be necessary. The General Assembly complied and set delegate elections for January 2, 1861.[25]

Speechmaking and debate about how to respond to the election of Lincoln was not confined to Milledgeville. Many towns across the state

---

[24] Johannsen, *Stephen A. Douglas*, 799 (the southern); Varon, *Disunion*, 322–23; The most detailed account of Georgia's secession remains M. P. Johnson's *Toward a Patriarchal Republic*, but several commentators have questioned "double revolution" theory and his quantitative analysis. See, e.g., B. Collins, "Governor Joseph E. Brown," 192–93, 222; and Carey, *Parties, Slavery, and the Union*, 323–24.

[25] Freehling and Simpson, *Secession Debated*, contains the principal speeches and an excellent introduction; see also Freehling, *Road to Disunion*, 2:429–44; Parks, *Joseph E. Brown*, 112–13 (strike); M. P. Johnson, *Toward a Patriarchal Republic*, 17–18; Hettle, "Ambiguous Democrat," 579–90; Wetherington, *Plain Folk's Fight*, 8; Wooster, "The Georgia Secession Convention," 21–22; McCash, *Thomas R. R. Cobb*, 186–93; Bates, "Last Stand," 455–67.

held mass meetings, and one such gathering brought tragedy to the Hill family. On Saturday evening, November 17, the congressman's brother Edward Young Hill, the former Whig gubernatorial candidate, took the stage at a large public meeting in LaGrange. About a half-hour into his oratory, the distinguished judge collapsed, probably from a stroke. The solemn memorial issued by the members of the local bar described the moment: "In the midst of an able and eloquent speech, his powers suddenly failed; his voice faltered, his vision grew dim, his frame quivered and sank into paralysis." Bystanders assisted the speaker from the stand and took him to the mayor's home where he lingered and then died. Judge Hill's body was scarcely cold when rivals began to claim the fallen jurist as a martyr for their respective positions on secession. It is not known how or when Joshua Hill learned of his brother's death. The absence of press coverage about the congressman around this time suggests that he may have withdrawn from his normal political activities and traveled to LaGrange.[26]

There was no clear consensus among Georgia's White elites about how to proceed. Some demanded immediate withdrawal from the Union; some wanted to set conditions and require cooperation from other states, and some were sorely distressed by the circumstances but calculated that secession and the war likely to follow would do more harm than good for their cotton-dependent plantation way of life. Poor Whites who held few or no enslaved workers were not among the politicians who debated, but they would be among the voters who selected convention delegates. Using whatever seemed to work—economic logic, emotional appeals to White manhood, or scare tactics about emancipation—the advocates of secession set out to convince all Whites that preserving slavery through secession was in their interests.[27]

---

[26] Memorial to E. Y. Hill, Troup Superior Court, November 21, 1860, E. Y. Hill vertical file, Troup County Archives, LaGrange, Georgia; *Columbus Enquirer*, November 27, 1860; *Columbus Times*, November 21, 22, 28; *Macon Telegraph*, November 22, 1860; *Columbus Enquirer*, November 27, [1860]; *Augusta Chronicle*, November 22, 1860; *Milledgeville Southern Recorder*, November 27, 1860; *(Athens) Southern Banner*, November 29, 1860.

[27] Merritt, *Masterless Men*, 290; Williams, *Georgia's Civil War*, 20; Levine, *Fall of the House of Dixie*, 24–26, 33–34; Manning, *What This Cruel War Was Over*, 22–

The vote for delegates to Georgia's convention to consider secession took place on a chilly, rainy January 2, 1861. Although the equivocal positions of some candidates and the lack of information about others make it difficult to assert definitive conclusions about the results, historians tend to conclude that immediate secessionists, who were better organized and more energized, carried the day by a narrow margin. Broadly speaking, the vote for delegates followed political and geographic divisions similar to the November elections. With some anomalies, areas that went for Breckenridge were more likely to choose immediate secessionist delegates; those chosen from places that voted for Bell or Douglass were more likely to be cooperationists. Despite their hesitations, most cooperationists were amenable to secession if efforts at compromise failed and/or if the Union undertook direct military action against the already seceded states. Benjamin Hill put it bluntly: "If we fail, then we are ready to join you."[28]

South Carolina kicked off the secession parade in December 1860 in the hope that other states would follow. On January 9, 10, and 11, Mississippi, Florida, and Alabama followed suit in quick order before the Georgia convention met. The nation's eyes then turned to see what Georgia, the largest and most important of the Deep South states, would do. Georgia's population of 462,000 enslaved people was second only to Virginia—first after Virginia lost its western portion.

Although there were very real disagreements among Georgia's elected convention delegates about the wisdom of immediate secession, they all supported the institution of slavery, and they all shared the fundamental Southern White racial, economic, and political assumptions of the day. None of the delegates who spoke piously about carrying out the will of the people gave any consideration whatsoever to the will of the more than four out of ten people of Georgia who were enslaved. The decision of Georgia's convention would determine if the lower South's stampede toward immediate secession would stall or accelerate. About three weeks before the

---

23, 148, 171–72; Wetherington, *Plain Folk's Fight*, 5–8; Ashworth, *Slavery, Capitalism, and Politics*, and his shorter synthesis, *The Republic in Crisis: 1848–1861*, stress the centrality of slavery and slave resistance to all peripheral causes of secession and Civil War.

[28] Bates, "Last Stand," 458 (if we fail); Coleman, *History of Georgia*, 150–51; M. P. Johnson, *Toward a Patriarchal Republic*, 17–27, 63–78, 108–17.

convention, Alexander Stephens received from the president-elect a "for your own eyes only" in which Lincoln tried to calm the storm:

> Do the people of the South really entertain fears that a Republican administration would, *directly, or indirectly*, interfere with their slaves, or with them, about their slaves? If they do, I wish to assure you, as once a friend, and still, I hope, not an enemy, that there is no cause for such fears.... You think that slavery is *right* and ought to be extended, while we think it *wrong* and ought to be restricted. That I suppose is the rub. It certainly is the only substantial difference between us.

However, as the convention progressed, it soon became crystal clear that the cooperationist/conditional group was overwhelmed by circumstances. On the third day, Herschel V. Johnson offered a cooperationist counter proposal similar to the compromise offered at the national level by Kentucky senator and Constitutional Union organizer John J. Crittenden. It failed, and by the clear but not overwhelming count of 166 to 130, the preliminary resolution in favor of secession passed. Two other intermediate votes revealed similar divisions. At that point, many of the delegates who had previously sought compromise began to jump on the disunion bandwagon. The final secession vote carried 208 to 89. In the end, all but six of the delegates, including Alexander Stephens, climbed on board by signing their names to the official secession ordinance on January 19.[29]

Hill Looks on from Washington

The state and national press followed Georgia events closely, so there is no doubt that when the final session of the 36th Congress convened on December 3, 1860, Joshua Hill knew what was going on back home. He made at least one overt effort to influence the outcome. On December 13, he sent to Georgia newspapers a public letter urging voters to elect convention delegates who would deliberate calmly and pledge in advance to submit the results to the state's voters for approval or rejection. Hill and

[29] Wooster, "The Georgia Secession Convention," *passim*; Abraham Lincoln to Alexander H. Stephens, December 22, 1860, copy in A. H. Stephens Family Papers, HRBML; B. Collins, "Governor Joseph E. Brown," 189–225. See Candler, *Confederate Records*, vol. 1, for the convention journal and other documents.

his fellow cooperationists hoped that requiring a plebiscite would buy time for passions to fade and compromise to emerge. There was reason for Hill's optimism about the election of cooperationist/conditional delegates because seven of the eleven counties in his congressional district had voted for Bell in November. Moreover, given that the combined statewide vote for Bell and Douglas slightly exceeded the total for Breckenridge, it was not unreasonable for Hill to think moderate delegate candidates could be chosen. Indeed, sixteen of the twenty-six convention delegates from his own Seventh District opposed secession on preliminary votes, but it would ultimately not be enough. After the delegate election was over, a pro-secession correspondent in an Athens paper acknowledged that Hill was "a patriotic gentleman and a true southern man" but strongly assailed his efforts at conciliation.[30]

Congress took a holiday on January 1, 1861. Worried members took advantage of the day off to seek out each other to commiserate about the impending crisis. Among those making the rounds was Representative Robert H. Hatton along with two fellow Tennessee Unionists. Hatton dropped in on Senators Crittenden and Douglas but did not find them at home. Next, he stopped at the lodging of Joshua Hill where he found folks eating, drinking, and talking of politics. Hill and Hatton were old Whigs, who had worked together on the floor to find compromise positions between Republicans and Democrats. After dinner Hatton sat down and wrote to his wife making a point to mention the other spouses. Mrs. Crittenden "was very polite and agreeable;" Mrs. Douglas was "beautiful and well behaved." Although he did not find Emily Hill physically, attractive, Hatton characterized her as "a pleasant little woman, full of talk." Aside from the social niceties, the Tennessean's letter spoke of despair. "The sky is dark, politically – dark as midnight," he began. "The company I met seemed all constrained and awkward – nothing approaching to pleasantry or gayety. The absorbing topic of conversation was the crisis. What is to be done? How long before the war will begin, etc., etc." Such was the mood

---

[30] *Milledgeville Southern Recorder*, December 25, 1860, letter dated December 13; L. Roberts, "Political Career of Joshua Hill," 54–55; *Richmond Whig*, January 4, 1861; *New York Times*, December 25, 1861; *Albany (NY) Evening Journal*, December 27, 1860; Williams, "Bitterly Divided" in Fowler and Parker, eds., *Breaking the Heartland*, 20–21.

of gloom in the household of Joshua Hill and all across the nation's capital city on New Years Day 1861.[31]

South Carolina had already withdrawn from the Union; so as the new year began all eyes were on the other deep South states, especially Georgia. The cover of the January 5th issue of *Harper's Weekly* featured a group drawing of all ten members of Georgia's congressional delegation and provided individual biographical snippets about each man. The description of Joshua Hill emphasized his American Party affiliation and noted correctly that he had "always refused to join in the discussion of slavery on the floor of the House, regarding it as a strictly local question, on the merits or demerits of which Congress has no right to talk or legislate." *Harper's* did not anticipate that Hill would soon break rank with his fellow Georgians, but it soon became clear.[32]

In those early days of 1861, Ohio Democrat Samuel S. Cox cited Joshua Hill as one of fifteen representatives from Southern states "whose zeal never flagged, and whose Unionism never wavered." Aside from these few, Cox lamented, "the whole array of Southern talent...was thrown in favor of precipitate action." Whenever Hill and that small band of unflagging unionists supported legislation or made statements perceived by secessionists to be anti-Southern, they suffered withering criticism. For example, Hill faced guilt by association when he supported a platitudinous resolution offered by Owen Lovejoy, an Illinois abolitionist and close friend of president-elect Lincoln. Later the same day, when he voted nay on a resolution that would have affirmed the right of secession, Hill assured the House that he was "as much in favor of the Union as I ever have been." That was not a sentiment that most Georgia politicians wanted to hear. Just days before Georgia's secession convention convened, Democratic representative Roger Pryor of Virginia presented a resolution declaring "that any attempt to preserve the Union between the States of this Confederacy, by force, would be impracticable and destructive of

[31] Hatton to wife, Jan. 1, 1861, in James V. Drake, *The Life of General Robert Hatton* (Nashville: Marshall & Bruce, 1867) pp. 316-317; Maury Klein, *Days of Defiance: Sumter, Secession, and the Coming of the Civil War* (NY: Knopf, 1997), pp. 190-191. Unlike his Georgia friend Joshua Hill, when TN seceded Hatton went with the CSA. He became a general and died in action.

[32] *Harper's Weekly*, January 5, 1861; Cox, *Eight Years in Congress*, 23; *Globe*, 36-2, 109, 111.

Republican liberty." The vote on the provocative resolution presented a test case to determine which members would be willing to use the federal military against the seceding South and which would not. Hill tried to avoid voting on the issue by calling for adjournment. His tactic failed, so the critical motion to table came to the floor, and Hill's hand was forced. Much to the dismay of almost all Southern members, Hill voted with the Northern majority in favor of the motion to table Pryor's provocative resolution. When the news of Hill's vote to kill the Pryor resolution reached Georgia, the reaction of secessionists was swift and overwhelmingly negative. The *Southern Banner* of Athens headlined its story "Enemies in the Camp. Milledgeville's *Federal Union* proclaimed in capital letters, "JOSH HILL FOR COERCION!!" The body of the editorial lamented, "Oh, Mr. Hill, this is too bad! It is worse than submission." Another article in the same issue cried, "Whilst the Black Republicans have the ascendancy in the Northern States, there is no reasonable hope of peace." By voting to table, Hill had not explicitly voted for coercion, but neither had he joined the rest of the Georgian delegation and most Southern representatives in vocally opposing it.[33]

A few of Hill's newspaper friends came to his defense. The *Savannah Republican* decried the effort of "a small portion of the press of Georgia, to excite indignation and ill-feeling against the Hon. Joshua Hill, the able and patriotic Representative from the Seventh District." Those angry editors, the *Republican* charged, fail to understand the "honest devotion to country, which Joshua Hill occupies." In response to the criticism, Hill distributed a public letter complaining of "the malignant assaults of certain ultra partisan prints of our State," and defending his decision on the Pryor resolution vote. "My object," the beleaguered congressman wrote, "was well understood in the House—it was to keep out all exciting topics." The account in the official *Congressional Globe* supports Hill's public explanation. His private motives can only be surmised:

> Mr. HILL. I move that the House do now adjourn. My object is to put a stop to all this resolution-making business in the House, as it is fraught with nothing but mischief. Every resolution on

[33] *Milledgeville Federal Union*, January 8, 1861 (Soon to be *Southern Union*). See also *(Macon) Georgia Journal and Messenger*, January 23, 1861; *Savannah Daily News*, January 12, 1861; *Globe*, 36-2, December 31, 1860, 220–21.

> the great subject, in my judgment, is unprofitable...I will endeavor to prevent all other resolutions of a like character coming in, either from one side or the other.... I want all resolutions touching the great question that is agitating the country to take the same course. I do not want the House to attempt to dispose of the question by resolution.

Hill's public letter stated: "I am satisfied with my action. I only regret that I have not always been successful. I have tried to pursue that course that I believed would best promote an adjustment of the unhappy strife now raging between a divided people." The parliamentary subtlety eluded Hill's most vocal critics and at least one later scholar, but the cooperationist press stood by him. "Were our halls of Legislation filled by such men as Mr. Hill," a Macon writer proclaimed, "we should be more hopeful of the country."[34]

A week after the kerfuffle over the Pryor resolution, Hill took essentially the same position in response to a resolution offered to approve President Buchanan's course of action and to commend Major Robert Anderson's decision to transfer his troops from indefensible Fort Moultrie on the mainland to Fort Sumter on an island in Charleston Harbor. Hill declared,

"It is well known that I am an advocate for peace.... It is with infinite pain that I have seen this resolution presented to the House. It is not, in my judgement a peace offering, and it is calculated to do nothing but harm."[35]

The naval appropriation bill presented another delicate situation for anti-secession Southern members like Hill. Representative Pryor tried to portray the bill as evidence that the North was readying to use force against the seceding states. He said of the federal navy, "I would sink it in the abyss of ocean before I would grant it a farthing." Other members, including leading Republican John Sherman of Ohio and even one of Pryor's

[34] *Milledgeville Southern Recorder*, January 15, 23, 25, 1861; *Augusta Chronicle*, January 16, 23, 1861; *Globe*, 36-2, December 31, 1861, 220; *Macon Telegraph*, February 1, 1861 (*Savannah Republican*); *(Athens) Southern Watchman*, January 23, 1861. Richard F. Bensel misleadingly wrote that Hill was the only member from the Deep South who "ever cast a vote for federal repression," apparently referring to the Pryor resolution (*Yankee Leviathan*, 80).

[35] *Globe*, 36-2, January 7, 1861, 280.

fellow Virginians, rose in opposition to his incendiary comments. Parliamentary maneuvering ensued, and Joshua Hill once again tried to steer the body away from contentious debate. Hill acknowledged "kind personal feelings" for Pryor and noted that both sides seemed to be anxious for confrontation, but then reminded the House, "It has been my policy from first to last to interpose objection to inflammatory debate."[36]

Hill's Whig-like efforts to eschew debate about slavery and secession appear naive in the heated context of those weeks, yet he had little alternative short of openly supporting the federal government or endorsing secession. At times Hill did imply that his Unionism was conditional. A Macon paper reported such words on January 14:

> If even now it be a crime to labor earnestly to preserve the Constitutional Union of the States, let me, by my own confession be adjudged guilty. But I am far from seeking its perpetuation by the subjugation of seceding States. My devotion to Georgia makes me unwilling to see her take to precipitate flight from the Union, before all honorable efforts to restore and preserve it, have been tried and failed.[37]

Perhaps he was still not sure in his own mind how he would react when and if Georgia actually seceded. Perhaps he felt that he needed to make such statements of "devotion to Georgia" in order to maintain some credibility with White Georgians whom he wanted to influence. He kept to himself just what the condition of "all honorable efforts" meant.

On January 18, 1861, aware that the secession convention in Milledgeville was nearing its decisive vote, Joshua Hill made his final speech as a member of the United States House of Representatives. The immediate reason for his statement was to reply to the call by John Sherman, brother of the general who would famously march through Georgia, to increase federal military appropriations in anticipation of possible conflict. Sherman asserted that the provocative occupation of several federal installations by the militia of Deep South states demonstrated that the time for conciliation had passed and that the Union must prepare for strong military response. Hill and others implored Sherman to yield the

---

[36] Ibid., January 12, 1861, 346.

[37] *(Macon) Georgia Journal & Messenger*, January 14, 23, 1861.

floor so that they could answer, but the influential Ohioan refused. At one point the Ohioan referred to Hill as his "friend from Georgia, whose patriotic feelings I know and appreciate," but he still refused to yield. To a subsequent request by Hill, Sherman replied, "There is no gentleman on this floor to whom I would sooner yield than to the gentlemen from Georgia, but I am under obligations not to allow myself to be interrupted." Finally, Sherman stood down and other members, Northern and Southern, rose to make comments. One of those statements came from Hill's fellow Georgian Martin J. Crawford of Columbus, an immediate secessionist. Crawford implored Congress to allow the Deep South "to retire in peace. That is all that we ask of the North." If the North refused, he warned, slave states would fight to the death if necessary. Crawford's very words proved Sherman's point.

After several commentators had been to the well, some members urged that further debate should be postponed. Joshua Hill did not want to wait—he wanted to have his say while he still had a chance. When a representative told Hill that he could speak another day, the Georgian replied ominously: "That may or may not be so; it depends very much upon circumstances." The chair granted Hill ten minutes. The thrust of his final argument was that compromise and conciliation were still on the table and that making a large federal military appropriation at that moment would be counterproductive to peace. Emphasizing the urgency of the situation but apparently unaware that the crucial vote in Georgia had already occurred, Hill expressed hope that "the convention of my own State, which is sitting to-day" would delay action until passions calmed. Hill wanted Georgia to "make her secession prospective, so as to afford ample time to intervene, and still save the great structure under which we live, and which has blessed us so long." By "prospective," cooperationists meant a secession that would go into effect only upon possible future events such as invasion. Alas, Joshua Hill's appeals were too little, too late, and too far away from action on the ground to make any difference at the state capitol.

In the final paragraph of Hill's allotted ten minutes, he seemed to turn from appeals for compromise to words of reluctant resistance to Union action. Rather than speaking like an unconditional unionist, Hill spoke for that moment like a conditional unionist who feared that his conditions would not be met: "When the time shall come, if it ever does come, when [Georgia] shall demand the allegiance and fidelity of her sons, though I shall regret in extreme sorrow the necessity, I say to every one who hears me here to-day, she shall not have a more faithful and devoted adherent to her fortunes that I shall be, despite my pleadings to her now to delay her action." With those words, Joshua Hill sounded more like Alexander Stephens and Benjamin Hill than like the submissionist his enemies thought him to be.

Hill's anguished words captured the full attention of the House. When his allotted time elapsed, many of the members wanted to hear more of what he had to say. The official record shows:

> The CHAIRMAN. The gentleman's ten minutes have expired. (General cries of "Go on!" "Go on")
>
> Mr. HINDMAN. I object. (Cries of "Oh, no!" and "Withdraw the objection!")

The chair relented and Hill proceeded. The Georgian implored Sherman "to make some distinct effort as conciliation; to present some plan such as that one, for example, as that offered by the venerable Senator [Crittenden] from Kentucky." In response to a question about whether he still stood by the platform of the Constitutional Union Party, Hill proudly reminded the questioner, "I happened to be one of the committee that made that platform." But he then added, "it will not do as a basis of settlement. It is not definite enough. We want something that will meet all of the exigencies that are presented to the country, and that are regarded as grievances by the southern people." Hill concluded, "Let every man go to work, and try to extinguish the flames that threaten destruction."[38]

One short line in Hill's discourse created an immediate backlash in Georgia that would vex him periodically for years to come. It was not his call for Northern conciliation and Southern compromise. Nor was it his implication that he would stand with Georgia if his state seceded. Instead, it was his almost offhand criticism of Georgia's first military action against the government of the United States. A brief account of events is necessary. On January 2, the very day that Georgians were casting their ballots for convention delegates, Governor Joe Brown took the provocative, and arguably treasonous, step of ordering state troops to take over Fort Pulaski,

---

[38] *Globe*, 34-2, January 18, 451–59. For the entire speech, see *Augusta Chronicle*, January 30, 1861, and others.

a federal installation near the mouth of the Savannah River. The huge brick fortification was part of the nation's coastal fortification plan along with Fort Sumter at Charleston, Fort Pickens at Pensacola, and others. Due to cost and the lack of current foreign threat, none of the forts was fully garrisoned at the beginning of 1861, but rumors were rife that the national government would soon move to reinforce, supply, and fortify these installations. Only caretakers and a few construction workers occupied Fort Pulaski, so Georgia's state troops were able to commandeer the federal post without resistance. Brown meanwhile urged his counterparts in South Carolina, Florida, and Alabama to take similar actions, which they soon did. Brown hoped that his bold move would help swing public opinion toward immediate secession, which it soon did.[39]

Joshua Hill was aghast at the governor's rash move, but it was not until his January 18 speech in the House that he publicly spoke of it. About halfway through his allotted ten minutes, Hill chastised South Carolina for seizing federal property and then immediately added the following brief indictment of Brown's action:

> The Governor of my own State may have erred—as I think he did—in seizing Fort Pulaski. I should have been better content for the State of Georgia to have bided her time, and not for him, who has assumed the peculiar guardianship of her defense, to have gone, without authority of her Legislature, or of her Convention, and while she was not even menaced, and done this deed.

Hill's comment was measured and unprovocative, but when his words hit the state's newspapers, all nuance was lost to secessionist ears. In one town, a mob burned the congressman in effigy. Georgia separatists were especially outraged that Hill's remarks had been cheered by Northern representatives and endorsed in Northern newspapers. The *Columbus Times* wrote,

> Hon. Joshua Hill disclaimed in Congress the act of Gov. Brown in taking Fort Pulaski. This elicited applause from the Republicans, and cries of "good." . . . The [Secession] Convention now in

---

[39] Freehling, *Road to Disunion*, 2:482–85; Parks, *Joseph E. Brown*, 124–26; Bryan, "Secession of Georgia," 96.

> session rebuked all such submissionists as Mr. Hill. Without a *dissenting* vote, it passed resolutions "highly approving the energetic and patriotic conduct of the Governor of Georgia in taking Fort Pulaski."...Mr. Hill does not represent his people. Not a delegate in the State [Convention] applauded or even voted for the sentiment he uttered on the floor of Congress. This is a very emphatic rebuke.[40]

Governor Brown's strategy of unifying support for secession in his own state and in other cotton-belt states by seizing the Fort had clearly served its purpose. Unlike the case of Hill's vote on the Pryor resolution just a few days earlier, no wave of support for the Madisonian's criticism of Brown appeared in the press—there was hardly any cooperationist press left. The *Atlanta Intelligencer* explained Hill's situation in folksy language:

> We publish to-day an account of the burning in effigy, at Geneva, Talbot county, Ga. of Hon. Joshua Hill. This feeling of indignation was the result of Mr. Hill's late speech in opposition to Gov. Brown's action in taking Fort Pulaski. *Personally*, we admire Mr. Hill—*politically*, we have always been opposed to him.... Mr. Hill mistook the way "the squirrel would jump," and got on the wrong side.... Everybody in Georgia now, seems to be in favor of secession.... Let Mr. Joshua Hill, of Georgia, stand alongside of "Andy Johnson," of Tennessee, and take the chances with him. If they have made their beds hard, they ought to be content to lie hard. "Them's our sentiments," as [Seminole war hero] Gen. [Duncan Lamont] Clinch once said.[41]

At about the same time that John Sherman and Joshua Hill were sparring on the floor of the House, the Ohioan was engaged in an exchange of private letters with Nathaniel G. Foster, Hill's mentor and predecessor in the House. Foster was frank and direct to Sherman, telling him that he believed that the president and his party intended to accomplish the eventual end of slavery in the South "by indirect action," despite

---

[40] *Columbus Times*, January 24 (Hon. Joshua), 29, 31, 1861; *Macon Telegraph*, January 31, 1861; *Milledgeville Federal Union*, January 29, 1861; *Savannah News*, January 31, 1861; *Washington (DC) Constitutionalist*, January 31, 1861.

[41] *Atlanta Intelligencer*, February 2, 1861 (quotations, quotation marks, emphasis, in original).

Lincoln's statements to Stephens and others that he would not disturb slavery where it already existed. Foster decried Northern "fanaticism" and declared that Georgia would not "tamely submit."[42] It can be assumed that Hill was not only aware of his close friend's opinions but that he also understood that Foster's sentiments reflected those of most of his fellow upper-class Georgians. Hill very likely felt the same way his friend did about slavery and Northern attitudes toward it except for one critical difference—he reasoned that secession and war were much more likely to result in the destruction of slavery than in its preservation.

Hill Makes His Choice

When Georgia's convention made the decision to secede, almost all of the state's political leaders fell in line, including almost all of the conditional Unionists who had for months and years cautioned against leaving the Union. The protestations of Hill and the most ardent Georgia Unionists had fallen on deaf ears. What was Joshua Hill to do? At times, his Unionism seemed unconditional; on other occasions, he had given the impression he, too, would follow his state if conciliation failed. Did he make these pledges sincerely, or did he make them strategically in order to give his appeals for compromise more weight? Most likely, his sometimes apparently contradictory rhetoric reflected his own genuine confliction. Other leading Unionists had to confront the same dilemma between state and nation—most chose differently. Hill's rhetorical assurances that he would support his state's decision contained important equivocations that placed conditions on Georgia as well as on the Union. He insisted that "all honorable efforts" to preserve the Union be exhausted. He had demanded a plebiscite that would reveal the "deliberate judgment of her people." He believed that secession should be considered "prospective" until future events unfolded. He had to decide if these caveats were sufficient to justify renouncing his state's decision to secede.

Joshua Hill was not making his choice in a vacuum. He was fully aware of what was happening in his state and among his political colleagues in Washington. Among the few staunch Unionists who did not go along was long-time United States Supreme Court associate justice James

[42] Foster-Sherman correspondence, January 1861, quoted in Crofts, *Lincoln and the Politics of Slavery*, 148–49.

Moore Wayne of Savannah, who defiantly remained on the court after secession. Wayne's biographer lamented that Wayne's voice "was neither loud enough nor strong enough" to slow the march to disunion. The same could be said of Joshua Hill. But Justice Wayne was the exception. Every other prominent Georgia politician had taken the other path. Howell Cobb had already relinquished his position as secretary of the treasury in President Buchanan's cabinet. Robert Toombs's family had already started packing up their Washington home, and the volatile senator gave an angry farewell speech to his chamber. Even Alexander Stephens, who had voted against secession at all key points in the convention came on board to sign the final document. Like Unionists elsewhere in the Deep South, Hill knew that if he refused to endorse the ordinance of secession, he would face unrelenting opprobrium from his state's press and political leaders.[43]

No contemporary private papers survive to reveal Hill's mental anguish in January 1861. The best insight comes via hindsight in a public letter he wrote in 1863 when he stood as the peace candidate for governor: "I had often expressed my honest conviction that the destruction of the Union would be followed by a long and bloody war, disastrous beyond precedent in its results, to every section." Similar fears of the horrors of war motivated other Southern Unionists as well. Hill was not alone in believing that war would be the worst possible outcome, but he did stand out from most other Georgia politicians in his expectation that the war would not result in Confederate triumph but would be "disastrous" to all.[44]

Finally, when Georgia's secession forced his decision, Joshua opted for a somewhat enigmatic middle course that reflected the mixed messages that he had been sending for years. He did not, like Andrew Johnson of Tennessee, opt to retain his seat in Congress, but neither did he endorse his state's course of action. On January 23, he sent a carefully worded letter to House Speaker William Pennington: "Satisfied as I am that a majority of the Convention of the people of Georgia, now sitting, desires that the

---

[43] McMahon, *Our Good and Faithful Servant*; W. C. Davis, *The Union*, 11; *Milledgeville Southern Recorder*, December 25, 1860; L. Roberts, "Political Career of Joshua Hill," 57; on Alabama, see M. Storey, *Loyalty and Loss*, 19–37.

[44] *Milledgeville Southern Recorder*, September 8, 1863. Hill expressed essentially the same thing in a letter to President Johnson (Hill to Johnson, May 10, 1865, in Johnson, *Papers of Andrew Johnson*; Varon, *Disunion*, 339–40).

State should no longer be represented on this floor, and in obedience to that will of the people, I hereby resign the seat I hold as a member of the House." His deft statement acknowledged political reality without accepting the legitimacy of secession.[45]

In contrast, the seven other Georgia members of the House sent Pennington a joint letter. Their statement began by affirming that the union between Georgia and the United States "is hereby dissolved" and then continued, "In view of the foregoing we hereby announce that we are no longer members of the United States Congress." It was deliberately an announcement rather than a resignation. To have resigned as Hill did would have constituted acknowledgment that they were bound by the formal process of Congress of the United States of which they believed they were no longer part. Georgia's two senators did essentially the same.[46]

The resignation of the gentlemanly Southern member who had so eloquently counseled delay and compromise to preserve the Union deeply saddened many Northern and border state representatives. Back in Georgia, the fact that Northern congressmen lamented losing Joshua Hill but had no kind words for the rest of the departing delegation made secessionists seethe. The *Southern Banner* responded sharply:

> The telegraph informs us that the parting of Hon. Joshua Hill from the members of the House of Representative at Washington, was "very affecting, and that many of them shed tears." but [the wire] does not mention that there was any "boohooing" on account of the rest of the Georgia delegation who withdrew the same day....

Crying over one was easy enough," the writer scoffed, "But for the other seven, 'the mourners put away their handkerchiefs.'"[47]

A few days later, some angry Republicans filed a case with the United States Supreme Court, charging that the senators and representatives from the first six seceding states had committed treason. Chief Justice Roger Taney quickly refused to entertain the action, but the specific wording of

---

[45] *Journal of the House of Representatives*, 36th Congress, 2nd session, Wednesday, January 23, 1861, 221; *Globe*, 36-2, 531; *(Athens) Southern Watchman*, January 30, 1861; Bryan, "Secession of Georgia," 95; Baggett, *Scalawags*, 31.

[46] Ibid.

[47] *(Athens) Southern Banner*, January 30, 1861.

the proposed lawsuit gave critics another chance to attack Hill. Georgia secessionists were rankled that the attorneys who filed the case made a special point of explicitly exempting Joshua Hill and a couple of other Unionists from Alabama and Texas from the inflammatory charge of "treason." The *Columbus Daily Times* cried that the exempting of Hill proved that he was a "friend to our enemies." The writer proudly countered, "We glory in our treason as did the patriots of the revolution when rebelling against their Mother Country."[48]

A little over a decade later, during debate about amnesty for former Confederates, then-senator Joshua Hill claimed that several of his fellow Southern congressman who had withdrawn in early 1861 did so very hesitantly under the false hope that there would be no war:

> I do know, of my own personal knowledge, that here were many members of Congress from the South who left these Halls with the very greatest reluctance to go home at the bidding of the conventions to participate in what they believed would be a harmless and useless contest. It terminated, however, in bloody war to the surprise and astonishment of a great many, because secession was commended to the people as a peaceful remedy, and the people were deluded with it as such.[49]

Hill himself had held no such delusions. He had very much feared the "long and bloody war" that in fact ensued.

The disappointed ex-congressman lingered in Washington for a while but soon returned to Madison to sit out the war in what might best be described as conflicted neutrality. A fitting coda to Hill's turbulent time in the House of Representatives was this small classified advertisement in the March 11, 1861, issue of the capital city's *Daily National Intelligencer*:

> FOR RENT The dwelling. 456 E St. between 6th and 7th, lately occupied by Hon. Joshua Hill. Has hot and cold water, range, bath & c.[50]

---

[48] *Columbus Daily Times*, January 28, 1861.

[49] *Globe*, 42-2, pt. 4, May 8, 1872, 3194.

[50] *(Washington) National Intelligencer*, March 11, 1861.

Chapter 4

Cautious Unionist in Confederate Georgia, 1861–1863

In town after town across the nascent Confederate nation, bravado held sway in gatherings reminiscent of the opening sequences of the motion picture *Gone with the Wind.* Two such scenes played out in Madison in spring 1861 just a few blocks from the home of Joshua and Emily Hill and their eight children. First to march off to war amid the cheering of a large crowd was a volunteer company of the existing state militia consisting of "the wealthiest young men in the county" under the leadership of Captain J. A. Billups. Soon, the Panola Guards left with perhaps even greater fanfare. The Panolas were composed of enthusiastic young men who rallied under the command of Dr. Gazaway B. Knight, who would later become a son-in-law of Joshua Hill. On the steps of the Madison Female College, young ladies ceremoniously presented each departing Panola boy with a special banner. Just over two years later, Hill would reflect on such bluster and declare, "I felt little comfort in the flippant assurances of sanguine orators, 'that the Yankees would not fight'.... In war, as in politics, it is unwise to underrate your adversary."[1]

Joshua Hill had long feared that bloody conflict would come and had endeavored in vain to prevent it. Now, in April 1861, war was upon him, and he had to determine how to live as a Unionist in the secessionist world that surrounded him. As he had done so often before, Hill tried to steer a

[1] "Nathan Massey: Recollections of the late war between the states and the incidents as they transpired," written 1876–1877 for his family, Civil War Miscellany Papers, Madison, microfilm 283-33, Georgia Archives, Morrow; L. Hicky, *Rambles through Morgan County*, 13 (*Madison Weekly Visitor*, July 31, 1861); *Augusta Constitutionalist*, September 6, 1863 (I felt).

middle-of-the-road course. He would not openly resist the Confederacy, but neither would he fully embrace it.

Unionist out of the Public Eye

For more than a hundred years after the Civil War, historians paid scant attention to Southern wartime Unionists. Lost Cause historians acted almost as if they did not exist because to acknowledge their existence would have been to cast doubt on the rectitude of the Confederate cause. More objective mid-twentieth-century historians intent on countering the myths of the Lost Cause devoted considerable attention to prewar Unionists and their resistance to immediate secession, but they typically gave less attention to White dissent within the Confederacy once the war had begun. At the risk of severely oversimplifying the historiography of the topic, it can be said that the turning point toward much wider attention to the issue of dissent within the confines of the Confederacy came in 1974 with the publication of Carl Degler's *The Other South: Southern Dissenters in the Nineteenth Century*. More studies followed, with Thomas G. Dyer's *Secret Yankees*, which told of clandestine interactions amongst Atlanta's most intense Unionists, emerging as the seminal work for Georgia. John Inscoe and Robert Kenzer gathered perspectives on Southern Unionists together in an important collection. David Williams soon followed with an anthology and two overviews focusing on Georgia's and the South's bitter inner battles. All of these studies and many others emphasize that White Southern support for the Confederacy was anything but unanimous. As Dyer put it, "There were, however, many shades of gray and blue—many many shades of loyalty." Inscoe stressed "the sheer diversity of the Unionist experience over the course of the war, and the importance of personal and local variables in providing a far more complex and colorful sense of who Southern Unionists were." This chapter seeks to probe those "shades of loyalty" and those "personal and local variables" as they apply to Joshua Hill.[2]

---

[2] Degler, *The Other South*; Inscoe and Kenzer, *Enemies of the Country*, 7; Dyer, *Secret Yankees*, 3; D. Williams, T. C. Williams, and Carlson, *Plain Folk in a Rich Man's War*; Williams, *Georgia's Civil War*; Williams, *Bitterly Divided*; Downing, *A South Divided*; Rubin, *Shattered Nation*; Sarris, *A Separate Civil War*; Bryan, *Confederate Georgia*; Levine, *Fall of the House of Dixie*; Freehling, *South vs. the South*;

The most extreme Unionists were those who left the South altogether, some of whom joined the Union army and literally bore arms against the seceded states. At the next level were those who remained home but openly spoke out at risk of social and economic ostracism and even bodily harm or death. Others were less bold, but still allowed their discontent and residual love for the Union to be known. Still more, like the Atlantans described by Dyer, held their public tongues yet kept close contact with like-minded souls behind the scenes. Most Unionists harbored deep resentment at secession and quietly longed for the war to end. However, they had to go along to get along—perhaps with a touch of subtle passive aggression. Thinking back on his days as a teenager whose mother opposed the Confederacy, one Atlantan recalled that Unionist families "simply wanted to be let alone, while events took their course."[3]

William G. Brownlow, the "Fighting Parson" of Knoxville, Tennessee, whom the Confederacy formally charged with treason, was probably the most famous wartime Unionist. Expelled from his home state in 1862, Brownlow toured the North giving impassioned lectures and wrote a best-selling anti-Confederate book. But men like Brownlow were the exception. Leading South Carolina Unionist James L. Petigru, who is said to have admired Joshua Hill's antisecession stance, was more typical of the men whose Unionism, historian Robert McKenzie observed, "was manifested primarily in 'prudent silence,' 'strict neutrality of conduct,' and a willingness to make money while awaiting federal deliverance."[4] Like Petigru, Hill's Unionist background was well known. He did not hide it, but he took care not to provide any overt aid, comfort, or endorsement to the Yankee cause. It was daily business as usual for his plantation and his law practice. For the most part, he remained circumspect in his public comments. At times he tiptoed a bit past prudent silence into the public eye but never in a way directly to challenge the Confederate government.

Sacher downplays the role of the draft in causing Confederate disunity; he especially mentions David Williams (*Confederate Conscription*, 1–7, 203–204).

[3] Dyer, *Secret Yankees*, 46–47, 84, and *passim*; Reed, *History of Atlanta*, 189.

[4] McKenzie, "Prudent Silence and Strict Neutrality," 90. An exception to the rule of Lost Cause historians ignoring Unionists is Coulter, *William G. Brownlow*; and Pease and Pease, *James Louis Petigru*. Family materials provided by Christina Wood-Smith quote a letter from Petigru to Hill; it is not in the published Petigru papers.

The 1850s had been prosperous years for the large planters of Georgia's lower Piedmont cotton belt. The upper crust of Madison took advantage of the decade's high cotton prices to erect several fine in-town homes and to remodel others. Their counterparts in Greensboro, Eatonton, Covington, and other surrounding towns of Georgia's lower Piedmont cotton belt did the same. By the beginning of the Civil War, Joshua Hill had become one of the wealthiest men in Morgan County. The 1860 Census valued his real estate at $22,500 and his personal estate at $50,000. The forty-eight-year-old lawyer-planter owned 2,060 acres of good countryside land plus $6,400 worth of in-town real estate according to the 1862 tax digest. Emily Hill was forty years old, and all eight of their children, from three to twenty years of age, were still living at home. Morgan County's 1860 population of 9,997 was about 70 percent enslaved, and Hill owned fifty-nine of the bondspeople, ranging from infant to sixty. The bulk of Hill's slaves worked his several-hundred-acre plantation near Seven Islands Road in the southeastern portion of the county, and others labored in town or on his other properties. Hill rented the balance of his land holdings to other farmers and planters who could utilize their own enslaved workers.[5]

When Southern White men headed to war from Madison in spring 1861, E. W. Evans was an enslaved six-year-old boy in the Hill household. His mother was a seamstress assisted by "aunt Lizzie." His "aunt Dinah" labored as the "washer-woman," and his "Aunt Caroline" served as "the nurse for Miss Emily's children." The 1860 Slave Schedule lists a half-dozen males of about his age among the Hill's property. Some seventy-five years later, the retired brick mason related his memories of childhood slavery to the New Deal–era slave narrative project. As was often the case in these narratives, Evans's story muddled some of the details and timeline, and there is no doubt that his story reflected a mixture of interviewer expectations and rosy memories shaped by decades of re-telling family lore.

---

[5] Mitchell, *Madison*, *passim*; 1862 Morgan County Tax Digest and Slave Schedules, accessed via Ancestry.com; Joshua Hill file, MCA; 1860 Census, Place, Town District, Morgan, Georgia, via Ancestry.com; The children were Anna (twenty), Clarence (seventeen), Hugh Legare (fourteen), Walter (eleven), John (nine), Louise (seven), Julia (five), and Isabelle (three).

Nevertheless, Evans provided the best available insight into slave life at the Hill town place and plantation:

> [Joshua Hill's] wife, our mistress, had charge of the slaves and plantation. She never seemed to like the idea of having slaves. Of course, I never heard her say she didn't want them, but she was the one to free the slaves on this place before surrender. Since that, I've felt she didn't want them in the first place.... I never worked as a slave because I wasn't old enough. In 1864, when I was about nine years old they sent me on a trial visit to the plantation to give me an idea of what I had to do some day.... At the age of ten years they were then sent to the field to work. They'd chop, hoe, pick cotton, and pull fodder, corn, or anything else to be done on the plantation. I stayed at the place a whole week and was brought home on Saturday. That week's work showed me what I was to do when I was ten years old. Well, this was just before Sherman's march from Atlanta to the sea and I never got a chance to go to the plantation to work again, for Miss Emily freed all on her place and soon after that we were emancipated.[6]

Although Joshua Hill did not keep a diary and no personal letters survive, snippets of evidence and his later remarks about the early years of the war tell of a relatively quiet life in Madison punctuated by occasional out-of-town business trips. He did face some ostracism from ardent Confederates such as Colonel Edwin Walker, whose house stood (and still stands) behind the Hill place. After the war began, Walker quit speaking to his old friend Josh, but others, including Walker's son-in-law, were more accommodating. Locals obviously valued Hill's political experience. In October 1861, just ten months after he resigned from Congress, the voters elected Hill to a one-year term on the Madison Board of Commissioners. Due to the loss of city records, it is not clear if Hill remained on the commission throughout the war, but at least one 1864 source refers to him as mayor. Even with two of his sons serving in the army, Hill refrained from giving direct aid to the Confederacy; but he did help his boys and contribute to a fund that assisted families needing relief. In January 1862,

[6] Tonsill and Evans, "E. W. Evans, Brick Layer & Plasterer," https://www.loc.gov/item/wpalh000565. The interviewer's use of dialect in transcription has been removed.

Hill wrote to Governor Brown to endorse "a personal friend" who was seeking a military appointment. He assured Brown that the endorsement was "wholly disconnected with politics," because he and the man wanting the position were "of different political persuasions."[7]

Although battles waged far from Madison, the realities of war still intruded on the home front. Charity drives raised funds for needy families who had fathers or sons serving away from home. Trainloads of troops and supplies passed through town on their way to and from Atlanta and Augusta. Morgan County had its own quasi-military body called the Silver Grays composed of men too old to fight. In 1862, townspeople got a close-up look at Union soldiers and some allegedly disloyal backcountry Whites when the Confederate military converted Madison's defunct steam-operated cotton mill into a stockade that admitted more than 850 prisoners, including at least two Union generals. In May 1862, Madison's town jail temporarily housed the Union spies of the famous Andrews Raid who were captured when the locomotive *General* ran out of fuel with the *Texas* in hot pursuit along the Western & Atlantic railroad north of Atlanta. One raider found Madison "a neat, prettily situated town," but the army soon returned the prisoners to incarceration in Northwest Georgia.[8]

Late in 1863, the grim reality of war became much more apparent to Morgan Countians when hundreds of sick and wounded Confederate soldiers began pouring into several local hospitals, including the old mill that had recently held Union prisoners and the two then-closed female colleges.[9]

Joshua Hill kept a low profile from February 1861 through July 1863, but it is evident that he kept up with wartime politics. During his business

---

[7] *Augusta Chronicle*, October 11, 1861 (*Madison Visitor*). Madison city records for the war period were lost in a postwar fire. *Augusta Constitutionalist*, October 25, 1862; Hill to Joseph E. Brown, January 25, 1862, Governor's Incoming Correspondence, Civil War, Gov. Joseph E. Brown, Georgia Archives, Morrow; Claim of Ida F. Rowland, administrator of the estate of John S. Rowland, Southern Claims Commission, Case No. 21746, NARA records, via Ancestry.com (Col. Walker). Hereinafter Rowland Claim testimony.

[8] Confederate States of America Prison (Madison, Georgia) Records of 1862, Arrivals, ms 1428, HRBML; B. Harris, *Confederate Hospitals*, 6; Bonds, *Stealing the General*, 220–21.

[9] B. Harris, *Confederate Hospitals*, 5, 474.

travels, Hill would have had ample opportunity to share political rumors and insights with both active Confederates and circumspect Unionists. Because he was often in Atlanta, he maintained contact with some of the Gate City's "secret Yankees." Hill kept his opinions to himself and his friends. His name had been often in the news from 1857 through early 1861, but from spring 1861 to the middle of 1863, the press wrote hardly a word about the ex-member of Congress, whom they had so recently vilified. In late summer and fall 1863 that would all change.[10]

Equivocal Candidate for Governor, 1863

The governmental structure of Confederate Georgia was essentially the same as it had been prior to secession—except, of course, for the removal of all reference to relationship with the federal government of the United States of America. In fall 1861, Governor Brown ran for a third two-year term. Tensions between Brown and the central government in Richmond had already begun to emerge, and some of the state's press opposed the incumbent. Several names, including Joshua Hill's friend Judge Augustus Reese of Madison, emerged as possible opponents. Opposition to Brown finally coalesced on Judge E. A. Nisbet, an ex-Whig who had formally introduced the secession resolution in January, but it was in vain. Incumbent Brown prevailed with just under 59 percent of the vote.[11]

During the following two years, Georgia's opinionated governor continued to be a thorn in the side of the Jefferson Davis administration because Brown opposed the usurpation of state prerogatives, mostly with regard to control of the Georgia state militia and conscription into the rebel army. Both of Georgia's Confederate senators, Hershel V. Johnson and Benjamin H. Hill, became disenchanted with Brown. Public discontent with the course of the war emerged among segments of the White population as early as 1862 and increased as 1863 began. Confederate vice president Alexander Stephens captured the essence of war weariness in a January 1863 letter to a friend: "The great majority of the masses, both North and South, are true to the cause of their side—no doubt about that. The great majority on both sides are tired of the war; want peace. I have no

[10] Dyer, *Secret Yankees*, 257; author's keyword search of newspaper databases.

[11] Parks, *Joseph E. Brown*, 157–58; Bass, "Georgia Gubernatorial Elections," 172–81; Bryan, *Confederate Georgia*, 33–36; Cook, *Governors of Georgia*, 67–70.

doubt about that. But as we do not want peace without independence, so they do not want peace without reunion. There is the difficulty."[12]

In the middle of 1863, three devastating Confederate defeats compounded the already existing political tensions in Georgia and other Confederate states. The thrust into the North failed at Gettysburg in early July. Simultaneously, the fall of Vicksburg gave full command of the Mississippi River to federal forces. Then, on September 8, the Union troops forced the Confederate army to pull back into far North Georgia from the important Tennessee River port at Chattanooga. The Union army held Georgia's sea islands, and the United States Navy's blockade proved highly effective—though not impenetrable. Discontent was rife, and Confederate desertions became more frequent, especially in North Georgia. Confederate money held little value, slave escapes were becoming more common, and food shortages plagued much of the state. Some better news for the Confederacy finally arrived in mid-September when victory at the Battle of Chickamauga thwarted further Union advance into Northwest Georgia. Although that battle provided a boost to White Southern morale and delayed further federal action, it did not result in the recapture of Chattanooga or any other territory for the Confederacy.[13]

Georgia's gubernatorial race of 1863 would be waged in this context of military and political anxiety. As they had in 1861, Brown's pro-Davis opponents searched for a viable candidate who would have a plausible chance to defeat him. Political wounds, suffered in the 1860 split between Douglas Democrats and Breckinridge Democrats, had not fully healed, and no political parties analogous to those of pre-secession years had yet emerged in Confederate Georgia. As a consequence, there was no natural path to produce a candidate. In order to discourage the formation of any such party, the governor made a belated show of cozying up to the Davis administration. In addition, Brown's relief efforts for destitute families who had boys on the fields of battle boosted his popularity at home and

---

[12] Alexander Stephens to R. M. Johnston, January 29, 1863, in C. Thompson, *Reconstruction in Georgia*, 33.

[13] Williams, *Georgia's Civil War*, 148–49; Levine, *Fall of the House of Dixie*, 206–207; McPherson, *Battle Cry of Freedom*, 666–81.

with the soldiers themselves. He further shored up his dwindling support in northern counties by suspending the draft there.[14]

Some three months after the governor's May announcement that he would run, the anti-Brown forces remained stymied. Out of the squabbling among current officeholders and military commanders, the strongest candidate who emerged to face Joe Brown proved to be neither an ally of Jefferson Davis nor an active Confederate soldier or politician. Rather it would be Joshua Hill, Brown's old nemesis from the Whig-American-Know-Nothing-Opposition days. Hill's potential candidacy came to public attention via a letter to the *Athens Watchman* and an article in the *Atlanta Gazette*. The reaction from anti-Brown forces was highly positive. Other newspapers reprinted or reported on the *Watchman* letter, and word soon spread that Hill had consented to having his name put forward. The *Augusta Constitutionalist* supported Governor Brown but conceded, "Hon. Colonel Hill is a high toned gentleman, and a man of acknowledged ability."[15]

The active effort to bring Joshua Hill out of retirement to face Governor Brown originated with Amos T. Akerman, who would eventually become Ulysses Grant's first attorney general. New Hampshire-born Akerman was an influential Atlanta attorney, but he was not yet well known across the state. As was the custom of the time, Akerman signed his letter of nomination with a pseudonym. The *Watchman* editor touted the writer's credentials: "The following communication, suggesting the Hon. Joshua Hill, as a candidate, is from the pen of an intelligent and patriotic gentleman, whose name, were we at liberty to publish it, would give great weight to his suggestion." It can be assumed that political insiders fairly soon learned of the actual authorship. Referring clearly to Brown and his secessionist friends, the letter charged, "We are learning by bitter experience that hotspurs and demagogues are unfit to govern a country." The lawyer's letter carefully avoided use of the then-toxic word "Unionist," but subscribers could read between the lines. He made it clear that he

---

[14] Bass, "Georgia Gubernatorial Elections," 181; L. B. Hill, *Joseph E. Brown and the Confederacy*; Sarris, *A Separate Civil War*, 99.

[15] *(Athens) Southern Watchman*, August 12, 1863; *Augusta Constitutionalist*, August 18, 1863 (*Watchman* and *Gazette*); L. Roberts, "Political Career of Joshua Hill," 50–72.

believed that the time had come to put the state in the hands of someone who had perceived the folly of secession. Referring to those whom he had called "hotspurs and demagogues," Ackerman continued:

> They were suffered to lead the country in 1861, and none of the blessings which they predicted have been realized, while most of the evils apprehended by more considerate men have come to pass. Our next Governor should be taken from the latter class. Men who were calm when others were excited, who saw clearly when others were blinded, who kept sober when others were intoxicated, have given evidence of the sagacity and soundness for which the public mind instinctively calls. Events are daily proving their wisdom. They, if any body, can deliver us from that gulf of trouble in which we are plunged.
>
> There is no worthier representative of this class than JOSHUA HILL, of the county of Morgan, and he is hereby proposed to the people as a suitable man for Governor. His tried capacity, his stainless integrity, his calm judgment, and his high personal bearing, all qualify him for that responsible office. He is well known to the people.[16]

A dozen years later, in sworn testimony, Hill explained why he consented to allow his candidacy to go forward. The occasion was his statement before the Southern Claims Commission in the case of the estate of John S. Rowland, whose widow was the daughter of Hill's neighbor Edwin Walker. The widow's case for compensation for damages caused by Sherman's troops in summer 1864 rested partly on the proposition that her late husband's support for Joshua Hill's gubernatorial candidacy constituted evidence of his Unionism. Hill testified that a gubernatorial vote for him would not in and of itself have constituted "an infallible test" of Unionism, but it was certainly a good indication because he doubted that "there was ever any democrat in the state who voted for me unless he sympathized with these peculiar views which I had." The commissioners pressed Hill for further details. One asked Hill directly if his candidacy was "distinctively a union movement or not—was it opposed to the confederacy?" His answer left little doubt:

---

[16] *(Athens) Southern Watchman*, August 12, 1863.

> **A.** Oh, yes sir. I was very open and avowed in my opposition and in my denunciation whenever I did speak at all, but I never attended a public meeting in four years. Whenever I spoke of the measures and tyrannies of Mr. Davis' administration, the conscription and impressment largely, I did it without any stint at all....
>
> **Q.** When you were candidate in 1863 for Governor of Georgia, were you known at that time as a union man, and were you voted for at that time as a union man, opposed to secession, opposed to the confederacy, and in favor of sustaining the integrity and supremacy of the union throughout the south, or were you a candidate of the party who were opposed to Davis as an individual, but with him in the measures of his administration?
>
> **A.** I will tell you how I was known. I was known in Georgia to have been the only representative who had or the only member of congress including the two senators and of ten who refused to sign a card of withdrawal.... That was published all over Georgia. I was burned in effigy in various counties for my [action]. I went home and took no part in anything and stayed there those years—1861, 1862, 1863. The first I ever heard of my candidacy for Governor was in the communication to a paper called the 'Athens Watchman' which Akerman afterwards told me he wrote. He was against the war and against secession and was then unknown as a public man.

Hill's testimony clarified that he knew in advance that his candidacy was primarily symbolic; he did not expect to win, but he wanted to give the opposition a chance to be counted. He explained that after the *Watchman* article and others appeared, "five men of distinction," including one former member of Congress, urged him to let his name be put forward:

> I said to them that if I should be elected Governor there was one thing I never would do—I never would take the oath to support the constitution of the confederate states or its government nothing on earth should induce me to do it. They then opened the code of the state saying that the Governor of Georgia was not required to take the oath to support the confederate government; it was simply that he would faithfully perform the duties of Governor of the state of Georgia—that was the oath. I did

> this for the purpose of showing them that if I was put in the position where it was necessary for me to do that, that I would not do it, and they had better take some other man.... So it went on but everybody, so far as I know, knew one thing of me; they knew I was a very uncompromising union man; everybody knew that who knew me at all personally.[17]

Many years later, in 1888, Hill related the same tale in a shorter and more colorful manner to a group at the Kimball Hotel: "In 1863 I was quite prominent in politics in Georgia. I was a union man, and my friends, more sanguine than I was, urged me to oppose Governor Brown for governor of Georgia. I did not hesitate to accept the place although I knew it was a desperate chance." The seventy-six-year-old told his younger listeners of an occasion during the campaign when he was in Atlanta and encountered two "former friends" who told him that they were not willing to support his candidacy. Hill replied, "I know what is right, and dare maintain it, and I don't care a d—n for your vote if you do not agree with me."[18]

At the last minute on September 15, 1863, about a month after Hill's announcement and about three weeks before the election, a pro-Davis candidate finally entered the field in the person of Timothy M. Furlow from Sumter County in Southwest Georgia. Furlow was a wealthy planter who rose to the rank of lieutenant colonel in his locally raised Confederate battalion, but he lacked statewide prominence. It was clear that Hill would present the more significant challenge. In a thinly veiled reference to Hill and Brown, respectively, Furlow announced, "This is no time for factious opposition or grudging support to the Administration [of President Davis]." Some backers of Furlow hoped that the three-way race would end with no candidate having a majority, thus throwing the choice into the legislature where anti-Brown members were in the ascendency.[19]

None of the candidates mounted an active canvas, so the gubernatorial race was carried out almost exclusively in the newspapers and in private communications. In addition to the normal advantages of incumbency, the

---

[17] Rowland Claim testimony.

[18] *Atlanta Constitution*, September 27, 1888.

[19] Bryan, *Confederate Georgia*, 43–44 (This is); Bass, "Georgia Gubernatorial Elections," 184–85; L. B. Hill, "Governor Brown and the Confederacy," 359–60; Rable, *Confederate Republic*, 217; Parks, *Joseph E. Brown*, 251–52.

low-key nature of the campaign benefitted the well-known Brown. Soldiers in particular lacked clear information about politics back home in September 1863. One soldier stationed in Virginia sought details about Hill from his brother-in-law in Southwest Georgia's Macon County:

> I learn that Gov. Brown of Georgia has an opponent in the field for Governorship. I am at a loss in this matter as for Brown he never can have my vote, and I know nothing of the principals on which Joshua Hill declares himself a candidate for the sufferages of the people of the State of Georgia, moreover I learn that Hill is a peace candidate or a reconstructionist, I don't know how true this is or what his principals is. If you know I want you to post me on the nature of the case. Just come out and tell me exactly what Hill stands for in this case. I shall have to depend on your judgment or the judgment of some good friend who knows something about affairs in general.

Another soldier, also writing from Virginia, was not as objective in his quest for information. First Lieutenant Irby Goodwin Scott of Putnam County, wrote:

> When you write give me a few notes about the politics in the county and State as I have very little chance of learning any other way. I have been opposed to Joe Brown for several reasons one, his opposition to Jeff Davis & and the administration. But if Joshua Hill is the candidate of the reconstructionist or union candidate I shall vote for Brown and regret that I am only allowed one vote for if I had ten thousand I would cast them all against Hill.

Unfortunately, in neither case is a reply from the correspondent available.[20]

A Confederate soldier stationed in Chattanooga had better access to timely "political balderdash" than his compatriots who were deployed in Virginia. The anonymous writer, apparently an officer and perhaps a former Know-Nothing, expressed his optimistic military observations and

[20] Jas. W. Smith to T. H. Morgan, September 8, 1863, in Hays, *History of Macon County*, 317–18 (sufferages, [*sic*]); Pearson, *Lee and Jackson's Bloody Twelfth*, 144.

negative political opinion about Joshua Hill in a long letter published in third person in the *Macon Telegraph*:

> The partisans of Mr. Joshua Hill at home have prejudiced him with the army by impliedly censuring a cause towards the success of which so many noble lives have been sacrificed, so much hardship endured and such unnumbered deprivations encountered. From the tone of that gentleman's professed organ, we understand him and them to be fishing for the votes of anti-war men, Unionists, reconstructionists, and all those who would dishonor their country… although the writer was once politically cliqued with Mr. Hill, he would feel it a shame to vote for him now, understanding him (through those who favor his election) to be the representative of the enemies to a successful prosecution of this war.… Mr. Hill declares that he will not define his own position. We of the army are left no alternative but to infer it from those who speak in his behalf.[21]

As the Chattanooga soldier's letter indicated, the tactic of Brown supporters was to question Hill's Confederate patriotism and to try to pin the Madisonian down on specific positions. One Atlanta writer put it bluntly: "Those who are not for us are against us." The *Macon Telegraph* declared, "it is universally known that in his official character, while a member of Congress from Georgia, [Hill] held on to the corrupt and rotten 'Old Union,' with tenacious purpose, until he stood 'solitary and alone' of all Georgia's senators and Representatives." The Macon writer astutely summarized Hill's electoral dilemma: "If Mr. Hill should proclaim himself a reconstructionist, this would lose him the votes of true men who might otherwise support him in a spirit of general opposition to Governor Brown. If [he stands] for war till independence is achieved, then the peace men are driven off." Indeed, the dilemma forced Joshua Hill to walk a middle-of-the-road political tightrope between his supporters who were loyal to the Confederacy but fed up with the administrations in Milledgeville and Richmond on the one hand and his backers who were motivated

[21] *Macon Telegraph*, September 1, 1863.

to seek peace and re-union on the other. Whichever position he took, he was bound to lose support.[22]

Hill's opponents sought to discredit him by outing him as a friend of Northern politicians and as a "reconstructionist." At this point in the war, there was considerable equivocation in the use of the word "reconstruction"—no one knew exactly what it would mean. For the most part, those who wanted the Confederacy to fight to the end used "reconstructionist" as an epithet to describe any man who was willing to end the war and seek some sort of compromise to put the Union back together. Soon after the announcement that Hill's name would be tendered, the *Dalton Times* asked and answered its own question:

> Can it be possible that there is a Reconstruction party in the State of Georgia, and that Mr. Hill is the candidate of that party? It would seem so.... We call upon Mr. Hill and his supporters to explain its meaning, to tell us in unequivocal language what they are for, and how they propose to take us out of our present difficulties—whether by a still more vigorous prosecution of the war, or by making overtures to the Lincoln Government for a reconstruction of the Union.... We call upon Mr. Hill, himself, to write out and publish to the people of Georgia his political sentiments.

Another columnist made the same point in countryfied dialect: "No I didn't say Mr. Hill wer a rekonstruktionist by no means. I said that if he were not, he would take down his sign—that's what I said.... Too steep a Hill, that, for us to climb."[23]

In his testimony in the Rowland case, Joshua Hill explained that his refusal to renounce his desire for reunion cost him support. The *Savannah Republican*, one of the most prominent dailies in the state, was anti-Davis and had endorsed Hill. James R. Sneed, one of the two editor-owners was, in Hill's own words, "a personal friend of mine." The other editor, however, demanded that if Hill wanted the paper's support, he must clearly

---

[22] *Macon Telegraph*, August 19, 1863; Rable, *Confederate Republic*, 216; *Atlanta Intelligencer*, August 29, 1863.

[23] *Atlanta Intelligencer*, September 2, 1863 (*Dalton Times*); *Macon Telegraph*, August 29, 1863, and *(Athens) Southern Banner*, September 2, 1863 (No, I didn't); *Macon Telegraph*, September 10, 1963; *Columbus Enquirer*, August 27, 1863.

state that he opposed restoration of the Union. Hill refused, and the *Republican* withdrew its endorsement.[24]

Joe Brown himself privately noted Hill's reluctance to be nailed down. "You have noticed," Brown wrote to Alexander Stephens on August 22,

> that I have opposition; I suppose Mr. Hill relies upon the failure of our own Government and disaster of our armies for his success. How ardently he desires our success in such case is not for me to know. I am reliably informed that he refused when in Atlanta to say whether he favored reconstruction or not, or to define his position one way or the other, leaving the people to take him upon his past record.[25]

Besides attacking Hill for his apparent equivocation, Brown's supporters used the former congressman's own words against him. They emphasized that Representative Hill had publicly condemned the governor's popular pre-secession seizure of Fort Pulaski. They revived the charge that Hill's vote to table Representative Pryor's resolution endorsing the right of secession had constituted disloyalty to the Southern states. They reminded voters that plaintiffs who raised treason charges against Southern congressmen had exempted Hill and other Unionists. Most often they emphasized and decried Hill's refusal to withdraw from the United States Congress in January 1861 along with Georgia's other representatives. The *Countryman* of Baldwin County charged:

> It would seem that Mr. Hill did not recognize that secession is a rightful, legal act.... There was great difference between "withdrawing," and "resigning." The men who "withdrew" recognized the secession of the State, and their withdrawal was a final severance of Georgia, as a sovereign State, from any connection through Congressional representation, with the Abolition government. The man who "resigned" instead of "withdrawing," implied that Georgia had not nor could not, through a sovereign

---

[24] Rowland Claim testimony; L. B. Hill, *Joseph E. Brown and the Confederacy*, 133–34.

[25] Joseph E. Brown to Alexander Stephens, August 22, 1863, in Phillips, *Correspondence*, 827.

> convention of her people secede from the Abolition government.[26]

All of these charges resonated with ardent Confederates.

Hill's backers took it upon themselves to defend and explain their candidate before he made any personal statement of his own. They contrasted the hotheaded nature of Brown with the more diplomatic style of Hill. One paid advertisement pulled no punches in making it clear that a negotiated peace was the goal of Hill's campaign. It is not certain that Hill specifically authorized the content, but the fact that it was placed by a Newton County Confederate soldier who had known Hill for twenty years and had supported him in previous elections indicates that it reflected Hill's sentiments. The endorsement declared that Hill "had the wisdom and prescience to perceive the troubles and difficulties ahead of us, which others did not." The Madisonian was said to possess "the sagacity to perceive the best and speediest method of piloting us out of our difficulties, and the ability to do it, which those in power have not." The ad contrasted Hill and Brown:

> No man in Georgia contributed more to bring about Secession than Governor Brown. He was a zealous advocate of the erroneous views and measures which I have already pointed out.... If we put men of worth and wisdom in power, and if we make no more ill-advised invasions of the territory of the Yankees [i.e., Gettysburg], we will, no doubt greatly dispose the minds of the people of the North to peace and the time may come sooner than we now suppose, when diplomacy can bring about a cessation of hostilities and an amicable adjustment of our difficulties.... I shall cast my vote for Joshua Hill. I shall require no long letter of acceptance from him defining his position—no canvassing, or stump speaking, or "platform" to stand upon.... I am willing to take the man upon his know wisdom, statesmanship and fidelity to the country."[27]

Efforts like the advertisement above were not enough to stop the heavy barrage of demands that Hill must speak for himself, so he finally felt

[26] *Augusta Constitutionalist*, August 29 (*Countryman*), September 8, 1863; *(Athens) Southern Banner*, September 2, 1863.

[27] *Macon Telegraph*, August 28, 1863 (ad dated August 22).

compelled to pen a personal response. Styling his August 31 public letter as a response to an interrogatory from three Atlanta gentlemen and "other friends," Hill explained that his name was put forth "without any agency or management of mine. Perhaps, it has proceeded," he offered, "from a few ardent friends who had determined to compliment me with their votes—without regard to any responsible prospect of success. That I have some such devoted friends, I have reason to know." His letter stressed that he had taken no active part in politics since his resignation from the House. He reiterated his principal reason for strongly opposing secession: "I had often expressed my honest convictions, that the destruction of the Union would be followed by a long and bloody war, disastrous beyond precedent in its results, to every section."[28]

Hill danced around the real question: "It is charged that I am in favor of a reconstruction of the Union—opposed to the prosecution of the war, and to the Administration of President Davis. I answer these charges to gratify a class of friends, who are really ignorant of my sentiments, and not with the hope or desire of appeasing the wrath of enemies." On the surface, Hill's answer read like the rhetoric of an ardent Confederate, yet there was an undercurrent of inscrutability. "I always regarded it [Reconstruction] as impossible, except by the success of the Northern arms, and then only the Union in name, and not the free Government of our fathers. I want no such Union as that, and will not accept it." He deftly avoided defining just exactly what "not accept it" meant.[29]

As the owner of five dozen enslaved people himself, Hill defended the institution: "The best argument in favor of disunion, and the one most relied on by its advocates, was apprehension for the security of our slave property." With a bit of an I-told-you-so tone, Hill charged that it was actually secessionists, not Unionists, who had put slavery "in extreme peril now." His observation was on target. Hill had been a strong advocate of the Crittenden compromise and similar proposals that had tried to avoid secession by extracting Northern guarantees of the continuation of slavery in the states where it existed. By the time Hill wrote this 1863 statement, it had been almost a year since President Lincoln had first promulgated

---

[28] *Augusta Constitutionalist*, September 6, 1863 (and numerous other Georgia newspapers).

[29] Ibid.

the Emancipation Proclamation and about nine months since it had gone into effect. Hill wrote, "So far as Mr. Lincoln and the Abolitionists are concerned, there is nothing left us but to resist to the last, by all the means at our command, their efforts to destroy and despoil us. They present us no alternative but ruin or victory.... Surely, no true Southerner can desire peace, with the surrender of our invaluable institution." What did he mean by "all the means at our command"? Was he implying the necessity of a fight to the death; or, more likely, was he hinting that because of his Unionist reputation that he might be the person best able to negotiate a peace settlement that would contain a guarantee of slavery even at this point? Was he suggesting that "ruin" was inevitable but blaming it on secession? Or was he, as he testified later in the Rowland case, just trying to stir things up and feed existing factionalism? With regard to Jefferson Davis, Hill admitted that he had "not approved of every act" of the president, but he did not know of any man who could do a better job. That was faint praise indeed.[30]

In response to those who argued that his candidacy was an affront to the fighting men of the Confederacy, Hill admitted that he had made no effort to encourage enlistment, but, he explained, "I denied them not my aid and my sympathy." He used his own family to establish his sympathy and support for the boys in the field: "Early in the struggle the youth of my own household, and those of my nearest kindred, flew to arms." Referring to the death of one of his nephews, Hill lamented, "The soil of Virginia had drank deep of the life-blood of my gallant young kinsmen."[31] A year later, Hill would lose his own son to battle in North Georgia.

The final paragraph of Hill's position paper added to its inscrutability. His preceding statements had supported soldiers, lamented that defeat meant the certain loss of slavery, and declined to criticize Jefferson Davis. Those were words that might have come from Joe Brown himself. But then he concluded with an extended if-then syllogism that opposed war and raised the possibility of an "honorable, lasting peace":

> If to mourn the fall of the thousands of youthful victims; if to pity the sufferings and trials of the maimed and wounded; if to lament the havoc and inhumanities wrought by a cruel foe; if to

[30] Ibid.

[31] Ibid.

> regret the pains and privations of the sick and war-weary soldier; if to desire that he should receive sufficient pay to supply his necessary wants; if to sympathize with wretched and helpless women and children; if to sigh for the return of peace, an honorable, lasting, peace, constitute opposition to the war, then am I opposed to it.[32]

The question, of course, was what might constitute "an honorable, lasting, peace."

Brown's supporters quickly attacked the letter, and Hill's later opponents would continue to cherry pick bits of it to use against him throughout the rest of his political career. The immediate criticism challenged both its substance and its opacity. One perceptive correspondent wrote, "Mr. Hill's letter certainly evinces much adroitness—a smooth, well written document—but, with others, I cannot help thinking that in portions of it he was 'using words to conceal his thoughts,' and that Mr. Hill has failed to satisfy the people of Georgia of his true position and views upon the momentous struggle."[33]

Joshua Hill was circumspect in his personal criticisms of Joe Brown. Hill's supporters, however, were not so reluctant to go after the governor for his allegedly imperious attitude. They sometimes sarcastically hailed him as "Joseph I." They called him an "oily flatterer of the masses" and accused him of having an enormous ego. Pro-Hill critics mocked the incumbent for claiming that it was mainly his efforts that kept Yankee troops out of the state, and they attacked him for favoritism toward his "pet" officers in the state militia. One pro-Hill newspaper charged that Brown was a tool of "bank influence." Perhaps the cleverest jab came from a writer who wryly observed that Joe Brown was "a swift historian when he himself is the hero."[34]

In the closing days of the gubernatorial race, Joshua Hill's candidacy received a boost from Confederate senator Benjamin H. Hill. A pre-secession unionist, Ben Hill was among the throng who rushed to join the

---

[32] Ibid.

[33] *Macon Telegraph*, September 9, 1863; *Atlanta Intelligencer*, September 12, 1863; *Augusta Constitutionalist*, October 4, 1863.

[34] Bass, "Georgia Gubernatorial Elections," 185–86 (Joseph I, pet, oily); Bryan, *Confederate Georgia*, 42–43 (bank, hero).

Confederacy once the die was cast. Politically aware Georgians knew that the two Hills had once been Know-Nothing and Constitutional Union allies and that Ben Hill had been a friend of Joshua's late brother in La-Grange. Still, it was unexpected that a sitting Confederate senator would openly stand against Brown. Ben Hill revealed his position in a pamphlet that was printed in the manner of a letter to J. A. Billups, a state senator from Madison who remained friendly with Josh despite their opposing views on secession. Ben Hill's letter attacked both Brown and Furlow and argued that Joshua Hill was the best man to overcome "the spirit of controversy" that enveloped the Richmond administration. Opponents of the apparent Hill-Hill alliance were aware of serious peace movements in North Carolina and other Confederate states, so they were especially anxious to make sure that a similar effort would not take root in Georgia. The day before the election, the *Atlanta Intelligencer* warned that "the election of Mr. Hill would prove prejudicial to every interest of the State and the Confederacy."[35]

Despite the paucity of open campaigning and notwithstanding the equivocal evasions in Hill's public letter, the stakes were clear. One Brown supporter from DeKalb County stated the anti-Hill sentiment as concisely as possible: "If we were right in seceding let us sustain President Davis and Gov. Brown in their efforts to defend our common country against the common enemy. If we were wrong, let us sustain the Hills and go back and live with the Yankees again." The venerable *Federal Union* newspaper of Milledgeville, then styling itself the *Confederate Union,* summarized the race and urged its readers to vote for Brown:

> The contest then will not be between Gov. Brown and Mr. Furlow, but between Gov. Brown and Mr. Hill. We believe that Mr. Hill will get the votes of all the disaffected, and those that are tired of fighting and want peace on any terms that we can get. We fear the vote of that class in some parts of the State will be large.... Every man then that does not want Joshua Hill for Governor should vote for Gov. Brown. Every man that does not want

[35] *Augusta Constitutionalist*, October 4, 1863; *Macon Telegraph*, September 9, 1863 (Mr. Hill); *(Athens) Southern Banner*, January 13, 1864; *Richmond (VA) Examiner*, January 13, 1864; *Raleigh Standard*, January 19, 1864; Schott, *Alexander H. Stephens*, 386–87.

> the war spirit of the country rebuked should vote for Gov. Brown, and every man that wants our soldiers and their families fed and clothed, should vote for Gov. Brown.[36]

Gubernatorial Results

The rumblings of Confederate discontent with the war and the Richmond government caught the attention of Northern politicians and journalists. Joshua Hill's 1863 gubernatorial candidacy was one of several developments that suggested that the South was not as unified as its leaders portrayed. Awareness of the growing dissension helped prompt Lincoln to announce his early reconstruction plan that would provide for postwar state governments organized by a core of Unionists and former Confederates who would pledge loyalty to the United States. Most of the attention, then and by later historians, focused on the North Carolina peace movement. William W. Holden, owner of the *Raleigh Standard*, was a prewar Unionist who had reluctantly acquiesced in secession. By 1863, however, he had become a strong advocate for a negotiated peace. In its coverage of the Georgia race, Holden's *Standard* wrote scathingly that Brown and Furlow were "Destructives" similar to those in his own state and optimistically predicted that Hill would carry the day. When the result favored Brown, the rival Raleigh paper taunted Holden, and a group of Confederate soldiers (allegedly from Georgia) ransacked the Raleigh office of the *Standard*.[37]

On the eve of the Georgia election, the *New York Herald* declared, and the *Chicago Tribune* echoed, that the race between "notorious radical secession fire-eater" Joe Brown and "old line Union whig" Joshua Hill "assumes some degree of national importance." The *Herald* and one major Boston paper went so far as to predict, wrongly as it turned out, that Hill would prevail. Another Boston paper printed substantial sections of Hill's letter of reply to his critics describing the remarks as "the opinions of one

---

[36] *Atlanta Intelligencer*, October 4 (If we were), 6, 1863; *Milledgeville Confederate Union*, September 29, 1863.

[37] McPherson, *Battle Cry of Freedom*, 695–98; *Raleigh Standard*, October 7, 1863; *Atlanta Intelligencer*, October 11, 1863; *Raleigh Register*, October 23, 1864; *Wilmington Journal*, October 22, 1863; W. Harris, *William Woods Holden*; Crofts, *Reluctant Confederates*, 142.

who resisted secession to the last, and now belongs to the moderate party at the South, and who is suspected by the violent secessionists of Union proclivities." In Washington, DC, the *National Intelligencer* also printed extracts from Hill's letter and accurately observed, "We judge from the tone in which the *Savannah News* and other Georgia papers comment upon his letter that the ultra-secessionists will vote against him, and the more moderate men will sustain him."[38]

Election day turned out to be, as Joshua Hill had expected, a sound victory for the incumbent. Due to a combination of apathy during a lackluster campaign and the disruptions of war, voter turnout was about 20 percent below the 1861 gubernatorial race and 40 percent less than the 1860 presidential election. Brown's margin of victory was solid but slightly less than his 59 percent versus Nesbit in 1861. More than four out of ten Georgia voters were dissatisfied enough to cast their ballots against him. Most of the dissatisfied were concentrated in North Georgia and in the Southern wiregrass region, both of which had relatively little slave population. The *Atlanta Intelligencer*'s immediate post-election observation has stood the test of time in voter analysis if not in tone. Repeating the question of whether it was possible that there were voters in Georgia "who want peace on any terms," the paper answered, "yes. There are some people in the counties bordering on East Tennessee and North Carolina, who, imbibing the Andy Johnson and [William H.] Holden sentiment of the sections of these States, are endeavoring to disgrace Georgia, as the tories of East Tennessee and North Carolina have disgraced their States."[39]

Hill could take both pride and a measure of self-satisfaction in the fact that he carried not only his own home county but also the home counties of both of his opponents, Cherokee (Brown) and Sumpter (Furlow). The endorsement of Ben Hill and fond memories of his late brother certainly accounted for Joshua Hill's victory in Troup County. In contrast,

[38] *New York Herald*, October 5, 1863; *Chicago Tribune*, October 8, 1863; *Evansville Daily Journal*, October 5, 1863 (Mr. Hill); *Philadelphia Illustrated New Age*, September 18, 1863. See also *Newark (NJ) Daily Advertiser*, September 26, 1863; (*Washington) National Intelligencer*, September 24, October 6, 1863; *Boston Advertiser*, October 5, 1863 (the opinions); *Boston American Traveller*, October 10, 1863; *Lancaster (PA) Inquirer*, October 12, 1863; *Chicago Tribune*, October 8, 1863; Avery, *History of the State of Georgia*, 261.

[39] *Atlanta Intelligencer*, October 11, 1863.

the support Hill received from his old friend Atlanta Mayor James Calhoun apparently helped little since Brown carried Fulton County with about three-quarters of the vote. As several observers had predicted, Brown's percentage was even higher from soldiers than it was at home; but it should be noted that voting in the field was difficult, and only a small percentage of soldiers cast ballots. Hill charged, but had only anecdotal evidence in support, that in some cases officers had coerced enlisted Confederate soldiers to vote for the governor.[40]

Table 4-1: Results of the 1863 Georgia Gubernatorial Election[41]

Candidate	**Total Vote***	**Percentage of Total Vote**	**Army Vote***	**Percentage of Army Vote**
Joseph E. Brown	36,679	57	10,012	66
Joshua Hill	17,939	28	3,334	22
Timothy Furlow	10,016	15	1,887	12

In the upcountry, the vote was much closer. As a whole, Governor Brown earned only 48 percent of that region's vote, approximately the same as Hill. Specifically in Pickens County, just north of Brown's home in Cherokee County, the governor polled only 55 votes to Hill's 426. A careful study noted that Brown had easily prevailed in Pickens in his two prewar elections, but once the war began, the county's voters rejected the governor twice. Another study contrasted the North Georgia counties of Fannin and Lumpkin and found that local peculiarities were critical to the result. In the former, Brown won, but turnout was only 29 percent. In adjacent Lumpkin, turnout exceeded 50 percent and Hill prevailed 331 to 121. The author asserted, however, that even in Lumpkin, the majority of White people "probably still supported the Confederacy."[42]

---

[40] L. B. Hill, "Governor Brown and the Confederacy," 357; Parks, *Joseph E. Brown*, 252; Williams, *Georgia's Civil War*, 150–52. Hill beat Brown 2:1 in Cherokee Co., 346–70; Bass, "Georgia Gubernatorial Elections," 185–88; Rable, *Confederate Republic*, 217–18; Wortman, *Bonfire*, 177 (Fulton vote).

[41] Parks, *Joseph E. Brown*, 252 (some sources use slightly different numbers); Avery, *History of the State of Georgia*, 260–61; Bass, "Georgia Gubernatorial Elections," 137; Bryan, *Confederate Georgia*, 60.

[42] Hahn, *Roots of Southern Populism*, 130; R. S. Davis, "War on the Edge," 5–6 (Pickens); Sarris, *A Separate Civil War*, 99 (probably).

In his 2017 comprehensive book about Georgia's wartime home front, David Williams found that "class-based political consciousness" manifested itself in the 1863 elections for governor and local offices. Even though voters were unclear about Hill's specific position, they had a general understanding that he would be more open to compromise with the federal government than would Brown. Due to local conditions and personalities, it is difficult to attribute the pattern of local results directly to the gubernatorial contest except possibly for a decline in legislative support for conscription. In the contest for Confederate senator, neither candidate carried the peace mantle, but the General Assembly did reject the bombastic Robert Toombs in favor of keeping the more moderate Herschel V. Johnson. Mid-war election results in other Confederate states also showed various levels of discontent, but, as in Georgia, none led to immediate efforts for a negotiated peace.[43]

When it comes to explaining voter behavior, what a candidate publicly says and what a candidate actually believes are not as determinative of the outcome as what the voters *perceive* that a candidate stands for. Regardless of the evasive and semicontradictory public statements in his own public letter and in the press comments of his supporters, the results confirm that most Georgia voters *perceived* that Joshua Hill was the Unionist peace candidate. It served the interests of Governor Brown for voters to think of Hill that way, so his supporters drove that message home. And it worked, especially with soldiers in the field.

Looking back just a few years after the war, Wallace Reed, the Atlanta journalist-historian, related a story that evokes the mood of the soldiery even though the details are likely more apocryphal than real:

> One day a soldier walked into a Whitehall Street store and asked the way to the home of Hon. Joshua Hill.
>
> "He lives at Madison," was the reply.
>
> "How far is that?"
>
> "About 60 miles."
>
> "That lets me out," said the soldier.

---

[43] Williams, *Georgia's Civil War*, 148–56; Bryan, *Confederate Georgia*, 60; Levine, *Fall of the House of Dixie*, 206–208.

"Our company from Mississippi is here for a day, and we thought we would hang old Josh."

"Hang him for what?"

"For disloyalty—he's a union man, you know."[44]

---

[44] *Atlanta Constitution*, June 24, 1888, July 9, 1902; Reed, *History of Atlanta*, 189–90; the 1888 and 1889 versions were in narrative form rather than the dialogue of the 1902 version, and the soldiers were from Kentucky, not Mississippi. Wortman quotes part of the 1902 version (*Bonfire*, 177).

Chapter 5

"Sorrowing Father" in Negotiations with Sherman, 1864

During the gubernatorial campaign in fall 1863, Joshua Hill faced harsh attacks from critics who felt that his reputation as the peace candidate constituted an affront to brave Southern soldiers in the field. Hill responded with empathy by sharing his own family's experience in Confederate service: "Early in the struggle the youth of my own household, and those of my nearest kindred, flew to arms." The youth of Hill's own household was his oldest son Clarence, soon to be followed by his younger brother Legare. About two months after the 1863 gubernatorial campaign, Hill expressed to a friend his deep anxiety about what the future might hold for his two boys in gray: "If the war could but end with as little damage to me as did the election I should be ready to rejoice. But that is impossible. It has already cost me several of my nephews that I know of and is likely to cost me my sons."[1] Just a few months later the father's worries came tragically true when Hugh Legare Hill fell to the bullet of a Union sharpshooter in the hills of Northwest Georgia.

The chain of events following the death of Legare led to Joshua Hill sitting down face-to-face in freshly conquered Atlanta to talk with William Tecumseh Sherman about the general's plans to remove Georgia from the war as a step toward peace. The conversations led to Hill becoming one of the emissaries who transmitted Sherman's offers to Georgia's unheeding leaders.

---

[1] *Augusta Constitutionalist*, September 6, 1863; Edward Y. Hill, Jr., vertical file biographical sketch, Troup County Georgia Archives, LaGrange, Georgia. Joshua Hill to Charles [C. S. Jordan, esq.], December 23, 1863, Reid & Jordan Family Papers (ms 749), Rose Manuscript Archives and Rare Book Library, Emory University, Atlanta.

Hugh Legare Hill:
"Victim of Political Madness and National Folly"

In her prize-wining account of the *Rise and Fall of the Confederacy*, Anne Rubin adroitly summarized the near instant creation of Confederate identity: "The speed with which white Southerners, many of them staunch Unionists through the election of 1860, shed their American identity and picked up a sense of themselves as Confederates was startling.... Most Southern whites seemed willing, if not eager, to turn their back on the Union in favor of this new nation."[2] As evidenced by his defiant separate letter of resignation and his 1863 gubernatorial candidacy, Joshua Hill was not among the most. He refused to embrace secession, he never endorsed the rebel cause, and he never pledged loyalty to the Confederate government; however, his two military-age sons were willing to put their lives on the line for the nascent nation that their father scorned. What combination of pride, patriotism, and peer pressure motivated them?

Many historians have sought to explain such motivations. Distilling the profusion of research, James M. McPherson, in *Battle Cry of Freedom*, concluded that Southern Whites "fought for abstractions—state sovereignty, the right of secession, the Constitution as they interpreted it [and] the concept of a southern 'nation' different from the American nation." Another synthesis stressed that many Southern White boys were driven by "individual local patriotisms" such as that expressed by the Georgia soldier who declared, "We fight for our homes, our firesides, our religion—every thing that makes life dear." David William's recent study of Georgia's home front identifies several factors that drew young men to fight for the "Stars and Bars." They feared invasion by Northern armies, they resented Lincoln's perceived abolitionist leanings, they desired to impress young ladies, and they sought adventure. All of these motivations were, of course, molded by a society based on chattel slavery and the assumption of White supremacy. Many Confederate volunteers expected that they, the strong White sons of the South, would win a quick and easy victory over the pale and feeble Yankees. Believing, or at least professing, that God was on the Confederate side, many preachers of the Christian gospel urged young men to take up arms against the Northern enemy. To be sure, some

[2] Rubin, *Shattered Nation*, 1, 11.

Southern White youths, especially those from poor farm regions in Georgia's Blue Ridge Mountains, had hesitations that would grow as the war progressed; but in the early days, volunteers came forward to enlist faster than the military authorities could accommodate them. As the war progressed, the Confederate draft (or fear thereof) swept even many doubters into the army.[3]

Without their own writings at hand, one cannot know for sure what motivated two sons of staunch unionist Hill to go to war, nor can it be determined with certainty what their sisters and younger brothers felt about the war and their father's Unionism. Some insight, however, can be drawn from the memories of the daughter of one of Hill's fellow old Whigs. Judge Garnett Andrews of Washington, Georgia, like Hill, never flagged in his "unflinching devotion to the Union." Writing in the 1908 preface to the publication of her wartime diary, Eliza Frances Andrews mused:

> How it was that the influence of such a parent, whom we all loved and honored should have failed to convert his own children to his way of thinking, I do not myself understand, unless it was the contagion of the general enthusiasm around us.... We caught the infection of the war spirit in the air and never stopped to reason or to think.... We sometimes forgot the respect due to our father's opinions.[4]

Similarly, despite their father's opinion, Hill's two older boys (and probably their brothers and sisters) caught the contagion of enthusiasm when they witnessed the wave of rebel patriotism that poured forth at the festive Madison send-offs when the townsfolk and the young ladies of the Female College said farewell to the first wave local volunteers. It all happened within earshot of the Hill's home. The younger sons, Walter and John, were preteens, but Clarence was already of military age and Legare soon would be. Eighteen-year-old Clarence enlisted in Company D, 63rd Georgia Infantry in June and went to Virginia. The peer pressure to join his fellow Morgan Countians was no doubt overwhelming, but as the war dragged on, the glory wore off. After Clarence came home on leave in

[3] McPherson, *Battle Cry of Freedom*, 309–11; Guelzo, *Fateful Lighting*, 233; Williams, *Georgia's Civil War*, 47–51; Sword, *Southern Invincibility*, 37–40; Sacher, *Confederate Conscription*, is the best overview of the draft.

[4] E. F. Andrews, *War-Time Journal*, 10.

December 1863, Joshua wrote a friend, "Poor Clarence, he is so tired of the army—and he is thinner than I ever saw him." Sometime in early 1865, Clarence returned to Madison "unfit for field service…on account of having pulmonary consumption." His death ten years later came from a combination of that affliction and alcoholism.[5]

The strong military tradition of the region is one of the reasons historians have cited to explain why the sons of the Southern gentry were so anxious to go off to war. That explanation proves apt for Hugh Legare Hill. In fall 1860, at about fifteen years of age, Legare entered the preparatory class at the United States Naval Academy along with five other youths from Georgia. The fact that the Georgia teenager went off to Annapolis only a few weeks prior to the election of 1860 indicates that his congressman father remained optimistic that the Union could be saved and that life in the United States would go on as normal. Legare's time at the academy turned out to be brief because he returned home soon after Georgia seceded. The disappointed youth then sought to join the Confederate Navy but was not admitted—perhaps because of his father's Unionist stance. Not to be thwarted, late in 1863, Legare enlisted in Company A of the 63rd Georgia Volunteer Infantry, known as the Oglethorpe Light Artillery. In the words of his obituary, "he left his happy home amidst the tears and apprehensions of his loved intimates, to seek the point of danger. 'He longed for the trumpet's clanger and the cannon's roar.'"[6]

Hugh Legare Hill's death came in the Atlanta Campaign during which the armies of Major General William Tecumseh Sherman left Chattanooga on May 5, 1864, and entered a conquered Atlanta on September 2. The historical literature about the campaign is truly voluminous, so only the briefest summary is offered here to put the loss of Joshua Hill's son in context. Sherman ventured forth with a force of about 110,000 men. His strategy was to use a series of flanking moves to force Confederate

---

[5] Hill to Jordan, December 23, 1863; Clarence Hill, in "Report to the Commissioner of Pensions, State of Georgia, January 10, 1916," from Compiled service records of Confederate soldiers from Georgia units (Fold3.com), NARA M266; Nathan Massey Recollections, Civil War Misc. Collection, Georgia Archives, Morrow; Scaife and Bragg, *Joe Brown's Pets*, 8–11.

[6] *Charleston (SC) Mercury*, October 29, 1860; Callahan's List of Navy and Marine Corps Officers from 1775 to 1900 (fold3.com); "Confederate Necrology," 293–94, quoting the *Augusta Chronicle*, June 15, 1864.

General Joseph E. Johnston back toward Atlanta. Johnston's strategy, knowing that he would be outnumbered, was to execute a series of defensive moves that would make Sherman pay for every inch of Northwest Georgia. He hoped to lure Sherman into costly frontal assaults against well-entrenched positions in order eventually to wear down the federal forces and thwart the invasion. Johnston kept the Western & Atlantic Railroad (W&ARR) open for supplies from Atlanta as needed but then destroyed the tracks as he fell back so that Union forces could not use them. The tactic managed to slow, but not stop, the federal onslaught.[7]

When Private Hill joined the Oglethorpes, the unit was posted to relatively safe coastal defense duty. It was later written that he longed for combat. If so, he soon got his wish. In May 1864, as Sherman began his move toward Atlanta, Company A was called to help bolster Johnston's defense as part of the 63rd in Brigadier General Hugh Mercer's brigade. On May 19, the company occupied a position near Cass Station (Cassville) about halfway from Chattanooga to Atlanta. While his unit supported the skirmish line, a Union rifleman's fatal bullet found Legare, who had been in the service just six months. The death of the son of a well-known figure such as Joshua Hill merited newspaper notice. Captain L. A. Picquet of the Oglethorpe Artillery wrote that young Hill "was shot through the head while fighting gallantly. He was a brave and noble boy. We feel his loss very much." The tone and level of detail in Legare Hill's obituary make it clear that if Joshua Hill didn't write it, it was submitted by a writer who knew his heart. "His sorrowing father," the obituary stated bitterly, grieved for the son who was the "victim of political madness and national folly."[8]

Soon after Joshua and Emily learned of Legare's death, they set about trying to locate his body to ensure that it would be given a proper interment. Joshua Hill reached out to his extensive contacts, both Union and

---

[7] See Castel, *Decision in the West*; McMurry, *Atlanta 1864*; S. Davis, "Atlanta Campaign," *What the Yankees Did to Us*, and *Texas Brigadier to the Fall of Atlanta*. For historiography of the campaign, see Fowler and Parker, *Breaking the Heartland*, 170–91.

[8] W. A. Clark, *Under the Stars and Bars*, 109–10 (Clark was a member of the 63rd); *Madisonian*, May 12, 1899 (by Clark). R. D. Jenkins provides a detailed account of the fighting and mentions Pvt. Hill's death (*Cassville Affairs*, 200–201, *passim*). Hugh Legare Hill (Fold3.com); *Columbus Enquirer*, May 29, 1864 (was shot); *Macon Telegraph* June 15, 1864; *Augusta Chronicle*, June 15, 1864.

Confederate, to seek information about how to find his son's temporary burial site. One poignant and highly specific letter from that effort has survived. The grieving father sought help from James R. Crew, superintendent of the Atlanta & West Point Railroad:

> You have doubtless heard of the cruel affliction this abominable war has brought to my hearthstone. I can't help thinking this was more than I merited. My poor boy met his death on Thursday morning the 19th of May, as I am informed, about 2½ miles above Cass Station to Kingston, about ½ mile from the R. road. He is said to have been brought by some comrades nearer the R. R. and left by the side of the public road, somewhere about or near a deserted cabin or perhaps nearer still to a small frame house near the R. R. *No one else was killed.* His name was Hugh Legare Hill, age 18 years—Complexion fair & ruddy. Light brown hair thick & inclined to curl a little—but was thin, rather short height about 5 ft. 8½ in. trim, erect figure eye-lashes long and dark. Had been sick and was rather thin in flesh, clothing all marked with his initials & name, thus "H. L. Hill," pants dark grey Janes—new (nearly) & lighter grey jacket, plaid domestic shirt—name on the front. His death wound was received in a retreat and entered at the back of the head. I write these particulars in the hope that with the shifting scenes through which we are passing you may see some chance to ascertain the fate of the poor boy's body—whether it was interred by some kind human or was left to waste away by the action of the elements. My object is to recover his remains—as perfectly as may be. Should any opportunity offer for you to obtain me this coveted information I know you will take pleasure in receiving it for me. Joshua Hill.... I forgot to state that my son had a beautiful set of regular and white teeth.[9]

Joseph T. Derry served alongside Legare in the 63rd Georgia. In the late 1890s, Derry visited the site and wrote of the day. He recalled that after Legare fell, Union sharpshooters held their fire while Confederate soldiers retrieved the body and placed a hastily scribbled identification on

---

[9] Hill to James Crew, June or July ?, 1864, Crew papers, Kennan Research Library, Atlanta History Center. Quoted in Hoehling, *Last Train from Atlanta*, 59–60, and Coletti, *Stone Mountain*, a well-researched historical novel.

it. Sometime soon after that, Union soldiers put up a crude headboard inscribed with Private Hill's name. Derry rendered the story in poetry as well as prose.

> O, never can my heart that day forget,
> When noble Legare Hill his death stroke met,
> One moment blooming in young manhood's pride,
> The next one dead, his sorrowing friends beside.

Joshua Hill's quest to locate his young son's body thrust the grieving Madisonian back into the intrigue of Georgia politics.[10]

Madison Threatened, Atlanta Falls

As Sherman closed in on Atlanta in late July, it became more and more clear to Joshua Hill and his fellow Morgan Countians that the war was no longer so far away. Rumors of Union forces raiding in and around Madison and other places east of Atlanta swirled among the citizenry. Towns along the Georgia Railroad had quick access to the two Augusta newspapers, and they were full of reports about federal military actions—verified and speculated. For example, a July 20 story falsely claimed that a thousand Yankees had entered Madison and burned the depot. Six days later, there was a report that three thousand raiders had reached Morgan County. The following day brought a warning that three brigades of cavalry were marching toward Madison on their way to Milledgeville. These particular newspaper stories turned out to be speculations shrouded in the fog of war, but the rumors had a basis in the reality of Union cavalry operations. Beginning on July 21, Brigadier General Kenner Garrard led the thirty-five hundred

---

[10] Joseph T. Derry, "The Strife of Brothers" (typescript, no date) in Joshua Hill vertical file, box 66, ms 3692, HRBML; *Atlanta Constitution*, July 28, 1899, contains part of the poem; Derry mentioned witnessing the death of Hill in the *Augusta Constitutionalist*, September 15, 1875; C. A. Evans, ed., *Confederate Military History*, 6:308 (Derry was the author of this volume). The WPA interview of E. W. Evans, who had been an enslaved boy of about nine in 1864, reported that Legare Hill had been found in a Yankee uniform. Evans's recollection does not comport with other evidence and likely reflects the confusion of passing years. It is probable that his memory stemmed from hearing the story about federal troops withholding fire and later marking the grave (Tonsill and Evans, "E. W. Evans, Brick Layer & Plasterer").

men of his division east from Atlanta to harass the Georgia Railroad. They burned depots in Conyers and Covington and severely damaged the trestles over the Yellow and Alcovy rivers, the latter of which was only about twenty miles west of Madison. The mounted federals foraged freely from farms and plantations in this bountiful and previously untouched region. By July 24, Garrard's men were back inside Union lines having covered a ninety-mile loop and having succeeded in disrupting Confederate logistics, gathering supplies, and spreading panic as far as Madison and beyond.[11]

Upon word that Garrard was approaching, the small Confederate post in Madison that guarded the three hospital buildings quickly brought together as many convalescing soldiers as it could to defend the town. Meanwhile, efforts began to evacuate. It was "a regular Yankee panic," according to one later comment. The head surgeon recorded the scene in his journal saying that the Yankees "threatened [every] moment to attack Madison." The doctor observed, "When the Citizens heard I was going to move the Hospital they became much more alarmed than before and began immediately to pack up and take out with them all their valuables into the Country."[12]

Scarcely a week after the much-anticipated raid on Morgan County by Garrard's cavalry failed to materialize, a large and unanticipated body of Union soldiers did swarm through the county, causing a great uproar and confiscating property, including that of Joshua Hill. The event became known in Madison as "Stoneman's Raid," but the defeated General George Stoneman himself was nowhere around. In late July, General Sherman sent Stoneman south on a mission to disrupt the railroad supplying Atlanta. In addition, Stoneman sought and received permission from Sherman to take his horsemen further south to free captive Union soldiers at Macon and further again at the infamous Andersonville Prison. Thousands of enslaved Black Georgians along the route got their first happy glimpse of Union soldiers, and many of them tagged along until the fighting got serious. Due to Stoneman's several tactical blunders, the action was a failure. Confederate defenders under Major General Howell Cobb, former Georgia governor and national cabinet member, turned Stoneman back at the edge of Macon on July 30. Stoneman held out long enough to facilitate the

---

[11] *Augusta Chronicle* July 20, 26, 27, 1864; D. Evans, *Sherman's Horsemen*, 175–92.

[12] B. Harris, *Confederate Hospitals*, 474; G. R. Matthews, *Basil Wilson Duke*, 172.

withdrawal back to Atlanta of two small contingents before he surrendered to the rebel army. The retreating force that headed north through Madison was composed of the remainder of two Kentucky brigades plus assorted stragglers who joined them. It was more of a panicked escape retreat than a raid.[13]

The first of the remnants of Stoneman's force reached Madison about nine o'clock in the morning on Monday, August 1. Local Baptist pastor J. R. Kendrick recalled the chaotic scene:

> On a hot July morning, I was sitting, Southern fashion, with a number of gentlemen before a store just outside of the public square. We were canvassing a strange rumor which had just reached us, to the effect that Yankee soldiers had been seen not far from the town.... The truth instantly flashed upon us, and with a cry of "*Yankees!*" we all sprang to our feet.... The strange intruders, coming upon us suddenly as if they had dropped out of the summer sky, now poured into the square and overflowed all the streets.

The retreating cavalrymen took horses and burned cotton stored near the railroad. The soldiers distributed boxes of Confederate shoes and clothes to a gathered crowd of slaves and then set fire to the balance. All but a few stragglers were gone by about three in the afternoon. Around midnight, a Confederate officer pursuing the federals awakened Kendrick seeking information about the enemy's whereabouts. The Kentuckian in gray had just left the home of a resolute Unionist who had declined to cooperate, and he remarked to the sleepy preacher that he had not expected to find "a Union man" so far south.[14]

About a week after Stoneman's retreating men had swept north through Morgan County and on to the outskirts of Athens, the *Augusta Chronicle & Sentinel* gathered information from "all accounts" and reported, "Among others who have suffered by the vandalism of the Yankee raiders at Madison, we learn that Hon. Joshua Hill was a heavy loser in horses, mules and other property." Hill was as incensed at the Confederate cavalry who pursued Stoneman's men as he was at the federals themselves. When the Union soldiers stripped his property of fresh mules and horses,

[13] D. Evans, *Sherman's Horsemen*, 291–340.

[14] Kendrick, "A Non-Combatant's War Reminiscences," 458–59.

they left their spent equines behind as compensation. Soon the Confederates came through in pursuit and confiscated the stock that the federals had abandoned. Hill protested their action to authorities in Richmond. Receiving no satisfaction, he angrily wrote to several editors complaining of both "the incursions of raiders, and the depredations of pretended defenders." Hill explained that, like his neighbors, he had "suffered from the rapacity of both these classes," but he was more upset with the rebels. "Justice to myself requires me to state that the last raid made upon me, was made in my absence, and by men in Confederate uniform. They took the greater portion of the horses left me by the enemy, and were offering them for sale in less than an hour afterwards." The deed was done, Hill wrote, by "ignorant and vicious men who disgrace the name of soldier."[15]

Thus, by the end of summer 1864, the war had become very real to Joshua Hill through the death of one son, the war weariness of another, the disruption of his hometown, and the confiscation of his property. For Hill and his fellow White residents of Morgan County, any and all illusions that their community was safe from attack and that the war was going well for the South were fast slipping away.

Meanwhile, by mid-July, about two months after Legare Hill fell at Cassville, Union forces crossed the Chattahoochee River and reached Peachtree Creek, only about five miles north of the very heart of Atlanta. With Sherman on Atlanta's doorstep, Jefferson Davis's frustration with Johnston culminated in his decision to relieve the cautious general and put the more bellicose and aggressive Texan John Bell Hood in charge of the Confederacy's Army of Tennessee. Atlanta's eleven-mile circumference of fortifications was too strong for direct assault, so Sherman surrounded the city, cut off communication and supplies, and began a bombardment. Hood's counterattacks failed, and the city fell. Most of Hood's army managed to slip away, but Sherman had Atlanta. On September 2, 1864, Mayor James M. Calhoun, Joshua Hill's friend from South Carolina youth, ally in the Constitutional Union Party, and supporter during the 1863 gubernatorial election, officially surrendered the city.[16]

---

[15] *Augusta Chronicle*, August 8 (all accounts), 28 (the incursions), 1864.

[16] Castel, *Decision in the West*, 528. Sherman tasked Gen. G. H. Thomas to pursue and defeat Hood, which he did just south of Nashville; see S. Davis, *Into Tennessee and Failure*.

Hill, Sherman, and Talk of Peace

The Union capture of Atlanta had political and psychological as well as military implications for the outcome of the war. The continued standoff in Northern Virginia, where General Grant had been unable to drive Robert E. Lee out of Richmond, taxed Northern patience and strengthened Lincoln's political opponents. But, as the authors of *Why the South Lost the Civil War* succinctly put it, "The fall of Atlanta changed the entire complexion of events." News of the accomplishment touched off celebrations in the North and lifted President Lincoln's spirit. Republican pessimism about the upcoming presidential election morphed into optimism. In the White South, especially in Georgia, gloomy despondency was the common response to Sherman's relentless offensive drive through Northwest Georgia. Desertions increased, and the will to fight waned. Governor Joseph E. Brown's desperate call for all men from ages sixteen to fifty-five to join the militia and come to Atlanta produced scant additional manpower. Even more disturbing, Alabama troops loyal to the Union accompanied Sherman, and some White Georgians assisted or even joined the invading force.[17]

Now safely occupying Atlanta and contemplating his next move, General Sherman concluded that the time might be right to seek negotiations with dispirited Georgians. This was not the first time that thoughts of a negotiated peace had arisen. In late 1863 and early 1864, when Union euphoria over the July victories at Gettysburg and Vicksburg had waned in the face of apparent stalemate in Virginia, it was Confederates who sensed that the time for negotiation might be at hand. Governor Joseph E. Brown and Alexander H. Stephens communicated with each other about ways to encourage President Jefferson Davis to take advantage of Northern war weariness by seeking a peace settlement that would somehow salvage Confederate nationhood and slavery. In March 1864, Brown went public with his thoughts by sending an address to the Georgia legislature in which he included suggestions for negotiations along with his calls for increased food production and harsh action against deserters. The peace that Brown and Stephens desired to achieve by such negotiation was one which would

---

[17] Beringer et al., *Why the South Lost*, 323–27; Bryan, *Confederate Georgia*, 164 (gloomy); Freehling, *South vs. the South*, 184–88. S. Davis, *All the Fighting They Want*, 118–22.

have allowed each Southern state to choose its own destiny—in the Union without slavery or in the Confederacy with slavery. Around the same time, Georgia Confederate Congressman Augustus R. Wright, a personal friend but frequent political rival of Brown, introduced resolutions calling for negotiations. Nothing much came of these early peace efforts, but there is no doubt that the Lincoln administration and his military command, including General Sherman, were well aware of the governor's general disgust with the government in Richmond. At that same time, several other CSA states, especially North Carolina, had their own flurries of peace interest.[18]

Sherman understood that September 1864 presented an even more auspicious time to extend peace feelers. The combination of Sherman's victory, Georgia's war weariness, and Joshua Hill's fatherly grief brought the Union general and the Madisonian Unionist together to talk about peace. Given the behind-the-scenes nature of the discussions between Hill and Sherman, there is little contemporary documentation of the details of their conversations. The same is true of Sherman and his other Georgia emissaries. The general sent some reports to officials in Washington, and there are a few contemporary press references, but for greater detail, the story must be pieced together from later accounts by Sherman, Hill, and the other principals. The key source is, of course, the *Memoirs of General W. T. Sherman*, which was first released in mid-1875. "Mr. Hill," Sherman explained, "resided at Madison, on the main road to Augusta, and seemed to realize fully the danger, said that that further resistance on the part of the South was madness...."[19]

Hill published his own January 1875 recollection of his encounter with Sherman in the *Atlanta Herald*, a short-lived competitor of the established *Constitution*. Hill's approximately two-thousand-word public letter comports with Sherman's account and adds significant detail, but it is scarcely known except indirectly through brief reference in I. W. Avery's 1881 history of Georgia in the Civil War era. In 1875 Avery worked at the

---

[18] Williams, *Georgia's Civil War*, 189–200; Hall, "Alexander H. Stephens and Joseph E. Brown," 50–63; Parks, *Joseph E. Brown*, 264–85; W. C. Davis, *The Union*, 210–11; McPherson, *Battle Cry of Freedom*, 692–98; Dixon, "Augustus R. Wright," 342–71; Guelzo, *Fateful Lighting*, 356–72.

[19] Sherman, *Memoirs*, 612–13. *Memoirs* originally appeared in 1875. The 1885 revision added appendices but did not change the narrative.

Herald and was apparently already at work on his tome. The reporter's boss and editor was Henry W. Grady, whose own special interest in the peace episode would have been piqued by the fact that his wife, Julia King Grady, was the granddaughter of William King, another of Sherman's 1864 messengers. Later, the *Constitution* purchased the *Herald* and brought Grady into its own editorial offices where the editor would embrace Sherman even more openly. Hill's letter is the most extensive firsthand account of what transpired in September and early October 1864.[20]

Hill began the letter by declaring that he had long owed the general "a public acknowledgement of his disinterested kindness shown me under circumstances of deep affliction" following the death of his son. But Hill had more in mind than just overdue appreciation. He believed that the White people of the South had been overly harsh in their attitudes toward Sherman:

> If I had only these graceful acts, prompted by sympathy for an unfortunate stranger to relate, I should limit the expression of gratitude to mere thanks, privately spoken. But when I reflect that so many candid and well-meaning people believe that a wanton disregard of human suffering is a leading characteristic of Sherman, I feel it my duty to make known a few facts, calculated to soften the harsh judgement.[21]

In 1875, most of Georgia's press was not yet ready to temper its judgment of Sherman. When Hill's letter appeared in the *Atlanta Herald* in early February, it received little in-state notice. The *Columbus Enquirer* was the only paper found by the author's search to have reprinted Hill's entire contents. The *Augusta Chronicle* ran a very brief summary that sneeringly dismissed the general's offer to reduce further damage if Georgia withdrew

---

[20] Hill's letter is dated February 20, 1875 (hereafter cited as "Hill's *Herald* letter, 1875"). Issues of the *Atlanta Herald* from that period are not available, so the quotations herein are drawn from the *Columbus Daily Enquirer*, which reprinted the article on March 2, 1875. The full letter or excerpts appeared in the *New York Times* on March 7, 1875, and in other papers. On Avery and Grady see H. E. Davis, *Henry Grady's New South*, 33–36; E. C. Clark, *Birth of a New South*, 17–42, 101; I. W. Avery refers to the very "Interesting and graphic account" he received from Hill (*History of the State of Georgia*, 303); Avery also received statements from other principals.

[21] Hill's *Herald* letter, 1875.

from the war as, "rather a small reward for such treachery." In notable contrast, the Northern press was pleased to learn that a well-known Southerner had kind words for their hero. The *New York Times* and the *St. Louis Post-Dispatch* ran the full letter, and publications in many other large Northern cities, including Cincinnati, Boston, Buffalo, and Pittsburgh, gave Hill's missive positive mention.[22]

Hill explained that he had used the good offices of Major General John A. Logan of Illinois, a Democrat with whom he had served in Congress, to make his connection with Sherman. Only a few weeks earlier, shortly before the city's fall, Logan had temporarily assumed field command upon the death of General James B. McPherson. Logan held high political ambitions, and he often clashed with Sherman, but his vouching for Hill nevertheless would have held considerable weight. Thanks to Logan, Hill explained, "I received from General Sherman in his own handwriting a permit to enter his lines, dated at Atlanta, Ga., and sent me to my home in Madison, with instructions to all officers of the army of the Tennessee and Ohio, to afford me any assistance I might ask for during my journey to recover the body of my son.... I was allowed to take with me a travelling companion and a servant." The traveling companion was Nathaniel G. Foster, Hill's family friend and immediate predecessor in Congress. The unidentified "servant" was effectively enslaved by circumstance even though by terms of the Emancipation Proclamation he was a free man in the eyes of the United States. Hill's party reached Atlanta sometime in the waning days of September and first met with Sherman on September 28.[23]

The account of the conversations in Sherman's *Memoirs* is consistent in essentials with Hill's letter:

> One day, two citizens, Messrs. Hill and Foster, came into our lines at Decatur, and were sent to my headquarters. They represented themselves as former members of Congress, and

---

[22] *Augusta Chronicle*, March 7, 1875; *Springfield Republican*, March 11, 1875; *Cincinnati Daily Gazette*, March 24, 1875; *Pittsburgh Daily Commercial*, March 13, 1875. Bassett contends that southern white demonization of Sherman began after the publication of Jefferson Davis's memoir in 1881; the reactions to Hill and Avery illustrate that it actually started earlier ("Birth of a Demon," 27–35).

[23] Hill's *Herald* letter, 1875; *OR*, ser. 1, vol. 39, pt. **[1, 2, or 3?]** 501, 514, 542.

> particular friends of my brother John Sherman; that Mr. Hill had a son killed in the rebel army as it fell back before us somewhere near Cassville, and they wanted to obtain the body, having learned from a comrade where it was buried. I gave them permission to go by rail to the rear, with a note to the commanding officer, General John E. Smith, at Cartersville, requiring him to furnish them an escort and an ambulance for the purpose.[24]

The official reason for their visit was Hill's quest to find his son's remains, but the talk soon turned to broader implications of war and peace. Sherman wrote, "I invited them to take dinner with our mess, and we naturally ran into a general conversation about politics and the devastation and ruin caused by the war." Hill's more extensive description adds depth. Soon after their party crossed federal lines at Decatur on the east side of Atlanta, the two former United States congressmen were "most hospitably entertained" by General J. D. Cox. Then they proceeded to Sherman's headquarters at Judge Lyon's house where they "became his guest for some days." Hill fondly recalled, "A more frank, cordial welcome, I do not remember ever to have received." The conversations with Sherman proceeded "with no one but himself present with ourselves." The commanding general, Hill wrote, "conversed freely on the current topics of the time, as well as of persons then prominent, both in civil and military life, without any apparent heat or vindictiveness." Those "prominent" persons no doubt included Joe Brown, Alexander Stephens, and Jefferson Davis.[25]

One of Sherman's goals in early fall 1864 was to use Hill and other emissaries to spread word about the vast swath of devastation that his troops had left along the route from Chattanooga and to Atlanta in the hope that knowing the strength of the mighty Union army would lessen enemy morale. Sherman said to Hill, "I want you to see as much as you can, my whole force if possible, and afterwards you may tell everybody what you saw." Sherman's *Memoirs* match Hill's recollections: "They [Hill and Foster] had been in a part of the country over which the army had passed, and could easily apply its measure of desolation to the remainder of the State, if necessity should compel us to go ahead."[26]

---

[24] Sherman, *Memoirs*, 612.

[25] Ibid., Hill's *Herald* letter, 1875.

[26] Ibid.

Hill did as the general requested and spread the word of Yankee might. In an October letter to railroad executive James Crew, whose help he had earlier sought in the search for Legare's body, Hill described the people of Atlanta as being "generally in a pitiable condition with small available means and no market." More broadly, he lamented, "as far as the eye can reach is one prolonged scene of desolation.... The silence that reigns is only broken by the sound of moving masses of men, trains of wagons, squadrons of cavalry & occasionally a railway train. I wish it could be seen by every war man in Georgia. But I doubt if it would do any good, so visionary & fanatical have they grown."[27]

Joshua Hill was one of three prominent Georgians whom Sherman enlisted to reach out to Governor Joseph E. Brown and Georgia's other Confederate leaders, and the general kept President Lincoln informed of his machinations. About ten days before he met Hill and Foster, Sherman wrote the commander-in-chief about his offer to Brown and of the contact that he had already initiated with Judge Augustus Wright and William King. On September 28, he updated the president that he had brought Joshua Hill and Nathaniel Foster, another former Unionist congressman, into his team of emissaries. Sherman knew that he was stepping from purely military concerns into the world of politics, and he acknowledged as much to Lincoln: "I am fully conscious of the delicate nature of such assertions, but it would be a magnificent stroke of policy if we could, without surrendering principle or a foot of ground, arouse the latent enmity of Georgia against [Jefferson] Davis."[28]

---

[27] Joshua Hill to James Crew, October 23, 1864, Crew Collection, Kenan Research Library, Atlanta History Center, quoted in Dyer, *Secret Yankees*, 204–205.

[28] *OR*, ser. 1, vol. 39, pt. 2, 501, 514, 542. The September 28, 1864, telegram in the *OR* (also in Lincoln papers, https://www.loc.gov/item/mal3679600/) incorrectly refers to "Nelson" rather than Foster. Sherman's *Memoirs* and all other sources reference Foster, not Nelson. Later on the same day (September 28), the *OR* error is corrected in Sherman's message to General Corse, which specifically mentions that Hill and "Foster" are headed to Rome (Sherman to Corse, Corse to Sherman, September 28, 1864, *OR*, ser. 1, vol. 39, pt. 2, 514). Sherman had previously notified Lincoln of contacts with Judge Wright (Sherman to Lincoln, September 17, 1864; Lincoln Papers [https://www.loc.gov/item/mal3642900/], Knox College version, Library of Congress, missed the later correction and incorrectly annotated Nelson as Rep. Thomas A. R. Nelson from East Tennessee).

William King was the son of Roswell King, founder of the cotton mill town of Roswell, Georgia. By 1864, the younger King had become an influential and wealthy industrialist in his own right. The other messenger, Augustus Wright, was a wealthy lawyer-planter from the Rome area whom Hill knew from Wright's two years in Congress, which coincided with Hill's first term. Wright was an antisecession Douglas Democrat in 1860, and he vocally opposed secession in early 1861. Like Hill, Wright argued that secession should require a direct vote of Georgia's citizens. However, when secession came, he, like most other conditional Unionists, sided with Georgia and the Confederacy. He raised a unit from Floyd County and served in the Confederate Congress wherein he initiated the unsuccessful negotiation resolution mentioned previously. All four of Wright's sons were wounded in Confederate army service, and he became disenchanted with the course of the war. He returned to Georgia and became as close to a full-fledged Unionist as his personal safety and the protection of his family would allow. To provide Wright with cover from his angry neighbors, Union officers sent a force ostensibly to arrest him before they delivered him to confer with Sherman. Wright later went to Washington, DC, to consult directly with President Lincoln. Since Joshua Hill's journey to Atlanta was a mission of mercy, he needed no such cover like the elaborate ruse that brought Judge Wright to Atlanta.[29]

The team of Hill, King, and Wright (with Foster playing a lesser role) represented a wide range of political Unionism, but none of them would have passed the litmus test of full-bore Unionism specified by William G. "Parson" Brownlow, the Knoxville editor who demanded that his fellows be willing to put their lives and property on the line to defend the United States. To some extent, these emissaries were embodiments of the "peace Unionists" whom historian Carl Degler profiled, but such classification is

---

[29] Sherman to Lincoln, September 17, 1864, Lincoln papers (https://www.loc.gov/item/mal3642900/); Dixon, "Augustus R. Wright," 342–71; *Cartersville Express*, September 21, 1876. Wright's son, who was present with his father during talks with Lincoln, recalled that the president had been willing to offer Georgia highly favorable terms of peace (*Atlanta Constitution*, May 20, 1895). King's visit to Sherman was known as early as September 27 per a letter in A. N. Skinner and J. L. Skinner, *Death of a Confederate*, 127; Marszalek muddled the story when he wrote that Hill, Wright, and King traveled to Atlanta together "under a flag of truce" (*Sherman*, 289).

imprecise at best. What can be said is that whatever they had believed before the war and whatever they had done up to late 1864, once Atlanta fell, these men were unified in their conclusion that continued resistance to federal authority was futile to the point of folly.[30]

The precise details of what conditions General Sherman asked his several envoys and correspondents to proffer in late September and early October 1864 are not recorded, but the basic parameters that he outlined and documented in his *Memoirs* have not been disputed. Sherman wanted Governor Brown to perceive the futility of further resistance, and he urged Brown to "withdraw his people from the rebellion, in pursuance of what was known as the policy of 'separate State action.'" Sherman's threat was clear—negotiate or face ruin.

> I told [Hill] if he saw Governor Brown, to describe to him fully what he had seen, and to say that if he remained inert, I would be compelled to go ahead, devastating the State in its whole length and breadth; that there was no adequate force to stop us, etc., but if he would issue his proclamation withdrawing his state troops from the armies of the Confederacy, I would spare the State, and in our passage across it confine the troops to the main roads, and would moreover, pay for all the corn and food we needed. I also told Mr. Hill that he might, in my name, invite Governor Brown to visit Atlanta; that I would give him a safeguard, and that if he wanted to make a speech, I would guarantee him as full and respectable an audience as he had ever spoken to. I believe that Mr. Hill, after reaching his home at Madison, went to Milledgeville, the capital of the State, and delivered the message to Governor Brown. I had also sent similar messages by Judge Wright of Rome, Georgia, and Mr. King. of Marietta.[31]

Hill's 1875 letter includes very similar language to Sherman's *Memoirs* concerning the invitation to Brown:

> I expressed the opinion that Governor Brown had the sagacity to perceive that the war was about to end disastrously to the Confederacy, and might counsel some course leading to a more favorable issue of the struggle. General S. then said: "I want you

---

[30] Inscoe and Kenzer, *Enemies of the Country*, 1–4; Degler, *The Other South*.
[31] Sherman, *Memoirs*, 613.

> to tell Governor Brown to come to see me. I want to talk with him. He shall have the kindest reception, and if he wants to make a speech, he shall have the largest and most respectful audience he ever saw. I will preside and preserve order for him, and he shall see my entire army and return to his home in safety."

After describing more of his trip, Hill's letter to the *Herald* further elaborated on his perceptions of General Sherman's attitude toward war and peace:

> I am well satisfied from all I heard from Gen. Sherman, that he was hoping for an abandonment of the struggle on the part of Georgia, and perhaps some other States of the Confederacy; thereby relieving him of the necessity of a hostile march through the South. He spoke of the morale effect of the disbanding of 'Governor Brown's militia,' as he styled the Georgia State troops, and of the utter absurdity of opposing a well appointed and powerful army like his, with a vastly inferior force, poorly disciplined. It was of this, that he desired to confer with Governor Brown.[32]

When Jefferson Davis got wind of the peace rumblings in Georgia, particularly the efforts of Judge Wright, he quickly arranged a trip to the state. The Confederate president's professed intention for coming to Georgia was to consult with General Hood about military matters, but the need to rally morale and blunt Sherman's peace effort was clearly the underlying motive. Davis's sojourn in the Empire State during the last week of September occurred just before Hill and Foster arrived in Atlanta, so Sherman wanted to make sure that his Madison visitors had heard about it. Hill recalled, "He handed me a Macon paper to read containing the celebrated war speeches of President Davis and Hon. B. H. Hill, made I think, the day before. He seemed amused that the promised strategic movement was to give fresh confidence the despondent Confederates." Unconcerned about Confederate action, Sherman remarked to Hill, "General Hood may go where *he can*, and I will go where *I please*."[33]

---

[32] Hill's *Herald* letter, 1875.

[33] Ibid.; Sherman, *Memoirs*, 613; Dixon, "Augustus R. Wright," 342–71; Bryan, *Confederate Georgia*, 164; McNeill, "Survey of Confederate Soldier Morale," 1–25.

Sherman was acutely aware of the ongoing dispute between Brown and the central command in Richmond over conscription and the control of the state troops sometimes known as "Joe Brown's Pets." He was also well informed about the lack of morale and the rising desertion rate amongst Confederate forces, so it was not at all unreasonable for the Union commander to think that he might be able to entice Brown to have his military stand down in exchange for reduced damage. As Brown's most thorough biographer put it, Sherman "had good reason to expect success." After the affair concluded, the ardently Confederate *Countryman* of Putnam County accused Brown of being "seriously afflicted with Davisophobia" and blamed the governor for making Sherman think that his plan might work. At the Confederate capital, the *Richmond Sentinel* agreed: "It is creditable to Gov. Brown to have spurned Sherman's proposition—it would have been far more so if Sherman had felt that he could not dare to insult his virtue by offering it."[34]

Following their late September conversations with Sherman in Atlanta, Hill and Foster took the train north just as Sherman was dispatching troops to divert General Hood from attacks on the tracks of the Western & Atlantic. Sherman directed General John M. Corse to notify Judge Wright to expect the visitors in Rome, and Corse confirmed that he had done so. Before reaching Rome, the two travelers got off at Cartersville to undertake their search for Legare Hill's remains. Upon examining Sherman's expansive order for full cooperation with the former US congressmen, Gen. John E. Smith chided Hill, joking that he hoped that the Madison delegation would not need him to supply a whole train of cars for his needs.[35]

Unfortunately, neither Hill's 1875 letter nor other available records indicate the result of the search for Legare's remains. The fact that Hill's letter described his return to Madison but omitted any reference to finding the body is a glaring omission that leads to the tentative conclusion that he did not retrieve it on this trip. About nine years had passed when a brief

---

[34] Parks, *Joseph E. Brown*, 296; *Countryman*, October 11, 1864; *Augusta Daily Register*, October 11, 1864 (*Sentinel*). The *Countryman* later tempered attacks on Brown on October 25 and December 6, 1864.

[35] Hill's *Herald* letter, 1875; Sherman to Gen. Corse, Corse to Sherman, September 28, 1864, *OR*, ser. 1, vol. 39, pt. 2, 514.

notice appeared in the Cartersville newspaper on May 1, 1873, declaring that remains identified as the body of Hugh Legare Hill, "son of United States ExSenator Joshua Hill," had been exhumed from "an abandoned graveyard" and moved to the Confederate "soldier's Cemetery in Cassville." A later inventory of the cemetery confirms that young Hill was among those reinterred.[36]

Presuming that the reinterred body was correctly identified, the evidence suggests, but does not fully confirm, the following course of events. After visiting with Sherman and receiving permission and Union support for his search, the grieving father may have learned of and possibly even observed Legare's temporary grave site with the wooden marker that the young private's comrades described in their recollections, and Hill may have determined to let the body remain there for the time being. It is likely, though again not confirmed, that officials at Cassville would have notified the Hill family of the reinterment. All of the other Hill children were still alive in 1873, so burial in an official soldier's cemetery may have been enough to satisfy the family. As explained more fully in the epilogue (chapter 14), Joshua and Emily's other three sons died in quick succession in from 1875 to 1877. It is possible that the agony of having lost all four sons motivated the family to bring their remains together at home, or at least to provide markers for them all. In any case, for as long as anyone alive today can remember or can recall having heard, the tombstone of the fallen young private of the 63rd Georgia Regiment has stood alongside his parents and his brothers in the Hill family plot in Madison's Historic Cemeteries. When, how, or even if, the body got there is not confirmed.

From Cartersville, the Madisonians went on to Rome, where they met with Judge Wright. According to the 1895 recollections of Wright's son, Hill and Foster urged his father to accept Sherman's suggestion that he travel to Washington for the meeting with Lincoln described earlier in this chapter. When the Hill and Foster party were heading home from Rome,

---

[36] *Cartersville Standard and Express*, May 1, 1873, reported the exhumation and relocation of six CSA soldiers including "Captain [sic] Hugh Hill, son of United States Ex-Senator Joshua Hill." The *Americus Sumter Republican*, May 9, 1873, ran a shorter version. The inventory, compiled in 1991 from RG 109 of NARA Confederate Military Service, is in the Cassville Cemetery file at the Mulinix Research Center of the Bartow History Museum. Sandy Moore of the Center and author Robert (Bob) Jenkins kindly assisted the author in this research.

they had a brief chance meeting with Sherman while they were changing cars in Kingston. During this railroad depot encounter, the commanding general took time to write an order for Hill to transmit to Major General Henry W. Slocum, directing the Twentieth Corps commander to make sure that Hill and Foster could obtain fresh horses when they reached Atlanta so that they could be sure to get back to Madison without trouble. (At that time the railroad was not operational East of Decatur.) Hill's *Herald* letter concluded, "Here I parted with Gen. Sherman, not to meet again until the war had ended.... I was deeply impressed with his simplicity and candor, and the generous tribute he paid to the gallantry of the Southern troops. He seemed to fully appreciate their courage and dash."[37]

Sherman's outreach to Governor Brown, Vice President Alexander Stephens, and others led to a flurry of correspondence among the state's Confederate leaders. Robert Toombs got wind of it and, on September 23, strongly advised Alexander Stephens not to visit the general. William King was the first peace emissary to get to Brown with Sherman's proposal even before the general had talked to Hill and Foster. Brown responded by releasing statements to the press. The governor first argued that neither he nor Sherman had any authority to act. The essence of that argument was that Brown was just a governor and that Sherman was just a general and that neither could commit their state or nation on such a momentous matter.[38]

Brown may have been constitutionally correct, but, of course, such niceties had never bothered him before. From the day that he ordered state troops to occupy the federal installation of Fort Pulaski on the eve of Georgia's secession convention to his abrupt withdrawal of the Georgia militia from Confederate service and sending them home to tend to crops after the fall of Atlanta, Governor Brown had never before felt constrained by constitutional or legal niceties. Brown's record to that point and later makes it clear that he was never afraid to act alone if he believed that he held the

[37] Dixon, "Augustus R. Wright," 342, 364–67; Wright's letter in Avery newspaper; Miller A. Wright's recollections in *Atlanta Constitution*, May 20, 1895 (Dixon does not cite this article.); Hill's *Herald* letter, 1875.

[38] Toombs to Stephens, September 23, 1864, in Phillips, *Correspondence*, 652–53. *Columbus Daily Sun*, September 29, 1864; *(Athens) Southern Watchman*, October 5, 1861; Sherman, *Memoirs*, 614–15; Morgan, "War and Rumors of War," 119–20.

political capital to do so. In short, Brown's constitutional argument amounted to a completely disingenuous cover for his fundamentally political calculation that the time was not right to pull Georgia out of the war. Alexander Stephens made the same lack of authority argument in his response to William King. Stephens's profession of lack of authority had somewhat more validity because even though he was vice president, he had little active involvement with the government's administration in Richmond.[39]

Governor Brown's confident public assertion that Georgia still had fight left in her and that if Sherman marched out of Atlanta he would meet ferocious military resistance amounted to nothing but bluster. Earlier speeches by Jeff Davis and Georgia Confederate senator Benjamin Hill were of the same order. Ben Hill played the patriotic hand: "Another reason why you cannot make peace with Sherman is our gallant army will not let you—you have not the power to make a dishonorable peace." Probably the most obviously political part of Brown's response was his claim that Georgia "is pledged by strong implication, to her Southern sisters, that she will not exercise this power without consent on their part, and concert of action with them." He had felt no such compulsion for the assent of sister states back in 1861 when he pushed for immediate disunion and adamantly opposed the suggestion of Hill, Herschel V. Johnson, and others that Georgia delay secession pending a conference of all slave states. Brown's response, like that of so many politicians before and after him, relied on his hope that his listeners would forget his own past words and actions. At this very time, a pro-Davis paper, speaking of Brown's use of the militia, asked the rhetorical question, "Who has usurped more authority than Gov. Brown, during this revolution, from its very beginning down to the present time?" By declaring that Brown was "afraid to act unless in concert with other Governors," Sherman's dispatch to the president perceptively communicated that the governor's motivation was not legal misgiving about Georgia going it alone but rather about his timidity to act without political cover.[40]

---

39 Bryan, *Confederate Georgia.*

40 *Columbus Daily Sun*, September 29, 1864; *Augusta Daily Register*, October 1, 1864 (usurped); *Milledgeville Confederate Union*, October 4, 1864 (B. Hill); Sherman to Lincoln, September 28, 1864 (afraid), Lincoln papers

Similarly, Brown's assertion that Sherman lacked authority to act was just as disingenuous. Brown was not, of course, privy to the specific late September correspondence that documents the high level of interest that Lincoln and chief of staff Henry Halleck had in Sherman's peace feelers with Hill and others, but it is clear that the governor was a savvy enough politician to have surmised even without documentary evidence that Sherman would not have extended such offers without the full confidence of Lincoln and the Union command structure. Joshua Hill certainly understood that Sherman had such authority. In his 1875 letter, Hill sought to make the record clear:

> While Gen. Sherman did not tell me that Mr. Lincoln was anxious to detach the State of Georgia from the Confederacy, and thereby to avoid the further destruction of the lives and property of its people, I was forced to conclude that such was the fact from the assurance of the General...Such a pledge, so earnestly made, would scarcely have been tendered by General S. without authority from his Government."[41]

Clara Mildred Thompson ably captured Brown's essence in her 1915 book *Reconstruction in Georgia*. The work was sympathetic to racist White redeemers and disdainful of Black Georgians and Radical Republicans, but her analysis of Joseph E. Brown's response to Sherman's peace overtures is insightful. Brown, she wrote, "had a rare facility for divining on which side of the bread the butter is spread.... The natural shrewdness of the Governor, sharpened by long political practice, made him see that the people of Georgia were not ready for such action as his own practical wisdom and regard for material consequence might dictate."[42] When Thompson referred "the people of Georgia," she, of course, meant only of the White people—the Black people of Georgia would have been delighted for the state to withdraw from the war.

(https://www.loc.gov/item/mal3679600/); Sherman, *Memoirs*, 617; Williams, *Georgia's Civil War*, 213; Parks, *Joseph E. Brown*, 296–99.

[41] Hill's *Herald* letter, 1875; Simpson documents that Grant wanted Lincoln to leave Georgia negotiations to Sherman. Simpson was wrong, however, when he wrote that Hill "floated a curious proposal" to Sherman; such a proposal was already in Sherman's mind (*Ulysses S. Grant*, 382).

[42] C. Thompson, *Reconstruction in Georgia*, 37–38.

Because of Hill and Foster's sojourn into Northwest Georgia to search for Legare's body and to talk to Judge Wright, several days passed between their initial conversations with Sherman and when they finally arrived in the state capital to plead the general's case for Georgia's withdrawal from hostilities. Both Hill and Foster called upon the legislators. Hill recalled his frustrating experience: "After my arrival at home, I visited Augusta and Milledgeville. In the latter city the Legislature was sitting; I sought at both places, to impress on influential persons, the certainty of Sherman's contemplated march, if not averted by some unforeseen event, or arrested by some interposition little less than miraculous." But it was not a message that most of the state's legislators or its governor wanted to hear or believe: "Many thought I exaggerated the danger and over-estimated his army," Hill wrote, "while others concluded, wisely perhaps, that it was too late to invoke public opinion to give direction in such a crisis." The loyal Confederates especially did not want to hear such a message from a staunch Unionist who had just spent several days amongst the enemy. As Hill remembered the effort, "It was well settled that I was not a fit person to advise in a matter so deeply affecting the safety if not the very existence of the Confederacy."[43]

After rejecting Sherman's offer for Georgia to withdraw unilaterally, Brown and his allies undertook to find political cover by suggesting a meeting of Southern states to discuss peace alternatives, but this last-minute effort, like the similar move the previous spring, failed to gain much traction in the face of opposition from Jefferson Davis. In the words of one of Joe Brown's biographers, the convention proposal failed "despite the Governor's wishes, Linton Stephens' eloquence, and Joshua Hill's lobbying." Newspaperman, Madison resident, and former legislative clerk Simeon Atkinson was on the scene in Milledgeville for the *Augusta Chronicle & Sentinel* during those hectic days just before Sherman began his infamous March to the Sea. Atkinson admired Davis and opposed peace negotiations, so his public reporting did not give much coverage to the efforts at foot. His private letters to his wife back in Madison revealed otherwise. On November 7, he explained. "I called on Gov. Brown, and he was as polite as ever. If he urges his plan for a convention of the States it will create a heated issue. Many regard it equivalent to reconstruction." On

[43] Hill's *Herald* letter, 1875.

November 13, after the multistate convention plan had gone down to defeat, Atkinson wrote, "Col Joshua Hill is here—Foster has been here—and there is earnest consultation for some means to stop the war."[44] Hill's earnest efforts were, of course, to no avail.

Even as Sherman was preparing for his March to the Sea, those whom Joshua Hill characterized as Georgia's "visionary and fanatical" leaders continued to profess that victory was possible. Maybe they believed it. Maybe they had to profess to believe it even if they did not. Joe Brown was surely among the latter group. Even those who had profound doubts would have had good reason to remain quiet due to fear of being branded traitors. The *Columbus Times*, for example, had written that speaking of "peace is criminal—he who entertains it with no abatement by the foe, is a traitor." David Williams has convincingly shown that many common White people had serious doubts about the course and worth of the war, but those common White people were being told otherwise by their leaders. Although many White Georgians were war weary and lugubrious, for most of them, the vision of Yankee victory was still too frightful to contemplate. One Columbus correspondent expressed such fears bluntly: "What sort of peace would Sherman or any other abolitionist give Georgia?... [E]very tender Georgia lady would be put to the wash tub, with a Yankee or negro mistress over her. The Abolitionists would delight in doing just this thing."[45]

A curious, but ultimately uneventful, sidebar to the fall 1864 peace episode is presented by a private letter of September 30 from Joe Brown to Alexander Stephens in which the governor tells the vice president that Hill is with them: "I learn that Hon. Joshua Hill agrees fully with us on the line of policy we have acted upon in Confederate politics. There is a vacancy in the [Georgia] Senate from his district by the death of Adams." Just a few days later, a letter suggesting Hill, a man of "unsullied personal character," for the Confederate senate vacancy appeared in Milledgeville's

[44] L. B. Hill, *Joseph E. Brown and the Confederacy*, 235; Simeon Atkinson to wife, November 7, 13, 1864. Atkinson letters, Judith Ulrich Collection in the custody of the Morgan County Landmarks Society, Madison, Georgia (copies in the MCA).

[45] Hill to Crew, October 23, 1864, quoted in Dyer, *Secret Yankees*, 204–205 (fanatical); *Columbus Times*, October 6, 1864, quoted in Bryan, *Confederate Georgia*, 164; Williams, *Georgia's Civil War*; *Columbus Daily Sun*, October 4, 1864.

Confederate Union. The near-simultaneous timing of the public and private letters suggests that some sort of movement was afoot to "lay aside all past party strife" and bring Unionist Hill into Brown's circle. It is unclear if Hill was even aware that his name was being bandied about for a place in the Confederate Senate because when the letter appeared in the newspaper, he was already on his trip behind Union lines in Atlanta. Though nothing came of it, the episode illustrates the landscape of political intrigue that enveloped Confederate Georgia after Atlanta came into Union hands.[46]

Why could Georgia's ardent Confederates not see that the end was near, and thus, it would be wise to cut their losses? Historians have speculated for a century and a half. The first historian to bring the efforts of Hill, Foster, Wright, and King to wide public attention was former *Atlanta Herald* reporter I. W. Avery in his *History of the State of Georgia from 1850 to 1881* and in newspaper stories published in advance of the book. He obtained statements from the key Georgia players of September–October 1864, including Joe Brown, Alexander Stephens, Augustus Wright, William King, and Joshua Hill. The unreconstructed rebel colonel concluded that Sherman's intrigue failed because neither Brown nor Stephens was capable of "deserting the fortunes of the Confederacy and leaving the other members of the compact to bear the calamities of failure." He added, "it was simply an impossibility that the soldiers or people of Georgia would have been willing to purchase exemption from the common peril and universal ruin by abandonment of the cause, thus securing safety by dishonor."[47]

---

[46] Brown to Stephens, in Phillips, *Correspondence*, 653; *Milledgeville Confederate Union*, October 4, 1864. Baggett incorrectly states that Joshua Hill served in the Georgia Senate in 1864 and was so serving when he met with Sherman; apparently, Baggett misinterpreted the Brown-Stephens letter (*Scalawags*, 75, 92). To confirm Hill's non-membership of the Senate, the author scanned three volumes of the *Journal of the [Georgia] Senate* (Milledgeville: Boughton, Nisbet, Barnes & Moore, State Printers) for the sessions beginning March 10, 1864, Nov. 3, 1865, and Feb. 15, 1865.

[47] Avery, *History of the State of Georgia*, 305.

The first appearance of Avery's work was in the form of long articles often headlined as "Unwritten History" in numerous newspapers in December 1879 and early 1880. The Georgia press also took specific notice of Avery's account of Sherman's meeting with Hill and company. One writer called it a "futile attempt of the wily federal General to divide and destroy the Confederacy." When Avery's highly anticipated full book came out in the latter part of 1881, White Georgians effusively praised the new work. The *Savannah Morning News* proclaimed that it will "be eagerly read by all lovers of Georgia's greatness and prosperity." Referring to Joshua Hill's role as revealed by Avery, the *Macon Telegraph* praised the Republican ex-senator's "admitted sincerity, firm convictions and manly intelligence" but felt compelled to remind the paper's readers that Hill "has not—especially since the war—been in harmony with the views of the majority of the white people." This conclusion that the governor had acted wisely and honorably in rejecting Sherman's message delivered by Hill and others remained the dominant White Southern interpretation for more than a century.[48]

Recent historians have paid more attention to rifts in Confederate politics and have unmasked the myth of Southern White wartime unanimity. In this context, the Georgia peace outreach of Joshua Hill and the other emissaries constitutes one of the most realistic of several steps toward negotiated settlements of the war that emerged from 1863 up to just before the very end. Alan Conway, in his comprehensive account of the state's postwar politics, called Sherman's outreach "the first step in the reconstruction of Georgia." In contrast, military historian Lee Kennett wrote that the whole episode demonstrated "a certain naivete on Sherman's part when it came to political realities." Writing of Hill and Foster without using their names and without a full understanding of Georgia politics or of the individuals involved, Sherman's most recent biographer, military historian Brian Holden Reid claimed, "Sherman certainly exaggerated both the audacity and credibility of the initial Georgia emissaries who knew his brother John." To be sure, Sherman may have been cautiously optimistic, but he was certainly not naïve as Kennett asserted, nor did he

---

[48] *Cincinnati Daily Enquirer*, April 24, 1880; *Macon Telegraph*, January 21, 1880; *New Orleans Item*, April 27, 1880; *Savannah Morning News*, August 30, 1881.

misunderstand either the "audacity" or the "credibility" of his visitors as Reid asserted. Joshua Hill was anything but audacious. He never promised Sherman that he could convince Governor Brown and the legislature to withdraw Georgia from the war—he only agreed to carry the message. It was not audacity that motivated Joshua Hill to use his contacts to reach out to Sherman in the first place—it was parental sorrow. Regarding the credibility of emissary Hill, Reid would not have made his assertion had he known of the Madisonian's intensive and long-standing, if often contentious, relationships with Brown, Robert Toombs, Alexander Stephens, and Benjamin Hill. Those leaders of Confederate Georgia did not usually agree with Hill, but they would never have doubted his credibility or his intentions. Reid also wrote that Sherman "exaggerated the extent of the Unionist sympathies of" Brown, Stephens, and others, but the biographer missed the fact that Sherman was not appealing to their latent Unionism—Sherman was appealing to their sense of realism and practicality in face of overwhelming military superiority. The general was not naive; he fully understood that his efforts constituted a long shot. He may have miscalculated the depth of Georgia politicians' attachment to the Confederacy, but Sherman knew that it would cost him nothing to try.[49]

Sherman's gambit was well worth the effort expended in his talks with Hill, Wright, and King. At the very least, any discord that Sherman could sow in Confederate circles would rebound only to his benefit. The general was astute enough not to put all his military eggs into the peace basket. Even as he was sending out feelers for peace, he was simultaneously dispatching forces to pursue Hood and planning for the march across Georgia. Given what he knew about Georgia politics and the mood of the state, it would have been irresponsible of Sherman not to have at least made the effort to accomplish a negotiated stand down of Georgia. Had the long shot succeeded it would have been, in the words of the general's September 28 letter to Lincoln, "a magnificent stroke of policy." As late as November

---

[49] Conway, *Reconstruction of Georgia*, 6; Parks, *Joseph E. Brown*, 299; Kennett, *Marching through Georgia*, 216; B. H. Reid, *Scourge of War*, 338. Reid misinterpreted Parks, *Joseph E. Brown*, 296–99, to support his point; Parks specifically wrote that Sherman "had good reason to expect success" (*Joseph E. Brown*, 296). See also McDonough, *William T. Sherman*, 557; Simpson, *Ulysses S. Grant*, 382; Venet, *Changing Wind*, 175; and Baggett, *Scalawags*, 75, 92.

13, just days before Union forces started toward the sea, Joshua Hill was at the state capital still striving gallantly for a path toward peace. Sherman's attempt to remove Georgia from the war through the good offices of Joshua Hill and others did not yield fruit, but it was a seed well worth planting.

Chapter 6

Unionist Hero in Confederate Madison, 1864

The literature about Sherman's march across Georgia to the sea is voluminous, but it lacks full exploration of the point of view of a prominent Southern White Unionist who spoke contemporaneously with Sherman about the war, who personally viewed the devastation of Atlanta and Northwest Georgia, who was able to offer first-hand observation of the strength of Union forces in and around Atlanta, who personally knew and conversed with the leaders of Confederate Georgia, who lost a son to Sherman's army in the Atlanta campaign, who had another son return home from the Confederate army with debilitating illness, who lost property to General Stoneman's retreating Yankees a few weeks before the March, who personally interacted with Union troops approaching his hometown, who invited a federal officer to lunch with his family in the dining room of his elegant in-town home, and who suffered the destruction of his large country plantation by the troops of the March. Joshua Hill had a unique perspective.

Union forces set forth on their March from Atlanta in mid-November 1864. When they reached Morgan County and Madison, they ripped up railroad tracks and destroyed war-related sites, including the depot and warehouses. There was some minor looting and other damage, but the residential district escaped significant damage. In the minds of contemporary locals who feared greater devastation and in the later memories of White Madisonians who regarded their community as specially spared, the relatively mild treatment by the Yankee invaders required explanation. Within just days of the march, newspaper stories gave credit to Joshua Hill. The narrative of Hill's role as his hometown's protector has persisted into the twenty-first century, alongside an equally persistent local mantra that Sherman's men spared Madison because the town was "too pretty to burn."

Some of the particulars of these stories are unique to Hill and Madison, but they also provide a case study of the process of mythmaking and myth-maintaining that continues to surround the March to the Sea.

The March to the Sea in Military Context

William Tecumseh Sherman wanted Joshua Hill and his other peace emissaries to make it very clear to Governor Joseph E. Brown, legislators, and other Confederate opinion leaders that if Georgia spurned his offers, the Union army "would be compelled to go ahead, devasting the State in its whole length and breadth." In other words, he would "make Georgia howl." However, when Sherman said that he would make the state howl, he did not mean that he wanted to make Unionists and Black people howl—he intended to make *Rebels* howl.[1]

Early in September, Sherman wrote to his chief of staff Henry Halleck: "If the people raise a howl against my barbarity and cruelty, I will answer that war is war and not popularity-seeking. If they want peace, they and their relatives must stop war." In Sherman's view, the majority of White people in the line of his intended march were not innocent civilians; they were complicit actors in the start and continuation of the war. The enemies were, in the words of prolific Civil War historian Wiley Sword, "Those with the strongest wills to break, those who dwelled in the Southern heartland and supported rebel resistance, from newspaper editors to planters to the humblest of farmers." Writing from Savannah at the end of the Georgia march but before the much harsher days in South Carolina, a New York reporter sympathetic to Sherman put the matter simply: "If the people along the line of march have suffered loss it has been the fortune of a war they voted for." To be sure, recent historians have documented that not all Southern Whites were supportive of the Confederacy and that civilian resistance was deeper than traditionally thought, but that discontent did not result in pro-peace legislatures or negotiation-minded executives. Efforts like Joshua Hill's pro-peace gubernatorial candidacy in 1863 documented discontent but failed to change the course of the war. Sherman understood

[1] Sherman, *Memoirs*, 612–13.

White man's democracy. He knew who started the war, who continued it, who could stop it, and who did not.[2]

Before Sherman could start his trek to Savannah, he had to deal with the remainder of General John Bell Hood's Confederate army. After regrouping south of Atlanta in the Jonesboro-Lovejoy area, Hood moved northward with the intention of threatening Sherman's supply line—the Western & Atlantic Railroad (W&A). On October 3, shortly after his meeting with Hill, Sherman left the Twentieth Corps as an occupation force in Atlanta and moved the rest of his army against Hood in Northwest Georgia. It was during this expedition that Joshua Hill had his brief second encounter with Sherman while he changed trains on his return from meeting Judge Augustus Wright in Rome. Under pressure, General Hood withdrew, and the Union secured full control of the W&A by early November. Confident that General George Thomas could dispose of Hood, Sherman returned to Atlanta to prepare for his march. In mid-December, Thomas won a decisive victory near Nashville.[3]

It was just a week after the fall of Atlanta that Sherman proposed to Grant his idea that he would sever his supply lines, march across the state destroying military targets, and live off the land. Grant knew that Sherman had previously employed a similar tactic in his Meridian, Mississippi, campaign, but the general-in-chief harbored serious doubts that such an undertaking would work on the much grander scale that Sherman now envisioned. President Lincoln, chief of staff Henry Halleck, and secretary of war Edwin Stanton harbored even more hesitations. The president, more politically confident after the capture of Atlanta but still nervous about his reelection, wanted any such risky action to wait until after the votes were cast. Ultimately, Grant's deep confidence in Sherman led him to give the order: "Go as you propose."[4]

---

[2] Vetter, *Sherman*, 222 (If the); Sword, *Southern Invincibility*, 309; J. C. Andrews, *North Reports the Civil War*, 577–78 (quoting *New York Herald*, December 28, 1864). See also Freehling, *South vs. the South*, 163; McNeill, "Survey of Confederate Soldier Morale," 1–25; McCurry, *Confederate Reckoning*; Williams, *Georgia's Civil War*.

[3] S. Davis, *Into Tennessee and Failure*; Wills, *George Henry Thomas*.

[4] Flood, *Grant and Sherman*, 263–68, 276; Trudeau, *Southern Storm*, 33–47; Brands, *Man Who Saved the Union*, 334–37.

General Sherman split his force of about sixty-two thousand soldiers into two roughly equal wings. Confederate defenders facing the onslaught consisted of only about ten thousand cavalry troops under Major General Joseph Wheeler plus roughly three thousand ill-equipped and poorly trained Georgia militiamen, mostly men too old, too young, or too infirm to be in the regular service. The right wing of the march under General O. O. Howard headed south along the Macon & Western Railroad through Jonesboro toward Macon and thus is not of direct relevance to Madison and Joshua Hill. The left wing, officially designated as the Army of Georgia and led by General Henry Warner Slocum, headed, in Sherman's words, "to the east by Decatur and Stone Mountain, toward Madison."[5] The two wings eventually merged around Milledgeville on November 23, three days after Slocum's men departed Morgan County.

Sherman kept his detailed plans on a need-to-know basis, but he revealed a key element of his strategy when he met in Atlanta with Hill and Foster in late September. The general pulled out a map, placed his finger on the important railroad junction at Millen, Georgia, and remarked, "I must go to this point." He spoke of cutting off Augusta and its powder works from Richmond and commented that he was aware that the Confederacy had "very little force to resist me." Madison stood about sixty miles east of Atlanta along the main railroad route, so the two Madisonians could have reasonably expected that their town would be on the route of the March even if Union troops did not have to go all the way to Augusta to accomplish their objective of neutralizing its importance. It is also reasonable to speculate that they urged the general to go easy on their hometown if the march happened to pass their way. There is, however, no evidence that they negotiated any specific agreement to spare their hometown.[6]

Lincoln, Halleck, and Grant knew the broad outlines of Sherman's plan, but after Union forces departed Atlanta, even the central command was mostly in the dark as to the day-to-day locations of the marchers of either wing. With telegraph lines cut or absent altogether, there could be no day-to-day reports as there had been during the summer campaign from Chattanooga to Atlanta. Sherman, who disliked and distrusted the

---

[5] Sherman, *Memoirs*, 654.

[6] Hill's *Herald* letter, 1875.

press, allowed only a few newspaper correspondents to accompany his columns; thus, anxious readers could glean only snippets of information and rumor about the march.[7]

The March to the Sea in Historical Perspective and Public Perception

There is a massive body of historical and popular literature about the March across Georgia to the Savannah and the subsequent campaign north through the Carolinas. As two journalism professors put it, "William Tecumseh Sherman has marched to the sea a million times in national memory." That biographies of Sherman continue to appear with regularity is further testimony to enduring interest in the war, the march, and the controversial general. Many of the books and articles mention Madison and Joshua Hill at various levels of detail in the context of their broader accounts. The White Southern effort to shape the memory of the war began even before it was over and continued well into the twentieth century. Writers influenced by the Lost Cause theory of Confederate defeat submitted Sherman's March to the Sea and northward through the Carolinas as the prime exhibit in their case to prove Yankee cruelty, venality, and blame. More recently, many professional Civil War historians and Sherman biographers have debunked Lost Cause historiography and have endeavored to present the march and its leader in the broader context of the war.[8]

---

[7] Marszalek, *Sherman's Other War*; Caudill and Ashdown, *Sherman's March*, 39–50.

[8] Caudill and Ashdown, *Sherman's March*, 1, 129–49; Rubin, *Through the Heart of Dixie*, 175, 224–31; Blight, *Race and Reunion*; Horwitz, *Confederates in the Attic*; Parker, "'To the Youth of the Southern Confederacy,'" 94–109; and W. C. Davis, *Cause Lost*, 191–205. General works on the March to the Sea include J. D. Dickey, *Rising in Flames*; Trudeau, *Southern Storm*; Marszalek, *Sherman's March to the Sea*; Bailey, *War and Ruin*; Miles, *To the Sea*; Kennett, *Marching through Georgia*; Glatthaar, *March to the Sea*; B. Davis, *Sherman's March*. Recent works on Sherman include B. H. Reid, *Life of William Tecumseh Sherman*; McDonough, *William Tecumseh Sherman*; O'Connell, *Fierce Patriot*; and Fellman, *Citizen Sherman*. For an overview of Sherman historiography prior to 2008, see Caudill and Ashdown, *Sherman's March*, 65–88.

The emphases and particulars of the many works that include extensive coverage of the March to the Sea vary widely, but common to many of them is an exploration of the dual interpretations of Sherman. Was the general a crass, unfeeling terrorist who wantonly and unnecessarily devastated much of Georgia and the Carolinas thereby embittering the White South and making national reconciliation even more difficult? Or, was Uncle Billy an efficient tactician who acknowledged that "War is hell" while doing what he had to do to reunite America? Was he a liberator of enslaved people or an unfeeling White supremacist? In 2019, Steve Huggins advanced the argument by using the March to the Sea as an example of how the United States itself has often resorted to the sort of terrorist tactics that it deplores when used by others. Conversely, some historians have downplayed the terroristic aspects of the march by pointing out that the number of rapes, murders, and physical assault were few. The author of a joint Sherman-Grant biography documented that in the minds of most of the men of Sherman's army, "the most comforting idea was that relatively bloodless violence, right then, could save much more bloodshed on both sides later." Both of these points of view draw from the same body of evidence, and, at least for scholars, if not for some of the more popular and polemic accounts, the differences are more of emphasis than essence.[9]

In the same 1875 letter in which he described Sherman's peace initiative, Joshua Hill confronted the already conflicting interpretations of the general and the march and came down firmly on the general's side. He began by acknowledging his personal debt to General Sherman for assistance in the search for his son's body and then continued:

> But when I reflect that so many candid and well-meaning people believe that a wanton disregard of human suffering is a leading characteristic of Sherman, I feel it my duty to make known a few facts, calculated to soften the harsh judgement.
>
> Notwithstanding his desolating march through Georgia and the Carolinas, and the wrongs and cruelties perpetrated by soldiers

---

[9] Huggins, *America's Use of Terror*, 99–23; Flood, *Grant and Sherman*, 271–73; Grimsley, *Hard Hand of War*, 172–222. Two earlier biographies that emphasize Sherman's terror are Vetter, *Sherman*, and Schenck, *"The General Who Marched to Hell"*; Caudill and Ashdown, *Sherman's March*, 129–49; Rubin, *Through the Heart of Dixie*, 204–31; and W. C. Davis, *The Cause Lost*, 191–205.

> of his command, subsequent to my meeting with him, I could never bring my mind to the belief, that such deeds were in keeping with the promptings of his heart, or that they received his approval. Nor did the destruction and despoilment of my own property during his march from Atlanta, for a single moment, excite in my breast a feeling of unkindness towards the commanding general of the great army to which my despoilers belonged. I felt, that it would grieve him to learn the havoc that his soldiers had made.[10]

The interpretation that Hill sought to debunk, i.e., "that a wanton disregard of human suffering is a leading characteristic of Sherman," was already well in place when he penned his letter in 1875, and it persists widely in the public mind more than a century and a half later. The popular image of the March to the Sea persistent in publications and media representations is that Sherman laid near total waste to a sixty-mile wide swath across Georgia, from Atlanta to Savannah. Postwar Whites dubbed the still-standing chimneys of burned homes as "Sherman's sentinels"—stark reminders of Union treachery. "As time passed," historian Lee Kennett wrote, "Georgians increasingly attributed the catastrophe that had struck them to a single man." In *Southern Storm*, one of the most popular recent studies of Sherman's march, Noah Andre Trudeau bluntly wrote, "The phrase *Sherman's March* has morphed into a comfortable metaphor for a scorched-earth policy, and its architect has become an accepted synonym for a pariah."[11]

There is no doubt that the march was highly destructive. On direct orders, Union soldiers destroyed some towns such as Millen, the railroad junction with an infamous prison nearby. They did torch some plantations—some, including that of leading Confederate Howell Cobb, by direct order. When the flames died down and the Union troops were gone, White residents in the path of the march could see for themselves that most of the structures in their towns and the great majority of the

---

[10] Hill's *Herald* letter, 1875.

[11] Kennett, *Marching through Georgia*, 321; Trudeau, *Southern Storm*, 537 (italics in original); Sword, *Southern Invincibility*, 311 (sentinels); Bassett, "Birth of a Demon," 27–35. Bassett dates the Southern White demonization of Sherman to 1881 following the publication of Jefferson Davis's book. It may have raised the level, but evidence herein shows anti-Sherman sentiment several years earlier.

homesteads in the countryside remained standing with limited or no damage. To be sure, "Sherman's sentinels" spotted the landscape here and there, but many more houses stood untorched, and even some of those burned had actually suffered at Confederate hands. How could that be? In the years after the war, the White citizens of several communities along the route of the March to the Sea constructed narratives to explain the supposedly unique circumstances that spared their homes and businesses while so many other places succumbed to severe destruction. These tales depend for their credence on the widespread acceptance of the impression that Sherman's troops devastated almost everything in their path except, of course, for the particular place in the particular tale. The local narrative could concede that their town's military targets met destruction and that their local residents suffered from some unruly soldiers, but the thrust of the story had to be that the minor damage at their specific town or plantation stood in stark contrast to near total mayhem elsewhere.

These two narrative threads, massive destruction and special exceptions, have coexisted for 160 years. The tales are nurtured especially by amateur historians and tourist offices that want their towns to seem special. No single place illustrates those contrasting legends more vividly than Joshua Hill's hometown of Madison—known in lore as the city that Hill saved and that Sherman found too beautiful to burn.

Many of the stories that sought to explain a community's relative good fortune in the face of Yankee onslaught did not emerge until after the end of the war, and most of them lack contemporaneous documentation. On the other hand, reports that Joshua Hill's intervention reduced damage in Madison appeared just days after the events. Union forces departed Morgan County on November 20, and on December 2, 1864, the following line appeared in the *Augusta Chronicle & Sentinel*: "The people of Madison are indebted to Hon. Joshua Hill for his strenuous exertions to have their property protected. It was owing to his efforts, solely, that they were spared."

The tale has scarcely abated. A 1951 article in the *Georgia Review* declared that Hill "heard that the soldiers were in town" and then urged the Union forces to spare it. The following year, Medora Field Perkerson, a close friend of *Gone with the Wind* author Margaret Mitchell, included several pages about Madison in *White Columns in Georgia*. When it came to the part about salvation from Union rage, she wrote, "Joshua Hill rode out on a horse to meet the general and to ask protection for the town." In her *Rambles through Morgan County, Georgia*, written in 1957 (and reprinted as late as 1989), Louise McHenry Hicky explained, "Madison was spared from the ravages of Sherman's raid because of an act of Representative Joshua Hill." These earlier publications laid the groundwork for dozens of later popular accounts. Travel writers for the *Washington Post* wrote it up at least twice without calling Hill by name but crediting a Hill-like character. From the 1960s into the twenty-first century, Madison-focused stories featuring references to Joshua Hill appeared in numerous newspaper travel articles and in such wide-circulation publications as *Southern Living*, *Antiques*, *Arthur Frommer's Budget Travel*, and *American Heritage*. *Garden & Gun*'s Summer 2007 issue explained that antebellum homes such as the grand 1850s Boxwood survived because Sherman thought the town "too pretty to burn," and because, "so the legend goes,.... Sherman was somehow swayed by the plaintive appeals of Madison's prominent resident Joshua Hill, a Union sympathizer." Authorized state and local tourist publications (and more recently websites) helped spread the story. The 2020 "Discover Morgan" official county guide encapsulated the persistent companion legends of widespread destruction and local exception succinctly:

> Madison's original claim to fame dates back to the Civil War when Union General W. T. Sherman's forces spared the city from a fiery fate during his infamous March to the Sea in which Sherman's troops torched communities ablaze from Atlanta to Savannah in 1864. It was the advocacy of a pro-union senator who hailed from Madison, who saved Madison's luxurious antebellum homes from being reduced to ashes.

These kinds of stories are consistent in portraying Joshua Hill as the hero even though they often muddle the details. The two most common errors include writing as if Sherman and Hill had met personally in Madison even though the general was actually with other units more than ten miles to the south and referring to Hill as a "senator" even though he did not earn that title until 1871.[12]

---

[12] Cumming, "Madison: Middle Georgia Minerva," 130; Perkerson, *White Columns in Georgia*, 52–53; L. Hicky, *Rambles through Morgan County*, 12–13; "Discover Morgan," *Morgan County Citizen*, June 10, 2020; Barth, "What

All of this extended attention to the story of Madison and Joshua Hill caught the attention of scholars in three early twenty-first-century articles from three different disciplines: folklore, journalism, and history. The folklore study documented how oral traditions about Sherman's ferocity and his occasional compassion persisted in Madison and other towns into the early twenty-first century. Madison residents told the folklorists anecdotes about horses being stabled in the Baptist church, Sherman having a girlfriend, ladies serving picnic baskets full of fried chicken, an old friend writing a letter to Sherman, and, of course, Sherman regarding the town to be too beautiful to burn and Joshua Hill saving it. One woman who resided in a restored antebellum family home across the intersection from Joshua Hill's former residence regaled her interviewer with fanciful tales about Sherman's infatuation with "the lovely daughter of the Mayor [i.e. Hill], who had been quite a favorite of General Sherman's in the years before the war." The interviewee added that the young lady with whom Sherman was supposedly smitten "sallied forth to the front line of the advancing Union troops."[13]

In 2009, two journalism scholars analyzed both contemporary and later press coverage of Sherman's March to the Sea with particular emphasis on "salvation mythology." They scoured newspaper stories from eight Georgia towns and found that the articles almost always portrayed their own communities as specific exceptions to the generality of massive destruction. Of all these legends they observed, "Perhaps the best-known salvation story is about Madison."[14]

Sherman Missed," 27; Banks, "History in Towns," 88–97; McCrady, "Boxwood," **[page?]**; Jeff Prugh, "The Town Sherman Refused to Burn," *Washington Post*, October 14, 1979; Mary Ann Anderson, "Georgia's Antebellum Trail, Meandering through the Towns that Sherman Spared," *Washington Post*, May 22, 2014; Bob Harrell, "The Town that Sherman Saved," *Atlanta Journal-Constitution*, September 16, 1978; Hicky, *Madison, Georgia and Her Homes*, 70; J. McDonald, *Georgia Off the Beaten Path*, 133; Propst and J. W. White, *Sidetracked*, 87; Benefield, "The Civil War in Georgia," 39; Grudowski, "Madison, Georgia Protects Its Historic Charms," 66; Mitchell, *Madison*, 16–17; Kennett, *Marching through Georgia*, 322; Rubin, *Through the Heart of Dixie*, 15–16, 63, 233.

[13] Henken, "Taming the Enemy," 289–307. It is clear from the context that one informant was Hattie Mina Hicky.

[14] Hume and Roessner, "Surviving Sherman's March," 119–37.

Whereas the folklorists and journalists thoroughly documented the persistence of tales about Joshua Hill saving Madison, historian Brian Melton sought to ascertain the factual accuracy of the basic story. His 2002 article classified the Civil War memories of Madison and other Georgia cities into four categories and then concluded that what happened in Madison was typical of what occurred in most other towns along the march, i.e., destruction of militarily relevant sites but little sacking of the rest of the town. He dubbed his interpretation as "realistic nonexceptionalist." In Melton's view, the activities of Joshua Hill in Madison made little, if any, substantive difference in how Madison fared. Melton was not too far from wrong, but further evidence using documents that Melton did not explore supports the conclusion Hill's intervention played a more determinative role than Melton posited.[15]

Sorting through the Joshua Hill Savior Story

The left wing of the March to the Sea departed Atlanta on November 15 and 16 under the overall leadership of General Henry W. Slocum. His force included two corps of more than ten thousand troops each: the Fourteenth, commanded by Brevet Major General Jefferson C. Davis (no relation to the Confederate president), and the Twentieth, led by Brigadier General Alpheus S. Williams. Sherman traveled with the Fourteenth, and Slocum's headquarters unit accompanied the Twentieth. For the first thirty-five miles, the Fourteenth and the Twentieth corps proceeded eastward in a parallel manner. The Twentieth marched mostly on the north side of the Georgia Railroad, and the Fourteenth proceeded primarily on the south side. (The tracks today still follow essentially the same roadbed just north of Interstate 20.) Around Covington in Newton County, the Fourteenth, including Sherman's HQ unit, moved away from the railroad and angled to the southeast directly toward Milledgeville. Meanwhile, the

---

[15] Melton, "'The Town that Sherman Wouldn't Burn,'" 201–30. Understandably, given that he wrote when online databases were not as robust, Melton underutilized newspapers and did not locate the letters and recollections of Atkinson, High, Reid, Pepper, or Harryman cited in this chapter. Melton inadvertently referred to Hill a prewar senator.

Twentieth Corps continued east along the tracks toward Madison. The Twentieth had become, in essence, the left wing of the Left Wing.[16]

The White residents of Morgan County and its county seat reasonably feared the worst. Their point of reference would have been the ghastly reports that they had so recently heard from newspapers and refugees about the burning of Atlanta and the thorough destruction that towns in Northwest Georgia including Rome, Cassville, Kingston, and Marietta had suffered not just once but in some cases twice—first during the Atlanta Campaign and then during Sherman's subsequent pursuit of Hood's army. It had been only a few weeks since General Sherman had exiled most remaining civilians from Atlanta, so it can be assumed that cowering Whites in the line of march feared the same fate for themselves. The last eastbound Georgia Railroad train left the village of Social Circle just ahead of the approaching federal force. Passengers and crew would have spread their fears as they passed through Madison about fifteen miles to the east.

A series of letters from Madison resident Simeon Atkinson to his wife and daughter testify to the level of confusion and concern in the face of the threat. Atkinson served as the capital correspondent of the main Augusta newspaper, and he wrote home from Milledgeville. On November 13, he warned that the family might have to flee Madison "since there is likely to be raids on the place, if it does not fall into the enemie's lines altogether." In the same letter, he noted that former Congressmen Hill and Foster, fellow Madisonians, were in the capital city continuing their last-minute efforts for a negotiated peace. Three days later, he wrote that Milledgeville was "in the midst of great excitement at the advance of the Yankees" and added "The Governor has news that parts of Rome, Marietta, Canton, Dallas, Atlanta, and all other towns and villages in their way are burned." Apparently thinking at that time that all of Sherman's army was headed directly to the capital, he assured his wife that "Madison is probably safe." The following day, the 17th, he had more news and wrote his daughter to calm her fears. "We are all much excited here about the Yankees. The Governor has been notified that they are at Jonesboro and Macdonough, about 80 miles from here, and are coming this way. They will probably come through Monticello and Eatonton. I don't think they will go to Madison." He was, of course, wrong since he was unaware that the left wing

[16] Melton, *Sherman's Forgotten General.*

had split in half with Slocum taking three divisions along the Georgia Railroad all the way to Madison while Sherman accompanied the balance on a more direct path toward Milledgeville where he would unite with the right wing.[17]

The troops of the Twentieth Corps pushed from Social Circle into Morgan County where they burned the depot at Rutledge. They were now in fresh territory outside the range that the Union army had foraged during the occupation of Atlanta. Union soldiers found such an abundance of food that they took only the best. A Connecticut commissary sergeant's letter home effused, "the country was overflowing with sweet potatoes, corn, syrup & hogs, and.... The boys wasted as much as they used, but no complaint was made, in fact I think Genl Sherman didn't intend to leave any thing for the Rebs." Farms near the line of march often hid cattle, horses, mules, corn, molasses, and valuables from the foragers—sometimes successfully, sometimes not. Occasionally, soldiers found the hidden bounty on their own; sometimes, slaves helped the foragers, and on at least one occasion, they discovered a clandestine stash due to the unwitting honesty of a young child.[18]

On the evening of November 18, the various units of the Twentieth Corps set up camps along the Atlanta Road and railroad tracks on the western fringe of Madison. Slocum's headquarters unit and Brigadier General William T. Ward's Third Division settled in on the plantation of Dr. John William Jones. The other two divisions encamped nearby. As dawn broke on November 19, 1864, one division after another, commencing with John W. Geary's Second, began marching toward Madison.[19]

---

[17] Simeon and Ethie Atkinson letters, Judith Ulrich Collection of the Morgan County Landmarks Society, Madison, Georgia, copies deposited in the Morgan County Archives. Hereafter, Atkinson letters, MCA.

[18] Padgett, "With Sherman through Georgia and the Carolinas," [Rufus Mead] 58; Merrill, *Seventieth Indiana Volunteer Infantry*, 224 [child]; Grunert, *History of the 129th Illinois*, 125; Bradley, *Star Corps*, 184; Morhous, *Reminiscences of the 123d*, 134; Byrne, *Uncommon Soldiers*, 205.

[19] Marvin, *Fifth Regiment Connecticut Volunteers*, 350; Bradley, *Star Corps*, 185; Byrne, *Uncommon Soldiers*, 206; McBride, *History of the 33rd Indiana*, 152; Boyle, *Soldiers True*, 56; Hurst, *Journal-History of the 73rd Ohio*, 155; *OR*, ser. 1, vol. 44, 491.

According to the standard story, Joshua Hill led a delegation out from town to meet with the Union command and ask their forbearance for the people and property of Madison. Because of Hill's reputation as an unwavering Unionist and his personal acquaintance with generals Sherman and Slocum, they granted his request. Madison was thereby spared greater destruction than would otherwise have occurred. That something akin to this scenario actually happened is entirely plausible and even highly likely. Having prominent citizens go forth to meet oncoming troops was not unusual. On September 2, 1864, Mayor James Calhoun, Joshua Hill's friend and political ally, met personally with elements of Union command to surrender the city of Atlanta. Just two days before the Union force reached the edge of Madison, a delegation of Covington's prominent citizens ventured forth to greet Sherman. The commanding general avoided meeting the Covingtonians personally, but other officers accepted the town's hospitality on his behalf. That a similar scene played out at Madison would not be unexpected.[20]

What makes the Madison story different from the other towns with salvation stories is that there is no question that the top command structure of the Twentieth Corps was aware of Joshua Hill's Unionist proclivities and that they knew that they were approaching his hometown. Only about six weeks had passed since Hill and Foster had met with Sherman in Atlanta and again briefly near Rome. Sherman specifically directed Slocum to facilitate Hill and Foster's return to Madison after they scoured Northwest Georgia battlefields for the remains of Legare Hill.

Unfortunately, neither the *Official Records of the War of Rebellion* nor any of the individual letters or memoirs that the present author has located explicitly describe a meeting between a Madison delegation and the generals of the Twentieth Corps. On the other hand, the likelihood that it did occur is supported by the fact that references to the meeting were already in wide circulation in Madison during and very soon after the war. A news story that appeared in the *Countryman* about two weeks after the troops passed through said that Hill "prevailed upon Gen. Slocum" to place guards about. Baptist minister J. R. Kendrick came to Madison in 1863 and "saw a good deal of Colonel Hill" during his time in the city. The pastor was in

[20] Kennett, *Marching through Georgia*, 200 and Castel, *Decision in the West*, 528 [Atlanta]; Trudeau, *Southern Storm*, 127 (Covington).

Southwest Georgia when the troops passed by his church on November 19, but he soon returned home. Kendrick recalled his experience in an 1889 article: "On reaching Madison we found the place substantially intact. Not a house had been destroyed, not a citizen harmed or insulted. Colonel Hill, as we learned, had gone out to meet the approaching column under Slocum, and if there had been any danger of violent demonstrations this pacific embassy removed it." Assuming that his published memories are accurate, Pastor Kendrick heard the reports of Hill's meeting with the commanders of the Twentieth Corps within just a few days of its occurrence.[21]

In 1864, Emma High was only about three or four years old. Many years later, she recorded her personal reminiscences, basing her account on stories that her mother had told her. High wrote, "The army reached the beautiful city of Madison on November 17th [*sic*] and were met, a few miles out of town, by a committee consisting of colonel Joshua Hill, colonel N. G. Foster, Major Woods, and Mr. Cohen. This committee surrendered the town, but pleaded with them not to burn it." Although High's childhood memories straddle the line between contemporary observation and later elaboration, the composition of the delegation that she specified is entirely plausible and is unquestionably evidence of Madison's late-nineteenth-century oral tradition. Foster died in 1869, but the other three men remained locally prominent well into the 1870s, so High would have known them during her teen and adult years. Major [William] Woods was Madison postmaster and an organizer of the local Panola Guards. He later served as mayor. Mr. Eleazer Hart Cohen, also a postwar mayor, owned a downtown store and had a son who married into the Foster family.[22]

Indirect evidence and reasonable supposition strongly indicate that Joshua Hill and company met with the Union command as they approached Madison, but the exact nature of the meeting remains unverified. Given that General Slocum was encamped on the Jones plantation with

---

[21] Kendrick, "A Non-Combatant's War Reminiscences," 449–63; *Countryman*, December 6, 1864.

[22] Emma High, in "Reminiscences of Confederate Soldiers" compiled by the United Daughters of the Confederacy (Georgia Division), 1940, 2:100–102, Georgia Archives, Morrow. Excerpts in K. M. Jones, *When Sherman Came*, 14–15; Kaemmerien, *General Sherman and the Georgia Belles*, 14.

Brigadier General William T. Ward's Third Division, it seems most likely that the encounter would have occurred there and that Slocum was directly involved or at least aware of the meeting. That Hill met later in the day with an aide-de-camp of Ward is confirmed by a contemporary letter written by Lieutenant Samuel K. Harryman of the Seventieth Indiana Infantry. The Third Division began entering Madison about nine and continued passing through the city well into the afternoon. They moved deliberately because, in addition to managing their own entourage, the Third escorted the supply wagons of the Second Division, which had hurried through town early in the morning on its way toward the Oconee River railroad bridge about ten miles further east.

Upon reaching the outskirts of Savannah in December, Lieutenant Harryman found time to write a long letter to a friend back home in Indiana in which he detailed his experiences on the march from Atlanta. The section of the letter about Madison began with the observation typical of his fellow soldiers that "Madison is the most beautiful town I saw on the march." He mentioned the "large yards well filled with the richest shrubbery and flowers the country north and south affords." Then he wrote of a very engaging luncheon:

> Joshua Hill the last Senator [*sic*] from Georgia in congress of the United States and the last Southern member leaving Congress when secession commenced resides in Madison. He claims to be a Union man yet, and claims the same for most of the citizens of his town. I had occasion to remain in town near half the day. Mr. Hill introduced himself to me, then took me to his house, introduced me to his family, and had me remain to dinner. I spent the time very pleasant for he has a pleasant family. One daughter [is] handsome and intelligent and a fine musician. [Probably Anna, the eldest.] On leave she presented me with a beautiful bouquet, finding it unhandy to carry I took it to pieces and pressed some of the roses. She also gave me a seed of the Tea plant. The plant is beautiful and ornamental.[23]

---

[23] Samuel K. Harryman to Margaret Moore (dateline "before Savannah") December 18, 1864, Samuel K. Harryman letters collection, Indiana State Library, Rare Books and Manuscript Repository (S-0603). The thirty-eight-year-old Lt.

Harryman's letter confirms that Hill was out and about among the troops on the morning of their arrival. Ward's young aide had to have been aware of Hill's reputation when he accepted the offer to join his family for the midday meal. It is reasonable to speculate that Hill might have brought the young man by the house to dine with the family and then excused himself to go back out again to further check on the actions of the troops.

Another soldier with connection to the command structure also wrote of Hill's impact on the Union's treatment of Madison. By virtue of his position as clerk at the regimental headquarters of the Twenty-second Wisconsin, Harvey Reid would have had opportunities to overhear conversations of superior officers to which the rank and file would not have been privy. He passed their observations along in a contemporaneous letter:

> Another remarkable feature of Madison is that it is the residence of at least three genuine Union men. They are General [George R.] Jessup, an old Mexican war officer, Colonel Hill, formerly a member of congress at Washington, and a Mr. [Nathaniel] Greene Foster. Colonel Hill visited General Sherman at Atlanta, his visit giving rise, I presume, to the reports of Georgia having made proposals of peace.... This town was well guarded from depredations by the soldiers, probably for the sake of the small leaven of righteousness it contained.[24]

Although his letter made no explicit reference to Hill meeting on site with Slocum or other high officers, it is clear that Sergeant Reid understood that it was the Unionism of Hill and his friends that constituted that "small leaven of righteousness" that helped protect Madison.

The 1866 *Recollections* of Captain George W. Pepper, a chaplain with the Twentieth Corps, was one of the earliest and most popular accounts of the March to the Sea. In writing of Madison, the reverend joined many others in remarking of the beauty of the town, and added, "I cannot forbear

---

Harryman was from Morgan County, Indiana; one presumes that this coincidence of place names would have come up in dinner conversation. The "handsome and intelligent" daughter was probably Anna, the oldest Hill child, who married a Union soldier after the war. Harryman made the common mistake of referring to Hill as a senator. Trudeau, *Southern Storm*, 145, mentions the encounter.

[24] Byrne, *Uncommon Soldiers*, 206–207 (Reid); Osborn, *Trials and Triumphs*, 177, also mentions Hill.

mentioning the name of the good and tried Joshua H. [*sic*] Hill.... Hill was always an old line Whig, and continued a staunch Unionist, when it was very dangerous to avow such sentiments." These five men—Hill, the two Unionists whom Reid mentioned, and Cohen and Woods—remain close today—all resting near each other in Madison's Old Cemetery.[25]

In addition to the contemporary letters of Union soldiers and the timely recollections of Madison residents, the impact of Joshua Hill's direct involvement with the command of the Twentieth Corps is supported by contemporaneous newspaper accounts. Simeon Atkinson, whose private letters about the approach of the march are quoted above, was both a resident of Madison and the capital reporter for the *Augusta Chronicle & Sentinel.* When Union troops approached Milledgeville and it became clear that the Confederacy would mount no defense, Atkinson fled north to his wife and children in Madison. His detailed description written for the *Chronicle* in the form of a letter dated November 24 and published on the 30th is the earliest printed account of his hometown's fate. Atkinson's account ran in full or part in Richmond, New Orleans, New York, Cleveland, Chicago, Indianapolis, Buffalo, Milwaukee, Columbus, Philadelphia, and lesser cities. Even readers in the British Isles could find reprints of the *Chronicle & Sentinel*'s report in the papers of London, Glasgow, and Liverpool. It was the mid-nineteenth-century equivalent of a post going viral. In the style of the day, the rabid Confederate newspaperman signed his published letter with a pseudonym—in this case a thinly veiled one—his middle name, Aristides.[26]

Atkinson told the world that Union soldiers had "burned the depot and one or two old warehouses, with the jail and market house. They gutted

---

[25] Pepper, *Personal Recollections of Sherman's Campaigns*, 268.

[26] *Augusta Chronicle*, November 30, 1864 (dateline November 24). Reprints of the *Augusta Chronicle & Sentinel* letter include *New York Times*, December 4, 1864; *Buffalo Commercial*, December 5; *Chicago Tribune*, December 6; *Milwaukee Daily News*, December 6, *Baltimore Sun*, December 6, *Philadelphia Inquirer*, December 5; *London (England) Guardian*, December 20; *Glasgow Herald*, December 21; and *Liverpool Mercury*, December 22, 1864. Atkinson started his career in 1846 as a typesetter for the *Madison Visitor*. From 1856 to 1867 he reported for, edited, and owned papers in Augusta. From 1867 to 1872 he ran the *Southern Banner* in Athens. Atkinson's biography files are maintained with the Ulrich collection in the MCA.

every store, and plundered more or less on every lot. They fired the drug store and several other houses." Given that he was describing the downtown district near the railroad, by "houses," Atkinson was apparently referring in nineteenth-century parlance to business houses and warehouses rather than to residences. Writing of the rest of town, he complained that "Yankees entered the house of my next door neighbor," but he admitted that his own "humble domicile escaped any serious depredations." Atkinson was almost certainly the writer of the line published a few days later that asserted that Joshua Hill was "solely" responsible for Madison's salvation from total destruction. Meanwhile, the correspondent's wife, Ethie Atkinson, related her own experiences in a private letter to her sister:

> The Yankees have been here and left. Nearly the whole of Sherman's army came through here and remained in the place two days. They did not disturb me much, and I felt very little fear or excitement. Indeed I wonder at my calmness for I never saw so many people at one time in my life. The officers conversed freely with us and I talked as freely and pleasantly as if in ordinary times. They saw too I was no Unionist either. I did not lose anything but some chickens and horses.... Well I found out the Yankees were not so bad after all. But they did commit depredation on many in the county and many negroes left with them. They took a great deal of provisions etc.[27]

A detailed description of Hill's relationship to Slocum and its influence on troop behavior appeared four days later in the *Countryman*, published by James Addison Turner on his Putnam County plantation near Eatonton.

> Mr. Hill is Mayor of the city (small) of Madison. When the 20th Federal army corps passed through that city, he prevailed upon Gen. Slocum to place a guard at every house in order to prevent any plundering or rude conduct on the part of the soldiers. Seeing Mr. Hill with Gen. Slocum very often, and seeing that that General always heeded the suggestions of Mr. Hill, the guards got so, finally, that they obeyed the Mayor of Madison just as they did their own General. By pursuing the course which he

[27] Ibid.; Ethie Atkinson to Alice [sister], December 11, 1864, Atkinson letters, MCA.

> did, Mr. Hill tendered the people of Madison great service, for which he deserves great credit.[28]

The ardent Confederate editor was no political ally of Joshua Hill, so Turner would have been disinclined to grant the strong Unionist more credit than he deserved. The paper explicitly attributed the story to "a gentleman in whom we have every confidence" who claimed a personal conversation with Hill. It can be assumed that the *Countryman*'s verbiage about Yankee troops treating Hill "just as they did their own General." Turner's account was probably somewhat exaggerated—colorful embellishment was characteristic of his florid style. Excerpts from the *Countryman* story, along with those from the slightly earlier *Augusta Chronicle & Sentinel* articles, soon appeared in several newspapers in Georgia, other Confederate cities, and the North. Thus, the story of Joshua Hill's role in the protection of Madison was in wide circulation within mere days of the actual events.

The lack of consistent sources and the varying perspectives makes detailed assessment of the actual level of destruction in Madison difficult. It is also impossible to make definitive conclusions about the comparative levels of destruction experienced by other towns along either wing of Sherman's notorious march. It is certainly true that all suffered some damage, yet it is also clear that few, barring extreme cases like Millen, were thoroughly burned or sacked. The *Official Records* are useful but spotty. Personal accounts are also fragmented. Each soldier or civilian letter writer or diarist observed only one point in time. One commentator's observation of "a little damage" and another's lament of "thoroughly devastated" could be descriptions of the very same incident depending on the timing and the observer's perspective. A store that appeared "ransacked" to a soldier who passed by soon after an incident could look just fine to another who went by a little later after the proprietor had cleaned up the mess. Soldiers who preceded later observers, even by moments, could have witnessed nothing of note.

---

[28] *Countryman*, December 6, 1864; this and subsequent accounts, probably relying on this reference, designate Hill as mayor of Madison. Certainly, he was the town's leading citizen; he had been elected to the city commission in 1861 (*Augusta Chronicle & Sentinel*, October 16, 1861). However, the loss of city records and absence of extant local papers make it difficult to confirm that he was officially serving as mayor in November 1864.

One commentator could describe a building as being engulfed in flames, but the actual damage could turn out to be fairly minor once the fire subsided. All of these considerations apply to Madison. With such caution in mind, the evidence permits a reasonably complete description of the events of November 19, 1864. It begins with the straight-forward, unelaborated, and uncontradicted statement from the pen of one of Sherman's staff officers: "At Madison the railroad buildings, the jail, several warehouses, and the market-house were burned."[29]

Other sources gave similar reports. In January 1865 *Harper's Weekly* magazine printed a lithograph of Madison's depot in flames. The accompanying story added the usual observation that Madison "is said to be the most picturesque" town in Georgia, but it did not mention any damage other than the railroad buildings and store houses.[30]

There is no doubt that Union soldiers, especially enlisted men out of the immediate supervision of their commissioned and noncommissioned officers, engaged in some destructiveness and petty theft in Madison as they did elsewhere. Much, but not all, such mischief was done by foragers (or bummers) ahead of or alongside the main column. The fullest account of such mayhem in Madison came from *New York Herald* correspondent Captain David P. Conyngham, author of the best-selling *Sherman's March through the South*, which was published in 1865. It should be noted that the captain misleadingly wrote in first person as if he had been in Madison and in the rest of the March to the Sea, but he was actually with General Thomas pursuing Hood and compiled this section of the book from other reporters' observations. In Madison, they reported that some stores were looted and offered colorful accounts of the looters prancing about. It is notable that the *Herald* reporters made a point to clarify that the miscreants were "stragglers, who manage to get to the front when there is plunder in view, and vagabonds of the army." Conyngham's account did not specifically mention Joshua Hill, but the account of what happened when the Third Division arrived are consistent with other reports that Madison

---

[29] Sherman, *Major-General Sherman's Reports*, v, 76.

[30] *Harper's Weekly Magazine*, January 7, 1865. The lithograph is incorrectly dated December 3; the burning occurred on November 19. On December 3, the 20th Corps was at Millen. The artist was Theodore R. Davis, who sketched many incidents along the march (Howe, *Marching with Sherman*, 153).

received protection beyond the usual: "The scene lasted until the head of the column under General Slocum arrived, when the town was at once cleared out of these marauders, and guards placed while the troops were passing."[31]

The soldiers of Ward's Division, who passed through from mid-morning to mid-afternoon, wrote little of the kind of early mayhem that Conyngham mentioned. Harvey Reid, the company clerk from Wisconsin who wrote of Hill and his fellow Unionists, observed that the "only exception" that he personally witnessed to the general rule of the lack of depredations was the sack of the office of a rebel doctor. Another soldier of the Third Division wrote in his journal that some men obtained old paper files and scattered them through the crowd while the band played on the Madison square in front of the county courthouse. Among the few documented thefts was the disappearance of the communion set from the Presbyterian church. The faux silver pieces were not highly valuable, but the miscreant probably assumed that they were sterling. A protest to Union command resulted in the eventual return of the set to the church.[32]

In his regimental history, the lieutenant colonel of the Third Division's Eighty-fifth Indiana also mentioned the band. "We marched through the beautiful town of Madison, bands playing Hail Columbia. Private property was respected but the depot and all R. R. property destroyed." Similarly, an Ohio chaplain who came through about midday recorded in his diary, "this is indeed a fine town, evidently a wealthy place. Many fine dwellings, abodes of luxury & ease! Town not damaged. Calaboose only burned." A New York sergeant called the town "quite a handsome place" and explained, "There was much railroad property in which was stored cotton and supplies for the confederate Army. After taking such things as we could use these

---

[31] Conyngham, *Sherman's March through the South*, 1, 248; J. C. Andrews places Conyngham with Gen. Thomas in north Georgia and Tennessee (*North Reports the Civil War*, 583). Trudeau concludes that Conyngham "did his homework" about the March leading to "sufficient truth" despite conveying the false impression of firsthand observation (*Southern Storm*, ix–x).

[32] Byrne, *Uncommon Soldiers*, 208 (Reid); *Augusta Chronicle*, November 30, December 2, 1864, and *Countryman*, December 20, 1864; Dunkleman, *Marching with Sherman*, 49; Fleharty, *Our Regiment*, 111 (102nd Illinois); Manos, *Madison Presbyterian Church*, 17. The communion set is in the museum of the Madison-Morgan Cultural Center.

buildings and the remaining supplies were burned." The account of a soldier from the 129th Illinois indicates that the conflagration spread to some nearby structures.[33]

A revealing example of the contrast between broad impression and specific cases came from the chaplain of the Twenty-second Wisconsin. When writing about the march as a whole he mentioned that Union forces consigned the homes of "thousands of families" to ashes. However, when he wrote specifically of Madison, he mentioned only the railroad buildings and the market house and made no reference to the burning of homes. After the common observation that the town was "one of the prettiest places I have seen in the South," the clergyman added that a local woman had remarked to him that the Union troops appeared "to be under excellent discipline.... much better than our soldiers."[34]

The Populace Encounters the Yankees

How did the people of Madison and Morgan County react to having thousands of Union soldiers march through the middle of their community? The first thing to keep in mind is that more than two-thirds of those people were enslaved men, women, and children of African descent. Joshua Hill owned about sixty people, including a nine-year-old boy who would come to be known as E. W. Evans. Some seventy years later, Evans recalled his memories of November 19, 1864:

> I was a small boy when Sherman left here at the fall of Atlanta. He came through Madison on his march to the sea and we children hung out on the front fence from early morning until late in the evening, watching the soldiers go by. It took most of the day.... The soldiers I mentioned while ago that passed with Sherman carried provisions, hams, shoulders, meal, flour, and other food. They had their cooks and other servants. I remember seeing a woman in that crowd of servants. She had a baby in her arms. She hollered at us children and said, "You children get off that

---

33 Brant, *History of the Eighty-fifth Indiana*, 77; diary of Lyman D. Ames, chaplain of the Twenty-ninth Ohio Volunteer Infantry, VFM 2972, Ohio History Connection, Columbus; Bauer, *Soldiering*, 185 (New York sergeant); Grunert, *History of the 129th Illinois*, 126.

34 Bradley, *Star Corps*, 187, 207.

> fence and go learn your ABC's. I thought she was crazy telling us that, for we had never been allowed to learn nothing at all like reading and writing. I learned but it was after surrender and I was over ten years old.[35]

Given that codes prohibited teaching slaves to read and write, firsthand accounts of how Black Georgians felt about the Union army are rare. Memories like those of Evans, which were recorded as part of a Works Projects Administration (WPA) program, are useful but clouded by decades of passed time and shaped by the cultural expectations of the times.

White observations also varied according to the perspective of the observers. The comments of two contemporaries then unknown to each other but now linked as common ancestors of the owner of Burge Planation provide a striking example. The diary of Dolly Lunt Burge, who spent much of her youth in Madison, is one of the most widely cited and excerpted accounts of White female civilian distress during the March to the Sea. On November 19, 1864, soon after the left wing split at Covington, soldiers of the Fourteenth Corps converged on Burge Plantation, less than twenty miles west and south of Madison. The young widow felt violated by Union forces, which confiscated much of her farm's livestock and foodstuffs. She stressed the fear and distress that she and some of her house slaves felt. She could not fathom that some of the enslaved young Black men would have left the plantation of their own accord, but go they did: "I had not believed they [Union soldiers] would force from their homes the poor doomed negroes, but such has been the fact here cursing them & saying that Jeff Davis was going to put them in his army.... No indeed! No! they are not friends to the slave."[36]

Meanwhile, the other Burge ancestor, Major Francis Lackner, was with the Twentieth Corps at Madison rather than the Fourteenth south of Covington. His diary of the Twenty-sixth Wisconsin Volunteer Infantry is much less known than that of Dolly Burge, and it presents an entirely

---

[35] Tonsill and Evans, "E. W. Evans, Brick Layer & Plasterer," https://www.loc.gov/item/wpalh000565. The interviewer's use of dialect in transcription has been removed.

[36] C. J. Carter, *Diary of Dolly Lunt Burge*, 160. See also Frank, *Civilian War*; K. M. Jones, *When Sherman Came*; Kaemmerien, *General Sherman and the Georgia Belles.*

different point of view. Major Lackner regarded his men as liberators, not conquerors.

> The joy of the Negroes at our arrival in the city [of Madison] was great; they came from far and wide to greet their friends, the Yankees, and while they laughed and grinned on the street, danced to the beat of the music, talked to the soldiers, and had a grand time, their white masters and mistresses locked themselves in their houses, cussing the common Yankees and the Negroes. And how superior they felt, in their stupidity, when they looked at the street from behind their window shades, and saw how the black and white "pack" mingled in colorful activity.

Lackner wrote particularly of one moment of intense emotion for Madison's enslaved people: "We burned the whipping-pen; amid the sounds of 'Yankee Doodle' and 'Hail Columbia' was the fire lit, to the greatest rejoicing of the blacks gathered there."[37]

Other Union soldiers had reactions like Lackner's to the burning of the slave pen. A Wisconsin chaplain recorded, "Our soldiers were quite loud in their denunciation of the vile system, and the torch was applied with a hearty good will." A New Yorker described the local commotion in his diary: "There were as usual Negroes by the hundreds, who came on the streets to see us." A soldier who came through town early wrote to his wife telling her that Madison was "a wealthy place, mostly all rich planters" and that "hundreds of slaves joined the Army, some with a half dozen children along with them." An Illinois soldier of the Third Division added colorful detail:

> At 1 o'clock we reached the beautiful town of Madison, where the Blacks welcomed us most kindly and sincerely. Having heard that a world of blue jackets was coming they had come to town and lined both sides of the road, slapping their hands and one "God bless you!" followed the other from the mouth of our recipients. After we had arrived in the center of the town a hollow

---

[37] A transcript of Francis Lackner's full diary is the possession of Sandy Morehouse, owner of Burge Plantation, Mansfield, Georgia, who, along with his wife, Betsy, kindly called the document to the author's attention. Lackner's regiment was part of the Third Division of Ward's Twentieth Corps, which is described in Pula, *Sigel Regiment*; Bradley, *Star Corps*, 186; Frank, *Civilian War*, 58.

> square was formed by our brigade, around the court house, and our band began to play. The negroes, and even whites, came flocking to us now.... The negroes, music-loving creatures as they were, commended dancing and jumping and shouting, saying "God bless the Yankees," and swearing that this was the happiest day of their life. They saw that the Yankees carried no horns as had been told them.... They got over these lies of their masters very quick.

A Wisconsin soldier wrote that many of the celebrating Blacks in Madison, "asked us if it was true that they were free. We told them they would be free if the North gained the war, which we were sure to do as the war was about over." General Slocum himself reviewed the men of the First Division as they passed the town square late in the day, so he would personally have witnessed the people who were beginning to taste the freedom of what came to be called the Day of Jubilee.[38]

Like Dolly Burge, many local Whites wrongly assumed that Black people who followed the Yankees did so only because they were duped or coerced by the invading army. For example, the *Southern Watchman* in Athens reported that marchers "carried off all stock, provisions, and negroes" from Joshua Hill's country place, reflecting the assumption that enslaved people were simply part of the list of property. In an unguarded snippet of hurried prose, journalist Atkinson's remark gave the lie to later legends of dedicated and loyal slaves: "Families of wealth have not a house servant left, and those who were the most trusted were often the first to leave." His wife's letter to her sister lamented that when the troops departed Madison,

---

[38] Bauer, *Soldiering*, 185 (New York); K. M. Jones, *When Sherman Came*, 14 (wealthy place); Grunert, *History of the 129th Illinois*, 126 (Illinois soldier); Stelle, *Memoirs of the Civil War*, 18 (Wisconsin soldier); New York State historian, Van Wagoner diary, 119 (141st New York); Morhous, *Reminiscences of the 123d*, 135; Parten stresses the importance of "Day of Jubilee" ("Somewhere toward Freedom," 124–25). The experience in Morgan County does not support the assertion that federal troops "pillaged Mansions and slave cabins with equal disregard" in Mohr, *On the Threshold of Freedom*, 94; diary of N. L. Parmater, Twenty-ninth OVI, Ohio History Connection (ms 246); Hurst, *Journal-History of the 73rd Ohio*, 155; Grunert, *History of the 129th Illinois*, 126; Bradley, *Star Corps*, 186–86. See also Priest, *John T. McMahon's Diary*, 111. Whipping stocks were also burned in Eatonton per Trudeau, *Southern Storm*, 171.

"many negroes left with them." The later wartime memories of White Southerners are full of stories of loyal enslaved servants who disdained the federals and remained home; however, their stories rarely tell of the thousands upon thousands of Black Georgians who cheered the Union arrival and the many who followed, temporarily or permanently. In the fond memories of the elderly E. W. Evans, his mistress Emily Hill was not the type of woman who would have been cowering as the Yankees passed by. He recounted that she was never entirely comfortable with slavery and that soon after Union forces left Madison, she told her female house servants that they were free and that they and their men could remain as employees or renters.[39]

Some recent historians have downplayed the number of slaves who followed the marchers and have discounted the sympathetic attitudes of Northern soldiers. The Madison experiences that Union soldiers reported present a more optimistic view of both. This does not, of course, excuse the fact that White supremacy and prejudice against Black people was ingrained in the mentality of Sherman and most of his army, but it puts that fact in context. Soldier interactions with the people who had been enslaved consisted of a mixture of heartfelt sympathy and heartless insensitivity. Indications are that most of the Union troops on the march either originally opposed slavery or had come to oppose it as they witnessed the institution firsthand. The historical point of comparison, however, should not be between what Northern White soldiers thought in November and December 1864 and what most twenty-first-century Americans wish they had thought. Instead, the March to the Sea presented the enslaved people of Morgan County and other communities in the soldiers' path with a brief opportunity to compare the actions and attitudes of the Union soldiers they encountered with the reality of the commitment to the institution of slavery expressed by the White Southerners around whom they had lived their whole lives. It is clear that the Black residents of Madison and the surrounding countryside did not see the federal forces as invaders; they saw them as liberators, as precursors to the Day of Jubilee. Even if the Union

---

[39] *(Athens) Southern Watchman*, December 8, 1864; *Augusta Chronicle & Sentinel*, November 30, 1864 (Atkinson); Ethie Atkinson letter, Atkinson letters, MCA.

Army was composed mostly of men whom historian Clarence Mohr called "reluctant liberators at best," they were liberators nonetheless.[40]

The experience of Madison confirms the findings of recent historians that enslaved people had come to understand that the war would lead to their freedom—even if they were not entirely sure what that freedom would entail. However, one would hardly be led to understand the perspective of the enslaved population by reading popular histories or tourist promotional materials. For example, in 1999 an *American Heritage* writer visited Madison and other towns on Georgia's designated "Antebellum Trail" to discover how the localities portrayed the March to the Sea. With the best of intentions, she observed,

> I had wondered if the trail might gloss over the uglier side of gracious antebellum living. As it turned out, it tends to overlook slavery altogether. Slavery may be ignored for the most part, but the Civil War is not. At every town on the trail, we were reminded again and again of Sherman's destructive force, which the residents speak of with the sort of bitterness usually reserved for more recent affronts.

Of course, when she wrote of "residents" speaking bitterly of Sherman, the author really meant only the White people with whom she had spoken.[41]

For most of the 30 percent of the people of Morgan County who were White, the real-time response to Sherman's men can be characterized as a sullen and angry but sometimes a grudgingly hospitable sense of resignation. The historian of the 111th Pennsylvania Regiment recounted that a group of old men watching from a Madison veranda "were evidently filled

---

[40] Rubin, *Through the Heart of Dixie*, 81–85; Kennett, *Marching through Georgia*, 288–96; Parten, "Somewhere toward Freedom," 117–46; Escott, "Context of Freedom," 79–104; Drago, "How Sherman's March through Georgia Affected the Slaves," 361–75; Downs, *After Appomattox*, 48–56, and Mohr, *On the Threshold of Freedom*.

[41] Levine, *Fall of the House of Dixie*, 126–30; Manning, *What This Cruel War Was Over*, 186–91, 216; Williams, *Georgia's Civil War*, 62–64, 144, 181–86, 206–209, 239; Glatthaar, *March to the Sea*, 64; Parten, "Somewhere toward Freedom," 117–46; Escott, "Context of Freedom," 79–104; Drago, "How Sherman's March through Georgia Affected the Slaves," 361–75; L. Barth, "What Sherman Missed," 27. The Morgan County CVB and the Antebellum Trail have recently revised some materials to be more sensitive to the perspectives of Black Georgians.

with a profound melancholy at the presence of the invading troops." Another Ohioan similarly observed that the Whites in town appeared "sour and sad." One soldier noted the reaction of the angrier Whites when he wrote of a woman who lived in a mansion and spat "spite and venom against the dirty Yanks." A chaplain commented on the vivid contrast between the Black and White reception: "Colored people are pleased to see the Yanks. Whites look sour & sad." The White response, however, was not entirely negative. The chaplain observed that there was a "little Union feeling manifest." Many Whites had fled town, but some stayed and engaged with the men whom they regarded as invaders. A private in an Illinois regiment noted that "the old gentlemen who were at home, while strong rebels, were gentlemen. The ladies were ladies neatly dressed, and the children were well behaved. The people were very hospitable even to their enemies. They were smart about it, too." The private went on to describe how the owner of a "splendid house" on the edge of town had served food and refreshments to soldiers all day long. Though she remained a staunch Confederate, Ethie Atkinson was one of the hospitable local ladies who "conversed freely" with the federal officers and who privately wrote that she "found out the Yankees were not so bad after all." Of course, it was with typical White Southern hospitality that the openly Unionist Joshua Hill invited General Ward's aide-de-camp for lunch, and his lovely and gracious daughter sent the officer away with floral keepsakes.[42]

One might wonder how people who had seen the power and force of the Union army march right past their homes could retain any hope at all for the success of the Confederacy. But many did. On the same page that it reprinted an article about the destructiveness of the March, the *Countryman* countered with an upbeat story that exuded unbounded (and unrealistic) optimism:

> The signs of the times are auspicious, and should inspire a high degree of hopefulness, and gratitudes. General Hood's great flank movement has proved a grand success, and this fact, alone,

---

[42] Boyle, *Soldiers True*, 256–58; Trudeau, *Southern Storm*, 37, 40 (sour); Lyman D. Ames diary, Ohio History Collection; Ashley Halsey, ed., *A Yankee Private's Civil War: Robert Hale Strong* (Mineola, NY: Dover Publications, Inc. 2013; orig. pub. 1961), 111–12. Ethie Atkinson to Alice [sister], December 11, 1864, Atkinson letters, MCA.

> should teach our people that the destinies of our army, and the defense of our cause is in competent, and sagacious hands, and that the same army, and the same leaders, who have already accomplished so much, may be trusted to finish the work so gloriously begun, in this fall campaign.[43]

Hill's Plantation and the Rest of Morgan County

Not until they left Madison did most of the rank-in-file federal soldiers come to realize that they were going to turn south toward Eatonton and Milledgeville rather than continue east along the Georgia Railroad toward Augusta as both sides had speculated. Geary's Second Division pushed another ten miles or so east of Madison, tearing up tracks along the way, burning the depot and cotton in Buckhead, and destroying the Oconee River railroad bridge. The next day they proceeded southward along the river on a path that took them slightly east of Joshua Hill's two-thousand-acre plantation.[44]

At the same time, the other two divisions headed directly south on the route to Eatonton (now Washington Street and Bethany Road). On the evening of November 19, they camped along and near Sugar Creek, about four miles from Madison. They took food and livestock from the Cousins plantation, but the grand, colonnaded 1832 home still stands. The Twentieth Corps was headquartered at the Harris farm a few miles north of Joshua Hill's plantation.[45]

Sometime during the night of November 19 or the morning of the 20th, Hill's plantation country house and surrounding outbuildings burned, thereby suffering the fate that his home and those of his neighbors in Madison had avoided. Simeon Atkinson came upon the scene some hours later. In the same widely-reprinted letter to the *Augusta Chronicle &*

---

[43] *Countryman*, December 6, 1864.

[44] The old Eatonton Road includes what is now Washington Street, Bethany Road, Bethany Church Road, and others (Dunkleman, *Marching with Sherman*, 49–53; G. K. Collins, *Memoirs of the 149th Regt. N. Y. Vo. Inft.*, 289; Trudeau, *Southern Storm*, 144; *OR*, ser. 1, vol. 44, 46–53, 214–18, 269–70; W. R. Johnson, "Enough to Make a Preacher Sware," 33; Walters, *Oconee River*, 246; J. M. Bryant, *How Curious a Land*, [page?]; Bartlett, *Dutchess County Regiment*, 137; diary of N. L. Parmater, Ohio History Connection).

[45] Ibid. The Cousins place is now known as Oaks Plantation on Bethany Rd.

Sentinel quoted above about in-town damage, Atkinson included a compelling description of how he and his companions fled from Milledgeville through the Union-infested countryside until he reached home in Madison. At the Credel place, they "found his fine house in ashes and his gin house burned, and every horse and mule gone." The men encountered a similar scene at the Hill plantation:

> [We] reached the fine farm of Hon. Joshua Hill. This is a perfect wreck. A large gin house full of cotton, corn cribs, dwelling—all a smouldering ruin. His loss was greater than that of any planter in this section. Besides the cotton, several thousand bushels of corn, potatoes, several hundred of wheat, and much other valuable property, with every horse and mule and many negroes are gone.

The roads the fleeing men traveled were "strewn with the debris of...dead horses, cows, sheep, hogs, chickens, corn, wheat, cotton, books, paper, broken vehicles, coffee mills, and fragments of nearly every specie of property that adorned the beautiful farms of this county." In the eyes of the angry newspaper man, the scene proved "the meanness, rapacity, and hypocrisy" of the federal invaders. It is worth noting, however, that even Atkinson's anti-Yankee rant conceded that with the exception of Credel and Hill, "no other dwelling houses were burned." When the exhausted traveler finally reached his own home in Madison on November 24, he found time to sit down and write his missive. The *Augusta Constitutionalist* beat its rival paper to print on the Hill plantation story by one day, albeit with scant detail: "HON. JOSHUA HILL.—At one time it was popular to classify this gentleman amongst the most luke warm of Southerners. The Yankees seem to have been of a different opinion, for they completely destroyed his plantation and home."[46]

Just days later, the *Countryman* claimed to have inside scoop as to why the Yankees singled out Hill's plantation. In the very next paragraph of the article that reported that General Slocum and Mayor Hill worked side-by-side to prevent in-town depredation, the paper wrote:

---

[46] *Augusta Chronicle*, November 30, 1864; *Columbus Sun*, December 3, 1864, and *Indianapolis State Sentinel*, December 6, 1864 (*Augusta Constitutionalist*, November 29, 1864).

> In order to wreak their vengeance upon Mr. Hill for preventing them from plundering the city of Madison, the Yankee soldiery determined to burn every house upon his plantation, and we understand they did so—including the dwelling, negro cabins, corn cribs and contents, stables, and everything else. Not satisfied with injuring his property, they endeavored, also, to injure his reputation, and spread the report, as they go that Josh Hill hoisted the Union flag over his plantation.... We are satisfied that it is not so. The course pursued by the Federal army towards the Mayor of Madison is another evidence of Yankee meanness. We understand the Yankee soldiers and, concerning Mr. Hill, that the "damned old rascal wouldn't let them plunder in Madison, and they meant to have their revenge by plundering and burning on his plantation.

That the plantation was ransacked and the house burned is certainly true. That revenge played some part of the motive is more difficult to confirm. Certainly revenge would not explain that the nearby Credel plantation also fell victim to the torch. Some of the bummers whose early morning activity in Madison had been curtailed by high command could have known of Hill and been angry enough at him to seek retribution when they came upon his plantation. The *Countryman* claimed a source who had had a conversation with Colonel Hill himself. Still, the tone of the paragraph rings more of confirmation bias than truth. It fit the editor's narrative of evil scheming Yankees and a somewhat tainted local Unionist, so it is not surprising that wags would have attributed the action to revenge. Hill himself never suggested the revenge motive in any published reports. On the other hand, Union soldiers exhibited at least some element of general revenge on both wings of the march, so the motive cannot be entirely dismissed.[47]

An alternative explanation is that foragers stripped Hill's plantation of food and livestock like they did others and then burned the outbuildings without at the time knowing much if anything about the absent owner. Whether by revengeful design, accident, or pyromania, the unoccupied country residence burned while Hill was at his in-town home in Madison.

---

[47] *Countryman*, December 6, 1864; also in the *Columbus Enquirer*, December 21, 1864; J. C. Andrews, *North Reports the Civil War*, 580.

It probably would not have happened if Hill or a supervisor had been present. As Atkinson wrote, "Those citizens who remained at home, and watched their premises, lost little, save horses, food and stock. Those who, from any cause, chanced to be away, lost all." This interpretation is strongly supported by the November 20 diary entry of an Ohio chaplain who noted that word of Hill's loyalty arrived too late to save the unoccupied plantation: "Passed many fine large plantations. Passed one belonging to Ex congressman Joshua Hill. He claims to be for the Union. I hear he obtained protection papers but he living in Madison, it was too late to save his Cotton and Gin House. They were all burned." A couple of weeks later, the press quoted the mayor of Greensboro: "I regret to state that our friends across the river in Morgan County lost heavily. Among them Col. Joshua Hill and Thomas Saffold." The mayor said nothing of revenge being a motive.[48]

Even if Joshua Hill suspected that his plantation had been singled out because he had prevented damage in Madison, he did not make that charge when he had a chance. About six months later, just days after the war finally ended, Hill wrote to General Sherman describing the destruction of his plantation. He absolved the Union command of responsibility for the transgression and asked if the general could help him be compensated for the damage:

> I hope you will find no difficulty in recalling our brief, but to me most agreeable acquaintance.... In the course of your march through middle Georgia without any fault of Gen. Slocum or the officers of his command, I was greatly injured by the burning of my plantation house, grain, cotton etc and the destruction of my stock. I am not aware of any act of disloyalty of mine to the Federal government. I think, I ought to be compensated for my losses. Will you be kind enough to advise me as to the best mode

[48] Williams, *Georgia's Civil War*, 204–206; Fleharty, *Our Regiment*, 113; *Augusta Chronicle*, November 30, 1864; Lyman D. Ames diary, Ohio History Connection. The Twenty-ninth Ohio regiment was part of Geary's Second Division. Most of the division went to the Oconee River bridge, but the supply train of the Second, including Chaplain Ames, went directly toward Eatonton with the Third Division. Fritsch cites the Ames diary but adds invented detail not therein including that Hill made a direct on-the-scene appeal to soldiers in response to lit torches (*Untried Life*, 354–55).

> of proceeding and if not too troublesome assist me in obtaining some redress.

Apparently the general was not able to help, and Hill continued unsuccessfully to press his claim for several more years.[49]

Three Days in Morgan County

The main body of men of the Left Wing was in Morgan County for fewer than seventy-two hours: one full day on November 19, 1864, plus the better part of the preceding and subsequent days. Those three days illustrate much about the times and the memories of those times. Unlike the cases of Atlanta and the burned cities of Northwestern Georgia where Johnston's and Hood's forces continually defended against Sherman's advance, the March to the Sea was unimpeded by significant Confederate resistance. The occasional capture of a forager and skirmishes in Morgan County along the Oconee River did nothing to slow the advance of the columns of the left wing. The annoyance caused by the muddy roads due to the scattered rain showers on November 19 and the steady downpour on the next day received much more attention in the soldiers' diaries and memoirs than any enemy action. Whites, especially those whose property the federals took or destroyed, were dejected and angry. As time passed, it was the anger rather than the sullen defeatism that dominated their memories and forged the obviously contradictory legends about the wide swath of destruction marked by Sherman's sentinels and about the various explanations for the many still-standing antebellum structures in Morgan County and all along the march.

The story of Joshua Hill's outreach to the command of the left wing of the march should not be placed in the same category as the many myths about girlfriends, Masonic pins, picnic lunches, and deference to beauty that arose in print and oral tradition after the march. The degree to which his intervention made a difference in what transpired in Madison cannot

[49] Joshua Hill to W. T. Sherman, May 5, 1865, William Tecumseh Sherman Papers, Library of Congress (reel 9, #290). Melton wrote that the destruction of Hill's plantation could not be completely confirmed, but Hill's own letter and Atkinson's firsthand accounts remove any doubt ("The Town that Sherman Wouldn't Burn," 224; *Globe*, 42-2, pt. 4, April 30, 1872, 2914).

be precisely determined, but the well-documented effort was real and most likely had a noticeable impact.

The enduring Lost Cause myth embraced by so many Southern Whites (and many Northerners as well) conveniently overlooked the fact of joyful Black Georgians welcoming Union troops, providing them with useful information, and, in thousands of instances, following them at least part way toward the sea. Instead, most White Southerners preferred to fashion memories of loyal servants working in a mostly benign institution. The reality that most of the federal troops on the march, including their leader, harbored White supremacist attitudes does not change the fact that the African-Americans of Morgan County and all along the march clearly preferred the liberation that the soldiers represented to the slavery that they had endured.

Looking back from 1889, Pastor Kendrick, who served the Baptists of Madison from 1863–1865, recalled that Josh Hill had been

> about as much at odds with the Confederate government as one could well be without provoking the stroke of its iron hand.... Though, naturally, well hated, he stood too high for assault. Preserving an external and entirely honorable loyalty to the existing government, and giving his sons to the army, he still did not disguise his hostility to what was going on, and employed a freedom of criticism which would hardly have been tolerated in a less formidable man.[50]

Joshua Hill's experience illustrates the delicate dance down the middle that staunch Unionists who remained in the South had to waltz. In the eyes of White chroniclers, contemporary and later, Hill could be not only a hero for saving Madison but also something of a rogue for the fact that he had placed himself in the favored position of having a degree of influence with Sherman and Slocum. The prominent Madisonian had to continue this dance between political extremes. It is revealing that during Reconstruction, when Hill played a significant role as Republican leader and eventual senator, neither he nor his political opponents made an issue of the Madisonian's wartime interactions with the Union army. His allies

---

[50] Kennett, *Marching through Georgia*, 33–34; Kendrick, "A Non-Combatant's War Reminiscences," 461.

most likely avoided the subject for fear of further offending potential White Southern voters. The fact that Hill opposed secession, sought the governorship on a peace ticket, counseled acceptance of defeat, and acquiesced in Black suffrage were bad enough in most Southern White minds without reminding them that he had cozied up with General Sherman in Atlanta and had welcomed the Union's Twentieth Corps to his own hometown. On the other hand, Georgia Radicals probably hesitated to mention it because they did not want to endear Hill to Black voters or to make him look even better in the eyes of moderate Northern Republicans. One exception to the rule appeared in February 1870. Addressing its Yankee readership, the *Boston Post* described Hill as an old Whig who "has been distinguished for his devotion to the Union and hostility to secession." The writer then added a line that Hill's friends and enemies would have left unsaid: "Gens. Sherman, Slocum and others bear testimony to his hospitality and valuable service to officers and soldiers of the federal army in 1864 and 1865."[51]

[51] *Boston Post*, February 17, 1870.

Chapter 7

Frustrated Unionist in Presidential Reconstruction, 1865–1866

The March to the Sea across Georgia ended on December 22, 1864, when William Tecumseh Sherman presented Savannah as a Christmas gift to President Lincoln. Another three and a half months would pass before Robert E. Lee surrendered to Ulysses S. Grant at Appomattox on April 9, 1865. When Confederate Georgia finally surrendered its remaining troops on April 30 in Macon, four years of Civil War finally ended for Joshua Hill and his state. Despite many public statements to the contrary, most Confederate leaders had come to realize well before those official surrenders that their struggle to establish a separate nation upon the cornerstone of slavery had come to an unsuccessful end. As Hill would soon find out, the end of the war did not mean the end of emotional attachment to the Confederacy for the great bulk of Georgia's White leaders. In fact, for many of them their attachment to the Lost Cause seemed to deepen as years passed.

When the end of the war neared, no one knew for sure what reconstruction would be like. Politicians in the Deep South states had hints from what had already transpired in Tennessee, Arkansas, Louisiana, and North Carolina. What they saw in those states was that to the extent politically possible, Lincoln hoped to build reconstruction upon a foundation of loyal ex-Whigs. Detailed plans remained unclear, so the defeated South and the rest of the nation waited for definitive answers. The tragedy at Ford's Theater upended everyone's calculations. Andrew Johnson, the former Democratic senator, Lincoln-appointed military governor of Tennessee, and Union ticket vice president, was now in the driver's seat. Thus, the first two years of Reconstruction in Georgia and the old Confederacy would be guided not by an antislavery Midwesterner who wanted to build a

Republican Party in the South but by a border state slaveowner who was a Democrat at heart.

Most histories of the Reconstruction period in the South have focused on the struggle between the eventually triumphant Democrats who sought to reassert White planter-businessman control on the one hand and a valiant but ultimately unsuccessful radical Republican coalition composed of so-called carpetbaggers and scalawags along with newly freed Blacks. White Southern conservatives such as Joshua Hill, who attempted to steer a middle course between the factions, have attracted limited attention. These men in the middle accomplished occasional and transient victories but ultimately failed to slow the political juggernaut that the Democratic Party victors called "Redemption."[1]

At three critical junctures in the early months of Andrew Johnson's presidential Reconstruction, Joshua Hill seemed to be on the verge of personifying Lincoln's vision of reconstruction government in the hands of loyal ex-Whigs: the appointment to the provisional governorship, the shaping of the state constitution, and the obtaining of a United States senatorship. In each instance, Hill's Unionist principles and his political moderation made him unacceptable to the old Democratic power structure, which was not ready to admit that secession and war had been great mistakes.

Potential Provisional Governor

Ex-Confederates were optimistic that Andrew Johnson would offer a more lenient and empathic approach to Reconstruction than they had feared from Lincoln. Many hoped that Johnson would allow the existing Confederate governors to retain their positions provisionally at least for a time of transition. Even Joshua Hill, who regarded Joe Brown more as a rival than an enemy, had suggested to General Sherman that it might be wise to leave the Georgia governor in office. Instead, Johnson decided to move forward immediately with the appointment of new provisional governors in Georgia and in the other states that had not already been organized by

---

[1] The classic accounts for Georgia are Conway, *Reconstruction of Georgia*; C. Thompson, *Reconstruction in Georgia*; Shadgett, *Republican Party in Georgia*; and Nathans, *Losing the Peace*. Recent national overviews include Summers, *Ordeal of the Reunion*; Foner, *Reconstruction*; and Fitzgerald, *Splendid Failure*.

Lincoln. In general, Johnson sought candidates who had opposed secession, who had refused active participation in the Confederacy, and who would strive to return their states to the Union in the most harmonious and moderate manner possible. It would seem that Joshua Hill fit that bill perfectly, but Johnson had one more characteristic in mind that disqualified the Madisonian. The president sought Democrats, or at least men who had not built their political careers around opposing Democracy.[2]

By May, a mad scramble for the several provisional governorships was underway. As his state's most prominent Unionist, Joshua Hill quickly emerged among the favorites for the Georgia spot. Hill wrote Johnson to apprise him of the situation in Georgia and to plead his own cause as one who stood alone among public men to condemn secession. His May 10, 1865, letter decried "the phantom of Southern independence," and firmly swore, "I am no sectionalist, and have never been a separatist in thought, act, or deed. I have never given a vote or taken an oath recognizing any other nationality than that of the United States." Though it was obvious that he was seeking favor with the new president, Hill claimed that his correspondence had "no other motive than a desire to see tranquility restored to a distracted land."[3]

Hill had solid support. A committee from heavily Unionist Cass County (now Bartow) urged Johnson to appoint Hill forthwith, "knowing him to be an able and loyal friend of the union of our fathers." An assemblage in Griffin asked the same, citing "the well known conservative views of Hon. Joshua Hill." David G. Cotting, later to become the first Republican to be Georgia's secretary of state, wrote to Hill on June 5. He flatteed the Madisonian by telling him that he was "seen now to be the only mediator between the people of Georgia and the Federal Government" and

---

[2] Joshua Hill to W. T. Sherman, May 5, 1865, W. T. Sherman Papers, Library of Congress (copy at MCA); Conway, *Reconstruction of Georgia*, 17; Perman, *Reunion without Compromise*, 43; Foner, *Reconstruction*, 186–88; and Guelzo, *Reconstruction*. On presidential Reconstruction, see McKitrick, *Andrew Johnson and Reconstruction*.

[3] Joshua Hill to Andrew Johnson, May 10, 1865, *Papers of Andrew Johnson*; Perman, *Reunion without Compromise*, 57–67; Parks, *Joseph E. Brown*, 334; Rubin, *Shattered Nation*, 153–54; Conway, *Reconstruction of Georgia*, 42.

suggesting that his appointment as provisional governor was highly anticipated.[4]

Although Hill appeared to be the leading candidate, his was not the only name put forth for the provisional governorship. He and several other aspirants and supporters traveled to Washington to press their cases in person. Three Atlanta Unionists, including Alexander N. Wilson, an old friend of Johnson from east Tennessee, were apparently the first Georgians to consult with Johnson. Wilson apprised the president that Hill's delegation and another group, headed by Judge O. A. Cochrane of Macon, were on their way. Wilson then returned to Georgia to gauge the political climate. The delegation headed by Hill met with Johnson on June 8. Although the details of the meeting are not available, indications are that the conversation was cordial but that the president made no commitments. Hill also had a long conversation with judge advocate general Joseph Holt, who was then involved in prosecuting the Lincoln assassination conspirators. Hill likely met with former congressional colleagues and other contacts as well.[5]

Rumors that Johnson had specifically requested the meeting with Hill led to widespread expectations that the former congressman would be the president's choice. The *Macon Messenger* jumped the gun and wrongly announced on June 7 that Hill had already been appointed. A few days later, the "Washington Gossip" section of the local rival *Telegraph* reported, "Washington is quite full of gentlemen from Southern States. Joshua Hill, it is thought, will be the Provisional Governor." A third Macon paper reported the same.[6]

---

[4] *Macon Telegraph*, June 20, 1865 (Cass), June 21, 1865 (Griffin); C. Thompson, *Reconstruction in Georgia*, 146; David G. Cotting to Hill, June 5, 1865, Confederate Applications for Presidential Pardons, 1865–1867, Records of the Adjutant General's Office, RG 94, National Archives (via ancestry.com and fold3.com). Hereinafter Confederate Applications.

[5] Dyer, *Secret Yankees*, 226–29; Alexander N. Wilson to Andrew Johnson, June 5, 1865, *Papers of Andrew Johnson*[**vol & page?**]; *Augusta Chronicle*, June 20, 1865; *New Orleans Times-Picayune*, June 20, 1865 (headed by); *Washington Evening Star*, July 16, 1865 (Holt); *OR*, ser. 1, vol. 49, pt. 2, 721 (Hill's permission to travel to DC).

[6] *Macon Messenger*, June 7, 1865; *Macon Telegraph*, June 13 (Gossip), 20, 1865; *Augusta Chronicle*, June 13, 1865 (*Macon Herald*).

Speculation was not confined to Georgia. The *Philadelphia Press* noticed that Hill was in the nation's capital and called him "probably one of the best of the Georgians." Papers in New Orleans, Boston, Cincinnati, and New York also reported on the Georgia situation. Confined at the time in federal prison, Alexander H. Stephens read news stories like these and recorded in his diary, "I see by the Boston paper that the Hon. Joshua Hill has reached Washington.... I do hope he will be the man. He is a gentleman of high tone and honor." Despite their differences, Stephens considered Hill to be an honorable opponent rather than an enemy. And vice-versa; Hill appealed directly to the president for Stephens's release from confinement.[7]

Georgia was, of course, not the only Confederate state to send delegations to meet with the new president. In fact, Johnson was overwhelmed with callers in the early weeks of his presidency. Many of the applicants were attempting to reclaim their prewar Unionist bona fides despite having supported the Confederacy after secession. The correspondent of the principal New Orleans newspaper mentioned several such visitors and reported that "Andy" was suspicious of the professions of loyalty from many of the supplicants because he believed "that most of them are as big rebels as ever."[8]

Joshua Hill's open disdain for secession, his war-time peace activities, his connections with congressional Republicans, and, most important, his long-time opposition to the Democratic Party produced opposition to his appointment even from some men who admired his reputation for integrity. On June 16, Johnson's trusted friend and frequent correspondent Alexander Wilson wrote from Atlanta to give the president his frank on-the-ground observations. He warned the chief executive that one aspirant was

---

[7] *Boston Traveller*, June 13, 1865 (*Philadelphia Press*); *New York Times*, June 8, 1865; *Cincinnati Tribune*, June 8, 1865; *New York World*, June 9, 1865; C. Thompson, *Reconstruction in Georgia*, 146–47; Avary, *Recollections of Alexander H. Stephens*, 183, June 6, 1865. Lists of prewar Unionists, including Hill, are in *Philadelphia Inquirer*, March 27, 1865; *New Orleans Times*, April 6, 1865, and *Springfield (MA) Republican*, March 27, 1865; Hill re Stephens, *Milledgeville Southern Recorder*, October 31, 1865, and *Columbus Enquirer*, November 1, 1865.

[8] *New Orleans Times-Picayune*, June 20, 1865; A. N. Wilson to Andrew Johnson, June 5, 1865, *Papers of Andrew Johnson*; Dyer, *Secret Yankees*, 219; Summers, *Ordeal of the Reunion*, 66–67.

"an ass, a lick spittle, and infernal secessionist" and that another had resisted secession but then "went over to the enemy." When it came to Hill, Wilson had mixed feelings:

> The impression is general that Hon. Joshua Hill will be made Provisional Gov. from the fact, as is said, that you had requested his presence in Washington. The people have confidence in his ability, also in his fidelity to the Government and interest in them. I am not personally acquainted with Mr. Hill, and consequently have but one fear in regard to him, and that is, he may play Brownlow.

He added that many observers "think that democrats will be kept on the back shelves by Hill."[9]

Wilson's comparison of Hill to the Reverend William G. Brownlow constituted a strong warning to the president. Brownlow was, like Johnson himself, an ardent Tennessee Unionist. The so-called "fighting parson" became governor in early April 1865, shortly before Lincoln's assassination. He almost immediately undertook harsh measures against former Tennessee Confederates. Brownlow's actions angered Johnson, who had himself served as the military governor of Tennessee before becoming vice president. Brownlow later moved toward alliance with the Radical Republicans in Congress.[10]

As Wilson's comments to the president about Hill reveal, all the various Georgia Unionists knew of each other by reputation even if they were not personally acquainted. It can be safely assumed that they interacted with each other in the hotels, cafes, and lobbies of Washington. By mid-

---

[9] A. N. Wilson to Andrew Johnson, June 5, 16, 1865, *Papers of Andrew Johnson* (W. F. Herrin [ass] and Richard Peters [went over]).

[10] See Coulter, *William G. Brownlow*. Two sources suggest that Pres. Johnson may have offered the provisional governorship appointment to individuals prior to James Johnson; the author doubts that the president did so (Shadgett, *Republican Party in Georgia*, 97 [to Wilson]; *Papers of Andrew Johnson*, 8:246n (to Alfred Austell). Austell later asked for patronage help, which makes it unlikely that he was first offered the governorship. Dyer says that Austell had been "unable to secure a position" that would pay enough (*Secret Yankees*, 225). Conway mentions that Alfred H. Colquitt and Henry L. Benning were proposed but it is unlikely that Johnson would seriously consider Confederate generals (*Reconstruction of Georgia*, 42).

June the various Georgians coalesced into something of a unified front with Judge O. A. Lochrane as spokesperson. By this time, it had become apparent that President Johnson found Hill too controversial, so in a widely rumored but undocumented compromise, the Georgians agreed to support Joshua Hill for one of Georgia's seats in the United States Senate and to endorse James Johnson of Columbus for provisional governor. Johnson was no relation to the president, but they had "messed together" when both were in Congress in the early 1850s. Having studied at Franklin College (University of Georgia) along with Alexander Stephens and George Crawford, Johnson was well-connected if not widely known. The choice was typical of President Johnson's tendency to avoid controversial appointments in the former Confederate states. Only in Texas and North Carolina did the gubernatorial appointees incur much pushback from local politicians. Provisional governor Johnson detested secession and never served the Confederacy, yet his Unionism had been much more low profile than Hill's, and he had not incurred the ire of leading Democrats. Joshua Hill had certainly desired the gubernatorial appointment for himself and was probably bitterly disappointed over not getting the nod even with a future senate seat dangled. He did not, however, harbor any personal animosity toward James Johnson. The new provisional governor and Hill had been political allies in their Know-Nothing/American Party days, and they continued to work closely together after Johnson's appointment.[11]

Constitutional Convention of 1865

For the next several months after the scramble for the provision governorship and before the constitutional convention convened in October, Joshua Hill concerned himself with making a living, obtaining pardons and patronage for his friends, and laying the groundwork for future political moves.

Despite Andrew Johnson having passed him over for a less controversial choice for provisional governor, Hill retained a good relationship with the president. Hill received a presidential pardon on June 22 even

[11] Perman, *Reunion without Compromise*, 62–63; Shadgett, "James Johnson," 3–4 (messed); Nathans, *Losing the Peace*, 6–7; Parks, *Joseph E. Brown*, 333–34; C. Thompson, *Reconstruction in Georgia*, 131–39; Baggett, *Scalawags*, 166–67; D. T. Carter, *When the War Was Over*, 40.

though as a staunch Unionist he professed not to need it. Taking advantage of his access to Johnson, Hill endorsed pardon applications for at least two dozen Georgians and recommended patronage appointments for others, some of whom were not his normal political allies. For example, in August he asked Attorney General James Speed for favorable action on the pardon application of a former member of the Confederate Congress, who was "an original Union man." He joined Judge Lochrane in urging the appointment of a candidate for federal marshal. Unionist David Cotting pleaded for Hill to assist him "if you can reach the ear of President Johnson or the authorities." Alfred Austell of Atlanta also used references from Hill and others to support his request to the president to be appointed federal marshal for Georgia.[12]

Two episodes in summer 1865 kept Hill, and his Unionist credentials, before the public. In a widely-reported Independence Day oration in Chicago, H. Winter Davis of Maryland, Hill's former Know-Nothing congressional colleague, urged that every effort must be made to prevent former Confederates from taking control because their "temper of mind" had not changed. Instead, he argued, the political future of the South should be placed in the hands of men like Joshua Hill and three others whom Davis hailed as "friends of the nation."[13]

Later that summer, Hill's praise of the union and the flag of the United States of America raised the ire of unreconstructed rebels. The occasion was the dedication of a flagpole in front of the headquarters of Union occupation troops in Augusta. Major General James B. Steedman called Hill to the speaker's stand and introduced him "as one having remained true and unwavering to the flag and the cause amid all the horrors of the past four years." Hill began his speech with the usual Whiggish praise of the founding fathers and an appeal to the memory of Daniel Webster. The former congressman then, "implored all to cling to the sacred emblem floating before him, whose stars were emblems of separate States,

---

[12] *New York Times*, June 23, 26, 1865; *Philadelphia Inquirer*, June 28, 1865, *Macon Telegraph*, June 30, 1865; Hill to Andrew Johnson, November 23, 1865, *Papers of Andrew Johnson*, p. 177 (marshal); Cotting to Hill, June 5; Austell to Hill, June 16, 1865; Hill to Speed, August 18, 1865; Hill application, June 22, 1865, Confederate Applications.

[13] *New York Times*, July 9, 1865.

bound together forever on the blue field of the common Union." The states of the Union were, in Hill's words, "many like waves, but one like the sea." Hill not only extolled the raising of old glory but also went on to extoll and defend the federal occupation troops standing before him. He told the audience, which probably included Black Augustans on the fringe of the crowd, that the soldiers were there "to protect and defend, and not to harass and destroy." Hill declared, as he had before and would again, that the Civil War had been "a blunder in its inception." He proudly concluded, "I am an American Citizen." One angry reporter claimed that by using the word "blunder," Hill had "applied with force the words of [French diplomat] Talleyrand—'*A blunder is worse than a crime.*'" The Unionist's open praise of flag and nation at this event came back to haunt him about six months later when opponents of his US Senate candidacy excoriated him for his veneration of the stars and stripes rather than the stars and bars of the Confederacy. Roughly 75 percent of military-age White men in the Confederacy served in the army, and many of them held strong resentment toward the flag that their opponents had carried.[14]

The most important responsibility of provisional governor James Johnson was to make arrangements for the constitutional convention. Like Hill, Johnson was not afraid to remind audiences that he had been a strong opponent of secession. "As a Southern man," he told a Macon audience, "I am bound to say, and history will say, we fired the first gun.... We have been impoverished by our own folly."[15] Had James Johnson earlier spoken so bluntly and so publicly of such "folly," Andrew Johnson might not have regarded him as a safe appointment. The state's Democrats were coming to realize that James Johnson was not that much different than Joshua Hill after all.

---

[14] *Columbus Sun*, September 17, 1865 (*Augusta Chronicle*); *Augusta Constitutionalist*, September 12, 1865. *Macon Telegraph*, September 14, 16, 1865. It is probable that some of the federal troops whom Hill addressed were Black, which would have made his speech even more controversial; see Cashin, *Story of Augusta*, 128–29; *Savannah Herald*, February 5, 1866. In his January 29, 1866, address to the legislature Hill (*Savannah Herald*, February 5, 1866), he referred to Gen. Steedman as a friend; that friendship may have stemmed from Steedman's being the House of Representatives printer while Hill served from 1856–1860. See Rable, *But There Was No Peace*, 11, on flag attitudes.

[15] Shadgett, "James Johnson," 4–5.

The election of constitutional convention delegates occurred on October 4, and the convention began three weeks later. Consideration of suffrage for freedmen was not in serious play at this stage of the state's reconstruction, so the basic age, gender, and race requirements for voting remained as they had been in 1861. There were, however, two additional requirement categories based on wartime actions. The first applied to White men who had supported the Confederacy but had not held high office or owned large estates. All they had to do was take an amnesty oath that promised future loyalty to the United States. Ex-governor Brown, provisional governor Johnson, and other leaders strongly urged them to do so. In the second category were major Confederate civil officials, high-ranking military officers, and planters with a taxable worth of more than twenty thousand dollars. The president's proclamation required these men to receive individualized presidential pardons before they would be eligible to take the loyalty oath. In Georgia, this provision affected about fifteen thousand potential voters, the bulk of whom were in the wealthy planter category. Joshua Hill fell into the planter category, but he had already received his pardon in June.[16]

An overwhelming number of pardon requests flowed into the White House from Georgia and the other ex-Confederate states. President Johnson apparently relished having such power to lord over men of prominence. Whenever a supplicant sought a pardon, Johnson usually granted it, especially if the application had the endorsement of a prominent Unionist or the provisional governor. As mentioned above, Joshua Hill and James Johnson recommended pardons for many of their acquaintances, some of whom were ex-Confederates who at least claimed that they were now willing to support the United States. President Johnson's goal was to use his pardon power to weaken the influence of the antebellum elite while at the same time enhancing the political power of the kind of yeoman farmer and small planters who had been the core of his Democratic Tennessee constituency. Unfortunately for the president's goals, his tendency to grant pardons to solicitous (and often duplicitous) wealthy and influential men such as Herschel V. Johnson undermined his own objectives and laid the groundwork for the ex-Confederate elite to regain their influence. The

[16] Ibid., 4–8; Conway, *Reconstruction of Georgia*, 43–44; Foner, *Reconstruction*, 183–87.

president's leniency in granting individual pardons also angered the Republican voters who had put him in office on the 1864 bipartisan ticket with Lincoln.[17]

Even given the large number of pardons, by the time of delegate elections, a considerable number of Georgia's political elite remained ineligible to vote or serve. A few men had their applications denied, some requests remained in process, and several hundred diehard rebels refused as a matter of principle even to seek pardons. To many of them the main stumbling point was that the oath required acquiescence in emancipation. Most of the highly prominent leaders of Confederate Georgia, including Alexander and Linton Stephens, Howell and Howell Cobb, Robert Toombs, Joe Brown, and Ben Hill did not or could not stand for election as convention delegates.[18]

As the delegate elections approached, federal troops were still stationed in Madison and in other key towns across the state. Fife player John W. Mambert and some of his fellow soldiers of the 159th New York arrived from Augusta and camped under a tree on the grounds of the Morgan County Courthouse where they kept a pet bear as their unit mascot. Mambert confessed that with no war to fight, the men had become a rowdy bunch. A few of their number were "in jail for robbing poor negroes and getting drunk, etc." The fifer and his comrades ate well but noticed that many locals were struggling to get by. Mambert was proud of what the Union army had accomplished by defeating the Confederacy and ending slavery: "We have raised our national banner.... We have subdued the rebellion, [and] we have wiped out an institution which has degraded our nation." Though they longed to be back in New York, Mambert noted that the Union soldiers in Madison understood why they would have to stay a few weeks more: "There is to be an election in this state on the 1st Wednesday in October and I suppose we are here for the purpose of keeping peace, etc." As it turned out, delegate election day passed smoothly, so federal troops found no reason to intervene.[19]

---

[17] Foner, *Reconstruction*, 190–91; Summers, *Ordeal of the Reunion*, 64–68; Guelzo, *Reconstruction*, 20–25.

[18] Parks, *Joseph E. Brown*, 341–42.

[19] John W. Mambert to family, September 5 (quotations), 28, 1865 (collection of Mike Kipp, third great-grandson of Mambert; transcripts in MCA).

The most populated counties (about a quarter of the total) elected three convention delegates each, and the rest, such as Morgan, sent two. Morgan County voters chose Joshua Hill and his friend Thomas P. Saffold, who owned a large plantation near the Hill property that Union forces had destroyed. Saffold's place had also suffered damage. On balance, the membership tended to be composed of men who had expressed hesitations about secession, but the majority of them had gone on to support the state's Confederate government by holding minor local offices or serving in the army. In the eyes of the *New York Times* correspondent, most of the delegates remained rebels at heart. "I am sorry to say," he wrote, "that these men, venerable and gray, did not bow gracefully to the stern logic of events." In contrast, the writer highlighted Joshua Hill and a handful of others who had opposed the war and remained loyal.[20]

The convention began on October 27 and ran for almost two weeks to November 8. Members of the state and national press thronged to Milledgeville, the tiny backwater state capital city where delegates were forced to meet in a hall far too small for their numbers. Thanks to disfranchisement, the convention did not include many of the major political leaders from the 1850s and the war years, so Joshua Hill and a few other men of some prominence attracted the preponderance of attention. The *Washington National Intelligencer* specifically identified six delegates considered to be "of State and Federal distinction" including Joshua Hill and convention president Herschel V. Johnson. Macon's *Georgia Journal & Messenger* listed Hill as one of eight distinguished personages who, the writer lamented in a reference to the English Civil War, had to labor along with "hundreds of village Hampdens and country Cromwells." Bostonian Sidney Andrews, who compiled his observations into an influential book, identified Charles J. Jenkins as the effective "leader" of the convention even though Herschel Johnson was the official presiding officer. Though he was

---

[20] "The Journal of the 1865 Constitutional Convention" in Candler, *Confederate Records of the State of Georgia*, 4:131–435. Some members, including Jenkins, required last minute pardons to serve (*New York Times*, November 17, 1865 [I am]; Shadgett, "James Johnson," 13; Perman, *Reunion without Compromise*, 68–69; Conway, *Reconstruction of Georgia*, 43–45; Nathans, *Losing the Peace*, 8–9).

not an official delegate, former governor Joe Brown was, in Andrew's words, "the leader of the lobby."[21]

The Unionist delegate from Morgan County made a strong impression on the Yankee journalist, and Andrews considered Hill to be "second in influence" to Jenkins:

> Mr. Hill is a fine type of physical manhood, over six feet in height, with deep chest, broad shoulders, erect figure, and a bearing that commands respect everywhere. He has a large mouth, large nose, high cheek-bones, forehead very prominent in the eyebrows,—in a word, his face is as rugged a one as could be found in a long day's travel. His intellectual ability is considerable, but his distinguishing characteristic, his friends say, is "plain horse sense."

Despite his popularity with the Northern press, Hill's influence extended mainly to the relatively small faction (perhaps a quarter) of loyal Unionists.[22]

Early in the proceedings a resolution urging President Johnson to release Jefferson Davis and other high Confederate leaders from federal confinement revealed the stark contrast between Hill's embrace of Union and the majority of the delegates' persisting affection for the late Confederacy. Hill strenuously but vainly opposed the resolution. His stated objection was that such an appeal was not germane to the business of the convention, but his real motivation was clear to all. The *New York Times* reporter wrote

---

[21] Clara Mildred Thomson's 1915 classic *Reconstruction in Georgia* established the enduring interpretation that the 1865 convention lacked the "distinguished" men of the 1861 convention (149). That point of view persisted in numerous sources, including Saye, *Constitutional History of Georgia*, 253. See also *Atlanta Intelligencer*, November 5, 22 (*National Intelligencer*), 1865; *(Macon) Georgia Journal & Messenger*, November 1, 1865 (hundreds); S. Andrews, *The South since the War*, 242 (see also Andrews in *Boston Advertiser*, November 8, 17, 1865); Shadgett, "James Johnson," 13–14; Baggett, *Scalawags*, 167. See *Newark Advertiser*, November 13, 16, 1865; *Philadelphia Press*, November 14, 1865; *New Haven Columbian Register*, November 4, 1865; *Springfield (MA) Republican*, November 22, 1865. Newspapers printed routine updates, e.g., *Augusta Constitutionalist*, October 29, November 1, 4, 1865.

[22] S. Andrews, *The South since the War*, 242; *New York Times*, November 17, December 1, 1865.

that Joshua Hill "is true blue, and bears a character without a stain, and hates JEFFERSON DAVIS with as much fervor as he loves his God." In later testimony before the Joint Committee on Reconstruction, Sidney Andrews cited the passage of the Jefferson Davis resolution and Hill's objection to it as strong evidence that rebel defiance had scarcely lessened.[23]

With the Jeff Davis resolution behind him, Hill chimed in often on specific constitutional details such as the method for selection of judges and the terms of office for executives and legislators. For the most part, however, the 1865 document carried over these kinds of provisions from the prewar Constitution with only minor adjustments. The issues that the bulk of the delegates really cared about were secession, slavery, and war debt. The delegates were not happy that President Johnson required the state to acknowledge the death of the Confederacy, the end of slavery, and the repudiation of Confederate debt. They were realistic enough, however, to know that they had to comply if they wanted to return to the Union. On all three matters, the great majority of Georgia's convention delegates insisted on language that indicated their distaste for the tasks.

When it came to slavery, the convention acknowledged only that the force of federal arms meant that the end of slavery had become a matter of "full practical effect." Other Deep South states used similar language to communicate their reluctant admission of the demise of the institution that sparked the war. Neither Hill nor James Johnson raised objection to the slavery provision. Hill had long ago come to grips with that inevitable outcome. In 1861, the Morgan County slaveholder had predicted and regretted that civil war would result in the destruction of the "peculiar institution." Shortly after becoming provisional governor, Johnson had declared

[23] *New York Times*, November 17, 1865 (true blue, caps in orig.); *Macon Telegraph*, October 27, 1865; *Columbus Enquirer*, October 28, November 1, 1865; *Savannah Herald*, November 1, 1865; *(Athens) Southern Watchman*, November 1, 1865; *New York Times*, October 28, November 9, 1865; *Boston Herald*, October 28, 1865; *Philadelphia Press*, November 14, 1865; S. Andrews, *The South since the War*, 247–50; Candler, *Confederate Records*, October 26, 1865, 4:143–44, 197, 211, 410, 430; Andrews testimony in House Report 30, 39th Congress, 1st Session, Serial Set vol. 1273.

that he had "no tears to shed" of the demise of slavery, so he too was willing to accept the tepid acknowledgment of its official end in Georgia.[24]

On day two, the delegates quickly voted to repeal the ordinance of session. All seemed harmonious until near the end of the session when Joshua Hill rose to declare his intention to submit on the following day a reconsideration motion that would change the official wording about secession from "hereby repealed" to the much more provocative "are now, and always have been, null and void." This rhetorical distinction was of no practical but much symbolic importance. Merely to repeal secession implied that dissolution of the Union was a legal option that could be employed again. In Hill's mind disunion had been an illegitimate act from the start which must be firmly and permanently repudiated. The next morning the gallery was packed with a crowd that expected an "exciting discussion." But it did not come to pass. Facing heavy pressure overnight, Hill relented. His acquiescence had come, he explained, because his Unionist allies had convinced him that the state's timely readmission was the greatest priority:

> On this occasion, at the solicitation of many friends who, four years ago, agreed cordially with me in opinion upon the subject of secession, and for a variety of reasons, the best of which is the harmony of this body, and the danger of distracting its counsels, I have been induced to reconsider that matter. The appeals of my friends, and the inducements they suggest do not fall unheeded upon me.... My labors in this body shall be bent to one single purpose, and that is the earliest admission of Georgia into the Union.... I am unwilling to be the first to produce dissension in this body, and therefore I withdraw my resolution to reconsider.

Hill later regretted that he had relented on this matter of principle.[25]

---

[24] Conway, Re*construction of Georgia*, 43, 47; Summers, *Ordeal of the Reunion*, 70; Foner, *Reconstruction*, 193–94; Candler, *Confederate Records*, 4:133–435.

[25] *Savannah Herald*, November 1, 3 (On this occasion), 1865; *New York Times*, November 17, 1865; *Columbus Enquirer*, October 28, 29, 1865; *Milledgeville Southern Recorder*, October 31, 1865; *Augusta Constitutionalist*, November 1, 1865; *Boston Herald*, October 28, 1865; *St. Louis Missouri Democrat*, October 28, 1865; *Ft. Wayne Gazette*, October 30, 1865; Candler, *Confederate Records*, 4:133–435; Summers, *Ordeal of the Reunion*, 69–70; Foner, *Reconstruction*, 194.

With the matter of the secession wording out of the way, the Convention could turn its attention to the most thorny and dominant issue, i.e., whether and how to repudiate the state's war debts. Unlike the slavery and secession issues, which were more theoretical than practical, the debt question involved both legal principle and real dollars—it was a pocketbook matter. Joshua Hill found the question simple. In his eyes, any debt incurred by the seceded state for the purpose of waging rebellion against the United States was illegitimate, and the new constitution must repudiate it. The dyed-in-the-wool secessionists and many of the conditional Unionists who had gone with the state to become ardent Confederates disagreed. They regarded the debt as an honorable obligation of the government of the people—the White people, of course. The *Milledgeville Federal Union* cried that if Georgia renounced its war debt, "the State is disgraced, and her fair fame and good character forever lost." It is very probable that self-interest as well as ideology influenced some individual delegates. Several of them and many of their friends held investments in the state's Confederate-era debt.[26]

Governor Johnson made it clear from the beginning that President Johnson would require debt repudiation as a condition of readmission. Similar scenarios played out in several other state conventions. Again, Hill stood out in Georgia's debate. In the words of a Northern reporter, Hill's speech on the debt "poured forth a burning denunciation of treason and its abettors, unparalleled by anything previously heard in the Convention.... [Delegate Hill] didn't want to reject this debt merely because the President demanded it, but because it was right. He didn't wish to incorporate a [debt repudiation] clause in the Constitution only because the Government dictated it, but because it is our duty to put it there."[27]

Faced with the reality that repudiation of war debt was necessary for readmission, the convention relented but sought loopholes to evade the spirit of the provision. None of the various options proposed was acceptable to Governor Johnson. Ex-congressman Hill used his legislative skill to

---

[26] *Chicago Inter Ocean*, November 8, 1865; Shadgett, "James Johnson," 13–17 (*Federal Union*, 15); Conway, *Reconstruction of Georgia*, 46–49; Perman, *Reunion without Compromise*, 76–77; Foner, *Reconstruction*, 194. On debt, see D. T. Carter, *When the War Was Over*, 136–37.

[27] *Newark Advertiser*, November 16, 1865 (*Cincinnati Gazette*).

craft compromise phraseology that narrowly defined war debt. The provision would allow the state to pay any debts incurred during the war as long as they were clearly "founded upon a consideration disconnected with any purpose of aiding or assisting the prosecution of the late war against the United States." The practical effect of this wording was virtually nil because there was little such debt, but including it in the debt repudiation ordinance preserved a face-saving element of dignity for the wartime actions of the Confederate legislature. Andrews admiringly reported that delegate Hill wanted the debt repudiation ordinance to "stand in the Constitution as a landmark for all coming generations of Georgia's children, to warn them against the mischiefs, evils, and curses of secession."[28]

The convention adjourned on November 8. By declaring slavery ended only through force of arms, by repealing rather than rejecting secession, and by repudiating the war debt with equivocal wording, the convention had done only the absolute minimum that it could get away with to facilitate Georgia's return to the Union.

Hill's efforts in the convention, limited though they were, attracted much praise from the Northern press. The *New York Tribune* editorialized, "We observe in the proceedings of the Georgia convention, that Hon. Joshua Hill continues to maintain his consistency as an unswerving Unionist." The *Philadelphia Press* credited Hill with standing up in the face of determined opposition: "During the whole time the convention was in session, many of the rebels were in the habit of making every conceivable mode of attack upon Hon. Joshua Hill, who, during the war, never wavered in his deadly sentiment of hostility to the whole Confederacy, and whose faith in the ultimate triumph of the Union he loved so well was never shaken." The *New York Times* admired Hill for his convictions but declared that he had been too often "conciliatory and vacillating." Observer Andrews agreed, and Hill himself later admitted as much, especially with regard to his having bowed to the pressure to withdraw his insistence that secession should have been declared null and void rather than merely repealed. Hill may have retreated on some specifics, but his rhetoric left no doubt where he stood. Such candor no doubt contributed to his limited effectiveness. During one encounter with a delegate, Hill retorted that he

---

[28] Candler, *Confederate Records*, 4:304–10, 341–42, 403; S. Andrews, *The South since the War*, 278.

held no "devotion to the ill-starred Confederacy. I regarded if from the first with open disfavor, and never abated my disproval of its insane origin." Later he lamented, "Seeing what I see, and hearing what I hear, I am bound to conclude that the spirit of enmity to the United States government is not yet extinct." That proved to be an understatement to be sure.[29]

The Senatorship Slips Away

No single action better epitomizes the lack of contrition and the presence of a spirit of defiance in the politicians of the Deep South than the Georgia General Assembly's decision in January 1866, only ten months after the end of the war, to select Alexander H. Stephens, the former vice president of the Confederate States of America, as the state's senior United States senator. Stephens was the most prominent among the many unrepentant rebels that the former Confederate states elected to high office. The debate that preceded and followed the election of Stephens provides a case study that conclusively illustrates the true motivations of the angry Southern White politicians who gathered in their state capital cities to write constitutions and set up new governments. Numerous historians have cited the choice of Stephens as evidence of Southern defiance, but few have emphasized that in the case of Georgia, the General Assembly had a clear and qualified alternative before it in the person of persistent Unionist Joshua Hill. Yet when presented with the clear option, the legislators made a knowing and deliberate decision to choose recalcitrance over cooperation.[30]

Even while the constitutional convention was in progress in fall 1865, there was considerable discussion about who would become the new governor and US senators once the readmitted state government got underway. Alexander Stephens declined to run for chief executive, so constitutional convention president Charles Jenkins won the governorship without serious opposition. In contrast, the choice of new United States senators was much less certain since it would be made by the newly constituted

[29] *New York Times*, November 17, 1865; *New York Tribune*, November 30, 1865; *Philadelphia Press*, November 20, 1865; S. Andrews, *The South since the War*, 283.

[30] Guelzo, *Reconstruction*, 25–26; Fitzgerald, *Splendid Failure*, 34–35; Foner, *Reconstruction*, 196.

legislature rather than by the electorate. The Civil War had disrupted the normal six-year senatorial cycle, so there were two positions to fill, a long-term and a short-term.[31]

Amid the speculation about who would take the senate seats, Joshua Hill's name appeared at the top of almost every list as it had since the June 1865 supposed compromise deal to support him for Senate in exchange for his endorsement of James Johnson as provisional governor. The Georgia correspondent of the *New York Times* reported on December 12, "Honorable JOSHUA HILL, once a member of congress, a consistent opponent of secession and the war, and an unwavering 'Union man,' will, it is thought be certainly elected." The paper expected James Johnson to fill the short term. Although many pundits were confident that those two would be the men, they also put forth other possible names, including S. J. Gartrell, Linton Stephens, Benjamin Hill, Herschel Johnson, and Joseph Brown. Always lurking above all of these men was the towering political presence of the physically frail Alexander H. Stephens.[32]

Joshua Hill and James Johnson stood at the top of the senatorial expectation lists because of the widespread and reasonable assumption that they, unlike the other prospects, would be acceptable to President Johnson and to the US Senate itself. In the minds of pragmatists who wished to see Georgia rapidly readmitted to the Union and represented on Capitol Hill, ex-governor Johnson and ex-congressman Joshua Hill were the obvious choices. On the other hand, those who were unwilling to admit that secession and support of the Confederacy had been errors harbored deep resentment against war-time Unionists, especially those like Hill who were of the slave-owning planter class. The disqualifications that kept many leading ex-Confederates from being qualified to vote for or serve as

[31] Conway, *Reconstruction of Georgia*, 50–52.

[32] *Augusta Constitutionalist*, November 4, December 5, 7, 1865; *Atlanta Intelligencer*, November 22, 1865 (*National Intelligencer*); *Milledgeville Southern Banner*, November 8, 1865; *Macon Telegraph*, November 30, 1865, January 24, 1865; *New York Times*, November 23, December 12 (Hon Joshua), 15, 1865; *Columbus Sun*, December 16, 1865; *Newark Advertiser*, December 15, 1865; *Philadelphia Press*, December 28, 1865; *New York Commercial Advertiser*, December 14, 1865. *Rome Courier*, January 30, 1866, added Linton Stephens and S. J. Gartrell to the list (Conway, *Reconstruction of Georgia*, 52–54; Nathans, *Losing the Peace*, 12–14; C. Thompson, *Reconstruction in Georgia*, 153–55).

constitutional convention delegates did not apply to legislative elections. As a consequence, the General Assembly that convened in December 1865 turned out to be even more pro-Confederate than the convention had been. The membership was overwhelmingly composed of men who were ex-Confederates even if they had been conditional Unionists prior to secession. A similar pattern emerged in the other Deep South states as they organized their first postwar civilian governments.[33]

In 1864 Congress established the so-called "Ironclad Oath" as a requirement for membership in its ranks. Accordingly, in addition to pledging future loyalty to the Union, any person selected by his state to be a United States senator or representative would have to swear that he had "never voluntarily borne arms against the United States," that he had not served in or sought office in the CSA, and, even more stringently, that he had not voluntarily given "aid, countenance, counsel, or encouragement to persons engage in armed hostility thereto." How did these provisions apply to Joshua Hill? He already held a presidential pardon, and no one doubted that he had been an unswerving Unionist who had not served in the Confederate military or government. But the other stipulation presented some questions. What about the assistance and support he provided to his sons who joined the Confederate army even though he had not wanted them to serve? What about the kindnesses that he afforded his friends and neighbors who chose to support the Confederacy even though he did not? And, most crucially, what about the fact that he had allowed himself to become a candidate for Georgia's governorship in 1863 even though he had not expected actually to take office? Despite these questions, Hill believed that he met the spirit of the law and could honestly take the Ironclad Test Oath (sometimes called the Test Oath).

In the eyes of the Republican majority in Congress, willingness to swear to the Ironclad Test Oath constituted a welcome measure of past and future loyalty to the United States. But to men who still believed that the quest for Confederate independence had been a noble if failed cause, willingness to take the oath constituted clear proof of disloyalty to hearth, home, and state. A Milledgeville paper contended that no true Southerner

[33] Guelzo, *Fateful Lighting*, 491–92; Foner, *Reconstruction*, 196–97; Nathans, *Losing the Peace*, 13–14; Perman, *Reunion without Compromise*, 155–81; C. Thompson, *Reconstruction in Georgia*, 155–56; Conway, *Reconstruction of Georgia*, 51–52.

would "willingly send any man to the National councils who could take the 'Test Oath.'" Benjamin H. Hill, agreed and proclaimed, "I would vote for no man to represent Georgia who could take this oath; because it is the highest evidence of infidelity to the sentiments of the people of the state." Sometime friends, sometime rivals, Ben and Josh Hill were now rivals again.[34]

Joshua Hill sensed that opposition to him was coalescing, and he understood that politics on the ground meant that his willingness to take the Ironclad Oath cut both ways. From the standpoint of pragmatism, it was the strongest argument in his favor; from the standpoint of electability, it stood in his way. In a late November note to Andrew Johnson, Hill asserted, "*I am one of the very few men in the State who can take the oath.* Men generally, know this." He proudly asserted that "the true Union men of the State desire me to be a candidate for the Senate," yet he candidly confessed that he thought it "doubtful, whether I could be chosen." Hill told the president that he faced frequent "denunciation of secessionists, unrepentant still of their efforts." To illustrate, he specifically cited his vociferous opposition to the constitutional convention's endorsement of a pardon for Jefferson Davis and his controversial "associations with Provl. Gov. Johnson & the Army officers, especially Genl. [James B.] Steedman." (It was Steedman who had introduced Hill at the American flag-raising ceremony in Augusta a few months earlier.) Despite the growing resistance to his candidacy and even though he professed that he did not really desire the office, Hill told Johnson that he nevertheless had resolved to have his name put forth to the General Assembly "in order to test the tone of the Legislature [and] to determine the actual state of feeling in Georgia." He accurately prophesied, "If the Legislature reject me—they will elect some one over me, who will make it matter of boasting, that he can not take the oath."[35]

---

[34] Foner, *Reconstruction*, 188–91; Summers, *Ordeal of the Reunion*, 65–88; Abbott, *Republican Party and the South*, 47–49; *Milledgeville Southern Recorder*, February 6, 1866; *Springfield (MA) Daily Republican*, December 2 (I would vote), 1865.

[35] Joshua Hill to Andrew Johnson, November 23, 1865, *Papers of Andrew Johnson*, 9:423–24. Hill appended a "confidential" note to a typical letter urging patronage for a friend (McKitrick, *Andrew Johnson and Reconstruction*, 208).

None of the seven men whom Georgia elected to the US House of Representatives was eligible to take the oath mainly due to having obtained high rank in the army of the Confederacy. One Massachusetts newspaper took note of the situation and offered the example of Joshua Hill in contrast: "The reconstructed Georgians give the preference, almost without exception, to candidates for office who have served in the rebel army.... But we suspect that nearly every Georgian fit to hold office—*the brave old Joshua Hill always excepted*—served in the confederacy in some way."[36]

Pragmatic Georgia journalists and politicians argued that the selection of Hill would please the president. An editorial in the *Macon Telegraph* astutely summarized, but did not necessarily endorse, this manner of thinking.

> We inferred that it had been pretty well determined to make choice of Hon. Joshua Hill to one of the vacancies. He has high qualifications, morally and intellectually, for the position, and it is understood that the President, to whom the people of the south feel under obligations, would be gratified by his election. In other respects, it would be an act eminently conciliatory in its character, and as such could not fail to be appreciated.

The *Southern Watchman* of Athens likewise explained to its readers that "the authorities in Washington" would welcome the selection of Hill and James Johnson. The Georgia correspondent of a New York paper observed that "The relations between [Hill] and President Johnson are said to be of the most amicable character." The *Chattanooga Gazette*, which had wide distribution in the Unionist region of Northwest Georgia, found even more practical reason that alliance with the "Andy's" preference would prove advantageous. It would, the paper argued, "strengthen the President in his war with the Radicals" to choose "men so favorably known to the Northern masses as Joshua Hill and Jas. H. Johnson."[37]

Until late January there was still a reasonable chance that the pragmatic strategy that Joshua Hill embodied would prevail over the distaste

---

[36] *Springfield (MA) Daily Republican*, December 18, 1865.

[37] *Macon Telegraph*, January 15, 1855; *(Athens) Southern Watchman*, December 13, 1865; *Newnan Herald*, January 6, 1866 (*Chattanooga Gazette*, December 27, 1865).

for his politics. Astute observers knew, however, that Hill's chances would be swept aside if Alexander H. Stephens were to become available. The immensely popular former vice president of the Confederacy was then on parole from federal prison. He had refused to run for governor and also professed not to be interested in the senatorship. Behind-the-scenes maneuvers belied Stephens's public statements. As early as December, the *Augusta Constitutionalist* announced, "We are authorized to state he would accept such a position, we feel fully justified in declaring that such a proffer may not be entirely in vain." Former governor Joseph Brown privately urged Stephens to put his name forward, and before the end of 1865, several newspapers were listing Stephens along with both Hills (Benjamin and Joshua) and both Johnsons (James and Herschel) as those who were "spoken of" for the senate positions. At about the same time, the *Chattanooga Gazette* floated the idea of electing both Joshua Hill and Alexander Stephens as a compromise that could satisfy both the pragmatic and the emotional choices. Hill, the *Gazette* conceded, "may not be the choice of a majority of the members of the Georgia legislature, but this fact should not permit them to ignore the more important consideration that he is recognized throughout the North as a consistent Union man, and he would, therefore, have more influence for good than any man Georgia could send to Washington, not excepting Mr. Stephens himself."[38]

General Steedman had become well aware of the rumors about Stephens's desire for the senate seat, so he decided that it would be prudent to ask the president for guidance. Johnson refrained from officially endorsing any candidate including Joshua Hill, but he made it crystal clear that he did not want Stephens to put his name forth because it would appear to be "something like defiance." When word of the president's concern

[38] *Chicago Inter Ocean*, December 4, 1865 (*Constitutionalist* and *Gazette*); *Augusta Constitutionalist*, December 7, 1865 (spoken of); *Macon Telegraph*, November 30, 1865. After the election, Brown wrote Pres. Johnson positively about Stephens, but he also commented that it would have been better if at least one of the defeated candidates (presumably Hill or James Johnson) had been elected (Parks, *Joseph E. Brown*, 349; D. Roberts, *Joseph E. Brown*, 38–39.

became widely known it may have temporarily slowed but did not stop the Stephens senatorial bandwagon.[39]

In January, as the legislative session approached, opposition to Joshua Hill and speculation about Stephens intensified. Martin J. Crawford, one of the Democratic congressmen who had withdrawn from the House of Representatives with the rest of the delegation while Joshua Hill resigned separately, wrote Stephens using the prospect of the election of Hill and James Johnson to put pressure on the former Confederate vice president to enter the fray. Crawford asserted that Governor Johnson was "thoroughly radical," and offered the judgement that Joshua Hill was "not so radical yet he is heart and soul against the friends of the South and would do all in his power to bring odium upon those who have earnestly desired our separate nationality—it won't do at all, at all—he hates the Democratic party with such intensity that he wouldn't give a cordial support to the President because he is a Democrat." Crawford's words were his own, but he expressed the insolent mood of the majority of the legislature when he made it clear: "My firm conviction is that it is far better not to have Senators at all, than to have such as I have described." The General Assembly and Stephens himself were well aware that the choice of Stephens would distress the president and result in almost certain rejection by the Senate.[40]

The legislative leadership postponed the senatorial choice to allow time to determine the intentions of the former Confederate vice president. On January 22 Stephens sent a letter to leading legislators declaring that he did not wish to be nominated. Within days, the purposely public letter appeared all over the Georgia press. It may have been a deliberate effort to inspire a draft—in any case, that is what resulted. A North Georgia weekly expressed the widely held thought that Stephens's friends might elect him "even in the face of his expressed wishes." Only a week after Stephens's public protestations that he did not want the position, word came that he had responded to inquiries by agreeing that he would not refuse to serve if drafted. That was all it took. Stephens was present in Milledgeville, and the *Atlanta Intelligencer* told its readers, "The election for the United States

---

[39] Johnston to Steedman, November 26, 1865, *Papers of Andrew Johnson*, 9:434; Schott, *Alexander H. Stephens*, 460–62; Downs, *After Appomattox*, 89–90; Nathans, *Losing the Peace*, 13; Conway, *Reconstruction of Georgia*, 52–53.

[40] Crawford to Stephens, in Perman, *Reunion without Compromise*, 163.

Senators takes place to-day. It seems to be well understood that Hon. A. H. Stephens will be elected." Some observers still thought that Joshua Hill might get one of the seats.[41]

On the evening of January 29, Josh Hill formally addressed a joint session. The aspiring candidate stood physically in the chamber of the Georgia House of Representatives, but he understood that he was speaking "by means of the press to the people of the whole country." Hill touted his qualifications and lauded his many efforts to help obtain pardons and relief for fellow Georgians in need. He and everyone listening was aware that Stephens had left the door open to a draft and that he would likely be chosen. With an unmistakable pique of frustration in his tone, Hill declared, "Rumor hath it, that I am to be defeated, nay, crushed, annihilated." His response was to stress the folly of electing anyone "prominently identified by either a military or civil capacity with the rebel government." Though Hill employed the rhetorical device of not speaking the name "Alexander H. Stephens," everyone knew exactly about whom he was speaking when he declared, "I have a right to insist that you do no hurt to the State by electing a man, who from any cause, cannot serve you if elected." The state's most prominent Unionist implored Georgia's legislators to realize that they would "be laboring under a delusion" if they thought that the United States Senate would accept a person who had occupied a position "in the defunct government of the Confederacy."[42]

Hill refused to apologize for his willingness to take the Ironclad Oath: "If it be matter of reproach to be able to take this severe oath, then denounce me, for I can take it. I am sorry to say that I know so few who are in my situation." The members were fully aware that President Johnson did not want Stephens to be chosen, so Hill challenged them: "Are you quite certain that your love for the President is heartfelt and sincere? If you would give evidence of your attachment, consult his wishes." Knowing that he was going to make little headway with the bulk of the legislators no

---

[41] Schott, *Alexander H. Stephens*, 460–62; *Savannah Herald*, January 29, 31, 1866; *Augusta Chronicle*, January 27, 1866; *Columbus Enquirer*, January 26, 1866; *Atlanta Intelligencer*, January 31 (and all that) February 1 (the election), 1866; *Dawson Journal*, February 2, 1866; *Newnan Herald*, February 3, 1866; *Cincinnati Enquirer*, January 27, 1866; *New York Times*, January 22, 1866.

[42] Transcript from the *Savannah Herald*, February 5, 1866; *Augusta Constitutionalist*, February 6, 1866; *New York Times*, February 18, 1866.

matter what he said, Hill chose not to hold back. He concluded, "I have sought to be explicit and frank, and have concealed from you no sentiment of mine.... I wish no man to be in doubt as to my opinions for my reputation for candor is more to me than the result of to-morrow's election."[43]

Southern Democratic reaction to the testy speech was swift and predictable. The state capital's *Southern Recorder* asserted that Hill's comments about taking the Test Oath were tantamount to calling supporters of the Confederacy "traitors." An Augusta commentator admired Joshua Hill's "pluck" but proclaimed, "We would rather see Georgia as a territory forever than an immediate State at his price. We do not believe that President Johnson would respect us for such shameful surrender as [Hill] depicts." An Atlanta correspondent succinctly stated Hill's key problem: "He thought the General Assembly ought to elect him. He could take the oath, which but few could do. For this very reason, many will not vote for him."[44]

The result went as expected. Stephens won the long term on the first ballot by a count of 152 to 38. The magnitude of the first ballot results against Hill made it clear that neither he nor former provisional governor James Johnson would be chosen for the short term. After several ballots, the members settled on former Confederate senator Hershel V. Johnson. Thus, the General Assembly selected for the Senate of the United States of America one man who, as vice president, served as the presiding officer of the Senate of the Confederate States of America and one man who had been a member of that body. Georgia's gesture of rebelliousness could not have been more blatant.[45]

Northern Republican reaction to the rejection of Hill and Johnson fell along partisan lines as usual. The opinion of the *New York Times* was typical:

> That two men should have been selected chiefly because of their prominence in the rebellion, and who cannot take the oath, simply embarrasses the work of restoration, and the Southern people in the end become the chief sufferers. The election of

---

[43] Ibid.

[44] *Southern Recorder*, February 6, 1866; *Augusta Constitutionalist*, February 2, 1866 (pluck); *Atlanta Intelligencer*, February 1, 1866 (He thought); *Newnan Herald*, February 3, 1866.

[45] Results in *Macon Telegraph*, January 31, 1866.

> Provisional Governor James Johnson and Joshua Hill would have been a very encouraging sign of the moral effect of which the South is very much in need.

According to the *Augusta Constitutionalist*, Northern Democrats held a contrary view: "The conservative party of the North have hailed their election with pleasure. They [Stephens and Johnson] were not chosen because of their connection with the late Confederacy, for it is well known that they were among the last to favor secession." The paper was probably correct that many Northern Democrats were pleased with Georgia's action, but the assertion that "their connection with the late Confederacy" was not the reason they were chosen was preposterous.[46]

President Lincoln, when he was alive, and his fellow Republicans thereafter, often made the error of overestimating the political strength of ex-Whig loyal Unionists in the South. Georgia's rejection of Hill and James Johnson constituted a prime example of that miscalculation. An Atlanta newspaper asserted that there was "not a corporal's guard" of Georgia politicians ready to renounce the Confederacy and cooperate with Reconstruction even under Lincoln's successor. In the General Assembly that "corporal's guard" amounted only to 38 of 190 voting members.[47]

The controversy did not go away after the vote. In his January 29 speech to the joint session, Hill leveled the bold and very likely correct accusation that Alexander H. Stephens had duplicitously engineered his own election: "I care not if a man be as pure as an angel.... Under the circumstances he cannot escape a suspicion of encouraging the act." In angry response, sixty-nine members of the General Assembly signed a widely-published letter emphatically declaring "that Mr. Stephens knew nothing of the movement until it was matured.... on Saturday previous to the election on Tuesday"; that is, on January 28. As a technicality, Stephens may not have been physically present in the rooms where legislative leaders mapped out the final details of strategy, but to deny that Stephens knew of and approved of what was going on constituted disingenuousness if not outright prevarication. The press, the legislature, the courthouse crowds

---

[46] *Macon Telegraph*, February 12, 1866 (*New York Times*); *Augusta Constitutionalist*, February 11, 1866; *New Orleans Times-Picayune*, February 23, 1866.

[47] Perman, *Reunion without Compromise*, 164 (there is not; from *Atlanta Intelligencer*, February 10, 1866).

across the state, the Union military commander of Georgia, the president of the United States, and Stephens himself had been fully aware of the possibility of his election for more than two months before it occurred. Even three weeks after his election Stephens still had the temerity to thank the legislature for electing him to "the position you know I did not seek." It defies credibility to assert that Stephens was drafted against his will, in the face of his sincere refusal, and without his own behind-the-scenes acquiescence, if not agency.[48]

The letter from the legislators combined with other personal attacks to motivate Joshua Hill to publish a sharp retort in newspapers and pamphlet form. In his response to the sixty-nine legislators, Hill dismissed the claim of Stephens's noninvolvement with a snide Shakespearean reference: "He did not refuse the high office as often as Caesar did the 'kingly crown' and yet Caesar was slain for his ambition." While the specifics of Hill's letter were about Georgia, his sentiments spoke the frustrations of unconditional loyalists across the lower South. He scathingly attacked the legislative majority for its false protestations of loyalty to the Union and its continuing adhesion to the right, if not the reality, of secession. He argued, as he had for weeks, that it was arrogant folly for Georgia to send to Washington senators who could not take the oath and would not be seated. He conceded that Stephens's pre-secession Unionism was "meritorious," but charged that any such merit was swept away the moment that he signed the Ordinance of Secession. As Thomas Schott, Stephens's most recent and thorough biographer wrote, "Hill was right on all counts."[49]

True to form, Republican-leaning papers in the North admired both the content of Hill's letter and its hutzpah.[50] On the other hand, several

---

[48] "Letter of Hon. Joshua Hill of Georgia on the Election of US Senators," (pamphlet by Joshua Hill, March 1866), hathitrust.org (hereinafter Hill letter, March 1866); *Savannah Herald*, February 5, 1866; *Augusta Constitutionalist*, February 11, 1866. The "Letter from the Friends of Hon. Alexander H. Stephens, in the Georgia Legislature, February 2, 1866" was widely reprinted, e.g., *Savannah Herald*, February 12, 1866; *Atlanta Intelligencer*, February 14, 1866; *Augusta Chronicle*, March 9, 14, 1866; *New York Times*, January 22, 1866; *Atlanta Intelligencer*, February 24, 1866 (the position).

[49] Hill letter, March 1866; Schott, *Alexander H. Stephens*, 463.

[50] *Boston Daily Advertiser*, March 20, 1866; *Augusta Constitutionalist*, March 21, 1866 (*National Intelligencer*).

Georgia newspapers lambasted Hill, and some refused to publish his letter at all or printed only excerpts. One wrote that Hill's outpourings were full of "ignorance, arrogance, self-glorification, and ridiculous vanity" and that the effect was to "further to fatigue public indignation." Another asserted that Hill's comments were "calculated to keep up old divisions." One central Georgia paper praised the Madisonian's character but bitterly assailed his politics: "Joshua Hill has, avowedly, been an enemy of the Confederacy since the commencement of the war, and though his private acts since the surrender have proven him to be a kind-hearted, generous, humane man, his public course, as a Georgian, is humiliating in the extreme."[51]

Among those who took after Joshua Hill was the virulently anti-Yankee humorist Bill Arp. He styled his comment as a letter to "Mr. Tammany Hall" and wrote, "We can't satisfy them Radikals. I don't care what we do.... We elected Mr. Stephens and Hershel Johnson to the Senate, and they are mad about that. They wanted Josh Hill and Jeems Johnson because they was *Union*." Addressing Hill directly, Arp concluded, "We haven't been runnin you down to give you offis, and we aint a goin to."[52]

Joshua Hill did not only speak and publish his frustrations for the public; he also expressed them directly to President Johnson and to General Sherman in private letters. He urged Sherman not to relax his guard about the intentions of most Southern White politicians. To the president, the Georgian lamented "that an effort was made by certain persons to depreciate me in your esteem. I was aware of it, but I was too proud to refute it—and suffered it to go on unresisted. I wanted nothing, but to be understood, *as not being a hypocrite*." He explained that even though former governors Joe Brown, Howell Cobb, and Henry Jackson and others had backed him and James Johnson "on grounds of expediency and propriety," that was not enough in face of the defiant mood of the bulk of the White populace:

---

[51] *Columbus Sun*, March 15, 1866; *Macon Telegraph*, March 14, 1866; *Milledgeville Federal Union*, March 30, 1866; *Sandersville Central Georgian*, February 21, 1866 (avowedly); *Augusta Constitution*, March 10, 1866; *Augusta Chronicle*, March 14, 1866.

[52] *Washington Review & Examiner*, March 14, 1866 (Arp, italics and dialect in original).

> I hear it continually from ultra secessionists, and particularly from soldiers. It takes a long time, for passion to cool, and reason to resume its sway. I am only tolerated myself by thousands, because of my supposed influence with government officials. The mails bring me many bitter and denunciatory anonymous letters.... Yet knaves and fools try to teach the people that I would injure them—and perpetuate military rule in the State. This would be to war against my own peace—and is therefore absurd.

Hill best summarized his frustrations when he wrote, "Jefferson Davis is today more popular in Georgia, than any other man." Unfortunately, none of those "bitter and denunciatory" letters to which Hill referred have survived. Some months later in July the episode was still on Hill's mind when he wrote from Washington to his friend T. P. Saffold: "The president & his cabinet have been kind & polite to me. I can not afford to be outdone in civility. I stand however, immovable, on every principle of my letter to the 69—which has been more generally read North than South."[53]

As Hill and pretty much everyone else had predicted, the Senate refused seats to Alexander Stephens and Herschel V. Johnson despite Stephens's assurances to Andrew Johnson that he would be loyal to the Union. Thus, Georgia remained unrepresented, unreconstructed, and unadmitted. Hill remained convinced that he and James Johnson would have been seated if the General Assembly had chosen the pragmatic route in late 1865 and early 1866. "I tell you what I know is true," he wrote to Saffold, "that had the Southern States elected to Congress none but Union men—they would be this day fully represented in Congress." But, as he lamented to his old friend, the door had closed: "You may feel assured, fully, that the defeat of Johnson & myself for the Senate clinched the nail—in the determination of Northern Union men—never, never to allow any disturber of the peace of the Union, to take a seat in either Ho[use] of Congress."

The 1866 Georgia senatorial race represented in a microcosm the region-wide political triumph of former Confederates over strong Union loyalists like Joshua Hill who had declined to serve in rebel administrations

---

[53] Joshua Hill to Andrew Johnson, March 19, 1866, *Papers of Andrew Johnson* [vol?], 273–74; Russ, "Was There a Danger," 39; Schott, *Alexander H. Stephens*, 462–63 (Hill to Sherman, February 5, 1866); Hill to Saffold, July 21, 1866, Saffold Family Collection, MCA.

or armies. Congress and the Northern Republican press had been watching, and in their eyes, Georgia had had its chance and had blown it. New York's *Jewish Messenger* was explicit: "While Georgia, for example, could have selected as senator a worthy and widely esteemed citizen of great legislative experience and consistent devotion to the Union, Joshua Hill, it has chosen prominent leaders in the secession movement." The *Boston Journal* wrote, "It will be remembered that the real Union men in the Georgia Legislature cast their votes for Hon. Joshua Hill."[54]

[54] *Boston Journal*, February 14, 1866; *New York Jewish Messenger*, February 16, 1866; *Vermont Journal*, March 17, 1866; *Springfield (MA) Republican*, February 8, 1866; *(St. Louis) Missouri Democrat*, February 13, 1866; Nathans, *Losing the Peace*, 13; Foner, *Reconstruction*, 196–97; Guelzo, *Reconstruction*, 25; Abbott, *Republican Party and the South*, 48–50.

Chapter 8

Conservative Republican in Congressional Reconstruction, 1866–1868

From the end of the Civil War in spring 1865 through early 1866, Joshua Hill's efforts to position himself for the provisional governorship and Senate seat dominated his political life and ended in frustration. In the meantime, he also had to rebuild his personal and professional life and, most importantly, figure out how to adapt to the South's new post-slavery racial order. But politics soon called, and once again Joshua Hill found himself trying to navigate a very narrow middle course. This time Georgia's middle ground lay between the radical wing of the emerging Republicans on the one hand and the re-emerging Democrats on the other. Even though Hill had little sympathy for either group, the conflict between them eventually led him to the Republican Party and to the United States Senate seat that had eluded him in 1866. Radical Republicans claimed a significant victory in the congressional elections in fall 1866. With a veto-proof Republican majority now assured in both houses, Congress moved quickly to pass a series of Reconstruction Acts beginning in March 1867 that together constituted the basis for "military" or "congressional" reconstruction.

Meanwhile, as politics simmered in Washington and Atlanta, Joshua Hill and other members of the Southern gentry endeavored to find ways to restore the foundations of their personal and economic lives in the absence of institutionalized chattel slavery. In late spring 1865, an Augusta Unionist wrote Hill to express his concerns. He worried about a possible "war of races" and mused, "There is absolutely no law outside the towns and cities occupied by Federal Forces.... The status of the black race is unsettled notwithstanding the action of the Federal Govt., and both blacks and Whites suffer from the uncertainty." It would take several years for the economic uncertainty to settle, but in the end, the planter class ensured its dominance over the formerly enslaved.[1]

Landowner and Lawyer in Reconstruction Georgia

With the end of hostilities, more than $700 million of slave value had evaporated, some $18 million in state war bonds had been repudiated, incalculable amounts of Confederate currency had turned into worthless paper, much property had been destroyed, and the worth of most real and personal assets had plummeted. The former slaves had gained their freedom, but they were not yet sure what that would mean for their daily lives. Rumors of the distribution of "forty acres and a mule" spread widely, but politically connected planters soon dashed that hope. Most planters in the Black Belt, such as Joshua Hill, hoped that emancipation would bring as little change as possible. Howell Cobb, whose plantation Sherman's men had burned, expressed the unrepentant rebel slaveowner's point of view in a June 1865 letter to General J. H. Wilson, the ranking Union commander in the state. Cobb opined, "The institution of slavery, in my judgment, provided the best system of labor that could be devised for the negro race." Cobb conceded that slavery had "passed away," but he urged that future labor relations be kept in the hands of the state. Troubled by the letter, Wilson told a colleague that planters like Cobb were "anxious to substitute a gradual system of emancipation, or a modified condition of Slavery, similar to Peonage." Wilson believed that "the whole system of Slavery and slave labor must be effectually destroyed, and the Freedmen protected from the injustice of evil men before the [White] people of Georgia get the State Government under their own control." This exchange epitomized the fundamental conflict.[2]

Joshua Hill was among those who favored, at least temporarily, the establishment of such a "modified condition of Slavery" as General Wilson

---

[1] David G. Cotting to Joshua Hill, June 5, 1865, in Cotting pardon file, NARA M1003, via Fold3.com.

[2] C. Thompson, *Reconstruction in Georgia*, 52–53. On Georgia's postwar economic disruptions see W. Range, *A Century of Georgia Agriculture*, 66–79; Wynne, *Continuity of Cotton*; Reidy, *From Slavery to Agrarian Capitalism*; Nathans, *Losing the Peace*; Conway, *Reconstruction of Georgia*; Gagnon, *Transition to an Industrial South*.

gloomily anticipated. On May 10, 1865, Hill wrote President Johnson to explain his concerns: "The disposition of these [formerly enslaved] people is of great consequence no matter when nor where it may occur, but its importance is greatest in the rural districts.... The general policy of the government is known to embrace emancipation, but the time and mode of retiring the institution are not so well understood." Hill elaborated on the urgency of having sufficient labor to get crops in on time and argued to the freed people must have "time to accommodate their actions to the novel condition of freedom. It is not to be expected that they can immediately comprehend their altered estate, its requirements and responsibilities."[3]

What Hill and many other planters endorsed was the contract labor system that General Nathan P. Banks had implemented in Louisiana soon after federal military occupation in 1864. Banks's plan sought to accommodate influential Bayou State Unionist planters, and Hill hoped it could do the same in Georgia. Referring to Banks's plan, Hill told Johnson "I can not see wherein its leading features could be improved." Under that system, which some former slave states incorporated into so-called "Black Codes," Black laborers worked for wages but were bound by contract for a year to one farm or plantation. Echoing slavery, the provost marshal could corral recalcitrant workers and return them to the contract holder. Even if one assumes that many White landowners like Joshua Hill would have acted fairly and honestly in making contracts with their former slaves, that assumption could not be widely applied to all. A careful study of Greene County documented widespread economic abuse of freedmen by most postwar planters. There is every reason to assume that the situation was similar in neighboring Morgan County.[4]

In Georgia as well as in other states, the Freedman's Bureau often proved to be of as much help to the planters as to the freed people. As late as August 1865 the bureau had no effective presence in Georgia beyond the coast and Augusta. Even as bureau activity increased in fall 1865 and into the next year, many of the local agents were White men steeped in the culture of slavery who promoted contract arrangements and coerced labor.

---

[3] Hill to Johnson, May 10, 1865, *Papers of Andrew Johnson*, 8:55–57.

[4] Ibid.; Abbott, *Republican Party and the South*, 44–45; McPherson, *Battle Cry of Freedom*, 711; J. M. Bryant, *How Curious a Land*. See also Foner, *Reconstruction*, 47–65; Levine, *Fall of the House of Dixie*, 295.

To be sure, the Freedmen's Bureau sometimes responded to complaints from African Americans and on occasion punished the most extreme abuses, but enforcement was spotty at best. More fundamentally, however, even if the contract system could have been operated honestly and fairly, it failed to recognize what the freed people in agricultural communities sought most—autonomy to work land that they controlled, preferably by ownership but alternatively by tenancy.[5]

Unfortunately, no day-to-day records of Hill's postwar agricultural operations survive, so it is not known how he dealt personally with freed people in the immediate aftermath of the war. There is no doubt that Hill continued to assume White superiority, yet based on the few comments available and judging from his later political positions and statements, he appears to have been more sympathetic and understanding of the freed people and their needs than most members of his class. In a wartime letter, Hill told a lawyer friend that he admired the farming skills and knowledge of the enslaved workers who kept plantation crops growing in the absence of White owners and overseers. In spring 1867, Hill commended fellow planter T. P. Saffold on his progress "at enlightenment of the freedmen." The 1930s narrative of the Hill's former slave E. W. Evans provides a retrospective glimpse of the Hill household's response to emancipation. Speaking from his childhood memories and decades of family tradition, Evans reported that Emily Hill called the formerly enslaved females together soon after Union troops passed through Madison and tried to explain what would happen: "She said they were free and could go wherever they wanted to.... She meant that they could rent from her if they wanted to." Soon the Freemen's Bureau established a school in a Baptist Church just a few hundred yards toward the railroad track from the Hill home, and Hill later donated land from his plantation for a rural Black church.[6]

---

[5] Cimbala, *Under the Guardianship of the Nation*, 4, 24, 52, 156–58, 221–24; Mohr, *On the Threshold of Freedom*, 296; Levine, *Fall of the House of Dixie*, 295–97; Wynne, *Continuity of Cotton*, 7–28; Conway, *Reconstruction of Georgia*, 76–94; and Downs, *After Appomattox*, 45–47.

[6] Joshua Hill to C. S. Jordan, December 23, 1863, Reid & Jordan Family Papers, ms 749, folder 21, box 2, Rose Manuscript Archives, Emory University; Hill to Saffold, April 7, 1867, Saffold Papers, MCA; Tonsill and Evans, "E. W. Evans, Brick Layer & Plasterer," https://www.loc.gov/item/wpalh000565;

Joshua Hill never abandoned farm ownership, but as his law practice and political ambitions expanded, he became more of a land investor than an active planter. The contrast is apparent. The 1860 agricultural census showed his properties producing 26 bales of cotton and 3,500 bushels of corn. He owned 189 head of livestock. Ten years later Hill raised no cotton, harvested only 800 bushels of corn, and kept only three head of livestock. The key to the transition was the 1867 sale of his main plantation on the Eatonton Road about seven miles south of Madison where, as related in earlier chapters, soldiers from both sides took much of the stock in August 1864 and Union marchers burned plantation structures in November 1864.[7]

The buyer of Hill's 2,367.5 acre plantation was Reuben Miller of Claverack, New York. Miller was one of the many Northerners who took advantage of the chance to buy large tracts of Southern land at attractive postwar prices. It is not clear exactly how Miller learned of availability of the Hill plantation, but it is possible that he heard of the opportunities through letters written home by soldiers from Claverack who occupied Morgan County after the war and wrote home about the cheap and fertile land of the lower Piedmont.[8]

In 1869 Joshua Hill wrote a section in the book *Where to Emigrate, and Why*, which compiled testimonies from many communities. He explained that his "pretty town" of about two thousand residents was "the principal cotton depot" on the Georgia Railroad and that it was surrounded by hinterland blessed with "fertile soil," a mild climate, and plenty of water. Hill mentioned his recent buyer as a prime example of successful and innovative immigrants from the North. All-in-all, Hill painted an optimistic word picture of postbellum life in his section of Georgia at the very time that Northerners were reading harrowing tales about the Ku

---

Conway, *Reconstruction of Georgia*, 89–94. The original building is gone, but the Mt. Zion Missionary Baptist Church (1868) still operates on the land Hill donated.

[7] Melton, "The Town that Sherman Wouldn't Burn," 216.

[8] Morgan County, Georgia, Deed Book M, 185, December 7, 1867, MCA; John W. Mambert to family, September 5, 28, 1865, private collection of Mike Kipp, copies in MCA; Goddard, *Where to Emigrate*, 425–26; *Eatonton Messenger*, March 5, 1904. On recruitment of immigrants, see Rubin, *Shattered Nation*, 179–87.

Klux Klan. He assured readers, "There is no apprehension of violence from any source. We enjoy a state of quiet and peace." Migrants, Hill claimed, "will find, in Georgia, a soil and climate to please them, and an intelligent, hospitable people to welcome them to new homes."[9]

In addition to his rosy portrayal of Morgan County's virtues, Hill provided a concise description of how the labor system was transforming from enslavement to sharecropping:

> These lands, in the days of slavery, fell into the hands of the large planters, and were cruelly abused by a system of bad culture, continuous crops of cotton, with shallow plowing. Since the close of the war there have settled among us a few Northern farmers, bringing with them improved farming implements.... These farms are still cultivated mainly by colored labor, especially the large tracts. There are many small proprietors who use white or mixed labor, and some who confine their work to the immediate family.... Most planters contract with their laborers, giving them a part of the crops produced.

Nine years later, the Madison newspaper reported that the old Hill properties that had once been worked by several dozen slaves were now "farmed mostly by freedmen on the shared principle" with about ninety-five workers housed in thirty settlements. The state of Georgia used Ruben Miller's testimony in an 1881 promotional publication: "I have always been treated as kindly and hospitality by the natives as if I was born and raised here." As evidence that his politics had not been an impediment to his economic success, Miller pointedly added, "I am Republican in politics to the backbone."[10]

Reuben Miller was not the only Northerner to take up postwar residence in the county. In 1868 one Morgan landowner wrote his son, "So it seems that we are to have Yankee neighbors a plenty." At least two Union soldiers from the Twentieth Corps, one from Ohio and one from New York returned to settle near Madison, the town they had found so attractive on their March to the Sea. One of them bought a large farm along the

---

[9] Goddard, *Where to Emigrate*, 425–26.

[10] Ibid.; Morgan County Landmarks Society, "Indigenous Architecture of the Georgia Piedmont: Plantation Plain Houses in Morgan County," April 17, 2016, MCA (farmed mostly); Fontaine, *State of Georgia*, 133.

Georgia Railroad west of town near where his division had camped. A young lieutenant from the 136th New York bought another Morgan County plantation in November 1865. He later sold most of it off to other planters and opened a newspaper in Madison. In 1871 he testified that there were about forty Northerners like him in the county and that they got along just fine. Several emigrants who came South as single men later married local women.[11]

Though he sold his main plantation and removed himself from day-to-day operations, Joshua Hill continued to buy and sell Morgan County farmland. In the mid-1880s the county tax digest showed that his various land holdings totaled over three thousand acres. He built a country home on land in the Kingston community to the east of his old place but did not regularly reside there. From 1866 to 1869 Hill also speculated in granite quarry land near Stone Mountain, about forty-five miles to the west of Madison.[12]

Following the war, Hill expanded his practice of law—and influence peddling—in Madison, Augusta, Atlanta, and Washington, DC. His lifeline to those Georgia cities and on to the nation's capital was the Georgia Railroad, so he was delighted to see it repaired and returned to service by late spring 1865, albeit in slow-moving dilapidated rolling stock. As described in the previous chapter, Hill endorsed and even prepared numerous pardon applications for his friends and even for his political rivals until his relationship with President Johnson began to wane in 1867. Among his last requests came in March of that year when he wrote on behalf of Alfred

[11] J. M. Perry to son, May 5, 1868, folder 1, box 1, J. M. Perry Family Collection, Kenan Research Center, Atlanta History Center; testimony of B. H. True, October 28, 1871, in US Congress, *Report...into the Condition of Affairs in the Late Insurrectionary States...and Testimony Taken* (hereafter KKK Hearings 1872), 2:717–18. Kennett, *Marching through Georgia*, 318–19, mentions B. H. True and James H. Ainslie. The latter's descendants remain active in Morgan County politics.

[12] Morgan County Georgia Tax Digests 1883–1887, MCA. The official 1897 map of Morgan County (MCA and Morgan Co. Court Clerk's Office) identifies Hill's postwar country home, which is now in ruin. Morgan Co. Landmarks, "Indigenous Architecture"; Coletti, *Stone Mountain*, addendum, 739–41; *Augusta Constitutionalist*, June 16, 1869, and *Macon Telegraph*, June 25, 1869, reported that Hill and his son-in-law were preparing to move to Stone Mountain; either the report was erroneous, or plans changed.

H. Colquitt, Ben Hill, and three other former members of the Confederate Congress. "Differing as I have widely with the gentlemen in their hearty embrace of the Rebel cause," Joshua Hill wrote, "I can perceive, at this distant day, no good that can come from a rejection of their petitions." Such magnanimity helped Joshua Hill maintain cordial person relations with his political opponents."[13]

Most of Hill's activity was, of course, in Georgia. However, at some period around late 1866, he also established a law office in Washington, DC, for the purpose of facilitating action for claimants against the federal government. This move, however, did not prove fruitful because Congress postponed all consideration of claims. In January 1867, Hill unsuccessfully sought a special exemption for himself. "Mr. Hill," the *New York Tribune* reported, "asserts that his is a case of peculiar merit, for in consequence of his undisguised Union sentiments during the progress of the war, he was granted by our armies a safeguard." When Congress declined to make the exception for Hill, the Democratic-oriented *Augusta Constitutionalist* taunted, "the Hon. JOSHUA HILL, of super-loyal memory, failed to get a greenback consideration for his friend SHERMAN'S frolicsome pranks upon his property." Writing from the nation's capital in spring 1867, Hill complained to Saffold that none of his efforts had brought him much money. After Congress established the Southern Claims Commission in the 1870s, Hill again asked for $25,491.75 for damage to his property, but

[13] Conway, *Reconstruction of Georgia*, 35–36; *Nation*, January 25, 1866; Records of the Adjutant General's Office, 1762–1984, Series: Amnesty Papers, 1865–1867, RG 94, (catalog.archives.gov); Joshua Hill to Andrew Johnson March 26, 1867 (Differing), in Benjamin H. Hill pardon file, NARA M1003 (fold3.com). My search found more than fifty individual pardon requests with Hill endorsements or letters, including at least eleven individuals from Morgan County, one of whom was his close friend, Nathaniel G. Foster (NARA M1003, Case Files of Applications from Former Confederates for Presidential Pardons, via Fold3.com; NARA RG 94, Records of the Adjutant General's Office, via catalog.archives.gov); *Columbus Enquirer*, July 8, 1866. On Johnson's pardon policy, see S. M. Lee, *Claiming the Union*, 4, 10, 15, 27–29; Perman, *Reunion without Compromise*, 122–31; and McKitrick, *Andrew Johnson and Reconstruction*, 48, 140–52.

the strict, Radical Republican-dominated commission disallowed his claim.[14]

In addition to advocating for pardons and claims, Hill was not oblivious to the fact that patronage might serve his personal needs as well. In March 1866, shortly after losing the US Senate contest, he wrote President Johnson about a friend and then turned to his own circumstances. Knowing that others had approached Johnson on his behalf about possible governmental appointments, Hill was not shy about telling the president that he had set his sights high: "There are very few that I could afford to accept. None that would not support a large family, genteelly." The request bore fruit. Johnson nominated and the Senate soon confirmed Hill to the post of United States Customs Collector in Savannah—a relatively lucrative position. The appointment met with general favor in the state, even from many of those who had opposed his senatorial candidacy. The *Columbus Enquirer*, for example, called Hill "honest, high-minded, and patriotic" even while noting that he had been "unduly vexed by his late defeat." The Northern press was, as usual, pleased that a consistent Unionist had apparently been treated well. After further consideration, however, Hill declined the appointment and never assumed the position. Apparently, he concluded that even a steady government salary would not merit giving up his law practice and local business interests to relocate to Savannah for the full-time collectorship. In April 1867, Hill was offered the lucrative collectorship in Mobile, but despite the urging of Treasury Secretary Hugh McCulloch and General Steedman, he decided to remain a Georgian.[15]

---

[14] *Springfield (MA) Republican*, November 21, 1866; *Augusta Constitutionalist*, January 23 (*New York Tribune*, January 16), February 6, 1867 (the Hon); *Boston Journal*, January 17, 1867; Hill to Saffold, April 7, 1867; *Consolidated Index of Claims*, Reported by the Commissioners of Claims to the House of Representatives, 1871–1880, 111 (Washington: GPO, 1892), National Archives, Atlanta Branch, microfilm P2257. Baggett wrongly declares that the Southern Claims Commission denied Hill's claim because he served in the state senate of Confederate Georgia, but Hill did not so serve (*Scalawags*, 92). Most likely it was Hill's candidacy for governor of Georgia in 1863 that stood in his way.

[15] Joshua Hill to Andrew Johnson, March 19, 1866, *Papers of Andrew Johnson*; *Journal of the Proceeding of the Senate of the United States*, 39th Congress, First Session, part 2, 713, 715, 840, 849; *Appointments to Office. Message from the President...Giving the names of all persons appoints to office, &c., February 1, 1867*, Serial

In June 1867, another patronage opportunity came Hill's way when Chief Justice Salmon P. Chase appointed him to be the register of bankruptcy for the state's First Congressional District, which included Atlanta. This was a position that a lawyer could hold while still maintaining his private practice. Hill returned to Georgia from Washington shortly after the appointment was announced, but sources differ as to whether he actually undertook the job. In mid-1867 Hill also received a prestigious but mainly honorific appointment to the fourteen-member Board of Visitors for the Military Academy at West Point. At the end of the year, there were reports that Hill was "very favorably considered" for appointment as solicitor of internal revenue but that he was not appointed because, according to reports, "he will be strongly pressed for United States Senator."[16]

Joshua Hill was not, of course, the only politician striving to advance in postwar Georgia. In October 1866 an Augusta journalist described the status of several politicians "once occupying high places, [who are] are now pursuing among us the even tenor of their ways, rebuilding broken fortunes, and sharing, in uncomplaining patience, the common loss of us all."

Set vol. 1292; *Columbus Enquirer*, April 7, 1866 (honest); *Augusta Constitutionalist*, April 4, 1866; *Boston Traveller*, March 31, 1966; *Augusta Chronicle*, April 10, 1866; *(Athens) Southern Watchman*, June 20, 1866; *Macon Telegraph*, August 1, 1866; *Philadelphia Illustrated New Age*, June 6, 1866; *Marshall County (IN) Republican*, June 14, 1866; *Crawfordsville (IN) Journal*, June 21, 1866; *Columbus Enquirer*, April 7, 1866; *Augusta Chronicle*, April 10, 1866; House Executive Document 67, Serial Set vol. 1292, February 1, 1867, lists Hill as "declined" and James Johnson as "accepted"; Hill to T. P. Saffold, July 21, 1866 (Savannah) and April 7, 1867 (Mobile), Saffold Family Papers, MCA; Northern, *Men of Mark in Georgia*, 3:72, and Mellichamp, *Senators from Georgia*, 150 (probably drawing from Northern) incorrectly state that Hill served.

[16] *Macon Telegraph*, June 14, July 9, 1867; *Augusta Chronicle*, June 19, 1867; *Columbus Enquirer*, June 18, July 8, 1867; *Chicago Inter Ocean*, June 14, 1867; *Richmond (VA) Whig*, July 19, 1867; *Milledgeville Federal Union*, June 11, July 9, 1867, and December 8, 1868 (*Savannah Republican*); Hill's entry in the Biographical Directory of the US Congress indicates that he declined both offices (US Congress, "Hill, Joshua"). The June 1867 report of the West Point board in *Message of the President of the United States and Accompanying Documents*, 40th Congress, 2nd Session, Serial Set vol. 1324, 500; *Boston Traveller*, June 3, 1967; *New York Times*, June 3, 1867; *Rome Courier*, June 14, 1867; "On Solicitor of Internal Revenue," *Chicago Tribune*, November 4, 1867 (very favorably); *(St. Louis) Missouri Democrat*, November 2, 1867; *Macon Telegraph*, November 15, 1867.

Joshua Hill was "quietly attending to the practice of law" as were Herschel Johnson, Ben Hill, Joe Brown, and Alexander Stephens. James Johnson was taking up the collectorship job in Savannah that the president had first offered to Hill. Robert Toombs was said to be "in foreign parts." All would soon be called back to politics in one way or another.[17]

Becoming a Republican

From mid-1866 to mid-1868, Joshua Hill worked to restore his political as well as his financial stature. Having turned down various patronage positions because they did not pay enough and would have restricted his other activities, Joshua Hill could concentrate on the practice of law in Georgia and Washington, DC, and keep a close eye on political developments. Despite his frustrations at the constitutional convention and his deep disappointment at not being chosen as senator, Hill still commanded a loyal following among a group of White Unionists who were loath to put their state in the hands of Democrats. Postwar frustrations eventually pushed many such men into some level of affiliation with Georgia's Republicans, but their inherent conservatism on property, class, and race restrained them from a full embrace of the Radical Republican agenda.

In summer 1866, Hill and James Johnson traveled to Washington to mend fences. The former congressman visited the floor of the House of Representatives where he "was greeted very cordially by many of the members" who had served with him before the war. Hill reported to T. P. Saffold, "The President & his cabinet have been kind & polite to me." In a telling comment that presaged Hill's political future, Hill told his friend, "I am greeted very kindly by all men, that did not sympathize with rebellion. It is true, however, that the Republicans, generally, are the most cordial." Along with a few other staunch Unionists, Hill had been one of the favorite Southerners of the non-Copperhead Northern press ever since his antisecession efforts in the weeks after Abraham Lincoln's election. Such adulation persisted into his visit to the nation's capital and reflected the continuing but mostly unfulfilled Lincoln-like vision that loyal Southern Unionists would form the basis of postwar Southern governments. Some

---

[17] *Memphis Avalanche*, October 26, 1866 (Augusta correspondent in *Cincinnati Enquirer*).

of the most effusive praise of the leading Georgia Unionist came from a Camden, New Jersey, column:

> Two worthies graced the Halls of Congress this week, who reflect honor upon the South, themselves, and the nation—Gov. [Jack] Hamilton of Texas and Joshua Hill, of Georgia, both of whom contend that white rebels should not be esteemed more highly than black patriots.... When Mr. Hill was forced to leave Congress at the outbreak of the rebellion, he shed bitter tears over the folly of his constituents.

In short, the writer concluded: "These men stood by the Government in its hour of peril."[18]

In the anticipation of the upcoming congressional elections in fall 1866, two different political groups scheduled summer conventions, both in Philadelphia. The National Union Convention supported President Johnson while the Southern Loyalists Convention, which met second, looked to build the Republican Party in the South. Joshua Hill found himself caught in the middle. The National Union convention presented him with an especially difficult dilemma. On the one hand, Hill had been supportive of Johnson's approach to Reconstruction, and he valued his fruitful relationship with the president. On the other hand, despite its pretensions of bipartisanship, the National Union movement was, in the words of a leading historian of Reconstruction, "essentially a front for the Democratic party." To make the event even more anathema to Hill, Alexander H. Stephens and Herschel V. Johnson were chosen to lead the Georgia delegation though in the end they did not attend. Alexander's brother Linton and a few others constituted the on-site Georgia delegation at the distinctly Democratic event. Up to that point Hill had been a supporter of Johnson's policies, so his absence at the National Union convention was conspicuous. Hill shared his misgivings about pro-Johnson convention with Saffold, and

[18] Hill to Saffold, July 21, 1866; *Cincinnati Enquirer*, June 27, 1866 (was greeted); *Macon Telegram*, July 1, 1866; *Augusta Constitutionalist*, July 3, 1866; *Newnan Herald*, July 7, 1866; *Federal Union*, July 10, 1866; *Springfield (MA) Republican*, July 14, 1866; *Camden West Jersey Press*, July 11, 1866.

a wire story confirmed, "Joshua Hill, the Union leader, emphatically denounces and repudiates the movement."[19]

Although Hill rejected the Democrat-dominated, pro-Johnson convention, he was not yet ready to go all the way to becoming a Republican. At first, it seemed that he was leaning toward supporting the Southern Loyalists Convention. A Pennsylvania paper listed Hill among those "patriots" who had endorsed the call. Just days before the convention opened, newspapers in Philadelphia still listed Hill among the anticipated speakers, along with Parson Brownlow and Jack Hamilton. However, at the last minute, the cautious Georgian calculated the political risk of being associated with a racially mixed Republican-dominated gathering and decided against attending even though some of his supporters did. Hill later wrote to Horace Greeley to explain that his attendance would have subjected him to "an avalanche of ridicule and contempt.... almost as great as it was in the days of the rebellion." Indeed, those Georgians who did attend faced the predicted avalanche of opprobrium. The *Atlanta Intelligencer* expressed outrage that the convention had given "its public adhesion to the doctrines of negro equality," and the state capital's leading paper hyperbolized that "So wicked, so disgraceful and mean a Convention [has] never before assembled in this country." The influential *Augusta Chronicle & Sentinel* referred to the meeting, at which Frederick Douglass and other Black leaders spoke, as the "N[—] Worshippers' Convention" and concluded, "There isn't a white man in the State but will rejoice if they [the Georgia delegates] never come back."[20]

---

[19] Hill to Saffold, July 21, 1866; *Macon Telegraph*, August 20, 1866; *Rome Courier*, July 14, 1866; Trelease, *Reconstruction*, 67 (essentially); *Philadelphia Evening Telegram*, August 11, 1866; *Newark (NJ) Advertiser*, July 23, 1866; *Burlington (VT) Daily Times*, August 13, 1866 (*Albany Evening Journal*); *Richmond (VA) Times*, August 8, 1866; *Augusta Constitutionalist*, July 10, 11, 1866; *Milledgeville Federal Union*, July 10, 1966; Abbott, *Republican Party and the South*, 66–71; Baggett, *Scalawags*, 179, 210; Conway, *Reconstruction of Georgia*, 137–38; Perman, *Reunion without Compromise*, 195–231; Parks, *Joseph E. Brown*, 363; Nathans, *Losing the Peace*, 14–15; Guelzo, *Fateful Lighting*, 496; McKitrick, *Andrew Johnson and Reconstruction*, 413–16.

[20] *Worcester Massachusetts Spy*, July 27, 1866; *Washington (PA) Reporter*, July 18, 1866 (patriots); *Philadelphia Evening Telegram and Inquirer*, August 31–September 4, 1866; Hill to Greeley, September 22, 1866, quoted in Foner,

In the November 1866 elections, Democratic congressional candidates carried Georgia but lost badly nationwide. Hill was "jolly over the glorious news" of Republican victories, according to a letter that an Augusta observer wrote to a friend. A Washington reporter declared that Hill now "stands with Congress, and against the President's policy." The Madisonian would soon become an open, if conservative, Republican.[21]

After the election, Hill headed for Washington again. In January 1867, he and his Texas friend Jack Hamilton were guests on the floor of Congress. They sat near Thaddeus Stevens and took "deep interest" in his argument that Southern states should be considered in the status of territories. His interest in Stevens's ideas may have been even deeper than the press suspected. Hill confided to Saffold that even though the Radical's arguments "called forth bitter reproaches," his critics had not provided "refutations of its historical facts, or of its logic. He is too bitter and relentless toward the President—and too credulous of wrongs done the Freedmen—but yet in his earnestness and arguments he is a man of power." The very fact that the Georgian had given an ear to Stevens was too much for Democrats to swallow. Even though he did not consider the case of much importance, Hill joined journalists and politicians in the gallery of the US Supreme Court to listen to arguments in the ultimately unsuccessful lawsuit to block military reconstruction by injunction. Meanwhile, Hill kept in touch with leading politicians and businessmen, even with those whom he normally opposed. He told Saffold that he had "introduced [Joe] Brown around here." Future governor Rufus Bullock wrote to him in spring 1867 to explain that he thought that "hearty acquiescence" with the Sherman bill (i.e., Congressional Reconstruction) would be good for Georgia business. In early 1867 Hill sat down with Ulysses S. Grant, and they "had a

---

Reconstruction, 270, and in Coulter, *South during Reconstruction*, 117; *Atlanta Intelligencer*, September 11, 1866; *Milledgeville Federal Union*, September 18, 25, 1866; *Augusta Chronicle*, September 19, 1866.

[21] *Belmont Chronicle* (St. Clairsville, OH), October 25, 1866 (jolly, *Springfield [OH] Republic*); *Chicago Tribune*, November 16, 1866; *Montpelier (VT) Daily Journal*, November 19, 1866, (stands); *Columbia (SC) Daily Phoenix*, November 16, 1866 (*New York Herald*).

good laugh" about how Southerners had "badly humbugged" the general on his fact-finding trip through the region in late 1865.[22]

The series of acts that constituted the basis of Congressional Reconstruction became law over Andrew Johnson's vetoes in March and July 1867. Taken together, the acts divided the Confederacy (except Tennessee, which was already readmitted) into five military districts, each to be overseen by a Union general. Georgia was in the Fifth District along with Florida and Alabama. Commanding general John Pope established his headquarters in Atlanta, which provided him excellent rail access to the whole district. The most far-reaching requirements of the acts were that the ex-Confederate states must enfranchise adult Black males and ratify the Fourteenth Amendment. The amendment was designed to enshrine the main principles of the Civil Rights Act of 1866 into the Constitution, i.e., citizenship and equal protection of the laws for the freed people. To carry this into effect, the Reconstruction Acts required states to call constitutional conventions in fall 1867 with delegates elected by a racially mixed electorate. The acts banned most high-ranking Confederate officials from holding government positions, allowed commanders to remove civil officials as needed, and empowered military courts to act when necessary. In short, the law required Georgia and most ex-Confederate states to repeat the process from late 1865, but this time with more explicit expectations and more federal supervision.[23]

The Georgia rolls for the convention included 190,000 voters, a bare majority of whom were White. Democrats were appalled by the thought of a constitutional convention that would be elected by a biracial electorate and would include some Black delegates. The convention call had to pass by a majority of the total number of registered voters, not just a majority of those voting. This provision provided Democrats in Georgia and other states facing reconstruction with the strategy of noncooperation since

[22] *Boston Herald*, January 4, 1867, and *Springfield (MA) Republican*, January 4, 1867 (deep interest); *Augusta Chronicle*, January 16, 1867; *Macon Telegraph*, May 10, 1867; *Augusta Daily Press*, April 27, 1867 (*Augusta Constitutionalist*); Bullock to Hill, March 7, 1867, in Duncan, *Entrepreneur for Equality*, 19–20; Edwards, *Legal History of the Civil War*, **[page?]**; Hill to Saffold, April 7, 1867 (Stevens & Grant**[clarify?]**).

[23] Downs, *After Appomattox*, 3–5, *passim*; Edwards, *Legal History of the Civil War*, 79–81, 98; Guelzo, *Reconstruction*, 40.

staying away from the polls would be tantamount to a "no" vote. The strategy, actively pressed by Ben Hill, almost worked, but Democrats were too dispirited to carry it to fruition. Enough Whites, mainly from the Northern mountain and Southern wiregrass regions, joined with Blacks to cast just enough votes in favor of the convention to achieve the requisite majority of all registered voters.[24]

Overwhelming Black support carried the day for conventions to be held in other states as well. However, Black men constituted a majority of the actual delegates in only three of ten. Despite freedmen constituting almost half of Georgia's eligible voters, only 35 of the state's 165 elected delegates were Black. In order to ensure the availability of decent housing accommodations for the Black delegates, General Pope ordered the convention venue to be changed from Milledgeville to Atlanta, soon to become the state capital. Although precise party classification is difficult to determine, it is clear that a majority of the delegates were avowed Republicans. Most of the White delegates had been born in Georgia, and several others had lived in the state for many years. Despite contemporary and subsequent claims to the contrary, neither so-called carpetbaggers nor Black people dominated the convention.[25]

The constitutional convention convened on December 9, 1867, and lasted into the early months of the next year. It wrestled with such issues as debt relief, homestead exemption from bankruptcy, legislative apportionment, and, most importantly, whether the granting of Black suffrage included the right of African Americans to hold elective office. Emphasis varied from state to state, but the same basic issues predominated in all ten conventions. Georgia Republicans understood that their long-term prospects would be doomed if all of the state's White males regained the franchise and united against them, so they endeavored (with mixed success) to keep the party unified on the surface. The convention ultimately left the

---

[24] Nathans, *Losing the Peace*, 45–55; Wynne, *Continuity of Cotton*, 30–32; Conway, *Reconstruction of Georgia*, 148–49; Perman, *Reunion without Compromise*, 308–36; Foner, *Reconstruction*, 314; Abbott, *Republican Party and the South*, 136–37; Summers, *Ordeal of the Reunion*, 130–34.

[25] Delegate numbers from Wynne, *Continuity of Cotton*, 29–34; Conway, *Reconstruction of Georgia*, 137–61; Nathans, *Losing the Peace*, 56–64; Fraser, *Savannah in the New South*, 36–37. On Atlanta becoming the capital, see Venet, *Changing Wind*; Russell, *Atlanta 1847–1890*; and Shingleton, *Richard Peters*.

question of Black office-holding unresolved because, in the words of one historian of late-nineteenth-century Georgia politics, "The Republicans hoped to work both sides of the street."[26]

The final document was not nearly as extreme as its opponents charged, but in their minds, any document that included Black suffrage was by definition outrageously radical. Ben Hill charged that the anticipated new constitution would permanently enthrone "Negro supremacy." Herschel Johnson described the palpable anger that he, and by extension most of the White elite, felt in December 1867: "At the end of such a career I find myself disfranchised and assigned by the dominant Despots in congress a position, politically subordinate to my former slaves, and a Convention is now in Session at Atlanta, whose object it to put my native State and all others of the South under negro Dominion!!!"[27]

Unlike in 1865, Joshua Hill was not a delegate to the 1867–1868 convention. While preparations were underway in summer and fall 1867, he had become "dangerously ill" while in Washington. In October he explained to a friend that he had been so sick that he found it difficult to concentrate and had been unable to walk. Fortunately, by early December, Hill had recovered enough to return to Madison "to take up abode in his old home" and to play a tangential role in convention proceedings.[28]

Just as he was recovering and only a few days before the convention began, Hill's name entered the political calculations of generals Pope and Grant. If all went well with ratification of the new Georgia constitution, Pope would appoint an interim caretaker provisional governor. However, there was a real possibility that ratification would fail, so the federal command needed a contingency plan to appoint a more prominent provisional governor to serve for a longer and more contentious period if needed. After Hill recovered but before he returned home, he met with General Grant to discuss affairs in Georgia. Presumably as a result of that meeting, on

---

[26] Wynne, *Continuity of Cotton*, 32–43, 39 (the Republicans); Nathans, *Losing the Peace*, 57–64; Summers, *Ordeal of the Reunion*, 130–34.

[27] Wynne, *Continuity of Cotton*, 32–33; Conway, *Reconstruction of Georgia*, 152 (Ben Hill); Johnson, "From the Autobiography of Hershel V. Johnson," 336.

[28] *Milledgeville Federal Union*, June 11, 1867 (dangerously ill); *Rome Courier*, June 14, 1867; *New York Herald*, June 16, 1867; *(Macon) Georgia Telegram*, September 27, October 18, 1867; *(Athens) Southern Watchman*, December 4, 1867 (to take up).

November 2, 1867, Grant telegraphed to Pope to "suggest the name of Joshua Hill" if the need arose. Back in Georgia, Hill made no secret of the recommendation, and one cynical Savannah writer called him a "restless politician" who was walking around "with a letter in his pocket" from the exalted general. Suspicious that Hill would be too accommodating to old Confederates if he were appointed, the Radical Republican faction urged General Pope to select Rufus Bullock of Augusta.[29]

Even though he was not a delegate and could not officially participate in debate, Hill went to Atlanta, and the body tendered him a seat on the floor "during his sojourn in the city." Despite some resistance from Democrats, Hill's friends convinced the convention to invite him to speak to the assembled delegates and other invited guests on the evening of December 17. He began by apologizing that he was still a bit weak from his lingering illness and could not speak at length, but he spoke long enough to argue that any leaders of the late rebellion who were not truly penitent should remain disfranchised and that freedmen should have the right to vote. Most provocatively, the unapologetic Unionist proclaimed that he would have left the South if the Confederacy had won the war.[30]

The response from anti-Reconstruction Democrats was swift, bitter, and overtly racist. The *Macon Telegraph* headline proclaimed: "Joshua Hill for White Disfranchisement." Another Macon writer charged that Hill's many friends were mortified by his "extreme positions," which showed that he had finally "parted with all his Southern sympathies and instincts during his brief residence at Washington." The *Atlanta Intelligencer* sneered that Hill showed "an attitude of hostility to the race whose blood swells

---

[29] U. S. Grant to John Pope, in Grant, *Papers of Ulysses S. Grant* (telegrams), 18:30; *Columbus Enquirer*, November 13, 1867; *Georgia Weekly Opinion*, November 15, 1867; *Savannah News & Herald*, December 24, 1867 (restless); *Columbus Enquirer*, December 21, 1867; *Atlanta Daily Opinion*, November 15, 19, 1867; *Augusta Constitutionalist*, December 27, 1867; Nathans, *Losing the Peace*, 70; *New York Times*, December 19, 1867; *Cincinnati Gazette*, December 18, 24, 1867; *Wilmington (NC) Journal*, December 27, 1867; *Washington Evening Star*, December 17, 1867.

[30] *Journal of the Proceedings of the Constitutional Convention of the People of Georgia* [1867–1868], 48 (during); *Augusta Constitutionalist*, December 19, 1867; *Chicago Tribune*, December 18, 1867; *Cincinnati Gazette*, December 19, 1867; Chicago *Inter Ocean*, December 21, 1867.

within [his] every vein" and was now in alliance with the "radical-negro party in its further disfranchisement and degradation of our people." To the editor, Hill was no longer a "Union man—honest and conscientious. We have now to view him in his new character." An Augusta columnist charged that Hill's speech "disgusted every Southern man who is not as degraded as himself.... It only pleased the negroes, to whom it was largely addressed." Hill's confession that he would have left Georgia upon Confederate triumph was, according to a widely reprinted article, "much to the delight of the Yankees present."[31]

Pro-Reconstruction Northern papers interpreted Hill and his speech far differently. A Concord, New Hampshire, editor explained that Hill had made it clear that "Georgia owed all her misery to her old politicians, who ought never again to be permitted to hold power." An optimistic Indiana Republican offered Hill as proof that even Black Belt plantation owners could be part of their party: "Mr Hill has always been a Union man, and notwithstanding Copperhead assertions than none but negroes and poor, mean Whites support reconstruction in the South, he is one of the foremost men of Georgia in character, intelligence and worth." As before, such popularity in Northern eyes did Hill no good at home.[32]

Andrew Johnson became irritated with General Pope for being too cozy with Republicans, so the president replaced him with General George G. Meade, who took office the first week of January 1868. Whatever plans that Pope and Grant had in mind for Joshua Hill were thereby swept aside. Meade removed both Governor Jenkins and the state treasurer from office and replaced them with military officers who reported directly to him. Once again, as it had been in 1865, Joshua Hill seemed to be on the verge

---

[31] *Macon Telegraph*, December 22, 27 (Joshua), 1867; January 3, 1868; *(Macon) Georgia Telegraph*, December 27, 1867 (extreme); *Atlanta Intelligencer*, December 25, 27, 1867; *Augusta Constitutionalist*, December 27, 1867(disgusted); *Athens Southern Recorder*, December 24, 1867 (much to, from *Atlanta Intelligencer*).

[32] *Concord (NH) Independent Democrat*, December 26, 1867; *Cincinnati Gazette* and *Chicago Tribune*, December 18, 1867; *Washington (PA) Reporter*, January 8, 1865; *Chicago Inter Ocean*, December 21, 1867; *(Plymouth, IN) Marshall County Reporter*, December 26, 1867.

of becoming provisional governor, but it slipped away because Andrew Johnson, via Meade, found him too controversial.[33]

Georgia's Divided Republican Party

Political party lines in Georgia were slow to solidify from 1865 to early 1868 but were becoming clear by the time the General Assembly convened in July 1868. By this time Georgia Democrats, like those in the other Deep South states, had begun to put aside their divisions and unify in angry resistance to military occupation and to Radical Republican demands to extend suffrage and civil rights to the former slaves. Any cooperative steps that they agreed to, such as ratification of the Fourteenth and Fifteenth amendments, were undertaken only as strategic necessities to obtain their twin goals of rapid readmission to the Union and White men's full control of state government. Republicans, meanwhile, remained fractured. At the broadest level there were three groups: (1) newly enfranchised Black men; (2) White Radicals who from conviction, opportunism, or both worked closely with Black people, and (3) White conservatives and moderates who opposed Democratic rule and acquiesced in Black suffrage but were hesitant to embrace extensive Black participation in governance and were solidly against interracial socialization. Joshua Hill stood in the third category. At any given time, the lines between Radical and moderate/conservative Republicans could blur depending on specific issues, personal agendas, and the level of Democratic threat.[34]

The pro-Democratic White supremacists who wrote the first published histories of Reconstruction used the highly oversimplified classification of "carpetbagger" and "scalawag" to describe the White Republican factions. At the most basic level, White Northerners who came South after the war and got involved with the Republican party were "carpetbaggers"

[33] Brig. Gen. Thomas H. Ruger became provisional governor, and Capt. C. F. Rockwell served as treasurer (Nathans, *Losing the Peace*, 70–72; Duncan, *Entrepreneur for Equality*, 37–49).

[34] Wynne, *Continuity of Cotton*; Conway, *Reconstruction of Georgia*; Nathans, *Losing the Peace*; Duncan, *Entrepreneur for Equality* (Bullock); Currie-McDaniel, *Carpetbagger of Conscience* (Bryant); Parks, *Joseph E. Brown*; Cimbala, *Under the Guardianship of the Nation* (Freedmen's Bureau); Drago, *Black Politicians*; Shadgett, *Republican Party in Georgia.*

while native White Southerners who voted Republican were "scalawags." Unfortunately, this overly simplistic interpretation persists even today in some circles. To be sure, contemporaneous journalists and politicians were not afraid to use the terms pejoratively when it suited their purposes, but they understood that the actual party divisions were more subtle and fluid than the simplistic "carpet bagger" versus "scalawag" labels implied. Joshua Hill's role in the Reconstruction-era Republican party illustrates such subtleties.[35]

South Carolina born Joshua Hill, who spent his entire adult life in Georgia, who never relented his opposition to secession, who eschewed involvement in the Confederate government, who advised cooperation with Reconstruction, and who affiliated with the Republican Party was, at the most basic level, the very definition of a scalawag. Still, even his opponents hardly ever classified him this way. The Democratic press often mentioned Hill alongside other native-South Republican politicians whom they dubbed scalawags while withholding the term from Hill. To be sure, one can readily imagine that when Georgia Democrats gathered privately they may have used words like "damn scalawag lawyer" to describe the Madisonian, but such language did not make its way into normal public discourse. A word proximity search of the Georgia Historic Newspapers database from 1867 to 1873 produced no examples of Hill being called a scalawag. One reference written by a fellow Madisonian came close but backed off. The anonymous correspondent decried that his native county "contains some '*manner born*' scalawags." Of Joshua Hill specifically, he wrote, "When I look upon that gentleman, who I know is a gentleman—

[35] During Reconstruction, only 13 percent of Georgia's more than 130 newspapers leaned Republican, the lowest percentage in the South, according to Abbott, *Republican Party and the South*, 93–94, 125–26. Baggett classifies all "white supporters of Congressional Reconstruction" as scalawags for the purposes of his "collective biography approach" (*Scalawags*, xi–xii, 7). This has the unfortunate effect of blurring intraparty differences. He mentions Hill several times but never acknowledges that contemporaries did not regard him as a "scalawag" (*Scalawags*, 9, 36–37, 51, 75, 92, 165–68, 172, 210). See Tunnell, "Creating 'The Propaganda of History,'" 791, 812–822, and Degler, *The Other South*, 198–99, 222–23, 228–33.

too much so to be in this scalawag crowd—I can but regret his *blindness* and his fatal error."[36]

Certainly, radical versus moderate and conservative is a more useful, if still fluid, way than carpetbagger versus scalawag to explain the fractionalization of Georgia's White Republicans. This distinction, however, was often obscured by Democrats who employed the term "radical" to refer to all Republicans. For example, in July 1868 a correspondent wrote, "There are two distinct Radical parties" in the state legislature. Or similarly, "The split in the Radical ranks seems to be widening daily." Occasionally such editors and writers would distinguish between radicals and "ultra Radicals." It served their partisan purpose to portray all Georgia Republicans as allies of the likes of true Radicals like Thaddeus Stevens and Charles Sumner. In fact, there were very real differences between Georgia's radicals and their more moderate and conservative rivals within the Republican Party.[37]

At the broadest level of explanation, Southern radical Republicans were more willing to bring freedmen into their ranks, albeit seldom in major leadership roles, than their moderate/conservative counterparts. Determining who was a moderate and who was a conservative is a much more difficult classification. Neither the press of the day nor the historians of the last 150 years have been consistent. In the case of Joshua Hill, he was unquestionably of conservative mindset in that he hoped that Reconstruction would bring as little change as possible to the social order of the South, yet he was not conservative enough to join the Democratic establishment. On the other hand, he was a political moderate in that he advocated for fair and honest, if subordinate, treatment of freed people, and he acquiesced in the necessity and reality of Black suffrage and limited Black office-holding. He balked at any suggestion of equal social interactions between the races during his lifetime, but he mused that the relationship might change with

[36] "Scalawag" and "Joshua/Josh Hill" proximity search was performed with the Georgia Historic Newspapers site of the Digital Library of Georgia (gahistoriannewspapers.galileo.usg.edu); *(Macon) Georgia Journal & Messenger*, September 8, 1868; *Dawson Journal*, September 10, 1868 (manor born), italics in original; *Dawson Journal*, August 6, 1868; *Columbus Sun*, August 4, 1868; D. Roberts, *Joseph E. Brown*, 58 (*(Athens) Southern Banner*).

[37] *Macon Telegraph*, July 10 (ultra), 24 (there are), 1868; *(Athens) Southern Watchman*, July 15, 1868.

time as future generations of African Americans became more experienced and educated. Was Joshua Hill a conservative moderate or a moderate conservative? It does not matter. When it comes to delineating between moderate and conservative Republicans one must simply accept equivocation and pay attention to context.

The election for ratification of the Constitution of 1868 and the election of a new governor and General Assembly was set for April. In January, even before the constitutional convention adjourned, Joshua Hill was among the several Republicans spoken of as possible nominees for governor. He discussed the possibility with Atlanta Republican Dr. N. L. Angier and others. However, the Radical faction controlled the party apparatus, so Hill stood little chance of being nominated. Rufus Bullock, leader of the so-called Augusta Ring of Radical Republicans, became the gubernatorial standard bearer. To oppose Bullock, the Democrats finally settled on war hero John B. Gordon. Despite being a Confederate general, Gordon was eligible because he had held no prewar office that had required him to take an oath of loyalty to the United States. When the choice eventually boiled down to Bullock or Gordon, Hill's distaste for Bullock was so intense that he and fellow Madisonians T. P. Saffold and A. G. Foster, as well as other "original Republicans and Union men of Georgia," decided to split their tickets by voting in favor of the 1868 constitution and for Gordon as governor even though the general had spoken out against ratification.[38]

Under the protection of federal troops and the Freedman's Bureau when available and courageously on their own when not, thousands of former slaves went to the polls, often in defiance of economic intimidation and threats of violence. Thanks primarily to those Black voters, the 1868 Constitution comfortably won, and Republican Rufus Bullock edged out John B. Gordon to become governor. The conservative strategy to both

[38] Hill to T. P. Saffold & A. G. Foster, January 28, 1868, Saffold Family Papers, MCA (Angier); *New York Times*, March 14, 1868; *Cincinnati Gazette*, March 7, 11, 1868; Chicago *Inter Ocean*, April 8, 1868; *Macon Telegraph*, March 13, 1868; Duncan, *Entrepreneur for Equality*, 36–50; Eckert, *John Brown Gordon*, 143–45; Conway, *Reconstruction of Georgia*, 156–58, 161; Nathans, *Losing the Peace*, 82–94; Hill to L. N. Trammell, March 17, 1868, in Conway, *Reconstruction of Georgia*, 157n; *Macon Telegraph*, April 17, 1868; *New York World*, July 31, 1868; *Savannah News & Herald*, April 3, 1868; *Newnan Herald*, April 11, 1868; *Macon Telegram*, April 17, 1868; *Atlanta Opinion*, March 22, 1868.

favor ratification on practical grounds and to support Gordon ultimately failed. It did, however, make enough difference that Bullock's total lagged almost five thousand votes behind ratification.[39]

Northern-born Bullock had not moved to Georgia until the late 1850s, but he had served the Confederacy in the quartermaster corp. Thus, in the eyes of contemporary opponents, the Augusta Republican stood on the cusp of being either a carpetbagger or a scalawag. Bullock led the so-called "August Ring" along with Foster Blodgett, Benjamin Conley, and John E. Bryant. Blodgett, Bullock's closest ally, was the postmaster and later mayor, and he controlled significant patronage. Conley was a prewar Unionist Whig, mayor of Augusta before Blodgett, and railroad executive. John E. Bryant was a quintessential carpetbagger who came to Georgia to work for the Freedman's Bureau and then helped form the Georgia Equal Rights Association that organized African American voters. Bryant remained moderate to Radical in politics, but he broke with the Augusta Ring by the end of 1868, partly at the urging of Joshua Hill and Henry Farrow, who approached Bryant in early 1868 to apprise him of their opinions of Blodgett's questionable character.[40]

The newly elected General Assembly included thirty-two Black Georgians (all Republicans). Radical-leaning Republicans won clear control of the state senate and elected Conley as the presiding officer. In the House of Representatives, however, there were enough moderate and conservative Republicans to keep either the Democrats or the Radical Republicans from dominating. The congressional delegation was also split.[41]

The first business of the new legislature was to comply with the requirement of the Reconstruction Acts by ratifying the Fourteenth Amendment. However distasteful they may have found it, most Democrats

---

[39] Wynne, *Continuity of Cotton*, 52–53; Abbott, *Republican Party and the South*, 160.

[40] Duncan, *Entrepreneur for Equality*, *passim*; Cashin, *Story of Augusta*, 130–35; Currie-McDaniel, *Carpetbagger of Conscience*, 88–89; *Columbus Enquirer*, July 12, 1868.

[41] Duncan, *Entrepreneur for Equality*, 50–51, counts sixty-seven Radical Republicans, twenty-six moderate Republicans, and eighty Democrats. Speaker R. L. McWhorter was a moderate Republican, friendly to the Democrats (Nathans, *Losing the Peace*, 112–13). The exact count of the number of Black members varies due to racial classification disputes regarding some members.

realized that they had no choice but to agree to the ratification if they wanted Congress to readmit the state. Unrepentant rebels, including Robert Toombs, continued to preach resistance to the federal mandate, but practicality and realism prevailed.[42] The next significant order of business was to select Georgia's two United States senators.

The "Earliest Traitor" Becomes Senator-elect

Just as in 1866, there were two senatorial seats to fill. This time, it was a long term of office ending in 1873 and a short term ending in 1871. Speculation about senatorial candidates began more than six months before the legislature convened. Joshua Hill and Joseph E. Brown were at or near the top of virtually every list.[43]

On June 15, 1868, about two weeks before the legislature was set to convene, Hill wrote Brown, his long-time but mostly cordial rival, a plaintive confidential letter. For the first time, they were in the same political party, albeit in different factions. Hill related to Brown that during his long and serious illness he had engaged in "sober reflection upon my own life":

> In analyzing my own character, I find that if no one had sought to depreciate me, I had never been a candidate for office. It was antagonism or the love of triumph over adversaries that lured me to political contests. I always felt that I erred in running for Congress.... I think I care less for place than I ever did —immeasurably less. And yet temptations assail me at many points. I have antagonists. They ascribe to me ambitions [and] aspirations and seek to depreciate me. Some of these come under the guise of friendship. They irritate and arouse me. I know not of your plans and I have not the right to inquire.

Hill regretted that the communication between the two of them had not been better in recent months. "I got sick. I came nigh of dying—no letter ever came. Why did you fail to write?" Then, in what was apparently a thinly veiled allusion to the Senate election, Hill declared, "It is not unlikely that I may conclude soon to say something to the public. Its tenor in

---

[42] *Columbus Enquirer*, July 10, 1868; Duncan, *Entrepreneur for Equality*, 52.

[43] *Savannah News & Herald*, November 13, 1867; *Atlanta Intelligencer*, June 6, 1868; *Macon Telegraph*, June 7, 24, July 17, 1868; *Augusta Chronicle*, June 12, 1868; *(Athens) Southern Watchman*, June 15, 1868; *Columbus Enquirer*, July 8, 1868.

some respect will depend on the course of others. Like most of my outpourings, it will be more candid than politic." Hill then turned to the intricacies of party politics: "I am satisfied that there is a fixed purpose, if possible, to destroy my influence in the Republican party of the State. Of course, it has origin in that party—though the Democrats will rejoice to see it done. I don't blame them for desiring it. Now, I feel that I can get along without a party if needed, as well as the party can without me." Whether it was for "love of triumph" or for other reasons, Hill soon found himself aligned directly against his recent correspondent and smack in the middle of Republican party strife.[44]

Like Joshua Hill, Joe Brown had maneuvered the political shoals and had hesitated to identify with either political party for more than two years following the end of the Civil War. But unlike Hill, the former governor's course seemed more motivated by political aspirations than ideological conviction. As a prewar Democrat, Brown's eventual transition to Republican identity was far more surprising than that of his old Whig/American (Know-Nothing) rival. Almost all of Brown's fellow high-level Confederate officeholders had come out strongly against the Reconstruction Acts of 1867 and had worked hard to help Democrats in the state elections of April 1868. Brown took a different track. He assessed the national political landscape and determined that cooperation with federal authorities offered him the best route to return to power. In the words of his principal biographer, Joe Brown was most concerned about "on which side of the bread was the butter." Brown supported Rufus Bullock over General Gordon in the contest for governor, thereby winning Bullock's cautious allegiance. He advised General Grant about patronage opportunities, and he served as a delegate to the Republican national convention in Chicago. All of this was to the great chagrin of Brown's old Democratic friends, who came to regard the former governor as a crassly opportunistic turncoat.[45]

The General Assembly convened July 4, 1868, at Atlanta City Hall. Later that afternoon, Joshua Hill, Joe Brown, and other Republicans gave speeches at a Republican rally for Grant. The local *Constitution*, which

---

[44] Hill to Brown, June 15, 1868, Brown Family Papers, HRBML. Hill dined with Brown in January 1868 during the constitutional convention (Parks, *Joseph E. Brown*, 423).

[45] Parks, *Joseph E. Brown*, 364 (on which), 367, 412–19.

leaned Democratic, estimated the crowd at about two thousand—80 percent Black. The reporter opined that Hill appeared uncomfortable addressing such a large mixed audience but acknowledged, "On the whole, there was not a great deal in his speech to condemn." In contrast, the *Constitution* was not so kind to Brown. It dismissed his whole address by declaring that he "did not have much to say."[46]

Atlanta, quite a contrast from sleepy Milledgeville, was abuzz with political activity. Action central for the Democrats was the United States Hotel while Governor Bullock and those following "the ascendant star of Radicalism" booked their rooms at the National. A Macon reporter described the chaotic scene:

> Private consultations, unofficial caucusing and button-holeing go on from morning to night, and almost from night to morning. The "mad hunt for office" was never madder, and it embraces everything from United States' Senator down to one of the three thousand Georgia Justices of the Peace.[47]

The Bullock faction in the legislature, which included almost all of the Black members, was large and influential, but the Augusta Radical could not be confident of a working majority in face of the conservative wing of his own party and a strong minority of Democrats. Bullock strategically decided to back the popular Joe Brown for the long-term Senate seat. For the short term, Bullock's faction put forth his Augusta Ring compatriot Foster Blodgett. Bullock implored General Meade to purge the General Assembly of several Democratic members whom he believed were ineligible to serve under the Test-Oath terms of the Reconstruction Acts. On July 14, Hill advised Saffold, "The *purging* will not be very thorough—it is generally believed." Hill was correct. Meade refused to do Bullock's bidding, so the legislature remained divided with a narrow Republican majority. One Georgia paper accurately observed, "The true key to this 'purging' business is the United States Senatorship." Meade's conduct in

---

[46] *Dalton North Georgia Citizen*, July 16, 1868 (*Atlanta Constitution*); *New York Tribune*, July 6, 1868.

[47] *Columbus Enquirer*, July 12, 1868; *New York Tribune*, July 6, 1868, *Cincinnati Gazette*, July 10, 1868; *Macon Telegraph*, July 10, 1868 (private); *Washington (GA) Gazette*, July 31, 1868 (*Republican Banner*); *Augusta Constitutionalist*, July 25, 1868.

evaluating legislator eligibility would later become an important issue in the controversial seating of Joshua Hill.[48]

On the Democratic side, the names of several possible nominees circulated, but the party soon turned to the ever-popular Alexander H. Stephens. Brown and Stephens were not only rivals for the Senate; they were also at the time facing each other as prosecuting and defense attorneys, respectively, in a high-profile trial in Columbus where alleged members of the Ku Klux Klan were charged with the murder of a "carpetbagger."[49]

The contest pitted two titans of Georgia Civil War politics, but Stephens had no chance of victory if the Republican majority stood united. The situation put Joshua Hill's faction of the Republican party in the driver's seat. A journalist styled as PINK aptly observed that "the conservative element" was "more than anxious to unite with the Democrats in electing what may be termed 'middle men.'…Josh Hill is its first choice." Supporting any Republican, even a conservative one, would be distasteful to Democrats, but their anger at Bullock, Blodgett, and the turncoat Brown was so visceral that they faced what one of their number characterized as "Hobson's choice." Another Democrat called Hill a "hard pill" to swallow but was willing to take the medicine. Another anti-Brown Democrat declared that he preferred Hill along with another conservative Republican because, unlike Bullock and company, they would be "gentlemen, whatever political views they may entertain."[50]

The days up to the final vote were filled with all sorts of rumors about behind-the-scenes maneuvers and possible deals. Some observers expected Hill to be elected along with John E. Bryant, the former member of Bullock's ring who was known to covet the senatorship. The names of several

---

[48] Nathans, *Losing the Peace*, 108–14; Duncan, *Entrepreneur for Equality*, 51–52; *Augusta Constitutionalist*, July 7, 1868; *Columbus Enquirer*, July 8, 1868; *Macon Telegraph*, July 10, 17 (true key), 1868; Hill to T. P. Saffold, July 14, 1868, Saffold Family Papers, MCA.

[49] Schott, *Alexander H. Stephens*, 477–81; *Augusta Constitutionalist*, July 29, 1868 (*New York Times*); *Augusta Chronicle*, August 5, 1868; *(Athens) Southern Watchman*, August 12, 1868; *Macon Telegram*, July 31, 1868; *Savannah News & Herald*, July 16, 1868; D. Roberts, *Joseph E. Brown*, 58.

[50] *Macon Telegraph*, July 24 (two), 31 (conservative), 1868; *Augusta Constitutionalist*, July 7 (Hobson's), 10 (hard pill), 1868; *Columbus Enquirer*, July 8, 1868 (gentlemen).

other Republicans to pair with Hill also circulated. Desperate to save at least one seat for their wing of the party, some Radicals apparently made a last ditch offer to sell out Blodgett and support Brown for the long-term seat and Hill for the short. Some commentators asserted that Hill rejected the bargain himself, and others claimed that Bullock had refused to abandon his ally Blodgett. In either case, no such deal was cut, and the chances for Republican unity remained elusive.[51]

The emerging deal was an ill-kept secret. The Radical-sympathizing *Cincinnati Gazette* expressed anger at the rumor that some Georgia Republicans had "stooped so low as to seek alliances with Democratic and semi-Republican candidates." Joshua Hill was, of course, the principal "semi-Republican." The writer lamented that Robert Toombs, Howell Cobb, and company had "stealthily" taken "advantage of the momentary Republican dismay." A day before the vote, a wire dispatch that appeared in the papers of Boston and several other Northern cities described precisely what was getting ready to happen: "Information from Atlanta, Georgia, is to the effect that a considerable number of the Republican members of the Legislature will support Joshua Hill for Senator in opposition to ex-Gov. Brown and Blodgett," and that a Democrat will get the short-term seat in return. Hill was optimistic. Just days before the vote, he wrote Saffold, "Things look cheering. My friends are in good spirits. Some curious things happening."[52]

Aware that they were not expected to prevail, loyalists on both sides got to vote for their favorites on the first ballot, and then the assembly adjourned. The initial count was Brown 102, Stephens 96, and 13 for Hill. This represented the high-water mark for Brown and Stephens, so the Hill forces held the balance. Desperate last-minute efforts overnight generated

---

[51] *Columbus Sun*, July 28, August 4, 1868; *Augusta Constitutionalist*, July 31, 1868; Currie-McDaniel, *Carpetbagger of Conscience*, 91–92.

[52] Hill to Saffold, July 14, 1868; *Cincinnati Gazette*, July 10, 1868; *New York Times*, August 4; *Augusta Constitutionalist*, July 29, 1868 (*New York Times*); *Boston Traveller*, July 29, 1868 (information); *Macon Telegraph*, July 24, 1868; *Columbus Enquirer*, July 29, 1868. On Toombs's role, see W. Thompson, *Robert Toombs of Georgia*, 229; W. C. Davis, *The Union*, 236; Conway, *Reconstruction of Georgia*, 164. A story in the *Macon Telegraph*, October 7, 1879, includes claims by Toombs that he bought the votes of Black legislators to defeat Brown. The claim was likely more retrospective bragging than truth since Hill won without Black votes.

rumors of various deals, but the basic arrangement that most observers had expected came to fruition the next morning. When the session opened, a few moderate Republicans switched from Brown to Hill and, more importantly, the Democratic delegation flipped almost en masse from Stephens to Hill. The final total was 110 for Hill, 94 for Brown, and one lone holdout for Stephens. Brown's opponents had jammed the gallery, and they burst into shouts of joy upon his defeat. A Washington correspondent colorfully summarized, "Brown fell between two stools, the dislike of original Unionists and the more virulent hatred of the rebels." In the hubbub that ensued following the defeat of Brown, the legislature chose lukewarm Democrat Dr. H. V. M. Miller to be the short-term senator. Miller was a low-profile prewar Unionist who had served the Confederate army as a physician.[53]

Democrats and conservative Republicans had thoroughly outmaneuvered the Radical Bullock-Brown coalition. Had the Radical and conservative Republicans managed to find some way to compromise on a unified ticket, they probably could have won both seats, but the divisions proved too great to overcome. Thus, the result was one moderate-to-conservative Republican in the person of Joshua Hill and one moderate Democrat in the person of Dr. Miller. The epilogue of Michael Perman's influential history of the early years of Reconstruction is titled "The Irrelevance of the Moderates." Perman was correct about the long run, but for at least this fleeting moment in Georgia's reconstruction, the moderates were relevant.[54]

In the speechmaking after the vote, the two senators-elect spoke glowingly of each other, but each man soon made it clear that he would remain loyal to his own political party. Dr. Miller endorsed the Democratic presidential ticket of Horatio Seymour and Francis P. Blair Jr. while Josh

[53] Parks, *Joseph E. Brown*, 422–23; Duncan, *Entrepreneur for Equality*, 63; Nathans, *Losing the Peace*, 114–16; C. Thompson, *Reconstruction in Georgia*, 209–10. The short-term count was Miller, 120, Blodgett 72, and a scattering of votes for others. The national press reported the results widely, e.g., *New York World*, July 31, 1868.

[54] Perman, *Reunion without Compromise*, 337–47.

Hill continued to stand strongly for Grant and spoke favorably of Black voting rights.[55]

Democratic newspapers almost unanimously approved of Dr. Miller even though they would have preferred Stephens. For the most part, they spun the election of Hill in a cautiously positive light as did a Macon editor:

> Mr. Hill was the choice of the more respectable and moderate Republicans, and it is to a combination of this element with the Democrats, that he owes his election. While he has always been a Union man, and since the war generally considered favorable to most of the Radical partisan legislation in reference to the South, he is well known to his fellow citizens as a gentleman of kindly impulses, of the highest personal honor, and of the most unblemished personal integrity. We are assured that if he does not act with the Democratic party at all times, he will not be found stabbing Georgia at Washington.

A central Georgia paper was more concise: "The former congressman is a Republican, but not of the radical stripe."[56]

It was almost de rigueur for Democratic writers to take great pleasure in the defeat of the ex-governor. One crowed that Hill was "immeasurably superior to Joe Brown." Another roundly criticized Hill but conceded that compared to Brown the Madisonian was "the lesser of the two evils." From the little town of Washington, Georgia, near Alexander Stephens's plantation came the shout: "All Christendom will rejoice that Joe Brown is defeated." From elsewhere in the South came the observation, "The election of these gentlemen is considered as a great triumph over Radicalism, and a still greater triumph over the treacherous Joe Brown and Foster

---

[55] *Providence (RI) Evening Press*, August 7, 1868; *Boston Traveller*, August 8, 1868 (necessary, *New Era*); *Augusta Constitutionalist*, August 19 (*Madison Auditor*), August 26, 1868. See *Indianapolis State Sentinel*, August 3, 1868; *Columbus Enquirer*, July 31 (*Atlanta Intelligencer*), August 1 (*Atlanta Constitution*), 1868; *Savannah Daily News & Herald*, August 1, 1868; *New York Herald*, August 2, 1868; *Augusta Chronicle*, August 5, 1868; *New York Tribune*, August 24, 1868; *Columbus Sun*, August 4, 1868; *Macon Telegraph*, August 7, 1868.

[56] *(Macon) Georgia Journal & Messenger*, August 4, 1868 (Mr. Hill); *Macon Telegraph*, July 31, 1868; *Savannah News & Herald*, July 30, 1868; *Sandersville Central Georgian*, August 5, 1868.

Blodgett." Augusta's leading paper proclaimed that the "Augusta ring…is considered hopelessly crushed by the defeat." The *Columbus Sun* exalted, "Two of the worst and most offensive scalawags have been consigned to the same political grave." Given Joe Brown's remarkable resilience, the notice of his political death proved highly premature.[57]

Although most Democrats acquiesced in the election of Hill and Miller as the best deal that they could negotiate, the angrier among them remained bitter. The *Milledgeville Federal Union* spoke for such thoroughly unreconstructed and unrepentant Democrats. It asserted that the election of Hill and Miller was "illegal, unconstitutional, and void…. The mulatto Legislature which elected them is itself the offspring of a negro Convention elected by fraud and military force and pinned together by the bayonet." The *Atlanta Intelligencer* expressed a similar but more circumspect opinion:

> [Democrats] can expect nothing favoring their views from that gentleman [Hill]. He is a "Republican" and favors the election of Grant and Colfax… this fact should be understood by the people of our State, and, recognizing it in its fullest force, we shall have to regard Mr. Hill in his Senatorial character, as not representing, in any degree, the Democratic party of Georgia, and, therefore, not representing the true interests of the State.[58]

The final comment is left to the acerbic pen of Robert Toombs in a postmortem letter to Stephens. In Toombs's worldview, all Republicans, even Joshua Hill, were Radicals, but Joe Brown was even worse because he was a Democratic turncoat: "I preferred that Brown should be beaten by Joshua Hill to almost any other man. It is impossible for you to think worse of the scoundrel [Brown] than I do but it could only be done by a Radical

---

[57] *Macon Telegraph*, July 31, 1868, and *Savannah News & Herald*, July 31, 1868 (immeasurably); *Columbus Sun*, August 11, 1868 (the lesser); *Washington (GA) Gazette*, July 31, 1868 (all Christendom); *Alexandria (VA) Gazette*, July 30 (the election); *Savannah News & Herald*, July 31, 1868 (Augusta ring, *Augusta Chronicle*); *Columbus Sun*, August 4, 1868. Governor Bullock soon appointed Brown to become chief justice of the Georgia Supreme Court as a consolation prize, and later he served as a Democratic US senator (Parks, *Joseph E. Brown*, 424, 475ff).

[58] *Milledgeville Federal Union*, August 4, 1868; *Macon Telegraph*, August 7, 1868 (*Atlanta Intelligencer*).

and *there was political justice in making the earliest traitor defeat the worst one*... I did my utmost to elect [Hill] and ask of him no other favor than not to join us or speak to me."[59]

[59] Toombs to Stephens, August 9, 1868, in Phillips, *Correspondence*, 703, emphasis added.

Chapter 9

Senator-Elect in Limbo, 1868–1869

To review, in April 1868 Georgia voters chose Radical Republican Rufus Bullock as governor and elected a General Assembly with narrow Republican majorities in both chambers. The body convened early in July and immediately ran into a snag. In an effort to seat even more Radicals, Bullock asked General George Meade, the district military commander, to remove the White Democratic members whom Bullock claimed had falsely sworn that they could pass the Test Oath. Meade directed the General Assembly to review the eligibility of the challenged members. The review ended with the legislature having removed none of the challenged members. Bullock's effort to bolster his majority had failed. Meade accepted the result and allowed the General Assembly to proceed as constituted. The members conducted routine organizational business, ratified the Fourteenth Amendment, and then on July 28, 1868, in the compromise described in chapter 8, they chose Joshua Hill and H.V.M. Miller to be Georgia's members in the United States Senate.

At that point, the senatorial controversy seemed resolved. Just three days earlier, the US House of Representatives seated Georgia's delegation without objection, and there was every reason to think that the Senate would do the same. However, a happenstance of time complicated the situation. Immediately after the House seated the Georgia members, both chambers of the 40th Congress went into recess until December and could not immediately welcome Georgia's new senators. Everyone assumed that the Senate would routinely seat Hill and Miller when it reconvened. But it was not to be. Events of the next few months turned a seating that was expected to be routine into a long, drawn-out controversy. The issues played out primarily in the form of bitter conflict between the Radical and the moderate/conservative wings of the Republican Party. Southern

Democrats looked on alternately bemused, angry, and smug knowing that their opponents' struggles would eventually work to their benefit. For those thirty-some months, Joshua Hill remained senator-elect but not senator.

As is almost always the case in politics, the personal aspirations and reputations of the politicians involved complicated the underlying matters of party, policy, and principle. At one time during the extended controversy, there were as many as seven men who laid claim to being rightfully elected as US senator from Georgia. Joshua Hill was the only one of them who ever held a seat for more than a few weeks. As historian Gregory Downs put it in his tome *After Appomattox*, the "furious debate" over Georgia's full readmission and the seating of Hill amounted to "the entire fight over Reconstruction in microcosm."[1]

Georgia Expels Its Black Legislators, September 1868

Thirty-two out of the more than 170 Georgia legislators elected in April 1868 were Black: twenty-nine in the House and three in the Senate. But that was thirty-two too many in the eyes of all Democrats and quite a few Republicans as well. The right of Black men to hold elective office had been a controversial topic at the 1867–1868 Georgia State Constitutional Convention and during the ratification campaign that followed. Democrats adamantly opposed Black office-holding, and the Republicans, with Joe Brown at the forefront, equivocated on the issue to avoid alienating White voters. Early in the legislative session, some Democrats had suggested removing Black members, but the topic was tabled until after the election of US senators and other matters were accomplished.

The topic finally reached the floor of the House for a vote on September 3. An overwhelming eighty-three members voted in favor of expelling the Blacks while only twenty-three White Republicans opposed the expulsion. More than forty White Republicans bowed to pressure from White constituents and yielded to their own racist assumptions either by voting for the purge or by abstaining. A parliamentary ruling prevented Black members from voting on their own fate, but the wide margin of defeat meant that their votes would not have mattered anyway. With similar

[1] Downs, *After Appomattox*, 226.

Republican support, expulsion passed in the Senate about two weeks later by a nearly two-to-one margin.

To compound the travesty, rather than calling for new elections to replace the expelled Black members, the General Assembly simply seated the runners-up from the April elections, all of whom were White Democrats. In many cases, the expelled members had defeated their now-seated White rivals by large margins in majority Black counties. Georgia's hapless White Republicans effectively handed full control of the House of Representatives to the Democrats. The immediate response from Governor Rufus Bullock was blustery but feckless.[2]

As would be expected, Georgia's Black Republican leaders and their remaining White allies were livid that so many of their supposed friends had abandoned them. As he walked out the door, expelled member Henry M. Turner angrily exclaimed, "White men are not to be trusted. They will betray you." Most of the expelled members and many of their supporters gathered in Macon and resolved that they were tired of being used by Whites who took them for granted. One result of the removal of the Black members and the anti-Black legislation that followed was to make Black political leaders even more militant.[3]

Georgia's purge was the most extreme of several anti-Black actions undertaken by the reconstructed states. In the eyes of Northern Republicans, the travesty constituted irrefutable evidence of persistent rebel recalcitrance and defiance. It was common for leading White Southerners to report that peaceful and equitable race relations prevailed in the old Confederate states, but Georgia's actions proved those claims false. Even the moderate-leaning Washington *National Republican* was appalled. The paper called attention to recent comments by the South's favorite general and wrote, "Look to excluding colored men from the Georgia Legislature because they are Black. In short, look to the general disquietude of the South, and the murderous deeds of the Ku-Klux, and then in the light of these

---

[2] Conway, *Reconstruction of Georgia*, 164–68; Duncan, *Entrepreneur for Equality*, 63–64; Nathans, *Losing the Peace*, 101–24; Currie-McDaniel, *Carpetbagger of Conscience*, 94; Drago, *Black Politicians*, 47–53; J. M. Matthews, "Negro Republicans," 152–53; Russ, "Radical Disfranchisement," 195–96. The vote counts and number expelled vary slightly among sources.

[3] Currie-McDaniel, *Carpetbagger of Conscience*, 95 (the white men); J. M. Bryant, "We Have No Chance of Justice," 25; Drago, *Black Politicians*, 51–53.

patent facts, observe what a flaunting lie is this statement of Mr. Robert E. Lee."[4]

Available sources do not provide direct evidence of how Joshua Hill regarded the purge of Black legislators as it was happening or immediately thereafter. He was on record in support of freedman suffrage, and his pre-expulsion joint appearances with Morgan County representative Monday Floyd and other Black legislators at rallies for Ulysses Grant indicated that he at least acquiesced in the reality of African Americans in office even if it might not have been his private preference. In any case, Hill would have fully realized that Republican participation in the purge would be seen on the national stage as a tremendous political blunder. Hill understood national-level politics as well as or better than any other politician in Georgia. Undoubtedly, he anticipated that the state would face stern repercussions from Congress and that the controversy could very well threaten his Senate seat.

Whatever Hill's private sentiments may have been in September 1868 when the purge occurred, the definitive public statement of his official position came on December 7 when Senator John Sherman (R-OH) presented the Georgian's credentials to the newly convened Senate. Anticipating pushback, Sherman carefully explained the timing of the purge and then declared on behalf of Hill:

> I am authorized to say by him, for he is not allowed to speak for himself, he disapproves of this highly.... It is the desire of the Senator-elect to participate with us in protecting these very people in the enjoyment of their clear right to hold office in the State of Georgia and throughout the United States, when they are duly elected by the qualified electors of a State.

From that point forward, Hill was publicly committed to the legitimacy of Black officeholding.[5]

The presidential election in November 1868 had a profound effect on how Congress viewed Georgia and its senators elect. In late May the Republican Party unanimously nominated Ulysses Grant for president. The equivocal Republican platform was more moderate than the Radical wing

---

[4] Foner, *Reconstruction*, 347; *Washington (DC) National Republican*, September 7, 1868.

[5] *Globe*, 40-3, December 7, 1868, 3–4.

desired, but it remained committed to Black suffrage in the South. After a long and bruising convention fight, Horatio Seymour of New York, a critic of congressional Reconstruction, emerged in July as the Democratic nominee. Although Seymour personally avoided overtly racist appeals, the vice-presidential nominee and many other Democratic campaigners, especially in the old Confederacy, were unafraid to make it clear that the Democratic Party stood for government by White men only.[6]

Joshua Hill's support of Grant, privately in a letter to the nominee and publicly at several rallies, solidified his Republican credentials. His appearances with Black speakers left no doubt that his support of the Republican Party included endorsement of Black suffrage. At a hometown rally in Madison about 250 Republicans, mostly Black, gathered to hear Hill and others speak on behalf of Grant. The gathering selected a three-man delegation composed of Monday Floyd and two Whites, A. J. Williams and T. P. Saffold, to represent the county at the upcoming Grant rally in Atlanta where Hill would be among the featured speakers. Reflecting on the event, one White Madisonian expressed his dismay that Hill had "placed his merit and influence against his race, his kindred, and his neighbors." Those characteristics—race, kindred, and neighbors—were indeed at play but not necessarily in the negative manner that the complainer foresaw. Monday Floyd, soon to be among the Black men expelled from the General Assembly, was a former slave of T. P. Saffold's uncle; Saffold's wife Sallie was a cousin of Joshua Hill, and Saffold and Hill had owned neighboring plantations in eastern Morgan County. At the rally in Atlanta, Hill shared the stage with other Republican luminaries, including Joe Brown. The *New York Tribune* admiringly reported that the senator-elect specifically directed some of his remarks to Black listeners, encouraging them to stand strong for the Republican ticket in the face of threats of reprisals sure to come. The *Atlanta New Era*, one of the state's few Republican newspapers, reported that Hill "spoke of the success of the Republican ticket as necessary in order to secure the full rights of the colored people." Hill was unable to attend a later Republican rally in Augusta due to illness, but he

[6] Foner, *Reconstruction*, 327–45; Summers, *Ordeal of the Reunion*, 141–51.

sent a letter reiterating his support of Grant and running mate Schuyler Colfax.[7]

It is important to note that all of these campaign events occurred before the General Assembly ejected Black members in September. The purge instantly changed the dynamic of the presidential election in Georgia. It emboldened Democrats, who now controlled the legislature. Given outright Democratic hostility to their interests, Black leaders had little practical choice but to remain in the Republican camp, but their enthusiasm had waned. The still splintered White Republicans also lacked electoral passion. Joe Brown, the one man who might have been able to engineer some party unity and bring North Georgia Whites to the Republican cause, was no longer available because he was now in a non-partisan role as chief justice of the state Supreme Court.

Joshua Hill stayed true to the Republican ticket through the fall, but he kept a low profile. He penned several public statements in support of Grant, but he pulled back from personal appearances in order to focus on securing his Senate seat. In one of his stronger pronouncements, Hill summarized the presidential race concisely: "Southern men who were loyal in the war are all for Grant; it is only the rebels who support Seymour and Blair." In late September and early October, the senator-elect spent several days in Washington attempting to shore up his relationships with key Republicans who were incensed at Georgia's legislative purge. When Hill returned home, he sent a letter to the *Atlanta New Era* in which he defended his low-key approach to the campaign.

> I have been invited to address large meetings of Republicans in this and other States, both North and South. In my solicitude

[7] Grant, *Papers of Ulysses S. Grant*, 18:268n, Hill to Grant, June 5, 1868; *(Macon) Georgia Journal & Messenger*, September 8, 1868 (placed his merit); *New York Tribune*, August 5, 13 (spoke of, *New Era*), 24, 1868; *Terre-Haute (IN) Weekly Express*, August 5, 1868; *Providence (RI) Press*, August 7, 1868; *Boston Traveller*, August 8, 1868 (*Atlanta New Era*); *New York Herald*, August 2, 1868; *Indianapolis State Sentinel*, August 3, 1868; *Macon Telegraph*, August 7, 14, 21, 1868; *Columbus Sun*, August 4, 1868; *Columbus Enquirer*, July 3 (*Atlanta Intelligencer*), August 1 (*Atlanta Constitution*) 1868; *Augusta Constitutionalist*, August 1, 19 (*Madison Auditor*, August 15, 1868), 21, 26, 1868; *Atlanta Intelligencer*, August 26, 1868; *Augusta Chronicle*, August 5, 26, 1868. *Savannah Daily News & Herald*, August 1, 1868; see Abbott, *For Free Press and Equal Rights*, 191.

> for the peace and quiet of the country, I have thought it best to decline speaking.... Much as I desire the election of Gen. GRANT—important as I believe his success is to the whole American people, and particularly to the Southern people, I would not, to secure it, sow discord and strife in a single family, White or black.

Hill accurately predicted that Grant would win the Electoral College easily and that the "voice of Georgia cannot, in my opinion, effect the result."[8]

In April 1868, Democrats had been caught off guard by the Black votes that resulted in Republican victories, and they were not about to let it happen again in the fall election. Speakers and editorialists roused White enthusiasm by warning that a victory by Grant and other Republicans would have the effect of ensuring Black and Radical political control of the South. They focused most of their rhetorical attacks on Radical Republicans, but Joshua Hill was not immune. An Augusta editor urged Democrats not to "seize upon Joshua Hill's honesty as a garment and rally for Grant." The paper later warned that even though the Madisonian was more restrained than his fellow Republicans, "he can not disguise the schemes of his political allies." To cover their options in case other approaches fell short, Democrats cynically attempted to take advantage of Black voters' lack of enthusiasm by having their own rallies featuring barbeques and African American speakers.[9]

Most historical analysis has concluded, however, that it was neither rousing rhetoric nor events courting Black voters that was most effective for Democrats. As Joshua Hill had warned in his Atlanta speech in August,

---

[8] *Point Pleasant (WV) Register*, September 24, 1868 (Southern men); *New York Times*, November 2, 1868 (*New Era*, I have been); *New York Tribune*, September 12, 1868; *Newnan Herald*, October 30, 1868; *Augusta Chronicle*, November 4, 1868; *Augusta Constitutionalist*, August 12, 21, 1868; *New York Times*, September 19 (Augusta), 22 (Raleigh), 1868; *Cincinnati Enquirer*, September 24, 1868; *Washington Evening Star*, September 22, 1868; *Baltimore Sun*, October 2, 1868; *Macon Telegraph*, October 2, 1868. See R. K. Brown, "Augusta's Other Voice," 592–607.

[9] *Augusta Constitutionalist*, August 12 (seize), 21 (he cannot), 1868; Nathans, *Losing the Peace*, 131–46; Duncan, *Entrepreneur for Equality*, 68–77; Drago, *Black Politicians*, 51–54; Currie-McDaniel, *Carpetbagger of Conscience*, 96–97; Conway, *Reconstruction of Georgia*, 168–79; J. M. Bryant, "We Have No Chance of Justice," 26; Perman, *Road to Redemption*, 4.

it was intimidation, threatened and actual, that made the most difference. In this era before the secret ballot, White landowners and employers could use thinly veiled threats to remind their tenants, sharecroppers, tradespeople, laborers, and domestics (mostly Black but including some sympathetic Whites) that casting a Republican ticket could impact the livelihood of their families. Violent intimidation in the form of the Ku Klux Klan and other paramilitary Klan-like groups could be applied if economic pressure failed to work. For the most part, the Democratic press turned a blind eye toward such activities. White Georgians understood that John B. Gordon, the Confederate general who had been the Democratic gubernatorial candidate in April (and who would later succeed Joshua Hill in the US Senate), was the titular head of Georgia's Klan if not the official grand dragon. Robert Toombs's son-in-law was one of the invisible empire's principal organizers.[10]

Efforts to counter the wave of intimidation were generally ineffective. General George Meade had the responsibility of protecting the franchise of Georgia's Black men, but he usually declined to dispatch his limited troops to rural and small-town trouble spots. This hands-off approach had the effect of giving Democrats a nearly free hand. The Freedmen's Bureau was likewise mostly ineffectual, and Governor Bullock had no effective state militia. Sporadic local attempts to counter the Klan by forming Black militias to protect voters often floundered, but they had some impact in a few places, such as Greene County immediately east of Morgan. Come November, Grant won the presidency, but Democrats won resoundingly in Georgia.[11]

Comparison between the spring vote and the November results constitutes striking evidence of the effectiveness of Democratic strategy. In April 1868, Republicans won slightly over half (54 percent) of Georgia's votes; in November they tallied less than a third (32 percent). Twenty-seven counties with Black majority registration switched from the Republican to Democratic column. Taliaferro, home county of Alexander H.

[10] Hahn, *Nation under Our Feet*, 286–92; Drago, *Black Politicians*, 51; J. M. Matthews, "Negro Republicans," 153–55; Wynne, *Continuity of Cotton*, 54–58; Clampitt, *Lost Causes*, 12–13, 186–88.

[11] J. M. Matthews, "Negro Republicans," 153; Cimbala, *Under the Guardianship of the Nation*, 218–20.

Stephens cast 627 votes for Rufus Bullock in the spring but only 187 for Grant in the fall. It was even worse elsewhere. In Columbia County, north of Augusta, more than a thousand voters went Republican in April, but only one—yes, *one*—did so in November. Incredibly, eleven counties recorded absolutely no votes for Grant whatsoever. Democratic assertions that it had been a free and fair election stretched credulity to the breaking point.[12]

Joshua Hill could take some solace in the fact that his home county and neighboring Greene County held for the Republicans. Morgan County's population was about two-thirds Black, and registration approximated that ratio. In April 1868, Bullock tallied more than double the vote of Gordon. By November the Republicans had lost ground, but Grant still prevailed 1046 to 635. Hill's cooperation with Monday Floyd and other African American leaders helped hold the county—for the time being. In 1869, Madison mayor Thomas J. Burney offered his explanation as to why his county was different: "The prevailing feeling toward the Blacks is one of sympathy and kindness, and a general disposition predominates to treat them fairly and justly; of course, there are exceptions to this rule in the case of bad white men." This rosy civic booster response was no doubt highly exaggerated, but the actual vote count meant that it rang closer to true for Morgan County than for most of the state.[13]

At the national level, Ulysses S. Grant did a masterful job of keeping both wings of the Republican party in his camp. Consequently, the general won a convincing electoral victory, 214-80. In six of the eleven former Confederate states, White disfranchisement and Black voting worked as Republicans hoped to carry the day for Grant (North Carolina, South Carolina, Alabama, Florida, Arkansas, and Tennessee). Democrats prevailed only in Georgia and Louisiana where few Whites remained disfranchised and where federal troops were unable to stop widespread voter intimidation. Three states were unreconstructed and did not participate in the

---

[12] Nathans, *Losing the Peace*, 143–46; C. Thompson, *Reconstruction in Georgia*, 375; Conway, *Reconstruction of Georgia*, 173–78; Duncan, *Entrepreneur for Equality*, 76–77; J. M. Matthews, "Negro Republicans," 153–54; Rable, *But There Was No Peace*, 69–79.

[13] US Congress, *Evidence before the Committee on Reconstruction*, 167. Hereinafter, *Condition of Affairs in Georgia.*

presidential election at all (Mississippi, Virginia, and Texas).[14] Radical Republicans, already disturbed by the expulsion of Black state legislators, were further enraged by Georgia elections results. They wanted to do something about it, and Joshua Hill became a convenient target.

Just a few weeks after the general election, the results of the city election in Augusta added further confirmation that Georgia was slipping away from Republican control. Political, business, and familial connections led Joshua Hill to become involved in the Augusta contest. A year earlier in December 1867, Hill's eldest daughter Anna married John Bowles, whom she apparently met while accompanying her father on business in Augusta. In November 1864, Miss Hill had lunched with a young Union officer in Madison and sent him away with flowers. Now another White Yankee caught her eye. An avowed abolitionist, Bowles rose to the rank of lieutenant colonel commanding the troops of the First Kansas Colored Regiment in Arkansas and Indian Territory (Oklahoma). After mustering out, he became the United States assessor of revenue for the district around Augusta. In the eyes of Democrats, Colonel Bowles was the very definition of carpetbagger—an abolitionist commander of Black troops who became involved in Republican politics, obtained a cushy federal patronage position, and married the daughter of an affluent Southern lawyer-planter-politician. Bowles became a political and business associate of his father-in-law and remained so until domestic discord scuttled the marriage in 1881.[15]

As the city election approached, Bowles, who was one of the several official election supervisors, wrote to the adjutant general in Washington saying that he had heard rumors that "Colored soldiers" would be brought to Augusta to supervise the election. Even though Bowles had led Black troops in battle, he strongly cautioned against using them for election supervision because he expected that "violence and bloodshed would result" and that such a result would only serve the interests of Radicals such as

---

[14] Chernow, *Grant*, 619; Perman, *Road to Redemption*, 4–6.

[15] *Augusta Chronicle*, October 15, 1865, September 29, 1866; *Atchinson (KS) Free Press*, January 4, 1868; *Lawrence Kansas Tribune*, December 22, 1867. Bowles had been married (and apparently widowed) before the war. The First Kansas became the Seventy-ninth Regiment, USCT. See *Augusta Constitutionalist*, January 3, November 11, 22, 29, 1868; Cashin, *Story of Augusta*, 135; Glatthaar, *Forged in Battle*.

Rufus Bullock and Foster Blodgett, who sought a pretense to return Georgia to federal military supervision. Bowles urged that the matter be called to General Grant's attention, adding that if Grant wanted "to know who I am and what amount of credence is to be placed in my statements, I refer you to Hon. Joshua Hill."[16]

No doubt at the urging of his son-in-law, Hill wrote a personal appeal to Grant. Hill acknowledged that "Troops under a discreet and gentlemanly officer may be of service," but he stressed, "prudent republicans prefer a company of white troops." At a time when Hill needed every high-placed friend he could get, it was a tactical mistake for him to write to Grant about a local matter rather than routing his request through General Meade where it ended up anyway. Meade replied to the president-elect, "I am not aware of the sources of information possessed by the Honorable Mr. Hill, but there was never any intention of sending colored troops to Augusta." Obviously piqued, Meade added that Hill would have already known that if he "had applied here direct." As it turned out, Meade sent two companies of White infantry, but to no avail. Democrats prevailed by over a thousand votes even though the nearly four thousand registered voters were almost exactly divided evenly Black and White.[17]

On December 7, just five days after the Augusta city election, Joe Brown wrote a long letter to Hill "in reference to our political affairs." Brown buried the hatchet regarding the Senate election and made it clear that he endorsed the seating of Hill:

---

[16] R. K. Brown, "Post-Civil War Violence," 196–213. The USCT units in Augusta 1865–1866 were the Thirty-third and 136th regiments (Bowles to Adjutant General, November 17, 1868, NARA M619, Letters Received by the Adjutant General's Office, 1860–1870, Main Series, RG 94, catalog 300368, file S 1054; and Adjutant General Office report, December 5, 1868, accessed via Fold3; Glatthaar, *Forged in Battle*, 214–17, 228–30; *Augusta Constitutionalist*, November 29, 1869). CSA veterans especially resented Black troops per Clampitt, *Lost Causes*, 13, 72.

[17] Joshua Hill to Grant, November 20, 1868, and Adj. Gen. Office report December 5, 1868, in Grant, *Papers of Ulysses S. Grant*, 19:306; *(Macon) Georgia Journal & Messenger*, December 1, 1868; *Savannah News*, December 2, 1868; *Augusta Chronicle*, December 9, 1868; *LaGrange Reporter*, December 11, 1868; *(Macon) Georgia Journal & Messenger*, December 8, 1868; *(Athens) Southern Watchman*, December 9, 1868; *(Sandersville) Central Georgian*, December 9, 1868.

> Our late race for the Senate produced some estrangement, which probably ought not to exist. The excess to which the democracy [party] carried their triumph over my defeat contributed to my mortification the more, because I thought you sympathized with it. If I know myself however, it is not in my nature to bear malice. I believe you will stand strongly by General Grant's administration and will be its faithful supporter. I shall do the same. I do not see, therefore, any just reason why we should quarrel or act as enemies. You and Dr. Miller were elected by a legislature which I consider loyal, and as the defeated party I do not hesitate to say that in my opinion it is best for the peace of our state and for the future of the Republican party in Georgia that you should be permitted to take your seat.[18]

With the personal matter out of the way, Brown proceeded to explain his concerns and his plans for Georgia's Republicans. It is clear that he and Hill were of similar thought. Brown said that recent elections "have demonstrated that we cannot rely on the negro vote unless we have a White party in the locality of the election of sufficient moral weight to lead them." He astutely foresaw that if Congress intervened forcefully it would unify the Democrats and that Republicans would be defeated "by an overwhelming majority which will become permanent in the state." His alternative plan was to try to build the Republican Party on an alliance between centrist White Republicans and disaffected White Democrats, especially from North Georgia. Black voters would play a subservient but essential role. In short, "we must divide the White people before we can hold power in the state." Brown authorized Hill to use the letter as needed in his upcoming discussions with senators, but, he cautioned, it was not for public release because of his nonpartisan position as chief justice. Hill himself showed the letter to president-elect Grant and others. The full text of the letter itself did not become public, but word soon came out that Brown backed Hill. Brown also sent a similar letter to Rufus Bullock though he unquestionably knew that, unlike Hill, the governor was of a different mind. As Brown's principal biographer put it, "Governor Bullock had not requested this advice; neither would he heed it." Historian Edmund L.

[18] Brown to Hill, December 7, 1868, ms 785, folder 4, box 2, Brown Family papers, HRBML.

Drago characterized Brown as a color-changing "chameleon" and interpreted the former governor's strategy as an unscrupulous long game to make himself "the savior of the white race."[19]

The long debate over the seating of Joshua Hill represents, with some caveats, a case study of what historian Michael Perman characterized as the struggle between Reconstruction-era Republicans who wanted the party to be "expressive" and those who preferred to be "competitive."[20] In Georgia, the expressive wing, led by Bullock and supported by Black activists such as Henry Turner, Tunis G. Campbell, and A. A. Bradley, professed to hold strong to the ideals of full Black participation. On the other hand, the competitive position, articulated by Joe Brown and exemplified by Joshua Hill, Amos T. Akerman, and others argued that the path to the Republican Party's long-term success in the South would require compromise and patient, evolutionary change. On the surface, this dispute between ideology and practicality was honorable, yet in practice, many of the choices made by the Whites in both factions were dictated by their personal aspirations for power and financial gain as well as by ideology and party loyalty. When politically expedient, the White leaders of both sides were willing to disregard the interests of Black Georgians to achieve their own ends. Even the expressive Bullock showed no willingness to go down in a flame of egalitarian righteousness.

The struggle between the factions of Georgia Republican Party reflected the broader national split between the Radical and moderate to conservative camps. As is typical in politics, the distinctions at the extremes were obvious, but the lines dividing the two sides were not always clear nearer the middle. President Grant endeavored, with varied success, to keep his party unified by trying to keep both sides happy and the Democrats at bay. The long, drawn-out dispute over the seating of Joshua Hill exemplified this struggle. Radical senators Charles D. Drake (R-MO) and John M. Thayer (R-NE) led the opposition to Hill's being seated. On the

---

19 Hill to T. P. Saffold, December 13, 1868, Saffold Family Papers, MCA; Duncan, *Entrepreneur for Equality*, 81–82; J. M. Matthews, "Negro Republicans," 154–56; *(Athens) Southern Watchman*, August 12, 1868 (*[Macon] Georgia Journal & Messenger*); *(Jackson, MI) Citizen Patriot*, February 1, 1868 (*New Era*); Parks, *Joseph E. Brown*, 431–32; Drago, *Black Politicians*, 49–50.

20 Perman, *Road to Redemption*, 20–32, 43–46; Duncan, *Entrepreneur for Equality*, 80–81.

other hand, the Georgian's consistent champions were moderate senators John Sherman (R-OH) and Lyman Trumbull (R-IL).[21]

When the Senate prepared to reconvene in December 1868, the president-elect and the sitting senators needed no introduction to Joshua Hill. Several knew him personally from his prewar service in the House of Representatives, and the others knew him by reputation from years of press coverage of his role as one of the South's most prominent Unionists. H. V. M. Miller, on the other hand, was a political unknown slated for the short term. Accordingly, the long dispute focused almost entirely on Hill, and the seating of Miller faded into the background as an afterthought that the Senate would not dispose of until February 1871. In his letter introducing Miller to Grant, General Meade urged that both men be seated:

> It is understood [that Hill and Miller] taking their seats has become questionable, in consequence of the Legislature subsequent to their election—and thru a considerable proportion of Republican votes—declaring the negro under the Georgia Constitution ineligible to office & ejecting the colored members of the Legislatures—I have reason to believe the admission of Mess Hill & Miller would be acceptable to the main body of the Republicans of the State—and I certainly believe, it is for the interest of the State, and the whole country, that all issues in the future should be avoided, and these gentlemen allowed to take their seats.[22]

When he referred to "the main body" of Georgia's Republicans, Meade was tacitly endorsing the interpretations of the moderate/conservative wing.

Hoping to get the ear of sympathetic senators, several Georgia Republicans traveled to Washington. Hill identified a group of "about ten" plus "colored gentlemen," including James M. Simms and Henry M. Turner. Hill told T. P. Saffold that he and Dr. Miller were "outsiders" to the group, but he added that he regarded Amos Akerman and Jonathan Bryant as friends. On the other hand, Hill added, "Southern Carpetbaggers generally are against me, as you would suppose. They hate any Southern gentleman." Those whom Hill called "Southern Gentlemen" might well have been dubbed "scalawags" by Democratic foes. Hill visited with Grant twice

---

[21] Foner, *Reconstruction*, 241.

[22] Grant, *Papers of Ulysses S. Grant*, 19:67n.

and introduced him to Dr. Miller. Hill pressed his case with Grant by telling the president-elect "that this movement against me is *aimed at him*." Hill optimistically concluded his letter to Saffold by urging him to come to Washington in January and stating optimistically, "I think I shall be admitted—but the delay is very annoying." Little did he know then that the delay would drag on for another two years and that his ultimate admission would come in January 1871 rather than December 1868.[23]

Senator John Sherman knew Hill well from their clash over the House speakership in late December 1859 and early January 1860. It can be presumed that he was aware of his brother's consultation with Hill prior to the commencement of the March to the Sea. When Sherman presented the Georgian's credentials to the Senate, the influential Ohioan made it clear that the controversy was about Georgia's actions in the latter part of 1868—not about the senator-elect himself:

> There can be no objection to the person, because Hon. Joshua Hill is well known to have been a Union man throughout the war, to be now able to take the oath, and to be one of the very few of those living in the South through the war who were not forced or who were not willingly in a condition to give aid to the rebels in arms. His is now prepared to take the oath of office, having been faithful and true during the whole war, and having been duly elected by the Legislature of the State of Georgia.[24]

After Sherman concluded, Senator Drake moved that the body table Hill's credentials pending investigation. Aware of the Georgian's positive reputation with many members and with the Republican press, Drake acknowledged that he had "no doubt that all that has been said of [Hill] by the Senator from Ohio is perfectly true." Drake's principal argument was that the exclusion of the Black members from the Georgia General Assembly meant that the legislature was under rebel control. After some discussion ensued, Senator Thayer rose to add Governor Bullock's argument to the mix, i.e., that General Meade had erred in not purging the legislature of White members ineligible to serve and that, therefore, it was illegally constituted from the start. Thus, Thayer concluded, Georgia's

[23] Hill to Saffold, December 13, 1868.

[24] *Globe*, 40-3, December 7, 1868, 2–5; US Congress, *Compilation of Senate Election Cases from 1789 to 1885*, Senate misc. doc. 47, January 1, 1886, 285–311.

government must be considered "provisional" and thereby not entitled to representation in Congress.[25]

Sherman, with some help from other moderates, responded to Drake and Thayer by touting Hill's support of the expelled Black members. He reminded the Senate that Hill had played no part in their expulsion and asserted that it would be unfair to block Hill "when really his desire is to secure these people against the very inflictions which have been put upon them." Sherman expressed sympathy with the feelings of the African Americans who were outraged at the removal of the Black legislators, but he contended that their complaints did "not conflict with the right of Mr. Hill to be sworn." He argued that Thayer's, and by extension Bullock's, contention that Georgia's government should be considered provisional was self-servingly disingenuous and hypocritical. He carefully laid out the chronology showing that Bullock had not considered Georgia to have had a provisional government in summer 1868 when he proudly participated in his own formal inauguration ceremony, when he proceeded to appoint numerous state officials, and when he signed bills that the legislature passed prior to the expulsion including the ratification of the Fourteenth Amendment. Most tellingly, Sherman called the attention of the upper house to the fact that Bullock had personally signed the very certificate of election that now lay before the body.[26]

With the respective positions having been presented and the key documents having been placed on record, the Senate consented to table the matter while the Judiciary Committee conducted its inquiries into Hill and Georgia politics. In anticipation of the investigation, the *Washington National Republican*, press organ of the moderate wing, published a long and detailed editorial that deftly laid out the case in favor of seating the Georgians. Several contemporary observers speculated that the unsigned piece came from the pen of Hill himself; their speculations ring true. In defense of the legitimacy of the July 1868 Georgia legislature, the writer stressed that General Meade's approval of the membership "was sustained by high military authority at Washington" and was "well known to Congress, then in session." The fact that the US House of Representatives swore

[25] Ibid.; Russ, "Radical Disfranchisement," 175–209, see 197–200.
[26] Ibid.

in Georgia's members was, the article asserted, prima facie evidence that Georgia's government was not provisional.[27]

The *National Republican* piece was especially hard on Rufus Bullock. It repeated and expanded John Sherman's argument that it was hypocritical for the governor to act for several months as if he were the regular governor of a fully readmitted state and then turn around later and contend that he and his state had been provisional all along. It was particularly notable that Bullock was drawing his salary from state funds as regular governor, "not from the United States Treasury as a Provisional Governor." The editorial concluded that refusing to seat Joshua Hill and declaring Georgia's government to be provisional would "undo the reconstruction of an important Southern State" and be tantamount to confessing that Reconstruction had failed. Anticipating the upcoming hearings about Klan-type violence, the author (whether Hill himself or a supporter) conceded that Georgia had neglected "to protect her people of all races, colors, and politics" and agreed that federal intervention was necessary to counter intimidation of Black voters. The seating of Hill, the piece argued, would facilitate rather than hinder congressional action to solve the problem.[28]

The next few weeks offered opportunities for both sides to lobby. Unlike most Southern military leaders and to their great distress, General James Longstreet had become a "Confederate Judas," i.e., a Republican, and he was among those working behind the scenes on Hill's behalf. Meanwhile, Democratic observers seemed smugly amused by the outrage expressed by some Northern Republicans whose own states had no African American legislators and few, if any, Black voters.[29]

---

27 *Savannah News*, December 17, 1868 (*National Republican*); *Augusta Chronicle*, December 30, 1868.

28 Ibid.

29 *New York Herald*, December 9, 1868; *New York World*, December 24, 1868; *Buffalo (NY) Post*, December 29, 1868; *Brooklyn (NY) Eagle*, December 7, 1868; *Savannah News*, December 11, 29, 1868; Duncan, *Entrepreneur for Equality*, 82–84; *Baltimore Sun*, December 18, 1868; *Charleston (SC) News*, December 22, 1868. On Longstreet, see Piston, *Lee's Tarnished Lieutenant*, pt. 2, 139, and Connelly and Bellows, *God and General Longstreet*. Longstreet's most recent biographer stresses his support for Grant and Republicans but does not specifically mention Hill (Varon, *Longstreet*, xiii [Judas]).

The Judiciary Committee reported on January 25, 1869, and it did not go Hill's way. The majority finding submitted by William M. Stewart (R-NV) reflected the Radical point of view that Hill should not be seated "for the reason that Georgia is not entitled to representation in Congress." The arguments put forth in the majority report were essentially the same that senators Drake and Thayer had raised. Conversely, Senator Trumbull's minority report embodied the moderate position and reiterated the points that Senator Sherman and the *National Republican* article had made on behalf of Hill. Not wanting to force a divisive full Senate vote at that time, the Radical-leading but cautious Senator Frederick Frelinghuysen (R-NJ) successfully negotiated the Judiciary Committee's final recommendation to read that Hill "ought not now to be permitted to take a seat in this body." That was a very important "now"! Frelinghuysen's compromise wording left the door open for the possible seating of the Georgia Unionist at some time in the future.[30]

At about the same time that the Senate committee used evasive wording to avoid the immediate seating of Joshua Hill, Congress sidestepped the challenges to Georgia's 1868 electoral vote, a move with implications for Hill's case. Accepting the votes of Georgia's electors for Seymour would have amounted to a de facto acknowledgment that the state was fully readmitted and entitled to Senate representation; rejecting them would have implied the contrary. Since Grant was the winner regardless of Georgia, Radical senator George F. Edmunds (R-VT) crafted a compromise that left the matter permanently moot by certifying the electoral both ways—with and without Georgia.[31]

As the 40th Congress drew to a close and the capital prepared for Grant's inauguration in March 1869, Senator Edmonds introduced legislation that would reinstate Georgia's purged Black legislators and reimpose military supervision. Again, both sides showed up to lobby. Governor Bullock was, in the words of the *Baltimore Sun*, "at the capital daily, and never

[30] *Report of the Committee on the Judiciary*, January 25, 1869, 40th Congress, 3rd Sess. Senate, Serial Set vol. 1362, Senate Report 192; US Congress, *Compilation of Senate Election Cases*, 285–311; *Springfield (MA) Republican*, January 27, 1869; *New York Times*, January 26, 1869; *Columbus Enquirer*, February 19, 1869; *Macon Telegraph*, January 8, 1869 (*Cincinnati Commercial*).

[31] Nathans, *Losing the Peace*, 159–61; *Nation*, February 11, 1868.

rests in his attempts to induce congressional action in such a way as to further the particular interests of is clique." To counter, Hill brought a delegation of six Georgia legislators to Washington to meet with Grant and to buttonhole member of Congress. Anxious to offend neither wing of his party, Grant wavered, and neither side could break the impasse before Congress adjourned. The matter did not come up in the very brief organizational session of the 41st Congress in March, so the status of Georgia's government and Hill's Senate seat remained in limbo until Congress reconvened in December 1869.[32]

The brief organizational session of the 41st Congress did, however, solve the thorny conundrum of Georgia being represented in the House but not in the Senate. When the House seated Georgia's members on July 25, 1868, everyone seemed to think that they had been elected for two-year terms, and the seating constituted a strong argument that Hill and Miller should be seated in the Senate as well. Fortuitously for the Radical position, it was noticed (by whom is not clear) that the official credentials of Georgia's House members did not explicitly indicate that their terms extended into the 41st Congress. Thus, an oversight became an excuse, and the House of Representatives sent the Georgians packing without the underlying issue being decided.[33]

Throughout the controversy over the seating of Joshua Hill, Senate Democrats were mainly sideline observers to an internecine Republican battle. They would, of course, have preferred for the Georgia legislature to have sent two Democrats to the Senate, but as things turned out they knew that they were lucky to have snagged even one. Knowing that Hill owed his election to the votes of Democrats and aware of Hill's conservative inclinations, Democratic senators raised no objections to his seating and maintained a low profile regarding H. V. M. Miller. As early as November Hill and Miller had reached a gentlemen's agreement that they would not

[32] *Baltimore Sun*, April 5, 1869; Russ, "Radical Disfranchisement," 199; *Mobile Register*, April 10, 1869; US Congress, *Compilation of Senate Election Cases*, 294; *Washington (DC) Daily Globe*, March 18, 1869; *Nation*, March 25, 1869; Nathans, *Losing the Peace*, 161–65; Farrow's April 13, long circular letter to Georgia senator John B. Dickey was printed as a nine-page booklet: Henry P. Farrow, "The Status of Georgia" (Washington, DC: M'Gill & Witherow, Printers and Stereotypers, 1869).

[33] Nathans, *Losing the Peace*, 161.

oppose the seating of each other. On January 11, Senator Trumbull officially presented Miller's credentials, and the Senate promptly referred the case to the Judiciary Committee along with Hill's. There was some Republican grumbling that Dr. Miller was ineligible for admission because he had served as a physician in the Confederate army; however, compared to the bruhaha over Hill, Miller's case attracted scant attention in the Senate or in the press.[34]

From December 1868 through the adjournment of the short session of the new 41st Congress, press reaction to the controversy over Hill's senate seat broke along factional lines. "No State was more thoroughly rebel than Georgia," claimed the moderate *Chicago Tribune*, but, the paper effused, "against that overwhelming tide of disloyalty, that swept everything before it, no man stood so firmly, no man breasted it so bravely, as Joshua Hill." The *Atlanta New Era* happily reported that Joe Brown, who had shifted from ally to opponent of Rufus Bullock, favored the seating of Hill. In New England, the *Springfield (MA) Republican* captured the moderate position succinctly: "Probably no better man than Joshua Hill could be elected to represent Georgia in the Senate, and while we desire to see his state forced to retract the foolish and wicked course she has taken, we agree with Mr. Frelinghuysen in the wish that the staunch old Union man may, *by and by*, be allowed to take his seat."[35]

A New York paper exemplified the Radical position when it proclaimed that for Hill to be seated "he would have to step over the prostrate bodies of the expelled colored members of the Legislature that elected him." The Democratic press used the Hill matter to take its usual potshots at Republicans. From the middle, the *Nation* magazine laid out the

---

[34] *Milledgeville Federal Union*, November 24, 1868.

[35] *Washington National Intelligencer*, March 5, 1869 (*Chicago Tribune*); *Jackson (MI) Citizen Patriot*, February 1, 1869 (*New Era*); *Springfield (MA) Republican*, January 27, 1869 (emphasis added); See *Burlington (VT) Sentinel*, December 25, 1868; 53; *New York Tribune*, April 12, 1869; *New York World*, March 2, 6, 1869; *New Orleans Tribune*, February 28, 1869; *Chicago Inter Ocean*, April 12, 1869; *Augusta Constitutionalist*, April 14, 1869; *Macon Telegraph*, April 16, 1869.

arguments with more detail and nuance than the partisan newspapers. That is where it stood when Congress went home in March.[36]

During the first half of 1869, while Grant organized his new administration and while Congress pondered the status of Georgia's senators-elect, two events back in Atlanta modified the political landscape in ways that would further complicate Joshua Hill's fight for his seat.

The first involved the controversy over whether the Georgia Constitution of 1868 granted Black citizens the right to hold elective office. In a move designed to conciliate congressional Republicans, the General Assembly voted in February 1869 to refer the question to the state Supreme Court and to abide by the decision. Governor Bullock vetoed the resolution because he wanted no part of any action that would mollify Congress and thwart his goal of keeping Washington Radicals angry at Georgia. Despite Bullock's efforts, the controversy reached the state supreme court. In the meantime, Joseph Brown's position had shifted—either out of conviction or convenience. In spring 1868, Brown had denied that the right to vote necessarily carried with it the right to serve. In December in his conciliatory letter to Hill, the chief justice privately declared that Black officeholding was "a question proper for the courts." Six months later the question came before him and the court. Brown joined in the two-to-one majority that allowed a light-skinned man classified as Black, to continue in office. This meant that if the General Assembly reinstated Black legislators, no constitutional question would stand in their way. It was the legal ruling that Bullock wanted, but he did not use it to act immediately because it served his interest to let the matter simmer.[37]

The other issue involved Georgia's failure to ratify the Fifteenth Amendment, which removed race as a legal reason to deny any man the right to vote. The amendment slipped through Congress in a watered-down version necessary to achieve the necessary two-thirds majority.

---

[36] *Troy (NY) Times*, January 30, 1869; *Atlanta Constitution*, February 4, 1869; *Mobile Register*, January 30 (*Montgomery Advertiser*), February 11, 1869; *New Orleans Times-Picayune*, February 6, 1868; *Augusta Constitutionalist*, January 30, February 5 (*Cincinnati Enquirer*), 1869; *Macon Telegraph*, January 29, February 5, 12, 1869; *New York Times*, January 26, 1869; *Nation*, February 4, 1869, 84–85.

[37] Brown to Hill, December 7, 1868, Brown Family Papers; Duncan, *Entrepreneur for Equality*, 86–87, 90–92; Parks, *Joseph E. Brown*, 435–37; Nathans, *Losing the Peace*, 152–54; Conway, *Reconstruction of Georgia*, 167n, 186.

Ratification was no certainty because several Northern states still restricted Black voting. The amendment's supporters counted on Republican-controlled legislatures in former Confederate states to provide the margin for ratification by the necessary three-fourths of the states. Some Georgia Democrats calculated that approval of the amendment was inevitable no matter what their state did, so they decided to support ratification in an effort to mollify moderate Republicans in Congress and thereby avoid a return to military supervision.[38]

Georgia Republican success depended heavily on the Black vote, so under normal circumstances, the state party would have heartily endorsed the Fifteenth Amendment, as did most of their fellow party members in other ex-Confederate states. But the situation in Georgia was not normal. Ratification would have made Georgia look reasonable to national Republicans and would, therefore, have lessened Governor Bullock's chances of obtaining congressional approval of his plan to keep his administration in power. Democrats pushed ratification through the state House, but pro-Bullock Republicans managed to block it in the Senate. The cynical gambit worked. Georgia's refusal to ratify the Fifteenth Amendment in March 1869 could now be advanced as a reason for Congress to reorganize the state's government.[39]

Not wanting to offend any faction, Joshua Hill remained publicly neutral about the Fifteenth Amendment. However, credible accounts indicate that he was quietly explaining to his Georgia allies that refusal to ratify would only intensify Radical resolve to re-reconstruct the state. The *New York Tribune* insinuated that Hill was equivocal about the amendment only because he was "hanging by the eyelids before the doors of the Senate." Hill responded to the perceived insult in a public letter that evasively danced around the question of whether he had been privately lobbying for the amendment's passage.[40]

---

[38] Foner, *Reconstruction*, 446–49; Conway, *Reconstruction of Georgia*, 185–86; Nathans, *Losing the Peace*, 153–54.

[39] Duncan, *Entrepreneur for Equality*, 87–88; Nathans, *Losing the Peace*, 153–54; Conway, *Reconstruction of Georgia*, 185–86; Parks, *Joseph E. Brown*, 436.

[40] *New York Tribune*, March 13, 16, 1869; *Macon Telegraph*, March 26, 1869 (Hill in *Tribune*); *Boston Herald*, March 17, 1869; *Cincinnati Gazette*, March 13, 1869; *Cleveland (OH) Leader*, March 16, 1869.

An Interlude in the Seating Struggle, April–November 1869

After nine months of political turmoil from July 1868 through the early days of the Grant administration in March 1869, Joshua Hill was disappointed that he remained in unseated limbo but was relieved not to have been rejected altogether. He had gone to Washington several times to argue his case, but now he was back home in Georgia where he could turn his attention to the practice of law and the managing of investments. It was time for him to put active politics on the back burner for a few months.

On April 8, 1869, a fire devastated downtown Madison. The flames started just after dark, and according to a reporter, "the conflagration progressed with such great rapidity, that scarcely anything was saved." Luckily, the Morgan County courthouse, standing protected in the center of the square, survived as did almost all residential structures. Relief funds and supplies flowed in from several towns across the state. Originally thought to be arson, the cause was later reported as accidental due to faulty storage of oil and cotton. Most of the nearly sixty wooden structures around and near the square lacked insurance coverage or were significantly underinsured. One of those buildings was the town hall, which Joshua Hill and other investors owned and leased to the municipal government. Their reported loss of nine thousand dollars exceeded that of any structure that did not also lose valuable inventory. By November, a local observer could write that the city "so recently destroyed by fire, is being rebuilt, and will very soon make a much finer show than ever before."[41]

On May 24, about six weeks after the devastating fire, Hill wrote a long letter to President Grant relating his assessment of "the present state of feelings now prevailing in this state." He reported that he had "seen a good many persons of all grades of intelligence and every political shade" including both "old political friends and lifelong adversaries." Hill was pleased that he had "been kindly met by nearly all," but he also lamented that "a few still retain their sworn hostility and estrangement. These were former allies. The probability is that we shall never *know* each other again." Hill conceded the accuracy of much of the recent congressional testimony

[41] *Augusta Chronicle*, April 10 (the breaking) and 11, 1869; *Atlanta New Era*, November 12, 1869 (so recently); *New York Times*, April 14, 1869; see 1869 Fire folder, MCA.

about violent conditions in the South but nevertheless optimistically claimed that "the tone of society in Georgia is rapidly improving." He told the president that when he conversed with politicians "disposed to reason" that could usually reconcile "them to distasteful appointments as have been dictated by the force of circumstances." Although Hill refrained from mentioning it specifically, Grant probably knew that one of the recent appointments that Hill found "distasteful" was that of Bullock-ally Edwin Belcher, a Black man who had been a member of the legislature at the time of the purge. The case hit home because Belcher replaced Hill's son-in-law John Bowles as district assessor in Augusta. To make matters worse, Bowles was facing accusations of malfeasance in office at the time of his removal. Hill's letter to Grant ended on a wistful note:

> And when it comes—I shall bless the day that makes it a matter of innocent choice for me to bid an eternal adieu to politics. Up to this time, neither I nor Misses [Emily Hill] have been benefitted by connection with public affairs, but have suffered thusly. I have not a wish beyond the tranquility of my country and simple independence.[42]

Joshua Hill continued to stay mostly behind the political scenes through summer and fall 1869 even as politics heated up around him. In October, the death of his dear friend and congressional predecessor Nathaniel G. Foster deeply saddened Hill. In good lawyerly fashion, the senator-elect busied himself with clients' needs, including helping some of them take advantage of the state's new debt relief and homestead provisions even though he had personally opposed them. Ever the civic booster, Hill made an appeal at a November railroad promotion meeting in Monticello that urged the building of a Griffin-to-Madison line. Several articles listed Hill as prominent among the moderates who resisted the

---

[42] Joshua Hill to Ulysses S. Grant, May 24, 1869, ms 1940, HRBML. On Bowles-Belcher, see *Augusta Constitutionalist*, April 23, 1869; *Savannah Morning News*, December 1, 1869; *Columbus Sun*, December 7, 1869; *Columbus Enquirer*, December 2, 1868; Currie-McDaniel, *Carpetbagger of Conscience*, 122–23.

Bullock wing of Georgia's Republican Party, but he made no public statements on the subject at this time.[43]

In his May 1869 private missive to the new president, Joshua Hill had portrayed Georgia as mostly peaceful despite a few instances of racially motivated violence. Nevertheless, persistent reports about White violence against Georgia's Black community captured Grant's attention. The beleaguered president referred the Georgia trouble to General Sherman, who in turn directed General Alfred H. Terry to investigate. Terry's August 1969 report detailed a string of politically motivated attacks on Black people and on White Republicans. He found that the state's efforts to prosecute the attackers had been ineffective because the Ku Klux Klan and similar groups intimidated local officials. Terry sympathized with Governor Bullock's suggestion that a reorganization of the Georgia General Assembly and that a reselection of US senators could help restore order and protect Republicans. When the document reached Major General H. W. Halleck, commander of the Division of the South, he apparently considered it too political and controversial for the military. He cautioned against rash action and recommended to Grant "that the matter be left for the action of Congress."[44]

Halleck was right about the political impact of Terry's report. It ignited optimism and activism in the ranks of Georgia Radicals and played an important role in developments over the next several months. African Americans seemed especially pleased that their grievances were finally receiving some official attention. About two hundred Black delegates gathered at a convention in Macon in October 1869 to demand economic and political change. The leaders of the gathering included several of the men whom the Georgia General Assembly had expelled fourteen months earlier. Meanwhile, using a legal technicality, Bullock kept what would have

---

[43] N. G. Foster memorial file, MCA; *Atlanta New Era*, November 12, 1869; *Augusta Chronicle & Sentinel*, November 10, 1869; *New York World*, September 21, 1869.

[44] Terry's report in *Report of the Secretary of War, Being Part of the Message and Documents Communicated to the two Houses of Congress*, 41st Cong., 2nd Sess., H. Exec. Doc. 1 pt. 2, vol. 1, es [esp.?] 93–95 (Halleck); Duncan, *Entrepreneur for Equality*, 92–93.

been a new Democratic majority legislature at bay by simply refusing to convene a session.[45]

The violence reported by General Terry and the president's desire to have the Fifteenth Amendment ratified would, by December, thrust Georgia, and thereby senator-elect Hill, back into the center of Reconstruction politics.

---

[45] Rable, *But There Was No Peace*, 103; Downs, *After Appomattox*, 219; Calhoun, *Presidency of Ulysses S. Grant*, 99–100; Nathans, *Losing the Peace*, 163; 10; Hahn, *Nation under Our Feet*, 262–63; Smith, "Reconstruction 'Triumph,'" 414–21; Russ, "Radical Disfranchisement," 198–99; *Macon Telegraph*, October 8, 1869 (*New York Tribune*).

Chapter 10

Senator-Elect to Senator in Georgia's Second Reconstruction, 1869–1871

Shortly before Congress convened in early December 1869, the *Nation* summarized the unique status of the Empire State of the South: "Georgia, as our readers may remember, is neither in nor out of the Union.... Georgia is in the Union to all intents and purposes, except that she has no representation in the Senate."[1]

As he would do throughout his administration, Ulysses S. Grant vacillated between supporting the two wings of the Republican Party. His treatment of individual states depended mainly on his assessment of the balance between long-term Republican strength and short-term political necessity. The urgency of securing ratification of the Fifteenth Amendment proved to be the principal factor in how the administration approached Georgia. The sitting General Assembly would be unlikely to approve a constitutional prohibition of using race to limit voting, but a reconstituted legislature with its Black members reinstated would be sure to ratify the pending amendment.

On December 6, 1869, early in his annual message to Congress, the new president proclaimed proudly that seven Confederate states had been fully restored to their places in the Union. Then he turned to Georgia. Grant lamented that the state legislature had "unseated the colored members of the legislature and admitted to seats some members who are disqualified by the third clause of the fourteenth amendment to the Constitution." He exhorted Congress to pass a bill that would reverse those actions. His request pointedly omitted any specific mention of the status of the senators-elect Hill and Miller, so it can be reasonably inferred that

---

[1] *Nation*, December 2, 1869.

the president deliberately wanted to avoid having that thorny question complicate his principal goals of calming the situation in Georgia and ensuring ratification of the Fifteenth Amendment. Nevertheless, passage of Grant's bill would be sure to affect the senatorial controversy.[2]

The opposition to Grant's proposal consisted of a very uneasy alliance between Democrats, who resisted everything that he stood for, and conservative Republicans, who usually backed the president but differed strongly with him when it came to remanding Georgia back to federal control. The opposition employed two argumentative thrusts. Unable to credibly deny the existence of political violence in Georgia, they contended that the incidents were isolated and highly exaggerated. They cited optimistic testimonials compiled by Democratic congressman Nelson Tift and highlighted reports from a group of Northern observers who, after attending the state fair in Macon, praised the "orderly, law-abiding, and enterprising character of the people of Georgia."[3]

The second and more compelling argument of the opponents was that Governor Rufus Bullock, who had recently begun referring to his position as "provisional," was guilty of complaining of his own lashes. They reminded Congress that Bullock had engineered Georgia's defeat of the Fifteenth Amendment, had vetoed the resolution that called for judicial clarification of the matter of Black office-holding, and had refused to convene the General Assembly to give it a chance to reinstate the Black members on its own in accordance with the state Supreme Court ruling. Despite those points, most of Georgia's Black Republicans continued to stand with Bullock. However, Jefferson Long, who would a year later serve about six weeks as Georgia's only Black member of Congress until the mid-twentieth century, had come to detest the governor. He believed that Bullock's efforts had more to do with his own personal ambition than with building

[2] President's Annual Message, December 6, 1869, in Grant, *Papers of Ulysses S. Grant*; Gillette, *Retreat from Reconstruction*, 80–88; Chernow, *Grant*, 654–55; Calhoun, *Presidency of Ulysses S. Grant*, 99–100; Smith, "Reconstruction 'Triumph,'" 414–19; Russ, "Radical Disfranchisement," 198–99.

[3] *New York World*, December 10, 1869 (orderly); Smith, "Reconstruction 'Triumph,'" 417; Hill to Grant, May 24, 1869, ms 1940, HRBML; *Augusta Chronicle*, December 22, 1869; *Columbus Weekly Sun*, December 21, 1869; Duncan, *Entrepreneur for Equality*, 92–94; *Atlanta Constitution*, September 30, 1869; *Augusta Constitutionalist*, October 27, 1869 (*Richmond Dispatch*).

the party. During the debates on the Georgia bill, Bullock scurried around the capitol simultaneously drumming up support and antagonizing opponents. At one dramatic Senate committee hearing, Representative Tift looked Bullock straight in the eye and called him a liar and a thief.[4]

Since Grant was so strongly in favor of the bill, critics made little headway, even with Republican moderates. The Act to Promote the Reconstruction of the State of Georgia passed handily on December 22, less than three weeks after the president's message. As Grant wished, the act made Georgia's full readmission contingent on restoring the expelled Black legislators, removing White assemblymen who could not honestly swear the Ironclad Test Oath, and ratifying the Fifteenth Amendment. Grant put General Alfred H. Terry, who had prepared the fall 1869 report about political intimidation in Georgia, in charge.[5]

Even though the Georgia act did not specifically mention the Senate seats, Joshua Hill realized that it would not portend well for his prospects of ever becoming a United States senator. One widely circulated article reported that Hill was "said to be specially incensed" about the law's passage. There was some speculation that Grant would appoint Joshua Hill as the new provisional governor, but he allowed Bullock to remain in office instead.[6]

The General Assembly convened in Atlanta on January 10, 1870. Determining which of the disputed White members would be rejected and who would replace them proved to be troublesome. Not trusting that White members would be honest and forthcoming about their eligibility

---

[4] Gillette, *Retreat from Reconstruction*, 87; Chernow, *Grant*, 690; Smith, "Reconstruction 'Triumph,'" 420; Currie, "The Reconstruction Congress," 488–89; J. M. Matthews, "Jefferson Franklin Long," 146; *Cincinnati Enquirer*, December 10, 1869; *Savannah Morning News*, December 3, 16, 1869; *Columbus Sun*, December 21, 1869; *Augusta Chronicle*, December 22, 1869; *Worcester (MA) Spy*, December 24, 1869; Nathans, *Losing the Peace*, 164–65; Duncan, *Entrepreneur for Equality*, 93–94; Currie-McDaniel, *Carpetbagger of Conscience*, 106–107; Conway, *Reconstruction of Georgia*, 186; J. M. Matthews, "Negro Republicans," 155.

[5] Downs, *After Appomattox*, 219–21; Russ, "Radical Disfranchisement," 200–201 (are about); Smith, "Reconstruction 'Triumph,'" 418–22.

[6] *Worcester (MA) Spy*, December 24, 1869; *Cincinnati Gazette*, January 13, 1870; *Augusta Constitutionalist*, January 25, 1870; *Memphis Appeal*, December 29, 1869.

to swear to the Test Oath, General Terry established a board of three military officers to investigate disputed cases. When Terry made inquiries to headquarters in Washington about how to proceed, General Sherman urged him to be vigilant about the most "flagrant" cases but left the case-by-case decisions to Terry's discretion. Joshua Hill telegraphed General Sherman and received the same answer. The process went fairly smoothly in the state senate, where Radicals had tight control. It was much tenser in the House where a Bullock ally supported by General Terry presided with a heavy hand as clerk pro tem. Bullock had opposed the seating of runners-up in September 1868 when it resulted in Democrats gaining seats, but he favored it now that it seated more Republicans. Critics rightly accused him of hypocrisy. The process resulted in the restoration of all but a few Black members and the replacement of about two dozen White members. Combining reinstatements with replacements, the reorganized General Assembly included, by most counts, thirty-six African Americans. An angry Democratic columnist quipped that the general was a "terry-ble man."[7]

The vote for Speaker of the House served as an approximate measure of the relative strength of Republican factions and the status of Joshua Hill. R. L. McWhorter, Bullock's man from Greene County, faced former Bullock ally John E. Bryant, who had come around to supporting Hill. Bryant was a former Freedman's Bureau official, an associate of Hill's son-in-law John Bowles, an ally of Black voters, and the editor of the *Loyal Georgian* newspaper. Originally a member of the so-called Augusta Ring, Bryant had opposed Hill for Senate in July 1868, and he was one of the twenty-three White Republicans who voted against the expulsion of Black legislators in September. However, Bryant's ties with Bullock and Blodgett and their radical Black allies had already begun to fray early in 1868. By the end of that year, he had broken completely from his previous Augusta Ring allies. Bryant opposed the act that remanded Georgia to military supervision, and he stated unequivocally to the *Atlanta New Era*, "I believe that

[7] Russ, "Radical Disfranchisement," 200 (flagrant); *Appendix to the Congressional Globe*, 42-2, pt. 6, 379; Hill mentioned the 1870 telegram in *Globe*, 42-2, May 20, 1872, 3646; *Augusta Chronicle*, January 5, 1870 (terry-able). Sources differ slightly; numbers cited come from Duncan, *Entrepreneur for Equality*, 96. See also Smith, "Reconstruction 'Triumph,'" 422–23; Currie-McDaniel, *Carpetbagger of Conscience*, 107–11; Gillette, *Retreat from Reconstruction*, 88; Nathans, *Losing the Peace*, 167–74; Conway, *Reconstruction of Georgia*, 186–88.

Messrs. Hill and Miller have been legally elected United States Senators from Georgia and are entitled to seats."[8]

Early in 1870 as the state legislature was convening, Bryant announced the formation of the National Republican Club with Hill as president and himself as chair of the executive committee. Some Radicals charged that Bryant and Hill were closet Democrats, to which Bryant replied, "We are working as members of the Republican party and will present our views from a Republican stand-point." Taking note that Joshua Hill was president of Bryant's group, the now pro-Bullock *New Era* of Atlanta dredged up statements from Hill's 1863 gubernatorial campaign to try to discredit him and his wing of Georgia Republicanism. The *Nation* observed, "the whole scene at Atlanta is one of the greatest confusion."[9]

It was not unreasonable for the Hill-Bryant faction to expect that some Democrats might cooperate with them in 1870 as they had to elect Hill back in July 1868. The influential *Augusta Chronicle* argued that the only way to prevent the nightmare of Radical rule was for Democrats to form some sort of alliance with the moderate and conservative Republicans "who have, from the first, opposed the extreme and violent measures of Bullock and Blodgett." The *Chronicle*'s list of men who might cooperate "to defeat the schemes of Bullock and of the extremists" began with Amos Akerman and Josh Hill. Once again, as in July 1868, when he had worked behind the scenes to help Hill prevail for the Senate seat, Robert Toombs became a strange political bedfellow with conservative Republicans. Bryant said that Toombs remarked, "while Bullock is killing the Republican party, by G-d he is killing the whole State as well." In a letter to Alexander Stephens, Toombs confirmed his behind-the-scenes role in the selection

[8] *LaGrange Reporter*, February 18, 1870; Currie-McDaniel, *Carpetbagger of Conscience*, 108–10; Nathans, *Losing the Peace*, 175–78; Smith, "Reconstruction 'Triumph,'" 421–23; *Augusta Chronicle & Sentinel*, December 9, 1868; *Savannah News*, December 11, 1868 (*New Era*); Duncan, *Entrepreneur for Equality*, 81–81; Drago, *Black Politicians*, 53–55. Currie-McDaniel, *Carpetbagger of Conscience*, 93–110, misses the importance of the city election in the break-up of the Augusta Ring.

[9] *LaGrange Reporter*, February 11, 1870 (*Augusta Chronicle*, we are working); *Columbus Sun*, February 25, 1870; Currie-McDaniel, *Carpetbagger of Conscience*, 108; *Atlanta New Era*, February 3, 1870; Duncan, *Entrepreneur for Equality*, 121; Abbott, "The Republican Party Press," 751; *Nation*, January 20, 1870.

of the new Speaker of the Georgia House of Representatives: "I and Joe Brown are trying to elect [Bryant]! Rather a strange conjunction is it not?"[10]

This time it did not work. Not enough Democrats followed Toombs's advice, and not enough Republicans followed the lead of Hill, Bryant, and company. Thus, without a unified bipartisan coalition to stop him, Bullock's pick, McWhorter, became Speaker by a 24-vote margin. With the three federal mandates of reinstating Black members, removing ineligible White members, and ratifying the Fifteenth Amendment out of the way, Bullock and the Radical Republican-dominated General Assembly could focus their aim on Georgia's two US senate seats and the state's full readmission.[11]

The legislature went into temporary recess in early February 1870 to give Bullock time to lead a delegation to Washington to lobby on behalf of his contention that the body was authorized to choose new senators. Knowing of Bullock's intentions, a group of conservatives and moderates hopped the train to the nation's capital so that they too could press their case. Neither group obtained definitive support for its interpretations. The Radical delegation composed of Bullock, Foster Blodgett, Ben Conley, and others reached the capital first. Their key argument was that the December 22 law had effectively voided the election of Hill and Miller and that a new selection must proceed apace. They contended that the voiding of the July 1868 Senate election was a necessary consequence of the required

[10] *Macon Telegraph* January 4, 1870 (*Augusta Chronicle*). See also *Augusta Chronicle*, January 5, 1870; *Columbus Enquirer*, January 14, 16, 1870; *LaGrange Reporter*, February 11, 1870 (*Augusta Chronicle*, while Bullock); Toombs to Stephens, January 24, 1870, in Phillips, *Correspondence*, 707; Nathans, *Losing the Peace*, 176.

[11] *Chicago Inter Ocean*, January 10, 1870; Currie-McDaniel, *Carpetbagger of Conscience*, 109–10; Duncan, *Entrepreneur for Equality*, 96–97, 124; Parks, *Joseph E. Brown*, 441–43; Nathans, *Losing the Peace*, 173–78; *Augusta Chronicle*, January 5, 12, 1870; *Columbus Enquirer*, February 22, 1870; *Milledgeville Southern Recorder*, January 25, 1870; *Sandersville Central Georgian*, January 12, 1870 (*Savannah Morning News*); *Columbus Enquirer*, January 16, 1870; *Boston Journal*, January 20, 1870; *Cincinnati Gazette*, January 20, 1870; J. M. Bryant, *How Curious a Land*, 117, 122–26, 134–37, 194–95.

reorganization of the General Assembly even though the December 1869 act was silent on the subject.[12]

Joshua Hill and John Bryant led the anti-Bullock delegation, which also included former congressman J. H. Caldwell, state treasurer N. L. Angier, John Bowles, and legislators C. K Osgood, and A. J. Williams. The pro-Hill group countered the Bullock-Blodgett argument by claiming that if Congress had meant to void the senatorial election, it would have done so explicitly as it did for the expulsion of Black legislators and the seating of ineligible White legislators. Thus, they contended, the act's silence should be interpreted to mean that the July 1868 senate election remained valid and no new election should proceed.[13]

The legislative history of the act was inconclusive. During the December debate, a congressman asked Benjamin Butler, the bill's principal sponsor, how the law would affect the Senate seats. The Massachusetts Radical replied, "This bill does not interfere with that matter at all." But then he immediately equivocated: "There may or may not be a new election of Senators after a loyal Legislature is assembled in the State."[14]

Both Georgia groups presented their cases to the Judiciary Committee and the public. Most of the national press reported that the Hill delegation fared better than Bullock's group. The Washington correspondent of the *New York Times* explained to his readers that even though some politicians argued that the December law mandated a new Senate election, "Nothing is further from the fact—and this is so understood by the president and by a majority of the Senate." A pro-Hill pamphlet published the opinion of one of the attorneys who had defended expelled legislators. He declared that the December act "does not, in express terms, or by reasonable implication, set aside anything that Georgia had done, except the act expelling the colored members from the Legislature." Like many other

[12] *Columbus Sun*, February 15, 1870; *Atlanta New Era*, February 10, 1870; *Augusta Constitutionalist*, February 13, 1870; *Augusta Chronicle*, February 16, 1870; *Savannah Morning News*, February 4, 14, 1870; *LaGrange Reporter*, February 3, 11, 1870 (*Atlanta Constitution*); *New York Herald*, February 14, 1870; *Nashville Tennessean*, February 25, 1870; *Chicago Tribune*, February 17, 1870; *Nation*, February 20, 1870.

[13] *New York Tribune*, February 9, 1870 (considerable); *Macon Telegraph*, February 22, 1870 (*Richmond Dispatch* of February 9).

[14] *Globe*, 41-2, December 20, 1869, 249.

commentators, the pamphlet's author asserted that if it had not been for the regrettable expulsion of Black legislators, "our Senators and Representatives long ago would have been in their places."[15]

Bryant and Caldwell, a former congressman and a member of the Republican National Committee, testified before the Senate Judiciary Committee and then published a forty-five-page booklet, which included their testimony along with supporting documents. The main focus of their case was that Rufus Bullock had changed his tune in late 1868 and that everything that he had done since that point constituted hypocritical machinations for his own cynical political purposes. They insisted Bullock had used the expulsion of the Black members to accomplish his own selfish political aims that went far beyond correcting the illegal expulsion itself. Their basic argument was essentially the same as that expressed in the Hill-inspired (or authored) *National Republican* editorial of December 1868, and then they added another year of alleged Bullock shenanigans to their case. To establish the authors' credibility and objectivity, Bryant explained to the committee that both he and Caldwell had been among the few Georgia legislators who voted against the expulsion of the Black members and that they had "appealed to Congress to reseat them." To further enhance his credence, Bryant pointed out that he had voted for Joe Brown rather than Hill in July 1868. Bryant testified that he and Caldwell had backed the Bullock administration "as long as we could conscientiously defend it," but that they now believed that the "ablest Republicans" in the state were Joseph Brown, A. T. Akerman, and "the great Union leader of Georgia" Joshua Hill.[16]

Bullock had his opportunity before the Senate Judiciary Committee as well. Reports emerged to the effect that Radicals tended to endorse the governor's conclusions but found him personally off-putting. The normally Radical-leaning senator Roscoe Conkling (R-NY) was said to be so irritated at the Georgia governor's crass opportunism that he "told Bullock to his face that he had deceived him and misled the Committee." Bullock countered the Caldwell-Bryant testimony and pamphlet by publishing his own fifty-seven-page booklet for distribution to Congress and the press. It

---

[15] *Augusta Chronicle*, February 9, 1870 (*New York Times*, Nothing); Lester, *Georgia Question*, 10 (does not).

[16] Caldwell and Bryant, *Georgia Question*, 6–8 (certified), 10, 21, 17.

included his point-by-point response plus several letters and documents, including General Terry's August report on disorder in Georgia. To support his case for new Senate elections, Bullock presented an analysis that demonstrated that Hill's July 1868 election had been dependent upon the votes of legislative members who were subsequently removed in accordance with the provisions of the December 1869 Act. J. E. Bryant and N. L. Angier countered by providing the committee with a twenty-page compilation of documents purporting to show that Hill and Miller would have prevailed even if ineligible members were removed from the count. The Senate committee itself made no definitive determination of the count.[17]

Both Georgia delegations obtained audiences with President Grant in February. Bullock's group went first. Following the meeting with Grant, the governor telegraphed to the press that the chief executive was in favor of having the General Assembly choose new senators. Joshua Hill's group reached the White House a couple of days later. Grant explicitly disclaimed Bullock's telegram and assured the delegation that he remained officially neutral. The moderates failed to obtain the open support that they sought from the president, but according to reliable reports, they found some solace in Grant's friendly parting remark to Hill: "I expect to see you very often."[18]

After they left the president, the Hill-Bryant group met with General Sherman, who, of course, knew Hill from their wartime relationship and subsequent correspondence. Sherman received the group warmly and reportedly laughed about Senator Conkling's stern put-down of Rufus

[17] "Georgia Before the Senate Judiciary Committee, Washington, DC, February 8, 1870" (no publisher listed; presumedly privately published by Bullock), HathiTrust.org; Angier and Bryant, *Georgia Legislature, Legally Organized in 1868*, copy in Hill file at MCA; *Bainbridge Southern Sun*, February 17, 1870 (told Bullock).

[18] *Columbus Sun*, February 15, 1870; *Savannah Morning News*, February 14, 1870 (*Baltimore American*, I expect); *Augusta Constitutionalist*, February 13, 1870; *Greensboro Herald*, February 17, 1870; *LaGrange Reporter*, February 11, 1870 (*Atlanta Constitution*); *Cleveland (OH) Leader*, February 12, 1870; *Richmond Dispatch*, February 10, 1870; *Springfield (MA) Republican*, February 10, 1870.

Bullock. The group inferred that the general favored the seating of Hill and Miller, but they departed without securing a formal public endorsement.[19]

Back in Georgia, the state's complicated half-in, half-out status presented a delicate legal and political challenge for Bullock and the Radical faction. If everything that the 1868–1869 legislature enacted and authorized had to be re-done, considerable legal confusion would ensue. Bullock's solution to the problem was to distinguish between "ordinary" laws which he classified as valid and acts "of a political character" which he considered to be void. Naturally, he classified the election of US senators as an act of political character. Unlike several of Bullock's other arguments, this one had a basis in legal precedents regarding routine matters undertaken by de facto legislatures. The challenge, of course, was where exactly to draw the line between the "ordinary" and the "political." The ordinary classification undoubtedly applied to administrative appointments, paying routine bills, conducting local elections, and the like. What was not so clear was on which side of the line the selection of US senators fell. A Columbus Democratic editorial regarded it "inconsistent to the extreme of absurdity" for Bullock to claim that the legislature could pass all sorts of valid laws "but could not elect United States Senators."[20]

To illustrate his "ordinary" versus "political" distinction, Bullock cleverly exploited the ratification of the Fourteenth Amendment. Moderate Republicans had contended that congressional acceptance of Georgia's mid-1868 ratification constituted strong evidence that all of the actions that occurred prior to the expulsion of the Black members, including the election of Hill and Miller, should stand. Tellingly, at the time that the 1868 ratification occurred, Bullock had raised no objections, but now he retroactively contended that it had been invalid. In a bold act of political theater, the governor persuaded the 1870 legislature to make a prominent show of re-ratifying the Fourteenth Amendment in order to buttress his

---

[19] *Macon Telegram*, February 22, 1870; *Savannah Morning News*, February 14, 1870; *Augusta Chronicle*, February 9, 1870; *LaGrange Reporter*, February 11, 1870, quoting *Atlanta Constitution*; *Augusta Constitutionalist*, February 13, 1870.

[20] Bullock letter of February 16, 1870 (*LaGrange Reporter*, February 18, 1870); *(Athens) Southern Banner*, February 18, 1870; *Columbus Enquirer*, February 20, 22 (inconsistent), 1870.

point that the senatorial election of July 1868 was similarly tainted and needed to be re-done.[21]

When he returned from Washington, Bullock called upon the General Assembly to choose new senators even though he had not received approval from the Judiciary Committee to do so. The situation was complicated by the fact that the vacancies caused by the Civil War and Reconstruction delays had disrupted the normal Senate rotation. The short-term position for which Miller had been elected would expire in March 1871, so whomever the Senate seated would be serve only briefly. Accordingly, Bullock asked the Republican caucus to nominee three men: one for the Miller term that would end in March 1871, one for the Hill term that extended to March 1873, and one for the full six-year term that would serve from 1871 to 1877.[22] Normally and legally, the choice for the full term would not be made by the legislature sitting in February 1870 but by the new legislature scheduled to be chosen in the upcoming fall elections. Bullock was rightfully fearful that Democrats would control that body, so he wanted to go ahead and make the choice when he could.

Some pundits suspected that Rufus Bullock wanted Hill's seat for himself, and other rumors were afoot that a secret party caucus would heal the Republican split by retaining Hill, letting Miller have his few months, and designating either Bullock or Blodgett for the full term. Such rumors may have been unfounded all along, but it is more likely that political reality led Bullock and the Radicals to change their minds. In any case, Bullock tapped his attorney general Henry P. Farrow for the Hill spot, and the caucus went along obligingly. The short-term Miller seat was more troublesome for the governor. Black caucus delegates had been led to believe that their White Radical allies would select an African American, but they were severely disappointed when neither Henry Turner nor any other Black man gained significant support. The Democratic press was quick to detect Radical Republican hypocrisy. Caucus votes for the short term scattered among several White candidates until attorney Richard H. Whiteley, a member of the 1867–1868 Georgia State Constitutional Convention and former Republican congressional candidate from southwest Georgia,

21 Duncan, *Entrepreneur for Equality*, 97; Nathans, *Losing the Peace*, 178, Russ, "Radical Disfranchisement," 198.

22 McClendon, "Status of the Ex-Confederate States," 706.

eventually won. The main prize was the full term slated to start in March 1871. As expected, the nomination went to the governor's highly controversial right-hand man Foster Blodgett, whom rival John Bryant called the "evil genius" of Georgia Republicans.[23]

The vote of the Republican legislative caucus was tantamount to election, so all three Republican caucus nominees were selected with only a few dissenting votes sprinkled among various African American candidates who felt disrespected. John Bryant joined with A. J. Williams of Morgan County and C. K. Osgood of Chatham to propose a House resolution that denounced the election of senators as illegal, but the Speaker summarily dismissed it. Democrats also vainly cried foul. The *August Chronicle*, long-time critic of Bullock and Blodgett, called the election a "farce" and an "outrageous fraud" accomplished only by "the instrumentality of the bayonet."[24]

Thus, by the end of February 1870, Georgia had five senators-elect: Hill, Miller, Farrow, Whiteley, and Blodgett. For the most ardent ex-rebels, but no one else, the count was seven to include Alexander Stephens and Herschel Johnson, whom the General Assembly had chosen in 1866. The Judiciary Committee of the US Senate had only four of the names officially before it because Bullock withheld Blodgett's credentials pending the resolution of perjury accusations against his compatriot. According to the *Savannah Morning News*, "the friends of Messrs. Hill and Miller here are confident that they will be admitted to their seats." The friends of Messrs. Farrow and Whiteley, of course, thought the opposite. The *New York World*

[23] *Augusta Constitutionalist*, January 8, 12, 1870; *Worcester (MA) Spy*, December 24, 1869; *Augusta Constitutionalist*, February 16, 1870; *Columbus Sun*, February 22, 1870; and *(Macon) Georgia Weekly Telegram* and *(Macon) Georgia Journal & Messenger*, February 22, 1870; Nathans, *Losing the Peace*, 178; Duncan, *Entrepreneur for Equality*, 123; Conway, *Reconstruction of Georgia*, 189; Rogers, *Scalawag in Georgia*, 58–60; Caldwell and Bryant, *Georgia Question*, 20 (evil).

[24] *Atlanta New Era*, February 17, 24, 1870; *Savannah Morning News*, February 16, 1870; *Springfield (MA) Republican*, February 17, 1870; *Augusta Constitutionalist*, February 22, 1870; *LaGrange Reporter*, February 18, 25, 1870 (*New Era*); *Augusta Chronicle & Sentinel*, February 23, 1870 (farce).

predicted that Hill would "doubtless go by the board" even though he was a friend of President Grant.[25]

For weeks the Judiciary Committee had endured countless hours of testimony, documents, newspaper stories, pamphlets, and face-to-face lobbying about Georgia affairs. Notwithstanding the fact that his son-in-law Johns Bowles and his most vociferous supporter, John Bryant, moved to Georgia after the war, Hill told T. P. Saffold that senators regarded input from native White Georgians more highly than that from "new citizens—or carpetbaggers."[26]

Finally in early March, a few weeks after the Georgia legislature selected its new set of senators-elect, the committee came to a compromise recommendation that satisfied neither side. The majority report accepted the moderate Bryant-Caldwell argument that the January 1870 reorganization of the General Assembly had been deeply flawed because the actions of Governor Bullock and General Terry had gone far beyond the authority and intentions of the December 22, 1869, law. However, that finding had no practical effect because the committee also decided that "it would be better for the peace and quiet of Georgia to overlook all these irregularities and let the Legislature stand as it was organized, rather than go over the whole subject again." The overall tone of the committee report and the word on the street seemed favorable to Hill and Miller, but the committee made no specific recommendation about the Senate seats. Congress did not formally adopt the Senate Judiciary report, but its conclusion shaped the course debate for the following several months. The immediate effect was to leave Governor Bullock in charge for the time being.[27]

The stage was thus set in March 1870 for the Senate controversy to drag on. The Senate had not officially rejected Joshua Hill and H. V. M. Miller, but neither had it rejected Henry P. Farrow and Richard H. Whiteley. It had not yet even considered Foster Blodgett. The *Southern Watchman* of Athens commented wryly, "However much our people may complain of

[25] *Savannah Morning News*, February 16, 1870; *New York World*, February 23, 1870; *Atlanta Constitution*, February 18, 22, 1870; *Greensboro Herald*, February 24, 1870, *Atlanta New Era*, February 24, 1870.

[26] Hill to Saffold, March 26, 1870, Saffold Family Papers, MCA.

[27] *Globe*, 41-2, pt. 3, 127 (On the whole); *(Athens) Southern Watchman*, March 2, 1870; *Atlanta New Era*, March 10, 1870; *Atlanta Intelligencer*, March 16, 1870; Russ, "Radical Disfranchisement," 204–205; Nathans, *Losing the Peace*, 180–81.

a scarcity of corn and other breadstuffs, of bacon and provender, there is certainly no lack of United States Senators." Also using an agricultural analogy, another Athens paper listed all seven: "Georgia has a pretty extensive crop of United States Senators. Stephens, Johnson, Hill, Miller, Blodgett, Farrow, Whiteley—and yet her Senatoral seats are vacant." Georgia would not see anything like this again until the infamous three governors controversy of 1946–1947.[28]

Congress Readmits Georgia, Joshua Hill Remains on Hold

The Senate could not move forward to determine who Georgia's rightful senators were until Congress as a whole resolved the more fundamental question of the state's position in the Union. By spring 1870, there was wide bipartisan consensus that the time had come for Georgia to be fully readmitted, yet there was nowhere near a consensus about how that was to be accomplished—the devil, as usual, was in the details.

Republican moderates and conservatives believed the details should be simple. Congress should accept Georgia's reorganized legislature and grant Hill and Miller their seats in the Senate. They wanted to end General Terry's supervision of state government, but they were amenable to some federal troops remaining in the state to protect Black voters during the scheduled November 1870 state legislative and congressional elections.

The party's Radical wing envisioned a different and more complicated scenario for readmission. In addition to wanting the Senate to seat Farrow and Whiteley (and eventually Blodgett), they wanted Congress to cancel Georgia's legislative elections scheduled for November 1870. They were almost certain that Democrats would sweep to victory even if federal troops supervised the polls. The Radical plan rested on the theory that the two-year terms of the current state legislators officially began not with the legislative election back in spring 1868 but with the General Assembly's reorganization in January 1870, some eighteen months later. Therefore, the Radicals contended, the current members should remain in office and not

---

[28] *(Athens) Southern Watchman*, February 23, 1870; *(Athens) Southern Banner*, February 18, 1870 (Whitely [*sic*?], Senatoral [*sic*]); *Atlanta Constitution*, February 22, 1870; *Augusta Constitutionalist*, December 2, 1870 (Stephens, Johnson). See Buchanan, "Three Governors Controversy."

have to stand for reelection until November 1872. This interpretation quickly came to be referred to as "prolongation."

On March 7, 1870, Radical representative Benjamin Butler (R-MA) introduced a bill that would readmit Georgia with prolongation of the sitting legislature to 1872 included. Moderate Republican John Bingham (R-OH) filed an amendment to the Butler bill, which provided for the readmission of Georgia but explicitly prohibited the prolongation of the sitting legislature by requiring Georgia to conduct its next legislative election in November 1870 as the state constitution provided.[29] Butler and Bingham had personified the differences between Radical and moderate Republicans since they tangled over the impeachment of Andrew Johnson in 1868.

The range of Congressional opinion on the Georgia question was wide even among Republicans. Some favored the simplest solution (i.e., that no bill was needed at all), and the Senate could just seat Hill and Miller and be done with it. At the other end of the spectrum, several Radicals in the Senate regarded even the Butler bill as too lenient. They desired to keep Georgia under strict military reconstruction because of the continuing politically motivated violence by the Klan and similar actors. Ultimately, the issue boiled down to admitting Georgia with the sitting General Assembly prolonged to 1872 (as Butler and mainstream Radicals advocated), admitting Georgia with the Bingham amendment attached (as moderates and conservatives preferred). This oversimplified summary captures the principal question but obscures a raft of personal, political, and constitutional issues that would keep the Georgia question before Congress and the nation for several more months. The Senate put off deciding among Georgia's competing senators-elect until they resolved the question of the Bingham amendment. A North Georgia wag observed the great political struggle and suggested Bible verses appropriate to the Georgia Republican luminaries involved: Joshua Hill, "Behold, I stand at the door

[29] *Globe*, 41-2, pt. 2, 1701–708; Nathans, *Losing the Peace*, 185; *Nation*, March 17, 1870; *Atlanta New Era*, March 17, 1870. The law provided that the term of the legislators elected in the April 1868 special election would considered as starting in fall 1868 when the general election would have been held.

and knock" (Rev 3:20), and Rufus Bullock, "When the wicked beareth rule, the people mourn" (Prov 20:2).[30]

Each Republican faction claimed that its position on the Bingham amendment would be best for the party, and each made valid points. All Republicans understood that the party could not survive in Georgia based on Black votes alone. It was a majority-White state, and by 1870 only a handful of Whites remained disqualified from voting. The Republicans' strategic challenge of how to support Black suffrage and office-holding while still retaining a significant portion of the White vote was not limited to Georgia—or even the South. In 1869, Massachusetts senator Henry Wilson, later to become Grant's second vice president, lamented that everywhere across the country where Republicans had advocated for Black rights, doing so had cost the party White votes. Radical Republicans correctly predicted that holding elections in 1870 would lead to Klan-like intimidation of Black voters and thus almost certain victory for the Democrats. Waiting until 1872, they argued, would give Republicans time to pass important legislation and consolidate their gains for the long run. On the other hand, moderate and conservative Republicans also expected a Democratic sweep, but they were convinced that canceling the elections to prolong the sitting Republican-majority legislature would make matters worse in the long run because it would enrage Whites who might otherwise be attracted to the party.[31]

The moderate viewpoint quickly prevailed in the House, so the Butler bill passed on March 7, 1870, with the Bingham amendment attached. The amended bill then went to the Senate, where it faced much more extended and contentious consideration than it had in the lower chamber. Senator Trumbull led the effort on behalf of the moderate Bingham amendment while Radical senator William M. Stewart (R-NV) became the principal spokesperson for passing the bill in the original form that Butler had proposed. Their arguments had a familiar ring. Trumbull continued to assert that the only purposes of the Georgia Act of December 1869 act were to

---

[30] Downs, *After Appomattox*, 225–36, portrays the struggle as between "peacetime" and "wartime" Republicans; *Dalton North Georgia Citizen*, March 10, 1870 (also included verses for Conley, Blodgett, Farrow, Brown, McWhorter, and Angier).

[31] *Globe*, 41-2, pt. 3, March 15, 1870, 1960 (I believe); Chernow, *Grant*, 687.

reinstate Black legislators, to remove and replace men who could not honestly swear to the Ironclad Test Oath, and to compel ratification of the Fifteenth Amendment. Trumbull's fellow moderate George Edmunds (R-VT) declared, "I believe as firmly as I believe anything that to strike out this [Bingham] provision and insert no other and leave [Georgians] to themselves would be to invite the very violence and disorder which Senators are so anxious, and sincerely anxious, to prevent." On the other hand, Stewart and the Radicals held to the position that Georgia's unseating of Black legislators tainted all political action before and after that point and that prolonging the legislature would give Republicans a fighting chance.[32]

During this March exchange and all through the rest of spring and early summer 1870, the question of who should be the senators from Georgia operated as a subtext of the immediate debate about prolongation and the personal character of Rufus Bullock. It was widely assumed in the press and in Congress that passage of the Butler Bill with the Bingham Amendment attached would bode well for the seating of Hill and Miller, and passage without the amendment would result in the seating of Farrow and Whiteley, followed later by Blodgett. Senator Stewart conceded that very point when he declared on the floor, "I believe this Bingham amendment is very strong evidence in favor of his [Hill's] right to a seat. I think it almost an enactment that Mr. Hill is entitled to it." During his arguments in favor of the Bingham amendment, Trumbull praised Hill as "a Union man all through the war, a loyal man who was here in Congress and upheld the Union here and went home and did everything that a man in that country could do to assist the cause of the Union all through the war." The Illinois senator stressed the stark contrast between consistent Unionist Hill and the newly chosen Georgia senators-elect, all three of whom had served the Confederacy in official positions before they switched to Radical politics for their own selfish purposes. To dent Hill's armor, Stewart brought up, as so many others had before and after him, Joshua Hill's equivocal statements about "reconstruction" from the 1863 gubernatorial campaign.[33]

---

[32] *Globe*, 41-2, pt. 3, 1925–930, March 14, 1870; 1953–954 (Stewart), 1960 (Trumbull), March 15, 1870; *Washington (DC) National Republican*, March 15–6, 1870; Nathans, *Losing the Peace*, 186.

[33] Ibid.

Georgians from both camps traveled in and out of the capital as the debate ebbed and flowed. Joshua Hill and his allies boarded at the Metropolitan Hotel while Rufus Bullock and company occupied accommodations at the fashionable Willard. In early May, Hill told T. P. Saffold that he had been very ill and lamented to his friend that further delay "seems inevitable." Hill reported that he had recently had "a long and earnest talk" with Grant and that the president opposed the reestablishment of military rule in Georgia and wanted the state to be admitted. "But under what particular terms I do not know…," he said; "I will not undertake to predict what will be done." Three weeks later, he wrote, "The Bullockites are alarmed," but he was still not sure what would happen. Congress, of course, faced many other issues besides Georgia, so the Butler bill and the Bingham amendment kicked around off and on in the Senate until the middle of July. All of the parliamentary maneuvering produced a legislative muddle that pleased no one completely. Despite all the peripheral issues, the Bingham amendment, i.e., prolongation of the sitting legislature, remained the principal sticking point between the Republican factions.[34]

Thomas Tipton, a who had become one of Nebraska's first two senators upon statehood in 1867, was not known for frequent Senate debate, but on April 12 he delivered a long and impassioned speech on behalf of the Bingham amendment that captured the essence of the moderate Republican position:

> I say to every Senator here and to every man everywhere in the United States that when we as Senators returned to our homes in the summer of 1868 and the question was put to us whether we had received the Senators from Georgia, we all replied that they were not elected until two or three days after our adjournment, but of course they would have been received just a members in the House of Representatives, if they had been elected in time. No man in the United States doubted in that hour that Georgia was admitted.

Tipton called attention to the critical "not now," wording of the 1869 Senate Judiciary report on Joshua Hill and argued in essence that "now" had finally come. "I desire the triumph of the Republicans of the State of

[34] Ibid.; Hill to Saffold, May 6, 27, 1870, Saffold Papers, MCA.

Georgia," the Nebraskan assured his colleagues, but he also explained to them that he resented being told what it meant to be a Republican. He mocked Rufus Bullock for holding forth like a regular governor until it served his selfish purposes to switch to the "provisional" mantle. With unnamed but unmistakable reference to Bullock, Tipton charged, "Everything that is low in the petty demagogism of party canvassers has been introduced here. The machinery was set in operation in this city. The wires were pulled from the State of Georgia." Tipton declared that he was strongly in favor of protecting Black voters, but he agreed with Bryant and others that prolongation of Bullock's pet legislature would actually prove contrary to that purpose. No one stated the moderate position more clearly.[35]

Not only did Bullock face allegations in Washington, but pressure on him also increased back home. State Treasurer N. L. Angier produced a report detailing Bullock's alleged malfeasance with government funds. The *New York Tribune* commented with apparent satisfaction that Angier was "evidently bent on making the State Capital as uncomfortable to the Governor as Mr. Hill has sought to make the National Capital."[36]

Both sides continued to spread their arguments in the press and in numerous pamphlets that could be put into the hands of reporters and placed on the desks of members of Congress. Hearing rumors of underhanded actions by Bullock, the Senate Judiciary Committee launched an investigation. One provocative charge was that by knowingly overpaying for the cost of printing his materials, Bullock had essentially bribed the editor of the *Washington Chronicle* to write news articles and editorials opposing the Bingham amendment. The details of charges about Bullock's alleged corruption in Washington and Georgia are tangential to this narrative, but the course of the investigation is relevant because Bullock made every effort to blame his Washington woes on the machinations of his rival Joshua Hill. The *Chicago Times* starkly contrasted the two men: "As Joshua Hill was an unflinching Union man in the darkest days of our civil war, Bullock's denunciation of him will have no effect with men who know

[35] *Globe*, 41-2, pt. 3, 2606–610, April 12, 1870.
[36] *New York Tribune*, May 30, 1870.

Bullock." Bullock seemed to have a knack for being disliked, even by many politicians who agreed with him politically.[37]

To some extent, Bullock was correct in blaming Hill for his most recent woes because the senator-elect had helped to facilitate the investigations of the governor. The story that Bullock operatives had offered ten thousand dollars in railroad bonds to secure votes against the Bingham amendment made it into the press when Hill passed along documentation to a well-known reporter with whom he often dined. Hill obtained the information from his long-time friend and former legislator Judge James Hughes, who had, in turn, acquired it from a local assistant postmaster. On March 4, Hill came before the Senate Judiciary Committee. His sworn testimony did not add anything of substance to the published reports about Bullock's actions, but it did add some personal context and insert some hometown connection. Hill explained that he had dropped by to see Judge Hughes while on the way to the theater with Albert G. Foster, brother of his late dear friend and congressional predecessor Nathaniel Green Foster. It was Foster's first visit to the nation's capital city, so Foster went on to the theater while Hill conferred with Hughes. A. G. Foster's son would soon become Hill's son-in-law. John Bowles, Hill's other son-in-law, was busy helping John Bryant advocate for the Bingham amendment. On May 6, Hill wrote Saffold, his cousin's husband, that he was not sure how the investigation would turn out but that "it is clear that some person or persons" had contacted senators "with a view of bribing them."[38]

Since January, public attacks and counterattacks had been flying between Bullock forces and Bryant's crowd. Bullock and his allies had good reason to consider Bryant to be "the tool of the Hon. Joshua Hill." The pro-Bullock *New Era* claimed "that model of intrigue, Joshua Hill, whose

---

[37] *Atlanta Constitution*, June 1, 1870 (*Chicago Times*, May 26). *Macon Telegraph*, March 22, 29, 1870, describes the flurry of pamphlets (Duncan, *Entrepreneur for Equality*, 126–30; Nathans, *Losing the Peace*, 188–90; Currie-McDaniel, *Carpetbagger of Conscience*, 112; Parks, *Joseph E. Brown*, 444–45). Albert W. Foster married Louise Hill in 1872.

[38] Hill to Saffold, May 6, 1870, Saffold Family Papers, MCA; Hill testimony in "Report of the Committee on the Judiciary," May 19, 1870, Senate Report 175, 41st Congress, 2nd Session, 65–68. The reporter was H. J. Ramsdell, an acquaintance of Hill who worked for the *New York Tribune* and the *Cincinnati Commercial.*

personal ambition is kept perpetually in view, is the author and instigator of the whole affair." The paper charged Hill with having "personal malevolence and enmity toward the Governor"—which, of course, he did. The *New Era* was heavily dependent on state printing contracts controlled by Bullock, and it published several excerpts from stories in the *Washington Chronicle*, the publication that the governor was accused of bribing for favorable coverage.[39]

As Hill had predicted to Saffold, the majority report of the Senate investigating committee was unable to prove direct evidence of bribery, but it was highly critical of Bullock and of recalcitrant witnesses who refused to testify against him. The Democratic *Atlanta Constitution* observed, "Of course Bullock did not himself offer money to senators. He is too shrewd for that. But…the lobbyists were acting with his knowledge if not by his authority, there can be no doubt whatever." Bullock defended himself in a ten-page public letter of May 21 that made it very clear whom he blamed:

> These infamous lies have a common origin, and have been coined and put into circulation by men who hypocritically pretend to belong to the Republican party, but who are, and have been, acting in concert with the rebel Democracy in Georgia.… So far as the assaults which have been made here are concerned, they are directly traceable to Mr. Joshua Hill.… It is established that the whole affair is founded upon the machinations of Mr. Hill.[40]

---

[39] Senate Report 175, 41st Congress, 2nd Session, 65–68; *New York Tribune*, May 20, 1870; *Atlanta New Era*, March 3 (the tool), April 21, 28 (that model), May 18, 25 (personal),1870; *Augusta Chronicle*, April 27, 28 (Washington *Chronicle*), May 5 (*Cincinnati Commercial*), 1870; *Atlanta Intelligencer*, April 27, 1870; *(Athens) Southern Banner*, April 29, 1870 (*New York World*); *Atlanta Constitution*, May 25, 1870; Duncan, *Entrepreneur for Equality*, 125–29.

[40] Hill to Saffold, May 6, 1870, Saffold Family Papers, MCA; *Atlanta Constitution*, May 31, 1870; *Worcester (MA) Spy*, May 27, 1870; Bullock, *Letter…to the Republican Senators*, 7–8, 10. All three capital papers, *Chronicle*, *National Republican*, and *Evening Star*, printed the letter on May 23, 1870, as did the *New York Times*; *Augusta Constitutionalist*, *Savannah Morning News*, May 26, 1870; J. R. Parrott, *Admission of Georgia*. Given Bullock's statement that the "whole affair" was due to Hill, it is puzzling that Bullock's biographer wrote very little about Hill's role (Duncan, *Entrepreneur for Equality*, 128–29).

Bullock, Butler, and Hill's other political enemies returned often to the Madisonian's equivocal statement from the 1863 gubernatorial campaign. In response, John Bryant redistributed the 1866 statement in which Hill explained that the term "reconstruction," as he used it in 1863, did not apply to the postwar use of the word. Hill's defense that the meaning of "reconstruction" had evolved was even truer in 1870 than it had been when he penned it four years earlier.[41]

John Bryant further articulated the perspective of Georgia's conservative and moderate Republicans in a twenty-two-page public letter addressed specifically to Senator Charles Sumner (R-MA) but intended for the eyes of all Republican members of Congress. The former Union soldier and Freedman's Bureau officer expressed regret that he now found himself opposing Sumner because he had admired the Massachusetts abolitionist since "boyhood." The main thrust of Bryant's letter was that it would be men like Joshua Hill, A. T. Akerman, T. P. Saffold, N. L. Angier, Alfred Austell "and other wealthy Republicans" who would save the party—not Rufus Bullock and the sitting legislators, Black or White. Bryant defended his own record as a strong friend of the Black man and then wrote an impassioned defense of the moderate to conservative Republican long-term strategy:

> Sir, you cannot force Republican ideas upon the Southern people at the point of the bayonet. If you desire the party to grow strong in the South, you must appeal to the brains and the wealth of the South. You must gain the affections of the people. I tell you today that if you force Bullock and Blodgett on to the people of Georgia against their will, you will cause the Republican party to be detested forever by a large majority of the people of that State, and then I pity the poor colored people.

[41] J. Hill, *Union Record of Hon. Joshua Hill*, 2 (Bryant), 16. Hill testified that he did not know in advance that Bryant was going to distribute the letter, but after he found out about it he appreciated the gesture enough to give Bryant fifty dollars to help defray the printing cost (Hill testimony in Senate Report 175, 41st Congress, 2nd Session, 65–68).

In a closing, Bryant wrote, "If you so legislate that the Republican party of Georgia is destroyed forever, you cannot say that I have not warned you."[42]

As they had since 1868, most of Georgia's Black politicians, including Henry Turner, supported Bullock. However, Turner and other prominent Black leaders, including Jefferson Long and Aaron A. Bradley, spoke highly of Bryant and Hill even if they often differed with them on specific matters. Long's break with Bullock in late 1869 gave some Northern Republicans cover to vote either way and still claim that they supported freedmen. Bullock summoned about a dozen Black Georgia legislators and supporters to come to Washington to tell senators of the abuses that they had endured in the past and feared in the future.[43]

To fill the void left when the *New Era* followed its printing contract profits into Bullock's camp, Joshua Hill, along with his Madison compatriots T. P. Saffold and A. G. Foster plus Alfred Austell of Atlanta encouraged and financed Samuel Bard, the former *New Era* editor, to revive the *True Georgian* in May 1870. They expected Bard to carry the moderate Republican banner by opposing prolongation and the Bullock administration. Joe Brown and J. E. Bryant also endorsed the new enterprise but were not directly involved. Hill helped draft the new paper's prospectus, and he told Saffold that he thought that the statement, "will attract some moderate men, of the present Democratic party." The Democratic *Macon Telegraph* responded to the prospectus of the *True Georgian* by describing Joshua Hill and his fellows as "comprising the decency and moderation of Georgia Republicanism, and who find themselves as much out of place in the party, as it exists in Georgia, as a band of Quakers on board of corsair.

[42] J. E. Bryant, *Letter to Hon. Charles Sumner*, 16, 17, 21–22, and *passim*. See also Bryant, *Col. J. E. Bryant of Georgia, and the Washington* Chronicle. *Macon Telegraph*, March 29, 1870, mentions another Bryant-Bowles pamphlet, "An Appeal to Republican Senators by Wealthy and Influential Republican Leaders of Georgia," including letters from T. P. Saffold and A. G. Foster of Madison plus other Georgians (Currie-McDaniel, *Carpetbagger of Conscience*, 111–12).

[43] J. E. Bryant, *Letter... to Hon. H. Hamlin*, includes a letter from Turner, 11; Drago, *Black Politicians*, 57–58; Nathans, *Losing the Peace*, 188; J. M. Matthews, "Jefferson Franklin Long," 146; *Atlanta New Era*, May 18, 25, 1870.

They can't go with the Radicals and say they can't go with the Democrats."[44]

In mid-June 1870 President Grant appointed Amos T. Akerman as attorney general, the only Southerner in his cabinet. Grant had endeavored to remain above the fray regarding Georgia's readmission and its Senate seats, but the appointment of Akerman was another signal that he was leaning toward the moderate faction. Hill had played a significant role in securing Akerman's earlier appointment as US attorney for Georgia, so the Georgian's elevation to national office portended well for the senator-elect. Akerman was a strong advocate for the legal protection of Black political rights, including the right to hold office; but he was no close ally of Bullock. The *Atlanta Constitution* reported that the new attorney general was "a warm friend of Hon. Joshua Hill, believing that he was legally elected, and that he is entitled to his seat in the Senate." The *Chicago Tribune* saw irony in the circumstance in which, "the State of Georgia [is] practically out of the Union, and yet a citizen thereof [is] in the Cabinet of the President." The writer saw further irony in Grant appointing Akerman, a New England born former Confederate officer while at the same time, "Joshua Hill cannot come to the Senate, though he was not even a Georgia rebel amongst rebels."[45]

As the Georgia debate stretched into late June, future president James A. Garfield (R-OH) proclaimed to the House of Representatives that the Georgia issue, i.e., the Bingham amendment, should be decided on principle, not partisanship. A few minutes later Kentucky Democrat James B. Beck was not so subtle. He recited the standard list of charges against

---

[44] "Prospectus of the True Georgian" in *Atlanta Constitution*, June 8, 1870; Hill to Saffold, May 27, 1870, Saffold Family Papers, MCA. Two other short-lived Republican papers started at about the same time (Abbott, "The Republican Party Press," 752–54; see also Abbott, *For Free Press and Equal Rights*, 93–94, 125–26; *Macon Telegraph*, June 14, 1870; *New Orleans Times-Picayune*, June 2, 1870; *Rome Courier*, July 8 [conservative], 15, 1870; *Atlanta New Era*, July 13, 15, 1870; *Savannah Morning News*, July 1, 1870).

[45] *Macon Telegraph*, July 5, 1870 (*Atlanta Georgian*); *Chicago Tribune*, June 24, 1870; *Springfield (MA) Republican*, June 18, 1870; Currie-McDaniel, *Carpetbagger of Conscience*, 112, 208n; Calhoun, *Presidency of Ulysses S. Grant*, 105–106; Chernow, *Grant*, 700; Hill to Grant, March 20, 1869, in Grant, *Papers of Ulysses S. Grant*, 20:174.

Rufus Bullock and asserted, "The whole scheme and its managers are reeking of corruption." From Beck's border state perspective, prolongation was a plan of "the extreme Radical senators, who seem anxious for a pretext to reject Messrs. Hill and Miller, the regularly elected senators, simply because they are gentlemen and would faithfully represent their State in the Senate."[46]

By the time that the Georgia bill finally reached the House-Senate conference committee with the Bingham amendment attached, the positions had not evolved much. The final act of July 15 frustrated both sides. It declared Georgia to be readmitted, but it watered down the explicit wording of the Bingham amendment to read "Nothing in the Act contained shall be construed to deprive the people of Georgia of the right to an election for members of the General Assembly of said state, as provided for in the constitution thereof." Supporters of the amendment agreed to the semantic change to please senators and representatives who held constitutional qualms about Congress telling any state exactly when to hold its elections, but they believed that it still sent the clear message that Georgia must hold fall elections and not prolong its sitting legislature. Like previous legislation, the readmission act avoided explicitly saying anything about the pending senate seats. Two full years had passed since Joshua Hill's election. He remained in "not now" limbo, but he seemed one step closer.

Six More Months of Delay

With encouragement from Ben Butler and General Terry, Bullock found enough wiggle room in the vaguely worded readmission act to proceed almost as if the Bingham amendment had been completely defeated rather than merely watered down. In late July, his supporters in the General Assembly introduced a resolution that called for delaying the fall election and prolonging the legislature just as the governor wanted. It passed quickly in the Senate, where Radicals predominated, but it faced a bigger hurdle in the House. That gave the opposition time to build.

It was to be expected that conservatives such as Joshua Hill and T. P. Saffold would oppose prolongation. They got a chance to make their point

---

[46] *Globe*, 41-2, pt. 6, 4785, 4789, June 24, 1870.

to senators when Henry Turner granted them access to the floor even though he and most other Blacks actually favored the resolution. Another Black politician, Aaron Bradley, was so estranged from Bullock that he openly opposed prolongation even though it would have retained several African Americans in office. Bullock's plan took an even bigger blow when H. P. Farrow and Richard H. Whiteley, his own hand-picked senators-elect came out publicly against it as well. They apparently reasoned that supporting prolongation would hurt their case before the US Senate. Rumor was rife that President Grant opposed extending the legislative terms past the elections in 1870. On the other side, Foster Blodgett, ever loyal to Bullock and vice versa, worked hard to line up House votes in favor of the resolution.[47]

The anti-prolongation forces organized a mass meeting in Atlanta to put pressure on the state House of Representatives. The Democratic press observation that "Democrats and Republicans mingled freely" and that the number in attendance was "reaching into the thousands" may have been hyperbole, but it was clearly a large event that featured addresses from both political parties. Mayor William Ezzard chaired the event, and Joshua Hill was the lead speaker. Hill urged unity against the governor's usurpation of power and cautioned that if elections were delayed now, then they could be delayed indefinitely. The senator-elect reported that he had spoken to many of the sitting legislators and that he had asked each one the same question: "When they were elected in 1868 did they believe, or their constituents believe, that they were elected for a term beyond 1870?" None, Hill proclaimed were cheeky enough to answer in the affirmative. Senator-elect H. V. M. Miller and former Confederate general H. L. Benning were among the Democrats who also spoke.[48]

When Hill was making an anti-prolongation speech in Madison, a Bullock supporter "thrust himself into the meeting" and spoke of Colonel Hill "in a very insulting manner." The hometown senator-elect, who

[47] *Athens Southern Recorder*, July 19, 1870; Downs, *After Appomattox*, 230; Currie-McDaniel, *Carpetbagger of Conscience*, 112; C. Thompson, *Reconstruction in Georgia*, 268; Foner, *Reconstruction*, 454; Nathans, *Losing the Peace*, 190–94; Duncan, *Entrepreneur for Equality*, 130–31; Drago, *Black Politicians*, 57–58, 63; Rogers, *Scalawag in Georgia*, 62–63; *Atlanta Constitution*, July 29, 1870; *Columbus Sun*, August 14, 1870.

[48] *Columbus Sun*, July 31, 1870 (*Atlanta Constitution*, July 29).

recognized the harasser as a former resident, responded, "Jesse, you know you lie." Reportedly, Jesse "submitted without a murmur." Some Black attendees left the meeting after this exchange, but others remained, and two made their own anti-prolongation speeches.[49]

The vote came to a head on August 11. Twelve White Republicans in the House broke ranks with Bullock and joined with Democrats to defeat the prolongation plan 73 to 63. The governor had lost, so the election would be held before the end of 1870 as the Bingham amendment had intended. Denied the extra time in office that they had sought, Georgia Radicals now had to calculate how to make the best of the situation.[50]

Attorney General Akerman opposed prolongation, but he still wanted Republican candidates to have the best chance possible in the upcoming vote. To that end he became the principal drafter of election legislation designed to enhance the Republican Party's admittedly slim chances for victory. The law changed election day from the typical one day in November to three days in late December and made other adjustments designed to attract Republican voters—especially Black voters. Most moderate Republicans, including Bryant and probably Hill, reasoned that the election measures might aid both party factions, so the bill passed. In another effort to help Republican turnout, Bullock waived the collection of poll taxes.[51]

As the fall campaign heated up, internal strife further weakened the Republican Party. White operatives made little effort to rally the Black vote, and the party's enhanced outreach to White voters alienated some Black leaders. In late October, after the Union League and the national party denied Georgia Republicans much help, Foster Blodgett wrote an angry public letter accusing Akerman and the Grant administration of abandoning them. Akerman testily responded to Blodgett in a widely

---

[49] *Macon Telegraph*, August 23, 1870 (*Madison Journal*). At this time, Southern newspapers normally specified race when mentioning African Americans, so it is presumed that Jesse W. Jackson was White.

[50] Duncan, *Entrepreneur for Equality*, 131–32; Nathans, *Losing the Peace*, 192–206; Conway, *Reconstruction of Georgia*, 190; Parks, *Joseph E. Brown*, 445–47.

[51] Ibid.; Currie-McDaniel, *Carpetbagger of Conscience*, 113; Parks, *Joseph E. Brown*, 445–47. On secret ballot, see Drago, *Black Politicians*, 146–48; Calhoun, *Presidency of Ulysses S. Grant*, 325–26.

published letter that said that good Republicans "ought not to pause to bicker with each other."[52]

Anticipating a huge Democratic sweep in the upcoming December elections, Sam Bard's new paper, the *True Georgian,* abandoned the floundering Republican Party altogether. Joshua Hill, despite having helped establish the *True Georgian* only six months earlier, quickly and publicly disassociated himself from Bard's return to the embrace of the Democratic Party and pledged himself "to the great Union party of the nation, and its peerless leader." Addressing himself directly to Bard, Hill declared, "It is easy for you to return to the Democratic party. [But] I have spent my life in opposing it. I have no facility for change." Several national newspapers took note of Hill's letter. The *New York World,* itself of Democratic leaning, called Hill, "an open Republican of suspected Democratic proclivities." A more favorable Boston paper admired Hill's strong words of support for Grant. Bard did not entirely abandon Hill. Leaning toward the more accommodating "New Departure" wing of the Democrats, *True Georgian* expressed admiration for the Madisonian's opposition to the Bullock wing of the Republicans by declaring, "Such honest men and patriots as Hon. Joshua Hill, for instance, never have and never can associate with such a rotten and factional concern." It was a familiar middle ground for Joshua Hill: entirely too Republican for the Democrats and entirely too cozy with Democrats for the most ardent Republicans.[53]

Some Democrats fretted that the Akerman-Bullock election rules might bring out enough Black votes to carry the day for the Republicans,

---

[52] Abbott, "Republican Party Press," 755–56; *Atlanta Intelligencer,* November 2, 1870.

[53] *The True Georgian* expired in mid-1871. *Americus Republican,* October 28, 1870 (*True Georgian,* October 18); *Augusta Constitutionalist,* December 2, 1870, *New York Tribune,* December 1, 1870 (*True Georgian,* November 30); Bard, *Letter from Governor Samuel Bard,* 4–5; *Albany News,* December 6 (Hill letter to Bard), 9 (*True Georgian*); *New York World,* December 6, 1870; *New York Times,* December 7, 1870; *Boston Journal,* December 8, 1870; *Bangor (ME) Whig & Courier,* December 10, 1870; *New York Times,* December 7, 1870. On the "New Departure" see Perman, *Road to Redemption,* 20, 58–86; Wynne, *Continuity of Cotton.* When Bard switched sides, he still owed money to Hill and Saffold, and they were working to reach a debt settlement in February 1871 (Hill to Saffold, February 9, 1871, Saffold Family Papers, MCA).

but they needed not to have worried. In most Georgia counties, Republican efforts were no match for the social, economic, and physical intimidation employed mainly by Democrats. It was a thorough rout. Republicans, Black and White, lost ground all across the South in fall 1870, but the results were most devastating in Georgia. Five of the state's seven districts sent Democrats to the US House of Representatives. Republicans won only eighteen of the 108 seats up for election in the General Assembly. Almost all Black legislators, including Henry Turner, lost their seats. For example, in Richmond County (Augusta), the party nominated Hill ally John Bryant plus two Black men, yet all three went down to defeat as Whites asserted control. Despite desperate appeals from Republicans, there were too few federal troops in too few places to make much of a difference. Unlike his counterparts in some other Republican-controlled ex-Confederate states, Bullock had no state militia under his control that could provide armed protection to voters. Without a military presence, the lack of a secret ballot made intimidation much easier than it would be today. Because eligible White voters outnumbered their Black counterparts, it is highly possible, as the *Savannah News* claimed at the time, that Democrats would have prevailed, though to a lesser extent, even in a fair and honest election. As long as Whites remained almost unanimous in their support of Democrats, Republicans stood little chance. To make matters worse, the rhetoric that Republicans sometimes used in their efforts to placate Whites had the effect of discouraging Black voters. The strategy of establishing Black-White alliance between moderate Republicans and disaffected Democrats might have had possibilities in 1867 when Joe Brown and Joshua Hill corresponded about it, but by December 1870 it was clearly too little, too late.[54]

---

[54] *New York World*, December 8, 1870; Nathans, *Losing the Peace*, 196–212; Duncan, *Entrepreneur for Equality*, 132–33; Parks, *Joseph E. Brown*, 447–49; Currie-McDaniel, *Carpetbagger of Conscience*, 113; Conway, *Reconstruction of Georgia*, 199; Drago, *Black Politicians*, 59–65; Downs, *After Appomattox*, 234; Rosenbaum, "Incendiary Negro," 507–508; Abbott, "Republican Party Press, 756; *New York Herald*, January 10, 1871 (Hill concurred); *Macon Telegraph*, January 17, 1871; Cashin, *Story of Augusta*, 138; J. M. Matthews, "Negro Republicans," 157; *New York World*, December 8, 1870 (*Savannah News*); Downs, *After Appomattox*, 234–35.

Joshua Hill's home county of Morgan was one of only five, all in the Black Belt, to elect a Republican delegation to the General Assembly in 1870. That about two-thirds of the population was African American was clearly the most important factor, but the result was no doubt assisted by influential White Republicans such as Hill, Saffold, and Foster, who discouraged White violence. Historian George Rable found that all across the South, the Klan tended to be strongest in jurisdictions where the racial balance was close to half Black and half White and weaker in places like Morgan County where African Americans strongly predominated.[55]

As 1870 ended, the ascendency of Rufus Bullock came to an end with it. It would be about ten more months before the governor fully lost power and slipped quietly out of the state, but Joshua Hill, J. E. Bryant, and their friends would no longer have to focus their energies on struggling with Bullock for control of the state party. The problem was that after the December 1870 election disaster, there was not much left of the Georgia Republican Party to control other than federal patronage.

Joshua Hill Finally Takes His Place in the Senate

As 1871 began, the US Senate could no longer kick Georgia's Senate seats further on down the road as it had done since the election of Stephens and Johnson five years earlier. All of the other issues had been decided, yet the lingering question of who would represent the state remained unresolved: Joshua Hill, H. V. M. Miller, Henry P. Farrow, Richard H. Whiteley, and Foster Blodgett were still knocking at the door.

Once again, the Senate Judiciary Committee took center stage. Credible reports continued to circulate that President Grant desired the seating of Hill even though he remained publicly neutral. There had been some rumors in fall 1870 before the December elections that a deal was afoot to re-do the Senate elections so that Bullock could take a seat for himself, but nothing came of that. After the Democratic sweep, there was a real possibility that the Senate seating issue could be further muddled if Georgia's new Democrat-majority legislature were to put forth its own crop of senators-elect. Senate Republicans did not want to deal with that eventuality,

---

55 County results from C. Thompson, *Reconstruction in Georgia*, 271; Rable, *But There Was No Peace*, 101–102; Cason, "Loyal League," 137, incorrectly stated that Morgan Co. never voted Republican.

so they settled the matter quickly before the new General Assembly convened.[56]

Senate Judiciary hearings began on January 11. Senator-elect Farrow presented the committee with a long and legalistic argument on behalf of himself and Whiteley. Farrow's lawyerly testimony encapsulated and recycled the anti-Hill arguments that Rufus Bullock and others had made for over two years. However, Farrow was aware of his competing senator-elect's popularity with the moderate Republicans who now dominated the committee, so he took a different rhetorical track than Bullock. He made a point of praising rather than attacking Hill: "I have not one word to say against him individually. I esteem his integrity of character, and regard him as one of the purest men within the bounds of my State. But," Farrow added in his last-ditch appeal, Joshua Hill's "untarnished character cannot, of itself, entitle him to a seat in the Senate." Because Farrow had served the Confederacy as a nitrate mine superintendent, he had the additional task of defending his own eligibility for the seat. He testified that his service was only "the result of the direct exercise of the physical power of the rebel Government" in face of conscription.[57]

The Judiciary Committee rejected Farrow's arguments and on January 23, 1871, recommended that Joshua Hill be admitted to his seat. The main conclusion of the majority effectively accepted the position that Hill's defenders such as John Sherman had been advancing since December 1868, *i.e.* that all of the acts of the Georgia legislature of 1868 prior to the expelling of Black members were valid. The majority unequivocally stated what many had declared before: "It is not believed that the act of December 22, 1869, would ever have been passed had the colored members been permitted to retain their seats and the peace of the State been preserved." The majority report concluded in words that the Madisonian had longed to hear for two and a half years: "Joshua Hill was duly elected by a legislature having authority to elect senators and is entitled to take his seat."[58]

---

[56] *Chicago Evening Mail*, December 28, 1870; *Chicago Tribune*, December 8, 28, 1870; Nathans, *Losing the Peace*, 195.

[57] Farrow, *Argument before the Judiciary Committee*, 18 (to assert), 8 (I have not), 32–33 (the result); *New York Times*, February 8, 1871 (*New Era*).

[58] Judiciary Committee Report of January 23, 1871, included in US Congress and Taft, *Compilation of Senate Election Cases from 1789 to 1885* (January 1, 1886,

The committee's minority report on the senate seat included a concise restatement of the Bullock-Farrow position and recommended that Farrow and Whiteley be admitted. The key vote came on January 30 when twenty of twenty-seven Republicans and all Democrats voted in favor of the majority report. After two-and-a-half years of debate, the anti-Hill Radicals could muster only seven votes against him. Roscoe Conkling illustrated the trend. The New Yorker loathed Bullock, yet in 1869 he had sided with the majority of the Judiciary Committee to recommend against immediate seating of Hill on the grounds that Georgia was not entitled to representation. Now, Conkling voted to seat him. The decline in Radical unity on the Georgia senate question was not an aberration. Votes on Reconstruction issues in Virginia and Louisiana illustrated similar shifts. Some parliamentary moves delayed the final vote for two more days, but on February 1, 1871, the final tally confirmed that no minds had changed. Joshua Hill was now the United States senator from Georgia.[59]

Five years had unfolded since his Senate loss to Alexander Stephens; two and a half years had gone by since his victory over Joseph E. Brown; almost a year had passed since the legislature chose Farrow to replace him, but finally the prize belonged to Senator Joshua Hill. "Not now" had finally become "now." Thanks to what the *New York Tribune* called Hill's "great persistence ever since 1868," Georgia had its first Republican United States senator. With the February 1871 seating of Hill and then of Miller, Georgia had full representation in the US Senate for the first time in ten years since the state's entire congressional delegation had left the capitol—Hill, of course, in his own special manner. An influential Baptist newspaper put it succinctly: "So will end reconstruction in Georgia."[60]

Senate Misc. Document 47, Serial Set vol. 2343), 285–311 (quotations 305–306). This report compiles all the key documents from 1868–1871.

[59] Ibid.; *Globe*, 41-3, 817–30, January 30, 1871; 848–51, January 31, 1871, 871–74, February 1, 1871. The total recorded vote was 36-9; to get the total of 27-20 among Republicans, two paired senators are counted as if they voted opposite each other (Downs, *After Appomattox*, 236; Foner, *Reconstruction*, 453; Calhoun, *Presidency of Ulysses S. Grant*, 399, *New York Tribune*, February 2, 1871).

[60] *Christian Index and South-western Baptist* (Atlanta), February 9, 1871.

Coda: Miller & Whiteley

When it came to the short-term seat, the Republican majority in the Senate was not enamored with seating a Democrat instead of Richard H. Whiteley, but the essential legal arguments for and against the seating of Dr. H. V. M. Miller for the short term were essentially the same as for Hill, so they acquiesced knowing that his service would be brief. Miller's case, however, added an additional complication. His service as a surgeon in the Confederate Army made him ineligible to hold federal office unless Congress removed his disabilities. Now a senator himself, Hill supported the seating of Miller and explained to his fellow Republicans that the doctor had gained election in July 1868 because he was "thought to be the least obnoxious of the number of prominent gentlemen who were regarded with favor among the Democratic party at the time." After short debate, Congress granted the necessary special dispensation, and Miller took his seat on February 24 to represent Georgia alongside Hill for the last couple of weeks of the 41st Congress. The Republican *New Era* of Atlanta characterized the short-time senator as "a 'Democrat' with good Republican principles."[61] Controversy over Foster Blodgett's eligibility for the full term to succeed Miller lay ahead.

Whiteley's situation added one more interesting wrinkle to the convoluted process. Knowing that his Senate term would have lasted for only a few weeks even if he had been admitted over Miller, Whiteley decided to cover his bases with a backup plan. He ran in December 1870 for election to a Southwest Georgia seat in the US House of Representatives at the same time that his Senate seat was still pending. His Democratic opponent appeared to have won on the first count, but the Republican challenged the result and eventually prevailed. Thus, in January 1871, the Senate turned Whiteley away, but the House granted him his seat.[62]

[61] Russ, "Radical Disfranchisement," 205–209. The article suffers from misidentifying Hill as a "rebel" and having a Dunning School point of view (*Globe*, 41-3, pt. 2, 1175, February 13, 1871 [thought to be]).

[62] Rogers, *Scalawag in Georgia*, 63–77; Rogers, "Not Reconstructed by a Long Ways Yet," 257–82; Conway, *Reconstruction of Georgia*, 199. Whiteley was reelected and served until 1875, after which he lost twice in face of Democratic dominance.

Chapter 11

Conservative Republican in the Radical Senate, 1871

Had Joshua Hill been seated immediately after he was elected to the Senate in July 1868, he would have served for a little over four years of the six-year term that he originally sought in 1866. Because of the drawn-out controversy over his seating and Georgia's readmission to the Union, Senator Hill served only two years and a month—all of February 1871 through the first three days of March 1872. His time in office constituted the last month of the 41st Congress and all of the 42nd. Hill knew from the day that he took the oath of office that no matter how tolerable Georgia Democrats might find him in comparison with the Radical wing of his party, he stood virtually no chance of returning to the Senate as long as he remained a Republican. Such awareness was liberating. Not having overly to concern himself with his own reelection gave Senator Hill a freedom to speak his mind and vote his conscience. The Madisonian sought to travel a middle road between Redeemer Democracy and Radical Republicanism. On that road, he found few traveling companions. When the lawyer from Madison entered the Senate, he was among twenty Republicans representing former Confederate states. Ten years later, there were none. His two years covered the beginning of the end of the Republican Party in the South for nearly a century.

During Hill's first year in the US Senate, he was Georgia's only senator except the few weeks that H. V. M. Miller held office at the very end of the 41st Congress. Aside from the usual matters of patronage and general legislative responsibilities, two issues consumed Hill's attention in 1871—the Ku Klux Klan bill (Third Enforcement Act) and the potential seating of senator-elect Foster Blodgett. The Blodgett struggle embodied the long-standing tension between the Radical and conservative/moderate wings of Georgia's Republicans, but it also reflected Hill's personal animosity toward his potential colleague. By the end of 1871, Bullock and Blodgett were out of the picture, and Georgia politics had profoundly changed.

The Business of Patronage and Pork

The Southern correspondent of a leading midwestern newspaper offered a succinct political and physical description of the new senator: "Joshua Hill, who is a conservative, and who attends the Republican caucuses, is a man with a long goatee of a whitish color, flurried, grizzled hair standing straight up, and gold spectacles." The Radical *Atlanta New Era* would have preferred a pro-Bullock senator of Radical stripe. Nevertheless, the paper offered a measured statement amounting to the conclusion that a conservative Republican is better than no Republican at all:

> Mr. Hill, as is well known, has always claimed to be a Republican. He so announced himself before his election in July, 1868, and has since then steadily disclaimed any affiliation, one way or another, with the Democracy. He claims a clear Republican record, and to have been, and to be still, a warm supporter of President Grant's administration. He must, therefore, be classed a Republican.[1]

In the eyes of the Democratic press, it was better to have an honest and conservative Republican senator like Joshua Hill than to be represented by someone of the Bullock-Blodgett stripe. The *Macon Telegraph* put it bluntly: "As between Hill and Miller, and Farrow and Whiteley, the people of Georgia could not hesitate in their choice.—While the former do not fully represent dominant political sentiment of the State, the latter so totally *misrepresent* it, that we are almost persuaded to congratulate the people, not only on their defeat, but on the triumph even of Mr. Hill." The editorial, which several papers reprinted, regrettably acknowledged that Hill would tend to support the Grant administration but added, "We do not believe, however, that he will give his aid to any more plots having for either object the further humiliation and oppression of the Southern

---

[1] *Cincinnati Gazette*, April 10, 1871; *New York Times*, February 8, 1871(*New Era*).

people—though we may be mistaken.... He is, if we know him at all, an honest man emphatically, and the filth of no job will soil his hands while he represents Georgia in the Senate." The *Columbus Enquirer* expressed a similar but more pessimistic assessment:

> He is, to be sure, a gentleman and a Southern man by birth, and we believe that he will support no measures proscriptive or invidiously oppressive or degrading to his State and section, but he is still a Republican, and we cannot count on his support or the influence of his position in favor of any distinctive Democratic measures. He will not, therefore, be a proper representative of the State of Georgia or the sentiments of a large majority of its people.

That "large majority" of which the editors wrote was, of course, White.[2]

Like any new senator in those days before the establishment of the civil service system, Joshua Hill sought to use federal patronage appointments office to reward his friends and frustrate his enemies. One Democrat observed that Hill possessed a very strong "memory for injuries received" from the Bullock and Blodgett faction: "They have fought a strong fight to crush *him*, and if we are not greatly mistaken he will make a stronger one to crush *them*." Knowing that none of its preferred party need apply, the *Savannah Morning News* urged the new senator to use his influence to fill federal offices with more "scalawags" and fewer "carpetbaggers." Obligingly, just weeks after being seated, Hill used his influence to help oust a Bullock-Blodgett ally from the postmaster position in Savannah. The new senator privately lamented to T. P. Saffold that he did not have to time to answer all of the some "50 letters for offices" and confided, "It is not easy to have influence and resist control. Ambitious partizans struggle for the control of the patronage of the government. Many of them, suspect my devotion to party."[3]

By far Hill's most difficult patronage case involved the Port of Savannah, which had more than seventy employees, most of whom, according to Hill, "are said to be carpetbaggers and colored people." Both Hill's

---

[2] *Macon Telegraph*, February 7, 1871 (emphasis original); *Columbus Enquirer*, February 2, 1871.

[3] *Macon Telegraph*, February 28, 1871 (scalawags, *Savannah News*); Hill to T. P. Saffold, March 12, 1871, Saffold Family Papers, MCA.

carpetbagger son-in-law John Bowles and his old friend and native Georgian T. P. Saffold coveted the top spot as collector of customs. The incumbent had enough political clout to hold on to his job, so Hill settled for getting Bowles the important but subordinate position of port surveyor. He told Saffold that Bowles wanted and needed the position and that he could not "be indifferent to his & Anna's appeals." Saffold's failure to obtain the plum created some tension between the two friends, especially between Hill and his cousin Sallie, wife of T. P. Emily Hill fired back at her husband's cousin: "You have sought to exercise an undue influence over Col. Hill, prejudicial to the interests of his own daughter. Viewing this one act from my standpoint you have perpetrated a most officious deed." (It is not known if Saffold wanted the secondary position that Bowles obtained.) Regardless of friendship and kinship, there was no escaping patronage and nepotism regardless of who had won; Foster Blodgett's son was reportedly slated to fill the surveyor position had the Augustan become a senator.[4]

In his first couple of months in office, Senator Hill had the chance to help steer some minor pork barrel Georgia's way. During the 1830s gold rush, the United States established a branch mint at Dahlonega in the North Georgia Blue Ridge Mountains. The Confederacy seized the mint at the beginning of the Civil War, and after the war, the federal government decided not to reopen it since gold production in the area had significantly declined. In spring 1871, Joshua Hill worked with the district's congressman in a bipartisan effort to transfer the mint to North Georgia Agricultural College. Although this transaction did not officially fall under the Morrill Land Grant Act, Vermont senator Justin Smith Morrill lent his prestige to the bill by introducing it. After Hill and Morrill conducted a quick sidebar with the one member who had questions, the bill passed

[4] April 18, 1872; *Savannah Morning News*, March 2, 3, 17, 27, May 5, 23, 1871; *Savannah Advertiser*, April 21, 1871; *Albany News*, February 28, 1871; Hill to Saffold, March 12, 1871 (indifferent); Hill to Cousin Sallie [Saffold], March 3, 1871, May 4, 1871; Hill to [?], March ?, 1871 (the post script directed to "Mr. S" from a longer letter from [?], possibly A. G. Foster); Mrs. [Emily] Hill to Mrs. [Sallie] Saffold, March ?, 1871, Saffold Family Papers, MCA.

by unanimous consent. The restored historic mint building still stands on the campus of the University of North Georgia.[5]

Hill also tried to steer some pork Georgia's way when he successfully offered a resolution by which Congress requested the secretary of war to expand the scope of a survey project to explore the feasibility of building a Great Southern Canal that would link Georgia's Etowah River with the Ocmulgee River system to provide a connection to the Atlantic. It turned out that the politically attractive idea was practically unrealistic, so it never got past the stage of speculation.[6]

The Ku Klux Klan Act, April 1871

The background of the Ku Klux Klan Act began with Republican rage over the violence and threats thereof perpetrated against potential Republican voters, mainly Black voters, in fall 1868. As the elections of 1870 approached, Republicans rightly feared the depredations would intensify. The political pressure to stop the outrages resulted in the passage of a series of Enforcement Acts. The first passed at the end of May 1870, a month after the final ratification of the Fifteenth Amendment and eight months before Joshua Hill took his seat. Had he already been a senator at the time, Hill very likely would have opposed the legislation that made interference with voting rights a federal crime. With the Ku Klux Klan and similar organizations clearly in mind, the act criminalized wearing a mask on public roads after dark. Unfortunately, the lack of vigorous enforcement meant that the act had little effect on elections in fall 1870. A Second Enforcement Act, which focused on voter fraud in Northern cities, passed on the last day of February 1871. Fearing that it would set precedent for federal action in the rural South, Hill opposed the bill.[7]

Among the Black leaders who raised their voices against voter suppression was Jefferson Franklin Long, Georgia's first, and until the mid-

---

[5] W. P. Roberts, *Georgia's Best Kept Secret*, 3–4; Head and Etheridge, *Neighborhood Mint*, 189; *Globe*, 41-1, 170, March 20, 1871, 402, April 3, 1871. Rep. W. P. Price was the cosponsor.

[6] *Globe*, 42-1, 326, March 29, 1871, 343, March 30, 1871; *Marietta Journal*, April 7, 1871.

[7] Farris, *Freedom on Trial*, 77–78; Bordewich, *Klan War*, 174–84; Abbott, *Republican Party and the South*, 211.

twentieth century, only Black member of the United States House of Representatives. Long served only a few weeks in early 1871. On February 1, he made history by making what was the first speech ever by an African American in the House. The specific issue concerned technicalities of the Test Oath, but more broadly his presentation was dedicated to decrying anti-Black violence and economic intimidation by opposing amnesty for the ex-Confederates most likely to commit such acts. Generally more conservative than other Black leaders, Long maintained a good relationship with Joshua Hill and remained a force in the Georgia Republican Party for another two decades.[8]

At the urging of Attorney General Akerman and others, President Grant promised the Union League, the primarily African American organization that advocated for equal voting rights, that he would crack down. He sent troops to North Carolina where the Republican governor had cried for action, and the Senate launched an investigation into Klan activities in the Tarheel state. Reports from the investigation intensified the demand for broad federal action. When the new session of Congress opened in March 1871, Congress established a joint House-Senate committee to examine conditions in the entire South, and President Grant asked for legislation that would enhance federal power to counter voter intimidation. Intense debate over the Third Enforcement Act, better known as the Ku Klux Klan Act, extended well into April.[9]

Democrats aligned overwhelmingly against any legislation that would authorize further federal intervention in the internal affairs of Southern states. Trotting out typical states' rights tropes, they charged that the Klan bill would make the commander-in-chief a despot who would suspend the right of *habeas corpus* and rule the South by bayonet—one wag dubbed him "Kaiser Grant." On the Republican side, Vice President Schuyler Colfax worked with Representative Ben Butler, the Massachusetts Radical, to

[8] J. M. Matthews, "Jefferson Franklin Long," 145–56 (148, If this); Rosenbaum, "Incendiary Negro," 498–530; D. L. Grant, *The Way It Was in the South*, 127–28.

[9] Bordewich, *Klan War*, 184–209; Calhoun, *Presidency of Ulysses S. Grant*, 313–19; Parsons, *Ku-Klux*, 172–73; Trelease, *White Terror*, 384–85; Summers, *Ordeal of the Reunion*, 266–67; Fitzgerald, *Splendid Failure*, 135; Gillette, *Retreat from Reconstruction*, 22–26, 168; Downs, *After Appomattox*, 238; Abbott, *Republican Party and the South*, 210–12.

rouse enthusiasm. Widespread Northern revulsion in response to the March race riot in Meridian, Mississippi, and other incidents increased constituent demands for action against excesses in the South. Black Republicans, including several from Georgia, brought what pressure they could bear in favor of the bill.[10]

As the debate unfolded, Senator Hill couched his words, as he had before, to downplay but not deny the existence of Klan-type violence in Georgia. On April 7 he spoke specifically about the bill to establish the joint investigating committee, but the Klan bill itself was clearly on his mind. Two Democrats who were vociferously opposed to the joint committee immediately preceded Hill, who followed with more temperate, but still skeptical, remarks. He conceded that he had "heard of outrages, of crimes that were very deplorable and very similar to those detailed in the testimony of the North Carolina witnesses, as having occurred in Georgia." However, he insisted, "these instances were not general, and they were limited in their extent; they were confined to a few counties, and I do not think there is any general spirit of lawlessness abroad in [my] State." Hill admitted to the existence of Klan-style atrocities in some counties but disputed the charge that they were the work of a well-organized invisible empire: "I am very sure that there is no general organization in the State of Georgia of this character. I am very glad to be able to assure the Senate of it."[11]

Unlike the Democrats who wanted to stop both investigation and legislation, Senator Hill took a characteristically cautious stance. He said was "not adverse" to investigating claims about Klan activity but added that it would be illogical to pass new enforcement legislation until all investigations were complete and the findings could be evaluated. In short, the Georgian's purposes were to delay action and to downplay the seriousness of the violence problem without sounding like either a hell-no Democrat or a gung-ho Radical.[12]

---

[10] Summers, *Ordeal of the Reunion*, 266–68; Egerton, *Wars of Reconstruction*, 299–300 (Kaiser); Rable, *But There Was No Peace*, 106 (Stephens); Foner, *Reconstruction*, 454–58.

[11] *Globe*, 42-1, pt. 1, March 18, 1871, 158–59; April 7, 1871, 535–36.

[12] Farris, *Freedom on Trial*, 104.

In addition to using more measured language, what distinguished Hill's remarks from those of angry Democrats was that Hill viewed the issue in economic terms. In the worldview of a Whiggish conservative Republican like Hill, talk of the Ku Klux Klan was bad for business. Hill correctly calculated that the Joint Select Committee to Enquire into the Condition of Affairs in the Late Insurrectionary States was going to be established and that some sort of Klan bill would be passed, so concluded that it was better to try to shape the narrative than resist the inevitable. Hill applied a chamber of commerce–type spin to the issue in order to benefit his own county where Republicans, including Black state representative Monday Floyd, still held local office. The new senator expressed "great objection" to the tendency for Northern politicians and journalists to treat all Southern communities alike. Confessing "some degree of selfishness," he admitted that the issues involved for him "a little of State pride and some pecuniary considerations." Hill called attention to some four dozen "gentlemen from northern States" who had already flocked to Morgan County, and he wanted more to come. The senator told a New York reporter, "I would dislike exceedingly for it to go abroad that there was generally in the State of Georgia a state of lawlessness that should deter any one from going there." With his mind on his law practice and extensive real estate holdings, Hill wanted to make sure that blame fell where it was due:

> If it should turn out, in four or five or six counties in the State—and if I chose I think I might specify what particular counties have been more distinguished than other for lawless outbreaks—that they do exist in those places, I have no particular objection, if the immigrants please, that they should shun the particular localities where these things have occurred.

The later testimony of an Augusta editor-lawyer supported Hill's perspective. Referring to Northern agricultural migrants who had brought capital to Georgia, he declared, "There are, perhaps, more in [Morgan] county than in any other of this class, but you can find some in all parts of the State." The editor specifically cited B. H. True of Madison, a former Union officer who held office in the state's agricultural society.[13]

[13] *Globe*, 42-1, pt. 1, April 7, 1871, 535–36; KKK Hearings 1872, 6:279.

Hill was technically correct that the Georgia KKK lacked the kind of tight-knit control that some advocates of enhanced enforcement legislation claimed. The work of historian Elaine Parsons has shown that semi-organized and geographically scattered Klan and Klan-like activity was typical of much of the South. In general, but with exceptions, heavily African American counties in Black Belt regions like Morgan County had less Klan activity than areas where the smaller Black population could be more easily intimidated. Hill's carefully measured comments, however, obscured the fact that the Klan did not have to be well-organized and widespread to cast an intimidating shadow on Black Georgians all across the state.[14] Later testimony would reveal that Hill's own hometown was not immune to Klan disturbance.

Georgia Democrats offered Hill some praise for his Senate floor comments about the Klan and his defense of his home state against Yankee attacks. The *Augusta Constitutionalist* headlined its story about the speech "A GEORGIA REPUBLICAN DEFENDS HIS STATE." Even the *Rome Courier*, a Klan-allied organ, reprinted an article that credited the senator with "a very calm, temperate earnest defence of the State." The *Atlanta Constitution* declared, "Mr. Hill has risen above partisan feelings." The editor in Blakely wrote, "We are glad to see that Georgia has at last a champion in the Senate, though a Republican." When the *New Era* chastised Hill for not endorsing what "enlightened Republicans" desired, the *Macon Telegraph* responded by writing that Hill "has made a manly and characteristic defence of his neighbors and fellow citizens against the shameful slanders of such papers as the Era."[15]

Some conservative Republican senators from Northern states, notably Lyman Trumbull of Illinois, opposed the KKK bill on the grounds that law enforcement against individuals should be left exclusively in local hands. Upon personal appeal from President Grant, the bulk of the party swept such concerns aside. At the Republican senatorial caucus three days before

---

[14] Parsons, *Ku-Klux*, 6–10, 13–5, 25, 203.

[15] *Augusta Constitutionalist*, April 13, 1871; *Rome Courier*, April 21, 1871 (very calm, *Constitution*); Trelease, *White Terror*, 326; *(Blakely) Early County News*, April 21, 1871; *Macon Telegraph*, April 18, 1871; *Columbus Enquirer*, April 20, 1871; *(Athens) Southern Watchman*, April 18, 19, 1871; *Savannah Advertiser*, April 18, 1871; *Atlanta Intelligencer*, April 18, 1871; *Columbus Enquirer*, April 13, 1871; *Atlanta New Era*, April 18, 1871.

the final passage of the Klan bill, Hill, along with John Sherman and some other moderate Republicans, urged the passage of an expanded amnesty bill that could be offered to the South as sort of an olive branch to offset the sting of the Klan bill. Administration supporters, including Hill's sometime ally George F. Edmunds (R-VT), voted down the proposition. Just before the final vote on the Klan bill, Senator Hill made one last but unsuccessful attempt to pass a broad amnesty bill.[16]

Various procedural votes weakened the so-called Force Bill somewhat to bring as many Republicans as possible on board. In a key vote on April 14, Joshua Hill joined the Democrats and four other Republicans in a final losing effort to block the measure. *Harper's Weekly*, normally supportive of Grant, considered the bill to be unconstitutional, but its opinion did not sway many votes. Carl Schurz and Lyman Trumbull, who would soon affiliate with the anti-Grant Liberal Republicans, were among the opponents motivated by constitutional concerns. Republican Party leaders exercised an extraordinary amount of discipline, including strong pressure by Attorney General Akerman, Hill's usual ally who had become much more inclined than the Madisonian to use federal force to protect Black voters. In the end, all Republican senators present except Hill and one other voted for the final legislation. The House followed suit, also along the partisan divide. With both the KKK Act passed and the Klan investigation committee authorized, it had become clear the cautious and conservative Georgia Republican was out of step with his party—even the moderates. As the *New York Herald* put it, "Hill is considered unsound on Republican principles."[17]

The Klan in Morgan County

For Morgan County Whites, life was returning to normal by spring 1871. The cotton crop of 1870 had been especially good. The Madison House

---

[16] *Memphis Public Ledger*, April 20, 1871; *Cincinnati Enquirer*, April 18, 1871; *Savannah Advertiser*, April 15, 1871; *Globe*, 42-1, pt. 2, 818, April 19, 1871 (I hope); Langguth, *After Lincoln*, 279–82.

[17] Farris, *Freedom on Trial*, 79–85; Abbott, *Republican Party and the South*, 212–18; Foner, *Reconstruction*, 454–58; *Savannah Morning News*, April 15, 1871 (*Harper's*); *Baltimore Sun*, April 15, 1871; Calhoun, *Presidency of Ulysses S. Grant*, 318–19; *New York Herald*, June 30, 1871.

Hotel had "lately changed hands" and was "being put into first class condition." The hotel's advertisement described Madison as "the handsomest, healthiest, and gayest city in the State."[18] Reality was, of course, different for the freed people who were striving to make the transition from slavery to sharecropping, tenancy, and, in a few cases, small-tract land ownership.

In his congressional speeches that portrayed Klan-like violence as sporadic rather than pervasive, Joshua Hill cited the relative calm of Morgan County. Given the fact that Republicans carried the county in 1868 and 1870, he was not entirely disingenuous. During floor debate, Hill offered the example of a local robbery in which thieves relieved a White Republican of his valuables. The ringleader of the highwaymen was soon caught and placed on trial. According to Hill, the defendant told the all-White jury "that he belonged to the Ku Klux," hoping that fact would get him off, but his purported Klan membership did not protect him from conviction. Under questioning from John Sherman, Hill had to concede to that he was "not prepared to say that the same offense committee anywhere else in Georgia would have met with the same prompt punishment" that it received in his home community.[19]

It was certainly true that Klan-like violence was more prevalent in some areas than in others, and it was probably accurate for Hill to portray his home county as one of the less-afflicted places. However, it would be a mistake to take the senator's conclusions about the Georgia Klan at full face value. Even if Morgan County Blacks did face fewer depredations than those in other parts of the state, the economic prosperity that Hill sought to encourage by downplaying violence would benefit the White elite much more than it would the Black tenants and sharecroppers who worked the land owned by Northern and native landowners. And even if Blacks in Morgan County fared better than those in the worst-afflicted areas, the advantage was only by comparison to the sorry state of affairs in most of Georgia.

As part his effort to sound reasonable to his Republican colleagues during floor debate, Hill remarked that if congressional investigators were to come to his state, "I will welcome them." He predicted that they would find that most instances of political violence were "traceable to a class of

[18] *Atlanta Constitution*, June 11, 1871.

[19] *Globe*, 42-1, pt. 1, March 18, 1871, 158–59; Bordewich, *Klan War*, 250–59.

men that never would have sprung up and would not have existed in Georgia or elsewhere but for the unfortunate war in which the country was involved." Sworn testimony both confirmed and refuted Senator Hill's rosy depiction of conditions in Morgan County and the surrounding Black Belt region of the lower Piedmont. The joint committee listened to dozens of White politicians and editors who mostly downplayed Klan activity. More importantly, however, the committee also heard from African Americans who had experienced or knew of violent acts and threats thereof. Many of the Black members of the legislature who had been expelled in summer 1868 were among those testifying. The testimony does not in any way constitute a random sample because all sorts of external political, social, and economic pressures and agendas influenced who testified and what they said. Despite those caveats, the 1872 report of the KKK Hearings constitutes the most comprehensive source of information about political violence in the Reconstruction era.[20]

A count of county and city names in the index of the two volumes of Georgia testimony provides some credence to Hill's assertions that Morgan County experienced fewer incidents than many others of comparable size, but Klan-style violence was not unknown in the senator's home territory. Monday Floyd was one of the Black legislators elected in April 1868, expelled in September of that year, and reinstated in January 1870. Floyd appeared with Joshua Hill at rallies supporting Grant's election in 1868, and his multicounty district reelected him and another Black man in 1870. When asked by a member of the Joint Select Committee if he knew of "acts of violence," Floyd replied, "Well sir, I do not know of any in my own immediate county, but I have heard of some in the adjoining counties of Clarke and Jasper." Although he did not recount local incidents of violence, he admitted that he had received some threatening letters addressed personally to him that were signed "KU-KLUX GANG, No. 1." The testimony of a White railroad man who was sympathetic to and personally acquainted with Floyd indicated that the Black politician may have faced more direct threats than he let on. Representative Abram Colby of neighboring Greene County had been severely beaten, and reports were that he and Floyd often stayed in Atlanta to avoid problems closer to

[20] *Globe*, 42-1, pt. 1, April 7, 1871, 535; Trelease, *White Terror*, 391–98; Parsons, *Ku-Klux*, 111, 128, 158–66, 194–95.

home. It is reasonable to assume that Hill knew of the threats against Floyd.[21]

Hill became tangentially involved in an episode from his former home county of Jasper. Thomas H. Allen, one of Floyd's fellow legislators, told investigators about the murder of his brother-in-law and about threats that he had faced at the time of the 1868 presidential election for organizing campaign groups called "Grant Rangers." Allen explained that he first went to Atlanta to seek assistance and "then went down to Madison and met with Joshua Hill," who at the time was still senator-elect:

> I told [Hill] some of the circumstances. He said he had heard of it and asked me what I was going to do about it. I said, "I am going back home [to Jasper County], my family is there, and all that I have in the world is there…." Said [Hill], "Allen, you are a good fellow, but you are going among mighty bad men if you go back there; it is hard, but if I was you I would go back." That was about 10 o'clock.

Allen then explained that Hill must have made some inquiries that changed his mind:

> At 2 o'clock Mr. Hill sent for me to come to his house, and I went. He said, "I see you have published that thing in Bryant's paper in Augusta." I said, "I have." [Hill] said, "Then I think you had better not go back there [to Jasper County], for they will kill you right in the day-time." I staid there [in Madison] until two days before the election for President. I said to [Hill], "I am going to vote for President sure." He said, "You can vote at Atlanta; if I was you I would not go back there [to Jasper County], and stay there; if you had not published this thing maybe you could have got along very well." I came back here [to Atlanta] and voted for President.

Later Hill sought out Allen to tell him that "it was a shame" that the coroner's jury had not been able to identify the White men who had killed his brother-in-law.[22]

---

[21] KKK Hearings 1872, 7:1060–1062 (Floyd); 6:249–64 (RR man, Andrew Rockafellow); 6:273.

[22] KKK Hearings 1872, 7:607–10.

Some witnesses were more inclined than Floyd to speak openly of stories they had heard of Klan-style whippings and killings in and around Morgan County. Some of the incidents happened or came to light after Hill made his mid-April 1871 floor comments about Georgia and local violence, but it is likely that he had heard rumblings of such occurrences. A Black Clarke County legislator reported that he had heard that some Blacks in surrounding counties, including Morgan, had been whipped and disarmed. He specifically told of a killing that took place in Morgan County "five or six miles from Madison" although the incident apparently stemmed from issues in Clarke County. Even B. H. True, the White transplant, reported hearing of "little disturbances occasionally," including the whipping of a Black man near Rutledge. A Black farmer, who might have been the individual that True mentioned, explained that White men claiming to be KKK had whipped him with hickory sticks because he had hired a Black woman who preferred to work for him rather than for a White plantation owner who had offered her a job. He also reported that "they" had burned a brush arbor where "colored folks met." Another interviewee testified that he had left Morgan County for Atlanta because he had been beaten at night and that the White man for whom he worked had been too scared to help him.[23]

The most notorious case of Klan-style violence in Morgan County was a lynching that occurred in September 1871. It happened while Hill was at home in Madison after the session so he would not have known of it earlier in the year when he made his statements about conditions in his own backyard. A White teenage girl claimed that she had been accosted by a Black man named Charles Clarke, and her siblings supported her report. The alleged harasser was apprehended and locked up. Local Blacks heard that Clarke might be lynched, so they organized to protect the jail over the weekend. One of the leaders of the protectors mentioned to the committee that while he was carrying his gun and heading toward the jail to take his turn as a guard, he passed by Senator Hill, who raised no objection to his being armed. After a couple of days, the impromptu group

[23] Ibid., 6:1–3 (Alfred Richardson, Clarke Co. legislator); 7:715–20 (True); 653–54 (Daniel Lane, Black farmer); 692–93 (Martin Anthony, left Morgan). Judge A. R. Wright of Rome said he had no recollection of hearing of incidents in Morgan County (6:137).

of Black men apparently thought that the threat of lynching had subsided, so they disbanded. With the protectors out of the way, a gang of White men obtained the keys from the jailer, opened the cell, and shot Clarke to death. Clarke's murderers remained officially unknown and thus went unpunished. The Joint Select Committee heard testimony from Black men who thought that Clarke was innocent or that he at least deserved a fair trial. Their remarks contrasted starkly with the White testimony and press accounts.[24]

Even though political violence declined somewhat after 1872, the result may have been as much a product of the success of the Klan as of its suppression. Fear of political violence lingered in the minds of freed people even as its incidence declined. Despite Joshua Hill's boosterism and his real personal concern for the fate of some Black men, Morgan County was no long-term exception.

Hill Leads the Opposition to Foster Blodgett

Upon the end of Senator Miller's brief tenure, Senator Hill extended to his Democratic colleague what a Democratic paper called "a worthy tribute" in a "gracious and magnanimous style."[25] Soon after praising Miller, Hill turned his attention to burying Foster Blodget. The senator from Madison had detested Blodgett personally and politically for years, and seldom, if ever, did a sitting senator play as large a role in the debate over who would be his in-state colleague as Joshua Hill did in the case of Rufus Bullock's Augusta Ring compatriot. The first round of the Blodgett fight raged in spring 1871 simultaneous with the debate over the KKK investigations and the Third Enforcement Act. The Augustan staggered, but he was not knocked out until the second round ended in December.

As explained in chapter 10, Foster Blodgett's claim to a seat in the US Senate rested on a convoluted process engineered by Rufus Bullock. A quick summary of the convoluted situation is in order. In February 1870, with most Black legislators re-seated, the newly reorganized Georgia

---

[24] KKK Hearings 1872, 6:655–63; *Greensboro Herald*, September 28, 1871; *Augusta Constitutionalist*, September 27, 1871. Investigators asked some questions in a manner that implied suspicion that Hill's son John might have been among the group that stormed the jail, but there was no direct testimony to that effect.

[25] *Augusta Constitutionalist*, March 4, 1871.

General Assembly elected its own three men for the Senate: Henry P. Farrow to replace senator-elect Hill for the long term ending in March 1873; Richard Whiteley to replace Miller for the short term ending in March 1871, and Foster Blodgett for the full Senate term scheduled to begin in March 1871. In January and February 1871, the Senate rejected the choices of the 1870 legislature and seated Hill and Miller, who had been elected in 1868. The Senate, however, did not at that time rule on whether Blodgett was duly chosen for the full term.

The legal issue regarding the seating of Blodgett turned on the question of which session of the Georgia General Assembly had the authority to make the choice. Because Congress had rejected Bullock's effort to "prolong" the reorganized January 1870 legislature to 1872, Georgia held new legislative elections in December 1870, and Democrats won a comfortable majority. Federal statute specified that the senatorial elections were to be conducted by the state legislature "*chosen next preceding the expiration of the time for which any Senator was elected*," so it seemed obvious that the body "chosen" in December 1870 would conduct the election for the March 1871 Senate seat, leaving Blodgett out in the cold. Bullock, however, found a parliamentary loophole that muddled the obvious. Under Georgia law, the outgoing lame-duck legislature (i.e., the January 1870 body) was empowered to set the date on which the incoming General Assembly (i.e., the December 1870 body) would convene. Normally, setting the date to convene was a mere housekeeping matter of picking a specific day in January of the new year, but January was not written into law. Thus, at Bullock's urging, the lame-duck legislature set the convening date for its successor to be in December 1871. This sly move meant that the new senate term for which Blodgett had been elected would commence *before* the newly-elected legislature ever convened. Bullock and his Radical Republican cohorts asserted that the men elected in December 1870 did not yet constitute a "legislature" within the meaning of federal law because they had not yet convened. Relying on this tortured semantic, Bullock and Blodgett argued that the legislature in place as of February 1870 was the body "chosen next proceeding," so its choice of senator had to stand.[26]

Democrats and conservative Republicans cried foul. Joshua Hill led the fight. When the 42nd Congress convened in March 1871, the Senate

[26] Duncan, *Entrepreneur for Equality*, 134; Nathans, *Losing the Peace*, 207–18.

referred the credentials of Blodgett to the Committee on Privileges and Elections, of which Hill was a member. Blodgett's supporters argued that he should be seated based on prima facie evidence that he was the state's only senator-elect and that he held certification from Governor Bullock. Opponents of Blodgett contended that the seat should remain vacant until the Georgia legislature "chosen" in December 1870 could finally convene to select a senator. To support the case against Blodgett, John Bryant prepared, and Hill submitted, a ten-page booklet that addressed the legal issues and added the additional charge that Blodgett should not be seated because he was of "well-known bad character." The character charges focused mainly on perjury accusations against Blodgett regarding his Civil War service for the Confederacy and on the allegations of his financial misdeeds as superintendent of the Western & Atlantic Railroad. The majority of the Judiciary Committee recommended that Blodgett should be seated on a temporary basis pending further investigation. Hill and Senator Allen G. Thurman (D-OH) produced a minority report that dissented vigorously. The battle then shifted to the full Senate, which would have to decide which report to adopt.[27]

Georgia's Democratic press had been doggedly attacking Blodgett for five years, and they were appalled that he now stood on the precipice of the Senate seat that he had long sought. The *Columbus Enquirer* editorialized, "We have more fear of Blodgett getting a seat that we have of either Farrow or Whitely." The *Herald* of Thomaston bemoaned that the Senate had waited too long to seat Hill and Miller and then added, "Let us hope that it will not imbue its hands with the greater stain of giving to Blodgett a seat!" Republican papers naturally took the opposite tack.[28]

When the Blodgett case reached the floor of the Senate for debate on April 10, considerations of law and constitution at first took a back seat to the personal issues. All Democrats and the most conservative Republicans

---

[27] US Congress and Taft, *Compilation of Senate Election Cases*, 331–37; "Memorial of John E. Bryant Protesting the Admission of Foster Blodgett to a Seat in the Senate," March 21, 1871, 42-1. Senate Misc. Doc. No. 30, HRBML; Conway, *Reconstruction of Georgia*, 192–97, 203; Currie-McDaniel, *Carpetbagger of Conscience*, 89; Nathans, *Losing the Peace*, 207–18; and Duncan, *Entrepreneur for Equality*, 137–38.

[28] *Columbus Enquirer*, February 2, 1871; *Thomaston Herald*, March 4, 1871; *Atlanta New Era*, March 21, 26 (*Macon Union*).

roundly opposed Blodgett from the start, so the relevant floor battle was between Radical and moderate Republicans. Senator William Stewart, the Nevada Radical who had earlier been at the forefront of the fight against Hill's admission, moved for the seating of both Blodgett and another disputed senator-elect, George Goldthwaite of Alabama. Senator Hill quickly sparked debate by agreeing to Goldthwaite but proposing an amendment to strike Blodgett's name. Georgia's sole senator held the floor well over two hours while he lambasted Blodgett. He referenced and expanded upon the pamphlet that Bryant had prepared, including accusations that Blodgett had bribed legislators to ensure his election. Hill put his greatest emphasis on the longstanding charge that Blodgett had committed perjury when he became the Augusta postmaster by swearing that he had served in the Confederate army only under duress when, in fact, he had donned his gray uniform with great enthusiasm. Blodgett's attorneys had managed to delay the perjury case for about three years, and he was eventually acquitted due to the lack of admissible contemporaneous evidence. The acquittal on such a technicality did not deter Hill, who continued to believe that Blodgett had perjured himself:

> It is not gratifying to me to enter into these personal assaults. It is my duty, however, to state what I believe to be the truth in the case. If I am asked in candor, with these things hanging over the head of any man, whether I personally think he is my peer if he be admitted upon this floor, I answer indignantly, no; I do not regard any man my equal who stands charged with crimes of this sort, who has not removed the suspicion by proofs that are conclusive to the mind of everybody.

"Even if the law favored his case," Hill proclaimed, the Senate should hesitate "to inflict upon her people as a representative in this body a man whose private reputation is not above reproach."[29]

Blodgett's defenders thought that Hill had gone too far. Senator Oliver Morton (R-IN) declared, "We have just listened to what I must call an extraordinary speech, the tendency of which is to blacken that man's character before the Senate and before the country." Morton's fellow Radical William Stewart proclaimed that he thought that Hill's speech was

[29] *Globe*, 42-1, pt. 1, April 10, 1871, 540–58 (547, it is not); "Memorial of John E. Bryant"; US Congress and Taft, *Compilation of Senate Election Cases*, 326–37.

"the most extraordinary attack I have ever heard made on any individual in this body before." Stewart asserted that the pending senator-elect stood accused only because he was a strong Republican. There was an element of truth in that assertion, but it did not fully explain why Democrats and conservative/moderate Republicans like Hill and Bryant went after the Augustan with so much more ferocity than they did other Georgia Radicals. The moderate Republican George Edmunds of Vermont responded to Morton's and Stewart's criticism of Hill by pointing out that his assertions about Blodgett were nothing new: "All that has been stated by the Senator from Georgia was public before; all the papers that [Sen. Hill] has read reflecting on Mr. Blodgett everybody has known about."[30]

The debate devolved into an intense exchange between Hill and Stewart in which the Nevadan once again harked back to Hill's 1863 letter and questioned his vaunted Unionism. Hill angrily responded, "I am not on trial, and if I were the guiltiest man under the sun of heaven, it does not excuse another. If the Senator will prefer charges against me before this body, I will meet him. I dare him to the encounter. Let him do it." Senator John Sherman tried to calm the waters by remarking that he believed "that questions of this kind ought to be decided without the slightest feeling either of a partisan or a personal character." Vice President Colfax finally brought an end to the long and intense exchange by ruling on a point of order that the personal details about Blodgett were irrelevant to the official question of which Georgia legislature had the authority to make the senatorial choice. The bickering between Hill and Stewart dragged on a bit longer, but the debate eventually shifted to the more mundane legal issues.[31]

The following day, the Senate kicked the issue down the road by tabling final consideration of Blodgett's case until December 1871—after the new Georgia Assembly would have convened and selected its own senator-elect. Republican senators were still divided, but seventeen voted to table, and only six opposed the motion, which showed that several Radicals were leaning toward Hill's interpretation. The vote to table Blodgett and not let him serve even temporarily foretold his probable eventual defeat. The *Boston Post* asserted that the "Radicals of the Senate" were pleased to

---

[30] *Globe*, 42-1, pt. 1, April 10, 1871, 547–78.

[31] Ibid., 552–58; US Congress and Taft, *Compilation of Senate Election Cases*, 334.

have found "some plausible pretext to get rid of Blodgett, who they regard as utterly unfit by character, reputation or talents for a seat in the Senate."[32]

Hill's attack on Blodgett and his sparring with Stewart and Morton attracted considerable attention in the state and national press. Observers took note, especially of the Madisonian's assertion that he was unwilling to consider Blodgett a peer. A Boston daily charitably described Hill's tone as "earnest but temperate." Horace Greeley's paper implied that it was inappropriate for Hill to attack the senator-elect's personal character "in a case in which he is also to vote in judgment." The short-lived *Washington Patriot* defended Hill's approach, writing that he "was very severe, and deservedly so, on the audacity displayed by Blodgett...and was not sparing in the portrayal of the crimes and misdemeanors with which that individual is charged."[33]

In-state Democratic papers relished Senator Hill's skewering of Blodgett, but they were simultaneously outraged by the fact that, in the process, the staunch Unionist Hill had once again characterized the Confederacy as "a vile concern." A *Macon Telegraph* writer cried that the senator was "by implication stigmatizing every man, woman and child who favored it as the endorsers and upholders of villainy." An angry Savannah editor feigned incredulity: "We cannot believe that he stood up in the United States Senate and uttered the language above attributed to him." The editors knew their readers. As a recent study of Confederate veterans concluded, "Those former Rebels were willing to concede defeat but, to be sure, expressed no remorse and admitted no wrongdoing."[34]

Knowing that the April 11, 1871, tabling of his admission probably meant that he would never serve, the enraged Foster Blodgett published a thirty-five-page pamphlet titled "Statement of Foster Blodgett and Evidence in Reply to the Charges of Joshua Hill." Addressed to the Senate, the statement went after Hill directly:

---

[32] *Globe*, 42-1, pt. 1, April 11, 1871; *Savannah Morning News*, June 19, 1871 (*Boston Post*).

[33] *Boston Advertiser*, April 11, 1871; *New York Tribune*, April 11, 1871; *Augusta Constitutionalist*, April 14, 1871 (*Patriot*); *Atlanta Constitution*, April 18, 1871.

[34] *Macon Telegraph & Messenger*, April 18, 1871; *Savannah Morning News*, May 5, 1871; *Quitman Banner*, April 28, 1871; Clampitt, *Lost Causes*, 186.

> Previous to the wanton, public attack upon my private character, by Joshua Hill...I had chosen to regard him as a fair opponent, who would deal in facts, and use the language of a gentleman in his opposition to me. But his fierce, vindictive attack, which surprised and disgusted honorable senators on that day, presents him to the world as a malignant falsifier, and were he not protected by his senatorial position, a slanderer of private character.

Even though in his April 10 speech and many times before, Hill had defended his Republican bona fides and explained the context of his 1863 gubernatorial contest letter, Blodgett once again dredged it up to question the legitimacy of Hill's Unionism. The pro-Blodgett *New Era* called the letter "a source of constant irritation" for Hill that "has stuck to him like the shirt of Nessus" that poisoned Hercules. Blodgett claimed that the senator acted like a Republican in Washington, but "while in Georgia, he is a sound democrat!"[35] In twenty-first-century parlance, Blodgett called the conservative Hill a RINO ("Republican in name only"). As in so many instances, Joshua Hill stood in the middle and took fire from both sides. Old rebels called him a Unionist traitor to his native South, and Radicals doubted that he was really a Unionist at all.

Hill was satisfied with having stalled the senator-elect's aspiration and chose not to respond publicly, but Blodgett's public statement led to another flurry of attention in the press. A New York City paper asserted that Blodgett had put out the document "with the avowed object of hurting Mr. Hill politically." The leading Macon paper contended that Blodgett's long anti-Hill statement succeeded only "in intensifying the wholesome contempt we, in common with all honest men, feel for the author." Senator Hill, the writer astutely concluded, had effectively committed Blodgett "to the tender mercies of the new Legislature of Georgia, which meets in November next."[36]

---

[35] Blodgett, *Statement of Foster Blodgett and Evidence*; *Atlanta New Era*, April 25, 1871.

[36] *New York Evening Post*, June 8, 1871; *Macon Telegraph*, June 6, 1871; *Washington National Republican*, June 2, 1871; *Augusta Chronicle*, June 7, 1871; and *Savannah Advertiser*, June 2, 1871.

Georgia Politics in Flux

After the eventful session closed on April 20, 1871, Joshua Hill returned to Georgia where the struggle within the Republican party continued while Congress was out of session and the new state legislature waited until December to convene. In June, four thinly anonymous White Georgia politicians spoke about Georgia politics with a special correspondent of Horace Greeley's *New York Tribune*. The men were a Republican Superior Court judge, a Democratic newspaper editor, a state legislator who had been a former Confederate colonel, and "a gentleman from Morgan County." Later testimony from Judge A. R. Wright confirmed that the "gentleman" was Joshua Hill himself desiring to remain anonymous. The judge told the *Tribune* that the Republican party in Georgia was "hopelessly ruined" because of the struggle between two factions, "one led by Bullock and Blodgett, and the other by Senator Joshua Hill and Attorney General Akerman." He posited that "there were now no White Republicans in the State except office holders" and that "any man who thought he could build up a party of negroes would be greatly mistaken." The jurist further explained that the Democrats were split between "progressive men" and "the reactionists or Bourbons, led by A. H. Stephens and Robert Toombs." In the judge's opinion, the only hope for any Republican success lay "in the division of the White men, which could only happen if the "New Departure" split the Democrats. Hill asserted as he had before that in Morgan County "the election [of 1870] had been perfectly fair, and that it was owing in a great measure to the influence of Northern men, who, to the number of forty or fifty, had settled in the county since the war, with their families." These were "substantial people, who could not be stigmatized as carpet-baggers and adventurers." Hill admitted that his county "was an exceptional case" because in most areas "it would be disagreeable for a northern man to attempt to live in them."[37]

What Georgians thought about the recent passage of the Ku Klux Klan Act (Third Enforcement Act) was clearly on the *Tribune* correspondent's mind. The Republican judge attributed Klan-like outrages to "low whites, who always had an antipathy to the negroes." He admitted, "In

---

[37] *New York Tribune*, June 9, 1871; *Augusta Chronicle*, June 22, 1871; KKK Hearings 1872, 6:117 (A. R. Wright), 264–95 (Ambrose Wright of *Augusta Chronicle*).

some counties they had established such a terrorism that no witnesses would testify against them" but that in other jurisdictions, "the land owners had organized to put down these gangs and protect the negro laborers." This explanation of the Klan tracked the conservative Republican line that Joshua Hill had expressed in his widely reported Senate speech in April. Illustrating the racist assumptions typical of even sympathetic Northern observers, the writer predicted that Democrats would find more effective ways than violence to influence "the ignorant mass of the negro voters." On the whole, the *Tribune* article offered accurate and timely insight into the actions and attitudes that characterized Hill and influential White men of both political parties.[38]

Rumors periodically circulated that Hill would leave the Republican Party and join the Democrats as so many opportunistic men like Joe Brown had already done or would soon do. In mid-1871 there was speculation that the Madisonian coveted the Georgia governorship under the banner of whichever party he would stand the best chances of winning. The gubernatorial rumors coincided with rumors that Hill was considering throwing in with the emerging New Departure Democrats, led by Benjamin Hill. Called by one contemporary "the most agile political acrobat in Georgia," Ben Hill continued to be a vociferous and unapologetic White supremacist even as he urged his party to seek more cooperation with Reconstruction. Ben Hill knew that Joshua Hill, his one-time Whig ally, was a lukewarm Republican, so the rumblings seemed credible. Several newspapers printed hearsay that Josh Hill, Joseph E. Brown, and even Rufus Bullock might jump on board with the New Departure Democrats if the party as a whole could break away from the grip of Robert Toombs and the old guard. The prediction of Joe Brown's switch eventually came true, but he returned to the Democratic fold as a member of the so-called Bourbon Triumvirate rather than as part of the New Departure movement.[39]

---

[38] KKK Hearings 1872, 6:117.

[39] *Atlanta Sun*, July 8, 12, October 28, November 1, 7, 8, 1871; *Atlanta New Era*, May 21, 1871; *Savannah Advertiser*, July 7, August 24, 1871; *Macon Telegraph & Messenger*, August 22, 1871; *Augusta Chronicle*, August 30, 1871; *Savannah Morning News*, October 25, 30, 1871; KKK Hearings 1872, 7:662; Parks, *Joseph E. Brown*, 462–63, 475–77; Perman, *Road to Redemption*, 64–65; Conway, *Reconstruction of Georgia*, 200–201; Nathans, *Losing the Peace*, 217; Wynne, *Continuity of Cotton*, 63–65.

Ben Hill himself soon put the quietus on any thought that Joshua Hill would join Democratic ranks as a New Departurist or in any other fashion. At the KKK Hearings in October 1871, an interviewer asked Ben Hill directly about the state's Republican senator: "The truth is," Ben Hill testified, "that there are a few gentlemen in the South so utterly anti-democratic that they would have gone anywhere on earth before they would have affiliated with the democratic party on any terms.... one is our present Senator, Joshua Hill."[40]

Other testimony at the Klan Hearings also revealed much about Georgia politics. Congressional Democrats made sure that the Joint Committee heard from White editors and politicians who would buttress their argument that the Grant administration should not push enforcement too hard. One of the interviewees was one of Hill's prewar Unionist allies who turned Confederate and Democrat, Ambrose Wright of the *Augusta Chronicle & Sentinel.* The editor roundly criticized Bullock, Blodgett, and other radical Republicans, but he went on to acknowledge that Democrats did not have a monopoly on what he regarded as good men: "Some of the best men we have in the State are republicans, but they are very few, and they are ostracized by their own party. They are Joshua Hill, Thomas Peter Saffold, and Albert Foster, men of prominence, of character, of ability, and of respectability; they have not lost the respect of their fellow citizens." In addition to listing the trio of Morgan Countians, Wright mentioned a couple of other names and added that there were other good Republicans across the state. "But," he emphasized, "they are not in good standing with the party."[41]

The committee also heard from A. R. Wright of Rome, who had met with Abraham Lincoln around the time that Joshua Hill was meeting with Sherman in fall 1864. Despite his presecession Unionist credentials and his efforts at peace negotiation, Judge Wright served in the Confederate Congress and remained a Democrat after the war. When asked if he considered Hill to be a Republican, Wright answered, "He now stands in a doubtful attitude," but recent indications are "that he intends to run in the republican line."[42]

---

[40] KKK Hearings 1872, 7:765.

[41] Ibid., 6:279.

[42] Ibid., 117.

From early 1868 forward, Republican Party politics in Georgia had revolved around the person of Rufus Bullock. Whether one was on his side, such as Foster Blodgett, or against him, such as Joshua Hill, Bullock could not be ignored—but in October 1871 the controversial governor quietly slipped away. His failure to convince Congress to prolong the term of the Republican legislature to 1872, his inability to shake charges of corruption, and his ineffectiveness at building a viable biracial Republican coalition that could stave off White Democratic dominance finally ended his political career. Not even Bullock's awarding of the lucrative lease of the state-owned but Joe Brown dominated Western & Atlantic Railroad provided enough political cover to save the governor from the inevitable. Bullock's railroad friends agreed to make efforts on behalf of Foster Blodgett in spring 1871, but they lacked enough influence to get the Senate to seat the governor's ally in face of intense pushback from Joshua Hill and others. Fearing the virtual certainty of impeachment and sensing the high probability of conviction, Bullock resigned the governorship and left the state to avoid prosecution.[43]

Bullock timed his resignation so that it would not only save his own neck but would also have the effect of handing the governorship to a close Republican ally. By Georgia law, the next man in the line of succession for governor was president of the senate Benjamin F. Conley, part of the old Blodgett-Bullock Augusta Ring. Even though the Senate was not in session, Conley still technically held the position because the new legislature had not yet convened due to the delay that Bullock engineered early in 1871.

Blodgett Pushed Aside and Norwood Joins Hill in the Senate

Democrats had a free hand in the new General Assembly that finally convened in December 1871. At the top of their priority list was filling the seat that Foster Blodgett claimed. They also called an election so that voters could replace Governor Conley with their nominee James M. Smith, Speaker of the House. Without Bullock at the helm, the Republican Party seemed unsure how to proceed. African American voters felt even more like neglected outsiders in the now Bullock-less Republican Party. Hoping

[43] Duncan, *Entrepreneur for Equality*, 134–40; Parks, *Joseph E. Brown*, 450–62; Nathans, *Losing the Peace*, 215–20; Conway, *Reconstruction of Georgia*, 200–203.

to build enthusiasm for the gubernatorial election, the party scheduled several meetings around the state including one in Atlanta where Joshua Hill spoke. Of this last-ditch Republican effort, the *Macon Telegraph* wrote, "We hope they will put up a man and make a fight. We only want one more chance to bury the crowd so deep that not even the ghost of a stench will be left to mark the spot." The Republican events failed to generate much excitement, so there was no real fight. Even more ominous for the party's long-term prospects, ex-governor Joe Brown openly supported Smith, thereby taking a crucial step on his path back to the Democratic Party. In the end, the dispirited Republicans did not even put forth a candidate to oppose Smith, who won the governorship in a low turnout runaway.[44]

When the General Assembly turned its attention to the US Senate, there might as well have been a "No Republicans Need Apply" sign on the wall. As the session prepared to open, Joshua Hill was in Atlanta attending to business before the state Supreme Court. Undoubtedly, rumors and speculations about who might be chosen to sit alongside him in the Senate abounded in the lobby and corridors of the grand Kimball House where the Madison lawyer-senator boarded. A Macon journalist listed the leading senatorial contenders and then, with tongue in cheek, added, "and thirty-nine others." By the time the Democratic members caucused, the list had narrowed to nine men, including John B. Gordon and two other former Confederate generals. Unexpectedly, Thomas M. Norwood of Savannah, who had served as a Confederate state representative, emerged from the middle of the pack to prevail on the eighth ballot. Caucus selection was tantamount to election. Norwood had built his political reputation with regular attacks against Bullock and company in widely circulated newspaper columns signed "Nemesis," Norwood's thinly veiled nom de plume.[45]

---

[44] *Savannah Advertiser*, December 9, 1871; *Macon Telegraph*, December 8, 12 (We hope), 1871; *Savannah Morning News*, December 9, 1871; *(Athens) Southern Banner*, December 15, 1871; Calhoun, *Presidency of Ulysses S. Grant*; Foner, *Reconstruction*, 458.

[45] *Macon Telegraph & Messenger*, November 9, 1871 (thirty-nine); *Atlanta Daily Sun*, November 11, 1871; *Covington Enterprise*, November 17, 1871; Bragg, "Junius of Georgia Redemption," 82–22; Mellichamp, *Senators from Georgia*, 152–55. (The Norwood entry muddles the account.)

Foster Blodgett waited in the wings in Washington for one final grasp at the seat. Now he faced a specific rival in addition to general opposition from Joshua Hill and others. With Bullock out of the picture, Blodgett needed help elsewhere. In early December, he wrote letters of mixed optimism and despair to Governor Conley. The Republican senator-elect told Conley that he had called on Attorney General Akerman and the president to seek their support. Blodgett admitted that Bullock's resignation had hurt his chances but added, "Still I will do my best and have some good friends in the Senate who will stick to me to the end." The Republican senator-elect knew that he needed something to get the edge, so he asked Conley to enlist a friend to dig into Norwood's Confederate legislative records where, "I am told I can find some of his acts and votes in them that will tell against him." Ten days later, in another letter, Blodgett explained to Conley that his past associations with Bullock were ruining his already slim chances at the senate seat. Apparently, he had finally figured out that Bullock tended to annoy even those who tried to help him. Blodgett confessed, "I am feeling rather blue about my case."[46]

Blodgett's sense of blue was justified. Norwood distributed a lengthy pamphlet that laid out his case against the seating of Blodgett using essentially the same arguments that John Bryant and Joshua Hill had used earlier in the year. The effort was hardly necessary. Even though the Committee on Privileges and Elections was composed of six Republicans (including Joshua Hill) and only one Democrat, it reported unanimously on December 18 in favor of the Democrat Norwood. The concise two-page document carefully sidestepped the matters of Blodgett's alleged perjury and corruption and stuck to the legal questions. The report soundly rejected the tortured semantic distinction between "chosen" and "elected" that Blodgett and his defenders had advanced to justify election by the January 1870 legislature. The next day, the full Senate accepted the committee's recommendation without debate and admitted Norwood. It was clear that Senate Republicans had grown so tired of Blodgett and his

---

[46] *Atlanta Sun*, November 1, 7, 8, 1871; *Atlanta Constitution*, November 5, 1872; Foster Blodgett to Benjamin Conley, December 4, 13, 1871, and J. W. Thomas to Conley, April 1, 1872; Benjamin Conley Papers, #1544, box 1, folder 16 (Blodgett), 17 (Thomas), HRBML; Duncan, *Entrepreneur for Equality*, 134, 137–38; Currie-McDaniel, *Carpetbagger of Conscience*, 121–22, 138.

patron, Rufus Bullock, that they were willing to accept a Democrat just to get it over with. Excepting the few weeks that Dr. Miller served early in 1871, Norwood's swearing-in marked the first time in a dozen years that the state of Georgia had full representation in both chambers of the United States Congress. Blodgett quickly faded from importance and died in 1877.[47]

The *Cincinnati Commercial* expressed, and approving Georgia papers reprinted, the Democratic view of Norwood's election: "By an extra streak of good luck, seldom run upon by a Southern State since the war, [Georgia] has escaped Blodgett, the notorious jobber; Farrow, the rebel saltpeter dirt digger, and Whitely[*sic*], the apostate Confederate Colonel, all of whom were elected to the Senate by the stupid and ignorant Legislature.... Both Norwood and Hill are men of good character." Norwood acted in the Senate as a dutiful Redeemer Democrat and did the same later when he served in the House. After leaving public life, Norwood published *A True Vindication of the South*, a tome firmly in the White supremacy, Lost Cause tradition.[48]

By the end of 1871 Georgia's Republican Party was weak and in disarray. The Radical wing was leaderless, and the moderate/conservative wing of Joshua Hill and compatriots held little or no electoral appeal with White voters and earned only lackluster support from Black citizens. Under pressure from railroad interests, Grant replaced Amos Akerman as attorney general in December with a former senator from Oregon, thereby reducing Georgia's and the South's already slight clout in the administration. Both houses of the General Assembly had strong Democratic majorities, and it would continue that way for a century. With the resignation of Rufus Bullock and the inauguration of Governor James M. Smith to replace the short-timer Benjamin Conley, Georgia would not have a Republican governor again until 2003, by which time the parties had

[47] *Atlanta New Era*, December 9 (*Washington Republican*), 17, 1871; *Savannah Morning News*, December 20, 1871 (Norwood pamphlet); *Macon Telegraph & Messenger*, March 7, 1871; US Congress and Taft, *Compilation of Senate Election Cases*, 334–35. Blodgett received expenses and back pay from March to December 1871.

[48] *Macon Telegraph & Messenger*, December 31, 1871 (*Commercial*); Mellichamp, *Senators from Georgia*, 153–55; Norwood, *True Vindication of the South*; Hobson, *Tell about the South*, 129–30.

effectively switched positions on many important issues. Republican senator Joshua Hill had only one more year to serve, so he would try to make the most of it.

Chapter 12

Lame Duck in the Republican Senate, 1872–1873

The big news of Georgia politics at the end of 1871—the resignation of Rufus Bullock and the consummation of the Democratic takeover of state government—had a profound, though not unexpected, effect on Joshua Hill's career. Radical Reconstruction in Georgia, already on life support, had breathed its last. Knowing for sure that his term was entering its final months, Hill could operate and speak without fear of compromising his chances of reelection. Alluding to politicians who dreamed of power and higher office, Hill dismissed such aspirations for himself and remarked that he could "afford to utter such sentiments in regard to them as I feel."[1]

Even though he was effectively a lame duck awaiting certain Democratic replacement, Georgia's first Republican senator retained some influence as a veteran legislator whom moderates of both parties respected and courted. During this period, Hill would tangle with quintessential Radical Charles Sumner in an important debate about the nature of civil rights and equality, toy with following liberal Republican Horace Greeley, and face being succeeded by Confederate war hero and reputed Ku Klux Klan leader John B. Gordon. In the meantime, the basic business of being a senator continued as he endeavored to influence a little more patronage for his friends and a little more pork for the state. Back in Georgia, Democratic control tightened, and pressure increased on the Madisonian to decide whether he would cling to his Republican identity or follow the great herd of conservative Whites into the party of Jackson.

Senator Hill and Senator Sumner Debate Civil Rights

Joshua Hill's interlocular with Charles Sumner was by far the most visible and controversial episode of his remaining months as a senator. The occasion arose when the Massachusetts Radical moved to amend the general

[1] *Globe*, 42-2, pt. 5, May 29, 1872, 4016.

amnesty bill for former Confederates by adding the essential provisions of the Civil Rights Act, which he had first introduced in 1870. The conservative drive for general amnesty and the Radical desire for stronger civil rights legislation fell at opposite ends of the Reconstruction-era political spectrum. Both ideas had languished for many months, but from December 1871 to March 1872 they were inextricably intertwined, and Joshua Hill found himself tangled up in the issue.

Democrats and some conservative Republicans like Hill had long favored broad amnesty for former Confederates, but no bill had passed because Radical senators resisted, and Grant equivocated. Following ratification of the Fourteenth Amendment in July 1868, Congress began passing hundreds and hundreds of special acts that removed the political disabilities still attached to Confederates who, in the words of the Amendment, "having previously taken an oath, as a member of Congress, or as an officer of the United States, or as a member of any State legislature, or as an executive or judicial officer of any State, to support the Constitution of the United States, shall have engaged in insurrection or rebellion against the same, or given aid or comfort to the enemies thereof." Each act required a two-thirds vote to pass. After some three years of this process, thousands of relatively easy cases had already been handled, and lawmakers had become tired of having to evaluate the long lists of applicants. The idea of passing a single bill that would relieve all but the very highest level of Confederate leaders in one fell swoop was always popular with Democrats, and by the end of 1871, it had gained significant Republican support as a convenience for Congress and as an olive branch to the White South. Once President Grant signaled his support, it became almost certain that a broad-based amnesty bill would soon pass.[2]

At the same time, the most ardent Radicals were disappointed at the lax enforcement of the existing Civil Rights Acts and of the voting and equal protection clauses of the Fourteenth Amendment. Their proposed solution was the supplementary civil rights bill introduced by Senator Sumner and Representative Benjamin Butler in 1870. Sumner hoped that the strengthened civil rights law would become his "crowning work," but it had been stalled in committee for nearly two years. In December 1871,

---

[2] Summers, *Ordeal of the Reunion*, 303–304; Abbott, *Republican Party and the South*, 214–17, 229; Foner, *Reconstruction*, 504–505.

the senator took advantage of the opportunity to hitch his civil rights bill onto the amnesty bandwagon. He knew that the tactic would draw attention to the crusade for equal rights even if the bill did not actually secure passage in the present session. A thorough study of President Grant and the Klan argues convincingly that Sumner knew that his amendment was too controversial to pass in the form he presented it and that his real intent was to use it as a "poison pill" to defeat amnesty, which the Radical feared would only strengthen the Democrats.[3]

The attempt to attach Sumner's bill to the general amnesty bill set the stage for an epic clash. Hill, who had previously endorsed the congressional relief of many specific individuals, entered the debate when he took the Senate floor to plead on behalf of amnesty. He began by assuring his fellow Republicans that he had not changed his Unionist stripes. Hill acknowledged that he still felt "bitterly towards those who originated the rebellion" and that he "had no sympathy, and I may say no toleration for the rebellion itself. I thought it unwise; I thought it unjust; I even thought it was wicked, and I so characterized it at the time." But, he then added, the passage of time "has soothed in some degree my own feelings, as it has toned down the feelings of others." The time had come, he argued, for broad-based amnesty.[4]

When he rose to speak on that occasion, Hill had no intention of entering into a philosophical debate over the substance of Sumner's amendment. His specific purpose was to make the parliamentary point that the Senate should strike Sumner's civil rights amendment from the amnesty bill because it violated the Senate rule that amendments must be germane to the principal bill. Civil rights for freed people, Hill contended, were not directly relevant to amnesty. Sumner's proposal, he said, should be considered on its merits "at the proper time."[5]

The New Englander, however, determined that "the proper time" was then, there, and now, so the face-to-face encounter began. Sumner rebuked

---

[3] Donald, *Charles Sumner*, 531 (crowning), 535 (a measure); Wilson, "Emerson, Transcendental Prudence," 468–69; McConnell, "Originalism," 997; Gudridge, "Privileges and Permissions," 83–130; Bordewich, *Klan War*, 276–78 (poison).

[4] *Globe*, 42-2, pt. 1, December 20, 1871, 241; 42-2, pt. 4, May 8, 1872, 3194.

[5] Ibid., December 20, 1871, 241.

Hill by declaring that he would "like to bring home to the senator that nearly one half of the people of Georgia are now excluded from those equal rights which my amendment proposes to secure, and yet I understand that the Senator disregards their condition, sets aside their desires, and proposes to vote down my proposition." With that rebuke, Sumner threw down the gauntlet. Hill set the matter of germaneness aside for the moment and replied as to substance: "There is a radical difference between the Senator from Massachusetts and myself; it is irreconcilable.... I will say that I think his definition of rights differs materially from my own.... I am one of those who have believed that when it pleased the Creator of heaven and earth to make different races of men it was His purpose to keep them distinct and separate." Sumner responded, "Now we see where the Senator is."[6]

Both Hill and Sumner professed to endorse the Fourteenth Amendment's guarantee of "the equal protection of the laws," so their differences focused on the meaning of "equal." Sumner presented his position succinctly and powerfully: "I may have whom I please as my friend, as my acquaintance, as my associate, and so may the Senator, but I cannot deny any human being, the humblest, any right of equality. He must be equal before the law or the promises of the Declaration of Independence are not yet fulfilled." Hill could fully agree with those literal words—but not with the syllogism that Sumner drew from them. In the Georgian's world view, equality before the law could be achieved concurrently with the physical separation of the races; in Sumner's it could not. That contrast was the crux of their encounters.[7]

Hill put forth a firm defense of what would come to be known as the principle of "separate but equal" though that exact phrase did not appear in the 1871–1872 exchange. Using examples to make his point, Hill declared, "I never can agree with [Sen. Sumner] in the proposition" that a dining establishment would have to serve travelers of both races side by side if it provided for each in a manner "alike in all respects." Unknowingly foreshadowing the majority ruling in *Plessy v Ferguson* some twenty-five

---

[6] Ibid., 241–42; Bordewich, *Klan War*, 278. Like most nineteenth-century orators, Hill was inclined to use the currency of religious reference such as "creator" even though indications are that he was agnostic himself (see ch. 14); see Kelly, "Congressional Controversy," 546.

[7] *Globe*, 42-2, pt. 1, December 20, 1871, 241–43.

years later, the Georgian declared, "I also contend that even upon the railways of the country, if cars of equal comfort, convenience, and security be provided for different classes of persons, no one has a right to complain." Then foreshadowing by more than eighty years the defense argument in *Brown v Board of Education of Topeka*, Hill explained, "Nor do I hold that if you have public schools, and you give all the advantages of education to one class as you do to another, but keep them separate and apart, there is any denial of a civil right in that."[8] The Madisonian had provided a clear and concise statement of the system that would come to be called Jim Crow—but with an emphasis on actual physical equivalence that soon got forgotten in practice.

The problem with Hill's position, Sumner argued, was that the Georgian mistook "substitutes for equality." In contrast, Sumner posited, "Equality is where all are alike. A substitute can never take the place of equality." In essence, he was putting forth the winning argument of *Brown v Board of Education*. Even without benefit of the sociological and psychological studies upon which the Warren court relied, the New Englander perceived the fundamental human problem better than his colleague: "The Senator [from Georgia] does not seem to see that any rule excluding a man on account of his color is an indignity, an insult, and a wrong." To Hill's comments that equivalently comfortable but separate facilities met the standard of equality, Sumner retorted, "Now let me ask the Senator whether in this world the personal respect that one receives is not an element of comfort? If a person is treated with indignity, can he be comfortable?" Hill answered, "No one can condemn more strongly than I do any indignity visited upon a person merely because of color." Sumner did not back down. "But when you exclude certain persons from the comforts of travel simply on account of color do you not offer them an indignity?"[9] The exchange was about transportation, but the principle spread across all accommodations, including public schools. Sumner grasped what Hill did not: that when separate facilities are authorized by law, they are inherently unequal.

In one of the sharpest and most widely reported exchanges, Sumner referred to former senator Hiram Revels and issued a challenge:

[8] Ibid.

[9] Ibid.

> Mr. SUMNER.... Why, sir, we have had in this Chamber a colored Senator from Mississippi, but according to the rule of the Senator from Georgia we should have set him apart by himself; he should not have sat with his brother senators. Do I understand the Senator from Georgia as favoring such a rule:
>
> Mr. HILL. No, sir.
>
> Mr. SUMNER. The Senator does not.
>
> Mr. HILL. I do not, sir, for this reason: it is under the institutions of this country that he becomes entitled by law to his seat here; we have no right to deny it to him.
>
> Mr. SUMNER. Very well, and I intend to the best of my ability to see that under the institutions of his country he is equal everywhere.[10]

This was certainly not the first time that Congress had heard discussion of such ideas. In fact, earlier that year Hill himself had engaged in a similar but much briefer and more obscure encounter with Senator Revels regarding Sumner's bill to integrate the public schools of the District of Columbia.[11] However, the Sumner-Hill encounter of December 1871 and its follow-up in the early months of 1872 constituted the first time that the concepts of separate but equal on the one hand and full racial integration in the public sphere on the other hand had been so clearly articulated on the floor of Congress and so widely reported in the national and regional press.

The *New York Tribune* characterized the December exchange as "an animated debate." A letter in Frederick Douglass's newspaper *New National Era*, found Sumner's position compelling: "Any one who has read the recent debate on Mr. Sumner's bill between that gentleman and Senator Hill, of Georgia, must have felt the potency of truth, the irresistible logic of justice, when confronted with half-awakened sympathies, defective reasoning faculties, and vulgar prejudices." The letter writer recognized that the "half-awakened sympathies" of Hill were at least preferable to the complete lack of sympathy he had experienced from other Southern Whites

---

[10] Ibid.

[11] *Globe*, 41–3, February 8, 1871, 1059–1061; *Columbus Enquirer*, February 18, 1871.

by adding, "Senator Hill means well to his 'humble' negro friends, if his logic is defective." A Pennsylvania paper declared that Sumner had demonstrated to Hill "that it was simply a question of right, and had nothing to do with social relations." In contrast, the Democratic *New York World* reported, "Most of the day was taken up with a colloquy between Senator Hill and Senator Sumner [who was] on his old hobby of negro equality."[12]

Back home, Democratic spokesmen praised Hill for standing up against Sumner, whom they detested. A Columbus paper headed its account "JOSH AFTER THE ENEMY" and reprinted the opinion of another paper, which wrote that Senator Hill had "acquitted himself in a running debate with great credit, considering who his antagonist was.... Mr. Hill met Sumner at all points, and showed himself well skilled and quick at repartee." A proud Savannah editor exclaimed, "The Georgian bore himself bravely in the fight with the great apostle of negrophilism." The *Greensboro Herald* wished that Hill had been even more assertive in the "spicy debate which was carried on with studied courtesy on either side." Reminding his readers of Hill's partisan affiliation, the editor wrote, "But it is very difficult for a member of the Republican party to stand up in a Radical Senate which has usurped and outraged the rights of the States.... The fact is Mr. Hill is no Radical. His antecedents and instincts, to say nothing of his practical good sense, are all against the doctrine and aims of the party of which he is only *nominally* a member." The writer predicted, wrongly as so many pundits had done before, that Hill would soon abandon his Republican ties.[13]

The sharp but gentlemanly clash of December 20 accomplished Sumner's goal of bringing discussion of his civil rights legislation out of committee and on to the floor. On January 15, Sumner made a major speech on behalf of his amendment and, in the words of Sumner's leading biographer, "For the next three weeks virtually all other Senate business had to be suspended while the debate upon the civil rights amendment

---

[12] *New York Tribune*, December 21, 1871; *(Washington, DC) New National Era*, December 28, 1871; *Harrisburg Telegram*, December 21, 1871; *New York World*, December 21, 1871.

[13] *Columbus Sun*, January 16, 1872 (acquitted, *Griffin Star*); *Columbus Enquirer*, January 9, 1872 (*Savannah Republican*); *Greensboro Herald*, January 11, 1872.

raged." A couple of days later, Sumner presented the Senate with several supportive letters and memorials from Southern Blacks and proclaimed, "I put this against the speeches of the Senator from Georgia [Mr. Hill], the Senator from Mississippi [Mr. Alcorn], and the Senator from South Carolina [Mr. Sawyer]…. and since Georgia has, through her Senator on this floor, been most conspicuous in opposing equal rights, I begin with Georgia."[14]

Whereas the December 20 encounter between Sumner and Hill had been face to face, the January interchange was less direct. Senator Hill took the floor a few days later to offer his response to Sumner's comments. He began by professing surprise that the December encounter with Sumner had attracted so much attention.

> Some three weeks ago, very much to my own astonishment, I was drawn into a colloquy with the Senator from Massachusetts [Mr. Sumner] upon his favorite policy. I had no anticipation of any such discussion, nor did I at the time or after it over attach to it any very great consequence…. But, as Lord Byron, I believe it was, said of himself, alluding to his sudden rise in the literary world, "I lay down to sleep, woke, and found myself famous." I thought what took place on that occasion was but a very innocent comparison of views between the Senator from Massachusetts and myself, I intervening in a simple way, from my practical knowledge of the character of the colored people of the south and my life-long association with them, to state what I thought was most expedient to be done, and the Senator rebuking with some severity many of the opinions that I advanced. *But that day's work has become important history.*"

Hill maintained that the recent speech by the Massachusetts senator had not changed the crux of the debate. Sumner maintained, Hill reminded the Senate, "that equivalents were not equality. There is the great point between him and myself, I maintaining the converse of his proposition that they are substantial equality…. I have seen no good reason for any modification of the views I expressed on the former occasion." Hill then turned to extolling

[14] Donald, *Charles Sumner*, 537; *Globe*, 42-2, pt. 1, 429, January 17, 1871, 491–92.

the amnesty bill and arguing once again that it should stand independent of Sumner's civil rights amendment.[15]

One of the letters of support that Sumner had entered into the record was from Henry M. Turner, a Black preacher, legislator, and political organizer whom a leading scholar of Georgia's African American politics characterized as "the state's most powerful black politician." Turner's letter roundly criticized Hill for saying that most Blacks in Georgia opposed Sumner's bill. Hill correctly pointed out that he had not made that assertion and then launched into a bitter attack on Turner. He characterized the reverend as a "demagogue" and claimed that Sumner was unaware that Turner "is not regarded as a decent man." To be sure, Turner had his detractors even among African Americans, but Hill's criticism was unduly harsh.[16]

In the January exchange, the two senators returned to the definition of equality. Sumner had cited the case of a distinguished Black man from Louisiana who had recently been separated from Whites while on a train to Washington. Referring to that example, Hill countered, "I still must insist that if it only consisted in putting him in a car that was designed for colored people, *and if the car was equal in comfort to a first-class passenger car*, there was no injustice done him. That is the distinction."[17]

The definition of equality was not the only issue upon which the senators sparred. They also articulated differing interpretations of what the Fourteenth Amendment meant when it stipulated that "no state" could deny equal protection to its citizens. The two senators agreed that no government at the local, state, or national level had the authority to enforce social equality in private matters such as whom one might choose as friends or whom one might invite into his parlor. They differed distinctly, however, about whether privately owned businesses (public accommodations, in current legal parlance) should enjoy the same rights to discriminate as private individuals. Sumner argued in favor of a broad interpretation of what constituted state action. "Show me, therefore, a legal

[15] *Globe*, 42-2, pt. 1, January 22, 1872, 491–93 (emphasis added).

[16] Angell, *Bishop Henry McNeal Turner*, 117–19; Drago, *Black Politicians*, 27 (the state's), 98, 100. Hill said at least once that many Black people preferred school segregation (Kelly, "Congressional Controversy," 546).

[17] *Globe*, 42-2, pt. 1, January 22, 1872, 492 (emphasis added).

institution, anything created or regulated by law, and I show you what must be opened equally to all without distinction of color." Hill's interpretation of legitimate state authority was much narrower than Sumner's:

> I am not well satisfied with the idea that a man's house ceases to be his castle whenever he chooses to convert it into a house of entertainment, and to take a license from the property authority as a hotel-keeper or a boarding-house keeper. Does he cease to have control over it? Does he become a slave of the public because he pays a tax? I think not. I think the hotel-keeper is entitled to all the discrimination in regard to his guests that other men have in admitting them into their houses.

Again Hill articulated a position that the Supreme Court would soon affirm, this time in the Civil Rights Cases of 1883.[18]

One thing that Hill seemed to understand better than Sumner was that fairness in business dealings and opportunities for economic sufficiency were of more pressing day-to-day concerns to most freedmen than politics and integration, a point that Booker T. Washington later made famous in his 1895 Atlanta Compromise speech. With that in mind, Hill challenged Sumner:

> If the Senator could devise an amendment that would secure to every colored laborer in the South fair and just remuneration for his toil, that would secure an honest settlement between him and every employer for whom he labors, he would do a work for the colored race far superior to this mere theoretical humanitarian project about which he seems to have such great consideration. There is something practical in that.

Hill was correct about the short run. As historian Edward Drago detailed, most Georgia Reconstruction-era Black politicians would have been willing to accept some short-term compromises regarding equality in exchange for economic security. Hill was wrong, however, to imply that

[18] *Globe*, May 14, 1872, 3424. Hill's concept of private vs. state action was not limited to race; he also used it in regard to labor legislation.

African Americans did not desire in the long run the sort of meaningful political influence and broad civil rights that Sumner offered.[19]

A few days later, Hill turned again to Sumner. This time he strayed somewhat from the civility that had previously characterized his references to the famous Radical. Hill had previously implied that the senator's motive for trying to attach the civil rights amendment to the amnesty bill was more political theater than serious effort to pass legislation, but this time his barb was sharp and direct. Hill charged that Senator Sumner "has at least achieved one great purpose: he has presented himself more prominently, if possible, than he ever did before to the entire colored race of the nation as their foremost, if not their excusive champion.... I have been prone to think that agitation for the sake of agitation had much to do with the Senator's movements."[20]

As popular as Sumner was with Black Americans, he was a New Englander who had little day-to-day contact with regular Black folks. Democrats and conservative Republicans were delighted when Hill pointed out on the Senate floor that Sumner's personal relationships with people of color did not match his rhetoric of equality. Hill's wife made her own allusions to the abolitionist's supposed hypocrisy in a private letter to a neighbor in Madison. Emily Hill began by extolling Washington's springtime weather and then turned her attention to a recent parade:

> I could have witnessed...the celebration of emancipation, being very near & opposite the whole procession, but as Charles Sumner was not to be conspicuous as he should have been on the occasion, the fact abated my curiosity. It seems strange, that from a man possessing his cultured mind & wealth, surrounded in his palatial home with Turkish lounges, rare, statuary, Turkish carpets & rugs, windows richly draped in brocade & the interior of this beautiful home forming a picture of Oriental

[19] *Globe*, 42-2, pt. 1, January 22, 1872, 491–92; Drago, *Black Politicians*, 86, 98–100, 117–18; 29; Gudridge, "Privileges and Permissions," 87, 116–19.

[20] *Globe,* 42-2, pt. 1, 879, February 7, 1872.

> magnificence almost inconceivable, should come the teachings of "equality."[21]

There is no question that Sumner loved the limelight and that he had filed his amendment knowing that it was unlikely to pass as presented. It is also true that he lived a life of ease insulated from everyday people, Black or White. Nevertheless, the Hills were wrong to imply that his long-time support for Black rights had been insincere.

An example of the esteem in which most Black politicians held Sumner came in response to pejorative remarks that Hill made about an unnamed Black office holder from Georgia. Edwin Belcher, Hill's son-in-law's rival for office, recognized himself as Hill's target and responded with a letter to the predominately Black readership of *New National Era*:

> I am charged with being a "pet" of Senator Sumner. If Mr. Hill means by that that I am devotedly attached to the noble champion of the rights of my race, he is correct, and where is the colored man—let him have more or less than one-eighth African blood—who does not revere and love Charles Sumner? If he means that I am a particular favorite of Mr. Sumner, I am indeed glad to be informed of that fact.[22]

For Radical and moderate White congressmen, the decision whether to endorse Sumner's civil rights legislation could be a matter of life and death—politically and literally. As the vote neared in March 1872, Representative Thomas J. Speer, the White man who succeeded Jefferson Long in the House, sought counsel from Ben Conley, the former short-time governor: "Can a man vote for the civil rights bill and live in Ga? What would you advise me to do regarding it? I am favorably inclined towards it and believe that in the main that it is right but still I hate to do a thing that would probably cost me my life." Luckily for Speer, it did not come to that.[23]

---

[21] *New York World*, December 21, 1871; *Augusta Chronicle*, Jan 17, 1872; *Gwinnett Herald* (Lawrenceville), Jan 24, 1872; Emily Hill to Eliza [Mrs. William Sanders] Stokes, April 22, 1872, Stokes-McHenry-Hicky Family Papers in the possession of Stratton Hicky, Madison, Georgia. (Mr. Hicky intends to transfer the collection to the HRBML.)

[22] *(Washington, DC) New National Era*, May 23, 1871.

[23] Thomas J. to Benjamin Conley, March 24, 1872, #1544, box 1, folder 17, Benjamin Conley Papers, HRBML.

In spring 1872, while other matters diverted Sumner's attention, the General Amnesty Act passed without the controversial civil rights provisions appended. At the last minute, Joshua Hill proposed his own amendment that would have given the amnesty bill even broader coverage, so he briefly sparred again with Sumner one last time. Hill soon withdrew his amendment in the interest of swift passage. Democrats, along with moderate and conservative Republicans like Hill, were pleased that broad-based amnesty with only a few hundred exceptions had finally passed and that Sumner's civil rights bill had once again been delayed.[24]

Charles Sumner persisted until his death. A weakened version of his bill finally passed as the Civil Rights Act of 1875, a year after its sponsor died and two years after Joshua Hill left the Senate. Less than a decade after its passage, the United States Supreme Court eviscerated the law's effectiveness in the Civil Rights Cases of 1883, which ruled that neither the Thirteenth nor the Fourteenth Amendment gave Congress the authority to regulate the actions of private individuals and corporations. Thirteen years later, in *Plessy v Ferguson*, the Supreme Court ruled that a state could accomplish "equal protection of the laws" and still require racial segregation on railroads (and by implication in all public accommodations) if it so chose. Both cases reflected the positions that Joshua Hill had articulated so forcefully in his confrontation with Sumner. At the time of the Hill-Sumner interlocular, racial segregation was already widespread (but not universal) in daily practice, but it was not yet widely enshrined in statute. Alas, by the end of the nineteenth century, Jim Crow had earned unequivocal judicial endorsement.[25]

Joshua Hill's statements during the December to March series of exchanges with Sumner provide insight into his own feelings about the nature of race. Hill's de facto lame-duck status allowed him to be frank and revealing, perhaps at times more so than he intended. He did not need to spout blatantly racist endorsements of White supremacy to please White

---

[24] *Globe*, 42-2, pt. 4, 3194–195, May 8, 1872.

[25] Fitzgerald, *Splendid Failure*, 181; Egerton, *Wars of Reconstruction*, 310–12; Scaturro, *Supreme Court's Retreat*, 115–16; McAfee, *Race, Religion, and Reconstruction*, 112; Gates, *Stony the Road*, 31–35. Historians have long debated the "Strange Career" of the origins and spread of Jim Crow; for a recent summary see Cobb, *C. Vann Woodward*, 154–206.

voters, but neither did he need to hide his true feelings in order to ingratiate himself with the Republican Party mainstream. One scholar of Sumner's rhetorical methods cited the example of the New Englander's colloquy with Hill to illustrate that Sumner had a remarkable ability to bring about the "unmasking" of his opponents. However, had the author known more about Joshua Hill, he would have realized that Sumner was not "unmasking" anything about this particular rival whose conservative views were already well known.[26]

There is no doubt that Hill's understanding of race relations was rooted in the White supremacist assumptions of his upcountry South Carolina boyhood and his Black Belt Georgia adulthood. Hill's assumption of White racial superiority carried with it a sense of obligation toward the enslaved and later the freed members of what he regarded as the lesser race. Hill told Sumner that he had "the reputation of being kind and humane" to Black people. As evidence of his benevolence, Hill specifically mentioned that he often assisted freed people of modest means and that he had personally given "a colored congregation an acre of ground for the erection of a church."[27]

Hill was by no means alone among affluent former enslavers in offering this sort of charity, especially for religious congregations, yet the Madisonian's version of White supremacy seems more nuanced than that of the typical Southern gentry. As a Unionist turned Republican, albeit a conservative one, Hill eschewed the overtly racist and hateful rhetoric characteristic of Georgia Democrats such as his new senate colleague Thomas Norwood, the unreconstructed Robert Toombs, or the bombastic New Departure advocate Ben Hill. Joshua Hill avoided openly denigrating Black people for political purposes, and he refrained from raising White supremacy to the height of noble and immutable principle. His endorsements of the separate but equal policy routinely gave lip service to the requirement of true physical equivalence. Neither did the Georgian decry the fact that other parts of the nation took differing approaches to equality. For example, he remarked during a debate that even though he confessed

[26] Wilson, "Emerson, Transcendental Prudence," 471.

[27] *Globe*, 42-2, pt. 1, January 22, 1872, 491–93. Mt. Zion Baptist still functions as a predominately Black congregation near the ruins of Hill's postbellum country house.

"a little penchant for the white race," it did not trouble him personally when he found himself on occasion seated next to Black people on the integrated streetcars of the nation's capital.[28] He had come to accept the right of political participation by African Americans, and he did not dispute their right to hold office. He did, however, question the current readiness of most, but not all, Blacks to assume office. By twenty-first-century standards, a politician who unabashedly expressed support for racial segregation as Joshua Hill did would be considered an extremist. By the standards of his time, however, Hill's very acceptance of Black political participation and legal equality, albeit with separation, placed him on the middle ground among White politicians—North and South.

Hill contended that African Americans, even those who opposed him, respected and trusted him:

> I believe that the colored people who know me in Georgia would rely, any of them, upon my benevolence and sense of justice as soon as they would upon that of the Senator [Sumner], or of any other man in any portion of this country.... I deny feeling prejudice or contempt for any man because he is black, for I have seen some colored men for whom I have the highest esteem, the greatest regard, and in whom I have the greatest confidence. It is not the fault of the race that, socially, they are not the equals of the white race to-day.

Other Southern Whites employed similar paternalistic tropes, but Hill's assertions ring differently. Intentionally or subconsciously, the last sentence of his statement suggests an important distinction between him and the more resolute racists who regarded inferiority as the immutable status of the Black race. His observation that existing inequality was "not the fault of the race" revealed a tacit acknowledgement that much of the blame for the state of racial affairs fell on Whites. His insertion of the qualifying word "to-day" at the end of the sentence implies that he harbored some doubt that racial inequality and racial animosity constituted permanent fixtures of the human condition. He later mused about the long-term future of race relations and how many years it might be before the order of things would change. "Perchance in a century," he wondered.

---

[28] *Globe,* 42-2, pt. 1, January 22, 1872, 491–93 (a little); B. Hill, *Senator Benjamin H. Hill of Georgia,* 278.

On another occasion, Hill made it clear that his musings about the future constituted speculation rather than conversion: "Call it prejudice if you will; it is the white man's prejudice this world over!…I shall never undertake to delude the black man of my State—and I live in a section overwhelmingly black and am a friend of all that are deserving—by endeavoring to persuade him that a new light, as miraculous as that which broke upon Saul of Tarsus, has fallen upon me."[29] There is no evidence that Hill ever had a road-to-Damascus moment about fundamental racial equality, but neither to his death in 1891 did he join his contemporaries in openly exploiting the rhetoric of racial animosity for political gain.

The Hill-Sumner colloquy of 1871–1872 has heretofore attracted scant attention from historians. On the other hand, the authors of several law review articles from the latter half of the twentieth century found the clear and unequivocal arguments of the rival senators to be critical in their interpretation of the legislative history of the Fourteenth Amendment and the Civil Rights Act of 1875. One article characterized Hill's statements as "the classic expression" of the argument that the Fourteenth Amendment did not grant federal government the right to regulate private businesses such as hotels, taverns, and railroads. By rejecting Hill's argument and agreeing with Sumner, Congress knew exactly what it was doing when it passed the act. The author concluded that the *Civil Rights Cases of 1883* were wrongly decided because the Supreme Court used "juridical slight [*sic*] of hand" to substitute "Hill's conception of discrimination as a matter of private choice for Sumner's Radical Republican conception of discrimination as a deprivation of rights." That was essentially the point (without reference to Hill) that Associate Justice John Marshall Harlan, the lone dissenter, made in his classic dissent.[30]

Hill's rejoinders to Sumner were also critical to the argument made by another law review article that contended that the Supreme Court ignored strong evidence of legislative intent. The professor contends that the Court erred by upholding "separate but equal" in *Plessy v Ferguson* (1896) and that when it effectively overruled *Plessy* in *Brown v Board of Education* (1954) it could have done so on an "originalist" basis rather than using modern social science evidence. Chief Justice Earl Warren and the

---

[29] *Globe*, 42-2, pt. 1, January 22, 1872, 492; May 14, 1872, 3424.

[30] D. M. Jones, "No Time for Trumpets," 2332.

unanimous court found historical sources to be "inconclusive" and refused to "turn the clock back" to the years of Reconstruction. The author disputed that conclusion by focusing not on the inconclusive debates from the time that the amendment was transmitted to the states for ratification in 1868 but rather on "a study of the legal thinking of the antagonists in the debate" over the legislative debates that led to the Civil Rights Act of 1875. The scholar contends that Hill and the other 1870s opponents of civil rights legislation defined the terms of "separate but equal" so clearly that the bill's eventual passage can only be interpreted to mean that Congress explicitly and intentionally rejected Hill's concepts and accepted Sumner's with regard to the whole range integration, including public schools. The author argues that Congress dropped school desegregation from the final Civil Rights Act of 1875 for reasons of political expediency not because it doubted its legal authority.[31]

Whether these two Constitutional interpretations are legally correct is not the concern of a biography of Joshua Hill. What these articles and others by legal scholars do accomplish, however, is to demonstrate the seminal importance of the Hill-Sumner interchange in the legislative history of the Civil Rights Act of 1875 and in the broader understanding of the meaning of federal authority and equal rights in the Reconstruction Era.

It is clear that the Massachusetts Radical occupied the moral high ground in his confrontation with the Georgia conservative. Yet, given the attitudes of most contemporary White Americans—North and South—both of their positions were more idealistic than practical. As Heather Cox Richardson and others have documented, neither "separate but equal" with the actual physical equivalence that Hill endorsed nor the full equality in the public sphere that Sumner envisioned were politically realistic options in the late nineteenth century. Hill argued on behalf of an honestly administered separate but equal society in which Black public schools would have resources equivalent to White and in which railroad cars for Black passengers would be the same as those reserved for Whites. As he said when

---

[31] McConnell, "Originalism," 947, 988–989, 1007–113; McConnell made the same point in a shorter article, "Originalist Case for *Brown v Board of Education*," 458, and in Balkin and Balkin, *What Brown v. Board of Education Should Have Said*, 163. See also Avins, "Civil Rights Act of 1875," 873–915; and Avins, "Anti-Miscegenation Laws," 1224–55.

speaking of a potential Black railroad passenger, "When he pays his money, he is entitled to as much comfort and as much convenience as I am." Decades of Jim Crow reality proved that Hill's vision of physical equivalence was unrealistic in face of intractable racism that cared naught for even the most basic definition of equal protection. On the other hand, it is also unlikely that Sumner's idealistic legislation would have eliminated racial prejudice and segregation in the nineteenth-century North, much less in the South. Even the watered-down version of Sumner's bill that finally passed in 1875 was only halfheartedly enforced. And the Supreme Court washed away even that limited protection less than ten years after it passed.[32]

In the historically fraught game of what might have been, one can wistfully speculate. If a strong civil rights act had passed both congressional and constitutional muster in the late nineteenth century and been even weakly enforced, racial distinctions might well have faded faster than they did under decades of Jim Crow in the South and persistent prejudice in the North. Maybe Whites in the South and in the rest of the country would have come around. If the "equal" aspect of the separate but equal doctrine had been enforced as Joshua Hill advocated, perhaps the "separate" part of the equation would have gradually faded away. But it was not to be for either. As late as the 1950s, Southern congressmen (and some non-Southern allies) were making essentially the same arguments that Joshua Hill had made in 1871 and 1872. At the same time, opponents of Jim Crow, White and Black, were still making essentially the same moral appeals that Charles Sumner and Frederick Douglass articulated in the 1870s and before. In 1872 Hill ruminated about such a future:

> As we are progressing in this great experiment of giving freedom to an enslaved race, we have yet to discover whether nature has implanted in the white man an ineradicable repugnance to equality with an inferior race.... Perhaps it may grow less; perchance in a century it may be obliterated, but it takes time to determine this question. Nature is more powerful than legislation.... I confess that I am open to conviction, but the conviction must come to me from time itself, and I do not know that I shall

---

[32] Richardson, *Death of Reconstruction*, 125–41, *Globe*, 41-3, pt. 2, 1060–1061, February 8, 1871.

> have time enough upon this earth to derive a great deal more enlightenment.[33]

To be sure, by 1972, when that century that Hill mused about had passed, race relations in America had improved, perhaps beyond even what Charles Sumer had thought possible. But "repugnance to equality" has yet to be fully "obliterated." It has been a long, long road full of potholes and detours, and the journey is not yet complete.

To Be Grant or to Be Greeley, That Was the Question

By spring 1872, Senator Joshua Hill found himself at a three-way fork in the political road. He could continue to stand by the Republican Party and the administration of Ulysses S. Grant; he could follow some of his non-Radical Republican friends into Horace Greeley's Liberal Republican movement, or he could emulate Joseph E. Brown and the parade of former Republicans who joined or returned to the Democratic fold.

Had Hill chosen to become a Democrat, he would have had to eat a lot of crow. He had detested Democrats ever since he became a Whig in the 1840s. Despite his long-time rejection of the party of Jackson and Calhoun, the ideas of the New Departure Democrats appeared in many ways to be a better fit for Hill than the Radical-dominated Republican Party. Certainly, Joshua Hill could have prolonged his political career by becoming a Democrat. A political profile published in the *Atlanta Constitution* and several other newspapers in mid-summer 1872 illustrates why Hill's party identification remained in doubt:

> The senior Senator, Hon. Joshua Hill, of Madison, Morgan county...is a grave and dignified gentleman of about sixty summers. Although Mr. Hill was elected as a Republican, he seldom votes or acts with that party, but almost in every instance, specially in the repression of harsh legislation toward the good true people, he uniformly co-operated with the Democrats. At this writing it is due to Mr. Hill to say, that we cannot call to mind in any instance where he has cast a vote, since a Senator from

---

[33] *Globe*, 42-2, pt. 1, January 22, 1872, 492; Richardson, *Death of Reconstruction, passim.*

Georgia, inimical to Southern interests, even from the standpoint of the most "unreconstructed." His character for probity is without blemish.[34]

Despite persistent rumors to the contrary, Hill could not abide becoming a Democrat. He lacked the predilection for slick political reinvention that Brown and the mercurial Benjamin Hill continually exhibited. Compared to that pair, the Madisonian valued consistency, even to the point of a stubbornness that sometimes served him ill, at least in terms of political attainment.

What road Hill would take within Georgia's Republican Party was a more difficult question. It certainly would not be the Radical route. The demise of Rufus Bullock, combined with Foster Blodgett's failure to win the Senate seat, shifted party leadership from the Radicals to the moderates/conservative wing, thereby leaving Joshua Hill, John Bryant, Henry P. Farrow, and Amos Akerman as the state's most prominent White Republicans. Even then, the party could not fully unify. Conflicts between conservatives and moderates, carpetbaggers and natives, Atlantans and outstaters, and, most crucially, Blacks and Whites divided the already struggling party. Just before the state legislative session opened, the solidly Democratic *Atlanta Sun* (owned by Alexander H. Stephens) stirred the simmering pot by reprinting the report of a Washington correspondent who claimed that Akerman was reorganizing his party in a way that "Joshua Hill is to be ignored, and the carpet-bag influence [is] to be thoroughly destroyed." The *New York Herald* commented, "Georgia politics have assumed a new phase and, if possible, a more muddled one than before." Some Black politicians such as Jefferson Long remained cautiously aligned with Bryant's moderate faction, but most would probably have agreed with Tunis Campbell, who wrote to Ben Conley early in 1872, describing Hill, Bryant, and their allies as "that sore head class" who thought that they could make the Republican Party "Respectable by Putting White Men in office."[35]

[34] *Atlanta Constitution*, July 2, 1872.

[35] *Atlanta Sun*, October 28, 1871; *Augusta Constitutionalist*, December 15, 1871 (*Herald*); Campbell to Conley, February 22, 1872, in Perman, *Road to Redemption*, 22. Attorney General Farrow broke with Bullock in early 1871.

The emerging Liberal Republican movement—despite use of the term "liberal"—offered a plausible alternative for conservative Southern Republicans like Hill who were ready to put the disruptions of Reconstruction behind them but were not ready to become Democrats. The two unifying forces of the Liberal Republicans were a long-standing desire to end Reconstruction and a deep-seated opposition to the renomination of President Grant. Joshua Hill's diminishing ties with the chief executive, and vice-versa, stemmed mainly from Hill's opposition to the Ku Klux Klan Enforcement Act. This growing disenchantment seemed to suggest that Hill might be willing to join the "reform" or "Liberal" movement. In addition, most of the Liberal program regarding Reconstruction aligned with Hill's positions on amnesty and the limitations of federal authority.

New York Tribune editor Horace Greeley was the face of the Liberal movement, and Senator Carl Schurz (R-MO) was its principal organizer. In February 1872, Hill approvingly distributed to Georgia newspapers copies of a Schurz speech that called for nearly universal amnesty for former Confederates. In addition, Illinois Republican senator Lyman Trumbull, who had been a strong advocate for Hill during his seating controversy, emerged as a Liberal Republican leader. The mainstream *New York Herald* characterized Trumbull as "more of a democrat at heart than a republican" and criticized him for having worked so hard on behalf of Hill.[36]

As early as May 1871, just three months after Hill joined the Senate, reports had already emerged in the press that the Georgian was among those who wanted Grant to be replaced on the Republican ticket. By the end of the year, the influential and normally strongly Republican *Chicago Tribune* printed an article that suggested several tickets for president and vice president to run in 1872 on a "Reform ticket." Leading the list of several pairings was "Horace Greeley (R.) of New York (the Empire State of the North) [with] Joshua Hill (D.) of Georgia (the Empire State of the South)." The capital D after Hill's name showed that many political observers had come to regard him as a Democrat despite his own self-

[36] *Macon Telegraph*, February 27, 1872; *New York Herald*, April 23, 1872; R. C. Williams, *Horace Greeley*, 279–303; Snay, *Horace Greeley*, 174–80.

identification and party caucus membership. Hill dismissed such hubbub as the work of "busybodies."[37]

Joshua Hill may have often aligned with Democratic sentiment about the supposedly "harsh legislation" of Reconstruction, but on other issues such as trade and foreign policy, he leaned more toward the Republican policies of Grant. Notably, in May 1871, Hill stood with the president on ratification of the Treaty of Washington, which sought to resolve outstanding claims and disputes with Great Britain. Approval of the treaty fell along distinct partisan lines. All but one Republican favored it, and all but two Democrats opposed it.[38]

There was no signature trade legislation while Hill served in the Senate, but when the question of tariffs did arise on such products as rice, tea, coffee, and crockery, he remained comfortable with the position of mainstream Republicans. The Liberal Republicans touted free trade, as did most Democrats, but Hill did not agree. He took the position that tariffs were a far superior way to raise "the largest amount of revenue practicable" as compared to direct taxes. Appealing to constituents in the northern reaches of his old congressional district, Hill singled out the disruptive effect of such direct taxes as those on the stills that "mountaineers" operated in the backwoods of the Georgia Blue Ridge. Regarding the "incidental protection" that would result from revenue tariffs, Hill remarked, "Then let it occur. I see no great evil in that. I do not belong to the extreme free trade school.... I belong rather to the opposite school." Expressing sentiments not likely to make him popular with Georgia Democrats, Hill explicitly rejected the "general opinion prevailing in the south that all duties were levied to the prejudice of the southern people." He also made a point of mentioning that, on the issue of diminishing the use of internal taxes, he agreed with Senator Sumner. As an old Whig turned Republican, Hill looked fondly back to the prewar days of Henry Clay and the American System. He expressed relief that arguments over tariffs no longer reached

---

[37] *Nashville Union & American*, May 17, 1871; *Chicago Tribune*, December 28, 1871 (from *Moore's Rural New Yorker*), March 18, 1872. Perhaps the use of D stemmed from the frequent confusion between Josh Hill and Ben Hill (*Globe*, 42-2, pt. 5, May 29, 1872, 4016 [There are]).

[38] Calhoun, *Presidency of Ulysses S. Grant*, 344, 363; *Journal of Executive Proceedings of the Senate*, 42nd Congress, Special Session, May 24, 1871, 106–109; *Globe*, 42-1, pt. 2, May 17, 1871, 856–65.

the "angry extent" and "national calamity" that they had during the nullification controversy of the 1830s, but he still laid much of the lingering problem at the feet of John C. Calhoun and his advocacy of direct taxes rather than tariffs. Despite his general position, when Hill advocated for the elimination of the duty on fertilizer so crucial to Georgia's farmers, he proved the axiom that tariffs are always a local issue.[39]

Neither Joshua Hill nor any other prominent Georgian attended the Liberal Republican Convention in Cincinnati in May. In fact, Hill questioned the very legitimacy of the Georgia delegation. He claimed that some if not all of the Empire State of the South's supposed delegates were not even Georgians. Across the South as a whole, many Liberal Republican delegates were men who had broken with the Grant administration over patronage issues. The Georgia delegation, legitimate or not, backed former Missouri senator B. Gratz Brown, the eventual vice-presidential nominee, but shifted to Greeley when Brown withdrew. Even after Hill denounced the composition of the Georgia delegation to the Liberal convention, word still circulated that he was either leaning toward Greeley or still undecided—and perhaps he was.[40]

In mid-May, shortly before the Liberal Republican and regular Republican conventions began, a Rome editor contended that "all the intelligence of the Republican party in Georgia is settled against Grant" and that the only Georgia politicians on Grant's side were those who held offices to which he had appointed them. Senator Hill, along with Joe Brown, James Johnson, and T. P. Saffold, were on the editor's list of those luminaries who had "declared strongly against" the president. Over the next couple of months, several sources continued to write as if it were a done deal that Hill would back Greeley. A Cincinnati paper reported that Hill had talked directly to Greeley and implied that he would support the New Yorker. The *New York Herald* observed that Hill and several other Constitutional Union Party organizers of the 1860 Bell-Everett ticket were on board for Greeley. The *Atlanta Sun* sarcastically remarked, "It was cruel on the part

[39] *Globe*, 42-2, pt. 3, March 21, 1872, 1859–1860, pt. 5, May 27, 1872, 3916; *Savannah Advertiser*, March 30, 1872.

[40] Downey, "Horace Greeley and the Politicians," 731–32, 744, 746; *Globe*, 42-2, pt. 3, March 21, 1872, 1859–1860, pt. 5, May 27, 1872, 3916; *Savannah Advertiser*, March 30, 1872.

of Mr. Hill to disappoint the hopes of his 'party,'" i.e., the Republicans. On the other hand, a man who claimed to have talked to Hill in Madison reported, "Whether [Senator Hill] will support Greeley or Grant in the coming election, is yet to be developed."[41]

Meanwhile, most Georgia Democrats had become reluctantly resolved to their party's embrace of Greeley on the fused Liberal Republican-Democrat ticket for president. (Fusion did not apply to state offices.) Leading Georgia Democrats justified the fusion ticket on the grounds that was that it was only a temporary expedient. Some in the press used the example of 1868 when Democrats cooperated with conservative Republicans to elect Hill to the Senate as proof of the contention that a fleeting alliance would not harm the party in the long run.[42]

Soon after the Liberal Republican convention, Republicans happily renominated President Grant. Since Schuyler Colfax did not run again, the second spot on the Grant ticket was wide open. Joshua Hill's name appeared on several speculative lists of vice-presidential possibilities, as did Amos Akerman even though Grant had eased him out as attorney general. Neither of them was a serious contender for the position, which went to Senator Henry Wilson of Massachusetts.[43]

Despite his dallying with the Liberals and the prospect of future office as a Democrat, Hill's default position was to remain a traditional, if conservative, Republican. Like most Southern Republicans in Congress, Hill was no doubt frustrated by the disinclination of his Northern colleagues to grant his state the level of patronage influence and economic support that they desired. But a little patronage was better than none. Even though

---

[41] *Gadsden (AL) Times*, May 16, 1872 (*Rome Commercial*); *(Selma, AL) Dollar Times*, July 9, 1872 (Whether); *(Athens) Southern Watchman*, May 29, 1872; *Columbus Enquirer*, May 28, 1872; *Cincinnati Times*, June 25, 1872; *New York Herald*, July 7, 1872; *Atlanta Sun*, July 9, September 25, 1872; *New Orleans Times-Picayune*, September 20, 1872.

[42] Parks, *Joseph E. Brown*, 475–77; Currie-McDaniel, *Carpetbagger of Conscience*, 127–28; W. C. Davis, *The Union*, 245–46 (Linton Stephens died in July 1872); see Donald, *Charles Sumner*, 516–20, 529–30.

[43] *Globe*, 42-2, pt. 4, 3292, May 8, 1872; *Cincinnati Times*, May 29, 1872; *New Orleans Times-Picayune*, May 26, 1872; *Buffalo Morning Express*, May 31, 1872; *Savannah Morning News*, March 16, 1872; Egerton, *Wars of Reconstruction*, 29S9 [299?].

Hill's relationship with Grant had cooled somewhat, he still admired the president and generally supported Republican economic policy. As the election neared, Senator Hill had to make his final choice. No doubt he agonized, and no doubt much of his sympathy lay with the Liberal Republicans and the more moderate Democrats, so it is not surprising that he wavered so long. Greeley pronouncements on race relations sounded close to Hill's when the New Yorker professed that full political equality would have to wait for many years and that "social equality will remain forever out of reach." Greeley told Black voters that their "best friends" were "sound, conservative, knowing white Southerners." Despite his affinity with Greeley's views and his disappointments from the administration, Senator Hill finally cast his lot with President Grant about seven weeks before the election. In the cautiously framed words of a widely circulated public letter, Hill explained his decision:

> I have seen too much of mankind to consent to become the zealous partisan of anyone. I shall not despair of the Republic, let who ever may be elected President. Personally it will likely be of small consequence to me who shall prove the successful candidate. And yet, I sincerely declare that unfettered by obligations in the past and without expectation of any personal advantage from the result, from all I know of the respective candidates and the condition of our public affairs, that duty to my country, and the best interests of my family impel me to the support of General Grant.

Many observers in Georgia and around the country were surprised. Even though the senator's statement had disavowed "expectation of any personal advantage," he had also referred to "the best interests of his family." Critics called attention to the fact that Hill's son and son-in-law held patronage positions, and one wrote snidely, "General Grant will prove a most ungrateful fellow if he fails to support Mr. Hill's family."[44]

Hill's endorsement of Grant did little to help the president's prospects in Georgia. Convinced that the incumbent had no chance to carry the state, the national Republican Party apparatus provided little financial or

[44] Kendi, *Stamped from the Beginning*, 251–52 (social equality, Greeley); *New York Times*, September 16, 1872 (I have seen); see *Buffalo (NY) Evening Post*, September 18, 1872; *Macon Telegraph*, September 12, 17, October 22 (Gen.), 29, 1872.

organizational assistance to their Georgia partisans despite earnest pleas. In several former Confederate states, the Black vote remained strong enough to carry their states for Grant—but not in Georgia where Greeley's fusion ticket handily bested the incumbent as Horatio Seymour had done four years before. Grant also lost in Texas and Tennessee, plus in the border states of Missouri, Kentucky, and Maryland. By endorsing President Grant when many other conservative Republicans did not, Hill found himself in company with the state's Black Republicans and moderate White Republicans such as John Bryant. As in 1868, Grant carried most of Georgia's heavily Black counties along the coast, in the cotton regions of the southwest, and in the lower Piedmont Black Belt, including Joshua Hill's home county. A few pockets of Republican support also remained in the Blue Ridge. Republicans won three Georgia seats in Congress, but the statewide vote went overwhelming for Greeley and the Liberal Republican/Democratic coalition. Compared to the state balloting in October, Black turnout increased in November when their champion Grant headed the ballot. Intimidation of Black voters persisted, but thanks to a combination of the reduction of Klan activity due to the Enforcement Act, the rise of Black protective organizations, and other factors, historians have concluded that the 1872 election in the South was somewhat less plagued by violence and fraud than the previous presidential contest had been. Therefore, the Democratic margin, though still substantial, was slightly lower than it had been in 1868.[45]

Georgia Republicans licked their local wounds but found some bright spots and cheered the national victory. Henry Turner claimed overly optimistically that Grant's victory meant that voters endorsed Sumner's civil rights legislation. John Bryant declared with more enthusiasm than truthfulness, "I rejoice that Republicans no longer fight each other." The Augustan pointed with pride to the three Republican congressional victories in Georgia. He could not, of course, have known then that those three men

[45] Abbott, *Republican Party and the South*, 218–22; J. M. Matthews, "Negro Republicans," 158–59; *Atlanta Constitution*, November 5, 1872; *Augusta Chronicle*, November 12, 1872. Grant carried Morgan County 742 to 541 (*Atlanta Sun*, December 4, 1872).

who prevailed in 1872 would be the last Republican congressmen elected from Georgia until the latter half of the twentieth century.[46]

As he had done four years before, Joshua Hill bet on the right horse in the national race but the wrong one in his state. Even though he had come around to back the president in the end, his flirtation with the Liberal Republicans had certainly done him no good with Grant.

General Gordon Becomes Senator Gordon

In mid-October 1872, after Democrats swept the state races, the *Augusta Chronicle* crowed, "We have, by an overwhelming majority, secured an able, patriotic Governor [James M. Smith], and an honest, intelligent Legislature. The election of a Democratic Senator in place of Hon. Joshua Hill is thus made certain." At first, incumbent Hill indicated that he would accept the Republican nomination despite the futility of the undertaking. Ultimately, however, he decided to stand aside and not seek reelection. With Hill out of the way, Amos Akerman earned the dubious honor of being the sacrificial Republican nominee. In response to a letter writer who urged the General Assembly to keep Hill in place, an Athens editor epitomized the widespread Democratic opinion of the incumbent: "We know Senator Hill well, and as a gentleman esteem him highly—believing him to be a man of rare ability and sterling integrity—but his sentiments are not in accord with those of a majority of the people of Georgia."[47]

Among the names advanced in various Democratic circles as possible replacements for Senator Hill were the ever-present Herschel V. Johnson, Alexander H. Stephens, and Benjamin Hill. Ex-senator H. V. M. Miller and former representative Thomas Hardeman were also mentioned. A whole raft of high-ranking Confederate officers, including Alfred H. Colquitt, Henry L. Benning, Lucious J. Gartrell, and George N. Lester,

[46] Angell, *Bishop Henry McNeal Turner*, 118; *Savannah Journal*, November 14, 1872. The *Journal* was a short-lived revival of Bryant's *Georgia Republican* (Currie-McDaniel, *Carpetbagger of Conscience*, 127–28; Nathans, *Losing the Peace*, 223).

[47] *Augusta Chronicle*, October 15 (We have), December 8, 1872; *(Athens) Southern Watchman*, December 18, 1872.

earned mention as well. Present on almost every list and leading on most was Confederate Major General John B. Gordon.[48]

Noting the long lists of potential senatorial aspirants and expecting even more, Hill sought "a special favor" from the Senate. With some sarcasm and a bit of grandstanding, he asked his colleagues if they would consider removing the political disabilities still attached to the potential Democratic contenders who were still disfranchised: "I think it rather graceful on my part to insist that the field should be wide open for as many contestants as choose to enter.... After the 'slaughter of innocents' that will take place on that occasion, I desire than none of them, or their apparitions, shall rise in the future, to rebuke me." Senator George F. Edmunds (R-VT) objected, so the bill was never officially considered. (Having sworn no prewar oath to the US Constitution, Gordon did not carry disability.)[49]

By the time that the legislature was ready to act on January 21, 1872, several contenders had withdrawn their names or been reduced to irrelevancy. A week before the vote, the *Augusta Chronicle* reported that it was clear that the real race to replace Joshua Hill, "that very excellent gentleman of bad political faith," had narrowed down to Gordon and Stephens with some residual support for Ben Hill, whom a Tennessee paper called Georgia's "most wordy and chameleonized politician." Gordon became the frontrunner by building a strong organization and by personally seeking support from many prominent White Georgians and new legislators, and his reputed Ku Klux Klan leadership was no handicap in Democratic circles. Even Josh Hill's hometown newspaper endorsed Gordon. Stephens remained popular with White voters, and he used his own newspaper, the *Atlanta Sun*, to promote his senatorial candidacy. The fact that the former vice president of the Confederacy had refused to endorse the Democratic

[48] *Atlanta Constitution*, December 24, 1872; *Cincinnati Commercial Tribune*, November 23, 1872; *San Francisco Bulletin*, October 4, 1872; *Savannah Morning News*, October 21, 1872; *Albany News*, October 25, 1872; *North Georgia Citizen*, March 7, 1872; *(Athens) Southern Watchman*, November 20, 1872; *Atlanta Sun*, December 4, 1872, January 9, 1873; *(DC) Evening Star*, December 7, 1872; *Pomeroy's Democrat* (New York), December 28, 1872; Shadgett, *Republican Party in Georgia*, 48.

[49] *Atlanta Constitution*, January 1 (I think), 7, 18, 1873; *Albany News*, January 3, 1873; *Macon Telegraph & Messenger*, January 15, 1873; *Baltimore Sun*, January 7, 1873 (It is); *Columbus Sun*, January 10, 1873; *New York World*, January 16, 1873.

fusion ticket with Horace Greeley was the principal impediment to his senatorial aspirations. In contrast, Gordon had worked hard to carry Georgia for the Greeley ticket and had won many friends by doing so. On the first ballot, Gordon led with 93 votes versus 104 for his combined Democratic opposition. Republican Akerman managed only 12 votes, and it is doubtful that Joshua Hill would have done much better. There were no longer enough Republican legislators, Black or White, to make a meaningful impact. On following ballots the gallery was packed, and the deal making became intense. In the final count, General Gordon carried the day 112 to 86 over Stephens. Georgia had a new senator-elect. In consolation, the Democratic establishment assured the former vice president of the Confederacy that they would arrange for him to get his old seat back in the US House of Representatives. Joshua Hill had been a de facto lame duck from the day that he was seated; now his status was official.[50]

During the Civil War, John B. Gordon had quickly risen from volunteer captain to major general becoming one of the best known and most popular Confederate war leaders. After the war, he parlayed his hero status, his opposition to Radical Republican policies, and his bellicose defense of White supremacy into political prominence. Despite the general's "masterfully vague responses" to congressional investigators, Gordon's scholarly biographer concluded "with reasonable certainty that he was at least titular head of the Georgia Ku Klux Klan." Gordon narrowly lost his race for the governorship to Radical Republican Rufus B. Bullock in 1868, but a bright political future lay ahead. Twenty years younger than Joshua Hill and also junior to most other contenders, Gordon represented a new generation of Georgia Democrats. In addition to becoming a United States senator in 1873, he served a term as governor, and then returned to the Senate. He stood with Joseph E. Brown and Alfred Colquitt as part of the so-called

[50] *Atlanta Sun*, January 9, 21, 1873; *Augusta Chronicle & Sentinel*, January 14, 1873 (that very); *Knoxville Chronicle*, January 21, 1873 (most wordy); *(Athens) Southern Watchman*, January 29, 1873; Knight, *Standard History of Georgia and Georgians*, 2:871 (quoting I. W. Avery). The first ballot totals come from Eckert, *John Brown Gordon*, 156. See also Tankersly, *John B. Gordon*, 265–66; W. C. Davis, *The Union*, 246; *Macon Telegraph & Messenger*, October 30, 1872 (*Madison Appeal*).

Bourbon Triumvirate of Democratic Party leaders who dominated Georgia's post-Reconstruction years.[51]

Meanwhile, in Congress

During Hill's time in the Senate, he served on three committees: Privileges and Elections, Claims, and Pensions. His experience as a Southern Unionist lawyer who had lost property in the war and who had to fight to claim his own seat was just right for these assignments, which, for the most part, dealt with cases regarding specific individuals rather than general policy. One highly publicized case involved the status of Senator S. C. Pomeroy of Kansas. The Republican faced serious allegations that his election had been accomplished by bribery of state legislators. Hill agreed with the committee's finding that cleared Pomeroy. Early in 1873, another Kansas bribery case, this time regarding Republican senator Alexander Caldwell, reached the Committee on Privileges and Elections. Hill urged immediate action, but resolution of the case was delayed until after his retirement.[52]

The most controversial and significant case that Hill faced in committee concerned the disputed Louisiana election of 1872. Both the Republican and the Democratic factions claimed victory in an election marred by violence, intimidation, and fraud on both sides, but most blatantly by Democrats. The two parties installed rival governors and formed competing state legislatures, each of which claimed the right to choose United States senators for the Bayou State. Early in the Louisiana controversy, Hill opposed the Grant administration's quick recognition of the Republican government and offered to act as a mediator. Hill explained to Senator Roscoe Conkling that his offer was "an invitation to the respective Legislatures and the people of Louisiana to come together like sensible men and see if they cannot bring order of the chaos that reigns there." Demonstrating once again that on Reconstruction-related issues Hill would buck his party, his compromise proposal received support only from Democrats and from Hill's Liberal Republican friend Lyman Trumbull. The issue lingered after Hill's Senate term expired early in March 1873.

---

[51] Eckert, *John Brown Gordon*, 143–57, 147 (masterfully), 149 (with). See also Tankersley, *John B. Gordon*, 263–67.

[52] *New York Times*, June 7, 1872 (to impugn); *(DC) National Republican*, February 25, 1873; *New Orleans Times-Picayune*, January 18, 1873.

Just over a month later, tension in Louisiana culminated in the infamous Colfax massacre in which a Klan-like band of White men, many of them former Confederate soldiers, killed at least 60 and as many as 150 Black Republicans who had gathered to defend the courthouse.[53]

In the first two months of 1873, lame-duck Senator Hill attracted attention for being involved in what some commentators, especially the Democratic press, called a "salary grab" or "salary steal." The *New York Tribune* singled out the Georgian, saying, "Senator Hill has a mania for increasing salaries." Indeed, Hill, had advanced unsuccessful appropriation amendments that would have increased the salaries of federal bureaucrats, district judges, members of Congress, and the president and vice president. The Committee on Privileges and Elections as a whole endorsed the congressional increase, so it was not just Hill's doing. Advocating for competitive federal salaries was, however, nothing new for Joshua Hill. Almost a year earlier, he had also proposed raises because he wanted to attract to federal office competent men rather than job-seeking hacks. Hill, a prosperous lawyer himself, told the Senate that "no man is fit to be chosen a district judge of the United States unless he has capacity and character enough to earn by his profession as much as $5,000 a year. I cannot think that the allowance is extravagant." In a move that calls to mind the assault on the capitol on January 6, 2021, Senator Hill urged the Senate not to delete from the House appropriations bill a raise in salary for the Capitol police force. The Senate, he said, "can very well afford not to be outdone in liberality toward a service which is so essential to the Capitol." He praised the officers' dedicated service and explained that one of their duties was showing "politeness to strangers" who were visiting the capitol and directing them to points of interest.[54]

---

[53] *Bangor Daily Whig*, February 25, 1873; *Savannah Morning News*, March 6, 1873; *New York Times*, February 21, 1873 (only such); *Globe*, 42-3, pt. 3, February 25, 1873, 1749–750 (mediator); February 27, 1867 (Sir), 1876, 1879, 1887–889; *Chicago Tribune*, April 17, 1873. Hill's full statement to the committee is in Senate Report 457; Serial Set vol. 1549, February 20, 1873; Foner, *Reconstruction*, 177–78; Summers, *Ordeal of the Reunion*, 293, 330–32.

[54] *New York Tribune*, February 5, 1873 (mania); *Cincinnati Enquirer*, September 27, 1873; *Pomeroy's Democrat* (New York), April 5, 1873 (salary steal); *Globe*, 42-3, pt. 2, 908, January 28, 1873, 1062, February 4, 1873; 42-2, pt. 2, March 14,

Hill's generosity in the expenditure of funds, raised, of course, by the tariffs he supported, was not limited to salaries. He joined with former vice president Hannibal Hamlin to advocate increased appropriations to beautify the capital city. When he was a representative, Hill had pressed for prewar measures to improve the Capitol, and now he continued in with a patriotic appeal:

> I have always thought it the duty of the national Legislature to provide a city that should be worthy of the national capital, and that should be the admiration of the citizen who should happened to come to it.... The Government is able and ought to be willing to make liberal appropriations for the ornamentation of these avenues. They ought to compare favorably with those of the most favored cities of Europe, to rival in beauty even those of Paris itself.[55]

Matters of pork and patronage concerned Hill all the way up to his final days in the Senate. He worked with his Democratic colleague T. P. Norwood to support funding for a "great inland canal" from New Orleans to St. Marys, Georgia. He met with General Sherman to discuss the matter from the military perspective, but like the earlier North Georgia canal idea, this far-fetched project never came to pass. In January the soon-to-retire senator obtained an audience with President Grant to advocate the removal of political disabilities remaining for some Georgians and possibly to discuss his own future. Hill even wrote a letter to the president on behalf of an "old and esteemed friend" who was "a lifelong democrat, but was independent enough and sensible enough to vote for you." Later in a "lively fight" over the Savannah post office, Hill backed the moderate Republican incumbent postmaster against an office-seeker whom the *Atlanta Constitution* called a "scalawag.... backed by the entire crowd of Radical representatives."[56]

1872, 1322–323, 1597–598 (can very well), 1643–645, 1670 (no man, have [*sic*]), 1672–675; *Atlanta Sun*, April 15, 1873.

[55] *Globe*, 42-3, pt. 3, 1975, February 28, 1873.

[56] *Savannah Morning News*, February 16, March 22, 1872; *Columbus Enquirer*, December 24, 1872; *Atlanta Constitution*, January 7, February 28 (scalawag),1873; *Atlanta Sun*, March 18, 1873; *Knoxville Chronicle*, January 25, 1873; Hill to Grant, January 22, 1873, in Grant, *Papers of Ulysses S. Grant*, 24:367.

Georgia's First Republican Senator Heads Home

Even as Joshua Hill was leaving the Senate, some people still wondered if he was really a Democrat at heart. A Republican-leaning paper from the Midwest offered the short answer: "Senator Hill of Georgia, naturally objects to being classed as a democrat, as he says he was a whig till he became a republican, was for the Union all through the war, and voted for Grant both times. That record settles the question, and if he is occasionally a little more independent than some other party men, he may be none the worse for that."[57]

An editorial in the *Atlanta Herald*, then managed and partly owned by the rising journalistic star Henry W. Grady, best expressed the Democratic establishment's evaluation of Hill's senatorial career. Grady's paper acknowledged its "irreconcilable differences of political opinion" with the Madisonian but still found his service "an agreeable surprise." It was pleased that Hill "has spoken and voted against the Radical oligarchy," specifically citing his blocking of Foster Blodgett and trying to mediate the ongoing Louisiana election controversy. Although it used the term "Radicals" to apply to all Republicans, the editorial made a point of exempting Joshua Hill from the sobriquets that Georgia Democrats so often applied to their other White Republican opponents.

> Of all the Southern men who joined the Radicals after the war, he is, perhaps, *the only one who has never sank to the level of the carpet-bagger and scalawag*. Placed in opposition to the great majority of his race, he has borne with dignity and silence much unfavorable criticism, and has never permitted anger to get the best of his judgement.... Of course, it is not likely that he will every again obtain high office from the people of Georgia, but it must be a matter of pride and satisfaction for him to know that he retires from public life with far more public esteem than he possessed when elected a Senator.

Several Georgia papers, including even Alexander Stephens's own *Atlanta Sun*, approvingly reprinted the *Herald*'s sentiments in whole or part.[58]

---

[57] *Cincinnati Times*, February 22, 1873; *Bangor Whig*, February 20, 1873.

[58] *Savannah Morning News*, March 3, 1873 (*Atlanta Herald*), emphasis added; *Atlanta Sun*, March 5, 1873.

On March 3, when the entire Senate knew that he would be gone the next day, Hill rose to speak once again on the salary issue and wistfully mused, "Perhaps it is the last word I shall ever say in the Senate." Then with tongue in cheek, he referred to his reputation as a big spender:

> For my own part I gave notice at the time I introduced a bill to raise these salaries, more than a year ago, that I knew that I did it at the hazard of all my prospects, whatever they might be, for the Presidency in the future; for I expected that if I ever attempted to reach that high position this would be brought up in the judgment against me, and yet utterly regardless of the danger I venture to encounter it.

The record shows that laughter ensued. Thus, Joshua Hill left the Senate not with a flurry of legislation or with a long and eloquent speech—he departed with a self-deprecating chuckle and the respect of his colleagues.[59]

[59] *Globe*, 42-3, pt. 3, March 3, 1873, 2183–184.

Chapter 13

Republican Senior Statesman in Democratic Georgia, 1873–1888

During his post-senatorial years, Joshua Hill could best be characterized as always prominent, often influential, but seldom powerful. A vigorous and active man of sixty-one years when he left the United States Senate in March 1873, the Madisonian concentrated most of his time on his land holdings, law practice, and family. Soon after Gordon entered the senate, Hill professed to have little interest in politics. He told T. P. Saffold that he had become "an indifferent observer—and have little to say for or against any man or party." Yet in the same letter, he commented on recent speeches by Gordon and Ben Hill, so it is clear that he never really lost his interest in politics. Hill's status as a Deep South White Republican with some degree of national renown kept his name in the political mix for high appointments in Republican administrations, but the call never came. Redeemer Democrats held a tight grip on Georgia politics, so there was not much that Joshua Hill could bring to the table to help his party other than his reputation. Closer to home, the conservative former senator tried to stand aloof from the racial tensions and petty personal infighting that characterized Georgia's small and fractionalized Republican organization in the 1870s and 1880s. He remained friendly with and often supportive of many Democrats. Even John B. Gordon praised his predecessor's "unblemished" character.[1]

Hill refused to join the dominant party and refused Congressional nominations from his own. He flirted with, but never embraced, the

[1] Hill to Saffold, undated partial letter (March or later 1873), Saffold Family Papers, MCA; *Congressional Record*, January 8, 1875, 341 (Gordon). The *Congressional Record* replaced the *Globe* in 1873.

Independent movement that sought to realign the state's politics. As he had for so long, Joshua Hill continued to steer a course down the middle as a moderate to conservative Republican. The only official political position that the Madisonian held after he left the US Senate in March 1873 was nonpartisan delegate to Georgia's constitutional convention in summer 1877. He was among the most prominent delegates, but his stance outside the state's political mainstream meant that he tended to exercise his influence mostly in a careful and lawyerly manner.

Declining Congressional Candidacy

Georgia Republicans hoped that they could take advantage of Hill's reputation, so in 1874 and again in 1876, they tried to convince the former senator to accept the party's nomination for Congress in the Ninth Congressional District, which stretched from the lower Piedmont around Morgan County northward toward the Blue Ridge, including the large towns of Athens and Gainesville. The district subsumed much of Hill's prewar congressional territory along with some counties where he had done well in the 1863 gubernatorial contest. Thus, it seemed to many Republicans that the former senator would present their best chance for a good showing in their uphill struggle. In May 1874, word on the street was that Hill would be the Republican candidate in the Ninth, but he declined to run. A few weeks later, the former senator was in Washington, where he met with President Grant. It is probable, but not known for sure, that the two men discussed the congressional seat and Hill's decision to eschew a hopeless campaign.[2]

As the election neared in September 1874, Hill's name returned to speculation for the Ninth District congressional seat. This time, however, rumors were that he would run as an Independent rather than as a Republican. The Independent movement began in the Seventh District around Rome and spread east. Neither district had a majority African American population although the southern part of the Ninth around Madison was heavily Black. The issue that motivated Independents in Georgia, and in similar movements in other Southern states, was resentment against

[2] *Macon Telegraph & Messenger*, May 12, 1874; *(Athens) Southern Watchman*, May 13, September 30, 1874; *Dawson Journal*, September 24, 1874; *(DC) Daily National Republican*, June 19, 1874; *Indianapolis News*, July 29, 1874.

domination by the Bourbon power structure, which ignored the interests of small farmers like those in the Georgia mountains. Democrats expressed concern that Hill might constitute a threat running as an Independent rather than as a Republican, but he ultimately declined to be a candidate—Republican or Independent.[3]

Anticipating a Democratic sweep and sensing that the Northern wing of the Republican Party neither respected nor understood their region, a group of Southern White Republicans called a convention to meet in Chattanooga in October 1874. Henry Farrow, who in 1870–1871 had challenged Hill for his Senate seat, was the meeting's leading Georgia organizer. Farrow listed the Madisonian on his slate of delegates along with former governor Benjamin Conley and former US attorney general Amos T. Akerman. It is not clear, however, if Hill actually attended. Blacks appointed as delegates included former congressmen Jefferson Long, H. M. Turner, and at least three others. Not much came of the meeting other than public statements of concern, but Joshua Hill's tangential involvement in the effort indicated that he was not yet entirely willing to leave politics alone.[4]

In determining not to seek a congressional seat in 1874 as either a straight-up Republican or as an Independent, Hill read the situation accurately. The nonpresidential election year proved to be a complete disaster for the Republican Party. Even if he had decided to run as an Independent, it would have been difficult for the former representative and senator to escape his Unionist and Republican past. Democrats won a nearly clean sweep. Even Hill's home county, which had voted Republican in 1868, 1870, and 1872, fell to the Democratic Party despite the fact that eligible Black voters outnumbered eligible Whites by about two to one; no longer was Morgan County that much different. Going into the 1874 elections, Georgia Republicans held three of the state's nine congressional seats; they emerged from the thorough whipping with none. Democrats even

---

[3] *Covington Georgia Enterprise*, September 25, 1874; *Rome Courier*, September 22, 1874 (*Athens Southern Watchman*); *Columbus Inquirer*, September 20, 1874; *Savannah Morning News*, September 23, 1874; Wynne, *Continuity of Cotton*, 120; Parks, *Joseph E. Brown*, 537; Currie-McDaniel, *Carpetbagger of Conscience*, 133–34; Shadgett, *Republican Party in Georgia*, 61–63.

[4] *New York Times*, October 13, 1874; *Macon Telegraph*, October 13, 1874; *New York Herald*, October 13, 1874.

defeated three-time incumbent Richard H. Whiteley, the White Republican who represented a majority Black district in the southwest part of the state. Representative Whiteley suffered vicious criticism for having voted in favor of Sumner's civil rights bill. It was the same sort of vitriol that had caused Representative Thomas J. Speer from the district just to the north to fear for his life if he had supported the legislation. Whiteley's opponents portrayed him as a particularly extreme Radical by contrasting the incumbent's favorable vote with the stance of conservative Hill, who had opposed the bill and stood up to Sumner. Meanwhile, Hill's ally John E. Bryant, who ran on a pro-Black platform in his Augusta-based district, went down to defeat once more. The congressional rout was so thorough and long-lasting that no Republican congressman would represent Georgia again until 1964, when Howard H. "Bo" Callaway turned the party tables on the race issue by railing against Lyndon Johnson, Democrats, and the Civil Rights Act of 1964.[5]

The 1874 Republican disaster was not unique to Georgia. In Alabama and all across the South, intimidation suppressed the Black vote. As a consequence, Democrats won thirty-seven of the region's fifty-four congressional seats at stake. Nationally, the civil rights issue combined with worries about the economic repercussions of the Panic of 1873 and growing dissatisfaction with the Grant administration to lead to widespread defeat for Republicans, who lost eighty-nine seats. Democrats won a majority in the US House of Representatives for the first time since secession.[6]

Soon after the 1874 Republican debacle, talk arose once again that Joshua Hill would abandon the Republican Party. The ex-senator's flirtation with the Independent movement gave credibility to the speculation, and John B. Gordon added further credence to the rumors by remarks he made on the floor of the Senate in January 1875 during debate over the Louisiana election controversy. Referring to Hill, who had previously

---

[5] Shadgett, *Republican Party in Georgia*, 52 (Morgan Co.); *Augusta Chronicle*, June 21, 1874 (will obtain); *Atlanta Constitution*, March 10, May 10, September 18 (*Athens Watchman*), 1874; *Macon Telegraph*, May 19, September 22 (*Athens Watchman*), 1874; Rogers, *Scalawag in Georgia*, 133–50; *Bainbridge Weekly*, October 29, 1874; Currie-McDaniel, *Carpetbagger of Conscience*, 128–34; Coleman, *History of Georgia*, 399.

[6] Abbott, *Republican Party and the South*, 229–32; M. Storey, *Loyalty and Loss*, 230–31.

advocated for compromise in the Pelican State, Senator Gordon declared, "For causes satisfactory to himself, he refuses to vote the republican ticket in Georgia. That is one change, and a quite prominent one, and the same reasons, whatever they were, which influenced him to abandon an organization, the record of whose acts in Georgia is enough to blacken the reputation of any citizen who sustains it, carried doubtless many of his followers with him." To be sure, Hill had often been critical of his fellow Republicans, and it is not unlikely that he voted for some Democrats in the October 1874 state elections. However, Gordon, as other commentators before him, was wrong to claim that Hill had abandoned his Republican affiliation.[7]

Ex-senator Hill continued his association with high-placed Republicans. In 1875, he penned the favorable and controversial letter about General William T. Sherman that is examined in chapter 5. In February 1876, he visited the Senate chamber and was "very cordially received by his former colleagues." Around the same time, a group of Republican senators, including John Sherman (R-OH) and Henry Dawes (R-MA), suggested to President Grant that he consider Hill for the office of collector of customs for Savannah, declaring that the Georgian "would reflect honorably upon your administration." This gesture may have been mainly honorific since it is doubtful that Hill was seriously interested in the position he had previously declined. In April 1876, Hill's name appeared in the press along with Ben Conley, James Johnson, and others as possible Republican candidates for governor. There is no indication, however, that he pursued this option.[8]

Anticipating higher African American voter turnout in the 1876 presidential election, Southern Republicans sensed a glimmer of opportunity. Unabashed Republican Richard Whiteley, who lost narrowly in 1874, ran again for his Southwest Georgia seat in the House. John E.

---

[7] *Congressional Record*, January 6, 275, January 8, 341 (Gordon), 1875; *Augusta Chronicle*, January 9, 1875; *New York Times*, January 9, 1875; *New York World*, January 9, 1875; *New Orleans Republican*, January 10, 1875.

[8] *New York Times*, March 7, 1875 (Hill letter about Sherman in the *Atlanta Herald*; see chapter 5 for details); *(Washington, DC) Evening Star*, February 23, 1876. Thomas J. Robertson (R-SC), Oliver Morton (R-IN), and John Logan (R-IL) were the other senators (Grant, *Papers of Ulysses S. Grant*, 27:383–84; *Savannah Morning News*, April 4, 1874).

Bryant also tried again in East Georgia. Bryant's biographer observed that the 1876 election "was the last one of the century in which Georgia Republicans had any chance for success." And a very slim chance it turned out to be.[9]

The only non-Democrat to win a Georgia congressional seat in 1876 was Dr. William H. Felton, who won reelection in the Seventh District by continuing to attract Republicans and disaffected Democrats to his Independent candidacy. Felton's racial views tracked more closely Democratic than Republican, but some Blacks, including ex-congressman Jefferson Long, nevertheless supported him as the lesser evil. Dr. Felton met his wife, Rebecca Latimer, in 1852 when he was the speaker at the ceremonies for her graduation from Madison Female College, so it is possible that Hill and Felton met on that occasion. In any case, there is no doubt that Hill had followed Felton's long career and that he understood the implications of the doctor's Independent victories.[10]

Republicans in the Ninth knew that that an openly Radical candidate, Black or White, would have no chance whatsoever, so in 1876 as they had two years previously, the party sought to draft conservative Joshua Hill. This time the Democratic incumbent in the Ninth District was the colorful and mercurial Benjamin H. Hill. A Hill vs. Hill contest would have pitted two old Whig allies who had split over secession, united again against Governor Joe Brown, and then split again over Reconstruction. Realizing that his prospects for victory were even worse than they would have been in 1874, Josh Hill again declined the nomination. The *Augusta Chronicle & Sentinel*, long opposed to but friendly with Joshua Hill, wrote, "We should dislike to see a clever man so badly beaten as the Republican candidate in the Ninth is bound to be." From a national perspective, a New York paper printed a succinct and accurate statement: "He is the ablest republican in Georgia and will poll the full party vote without any chance of defeating Ben Hill." As expected, the always ambitious Ben Hill cruised to reelection even as it was widely known that he was simultaneously lobbying

---

[9] Rogers, *Scalawag in Georgia*, 160–71; Currie-McDaniel, *Carpetbagger of Conscience*, 139.

[10] Currie-McDaniel, *Carpetbagger of Conscience*, 134–40; Shadgett, *Republican Party in Georgia*, 61–75; Ward, "Republican Party," 197–98.

legislators to choose him to replace Senator Norwood when they convened in January.[11]

Long before 1876, Joshua Hill had concluded that the goal of establishing and sustaining a viable long-term Southern Republican Party based on the leadership of old Whigs and sustained by the votes of compliant freedmen had been in vain. Sadly, he understood from his own experience and observations that no man could succeed in Southern politics unless he were willing to give lip service to the glory and rectitude of the Lost Cause of the old Confederacy. That was something that Joshua Hill was resolutely unwilling to do. The occasion of declining the 1876 congressional nomination gave the Madisonian an opportunity to make it firmly and publicly clear that would never disavow his Unionism. He sent a very public, very frank, and very melancholy letter to Henry Farrow and other Republican committee leaders. "However well meant," Hill began, "this appeal to an old man's vanity is a questionable kindness." He conceded some temptation to yield to "the latent desire for popular applause," but he firmly declined. With men such as Ben Hill and Alexander Stephens as his rhetorical targets, Hill expressed bitter wonderment that followers of the great Kentuckian Henry Clay had become "the advocates or apologists of the most stupendous folly since the revolt in Paradise." He poured his heart out when he wrote plaintively, "*The sin of secession took away half the joys of existence.*" The heartfelt missive ended with an appeal to bipartisanship: "It would be deplorable indeed if all the virtue belonged to onc party and all the vice to the other." The widely reprinted letter signaled clearly that no matter how much he might cozy up to individual Democrats and regardless of how much he might shy away from the more radical stances of his own party, Josh Hill was never going to embrace either the Democratic Party or the Lost Cause.[12]

---

[11] *Savannah Morning News*, April 4, 1874; *Marietta Journal*, September 9, 1876; *Atlanta Constitution*, September 22, 1876; B. Hill, *Senator Benjamin H. Hill of Georgia*, 67–68; *Augusta Constitutionalist*, June 28, 1874; *Augusta Chronicle*, October 4, 1876; *New York Herald*, September 23, 1876; *Monroe Advertiser* (Forsyth), October 10, 1876 (He is). Ben Hill obtained his congressional seat due to the untimely death of the original Democratic nominee.

[12] *Augusta Chronicle*, October 25, 1876 (emphasis added); *Madison Home Journal*, November 3, 1876; *New York Times*, October 20, 1876.

Reaction to Hill's public letter showed once again that he was Democratic Georgia's favorite Republican. The *Augusta Chronicle & Sentinel* reminded its readers that it did "not agree with Mr. Hill in politics" but stressed that he was "an honorable and distinguished citizen of Georgia." The paper reiterated its praise of Hill for his persistent opposition to Rufus Bullock and Foster Blodgett and commended him for his opposition to the civil rights bill of the "fanatical Sumner." The editorial concluded, "In shaping his course as he did, we think—his best friends think—Mr. Hill made a great mistake. But it was nothing more than a mistake. It was an error of judgment, not an error of the heart."[13] Joshua Hill himself would have agreed that his resolute stance was "of the heart," but he would not have regarded it as an error.

The results of the 1876 election extinguished any remaining glimmer of optimism that Georgia Republicans might have seen. Democrats carried every important office in Georgia, and, as expected, the newly elected General Assembly sent Benjamin Hill to the US Senate to join John B. Gordon. Georgia gave Democrat Samuel J. Tilden the highest percentage of official popular vote of any state—North or South. The popular vote for Rutherford B. Hayes in Georgia and across the South unquestionably would have been significantly higher had Black Republicans been allowed fair and unfettered access to the polls, but it is highly unlikely that a Republican presidential candidate could have carried Georgia even in such a hypothetical scenario of fairness. The well-known dispute over Electoral College results gave Georgia Democrats hope that Tilden might yet capture the White House, but Hayes eventually prevailed. The set of Republican and Democratic concessions necessary to avoid dragging out the controversy beyond the designated inauguration day are still often referred to as "the Compromise of 1877" although most professional historians now eschew that overly simplistic term. In any case, the peaceful settlement of the presidential election of 1876 remains the convenient mark of the coup de grace of the Reconstruction period. For all practical purposes, however, Reconstruction in Georgia had been over long before 1877. Senator Hill had already recognized that fact when he determined that it would have

[13] *Augusta Chronicle*, October 25, 1876; Mellichamp, *Senators from Georgia*, 185–89.

been a waste of his time to seek reelection to the Senate. The elections of 1874 and 1876 further confirmed the accuracy of his foresight.[14]

Considered for Cabinet and Court

After 1876, it was clear that neither Joshua Hill nor any other Georgia Republican would for the foreseeable future return to Washington as a senator or representative. However, throughout the later 1870s and even into the early 1880s, Hill's name continually appeared on lists of potential Deep South appointees in Republican administrations. With the exception of former attorney general Akerman, Hill remained the best-known Georgia Republican on the national scene. The wealthy and prosperous Madison lawyer was not personally interested in any run-of-the-mill in-state patronage offerings, but the possibility of a significant position in the Hayes administration thrust him back into the news—though not into office. Some advisers urged the president-elect to give cabinet positions to one or two ex-Whig Unionists who had never served the Confederacy as a gesture toward building a viable Southern Republican party bereft of carpetbaggers. Hill fit that bill precisely, and his name appeared in the press on many such lists, including postmaster general. The suggestion that the former senator might sit in a Republican cabinet was palatable to Georgia Democrats. The *Columbus Times* wrote, "We would regard the appointment of Mr. Hill as a very good and significant one for a Republican President to make, for Joshua Hill was never accused of a base or malignant act."[15]

As it turned out, the old vision of building Southern Republicanism on Unionist ex-Whigs was not nearly as determinative for Rutherford B. Hayes as was his own political hide. As part of the flurry of behind-the-

---

[14] *Columbus Times*, November 24, 1876; *Macon Telegraph & Messenger*, November 23, 1876. Norwood later served in the US House of Representatives (*Columbus Enquirer*, December 29, 1874). On the 1876 election, see Summers, *Ordeal of the Reunion*, 372–86; Trefousse, *Rutherford B. Hayes*, 65–83; Hoogenboom, *Rutherford B. Hayes*, 256–94; Abbott, *Republican Party and the South*, 205–44.

[15] *(DC) National Republican*, March 4, 7, 16, 1877; *Columbus Times*, March 2, 1877; *Atlanta Constitution*, February 27, March 6, 1877; *Macon Telegraph*, March 6, 1877; *Memphis Appeal*, February 24, 1877; *New Orleans Times-Picayune*, February 28, 1877; *Augusta Chronicle*, March 7, 1877 (ref. *Louisville Courier-Journal*); *New York Herald*, March 3, 1877; *Boston Journal*, March 3, 1877; Hoogenboom, *Rutherford B. Hayes*, 289–96; Shadgett, *Republican Party in Georgia*, 139–40.

scenes negotiations to remove congressional obstacles to his inauguration, Hayes calculated that bringing moderate Southern Democrats and border-state Republicans into his cabinet would do more for his presidency than granting appointments to men, no matter how loyal they had been, from states that held no prospects for his party. Accordingly, the president-elect passed over Hill and other aspirants from the Deep South for the cabinet or other top spots in his administration.[16]

The president's filling of a vacancy on the US Supreme Court presented a similar pattern of widespread rumor. Just a few days after Hayes took office, a widely published wire release reported, "The most influential recommendations from the South" for the high court were "about equally divided between Herschel V. Johnson and ex-Senator Joshua Hill of Ga." Some sources claimed that Hill had the inside track. The vacancy occurred when Associate Justice David Davis, who had been on the commission deciding the 1876 electoral vote controversy, resigned in January 1877 to become the US senator from Illinois.[17]

In late May 1877, an ostensibly private letter written by Joshua Hill found its way into wide public distribution in newspapers in New York, Philadelphia, and across the country. In it the ex-senator effusively praised Hayes and wrote that the new president's policy regarding the South met with his "hearty approval." Press accounts declared that Hill had written the letter to a "friend." In fact, the friend to whom Hill had written was John Bowles, then still in good stead as Hill's son-in-law. The letter, originally dated Madison, April 29, 1877, and on the surface mainly about real estate matters, ended up in the hands of the Hayes administration. Exactly how a supposedly personal letter from Hill to Bowles got to Hayes and the newspapers is not clear. One possibility is that the son-in-law leaked it to the press and then forwarded the original to Hayes. The other possibility is that Bowles sent the correspondence to the White House and that the

---

16 Abshire, *South Rejects a Prophet*, 143–60; Hoogenboom, *Rutherford B. Hayes*, 281, 291, 297, 301; Trefousse, *Rutherford B. Hayes*, 87; Barnard, *Rutherford B. Hayes*, 417–18; *(DC) National Republican*, March 7, 1877; Foner, *Reconstruction*, 578–81.

17 *New York Times*, March 16, 1877 (The most); *Chicago Tribune*, March 16, 1877; *Boston Journal*, March 16, 1877; *Galveston News*, March 16, 19, 1877; *Atlanta Constitution*, March 16, 1877; *Columbus Enquirer*, March 16, 1877; *Milledgeville Union & Recorder*, March 20, 1877; Trefousse, *Rutherford B. Hayes*, 88.

Hayes administration then leaked the obsequious letter for its own purposes. How much direct agency Hill himself had in the distribution is unknown. In any case, given that the pro-Hayes excerpts from the long missive appeared in newspapers across the country, the result no doubt boosted the ex-senator's visibility with the administration at a time when the Morgan County lawyer was still in the rumor mill for high judicial appointment.[18]

Josh Hill found another opportunity to praise the president when Hayes made a good will tour of the South in September 1877. The trip included a stop in Atlanta where the crowd graciously greeted the Ohioan. Hayes told Blacks in the audience that he would stand by their constitutional rights, but he also paternalistically declared that "the great mass of intelligent white men" would make it happen if left alone by the national government. Hill, presumably one of those "intelligent" men, was not able to attend, but he sent a telegram of best wishes that sounded a lot like it came from a man seeking favor.[19]

It was not to be for Hill. Hayes selected former Union general John Marshall Harlan from Kentucky. As he had for executive appointments, the president decided to pick someone from an upper South or border state rather than the Deep South. Hayes was beholden to Harlan because he had helped swing his state's Republican convention delegation to the Ohioan when his nomination was still in doubt. Harlan's later vigorous dissents in the *Civil Rights Cases of 1883* and *Plessy v Ferguson* (1896) attested that he was much more in line with Hayes's views on race than Hill's.[20]

In December 1877, President Hayes appointed a new US marshal for Georgia upon the recommendations of Senator John B. Gordon and

---

[18] Joshua Hill to Col. John Bowles, April 29, 1877, Executive Files, Rutherford. B. Hayes Presidential Library, Fremont, OH; *Chicago Tribune*, May 29, 1877; *Boston Journal*, May 24, 1877; *Philadelphia Times*, May 24, 1877; *Galveston News*, June 4, 1877.

[19] Hoogenboom, *Rutherford B. Hayes*, 317 (great mass); *New York Tribune*, September 29, 1877; *Atlanta Constitution*, September 26, 27, 1877; *Chicago Tribune*, October 7, 9; *Indianapolis News*, October 8, 1877; *(DC) National Republican*, October 8, 1877; *Cincinnati Star*, October 4, 1877.

[20] Hoogenboom, *Rutherford B. Hayes*, 361; Hoogenboom, *Presidency of Rutherford B. Hayes*, 15, 64, 137; Foner, *Reconstruction*, 579–80; *New York Times*, March 16, 1877; *Chicago Tribune*, March 16, 19, 1877.

Representative Alexander H. Stephens. This choice further demonstrated that Hayes preferred to curry the favor of influential Democrats rather than to pursue the hopeless task of building a viable Republican Party in Georgia. Senator Roscoe Conkling of New York attacked the president in a "striking tone and manner," lamenting that Hayes had not consulted with leading Republicans Joshua Hill, Amos T. Akerman, and James A. Longstreet to find a suitable party member for the Georgia position. Hayes also faced criticism from Georgia's Black Republicans, who claimed that despite the president's supportive rhetoric, he slighted them in appointments.[21]

Joshua Hill lowered his sights a bit in his next flirtation with a Hayes appointment. It is not likely that the wealthy Georgian would have been enticed by the thought of a district-level federal judgeship, but in July 1879 he did write the president to express his interest in an appointment to fill a vacancy on the Supreme Court of the District of Columbia, then widely considered second in prestige to the US Supreme Court. As always in this era, sectional politics mattered, so Hill began his letter to the president carefully: "If it should not conflict with the policy of the administration to fill the vacancy...with a southern man, I will ask the favor of having my name considered." He knew that his request was a long shot, so Hill assured Hayes that if he did not receive the appointment, "It shall not affect, in the slightest, my respect and kind feeling for you." Again, he was disappointed.[22]

Joshua Hill appeared in one last episode of Hayes administration politics in spring 1880 when David M. Key resigned as postmaster general to take a federal judgeship back in Tennessee. Again Hill and fellow Georgians Hershel V. Johnson and James Longstreet entered the speculation to replace Key. Instead, the position went to a loyal Upper South Republican. Despite all the rumors and speculation involving Hill and others, Hayes

---

[21] The appointee was O. P. Fitzsimmons (*New York Tribune*, December 3, 1877; *Atlanta Constitution*, December 6, 1877 [*New York World* and *Philadelphia Times*]; Shadgett, *Republican Party in Georgia*, 142–43).

[22] Hill to Hayes, July 21, 1879, Hayes Presidential Library, Fremont, OH. The *Atlanta Constitution*, August 7, 1886, declared that Hill had "refused a lifetime federal judgeship," but it is not clear what judicial appointment he may have declined. It may have been an informal offer for a lesser court, but the author has found no other documentation.

never did appoint a Deep South Republican to a prominent position in his administration. As far as prestigious and influential federal appointments in the Hayes administration for Joshua Hill went, it was case-after-case of bridesmaid rather than bride.[23]

The Constitution of 1877

Joshua Hill's last official political position was serving as one of Morgan County's two delegates to the 1867–1868 Georgia State Constitutional Convention. It was his third chance to have some influence on his state's most fundamental document. First, he was a delegate to the convention that crafted the state's 1865 Constitution during the period of presidential Reconstruction under Andrew Johnson. In the second case, illness prevented Hill's being chosen as a delegate to the 1867–1868 convention, but the racially integrated, Republican-dominated body granted him access to the floor where he had some sway with the moderate to conservative faction. In 1877, the third instance would be an entirely different affair. The officially nonpartisan gathering was overwhelmingly dominated by Democrats. Neither Black men nor Republicans of a radical stripe were among the 194 delegates in attendance.

Most White Georgians perceived the existing 1868 constitution to be, in the words of the petulant Robert Toombs, the work of "negroes, thieves, and Yankees." That was hardly a fair assessment, but Toombs's statement accurately reflected the visceral feeling of Democrats that the state deserved a new constitution crafted exclusively by native White men who would wipe away the hallmarks of Radical Reconstruction. As the June 12, 1877, referendum approached, Democratic leaders uniformly favored the convention call whereas White Republicans were split along typical lines with the press listing Joshua Hill as supportive but Rufus Bullock (who had returned to the state), John Bryant, and Ben Conley in

[23] *Atlanta Constitution*, May 7, 11, 1880; *Raleigh Observer*, November 30, 1879 (ref. *New York World*); *Augusta Chronicle*, November 30, 1879; *Chicago Inter Ocean*, May 5, 1880; *Augusta Chronicle*, May 8, 1880; *Memphis Appeal*, May 7, 1880; *(DC) National Republican*, June 11, 1880. Hayes appointed Horace Maynard of Tennessee. Out of the episode, Longstreet became minister to Turkey, a position that Hill would not have wanted (Varon, *Longstreet*, 244).

opposition. In a turnout low relative to typical state elections, voters narrowly approved holding the convention.[24]

When the convention opened on July 11, a Columbus writer succinctly expressed the prevalent Democratic anger at the past and the party's optimism for the new day:

> The so-called Convention of 1867 [and 1868] was composed almost exclusively of renegades and aliens.... They met in accordance with the provisions of the iniquitous Reconstruction Acts, and under the protection of United States bayonets. Their object was oppression and rapine.... One who is familiar with the dark days of ten years ago can scarcely realize the change that has taken place. The carpet bagger, the scallawag, and the negro have disappeared. There is not one of either genus in the whole body. In their stead we see a body of men who worthily represent the flower of Georgia.

The editorialist listed eighteen such leading flowers by name—for better or worse, Joshua Hill was among them.[25]

Morgan County delegates Joshua Hill and Augustus Reese were of long acquaintance even though they had differed over secession and had diverged in postwar party affiliation. Despite their partisan differences, the lawyer and the judge sat side by side in the convention hall. That Morgan County, now firmly back in Democratic control, had elected Hill was evidence of his longstanding bipartisanship. A Northwest Georgia editor took note of the senator as "one of the most honest and consistent Republicans since the war." During proceedings, party affiliation played little direct role although Hill did suffer the occasional partisan jab. On opening day, one reporter surveyed the membership and cracked, "Joshua Hill *in spite of his naughty record* of a few years back claimed general attention." Later, in the midst of debate, a delegate made snide reference to Hill's Republicanism: "I must confess, Mr. President, that I have less confidence in

---

[24] H. E. Davis, *Henry Grady's New South*, 55–60; Scroggins, *Robert Toombs*, 181–86; Coleman, *History of Georgia*, 219 (negroes); E. K. Ware, *Constitutional History of Georgia*, 159–67; Saye, *Constitutional History of Georgia*, 279–309; Wynne, *Continuity of Cotton*, 95–17.

[25] *Columbus Enquirer-Sun*, June 12, 1877; Saye, *Constitutional History*, 279; *Augusta Chronicle*, July 12, 1877.

his party than in himself." Judge Reese, on the other hand, was a strong conservative Democrat. His resistance to allowing African Americans on his juries had led to his removal from the bench during the military occupation period.[26]

The delegates convened in the bustling new capital city of Atlanta, now more than a dozen years removed from its near destruction in 1864. The convention brought to town virtually all of the state's influential White politicians along with dozens of journalists and uncounted numbers of men who sought to shape the constitution to serve their interests. As the delegates prepared to gather in Atlanta, several newspapers identified a dozen or more members in whom they had particular confidence and whom they expected to assume leadership roles. Both Morgan delegates were on the lists along with Toombs, Charles J. Jenkins, and others. In an article that included Hill, a Milledgeville writer optimistically claimed, "With such men for leaders, the Convention cannot go far wrong." Ten days into the proceedings, the special correspondent of a Columbus daily observed, "Leaving aside Gen. Toombs and Gen. [Alexander R.] Lawton, Hon. Joshua Hill promises to be the most useful member." Another reporter scanned the hall for "conspicuous personages" among the "collection of gray beards" and noticed the "Roman face" of Hon. Joshua Hill. Years later, Timothy M. Furlow fondly recalled a chance meeting of old rivals amid the hubbub:

> One day during the session of that convention I was walking down Marietta street with Mr. Hill when we met Governor Brown. After a cordial greeting, Governor Brown smiled and said, "Well, gentlemen, this is certainly a coincidence—something that has never happened before or may never happen again—the three candidates for governor of Georgia in 1863 meeting at one and the same time."[27]

---

[26] *Savannah Morning News*, July 17, 1877; *Cartersville Express*, June 8, 1877 (one of); *Greensboro Herald*, July 13, 1877 (emphasis added); *Augusta Chronicle*, March 15, 1886; State of Georgia, *A Stenographic Report of the Proceedings of the Constitutional Convention*, 249 (I must), hereafter cited as *Proceedings 1877.*

[27] *Atlanta Constitution*, May 31, June 7, 1877; August 31, 1888 (One day); *Milledgeville Union & Recorder*, June 19, 1877 (with such); *Columbus Times*, July

Presiding officer Jenkins had been an ardent opponent of Radical Reconstruction. He served on the Georgia Supreme Court during the Civil War and was the state's first elected governor after the war. Like so many conservative Democrats, Jenkins remained friendly with Republican Hill, who was one of the three delegates chosen to escort Jenkins to the podium on opening day. Both Jenkins and Hill had ties to the plantation's past as well as to the New South future. Jenkins was a bank president who served as a trustee of the University of Georgia. Hill represented wealthy clients and invested heavily in real estate. This put the two men in the ideal position to lead what historian Nick Wynne called the "swing faction" that strove mightily, though often unsuccessfully, to engineer compromise between the two principal convention factions, broadly classified as the antebellum planters led by Robert Toombs versus the business-corporate class led by James R. Brown, brother of ex-governor Joe Brown.[28]

The planter faction was anti-Reconstruction, anti-taxation, anti-monopoly, anti-Atlanta, and anti-Black. Toombs declared that blocking subsidies and loan guarantees for railroads "was one of the main objects of my coming here." On the issue of the repudiation of state bonds that had been issued to help railroads, Jenkins, Hill, and fourteen others voted opposite of Toombs and the overwhelming majority of delegates. When some pundits suggested that the votes of the pro-railroad delegates might have been corrupt, the *Augusta Chronicle* jumped to the defense of Hill, Jenkins, and five of the others "whose purity and integrity has never been and can never be questioned. They own none of the bonds affected by the resolution, and their vote upon it was simply governed by the dictates of their conscience."[29]

Northern Republicans took a dim view of the goings on in Atlanta. The *Chicago Inter Ocean* declared that "the convention represents the old anti-national or rebel sentiment in the State." The writer complained that Toombs's "influence has always been cast against the Union," and

---

24, 1877 (leaving); *Macon Telegraph*, July 13, 1877; *Augusta Chronicle*, April 8, 10 (*Madison Home Journal*), 14, 18, 19, June 8, 13, 27, 1877.

[28] *Savannah Morning News*, July 12, 14, 1877; *Proceedings 1877*, 2 (June 11); Cook, *Governors of Georgia*, 144–47; Wynne, *Continuity of Cotton*, 105–106.

[29] *Proceedings 1877*, 284 (was one); *Columbus Times*, August 21, 1877 (Gen. Toombs); *Augusta Chronicle*, August 17, 1877; *Chicago Inter Ocean*, August 13, 1877; Scroggins, *Robert Toombs*, 181–86.

explained that Senator Benjamin Hill was urging his delegate friends to strike all references to the perpetuity of the national union. "Opposed to these hot-headed reactionists," the *Inter Ocean* explained, "is a faction of conservatives acting under the leadership of ex-Senator Joshua Hill." Unfortunately, the article correctly concluded, Joshua Hill and "others of the old-school will be so much in minority it is feared that they can exercise but little influence" against the "schemes" of Toombs and Ben Hill.[30]

The convention opened on July 11 and ran through August 25. Much of the work occurred in committee meetings and in behind-the-scenes negotiations in lobbies, taverns, and hotels after hours, so it is difficult to isolate the influence of any one delegate or group. However, as the proceedings unfolded, it became clear that the loosely organized planter faction would prevail on most issues, especially those involving the limitation of state taxing and spending. They sought to constrain the discretion of state government by weakening the governor's appointment powers and writing into the constitution detailed restrictions on expenditures. Planters, who sent their own children to academies and who relied on ill-educated agricultural labor, tended to be lukewarm about public education. Thus, they limited state financial aid to the study of basic subjects only—and then only in schools rigidly segregated by race. The requirement for racial separation was consistent with Joshua Hill's philosophy. The system soon evolved into separate but very unequal. Hill consistently, but only occasionally successfully, opposed most efforts to adopt provisions that would hamstring future legislators. His objections presaged the later criticisms of historians and political scientists who regarded excessive length and excruciating detail as the critical flaws of the 115-page 1877 constitution. On one occasion, specifically regarding restrictions on the salaries of executive officers and judges, Hill took the opportunity to express his broader philosophical objections to the direction the convention was taking.

> It seems to be policy of this body to withhold from the legislature powers worthy of the discretion of honorable men. I hoped when we came here that it would be the sense of this convention to abstain from the business of the legislature.... There seems to me a disposition in this house to deprive the representatives of

---

[30] *Chicago Inter Ocean*, July 12, 13, 1877.

the people, who are to be chosen under this constitution, of their legitimate power.

Others rose to agree with the Madisonian in theory, but when it came to specific issues the convention time and again adopted restrictive provisions. Even Hill was not entirely consistent in applying the principle that the state constitution should deal only with the broad, fundamental structure of government and leave wide discretion to the General Assembly. When provisions that barred the General Assembly from granting future "subsidies and the credit of the state to railroads and other corporations" came to a vote, Hill tended to side with Toombs and the planter interests.[31]

Near the end of the convention, one journalist gave his impressions of the men who had been most prominent in the proceedings. He observed, "When Hon. Joshua Hill rises, the Convention is prepared to hear both sides fairly given, rather than an effort to have his own opinions adopted." Hill's approach sometimes resulted in his specific motions being rejected even though his broader goal of shaping the outcome prevailed at least in part. One example that received considerable press attention involved state rights. The 1868 State Constitution, adopted during the period of congressional reconstruction, explicitly declared that Georgia "shall ever remain a member of the American Union" (art. I, § 23). There was no way that this rousing nationalistic statement rejecting the right of secession and acknowledging the perpetuity of the Union would survive the mood of the 1877 convention. In its place, the committee report proposed a mild statement to the effect that the people of Georgia had the "right of regulating their internal government…and of altering and abolishing the Constitution" if necessary (1877, art. I, § 5). Some delegates mounted an effort to strengthen the clause. Using several parliamentary maneuvers, Hill, with the help of Judge Reese, avoided the inclusion of a Bill of Rights provision that asserted unfettered state sovereignty. The Republican press praised Hill for keeping the hot-button issue out of the document.[32]

---

[31] *Proceedings 1877*, 248–49 (subsidies), 280–81; *Savannah Morning News*, August 6, 8, 1877; Coleman, *History of Georgia*, 219; Joiner, *History of Public Education*, 89.

[32] *Columbus Times*, August 21, 1877 (When); *Augusta Chronicle*, July 26, 1877; *Savannah Morning News*, July 26, 1877; *Pittsburgh Post*, August 28, 1877; *Proceedings 1877*, 98–100.

Aside from the provision requiring school segregation, the convention did very little that directly affected race relations. Because scant if any enforcement of the Civil Rights Act of 1875 took place in Georgia anyway, the delegates saw little need to include provisions that would openly appear to contradict federal law. For the most part, the delegates avoided taking any actions that would have risked attracting congressional ire.

The referendum to approve or reject the proposed constitution did not occur until December 5, more than three months after the close of the convention. The convention had avoided the potentially inflammatory question of whether to move the state capital back to Milledgeville by referring that matter to a separate vote at the same time as ratification. The pro-business *Constitution* did not want to risk Atlanta's status by opposing the constitution itself, so it offered the tepid endorsement that the new document was "worthier of commendation than of condemnation." Voters approved the constitution by more than two to one, and Atlanta retained capital status by a comfortable but slightly narrower margin. Black voters were rightly suspicious of the document that the all-White body had drafted. Several counties with a high proportion of Black voters, including Hill's home county of Morgan, rejected ratification. Adjacent Greene County also voted against the new constitution along with several counties in the southwestern part of the state and Camden and McIntosh counties along the coast. Black turnout was proportionally higher in the constitutional referendum than in normal partisan elections because the White power structure was confident of victory and therefore had less incentive to intimidate Black voters.[33]

Politically attuned Georgians recognized Joshua Hill's role of quietly working to shape the new document even though he did not always prevail. On the other hand, the most publicized episode of his role as delegate had little to do with the substantive provisions and everything to do with his own views about the proper role of Christian prayer in the public sphere and about the efficacy of prayer itself. The following chapter explores that controversial episode.

---

[33] H. E. Davis, *Henry Grady's New South*, 59–60 (worthier); See Wynne, *Continuity of Cotton*, 95–17; Ward, "Republican Party," 198–209; Abbott, *Republican Party and the South*, 229–32.

Final Flurries of Political Attention

After the 1877 Georgia State Constitutional Convention, Joshua Hill settled back into the role of elder statesman. He maintained a nominal relationship with the Republican Party, but he backed ever further away from the bitter infighting that characterized the state committee. He did not need a state-based patronage position to make a living, and he did not need to hold party office to continue to be regarded as one of the most prominent and respected Republicans in Georgia. The former senator remained well known enough that politicians and press would occasionally drop his name into the conversation just to demonstrate that neither Josh Hill in particular nor White Republicans in general had completely disappeared from the state's political universe. Georgia politics, however, was no longer played out in Democratic vs. Republican—or even Black vs. White—terms. Economic, physical, and social intimidation had so reduced the Republican voter base that the Democratic Party did not have to worry about defeat. At least until the brief Populist upsurge in the 1890s, the assumption of White supremacy and the myth of the Lost Cause so thoroughly united Democrats that they could squabble among themselves without fear that their divisions would open the door for the triumph by the opposition. It was not just a Georgia phenomenon; the party of Jackson was in the ascendancy all across the South. As the 1880 elections approached, the *New York Times* took notice that Democrats held almost all Southern senate and house seats and headlined one story, "The Lost Cause Regained: Secession's Great Power in the Nation's Councils."[34]

Georgia Republicans wanted to find a modicum of relevance even if they had no hope of gaining important elective offices. Despite President Hayes's efforts to enact some semblance of civil service reform, there would still be still a raft of patronage positions available in the South as long as a Republican sat in the White House. Atlanta launched a long-shot effort to bring the Republican National Convention to the Gate City. Hill joined Amos Akerman and others in that ambitious but unsuccessful exercise in boosterism. Even more audacious was the editorial in the short-lived *Atlanta Republican* that put forth for consideration the pairing of General William T. Sherman for president with Joshua Hill for vice president.

[34] *New York Times*, August 30, 1880.

Newspapers around the country dutifully reported several Southern contenders for the vice-presidential nomination, including Hill. One concluded, "But it is evident to the unprejudiced observer that the man to look out for is ex-Senator Hill. A very powerful movement has been started in his behalf." The *Baltimore American* observed, "It is argued that Mr. Hill will make a better run than any other southern man," and the *New York World* reported that some authorities found Hill the most likely name for second place if Grant were to run again. Hill's strongly Democratic hometown paper expressed of Madison's favorite son, "There is no man in Georgia for whom we entertain a more exalted opinion than Joshua Hill. He is the embodiment of honor, and *if we are to have a republican vice-president* we prefer him to any man on the continent." The national convention was still half a year away, and the mini-boom for Hill soon faded.[35]

According to a wire report from Washington, the optimistic ex-senator believed his party could actually out-vote the Democrats in Georgia in the presidential election of 1880 if a "fair and unfettered count of both white and black Republicans could be made." But, of course, such a count was not possible in the prevailing atmosphere of intimidation, so as usual the Democratic nominee carried the state while the GOP prevailed nationwide.[36]

With each new Republican administration in Washington came speculation about and prominent Southerners assuming cabinet and judicial positions. Of course, if a Democrat had won in 1880, the patronage river would run dry for Republicans in all sections of the country. Just a few weeks before the election, Joshua Hill returned from one of his many trips to the nation's capital city and remarked to a reporter, "It depends on what company you keep, as to who is to be elected president." In the exceedingly close election, James A. Garfield prevailed, marking the sixth consecutive win for a Republican. As Garfield began to assemble his cabinet early in 1881, Joshua Hill's name once again appeared on several lists

---

[35] *Macon Telegraph*, October 7, 1879 (*Augusta News*); *Atlanta Constitution*, October 7, 1879; *Cincinnati Gazette*, December 9, 1879; *Chicago Tribune*, December 9, 1879; *(DC) Evening Star*, November 22, 1879; *Springfield (MA) Republican*, December 5, 1879; *Philadelphia Times*, November 29, 1879 (it is evident); *Atlanta Constitution*, November 4 (there is no man, *Madisonian*), December 2 (It is argued, *Baltimore American*), 1879.

[36] *Wilkes-Barre Record of the Times*, August 7, 1880.

of potential appointees. He was most often mentioned as a possible attorney general, but there was considerable doubt that the president-elect would select any Deep South man, and he did not.[37]

The frustration of Georgia's White Republicans led to efforts as early as 1876 to establish separate but parallel party organizations for Blacks and Whites. Their hope was that they would stand a better chance of attracting White voters to the party if the two races could operate separately but cooperate at election time. In the 1880s these long-simmering tensions between White and Black Republicans became more open. A younger generation of African Americans was emerging, and the Republican central committee elected twenty-eight-year-old Black Atlanta newspaper editor and lawyer William A. Pledger chairman. Conservative Whites such as Hill fully accepted Black voting and acquiesced in limited office-holding by African Americans whom they regarded as competent and compliant, but they were suspicious of independent-minded Black politicians like Pledger and believed that White men should retain ultimate control of the party.[38]

In 1882 and 1884, General Longstreet and Atlanta-area businessman Jonathan Norcross, both of whom Hill knew well, revived the idea of separate Black and White Republican organizations. The *Macon Telegraph* observed, "Indeed, General Longstreet, *if we except Hon. Joshua Hill*, is the most respectable and upright member of his party in the Southern States." (Amos Akerman died shortly after the 1880 election.) In 1884, the organizers of the self-named "Whig Republicans" tried their best to attach Hill's prestige to their effort. They suggested in the press that he would attend the national Republican convention as part of their group, and they listed him on the executive committee as one of several regional vice presidents. In return the movement received only tepid public endorsement from the ex-senator. Hill wrote that he had originally planned to attend their meeting but later discovered (without specific explanation), "I cannot spare the time from my private affairs." The best he would offer was his acknowledge

[37] *Macon Telegraph*, September 7, 1880 (it depends); *Atlanta Constitution*, February 1, 19, 1881; *Washington Post*, February 20, 1881; *Minneapolis Star Tribune*, February 20, 1881; *(Springfield) Illinois State Journal*, February 18, 1881; Rutkow, *James A. Garfield*, 67–69.

[38] Shadgett, *Republican Party in Georgia*, 141–43.

that the general points expressed in Whig Republican pronouncements were "in accord with" the positions that he had entertained since 1868. He advised, however, against the plan to send a separate delegation to the upcoming convention in Chicago. Hill, then seventy-two years old, concluded his letter by urging the leaders of the reform movement to attract younger men who could persevere with the goal "to purify the political tone of the state by placing in prominent positions the highest intelligence and most deserving citizens." At that time, "purify" was often a euphemism for reducing or removing Black influence. Nothing much came of the Whig Republican effort, so the Georgia Republican Party continued to muddle along in an uneasy alliance of most of the state's Blacks and a few of its Whites. It is doubtful that a more enthusiastic embrace of the "Whig Republican" scheme by Josh Hill would have changed that result, and the Madisonian was surely aware of that when he decided to keep his distance. Democrat Grover Cleveland won the presidency in 1884, so already bereft of elective office, Georgia Republicans temporarily lost their patronage access as well.[39]

Fellow Madisonians of both parties encouraged Hill to stand for the legislature in 1886 in order to be in a position to help his hometown on proposed railroad legislation. Hill had been a strong advocate of private railroad development for his entire career, but he resisted the draft.[40]

The frustrated dreams of Southern White Republicans surfaced again in 1887 and 1888, which led to the final mentions of Joshua Hill as a political candidate or major appointee. It started with a bout of interest in Robert Todd Lincoln, son of the president, making a run for the presidency. Lincoln's possible candidacy had been mentioned before, and now a short-lived Atlanta newspaper ran a letter suggesting the fanciful idea of a Lincoln-led ticket with Joshua Hill in the second spot. The widely circulated Chicago *Inter Ocean* picked up the story and remarked that Hill "has the respect of all classes, inclusive of the Bourbon Democrats." The article drug out one more time the faded Lincolnesque hope that having an old

[39] *Macon Telegraph*, May 9, 1884 (emphasis added); *New York Times*, May 1, 1884; *Columbus Enquirer*, April 11, 1884; *Atlanta Constitution*, March 26, 27, April 2, 3, 4, 9, 10 (I cannot spare; Hill to Longstreet, April 7, 1884), May 1, 1884, March 27, 1890; *Augusta Chronicle*, April 5, 1890; Shadgett, *Republican Party in Georgia*, 76–89; Ward, "The Republican Party," 208–209; Varon, *Longstreet*, 277–79.

[40] *Atlanta Constitution*, August 5, 7, 10, 1886.

Southern Whig on a presidential ticket could "shatter the solid South." The idea attracted no further attention. A more reasonable, but still unrealistic, suggestion was that Joshua Hill, James Longstreet, Jonathan Norcross, or even Rufus Bullock might make credible Republican candidates for the governorship. The general and the former senator replied to party officials that they were too old and unwell to serve—though both would probably have refused the sacrificial honor of Republican nomination had they been in the best of health. When a Republican returned to the White House with Benjamin Harrison's 1888 victory over incumbent Democrat Grover Cleveland, it was almost pro forma for the press to trot out Hill's name for a possible cabinet position. The *Augusta Chronicle* conceded, "As Democrats, we have no claims upon the new administration," but nevertheless the editor offered up Hill for Harrison's cabinet, arguing that the former senator was "venerable but still a vigorous man…[who] was always an honest and honorable opponent."[41] That was the final gasp in the long effort to put another Georgian in the cabinet of a Republican president. None had served since Amos T. Akerman under Grant.

The elder statesman from Madison may have been flattered by having his name trotted out so many times in the fifteen years after he left the Senate. It is doubtful, however, if he ever had serious expectations that any of the efforts would come to fruition. The most serious opportunities came with presidents Hayes in 1877 and Garfield in 1881, but in both cases the administrations concluded that other men from other states (and in some cases from the other party) brought more to the national table than an old Whig-Know-Nothing-Republican Unionist from a solidly Democratic state.

At any time during his post-senatorial career, Josh Hill could have moved from being prominent but not powerful to being both if only he had been willing to extoll the Lost Cause and embrace the Democratic Party as so many of his planter-professional class had done. He had many chances to do so, and few people would have been surprised had he done so. Instead, he chose to remain in the middle—cozy with the party of Jackson but officially aligned with the party of Lincoln.

---

[41] *Chicago Inter Ocean*, April 20, 1887; *Cleveland Leader*, April 22, 1887; *Public Opinion* (NY and Washington), April 23, 1887; *Atlanta Constitution*, August 3, 1888; *Perry Home Journal*, August 2, 1888; *Augusta Chronicle*, March 13, 1888; January 4, 1889 (As Democrats); *Macon Telegraph*, July 29, 1888, January 5, 1889.

Chapter 14

Epilogue: Family, Religion, and Death, 1873–1891

For the last eighteen years of Joshua Hill's life, most of his energy went into his law practice, business investments, and family affairs with some dalliances in politics. His personal life had moments of joy highlighted by the marriages of his three youngest daughters and the pleasures of grandfathering. But these good times were clouded by the pall of his wife's frequent bouts of illness, the divorce of his eldest daughter, and, most tragically, the sudden deaths of his three remaining sons by the age of thirty.

There are few extant records of these Hill family tragedies, but what can be known for sure is that Hill's post-senatorial years were filled with episodes of great personal anguish. He suffered blows that would challenge the mettle of any man, but he kept his pain to himself and those closest to him. After his death, a committee of Hill's fellow lawyers wrote, "He never paraded his success, defeats or griefs before the public."[1]

The Loss of Three Adult Sons, 1875–1877

As recounted in chapter 5, eighteen-year-old Hugh Legare Hill, a Confederate soldier despite his father's Unionism, fell to a sniper's bullet during the Sherman's advance toward Atlanta in 1864. Just over ten year later, his three brothers died in quick succession.

Clarence was the first of the three to go. He was the eldest boy and second-oldest child. Five years younger than Anna, Clarence Hill was born

---

[1] "In Memoriam" [Joshua Hill], a memorial prepared by attorneys of the bar of the Morgan Superior Court, Ocmulgee Circuit, September Term 1891 (hereafter, Hill bar memorial), MCA (also Joshua Hill folder, HRBML). The author has found no record to indicate that the Hills lost any children in infancy.

in 1845 prior to his parents' move from Monticello to Madison. In the Civil War, he volunteered for the Confederate army with Company D of the 3rd Georgia infantry. He saw service first in Virginia as a courier then went to Georgia and served with the Home Guard. Near the end of the war, Clarence, unfit for service due to "pulmonary consumption" (tuberculosis), left the military. Clarence's persistent illness kept him confined to his parents' residence in Madison, and there he died in May 1875 while Joshua and Emily were away in Washington, DC. The members of Company D remembered and eulogized their fallen comrade: "He was our companion in the field, in the late terrible conflict between the sections, during which trying ordeal he proved himself a true and gallant soldier.... In disposition he was amiable and cheerful, with great fondness for the humorous; as a companion, uniformly courteous and agreeable."[2]

Clarence Hill's long-term illness probably contributed to his demise, but in an anguished letter to T. P. Saffold, Hill placed the blame for Clarence's passing squarely on "that Prince of devils, Alcohol." The distraught parent, whose son was "lying dead in my desolate home" as he wrote, lamented that his remaining two sons were hopeless alcoholics as well. One of them "was worse than dead; a poor shrinking lunatic," and the other was "not able to resist the tempter Drink." The father's agony dripped from the page.

Then, in a frank manner that only an old and trusted friend would dare, Hill used the occasion of his own family's tragedy to beseech Saffold to "abandon the habit of excessive indulgence in the deadly vice of the age. Stop! Oh! For God's sake, shove aside the draught." The former senator implied that he, too, faced the temptation to overindulge: "Your efforts will assist me—mine will strengthen you."

Scarcely a year later, on August 22, 1876, death again struck the Hill household. Little is known of John Edward Hill's youth (b. 1851), aside from the fact that during the 1871 Ku Klux Klan Hearings a questioner implied that John had been involved in the lynching of a jailed Black man in Madison. The committee did not pursue the matter. The only confirmed

---

[2] *Augusta Constitutionalist*, June 6 (*Madison Home Journal*), 11(He was), 1875; *Macon Telegraph*, June 8, 1875; *Madison Home Journal*, February 2, 1878; Georgia Commissioner of Pensions statement, January 10, 1916, via fold3.com; *Madisonian*, August 12, 1887.

details of John Hill's death are that the twenty-five-year-old was in in Washington, DC, at the time and that his remains were brought back to Madison for burial. Given the allusions about all three boys in Hill's 1875 letter to Saffold, alcohol dependence was likely the root of his demise as it had been for Clarence and would soon be for Walter.[3]

Only fifteen more months passed before the last of the Hill sons died—this time under mysterious circumstances unquestionably connected to the alcoholism that also plagued the two brothers who had died so recently before him. In 1870, no doubt upon the connections of his father, the promising young Walter S. Hill (b. 1849) received appointment as a junior clerk in the office of US Attorney General Amos T. Akerman. Little can be confirmed of his career after that except that he returned to Georgia. In the wee hours of Tuesday, November 20, 1877, Walter's lifeless body was discovered lying alongside the tracks of the Georgia Railroad, not far from the family home. No coroner's report survives, and no arrest is recorded; so the details must be gleaned from press reports. The death remains unsolved; was it murder, suicide, or drunken accident? According to one report, "The head was nearly severed from the body and one of the arms was broken. The body was cold when found. It had evidently been run over by a train, but it is not known whether before or after death." In the words of another account, Walter Hill had been "effectually guillotined." That writer related the events of the night as best he could:

> [Walter Hill] had been dissipating somewhat and was last seen about the depot, near midnight, in company with other parties. When found, we learn, there were a couple of wounds near the jaw and in the forehead that seemed to indicate the passage of a bullet through the head.... The grave suspicion was aroused that the young man might have been murdered and placed on the track with a view to the train mashing out all traces of the crime. Others doubted whether the unfortunate youth had committed suicide or accidently shot himself, while intoxicated.

A Milledgeville newspaper's story about the incident cautioned, "Verily, whiskey is no respecter of persons." That Joshua Hill emerged sane and rational from losing one son in a tragic war that he had vainly endeavored

---

[3] *Atlanta Constitution*, September 12, 1876; "District of Columbia Deaths, 1874–961" via FamilySearch.org; *Madison Home Journal*, September 1, 1876.

to avoid and then just over a decade later losing three more in battles with alcoholism is a wonder. The toll on their mother was too much to bear.[4]

Anna's Divorce

While Joshua Hill was still reeling from the deaths of Clarence, John, and Walter, he was struck in 1881 with another deep personal disappointment. As described in chapter 9, Anna Hill occasionally accompanied her father on postwar trips to Augusta where he had extensive professional and political connections. There she met and fell in love with John Bowles, a former Union officer who had commanded the First Kansas Colored Regiment during the Civil War and later became involved in Republican Party politics. They wed at the Hill home in Madison on December 10, 1867, and one can only imagine the clucking of many local tongues as Anna stood in the parlor with her carpetbagger groom. Bowles used the influence of his new father-in-law to obtain well-paying patronage positions and often traveled with Hill for politics and business. They invested together in Stone Mountain quarry property, and Bowles served as Hill's agent for real estate investments in the nation's capital.[5]

The Bowles had two children born in Madison in 1872 and 1873, respectively, while their father served as surveyor of customs in Savannah. As Republican opportunities faded in Georgia, Colonel Bowles and Anna moved in May 1874 to Washington, DC. When Anna's unmarried younger sisters Belle and Julia spent time with "Mrs. Colonel Bowles" in Washington, they were quite a hit. A society paper called one of the girls an "accomplished and noble type of Southern beauty." Another capital publication reported that "the accomplished and beautiful Misses Hill, daughters of ex-Senator Hill…will leave soon for their sunny home in

---

[4] *Macon Telegraph*, August 16, 1870; *Augusta Chronicle*, November 22, 1877 (The head); *Atlanta Constitution*, November 24, 1877 (He had); *Milledgeville Union Recorder*, November 27, 1877 (Verily). There were several other news reports in Georgia and nationally, which drew from the early accounts in Atlanta and Augusta papers. Joshua Hill's son Walter S. Hill should not be confused with his contemporary Walter B. Hill, who practiced law in South Georgia.

[5] *Atlanta Constitution*, May 7, 1869; April 4, 1876; Hill to President R. B. Hayes, January 22, 1878, Madison, Executive Files, Rutherford B. Hayes Presidential Library, Fremont, OH.

Georgia, much to the regret of the Washington beaux, with whom they are universal favorites."[6]

Over time, however, it became clear that life in Washington was not good for the Bowleses' relationship. In 1881, Anna filed for divorce, charging John with "cruelty, neglect, misconduct, and finally desertion." He countered that "life was unbearable with her" because she had a violent temper. The *Washington Post* reported, "The case has attracted considerable attention, on account of the social position and standing of the parties." The details that led to the competing charges are not known, but the Equity Court judge apparently found Anna's claims credible. In April 1881, he not only granted the divorce but also restored her maiden name after fourteen years of marriage. The court awarded the disputed guardianship of the children to their maternal grandfather. Joshua and Emily already had de facto custody of the grandchildren, who lived with them in Madison. Taking note of the wave of four divorces on one day, a New York reporter wryly commented, "There seems to be something in the atmosphere of Washington which is at variance with happy marital relations." The bitter divorce severed the Hill-Bowles political and business alliance. Soon after the split was finalized, Joshua Hill sold much of the Washington property ("worth $50,000 now, with an upward tendency") that John Bowles had been managing. Anna Hill remained in the capital and obtained a "responsible and lucrative" position in the US Treasury Department.[7]

Anna's son Joshua spent some time with her in Washington before returning to Madison to practice law like his esteemed grandfather who had raised him. On February 26, 1891, shortly before her father's death,

---

[6] *Macon Telegraph*, December 31, 1874 (accomplished and noble); *Salisbury Carolina Watchman*, March 18, 1875 (accomplished and beautiful); *(DC) National Republican*, January 1, July 2, 1875; *Americus Sumter Republican*, March 5, 1875.

[7] *Washington Post*, April 12, 1881; *Washington Evening Star*, April 12, 15, 1881; *Macon Telegraph*, April 22, 1881; *New York Truth*, April 14, 1881. The grandchildren spent their youth living in Madison with their grandparents. Grandson Joshua Hill died at twenty-five; his obituary made no mention of his father (*Madisonian*, March 18, 25, 1898; *Atlanta Constitution*, April 6, 1881 [worth]; *New York Herald*, April 13, 1881; *Washington Evening Star*, June 29, 1881; April 2,7, 15, 1882, June 19, 1883; *Marietta Journal*, December 24, 1882; *Augusta Chronicle*, April 5, 1890 [responsible]).

Anna married again. The romance began when an old friend whom she had not seen in some twenty-five years since they met in New York City reached out. The groom, Captain James H. Hays, was a Confederate veteran and widower who came from a prominent Tennessee family. A former governor was among the several Volunteer State friends who traveled to Madison for the ceremony at the Hill home. In deference to appearances, the *Atlanta Constitution*'s account of the wedding referred to the bride as a "widow" even though her ex-husband remained very much alive.[8]

Louise, Belle, and Julia

Life was less challenging, or at least it would appear so, for the three other Hill daughters. When Louise Hill was barely nineteen and her father was in the Senate, she married lawyer Albert W. "Abbo" Foster, son of Albert G. Foster and nephew of the late Nathaniel Greene Foster, Hill's close friends and allies. The couple resided in Madison and later in Atlanta. Following Abbo's death, Louise married L. H. Turnbull in 1895 and resided in Madison until 1920 in the large 1824 Greek Revival mansion on the west side of town known as the Anchorage. Louise Hill Foster Turnbull died in 1939.[9]

The postwar shortage of marriageable young men for young White women of high social standing in Southern small towns apparently affected Isabelle Hill's marriage prospects. Shortly before Christmas in 1884, twenty-eight-year-old Belle married Dr. Gazaway B. Knight, a widower three decades her senior. Back in 1861, Dr. Knight had organized and

---

[8] *Madisonian*, November 12, 1886; **[also the *Madisonian*?]** November 12, 1888; *Atlanta Constitution*, February 26, 1891; *Nashville Banner*, February 26, 1891; *New Orleans Times-Democrat*, February 27, 1891, did mention the divorce. As late as 1906, she was still living in Washington, DC (*Atlanta Georgian*, October 16, 1906). Col. John Bowles was listed as a "widower" in the 1880 Census. His first wife was apparently dead, but he was still married to Anna. He returned to Augusta, considered himself a Southerner, and in 1894 wrote *The Stormy Petral*, a novel set in the Civil War. He died in 1900.

[9] *Atlanta Constitution*, November 15, 1872, November 7, 1895; September 10, 1899; "History of the Anchorage, 2011" files of the Madison Historic Preservation Commission; *Madisonian*, February 12, 1932. Hill's granddaughter Legare Hill Obear, niece of Louise, later owned the house, which stood not far west of the railroad depots. It was moved to Walton County, Georgia, around 1985.

became captain of the local Panola Guards, part of Thomas R. R. Cobb's infantry legion. A veteran of several battles, Knight rose to the rank of lieutenant colonel. He fell ill and returned to Madison before the end of the war. Dr. Knight resumed the practice of medicine and died in 1902. Belle lived until 1938.[10]

In 1916, Isabelle Hill Knight gifted family land on the south side of town to the City of Madison for the establishment of a park. Consistent with the Jim Crow practice of the day, enjoyment of the park was limited to Whites. While Belle still lived, the city built a swimming pool in Hill Park so that local White children could enjoy summer fun in the water. Ironically, Madison's original Confederate monument now stands on a corner of the park named for Joshua Hill where the city relocated it in 1957 because its previous prominent location in the middle of a downtown intersection had become a traffic hazard. In 1908 the local chapter of the United Daughters of the Confederacy (UDC), of which Belle Hill Knight was an honorary member, selected the inscription for the pedestal, which was extracted from a poem dedicated to Robert E. Lee. In the tradition of the Lost Cause it says of the Confederacy in capital letters, "NO NATION ROSE SO WHITE AND FAIR. NONE FELL SO PURE OF CRIME." No such words would ever have come from the mouth or pen of Belle's father, who had called secession "the most stupendous folly since the revolt in Paradise" and who had proclaimed of the "ill-starred" Confederate States of America, "I regarded it from the first with open disfavor, and never abated my disproval of its insane origin."[11]

In 1886, two years after Belle's wedding, thirty-one-year-old Julia Hill married the up-and-coming Edward W. Butler. An 1873 graduate of Mercer University, Butler farmed in Morgan County with his uncle before being admitted to the bar and becoming junior partner in the influential Foster & Butler law firm. Butler joined the board of the Georgia Railroad & Banking Co. and served as Madison's mayor. Julia's marriage to the partner

---

[10] *Atlanta Constitution*, January 3, 1902; *Madisonian*, June 13, 1902, August 12, 1938, September 16, 1938.

[11] *Madisonian*, November 24, 1916, June 1, September 7, 1928; *Morgan County Citizen*, August 20, 27, 2020, by the author (a typo in the August 20 article, corrected August 27, used DAR in one place that should be UDC); *Augusta Chronicle*, October 25, 1876 (The most); "The Journal of the 1865 Constitutional Convention" in Candler, *Confederate Records*, 4:131–435 (ill-starred).

of her brother-in-law solidified her standing at the center of Madison's White society and further cemented the Hill-Foster family connection that stretched back to the early 1850s.[12]

Emily Hill's Struggles

Emily Reid Hill, eight years younger than Joshua, gave birth to eight children from 1840 to 1856. Joshua's affluence meant that Emily had a household staff (enslaved until 1865 and then free) to care for the young children and perform other domestic chores. Yet, even with such help, raising a family of eight would have been a challenge. The youngest, Belle, was born in 1856, shortly before her father went off to Congress. From that point forward, Emily's life became enmeshed in her husband's political and business career. The realities of war included the death of a son and the disruption of the lifestyle to which she had become accustomed. According to the decades-later recollections of the son of two household slaves, Emily was never entirely comfortable with the "peculiar institution." The narrator recounted the oral tradition, likely grounded in truth but romanticized with time, that as soon as Union troops departed Madison in November 1864, Miss Emily, then forty-four years old, gathered the enslaved house servants to tell them that they were free. She said that she hoped that they would stay on and work for the family. Indications are that many did.[13]

The record tells little of Emily's life during Reconstruction other than the snide remark about Charles Sumner and her pique at her husband's cousin (see chapters 11 and 12). She does appear in occasional press references to a series of recurring illnesses that required her husband's attention. The notices of several 1872–1873 social events that included Washington luminaries and their wives listed Senator Hill as attending alone. During summer that year, the Hills spent extended time for the benefit of Emily's recuperation at the Indian Springs resort about forty-five miles southwest of Madison. Early that fall in a letter to a friend, the senator explained that Emily's health had been precarious for several years and that she was mostly confined to bed, keeping him often occupied at home with her. Hill

---

[12] *Macon Telegraph*, November 18, 1886; *Madisonian*, November 19, 1886. Julia died in 1906 (*Atlanta Georgian*, October 16, 1906). Butler later remarried (Edward W. Butler file, MCA).

[13] Tonsill and Evans, "E. W. Evans, Brick Layer & Plasterer."

arrived in Washington late for the opening of the new session in December 1872 because of the "ill health of Mrs. Hill and pressing business."[14]

Joshua was at Emily's bedside in Washington, and she was not expected to live when they received news of Clarence's death in June 1875. She survived that episode, but Clarence's death followed closely by the passing of John and then the loss of her youngest under mysterious circumstances weighed heavily on her. In spring 1878, the local Madison paper reported that Emily faced serious illness again.[15] Anna's 1881 divorce, certainly sad for all involved and no doubt highly embarrassing to her parents, added an additional strain, including the guardianship of two grandchildren. It is probable that household staff managed most of the youngsters' care.

The burdens of illness, death, and disappointment were so great that Emily Hill become a recluse. In early May 1889, reports from Madison indicated that Emily's "family entertain no hope of her recovery." Joshua himself had "just recovered from a severe spell of sickness." Their more than fifty-two years of marriage came to an end on May 24, 1889, after "a lingering illness of ninety-nine days." She was just short of seventy. The death notice revealed the depth and length of her travails:

> Mrs. Joshua Hill died at her home in this city after a long illness. She was a most excellent lady, the beloved wife of one of Georgia's most illustrious citizens, ex-United States Senator Joshua Hill. Although a resident of this city for nearly fifty years, few of our people have ever seen her face, and she has led a retired life at her elegant home not having been out of the house in years.[16]

Man "Without a Creed"

Like most orators of the period, Hill was adept at employing biblical references and the language of civil religion in his writings and public utterances, but he never publicly revealed his own religious views until the early

[14] *Atlanta Constitution*, March 7, 1891, September 20, 1872; *Washington Evening Star*, June 6, 1872; *(DC) National Republican*, September 20 (Hill letter), December 5 (ill health) 1872, February 6, 1873.

[15] *Madison Home Journal*, February 2, March 16, 1878.

[16] *Atlanta Constitution*, May 11 (family), 25, 1889; *Macon Telegraph*, May 25, 1889 (lingering).

days of the 1877 constitutional convention brought religion to the fore. He did not set out for the 1877 constitutional convention to be his coming out, but that is what happened. Mainly as a result of that controversy, later biographical sketches often identified Hill as either an atheist or an agnostic. For example, in 1980, when Georgia finally elected its second Republican senator, an Associated Press story recounted the first Republican senator's staunch Unionism and then added somewhat incredulously: "Moreover, Hill was an atheist. But somehow, he managed to retain the respect and the admiration, perhaps grudging, of his fellow Georgians." It is difficult to ascertain if Hill was a full-fledged atheist or whether "agnostic" would be more precise. Either way, there is no doubt that he fully rejected the concept of there being an activist deity who regularly intervenes in the course of human events in response to prayer. Unquestionably, by the time of his post-senatorial years, Joshua Hill had become nonorthodox, ecumenical, and secular.[17]

Joshua Hill, like virtually all Southern White people of his generation, grew up in a strongly religious household, and the author has been found no evidence to indicate that he rebelled against the church as a young man. Many of Joshua Hill's close associates, such as Nathaniel Greene Foster, were clergy or active church members. An up-and-coming young lawyer would, of course, endeavor to fit in with the civic religion of his community. In 1851, shortly after he relocated to Madison, Hill was on the committee that drew up the incorporation papers for Madison's Advent Episcopal Church. In fact, the document appears to be in his handwriting, so it is likely that he did the legal work. Hill was listed as one of the members of the congregation's original board of vestrymen, but church records indicate no further involvement.[18]

---

[17] *Atlanta Constitution*, November 10, 1980 (AP); Knight, *Georgia's Landmarks*, 2:805, described Hill as "strongly inclined toward agnosticism." Northern, *Men of Mark in Georgia*, 3:75, called Hill "an open theist, of the agnostic order." "Open theist" is an odd construction, which makes one speculate that the phrase was edited from "atheist" to be softer. Allen and Malone, *Dictionary of American Biography*, 5:42–43, used "atheist." Mellichamp, *Senators from Georgia*, 151, used "atheist," drawing from older accounts.

[18] Superior Court of Morgan Co., Georgia, September Session, 1851. The original document is in the possession of the Episcopal Church of the Advent in

Hill lost a son in the bloody war he so bitterly opposed, and he observed his neighbors pray in vain for Confederate victory. While he was still in the Senate and for several years afterward, a series of serious illnesses plagued his wife, Emily. Two more of his sons died in 1875 and 1876 respectively, and the last succumbed to alcoholism. All of this would have been fresh in the Madisonian's mind when circumstances led him to pour out his private religious views in the very public setting of the 1877 Georgia State Constitutional Convention. The controversial episode had nothing to do with the substance of the document—yet it spoke volumes about Joshua Hill.

On the second day of the convention, just before he called upon a delegate to open the session with a prayer, President Jenkins declared, "I have no doubt that it will be the pleasure of this convention to appoint a chaplain." Jenkins was wrong. Expecting no opposition, Lucius J. Gartrell, who had served in the House of Representatives with Hill before the war, offered a resolution to appoint a paid chaplain. Hill immediately rose to move to table Gartrell's resolution. The former representative and senator explained that he recalled from his days in Washington that few members ever paid much attention to the opening prayer even though the chaplain was often a distinguished cleric; therefore, he saw "no reason why the state of Georgia should pay for" an official clergyman. Several delegates argued in response that having a paid chaplain for such bodies was routine and that Georgia should follow suit. Hill replied that there were several delegates who were "preachers of distinction" who would be happy to pray for free. It appeared on the surface that Hill was merely taking a parsimonious approach toward governmental expenditures. In this spirit Hill's motion to table passed 100 to 60, and the agenda of the second day moved forward.[19]

Following a period of routine business, the ardent proponents of appointing an official paid Christian chaplain tried again, forcing Hill to reveal his true motive. Hill's opposition to the chaplaincy was not just about saving money—it was about the very nature of prayer itself: "I might as well be frank and say that I am opposed on principle to the appointment

Madison. The author thanks Richard Simmons, long-time Church of the Advent historian, for carefully reviewing nineteenth-century congregational records for mention of Hill.

[19] *Proceedings 1877*, 11–12.

of a chaplain to bodies of this sort." He asked rhetorically, "Why is it necessary to have these sessions daily opened with prayer?" Then Hill spoke the words that challenged the prevailing belief and practice of public prayer: "I believe with the great Napoleon Bonaparte, who said that *prayer never won a battle* but that success was with those who had the heaviest artillery." The remark "brought down the house" and hit the next day's press. Hill then went further. He had no objection to a man who prayed "in his closet," but he did "object to this formality, this advertising that we start out as a devout body of men." The delegates knew their King James Bible, so they would have fully understood the intent and relevance of Hill's reference to the occasion when Jesus of Nazareth admonished men not to pray aloud in the temple where "they may be seen" but rather "when thou prayest, enter into thy closet" (Matt 6:5-6).[20]

After some discussion, a compromise resolution passed. There would be no paid chaplain, but the presiding officer would call upon a delegate with ministerial credentials to open each morning with prayer. Hill offered no further objections. The compromise satisfied the plea of one frustrated delegate who had cried to appreciative clapping, "I want prayer, I don't care who offers it."[21]

The normal business of the second day resumed, but the prayer issue would not go away. The discussions about the appointment of a paid chaplain caused, in the words of one reporter, "a good deal of excitement among some few of the faithful, who were greatly scandalized by the defeat of the measure." As soon as the third day's opening proceedings concluded, including a prayer delivered by a volunteer delegate, Judge A. R. Wright of Rome rose to move reconsideration of the compromise reached the previous day. This time the debate raged with more intensity. Wright, who like Hill had been an emissary in General William T. Sherman's efforts to remove Georgia from the Civil War, began with courteous words of "high respect" for his colleague and then declared, "When he says that he doubts that anything is accomplished by prayer, it is his doubt and not that of this assembly." Protesting at least twice, "I do not care to discuss this question at length," the judge nevertheless continued to argue at length that the

---

[20] Ibid., 20–22 (emphasis added); *Atlanta Constitution*, July 13, 1877 (brought).

[21] *Proceedings 1877*, 22.

American union and its states were "Christian governments...founded upon the precept of Moses." Advocating the controversial doctrine of what is today known as Christian Nationalism, Wright implored the delegates to make it clear "that this is to be a Christian, and not a heathen, government." Presuming a civic consensus that few men other than Joshua Hill were brave enough publicly to dispute, Wright asserted, "Every representative here agrees with me that our government is a Christian government and is founded upon the principles of the Christian religion.... Although some of us may not think that the prayers will reach to heaven and bring down a blessing, still let us have them." He ended by urging delegates "to follow in the footsteps of our fathers."[22]

In his reply to Wright, the secular Madisonian revealed even more of his personal feelings. He declared that his feelings were "liberal toward all sects of men" and reminded the convention that Georgians represented numerous different Protestant denominations as well as Jews. Hill opposed "the employment of one of them to the exclusion of all others" and added, "*If that be irreligious, then I am irreligious.*" Wright had urged the delegates "to follow in the footsteps of our fathers." Hill had that phrase clearly in mind when he explained that his own father had been a "Hard-shell" Baptist but that he had taught his son "to keep church spirit separate from the other affairs of society." Accordingly, Hill proclaimed that it seemed to him "that in this matter of forming a secular government for civil purposes, this convention does well to keep itself distinct from all religious alliances." Turning to the religious thoughts of the Founding Fathers (as all arguments of this sort tend to do), Hill extolled the ecumenicalism of Charles Carroll, the staunch Roman Catholic from Maryland, and urged Judge Wright to recall that that Thomas Jefferson "was not very rigid in his religious views."[23]

As to the efficacy of prayer, the former senator needled Judge Wright by turning his arguments around on him. In Wright's zeal to refute Napoleon's dictum that large armies were more powerful than prayer, he cited the example of a recent Turkish victory in a battle against Christian forces of greater might. Hill cheekily reminded Wright that if prayer worked for the Turks, then it must work for infidels (Muslims) as well as for

---

[22] Ibid.; *Augusta Chronicle*, July 14, 1877 (caused).

[23] *Proceedings 1877*, 19–22.

Christians. It was obvious without Hill explicitly saying it that there would be no Islamic prayers delivered at Georgia's convention. (Incidentally, it turned out that the stronger forces eventually won that war.) When it came to America's Civil War, Hill's remarks hit closer to home. The success of Confederate armies, Hill recalled for the delegates, "was the constant burden of the people's prayers for years and its failure is a theme of constant lamentation throughout this section of the country." If Judge Wright's logic was correct, Hill boldly advanced, either the Confederacy "was wrong, or Divine aid would have been given to it." Hill then proceeded to validate Napoleon's dictum by attributing Northern victory to the large and well-supplied Union army under the leadership of generals Sherman and Grant. Such an argument for the futility of intercessory prayer was not a tack that a man who coveted future elective office in Georgia would have taken.[24]

In response to the charge that he was irreligious, Hill professed a spiritual ecumenicalism of the broadest sort: "I devote more time to the study of religion than a majority of men professing a faith do. If my communion is with nature and in her grooves and solitudes I seek to know my Creator, it is not in keeping to call me an irreligious man." His toleration of religious diversity was expansive, including even Islam: "Look at that beautiful pattern of devotion, the Mohammedan, who with his face turned toward Mecca, three times a day, utters his aspirations to God.... He may be wrong in his faith, but he is not irreligious." Hill concluded his refutation of Judge Wright's speech by pledging that if he "could call down the choicest blessings of Heaven upon my country, it would be that God should forever keep it free from religious bigotry and intolerance."[25]

The intense Hill-Wright confrontation became the story of the hour in the Georgia press. The dispatch from the Atlanta reporter of the *Savannah Morning News* described Wright's remarks as "severe, but good tempered" and then added that Joshua Hill "replied in a masterly and scorching vindication of religious toleration." "A RUNNING DEBATE ON THE EFFICACY OF PRAYER" proclaimed the headline in the *Atlanta Constitution*. As would be expected, much of the reaction was highly critical of Hill's position. In possibly the most bitter attack, a Sandersville editor extolled

---

[24] Ibid.

[25] Ibid.

prayer, quoted scripture, and proclaimed, "Joshua Hill, and those of his ilk, are in error—yea, are in battle array against the experience of the religious world, the providence and revelations of God, and have allied themselves with [unclear name] and other scoffing infidels." Not content to tag the ex-senator as an ally of infidels, the writer went on to employ the epithets of Reconstruction, charging that Hill had "during the last several years, shown signs of either mental aberration or moral blindness by his overweaning anxiety to affiliate with the carpet-baggers and scallawags who have devastated the South." It pained the writer deeply that so many delegates had sustained Hill's argument.[26]

Several Georgia journalists supported Hill's contention that there should be no official paid chaplain, but they did so cautiously and carefully. Some limited their agreement to the point that voluntary prayer was preferable to paying an official chaplain. Some agreed on the grounds of religious pluralism that no chaplain representing a single denomination should be hired. Others asserted that the whole effort on behalf of appointing a paid chaplain stemmed from the schemes of a few delegates who had a particular person in mind for the sinecure. But no in-state writer was so bold as to defend Hill's rejection of the efficacy of prayer on principle. For example, the editorialist of the *Augusta Chronicle* clarified that the convention had not banned prayer; it had "simply declined to employ a chaplain at a regular salary." The editor assured his readers, "We believe as much as any one does in the efficacy of prayer." Henry W. Grady, who covered the convention for several papers, quipped, "The day they met they declared themselves independent of the United States Government. The second day they declared themselves independent of the Governor.... The third day they declared themselves independent of God Almighty by refusing to appoint a chaplain."[27]

The national press also took notice of the Georgia convention's debate about prayer. A Memphis writer saw the choice to use volunteer rather than paid preachers as good evidence of economy in government and acknowledged Hill's point that legislators often pay little attention to the

---

[26] Ibid.; *Savannah Morning News*, July 14, 1877; *Atlanta Constitution*, July 17, 1877; *Macon Telegraph*, July 13, 1877; *Sandersville Herald & Georgian*, July 19, 1877.

[27] Nixon, *Henry W. Grady*, 144.

day's invocation, but he still concluded that those were not good enough reasons to abolish the practice. To the contrary, the paper argued, "more praying is needed." On the other hand, much out-of-state commentary tended to favor Hill's position. A Philadelphia publication called legislative prayers "a sacrilegious farce." On two occasions the *New York Times* printed several paragraphs of Hill's remarks, including his reference to Napoleon's dictum on prayer and armies. An Indiana paper commented on Hill's reasons for opposing an official chaplain and noted, "It does not necessarily follow that the ex-Senator is a heathen." A column that appeared in several papers celebrated Hill for striking a blow "at one of the time-honored superstitions of American politics." The author decried that "Atheists, Jews, Catholics and Quakers" could not "escape the regulation prayer with which our legislative proceedings are invariably opened.... To everybody except the Protestant Church members, the appearance of the chaplain is simply an insult." Delegate Hill, the column concluded, "showed much more reverence for religion in objecting to official chaplains than is usually shown by the supporters of the chaplains." The writer hoped that Hill's "good example might find many imitators." The *American Israelite* approvingly published a letter from a Rome, Georgia, writer (presumedly Jewish) who wrote of Hill, "Noble words nobly uttered. If all our statemen and lawmakers were animated by the same patriotic sentiments, religious intolerance would never stain the pages of our country's history, nor mar the glory of her free institutions."[28]

Knowing that daily prayers delivered by a fellow delegate were going to continue regardless of whether the convention appointed an official chaplain, the delegates just wanted to get on with other business. Thus, Judge Wright's motion to reconsider was tabled by a vote of 101 to 64. Hill

---

[28] *Augusta Chronicle*, July 14 (simply), 18, 1877; *Macon Telegraph*, July 15, 1877; *Columbus Enquirer*, July 15, 1877; *Columbus Times*, July 15, 1877; *Savannah Morning News*, July 16, 1877; *Meriwether County Vindicator* (Greenville), July 20, 1877; Nixon, *Henry W. Grady*, 144; *Memphis Evening Herald*, July 24, 1877 (mistakenly wrote "Ben" Hill but clearly meant Joshua); *(Jefferson, GA) Forest News*, September 29, 1877 (*Philadelphia Public Record*); *New York Times*, July 14, 17 (Turks, lamentation) 1877; *Cincinnati Commercial Tribune*, July 20, 1877 (Turks); *Fort Wayne Gazette*, July 25, 1877; *St. Louis Globe-Democrat*, July 22, 1877, and *Princeton (Minnesota) Union*, August 3, 1877 (at one); *(Cincinnati) American Israelite*, July 27, 1877.

prevailed on the specific minor point of opposing a paid chaplain, but it is doubtful that he changed many minds about the efficacy of prayer.[29]

Hill's secular and ecumenical philosophy also emerged on other issues, but they attracted considerably less attention compared to his pronouncements on the efficacy of prayer and its place in the public forum. He supported inclusion of a Bill of Rights provision that would prevent the state from funding religious institutions. Georgia's wording tracked closely to the wave of so-called Blaine Amendments, named for Republican James G. Blaine, who had unsuccessfully proposed a similar provision for the US Constitution. Georgia became one of the sixteen states that inserted similar provisions in their state constitutions after 1875. The Blaine Amendment movement derived from an uneasy mix of Protestant anti-Catholicism and freethinking agnosticism. Hill, like Blaine and even Grant, believed that church property should be taxed like any other asset or at least that any religious tax exemption be limited so that it would cover only the most basic house of worship. His proposal to that effect gained little traction in the convention. Regarding freedom of worship and assurances that no religious test could be required for public office, Hill worked with like-minded delegates to tweak language to ensure that protections included in previous state constitutions would be carried over and strengthened in 1877.[30]

The mid-1870s fell at the beginning of the Golden Age of Freethought, and it seems that Hill had absorbed some of its attributes. Unfortunately, neither a record of his personal periodical subscriptions nor a full inventory of the contents of his home library survives to reveal what specific influences shaped his thoughts. Some insight can be derived, however, from the books that he willed to his son-in-law Abbo Foster. The bequest included the eight-volume Library of Choice Literature, a collection of Shakespeare, and a work by Charles Lamb, a British author whose life and writings, including poetry, reflected struggles with religious belief. The secularly inclined former senator unquestionably knew of the reputation of Robert Ingersoll, if only from the famous agnostic's nomination of Senator James G. Blaine (R-ME) at the 1876 Republican National Convention.

---

[29] *Proceedings 1877*, 20–22.

[30] Ibid., 83–84; *Columbus Times*, August 9, 1877; *Atlanta Constitution*, July 31, 1877; Jacoby, *Freethinkers*, 166.

Ingersoll's open agnosticism kept him from significant political appointment, despite his fame. Perhaps Hill knew of *Truth Seeker* magazine, which, according to freethought historian Susan Jacoby, brought discourse to "'village atheists' in small towns, particularly in the South, where religious unorthodoxy could lead to social ostracism or worse." Hill strongly advocated for the strict separation of church and state, which Jacoby identified as the unifying principle of the late-nineteenth-century freethought movement.[31]

In 1879 Joshua Hill wrote a revealing poem titled "Without a Creed." By this time, Joshua and Emily had suffered the loss of their youngest son Walter, whose gruesome death came just a few months after the close of the constitutional convention in 1877. The poem rejects traditional Christianity and confronts the reality of the poet's own inevitable demise. Although many of the lines are dedicated to specific instructions about how he wished to be buried and remembered, the most revealing stanzas reflect Hill's distinct agnosticism:

> The doubts and hopes that fill my breast
> Vainly I've sought to solve in Christian Creeds!
> Content I am to think at last
> That man's only merit consists in deeds.
> I know not where power resides,
> I know not in whom rests supreme control;
> I know not where man's soul abides,
> Nor am I certain that man has a soul

The brooding poem remained private until after the ex-senator's death in 1891 when the *Madisonian* published it, and at least one other Georgia paper reprinted it. With no copy in his hand surviving, the certainty of Hill's authorship cannot be unconditionally confirmed, but the words ring authentic. Given Hill's prominence and the widespread local knowledge of his secular philosophy, it is highly unlikely that the *Madisonian* would have ventured to print the poem unless it had been handed to the editor directly by a family member who attested to its authorship. The authenticity of the

---

[31] Last Will and Testament of Joshua Hill, Clause 3, September 28, 1889, copy in Hill File, MCA; Jacoby, *Freethinkers*, 149–57; Wright, "The Religious Opinions of Charles Lamb," 641–47.

poem is further confirmed by the internal consistency of the lines with Hill's personality and his public statements at the 1877 Georgia State Constitutional Convention. The *Madisonian*'s headnote to the poem read, "The following lines were written Sunday, Feb. 23, 1879, in view of death by the late Joshua Hill, US Senator from Georgia." The publication of "Without a Creed" upon Hill's death in 1891 entrenched his reputation as a religious doubter. The *Atlanta Constitution* printed the poem with the following header: "Twelve years ago, when the late Hon. Joshua Hill, of Madison, was ill, and expecting to die, he wrote the following agnostic lines." In 1938, five weeks before Hill's daughter Belle Knight died, the *Madisonian* reprinted the poem and followed it with an explanatory note, which was clearly intended as a defense of the local hero's character despite his unorthodox, creedless philosophy:

> Note: Mr. Hill was honorable and just in his dealings with all. He was a true friend, in helpfulness, the hospitality of his home was known by all who entered it. He was a true friend to Madison, Morgan County, in his helpfulness, in her moral, intellectual, and material development.[32]

WITHOUT A CREED
by Joshua Hill (1879)

When death shall claim me for his own,
    And of this world I cease to be a part,
To those I love I would make known
    The oft expressed desire of my heart.

When well assured that I do sleep
    The peaceful slumber that knows no waking,

[32] *Macon Telegraph*, March 30, 1891; *Atlanta Constitution*, April 1, 1891; *Madisonian*, July 1, 1938. The author used grammerly.com to scan the poem and detected no plagiarism. Hill's daughter Isabelle Hill Knight died on August 8, 1938, five weeks after the reprint. Her lingering terminal illness may have inspired the paper to run the poem when it did. Reprinting the poem while Hill's daughters Belle and Louise were still alive further attests to the authenticity of Hill's authorship.

Then no longer my body keep,
  To allow of idle, empty leave taking.

Apparel, such as now I wear,
  Plain and modest, avoiding all display,
Clothe me with, but let me cease to hear
  A gem or jewel, when I am laid away.

Without lesson, prayer or song
  Bear me to my appointed resting place,
In profoundest stillness—Earth's throng
  Will neither miss nor mourn my absent face.

I ask no monumental stone
  To proclaim and magnify my poor worth,
But something simple, meant alone
  To tell the story of my death and birth.

The doubts and hopes that fill my breast
  Vainly I've sought to solve in Christian Creeds!
Content I am to think at last
  That man's only merit consists in deeds.

I know not where power resides,
  I know not in whom rests supreme control;
I know not where man's soul abides,
  Nor am I certain that man has a soul.

If to reverence Nature be a test
  Of man's devotion to creative power,
Then should I feel supremely blest,
  Nor fear to meet the inevitable hour.

Go hence: I know not whether
  To bright scenes of bliss or dark cares of Woe:
Or, it may be that to neither,
  Nor elsewhere, that I am destined to go.

Without a creed I leave the world,
  Wholly ignorant of a future state:
Like a ship with sails unfurled
  I leave the shore; my only pilot, Fate.

The Death of Joshua Hill

One day in early 1888 when he was in Atlanta and in good spirits, Joshua Hill told a newspaperman, "I feel splendidly, and am in fine health, but I am not as young as I was many years before the war, when [a friend] and myself ran down a passenger train in Washington that had forty yards the start of us." Later that year he regaled a party of young men at the Kimball Hotel with stories of the 1863 gubernatorial campaign. When asked about current events, Hill was reported to have remarked that hypocrisy was "the prevailing evil of the day." At that time, Hill was still active in real estate and was in the process of subdividing and selling his property in Shady Dale, the tiny village southwest of Madison where he had presented his first political oration some fifty years before. Later that year, lawyer Hill went before the railroad commissioners in Atlanta to argue that the regulators should mandate that the Macon & Covington Railroad Co. continue to maintain a depot in Shady Dale near his property. In very early 1889, Hill sold for a nice gain the last part of a plot he had held for many years along Connecticut Avenue near DuPont Circle in Washington, DC.[33]

Those may have been the Madisonian's last trips to the state capital and some of his final business dealings. Emily died later in 1889, and soon Joshua was in severe decline. The death of his wife of fifty-plus years, one death notice explained, "was a great shock from which he never fully recovered." By early spring 1890, Joshua was confined to home. Reports were that "his death is daily expected," but he lingered for nearly a year more. He lived long enough to receive a string of visitors and to witness Anna's remarriage. As the end neared and Joshua Hill's faculties declined, the family prepared guardianship papers, but he died before they were needed. He left an estate of real estate, stock, and cash variously estimated at from

[33] *Macon Telegraph*, February 7, May 22, 1888; *Atlanta Constitution*, September 26, 27, 1888; *(DC) Evening Star*, February 6, 1889.

$250,000 to "at least" $500,000 (about $7.5 million to $15 million in 2023 dollars).[34]

Death came to the seventy-nine-year-old former senator at home with family gathered around on March 6, 1891—just over twenty years after he took his seat as Georgia's first Republican senator and almost thirty-five years after he entered Congress as a freshman in 1857. The *Augusta Chronicle*'s final assessment was consistent with the sentiments it had printed so many times over the previous thirty-five years: "Mr. Hill maintained the confidence and respect of the people of Georgia in spite of his politics. He was Republican, but an honest man and a conservative one." The *New York Times* echoed that evaluation writing that Hill had been "the one prominent Southern man who, becoming a Republican, commanded the devotion and admiration of his old Democratic friends to the last." One of those "old Democratic friends" spoke about his departed colleague. Lucious J. Gartrell and Hill's relationship went back to the late 1850s when they served together in the US House of Representatives. Their paths crossed again as delegates at the 1877 constitutional convention, where they butted heads over the chaplaincy controversy. Gartrell recounted the tense days of January 1861 when he and all his colleagues except Joshua Hill renounced the Union and joined the Confederacy. The former Confederate general told the *Atlanta Constitution*, "Between him and the other Georgians in congress there was no personal ill-feeling whatever. He was a perfect gentleman, of inflexible honesty, and of very decided opinions and great will power. He was conscientiously opposed to secession. It was a matter of principle with him." The committee of local lawyers who memorialized their elder colleague concluded, "Were we called on to designate his most prominent characteristics, we would say, love of home, justice, nature and uncompromising courage of his convictions."[35]

---

[34] *Augusta Chronicle*, March 2, April 5 (his death), 1890; March 7, 1891; *(DC) Evening Star*, April 9, 1890; *Macon Telegraph*, April 5, 1890; *Atlanta Constitution*, March 7, 1891 (was a great) 1890; *Savannah Morning News*, June 1, 1891; Northern, *Men of Mark*, 75 (at least). Guardianship, will, and other documents in the Joshua Hill estate file, MCA.

[35] *Augusta Chronicle*, March 8, 1891; *New York Times*, March 7, 1891; *Atlanta Constitution*, March 7, 1891 (Gartrell); Hill bar memorial; see *Washington Post*, March 7, 1891; *Chicago Tribune*, March 7, 11, 1891; Boston *Globe*, March 7, 1891;

The fifth stanza of Hill's "Without a Creed" reads:

I ask no monumental stone
    To proclaim and magnify my poor worth,
But something simple, meant alone
    To tell the story of my death and birth.

As he wished, engraved on the simple slab over Joshua Hill's body in Madison's Old Cemetery are the basic facts of birth, marriage, death, and public service followed by this succinct epitaph:

"A STAUNCH SOUTHERN FRIEND OF THE UNION"

Boston Herald, March 7, 1891; *New York Tribune*, March 9, 1891; *Baltimore Sun*, March 9, 1891; *New Orleans Item*, March 7, 1891; *New Orleans Times-Picayune*, March 7, 1891. Coincidentally, Thomas Hardeman, who had served alongside Hill and Gartrell in January 1861, died the day after Hill (*Milledgeville Union-Recorder*, March 10, 1891). On estate value: *Columbus Enquirer*, May 30, 1891, and Hill file at MCA. Current dollar equivalents prior to the establishment of Federal Reserve data in 1913 are somewhat unreliable. The estimate herein comes from www.officialdata.org/us/inflation/1891? (accessed July 19, 2024).

Afterword and Acknowledgments

As a retired history professor newly moved to Madison in late 2010, I soon heard the legends about how Joshua Hill's Unionist sympathies saved the town "too pretty to burn" from the torches of General Sherman's troops on their March to the Sea. Immediately, I sensed that the story had to be more complicated than that, so I set out to find out. I got involved with the Madison-Morgan Cultural Center, met the owners who were expanding and restoring the Joshua Hill house, got to know local archivist Woody Williams, and went to work.

My first step was to help organize a Cultural Center symposium to commemorate the 150th anniversary of the days that the Union "March to the Sea" passed through Morgan County in November 1864. By then I was hooked; I wanted to know everything that there was to know about Hill and the politics of his era. For the next ten years, Joshua Hill often took a back seat to my other civic, history, and business activities and to travels with my wife, Deneice, but I always came back to ol' Josh until I finally got it done. Deneice was the happiest of all when the completed manuscript went off to Marc Jolley and his very supportive staff at Mercer University Press.

From the earliest stages of this project, the staff and volunteers at the Morgan County Archives were unfailingly helpful and unflaggingly encouraging. The legendary archives founder Marshall "Woody" Williams, now a still-alert 101, told me stories and pointed me to sources. His daughter-in-law Linda Williams carried Woody's archival work and was extremely helpful to me. Most dedicated to making sure that I left no stone unturned were Terry Tatum and Patsy Harris. They constantly kept their eyes out for helpful sources, and their persistence with potential document donors resulted in my access to invaluable letters not available when I began.

Steve Schaefer, the now-retired director of the Azalea Regional Library System (formerly Uncle Remus), helped me even before he knew me by building an exemplary organization and spearheading the creation of the library system's invaluable online repository of regional newspapers. Steve is a Lincoln bibliophile who brought his knowledge of the period to the fore as he read and deftly critiqued drafts of every chapter of this book. The current staff of the Morgan County Library were always supportive as they processed dozens upon dozens of interlibrary loans for me from the Georgia PINES network and other libraries.

Fellow academic and public historians living in Madison (James "Trae" Welborn, Glenn Eskew, Steve Huggins, and Ken Kocher) served as my colleagues down the hall by reading parts of the manuscript, pointing me toward important documents and secondary works, and being steadily supportive. Dear friend and distinguished historian Hardy Jackson kept telling me to keep at it. Madisonians Stratton Hicky, Jan Manos, Richard Simpson, Joe Smith, Frank Walsh, and Christine Watts provided key help along the way. Hill descendant Christina Wood-Smith filled me in about her family's genealogy and history. Suggestions from David Worley and Heather Cousins improved my prose. Historians Lee Ann Caldwell, James C. Cobb, George Coletti, Robert S. Davis, Edward Hatfield, Robert D. Jenkins Sr., Brian Melton, and Noah Trudeau offered advice and direction on various specifics along the way. In addition, the staff at the traditional archives I visited in person were always professional and welcoming. Finally, an impersonal but very sincere thank you is due to the myriad archivists, programmers, technicians, and institutional leaders who have made online research a twenty-first-century reality for this old historian, who cut his teeth in the era of typewriters, microfilm readers, and very literal cut and paste.

The suggestions and encouragements from these wonderful people and more were theirs; the responsibility and any errors are mine.

Note on Sources, Abbreviations, and Selected Bibliography

Note on Sources

Joshua Hill left no collection of personal papers. Neither did he keep a journal nor author a memoir. Indeed, immediately upon his death, the committee of the local bar association which memorialized the former senator "regretted...that he failed to put on record his many memories" (Hill file, Morgan County Archives). Historians are attracted to troves of personal papers, and the lack thereof in the case of Hill may explain why no previous biographer has undertaken a full study of Georgia's leading Unionist and first Republican senator.

Advances in twenty-first-century computer technology have greatly facilitated the search for and the access to evidence about Joshua Hill in the archival collections of other figures, government documents, journals, books, and, most important for this study, contemporary newspapers. Fittingly, the occasion of the death of Joshua Hill and another influential Georgian inspired an appeal in the *Atlanta Constitution* (April 19, 1891) for old newspapers to be preserved for posterity. "The files of old Georgia newspapers are the sources to look for facts worthy of being preserved, but where are they?" The writer asked and answered: "Either lost, destroyed or inaccessible from some cause." He urged the state library to rescue them "from oblivion" and to bind as many as it can obtain "for the future historian." That is exactly what the online collection of Georgia Historic Newspapers project of the Digital Library of Georgia has accomplished—virtual binding. Also important to this study were the regional newspaper collection of the Azalea Regional Library of the Georgia PINES System, Newspapers.com, and the Chronicling America collection of the Library of Congress. Moreover, thanks to hathitrust.org, internetarchives.org, books.google.com, catalog.archives.gov, and various genealogy services (ancestry.com, fold3.com, findagrave.com), it is possible to access books, documents, and ephemera that would otherwise have required physical trips to dozens and dozens of individual libraries and archives. Without these online resources, the present work could not have been nearly so comprehensive. The words of contemporary politicians, editors, reporters, soldiers, and ordinary people bring the period to life.

Abbreviations

Journals

AHR	*American Historical Review*
GHQ	*Georgia Historical Quarterly*
JAH	*Journal of American History*
JSH	*Journal of Southern History*

Archives

HRBML	Hargrett Rare Book and Manuscript Library, University of Georgia, Athens
MCA	Morgan County Archives

Newspapers in footnotes: For consistency, the various iterations in newspaper titles are cited in footnotes by the common and consistent key word used over time, e.g. *Constitution*, *Telegraph*, *Chronicle.*

Selected Bibliography

Books: Georgia-specific

Andrews, Eliza Frances. *The War-Time Journal of a Georgia Girl, 1864–66.* New York: D. Appleton & Co., 1903. Reprint, Orlando: 2023.

Andrews, J. Cutler. *The North Reports the Civil War.* Pittsburgh: University of Pittsburgh Press, 1955.

Angell, Stephen Ward. *Bishop Henry McNeal Turner and African-American Religion in the South.* Knoxville: University of Tennessee Press, 1992.

Avery, I. W. *The History of the State of Georgia from 1850 to 1881.* New York: Brown & Derby Publishers, 1881. Facsimile reprint, New York: AMS Press Inc. 1972.

Bailey, Anne J. *War and Ruin: William Tecumseh Sherman and the Savannah Campaign.* Lanham, MD: Rowman & Littlefield, 2002.

Bonds, Russell S. *Stealing the General : The Great Locomotive Chase and the First Medal of Honor.* Yardley, PA: Westholme, 2007.

Bryan, T. Conn. *Confederate Georgia.* Athens: University of Georgia Press, 1953, 1964.

Bryant, Jonathan M. *How Curious a Land: Conflict and Change in Greene County, Georgia, 1850–1885.* Chapel Hill: University of North Carolina Press, 1996.

Carey, Anthony Gene. *Parties, Slavery, and the Union in Antebellum Georgia.* Athens: University of Georgia Press, 1997.

Cashin, Edward J. *The Story of Augusta.* Augusta: Richmond County Board of Education, 1980.

Castel, Albert. *Decision in the West: The Atlanta Campaign of 1864.* Lawrence: University of Kansas Press, 1992.

Caudill, Edward, and Paul Ashdown. *Sherman's March in Myth and Memory.* Lanham, MD: Rowman & Littlefield Publishers, Inc., 2008.

Cimbala, Paul A. *Under the Guardianship of the Nation: The Freedmen's Bureau and the Reconstruction of Georgia, 1865–1870.* Athens: University of Georgia Press, 1997.

Clark, E. Culpepper. *The Birth of a New South: Sherman, Grady, and the Making of Atlanta.* Macon: Mercer University Press, 2021.

Clayton, Sarah "Sallie" Conley. *Requiem for a Lost City: A Memoir of Civil War Atlanta and the Old South.* Edited by Robert S. Davis Jr. Macon: Mercer University Press, 1999.

Coleman, Kenneth, ed. *A History of Georgia.* 2nd ed. Athens: University of Georgia Press, 1991.

Conway, Alan. *Reconstruction of Georgia.* Minneapolis: University of Minnesota Press, 1966.

Cooper, Walter G. *The Story of Georgia.* New York: American Historical Society, 1938.

Currie-McDaniel, Ruth. *Carpetbagger of Conscience: A Biography of John Emory Bryant.* New York: Fordham University Press, 1999. Revised from the 1987 original published by the University of Georgia Press.

Davis, Burke. *Sherman's March.* New York: Random House, 1980.

Davis, Harold E. *Henry Grady's New South: Atlanta, a Brave and Beautiful City.* Tuscaloosa: University of Alabama Press, 1990.

Davis, Stephen. *All the Fighting They Want.* El Dorado Hills, CA: Savas Beatie, 2017.

———. *Into Tennessee & Failure: John Bell Hood.* Macon: Mercer University Press, 2020.

———. *Texas Brigadier to the Fall of Atlanta: John Bell Hood.* Macon: Mercer University Press, 2019.

———. *What the Yankees Did to Us: Sherman's Bombardment and Wrecking of Atlanta.* Macon: Mercer University Press, 2012.

Davis, William C. *The Union that Shaped the Confederacy: Robert Toombs and Alexander H. Stephens.* Lawrence: University Press of Kansas, 2001.

DeBats, Donald A. *Elites and Masses: Political Structure, Communication, and Behavior in Ante-Bellum Georgia.* New York: Garland Publishing Co., 1990.

Dickey, J. D. *Rising in Flames.* New York: Pegasus Books, 2018.

Drago, Edmund L. *Black Politicians and Reconstruction in Georgia: A Splendid Failure.* Athens: University of Georgia Press, 1992.

Duncan, Russell. *Entrepreneur for Equality: Gov. Rufus Bullock, Commerce, and Race in Post-Civil War Georgia.* Athens: University of Georgia Press, 1994.

Dunkelman, Mark H. *Marching with Sherman: Through Georgia and the Carolinas with the 154th New York.* Baton Rouge: Louisiana State University Press, 2012.

Dyer, Thomas G. *Secret Yankees: The Union Circle in Confederate Atlanta.* Baltimore: Johns Hopkins University Press, 1999.

Eckert, Ralph Lowell. *John Brown Gordon: Soldier-Southerner-American.* Baton Rouge: Louisiana State University Press, 1989.

Evans, Clement A., ed. *Confederate Military History: A Library of Confederate States History.* Vol. 6. Atlanta: Confederate Publishing Co., 1899.

Evans, David. *Sherman's Horsemen: Union Cavalry Operation in the Atlanta Campaign.* Bloomington: Indiana University Press, 1996.

Flippen, Percy S. *Herschel V. Johnson of Georgia: State Rights Unionist.* Richmond: Dietz Printing Co., 1931. https://catalog.hathitrust.org/Record/000197519.

Fowler, John D., and David B. Parker, eds. *Breaking the Heartland: The Civil War in Georgia.* Macon: Mercer University Press, 2011.

Fraser, Walter J., Jr. *Savannah in the New South: From the Civil War to the Twenty-First Century.* Columbia: University of South Carolina Press, 2018.

Freehling, William W., and Craig M. Simpson, eds. *Secession Debated: Georgia's Showdown.* New York: Oxford University Press, 1992.

Gagnon, Michael J. *Transition to an Industrial South: Athens, Georgia, 1830–1870.* Baton Rouge: Louisiana State University Press, 2012.

Grant, Donald L. *The Way It Was in the South: The Black Experience in Georgia.* New York: Carol Publishing Group, 1993.

Hahn, Steven. *The Roots of Southern Populism: Yeoman Farmers and the Transformation of the Georgia Upcountry: 1850–1890.* New York: Oxford University Press, 2006.

Harris, Bonnie P. *The Confederate Hospitals of Madison, GA: Their Records and Histories 1861–1865.* Buckhead, GA: by the author, 2014.

Hays, Louis Frederick. *History of Macon County Georgia.* 1933. Spartanburg: The Reprint Co., 1993.

Head, Sylvia Gailey, and Elizabeth W. Etheridge. *The Neighborhood Mint: Dahlonega in the Age of Jackson.* Macon: Mercer University Press, 1986.

Hebert, Keith S. *The Long Civil War in the North Georgia Mountains: Confederate Nationalism, Sectionalism, and White Supremacy in Bartow County, Georgia.* Knoxville: University of Tennessee Press, 2017.

Hicky, Hattie Mina Reid. *Madison, Georgia, and Her Homes: As It Was Told to Me.* Atlanta: United Writers Press, 2011.

Hicky, Louise McHenry. *Rambles through Morgan County, Georgia.* Madison: Morgan County Historical Society, 1971; reprint Walton Press Inc., Monroe, Ga., 1989.

Hill, Louise B. *Joseph E. Brown and the Confederacy.* Chapel Hill: University of North Carolina Press, 1939.

Hills, Tommy. *Red State Rising: Triumph of the Republican Party in Georgia.* Macon: Stroud & Hall Publishers, 2009.

Hodler, Thomas W., and Howard A. Schretter. *The Atlas of Georgia.* Athens: University of Georgia Institute of Community and Area Development, 1986.

Hoehling, A. A. *Last Train from Atlanta.* New York: Thomas Yoseloff, 1958.

Inscoe, John C., ed. *Georgia in Black & White: Explorations in the Race Relations of a Southern State, 1865–1950.* Athens: University of Georgia Press, 1994.

———, and Robert C. Kenzer, eds. *Enemies of the Country: New Perspectives on Unionists in the Civil War South.* Athens: University of Georgia Press, 2001.

Jasper County Historical Foundation. *History of Jasper County, Georgia.* Roswell, GA: W. H. Wolfe, 1984.

Jenkins, Robert D., Sr. *The Cassville Affairs: Johnston, Hood, and the Failed Confederate Strategy in the Atlanta Campaign, 19 May 1864.* Macon: Mercer University Press, 2024.

Joiner, Oscar, et al., eds. *A History of Public Education in Georgia 1734–1876*. Columbia, SC: R. L. Bryan Co., 1979.

Johnson, Michael P. *Toward a Patriarchal Republic: The Secession of Georgia*. Baton Rouge: Louisiana State University Press, 1977.

Kaemmerien, Cathy J., ed. *General Sherman and the Georgia Belles: Tales from the Women Left Behind*. Charleston: History Press, 2006.

Kennett, Lee. *Marching through Georgia: The Story of Soldiers and Civilians during Sherman's Campaign*. New York: HarperCollins Publishers, 1995.

Knight, Lucian Lamar. *A Standard History of Georgia and Georgians*. Vol. 2. New York: Lewis Publishing Co., 1917.

———. *Georgia's Landmarks, Memorials and Legends*. Vol. 2. Atlanta: Byrd Printing Co, 1914.

Link, William A. *Atlanta, Cradle of the New South*. Chapel Hill: University of North Carolina Press, 2013.

Little, Windee A. *Reminiscent: A Pictorial History of Eatonton/Putnam County, Georgia*. Virginia Beach: The Dorning Co., 1999.

Marszalek, John F. *Sherman's March to the Sea*. Abilene, TX: State House Press, 2005.

McCash, William B. *Thomas R. R. Cobb: The Making of a Southern Nationalist*. Macon: Mercer University Press, 1983.

McDonough, James Lee, and James Pickett Jones. *War So Terrible: Sherman and Atlanta*. New York: W. W. Norton & Co., 1987.

McMahon, Joel. *Our Good and Faithful Servant: James Moore Wayne and Georgia Unionism*. Macon: Mercer University Press, 2017.

McMurry, Richard M. *Atlanta 1864: Last Chance for the Confederacy*. Lincoln: University of Nebraska Press, 2000.

Mellichamp, Josephine. *Senators from Georgia*. Huntsville: Strode Publishers, 1976.

Miles, Jim. *Civil War Sites in Georgia*. Nashville: Rutledge Hill Press, 1996.

———. *To the Sea: A History and Tour Guide of Sherman's March*. Nashville: Rutledge Hill Press, 2000.

Mitchell, William R. *Madison: A Classic Southern Town*. Madison, GA: Historic Madison-Morgan Foundation, 2009.

Mohr, Clarence L. *On the Threshold of Freedom: Masters and Slaves in Civil War Georgia*. Baton Rouge: Louisiana State University Press, 2001.

Montgomery, Horace. *Cracker Parties*. Baton Rouge: Louisiana State University Press, 1950.

Morgan County Heritage, 1807–1997. Madison: Morgan County Heritage Book Committee, 1997.

Murray, Paul. *The Whig Party in Georgia: 1825–1853*. Chapel Hill: University of North Carolina Press, 1948.

Nathans, Elizabeth Studley. *Losing the Peace: Georgia Republicans and Reconstruction, 1865–1871*. Baton Rouge: Louisiana State University Press, 1969.

Nixon, Raymond B. *Henry W. Grady: Spokesman of the New South.* New York: Alfred A. Knopf, 1943.

Parks, Joseph H. *Joseph E. Brown of Georgia.* Baton Rouge: Louisiana State University Press, 1977.

Pearce, Haywood J., Jr. *Benjamin H. Hill: Secession and Reconstruction.* Chicago: University of Chicago Press, 1928.

Perkerson, Madora Field. *White Columns in Georgia.* New York: Bonanza Books, 1951.

Phillips, Ulrich B. *Georgia and State Rights.* 1902. Yellow Springs: Antioch Press, 1968.

Propst, Milam McGraw, and Jaclyn Weldon White. *Sidetracked: Two Women, Two Cameras, and Lunches on Sherman's Trail.* Macon: Mercer University Press, 2016.

Range, Willard. *A Century of Georgia Agriculture: 1850–1950.* Athens: University of Georgia Press, 1954.

Reed, Wallace P. *History of Atlanta, Georgia.* Syracuse: D. Mason & Co., 1889.

Reidy, Joseph P. *From Slavery to Agrarian Capitalism in the Cotton Plantation South: Central Georgia, 1800–1880.* Chapel Hill: University of North Carolina Press, 1992.

Roberts, Derrell C. *Joseph E. Brown and the Politics of Reconstruction.* Tuscaloosa: University of Alabama Press, 1973.

Roberts, William P. *Georgia's Best Kept Secret: A History of North Georgia College.* Dahlonega: Alumni Association of North Georgia College, 1998.

Rogers, William Warren, Jr. *A Scalawag in Georgia: Richard Whiteley and the Politics of Reconstruction.* Champaign: University Illinois Press, 2007.

Rubin, Anne S. *Through the Heart of Dixie: Sherman's March and American Memory.* Chapel Hill: University of North Carolina Press, 2014.

Russell, James Michael. *Atlanta 1847–1890: City Building in the Old South and the New.* Baton Rouge: Louisiana State University Press, 1988.

Sarris, Jonathan D. *A Separate Civil War: Communities in Conflict in the Mountain South.* Charlottesville: University of Virginia Press, 2006.

Savas, Theodore P., and David A. Woodbury. *The Campaign for Atlanta & Sherman's March to the Sea: Essays on the 1864 Campaign.* Campbell, LA: Savis Woodbury Publisher, 1992.

Saye, Albert B. *A Constitutional History of Georgia, 1732–1945.* Athens: University of Georgia Press, 1970.

Scaife, William R., and William H. Bragg. *Joe Brown's Pets: The Georgia Militia, 1861–1865.* Macon: Mercer University Press, 2004.

Shadgett, Olive Hall. *The Republican Party in Georgia: From Reconstruction through 1900.* 1964. Athens: University of Georgia Press, 2010.

Schott, Thomas E. *Alexander H. Stephens of Georgia: A Biography.* Baton Rouge: Louisiana State University Press, 1988.

Scroggins, Mark. *Robert Toombs: The Civil Wars of a United States Senator and Confederate General.* Jefferson, NC: McFarland & Co., 2011.

Shingleton, Royce. *Richard Peters: Champion of the New South.* Macon: Mercer University Press, 1985.

Tankersley, Allen P. *John B. Gordon: A Study in Gallantry.* Atlanta: Whitehall Press, 1955.

Thompson, Clara Mildred. *Reconstruction in Georgia: Economic, Social, Political 1865–1872.* 1915. Atlanta: Cherokee Publishing Co., 1971.

Thompson, William Y. *Robert Toombs of Georgia.* Baton Rouge: Louisiana State University Press, 1966.

Trudeau, Noah Andre. *Southern Storm: Sherman's March to the Sea.* New York: Harper Collins, 2008.

US Congress. House Committee on Reconstruction. *Evidence Before the Committee on Reconstruction, Relative to the Condition of Affairs in Georgia.* House Miscellaneous Document no. 52, 40th Congress, 3rd Session. Washington, D.C.: United States Government Printing Office, 1869.

Varon, Elizabeth R. Longstreet. *The Confederate General Who Defied the South.* New York: Simon & Schuster, 2023.

Venet, Wendy Hamand. *A Changing Wind: Commerce and Conflict in Civil War Atlanta.* Athens: University of Georgia Press, 2014.

Walters, Katherine Bowman. *Oconee River: Tales to Tell.* Spartanburg: Reprint Company, 2000, for the Eatonton-Putnam County Historical Society.

Wetherington, Mark V. *Plain Folk's Fight: The Civil War and Reconstruction in Piney Woods Georgia.* Chapel Hill: University of North Carolina Press, 2005.

Williams, David. *Georgia's Civil War: Conflict on the Home Front.* Macon: Mercer University Press, 2017.

———, Teresa Crisp Williams, and David Carlson. *Plain Folk in a Rich Man's War: Class and Dissent in Confederate Georgia.* Gainesville: University Press of Florida, 2002.

Woolley, Edwin C. *Studies in History, Economics, & Public Law: The Reconstruction of Georgia* 8/36 (1901). New York: Columbia University Press, 1901. https://dlg.galileo.usg.edu/id:dlg_zlgb_gb0299.

Wortman, Marc. *The Bonfire: The Siege and Burning of Atlanta.* New York: Public Affairs Press, 2009.

Wynne, Lewis Nicholas. *The Continuity of Cotton.* Macon: Mercer University Press, 1986.

Books: Not Georgia-specific

Abbott, Richard H. *The Republican Party and the South, 1855–1877: The First Southern Strategy.* Chapel Hill: University of North Carolina Press, 1986.

Abbott, Richard H. *For Free Press and Equal Rights: Republican Newspapers in the Reconstruction South*. Edited by John W. Quist. Athens: University of Georgia Press, 2004.

Abshire, David M. *The South Rejects a Prophet: The Life of Senator D. M. Key, 1824–1900*. New York: Frederick A. Praeger, 1967.

Anbinder, Tyler G. *Nativism and Slavery: The Northern Know Nothings and the Politics of the 1850s*. New York: Oxford University Press, 1992.

Anderson, Carol. *White Rage: The Unspoken Truth of Our Racial Divide*. London: Bloomsbury, 2016, 2020 ed.

Andrews, J. Cutler. *The North Reports the Civil War*. Pittsburgh: University of Pittsburgh Press, 1955.

Ash, Stephen V. *When the Yankees Came: Conflict and Chaos in the Occupied South, 1861–1865*. Chapel Hill: University of North Carolina Press, 1999.

Ashworth, John. *Slavery, Capitalism, and Politics in the Antebellum Republic*. 2 vols. New York: Cambridge University Press, 2007.

———. *The Republic in Crisis, 1848–1861*. New York: Cambridge University Press, 2012.

Baggett, James Alex. *The Scalawags: Southern Dissenters in the Civil War and Reconstruction*. Baton Rouge: Louisiana State University Press, 2003.

Balkin, Jack, and J. M. Balkin, eds. *What Brown v. Board of Education Should Have Said: The Nation's Top Legal Experts Rewrite American's Landmark Civil Rights Decision*. New York: New York University Press, 2002.

Barnard, Harry. *Rutherford B. Hayes and His America*. 1954. Newtown, CT: American Political Biography Press, 1992.

Barreyre, Nicolas. *Gold and Freedom: The Political Economy of Reconstruction*. Charlottesville: University of Virginia Press, 2015.

Behrend, Justin. *Reconstructing Democracy: Grassroots Black Politics in the Deep South after the Civil War*. Athens: University of Georgia Press, 2015.

Bensel, Richard F. *Yankee Leviathan: The Origins of Central State Authority in America, 1859–1877*. New York: Cambridge University Press, 1991.

Beringer, Richard E., Herman Hattaway, Archer Jones, and William N. Still, Jr. *Why the South Lost the Civil War*. Athens: University of Georgia Press, 1986.

Beth, Loren P. *John Marshall Harlan: The Last Whig Justice*. Lexington: University Press of Kentucky, 1992.

Blight, David W. *Frederick Douglas: Prophet of Freedom*. New York: Simon & Schuster, 2018.

———. *Race and Reunion: The Civil War in American Memory*. Cambridge: Belknap Press of Harvard, 2001.

Bonner, Robert E. *Mastering America: Southern Slaveholders and the Crises of American Nationhood*. New York: Cambridge University Press, 2009.

Bordewich, Fergus M. *Congress at War: How Republican Reformers Fought the Civil War, Defied Lincoln, Ended Slavery, & Remade America.* New York: Alfred A. Knopf, 2020.

———. *Klan War: Ulysses S. Grant and the Battle to Save Reconstruction.* New York: Alfred A. Knopf, 2023.

Boritt, Gabor S., ed. *Why the Confederacy Lost.* New York: Oxford University Press, 1993.

Bowman, Shearer Davis. *At the Precipice: Americans North and South during the Secession Crisis.* Chapel Hill: University of North Carolina Press, 2010.

Brettle, Adrian. *Colossal Ambitions: Confederate Planning for a Post-Civil War World.* Charlottesville: University of Virginia Press, 2020.

Simpson, Brooks D. *Ulysses S. Grant: Triumph over Adversity, 1822–1865.* Minneapolis: Zenith Press, 2014.

Burlingame, Michael. *Abraham Lincoln: A Life.* Vol. 2. Baltimore: Johns Hopkins University Press, 2008.

Calhoun, Charles W. *The Presidency of Ulysses S. Grant.* Lawrence: University Press of Kansas, 2017.

Carr, Matthew. *Sherman's Ghosts: Soldiers, Civilians, and the American Way of War.* New York: New Press, 2015.

Carter, Dan T. *When the War Was Over: The Failure of Self Reconstruction in the South, 1865–1867.* Chapel Hill: University of North Carolina Press, 1985.

Chernow, Ron. *Grant.* New York: Penguin Press, 2017.

Clampitt, Bradley R. *Lost Causes: Confederate Demobilization & the Making of Veteran Identity.* Baton Rouge: Louisiana State University Press, 2022.

Cobb, James C. *C. Vann Woodward: America's Historian.* Chapel Hill: University of North Carolina Press, 2022.

Coburn, Mark. *Terrible Innocence: General Sherman at War.* New York: Hippocrene Books, 1993.

Connelly, Thomas L., and Barbara Bellows. *God and General Longstreet: The Lost Cause and the Southern Mind.* Baton Rouge: Louisiana State University Press, 1982.

Coulter, E. Merton. *William G. Brownlow: Fighting Parson of the Southern Highlands.* 1939. Knoxville: University of Tennessee Press, 1999.

Crofts, Daniel W. *Lincoln and the Politics of Slavery.* Chapel Hill: University of North Carolina Press, 2016.

———. *Reluctant Confederates: Upper South Unionists in the Secession Crisis.* Chapel Hill: University of North Carolina Press, 1989.

Davis, William C. *The Cause Lost.* Lawrence: University Press of Kansas, 1998.

Degler, Carl. *The Other South: Southern Dissenters in the Nineteenth Century.* New York: Harper & Row, 1974.

Dew, Charles B. *Apostles of Disunion: Southern Secession Commissioners and the Causes of the Civil War.* Charlottesville: University of Virginia Press, 2002.

Donald, David. *Charles Sumner and the Rights of Man.* New York: Alfred A. Knopf, 1970.

Downing, David C. *A South Divided: Portraits of Dissent in the Confederacy.* Nashville: Cumberland House, 2007.

Downs, Gregory P. *After Appomattox: Military Occupation and the Ends of War.* Cambridge: Harvard University Press, 2015.

———, and Kate Masur. *The World the Civil War Made.* Chapel Hill: University of North Carolina Press, 2015.

Edwards, Laura F. *A Legal History of the Civil War and Reconstruction.* New York: Cambridge University Press, 2015.

Egerton, Douglas R. *The Wars of Reconstruction: The Brief Violent History of America's Most Progressive Era.* New York: Bloomsburg Press, 2014.

Etcheson, Nicole. *Bleeding Kansas: Contested Liberty in the Civil War Era.* Lawrence: University Press of Kansas, 2004.

Farris, Scott. *Freedom on Trial: The First Post-Civil War Battle Over Civil Rights & Voter Suppression.* Guilford, CT: Lyons Press, 2022.

Fellman, Michael. *Citizen Soldier: A Life of William Tecumseh Sherman.* New York: Random House, 2013.

Fitzgerald, Michael W. *Reconstruction in Alabama: From Civil War to Redemption in the Cotton South.* Baton Rouge: Louisiana State University Press, 2017.

———. *Splendid Failure: Postwar Reconstruction in the American South.* Chicago: Ivan R. Dee, 2007.

———. *The Union League Movement in the Deep South.* Baton Rouge: Louisiana State University Press, 1989.

Flood, Charles Bracelen. *Grant and Sherman: The Friendship That Won the Civil War.* New York: Farrar, Straus & Giroux, 2005.

Foner, Eric. *Reconstruction: America's Unfinished Revolution: 1863–1877.* 1988. New York: HarperPerennial, 2014.

Frank, Lisa Tendrich. *The Civilian War: Confederate Women and Union Soldiers during Sherman's March.* Baton Rouge: Louisiana State University Press, 2015.

Freehling, William W. *The South vs. the South: How Anti-Confederate Southerners Shaped the Course of the Civil War.* New York: Oxford University Press, 2001.

———. *Secessionists Triumphant: 1854–1861.* Vol. 2 of *The Road to Disunion.* New York: Oxford University Press, 2007.

Fritsch, James T. *The Untried Life—The Twenty-Ninth Ohio Volunteer Infantry in the Civil War.* Athens: Swallow Press of Ohio University Press, 2012.

Gaines, Wesley J. *The Negro and the White Man.* Philadelphia: AME Publishing House, 1897.

Gates, Henry Louis, Jr. *Stony the Road: Reconstruction, White Supremacy, and the Rise of Jim Crow.* New York: Penguin Random House, 2019.

Gillette, William. *Retreat from Reconstruction, 1869–1879.* Baton Rouge: Louisiana State University Press, 1979.

Glatthaar, Joseph. *Forged in Battle: The Civil War Alliance of Black Soldiers and White Officers.* Baton Rouge: Louisiana State University Press, 2000.

Gould, Lewis L. *Grand Old Party: A History of the Republicans.* New York: Random House, 2003.

Grimsley, Mark. *The Hard Hand of War—Union Military Policy Toward Southern Civilians, 1861–1865.* New York: Cambridge University Press, 1995.

Guelzo, Allen C. *Reconstruction: A Concise History.* New York: Oxford University Press, 2018.

———. *Fateful Lighting: A New History of the Civil War & Reconstruction.* New York: Oxford University Press, 2012.

Hahn, Steven. *A Nation under Our Feet: Black Political Struggles in the Rural South from Slavery to the Great Migration.* Cambridge: Harvard University Press, 2005.

Harris, William C. *With Charity for All.* Lexington: University Press of Kentucky, 1997.

Harrison, Robert. *Washington during Civil War and Reconstruction: Race and Radicalism.* New York: Cambridge University Press, 2011.

Hebert, Keith S. *Cornerstone of the Confederacy: Alexander Stephens and the Speech that Defined the Lost Cause.* Knoxville: University of Tennessee Press, 2021.

Herek, Raymond J. *These Men Have Seen Hard Service: The First Michigan Sharpshooters in the Civil War.* Detroit: Wayne State University Press, 1998.

Hobson, Fred. *Tell about the South: The Southern Rage to Explain.* Baton Rouge: Louisiana State University Press, 1974.

Holt, Michael F. *The Fate of Their Country: Politicians, Slavery Extension, and the Coming of the Civil War.* New York: Hill and Wang, 2004.

———. *The Rise and Fall of the American Whig Party: Jacksonian Politics and the Onset of the Civil War.* New York: Oxford University Press, 2003.

Hoogenboom, Ari. *The Presidency of Rutherford B. Hays.* Lawrence: University Press of Kansas, 1988.

Huggins, Stephen. *America's Use of Terror from Colonial Times to the A-Bomb.* Lawrence: University Press of Kansas, 2019.

Hume, Richard, and Jerry B. Gough. *Blacks, Carpetbaggers, and Scalawags: The Constitutional Conventions of Radical Reconstruction.* Baton Rouge: Louisiana State University Press, 2008.

Huston, James L. *The British Gentry, The Southern Planter, and the Northern Family Farmer.* Baton Rouge: Louisiana State University Press, 2015.

Inscoe, John C., and Robert C. Kenzer, eds. *Enemies of the Country: New Perspectives on Unionists in the Civil War South.* Athens: University of Georgia Press, 2001.

Jacoby, Susan. *Freethinkers: A History of American Secularism.* New York: Henry Holt and Company, 2004.

Jenkins, Jeffery A., and Charles H. Stewart. *Fighting for the Speakership: The House and the Rise of Party Government.* Princeton: Princeton University Press, 2013.

Johannsen, Robert W. *Stephen A. Douglas.* New York: Oxford University Press, 1973.

Keith, LeeAnna. *When It Was Grand: The Radical Republican History of the Civil War.* New York: Hill & Wang, 2020.

Klein, Maury *Days of Defiance: Sumter, Secession, and the Coming of the Civil War* New York: Knopf, 1997.

Langguth, A. J. *After Lincoln: How the Union Won the Civil War and Lost the Peace.* New York: Simon & Schuster, 2014.

Klein, Maury. *Days of Defiance: Sumter, Secession, and the Coming of the Civil War.* New York: Knopf, 1997.

Klingberg, Frank W. *The Southern Claims Commission.* Berkeley: University of California Press, 1955.

Lee, Susanna M. *Claiming the Union: Citizenship in the Post-Civil War South.* New York: Cambridge University Press, 2014.

Leigh, Philip. *Southern Reconstruction.* Yardley, PA: Westholme Publishing, 2018.

Levine, Bruce. *The Fall of the House of Dixie.* New York: Random House, 2013.

Lundberg, James M. *Horace Greeley: Print, Politics, and the Failure of American Nationhood.* Baltimore: Johns Hopkins University Press, 2019.

Lyons, Philip B. *Statesmanship and Reconstruction: Moderate versus Radical Republicans on Restoring the Union after the Civil War.* Lanham, MD: Lexington Books, 2014.

Manning, Chandra. *What This Cruel War Was Over: Soldiers, Slavery, and the Civil War.* New York: Alfred A. Knopf, 2007.

Marszalek, John F. *Sherman: A Soldier's Passion for Order.* Carbondale: Southern Illinois Press, 2007.

———. *Sherman's Other War: The General and the Civil War Press.* Kent: Kent State University Press, 1999.

Mason, Matthew. *Apostle of Union: A Political Biography of Edward Everett.* Chapel Hill: University of North Carolina Press, 2016.

Matthews, Gary R. *Basil Wilson Duke, CSA: The Right Man in the Right Place.* Lexington: University Press of Kentucky, 2005.

McAfee, Ward. *Religion, Race, and Reconstruction: The Public School in the Politics of the 1870s.* Albany: SUNY Press, 1998.

McCurry, Stephanie. *Confederate Reckoning: Power & Politics in the Civil War South.* Cambridge: Harvard University Press, 2010.

McDonough, James Lee. *William Tecumseh Sherman: In the Service of My Country: A Life.* New York: W. W. Norton & Co., 2016.

McKitrick, Eric L. *Andrew Johnson and Reconstruction.* New York: Oxford University Press, 1988.

McMurry, Richard M. *John Bell Hood and the War for Southern Independence.* Lincoln: University of Nebraska Press, 1982.

McPherson, James M. *The Battle Cry of Freedom: The Civil War Era.* New York: Oxford University Press, 1988.

Melton, Brian C. *Sherman's Forgotten General: Henry W. Slocum.* Columbia: University of Missouri Press, 2007.

Meriwether, Jeffrey Lee, and Laura Mattoon D'Amore, eds. *We Are What We Remember: The American Past through Commemoration.* Newcastle Upon Tyne, UK: Cambridge Scholars Publishing, 2012.

Merritt, Keri Leigh. *Masterless Men: Poor Whites and Slavery in the Antebellum South.* New York: Cambridge University Press, 2017.

Miers, Earl Schenck. *The General Who Marched to Hell: William Tecumseh Sherman and His March to Fame and Infamy.* New York: Knopf, 1951.

Oakes, James. *Freedom National: The Destruction of Slavery in the United States, 1861–1865.* New York: W. W. Norton, 2012.

———. *The Scorpion's Sting: Antislavery and the Coming of the Civil War.* New York: W. W. Norton & Co., 2014.

O'Connell, Robert L. *Fierce Patriot: The Tangled Lives of William Tecumseh Sherman.* New York: Random House, 2014.

Overdyke, W. Darrell. *The Know-Nothing Party in the South.* Baton Rouge: Louisiana State University Press, 1950.

Parks, Joseph Howard. *John Bell of Tennessee.* Baton Rouge: Louisiana State University Press, 1950.

Parsons, Elaine Frantz. *Ku-Klux: The Birth of the Klan During Reconstruction.* Chapel Hill: University of North Carolina Press, 2015.

Pease, William H., and Jane H. Pease. *James Louis Petigru: Southern Conservative, Southern Dissenter.* Athens: University of Georgia Press, 1995.

Perman, Michael. *The Road to Redemption: Southern Politics, 1869–1879.* Chapel Hill: University of North Carolina Press, 1984.

———. *Reunion without Compromise: The South and Reconstruction: 1865–1868.* New York: Cambridge University Press, 1973.

Pickenpaugh, Roger. *Captives in Blue: The Civil War Prisons of the Confederacy.* Tuscaloosa: University Alabama Press, 2013.

Piston, William Garrett. *Lee's Tarnished Lieutenant: James Longstreet and His Place in Southern History.* Athens: University of Georgia Press,1987.

Potter, David M. *The Impending Crisis: 1848–1861.* Compiled and edited by Don E. Fehrenbacher. New York: Harper & Row, Pub., 1976.

Pula, James S. *The Sigel Regiment: A History of the Twenty-Sixth Wisconsin Volunteer Infantry 1962–1865.* Campbell, CA: Savas Publishing Co., 1998.

Rable, George. *But There Was No Peace: The Role of Violence in the Politics of Reconstruction.* Athens: University of Georgia Press, 1984.

———. *The Confederate Republic: A Revolution against Politics.* Chapel Hill: University of North Carolina Press, 1994)

Rawley, James A. *Secession: The Disruption of the American Republic, 1844–1861*. Malabar, FL: Krieger, 1990.

Reid, Brian Holden. *The Scourge of War: The Life of William Tecumseh Sherman*. New York: Oxford University Press, 2020.

Reid, Whitelaw. *After the War—A Tour of the Southern States 1865–1866*. New York: Harper & Row, 1965.

Richardson, Heather Cox. *The Death of Reconstruction: Race, Labor, and Politics in the Post-Civil War North, 1865–1901*. Cambridge: Harvard University Press, 2009.

———. *To Make Men Free: A History of the Republican Party*. New York: Basic Books, 2014.

Rogers, William Warren, Jr. *Black Belt Scalawag: Charles Hays and the Southern Republicans in the Era of Reconstruction*. Athens: University of Georgia Press, 1993.

Rosen, Hannah. *Terror in the Heart of Freedom: Citizenship, Sexual Violence, and the Meaning of Race in the Postemancipation South*. Chapel Hill: University of North Carolina Press, 2009.

Rubin, Anne Sarah. *A Shattered Nation: The Rise and Fall of the Confederacy, 1861–1868*. Chapel Hill: University of North Carolina Press, 2005.

Sacher, John M. *Confederate Conscription and the Struggle for Southern Soldiers*. Baton Rouge: Louisiana State University Press, 2021.

Sands, Eric C. *American Public Philosophy and the Mystery of Lincolnism*. Columbia: University of Missouri Press, 2009.

Scaturro, Frank J. *The Supreme Court's Retreat from Reconstruction—A Distortion of Constitutional Jurisprudence*. Westport, CT: Greenwood Press, 2000.

Schoen, Brian. *Fragile Fabric of the Union: Cotton, Federal Policy, and the Global Origins of the Civil War*. Baltimore: Johns Hopkins University Press, 2009.

Simpson, Brooks D. *Let Us Have Peace: Ulysses S. Grant and the Politics of War and Reconstruction, 1861–1868*. Chapel Hill: University of North Carolina Press, 1991.

———. *Ulysses S. Grant: Triumph over Adversity, 1822–1865*. Minneapolis: Zenith Press, 2014.

Slap, Andrew. *The Doom of Reconstruction: The Liberal Republicans in the Civil War Era*. New York: Fordham University Press, 2006.

Snay, Mitchell. *Horace Greeley and the Politics of Reform in Nineteenth-Century America*. Lanham, MD: Rowman & Littlefield, Inc., 2011.

Storey, Margaret M. *Loyalty and Loss: Alabama's Unionists in the Civil War and Reconstruction*. Baton Rouge: Louisiana State University Press, 2004.

Summers, Mark Wahlgren. *The Ordeal of the Reunion: A New History of Reconstruction*. Chapel Hill: University of North Carolina Press, 2014.

Sword, Wiley. *Southern Invincibility: A History of the Confederate Heart*. New York: St. Martin's Griffin, 1999.

Trefousse, Hans L. *Rutherford B. Hayes.* New York: Henry Holt and Company, 2002.
———. *The Radical Republicans.* New York: Knopf Doubleday Publishing Group, 2014.
Trelease, Allen W. *Reconstruction: The Great Experiment.* New York: Harper & Row, 1971.
———. *White Terror: The Ku Klux Klan Conspiracy and Southern Reconstruction.* Baton Rouge: Louisiana State University Press, 1971.
US Congress. Joint Select Committee on the Condition of Affairs in the Late Insurrectionary States. *Report of the Joint select committee appointed to inquire into the condition of affairs in the late insurrectionary states, so far as regards the execution of laws, and the safety of the lives and property of the citizens of the United States and Testimony taken.* 13 vols. Washington: Government Printing Office, 1872.
US Congress. Senate Committee on Privileges and Elections, and George S. Taft. *Compilation of Senate Election Cases from 1789 to 1885.* Washington, D.C.: Government Printing Office, 1903. Accessed July 12, 2024. https://www.loc.gov/item/03011928/.
Varon, Elizabeth R. *Armies of Deliverance.* New York: Oxford University Press, 2019.
———. *Disunion! The Coming of the American Civil War 1789–1859.* Chapel Hill: University of North Carolina Press, 2008.
Vetter, Charles Edmund. *Sherman: Merchant of Terror, Advocate of Peace.* Gretna, LA: Pelican Publishing Company, 1992.
Ware, Lowry. *Chapters in the History of Abbeville County, the "Banner County" of South Carolina.* Berwyn Heights, MD: Heritage Books, 2012.
———. *Old Abbeville: Scenes of the Past of a Town Where Old Time Things Are Not Forgotten.* Columbia, SC: SCMAR, 1992.
Wiggins, Sarah Woolfolk. *The Scalawag in Alabama Politics, 1865–1881.* Tuscaloosa: University of Alabama Press, 1977.
Williams, David. *Bitterly Divided: The South's Inner Civil War.* New York: The New Press, 2010.
Woods, Michael E. *Bleeding Kansas: Slavery, Sectionalism, and Civil War on the Missouri-Kansas Border.* New York: Routledge, 2017.

Articles, Chapters, and Pamphlets Specific to Georgia

Abbott, Richard H. "The Republican Party Press in Reconstruction Georgia, 1867–1874." *JSH* 61/4 (November 1995): 725–60.
Banks, William N. "History in Towns: Madison, Georgia." *The Magazine Antiques* (April 2009): 88–97.
Bard, Samuel. *A Letter from Governor Samuel Bard to President Grant, on the Political Situation in Georgia and the South.* Atlanta, 1870. Ya Pamphlet Collection, Library of Congress. https://www.loc.gov/item/11026674/.

Bass, James Horace. "The Georgia Gubernatorial Elections of 1861 and 1863." *GHQ* 17/3 (September 1933): 167–88.

Bates, William M. "The Last Stand for the Union in Georgia." *Georgia Review* 7/4 (Winter 1953): 455–67.

Benefield, Kevin. "The Civil War in Georgia: 1864 Total War." In *Georgia Travel Guide*. Atlanta: Georgia Department of Economic Development, Tourism Division, 2014.

Bonds, Russell S. "Sherman's First March through Georgia." *Civil War Times* 46/6 (August 2007): 30–37.

Bragg, William Harris. "The Junius of Georgia Redemption: Thomas M. Norwood and the 'Nemesis' Letters." *GHQ* 77/1 (Spring 1993): 86–122.

Brooks, R. P. "Howell Cobb Papers." *GHQ* 6/2 (June 1922): 147–73.

Brown, Russell K. "Augusta's Other Voice: James Gardner and the *Constitutionalist*." *GHQ* 85/4 (Winter 2001): 592–607.

———. "Post-Civil War Violence in Augusta, Georgia." *GHQ* 90/2 (Summer 2006): 196–213.

Bryan, T. Conn. "The Secession of Georgia." *GHQ* 31/2 (June 1947): 89–111.

Bryant, Jonathan M. "'We Have No Chance of Justice before the Courts': The Freedmen's Struggle for Power in Greene County, Georgia, 1865–1874." In *Georgia in Black & White*, edited by John C. Inscoe. Athens: University of Georgia Press, 1994.

Carey, Anthony Gene. "Too Southern to be Americans: Proslavery Politics and the Failure of the Know-Nothing Party in Georgia, 1854–1856." *Civil War History* 41/1 (March 1995): 22–40.

Cason, Roberta F. "The Loyal League in Georgia." *GHQ* 20/2 (June 1936): 125–53.

Collins, Bruce W. "Governor Joseph E. Brown, Economic Issues, and Georgia's Road to Secession, 1857–1859." *GHQ* 71 (Summer 1987): 189–225.

"Confederate Necrology." Notes & Documents. Hugh Legare Hill Obituary. *GHQ* 25/3 (September 1941): 293–94.

Coulter, E. Merton. "Aaron Alpeoria Bradley, Georgia Negro Politician during Reconstruction Times, Part I." *GHQ* 51/1 (March 1967): 15–41.

Cumming, Inez Parker. "Madison: Middle Georgia Minerva." *Georgia Review* 5/1 (Spring 1951): 121–36.

Davis, Robert Scott. "War on the Edge: Civil War Era Politics and Its Legacy in an Appalachian County." In *Breaking the Heartland: The Civil War in Georgia*, edited by John D. Fowler and David B. Parker, 1–18. Macon: Mercer University Press, 2011.

Doherty, Herbert J., Jr. "Union Nationalism in Georgia." *GHQ* 37/1 (March 1953): 18–28.

Dixon, David T. "Augustus R. Wright and the Loyalty of the Heart." *GHQ* 94/3 (Fall 2010): 342–71.

Drago, Edmund L. "How Sherman's March through Georgia Affected the Slaves." *GHQ* 57/3 (Fall 1973): 361–75.

Escott, Paul D. "The Context of Freedom: Georgia's Slaves during the Civil War." *GHQ* 58/1 (Spring 1974): 79–104.

Grudowski, Mike. "Madison, Georgia Protects Its Historic Charms." *Garden & Gun* (April/May 2020): 166.

Hall, Mark. "Alexander H. Stephens and Joseph E. Brown and the Georgia Resolutions for Peace." *GHQ* 64/1 (Spring 1980): 50–63.

Henken, Elissa R. "Taming the Enemy: Georgian Narratives about the Civil War." *Journal of Folklore Research* 40/3 (September–December 2003): 289–307.

Hettle, Wallace T. "An Ambiguous Democrat: Joseph Brown and Georgia's Road to Secession." *GHQ* 81/3 (Fall 1997): 577–92.

Hill, Louise Biles. "Governor Brown and the Confederacy, Part II." *GHQ* 21/4 (December 1937): 345–72.

Hubbell, John T. "Three Georgia Unionists and the Compromise of 1850." *GHQ* 51/3 (September 1967): 307–23.

Hume, Janice, and Amber Roessner. "Surviving Sherman's March: Press, Public Memory, and Georgia's Salvation Mythology." *Journalism and Mass Communication Quarterly* 86/1 (Spring 2009): 119–37.

Johnson, Forest C. "LaGrange, GA." *New Georgia Encyclopedia.* https://www.georgiaencyclopedia.org/articles/counties-cities-neighborhoods/lagrange/. (October 8, 2015). Accessed June 21, 2024.

Matthews, John M. "Negro Republicans in the Reconstruction of Georgia." *GHQ* 60/2 (Summer 1976): 145–64.

McCrady, Allston ."Boxwood: An Antebellum Garden." *Garden & Gun* (Summer 2007).

McNeill, William J. "A Survey of Confederate Soldier Morale during Sherman's Campaign through Georgia and the Carolinas." *GHQ* 55/1 (Spring 1971): 1–25.

Melton, Brian C. "'The Town that Sherman Wouldn't Burn': Sherman's March and Madison, Georgia, in History, Memory, and Legend." *GHQ* 86/2 (Summer 2002): 201–30.

Morgan, Chad. "War and Rumors of War: Hearsay as Information on Georgia's Civil War Home Front." In *Breaking the Heartland: The Civil War in Georgia*, edited by John D. Fowler and David B. Parker. Macon: Mercer University Press, 2011.

Parker, David B. "'To the Youth of the Southern Confederacy': Georgia's Confederate Textbooks." In *Breaking the Heartland: The Civil War in Georgia.* Edited by John F. Fowler and David B. Parker, 94–109. Macon: Mercer University Press.

Roberts, Lucien E. "The Political Career of Joshua Hill, Georgia Unionist." *GHQ* 21/1 (March 1937): 50–72.

Rogers, William Warren, Jr. "'Not Reconstructed by a Long Ways Yet': Southwest Georgia's Disputed Congressional Election of 1870." *GHQ* 82/2 (Summer 1998): 257–82.

Rosenbaum, Ephraim Samuel. "Incendiary Negro: The Life and Times of the Honorable Jefferson Franklin Long." *GHQ* 95/4 (Winter 2011): 498–530.

Russ, William A., Jr. "Radical Disfranchisement in Georgia, 1867–71." *GHQ* 19/3 (September 1935): 175–209.

Shadgett, Olive Hall. "James Johnson, Provisional Governor of Georgia." *GHQ* 36/1 (March 1952): 1–21.

Smith, W. Calvin. "The Reconstruction 'Triumph' of Rufus B. Bullock." *GHQ* 52/4 (December 1968): 414–21.

Storey, Steve. "Railroads." *New Georgia Encyclopedia*. https://www.georgiaencyclopedia.org/articles/business-economy/railroads/ (September 14, 2018). Accessed June 21, 2024.

US Congress. "Hill, Joshua." *Biographical Directory of the United States Congress*. Accessed July 11, 2024, https://bioguide.congress.gov/search/bio/H000599.

Venet, Wendy Hamand. "From Gate City to Gotham: Sam Richards Chronicles the Civil War in Atlanta." In *Breaking the Heartland: The Civil War in Georgia*, edited by John D. Fowler and David B. Parker, 150–68. Macon: Mercer University Press, 2011.

William, David. "Bitterly Divided: Georgia's Inner Civil War." In *Breaking the Heartland: The Civil War in Georgia*, edited by John D. Fowler and David B. Parker, 19–45. Macon: Mercer University Press, 2011.

Ward, Judson C., Jr. "The Republican Party in Bourbon Georgia, 1872–1890." *Journal of Southern History* 9/2 (May 1943): 196–209.

Wooster, Ralph. "The Georgia Secession Convention." *GHQ* 40/1 (March 1956): 21–55.

Articles and Chapters: Not specific to Georgia

Alexander, Thomas B. "Persistent Whiggery in the Confederate South." *JSH* 27/3 (August 1961): 305–29.

Avins, Alfred. "Anti-Miscegenation Laws and the Fourteenth Amendment: The Original Intent." *Virginia Law Review* 52/7 (November 1966): 1224–255.

———. "The Civil Rights Act of 1875: Some Reflected Light on the Fourteenth Amendment and Public Accommodations." *Columbia Law Review* 66/5 (May 1966): 873–915.

Castel, Albert. "Liddell Hart's 'Sherman' Propaganda as History." *Journal of Military History* 67/2 (April 2003): 405–26.

Currie, David P. "The Reconstruction Congress." *University of Chicago Law Review* 75/1 (Winter 2008): 383–495.

Dante, Harris L. "The *Chicago Tribune*'s 'Lost' Years, 1865–1874." *Journal of the Illinois State Historical Society* 58/2 (Summer 1965): 139–64.

Downey, Mathew T. "Horace Greeley and the Politicians: The Liberal Republican Convention in 1872." *JSH* 53/4 (March 1967): 727–50.

Etcheson, Nicole. "'Our lives, our fortunes, and our sacred honors': The Kansas Civil War and the Revolutionary Tradition." *American Nineteenth Century History* 10/1 (Spring 2000): 62–81.

Green, Don. "Constitutional Unionists: The Party that Tried to Stop Lincoln and Save the Union." *Historian* 69/2 (Summer 2007): 231–53.

Grow, Matthew J. "The Shadow of the Civil War: A Historiography of Civil War Memory." *American Nineteenth Century History* 4/2 (Summer 2003): 77–103

Gundridge, Patrick J. "Privileges and Permissions: The Civil Rights Act of 1875." *Law and Philosophy* 8/**[issue no.?]** (April 1989): 83–130.

Huston, James L. "Southerners Against Secession: The Arguments of Constitutional Unionists in 1850–1851." *Civil War History* 46/4 (Fall 2000): 281–99.

Johnson, Herschel V. "From the Autobiography of Hershel V. Johnson, 1856-1867." *American Historical Review* 30/2 (1915): 294–309.

Jones, D. Marvin. "No Time for Trumpets: Title VII, Equality, and the *Fin de Siècle*." *Michigan Law Review* 92 (August 1994): 2311–369.

Kelly, Alfred H. "The Congressional Controversy over School Segregation, 1867–1875." *AHR* 64/3 (April 1959): 537–63.

McClendon, R. Earl. "Status of the Ex-Confederate States as Seen in the Readmission of United States Senators." *AHR* 41/4 (July 1936): 703–709.

McConnell, Michael W. "The Originalist Case for Brown v. Board of Education." *Harvard Journal of Law and Public Policy* 19 (Winter 1996): 457–65.

McKenzie, Robert T. "Prudent Silence and Strict Neutrality: The Parameters of Unionism in Parson Brownlow's Knoxville, 1860–1863." In *Enemies of the Country: New Perspectives on Unionists in the Civil War South*, edited by John C. Inscoe and Robert C. Kenzer, 73–96. Athens: University of Georgia Press, 2001.

McMurry, Richard M. "The Confederate Newspaper Press and the Civil War: An Overview and a Report on Research in Progress." *Atlanta History: A Journal of Georgia and the South*, 42 (Spring–Summer 1889): 59–75.

Russ, William A., Jr. "Was There Danger of a Second Civil War during Reconstruction?" *Mississippi Valley Historical Review* 25/1 (June 1938): 39.

Simpson, Brooks D. "Olive Branch and Sword: Union War-making in the American Civil War." In *Aspects of War in American History*, edited by David K. Adams and Cornelis A. Van Minnen, 63–79. Keele, Staffordshire, UK: Keele University Press, 1997)

Smith, Stephen Eliot. "Barbarians within the Gates: Congressional Debates on Mormon Polygamy, 1850–1879." *Journal of Church and State* 51/4 (Autumn 2009): 587–616.

Stanley, Amy Dru. "Slave Emancipation and the Revolutionizing of Human Rights." In *The World the Civil War Made*, edited by Gregory P. Downs and Kate Masur, 269–303. Chapel Hill: University of North Carolina Press, 2015.

Tunnell, Ted. "Creating 'The Propaganda of History': Southern Editors and the Origins of 'Carpetbagger and Scalawag.'" *JSH* 72/4 (November 2006): 789–822.

Wilson, Kirt H. "Emerson, Transcendental Prudence, and the Legacy of Senator Charles Sumner." *Rhetoric & Public Affairs* 2/3 (Fall 1999): 453–79.

Dissertations and Theses

Allen, Leslye Joy. "For Union and Slavery, for Slavery and Union: Know-Nothings in Georgia, 1854–1860." Master's thesis, Georgia State University, 2006.

Cleveland, Len Gibson. "George W. Crawford of Georgia: 1798–1872." PhD diss., University of Georgia, 1974.

Reference Works and Directories

Cook, James F. *The Governors of Georgia: 1754–2004*. Macon: Mercer University Press, 2005.

Henderson, Lillian, comp. *Roster of the Confederate Soldiers of Georgia, 1861–1865*. Vols. 1 and 6. Hapeville, GA: Longino & Porter Inc., 1964.

Nathans, Elizabeth S. "Joshua Hill." *American National Biography*. New York: Oxford University Press, 2010.

Massey, R. J. "Joshua Hill." In vol. 3 of *Men of Mark in Georgia*, edited by William J. Northen, 71–76. Spartanburg, SC: The Reprint Co., 1974.

Martis, Kenneth C. *Historical Atlas of United States Congressional Districts: 1789–1983*. New York: Free Press, 1982.

———. *The Historical Atlas of the Congresses of the Confederate States of America, 1861–1865*. New York: Simon & Schuster, 1994.

Martis, Kenneth C., and Gregory A. Elmes. *The Historical Atlas of Political Parties in the United States Congress, 1789–1989*. New York: Macmillan Publishing Company, 1989.

Miller, Stephen F. *The Bench and Bar of Georgia: Memoirs and Sketches*. Vol. 2. Philadelphia: J. B. Lippincott & Co., 1858.

Published Primary Sources

Andrews, Sidney. *The South since the War*. Boston: Ticknor & Fields, 1866.

Avary, Myrta Lockett, ed. *Recollections of Alexander H. Stephens: His Diary Kept When a Prisoner at Fort Warren, Boston Harbour, 1865; Giving Incidents and Reflections of His Prison Life and Some Letters and Reminiscences*. New York: Doubleday, Page & Co., 1910.

Bauer, K. Jack, ed. *Soldiering: The Civil War Diary of Rice C. Bull.* San Rafael, CA: Presidio Press, 1977.

Blaine, James G. *Twenty Years of Congress, Lincoln to Garfield: The Events Which Led to the Political Revolution of 1860.* Vol. 2. Norwich, CT: Henry Bill Publishing, 1886.

Boyle, John Richards. *Soldiers True: The Story of the One Hundred and Eleventh Regiment Pennsylvania Veteran Volunteers and of Its Campaigns in the War for the Union 1861–1865.* New York: Eaton & Mains, 1903.

Bradley, G. S. *The Star Corps: Or Notes of an Army Chaplain during Sherman's Famous "March to the Sea."* Milwaukee: Jermain & Brightman, Book & Job Printers, 1865.

Brant, J. E. *History of the Eighty-Fifth Indiana Volunteer Infantry.* Bloomington, IN: Cravens Bros., Printers and Binders, 1902.

Byrne, Frank L., ed. *Uncommon Soldiers: Harvey Reid and the 22nd Wisconsin March with Sherman.* Knoxville: University of Tennessee Press, 2001.

Candler, Allen D. *The Confederate Records of the State of Georgia.* Vol. 1, *Journal of the Secession Convention of 1861*, and vol. 4, *Journal of the Constitutional Convention of 1865.* Atlanta: Chas. P. Byrd, State Printers, 1909–1911.

———, and Clement A. Evans, eds. *Georgia: Comprising Sketches of Counties, Towns, Events, Institutions, and Persons, Arranged in Cyclopedic Form.* 3 vols. Atlanta: State Historical Association, 1906. Commonly called the *Cyclopedia of Georgia.*

Carter, Christine Jacobson, ed. *The Diary of Dolly Lunt Burge 1848–1879.* Athens: University of Georgia Press, 1997.

Clark, Walter A. *Under the Stars and Bars or Four Years of Service with the Oglethorpes of Augusta, Georgia.* Augusta: Chronicle Printing Co., 1900.

Clayton, Sarah "Sallie" Conley. *Requiem for a Lost City: A Memoir of Civil War Atlanta and the Old South.* Edited by Davis, Robert Scott Jr. Macon: Mercer University Press, 1999.

Collins, George K. Capt. *Memories of the 149th Regt. N.Y. Vol. Inft., 3d Brig., 2 Div., 12th and 20th A.C.* Syracuse, NY: publ. by the author, 1891.

Congressional Globe. Herein cited as *Globe*, by Congress and session, e.g., *Globe* 36–2.

Conyngham, David P. *Sherman's March through the South.* New York: Sheldon & Co., 1865.

Cook, S. G., and Charles E. Benton, eds. *The "Dutchess County Regiment."* Danbury, CT: Danbury Medical Printing Co., 1907.

Cox, Samuel S. *Eight Years in Congress from 1857–1865 Memoir and Speeches.* New York: D. Appleton & Co., 1865.

Drake, James V. *The Life of General Robert Hatton.* Nashville: Marshall & Bruce, 1867.

Fleharty, S. F. *Our Regiment. A History of the 102d Illinois Infantry Volunteers.* Chicago: Brewster & Hanscom, Printers, 1865.

Geer, J. J. *Beyond the Lines, Or, A Yankee Prisoner Loose in Dixie.* Scituate, MA: Digital Scanning Inc., 2000.

Genoways, Ted, and Hugh H. Genoways. *A Perfect Picture of Hell: Eyewitness Accounts by Civil War Prisoners from the 12th Iowa.* Iowa City: University of Iowa Press, 2001.

Grant, Ulysses. *The Papers of Ulysses S. Grant.* 31 vols. Edited by John Y. Simon. Carbondale: Southern Illinois University Press, 1967–2009.

Grunert, William. *History of the One Hundred and Twenty-Ninth Regiment Illinois Volunteer Infantry.* Winchester, IL: R. B. Dedman, Printer, 1866.

Halsey, Ashley, ed. *A Yankee Private's Civil War: Robert Hale Strong.* 1961. Mineola, NY: Dover Publications, 2013.

Harris, Bonnie P., comp. *Minutes of the Board of Commissioners, Madison, GA 1864–1853.* Madison, GA: Bonnie P. Harris, 2003.

Hayden, Rene, et al. *Freedom—A Documentary History of Emancipation, 1861–1867.* Chapel Hill: University of North Carolina Press, 2013.

Hill, Benjamin H., Jr. *Senator Benjamin H. Hill of Georgia: His Life, Speeches, and Writings.* Atlanta: H. C. Hudgins & Co., 1891.

Howe, M. A. DeWolfe, ed. *Marching with Sherman: Passages from the Letters and Diaries of Henry Hitchcock.* New Haven: Yale University Press, 1927.

Hurst, Samuel H. *Journal-History of the Seventy-Third Ohio Volunteer Infantry.* Chillicothe, OH: [no publisher listed], 1866.

Johnson, Andrew. *The Papers of Andrew Johnson.* Edited by LeRoy P. Graf, et al. Knoxville: University of Tennessee Press, 1967–2000. Cited herein as *Papers of Andrew Johnson.*

Johnson, W. R., ed. "Enough to Make a Preacher Sware: A Union Mule Driver's Diary of Sherman's March." *Atlanta History: A Journal of Georgia and the South* 33 (Fall 1989): 20–36.

Jones, Katharine M. *When Sherman Came: Southern Women and the "Great March."* New York: Bobbs-Merrill, 1964.

Kendrick, J. R. "A Non-Combatant's War Reminiscences." *Atlantic Monthly* 384 (October 1889): 449–63.

Marvin, Edwin E. *The Fifth Regiment Connecticut Volunteers.* Hartford: Press of Wiley, Waterman, & Eaton, 1989.

McBride, John R. *History of the Thirty-Third Indiana Veteran Volunteer Infantry.* Indianapolis: Wm. B. Burford, 1900.

Merrill, Samuel. *The Seventieth Indiana Volunteer Infantry in the War of the Rebellion.* Indianapolis: Bowen-Merrill, 1900.

Morhous, Henry C. Sgt. *Reminiscences of the 123d Regiment, N.Y.S.V.* Greenwich, NY: People's Journal Book and Job Office, 1879.

New York State Historian. *Third Annual Report of the State Historian of the State of New York,* 1897. New York and Albany: Wynkoop Hallenbeck Crawford Co., State Printers, 1908. Van Wagoner Diary.

Osborn, Capt. Hartwell, et al. *Trials and Triumphs: The Record of the Fifty-Fifth Ohio Volunteer Infantry.* Chicago: A. C. McClurg & Co., 1904.

Pearson, Johnnie Perry. *Lee and Jackson's Bloody Twelfth.* Knoxville: University of Tennessee Press, 2010.

Pepper, George W. *Personal Recollections of Sherman's Campaigns in Georgia and the Carolinas.* Zanesville, OH: Hugh Dunne, 1866.

Padgett, James A., ed. "With Sherman through Georgia and the Carolinas: Letters of a Federal Soldier [Rufus Mead], Part II." *GHQ* 33/1 (March 1949): 49–81.

Phillips, Ulrich B., ed. *The Correspondence of Robert Toombs, Alexander H. Stephens, and Howell Cobb.* 1913. New York: Da Capo Press, 1971.

Potter, Rev. John. *Reminiscences of the Civil War in the United States.* Oskaloosa, IA: Globe Presses, 1897.

Priest, John Michael, ed. *John T. McMahon's Diary of the 136th New York: 1861–1864.* Shippensburg, PA: White Mane Publisher, 1993.

Shally-Jensen, Michael. *Reconstruction Era, 1865–1877.* Ipswich, MA: Grey House Publishing, 2014.

Sherman, John. *John Sherman's Recollections of Forty Years in the House, Senate, and Cabinet: An Autobiography.* Chicago: Werner Co., 1896.

Sherman, William Tecumseh. *Major-General Sherman's Reports.* New York: Beadle & Co., 1865[?].

———. *Memoirs of General William Tecumseh Sherman.* 1875. 2nd edition, 1885. New York: Library of America, 1990 (reprint of 2nd edition).

Skinner, Arthur N., and James L. Skinner. *The Death of a Confederate.* Athens: University of Georgia Press, 1996.

Stelle, Abel C. *Memoirs of the Civil War.* New Albany, IN: [no publisher identified], 1904.

Thorndike, Rachel Sherman. *The Sherman Letters: Correspondence between General and Senator Sherman from 1837 to 1891.* New York: Charles Scribner's Sons, 1894.

Tonsill, Geneva, and E. W. Evans. "E. W. Evans, Brick Layer & Plasterer." WPA Slave Narratives, Georgia. Manuscript/Mixed Material. https://www.loc.gov/item/wpalh000565/.

US War Department. *The War of the Rebellion: A Compilation of the Official Records of the Union and Confederate Armies.* 1880–1901. Cited as *OR.*

Waddell, James D. *Biographical Sketch of Linton Stephens Containing a Selection of his Letters, Speeches, State Papers, Etc.* Atlanta: Dodson & Scott, 1877.

Wakelyn, Jon L., ed. *Southern Unionist Pamphlets and the Civil War.* Columbia: University of Missouri, 1999.

Welcher, Frank Johnson, and Larry G. Liggett. *Coburn's Brigade: The 85th Indiana, 33rd Indiana, 19th Michigan, and 22nd Wisconsin in the Western Civil War.* Carmel, IN: Guild Press of Indiana, 1999.

Wheeler, Richard. *Sherman's March.* New York: Ty Crowell Co., 1978.

White, George. *Statistics of the State of Georgia: including an account of its natural, civil, and ecclesiastical history: together with a particular description of each county.* Savannah: W. Thorne Williams, 1849.

———. *Historical Collections of Georgia: Facts, Traditions, Biographical Sketches, Anecdotes, Etc.* New York: Pudney & Russell Publishers, 1855.

Woods, Brett F., ed. *Abraham Lincoln Letters to His Generals 1861–1865.* New York: Algora Publishing, 2013.

Archival Collections

1869 Fire Folder. Morgan County Archives, Madison, GA.

Ames, Lyman D. Diary. Ohio History Connection Archives & Library. Ohio Historical Society, Columbus, OH.

Atkinson Family Papers. Courtesy Morgan County Landmarks Society, held for Judith Ulrich. Morgan County Archives, Madison, GA.

Brown Family Papers. University of Georgia, Hargrett Rare Books Library and Archives, Athens, GA.

Brown, Joseph E. Incoming Governor's Correspondence. Civil War Miscellany. Georgia Archives, Morrow, GA.

Cassville Confederate Cemetery file. Mulinix Research Center. Bartow History Museum, Cartersville, GA.

Civil War Misc. Collections, Georgia Archives, Morrow, Georgia.

Confederate States of America Prison Records, 1862. University of Georgia, Hargrett Rare Books Library and Archives, Athens, GA.

Conley, Benjamin. Papers. University of Georgia, Hargrett Rare Books Library and Archives, Athens, GA.

Crew, James H. Papers. Kenan Research Center. Atlanta History Center, Atlanta, GA.

Fleming, Jordan. Papers. University of Georgia, Hargrett Rare Books Library and Archives, Athens, GA.

Foster, N. G. File. University of Georgia, Hargrett Rare Books Library and Archives, Athens, GA.

Hambleton, James Pinckney. Papers. Stuart A. Rose Manuscript, Archives & Rare Book Library, Emory University, Atlanta, GA.

Harryman, S. K. Letters Collection (S-0603), Indiana State Library.

Hill, Edward Y. Vertical Files. Troup County Archives, LaGrange, GA.

Hill, Joshua. File. University of Georgia, Hargrett Rare Books Library and Archives, Athens, GA.

Hill, Joshua. Folders. Morgan County Archives, Madison, GA.

Mambert, John. W. Courtesy Mike Kipp. Morgan County Archives, Madison, GA.

Memorial of Putnam County Citizens. Abraham Lincoln Library, Springfield, IL.

Parmeter, N. L. Diary. Ohio History Connection Archives & Library. Ohio Historical Society, Columbus, OH.

Reid & Jordan Family Papers, rose Manuscript Archives, Emory University, Atlanta.

Saffold Family Papers. Courtesy family of Ms. Mattie Saffold. Morgan County Archives, Madison, GA.

Sherman, W. T. Folder. Morgan County Archives, Madison, GA.

Sherman, William T., to Abraham Lincoln. Saturday, September 17, 1864. *Abraham Lincoln papers: Series 1. General Correspondence. 1833 to 1916: Telegram concerning political situation in Georgia*. 1864. Manuscript/Mixed Material. Library of Congress. https://www.loc.gov/item/mal3642900/.

Sherman, William T., to Abraham Lincoln. Wednesday, September 28, 1864. *Abraham Lincoln papers: Series 1. General Correspondence. 1833 to 1916: Telegram concerning affairs in Georgia*. 1864. Manuscript/Mixed Material. https://www.loc.gov/item/mal3679600/.

Stephens, Alexander H. Family Papers. University of Georgia, Hargrett Rare Books Library and Archives, Athens, GA.

Index